Irina Gorbach
Alexander Berger
Edward Melomed

Microsoft® SQL Server™ 2008 Analysis Services

UNLEASHED

SAMS | 800 East 96th Street, Indianapolis, Indiana 46240 USA

Microsoft® SQL Server™ 2008 Analysis Services Unleashed

ISBN-13: 978-0-672-33001-8
ISBN-10: 0-672-33001-6

Library of Congress Cataloging-in-Publication Data:

Melomed, Edward.

Microsoft SQL server 2008 analysis services unleashed / Edward Melomed, Alexander Berger, Irina Gorbach.

p. cm.

ISBN 978-0-672-33001-8

1. SQL server. 2. Client/server computing. 3. Relational databases.

I. Berger, Alexander. II. Gorbach, Irina. III. Title.

QA76.9.C55M483 2008

005.75'65–dc22

2008049303

Printed in the United States of America

First Printing December 2008

Trademarks

All terms mentioned in this book that are known to be trademarks or service marks have been appropriately capitalized. Sams Publishing cannot attest to the accuracy of this information. Use of a term in this book should not be regarded as affecting the validity of any trademark or service mark.

Warning and Disclaimer

Every effort has been made to make this book as complete and as accurate as possible, but no warranty or fitness is implied. The information provided is on an "as is" basis. The authors and the publisher shall have neither liability nor responsibility to any person or entity with respect to any loss or damages arising from the information contained in this book.

Bulk Sales

Pearson offers excellent discounts on this book when ordered in quantity for bulk purchases or special sales. For more information, please contact:

U.S. Corporate and Government Sales
1-800-382-3419
corpsales@pearsontechgroup.com

For sales outside of the U.S., please contact:

International Sales
+1-317-581-3793
international@pearsontechgroup.com

Editor-in-Chief
Karen Gettman

Executive Editor
Neil Rowe

Acquisitions Editor
Brook Farling

Development Editor
Mark Renfrow

Managing Editor
Patrick Kanouse

Project Editor
Jennifer Gallant

Copy Editor
Keith Cline

Indexer
Ken Johnson

Proofreader
Water Crest Publishing, Inc.

Publishing Coordinator
Cindy Teeters

Book Designer
Gary Adair

Compositor
Mark Shirar

Graphics
Laura Robbins

Contents at a Glance

Table of Contents

Foreword

I am pleased to see this book being updated for a second edition, to cover the changes in Analysis Services 2008, and also to clarify some of the more difficult material in the first edition. This should make the book even more useful to its target users.

Now that Analysis Services is in its fourth major release, it has become a big, complex product, far removed from the relatively simple first release of a mere decade earlier. To make the most of it, model designers need much more knowledge than is available in the online documentation, which makes books like this all the more necessary. And, of course, now that the product is so widely used, sometimes for quite challenging applications, there is much more experience of the best practices to follow. Some of these are now baked into the product itself, but books like this can provide much more context for their use.

The authors are to be highly commended for putting in the effort to comprehensively update a substantial work like this; I know from my own experience how much extra motivation you need to update an existing publication after just two years, compared to the excitement of creating the first edition. All too often, publications like this remain frozen when new versions of the software they describe are released, leaving users to guess which parts remain true, and which have been superseded. In this case, this second edition actually follows more closely on the heels of Analysis Services 2008 than did the first edition on Analysis Services 2005.

Microsoft is also to be commended for continuing to permit or even encourage the disclosure of this level of detail about one of its major products; with the consolidation of the BI industry, some of the other major vendors have become much less willing to provide detailed information about the inner workings of their products. In any case, I have never known any other OLAP server vendor to be so open.

Users of Analysis Services are fortunate in the range of books available to them: more than for all the other OLAP servers combined. This is clearly the book for the most technical users who really need and want to understand exactly how Analysis Services works.

There are many other books for those just getting started with Analysis Services, or who want a clear 'how do I?' guide. The many application developers who just want to improve their Analysis Services skills will probably find this book overwhelming; there are at least a dozen simpler books to choose from. And, needless to say, this book is definitely not aimed at business users who want to understand what Analysis Services can do for them.

Nigel Pendse
Editor of *The OLAP Report*
Author of *The OLAP Survey*

About the Authors

Irina Gorbach is a senior development lead at Microsoft. She joined the Analysis Services team soon after its creation over 11 years ago. During her work at Microsoft, Irina has designed and developed many features of the Analysis Services product, and was responsible for client subsystem: OLEDB and ADOMD.Net. Irina was in the original group of architects that designed XML for Analysis specification; she worked on the architecture and design of calculation algorithms and currently is working on scalability of Analysis Services.

Alexander Berger was one of the first developers to work on OLAP systems at Panorama, prior to their purchase by Microsoft. After the acquisition, Alexander led the development of Microsoft OLAP Server through all of its major releases prior to SSAS 2008. Currently, Alexander leads the Business Intelligence department for Microsoft adCenter. He is one of the architects of OLEDB for the OLAP standard and MDX language, and holds more than 30 patents in the area of multidimensional databases.

Edward Melomed is one of the original members of the Microsoft SQL Server Analysis Services team. He arrived in Redmond as part of Microsoft's acquisition of Panorama Software Systems, Inc., which led to the technology that gave rise to Analysis Services 2008. He works as a program manager at Microsoft and plays a major role in the infrastructure design for the Analysis Services engine.

Acknowledgments

We are incredibly grateful to many people who have gone out of their way to help with this book.

To Py Bateman, our co-author, for making this book possible.

To Mosha Pasumansky, MDX guru, for answering all our questions and providing us with your expertise. Your mosha.com served as a terrific tool in our research.

To Marius Dimitru, formula engine expert, for helping us explain the details of the formula engine architecture and exposing power of the latest improvements.

To Akshai Mirchandani, engine expert, for support and help with writeback, proactive caching, and drillthrough.

To Michael Vovchik, storage engine expert, for support and help with DMVs.

To Oleg Lvovitch, expert in Visual Studio integration—thanks for help with the inner workings of Analysis Services tools.

To Adrian Dumitrascu, AMO expert, for answering numerous questions.

Thanks to Bala Atur, Michael Entin, Jeffrey Wang, Ksenia Kosobutsky, and Vladimir Chtepa, for your extensive reviews and feedback.

To Brook Farling, our talented and professional editor—thanks for your help to publish this book and publish it on time.

We would like to give special thanks to the publishing team at Sams: Neil Rowe, Mark Renfrow, Brook Farling, and Jennifer Gallant for all your support and patience for this project.

To Denis Kennedy, technical writing guru, for improving our writing skills and fixing all the errors we made.

Dedication

Edward Melomed

To my beautiful wife, Julia, who supported me through late nights and odd working hours. To our little sunshine, Anna. To my parents, Raisa and Lev, and to my sister Mila, whose guidance helped shape my life.

Irina Gorbach

To my husband Eduard, who is my best friend and biggest supporter.

To my wonderful children Daniel and Ellen, who constantly give me joy and make everything worthwhile. To my parents Eleonora and Vladimir, for their support and love: without you, this book wouldn't be possible. To my grandparents Bronya and Semen, for their unconditional love.

Alexander Berger

To my family and friends in Russia, Israel, and America.

We Want to Hear from You!

As the reader of this book, *you* are our most important critic and commentator. We value your opinion and want to know what we're doing right, what we could do better, what areas you'd like to see us publish in, and any other words of wisdom you're willing to pass our way.

You can email or write me directly to let me know what you did or didn't like about this book—as well as what we can do to make our books stronger.

Please note that I cannot help you with technical problems related to the topic of this book, and that due to the high volume of mail I receive, I might not be able to reply to every message.

When you write, please be sure to include this book's title and author as well as your name and phone or email address. I will carefully review your comments and share them with the author and editors who worked on the book.

Email: feedback@samspublishing.com

Mail: Neil Rowe
Executive Editor
Sams Publishing
800 East 96th Street
Indianapolis, IN 46240 USA

Reader Services

Visit our website and register this book at www.informit.com/title/9780672330018 for convenient access to any updates, downloads, or errata that might be available for this book.

Introduction

Analysis Services began as the project of a small Israeli firm named Panorama, which had responded to a request from a British publishing company to develop an application that would analyze the data stored in its relational database. By the end of 1994, Panorama developers began work on a more general application that would make it possible for business managers to analyze data with relative ease.

With its first release in 1995, Panorama deployed the application to several dozen customers. As the next release moved the application more deeply into the Israeli market, the Panorama team began to develop a new client/server analytical application. The server would process the data and store it in a proprietary format, and the client would also offer users an easy-to-use, rich graphical interface.

By 1996, the application had come to the attention of Microsoft, which acquired the technology by the end of that same year. In early 1997, a small Panorama team comprised of Alexander Berger, Amir and Ariel Netz, Edward Melomed, and Mosha Pasumansky moved from Tel Aviv to Redmond to start work on the first version of Microsoft OLAP Server. After the move to the United States, the team added new developers Irina Gorbach and Py Bateman.

To make the application attractive to enterprise customers, the team took on the challenge of formalizing and standardizing data exchange protocols, and they eliminated the client side of the application in favor of supporting a variety of third-party client applications. In early 1997, a small group including Alexander Berger retreated to a Puget Sound island to brainstorm the foundation of what would become SQL Server Analysis Services.

That retreat produced a plan for developing a standard protocol for client applications to access OLAP data: OLEDB for OLAP. More important, and more challenging, was the plan for developing a new query language that could access multidimensional data stored in the OLAP server—MDX (Multidimensional Expressions). MDX is a text language similar to SQL. MDX makes it possible to work with a multidimensional dataset returned from a multidimensional cube. From its inception, MDX has continued to change and improve, and now it is the de facto standard for the industry.

The original release plan was to include the OLAP server in the 1997 release of SQL Server 6.5. However, instead of rushing to market, Microsoft decided to give the development team more time to implement MDX and a new OLEDB for OLAP provider. Microsoft's first version of a multidimensional database was released in 1998 as part of SQL Server 7.0. That version was integrated with Microsoft Excel PivotTables, the first client for the new server.

Under the slogan, "multidimensionality for the masses," this new multidimensional database from Microsoft opened the market for multidimensional applications to companies of all sizes. The new language and interface were greeted favorably. The simplicity (and, one could say, elegance) of the design made it possible for users to rapidly become proficient with the new product, including users who weren't database experts. Technology that used to be available only to large corporations was now accessible to medium-sized and small businesses. As a result, the market for new applications that use multidimensional analysis has expanded and flourished in an environment rich with developers who write those applications.

But, of course, we were not satisfied to rest on our laurels. We took on a new goal—turn Analysis Services into a new platform for data warehousing. To achieve this, we introduced new types of dimensions, increased the volume of data the server can process, and extended the calculation model to be more robust and flexible. Even though no additional personnel joined the team for this effort, by the end of 1999 we brought the new and improved Analysis Services 2000 to market.

For the next five years, more and more companies adopted Analysis Services until it became a leader in the multidimensional database market, garnering a 27% market share. Now, multidimensional databases running on OLAP servers are integral to the IT infrastructures of companies of all sizes. In response to this wide adoption of multidimensional database technology, Microsoft has increased the size of the team devoted to OLAP technology in order to continue to develop the platform to meet the requirements of enterprise customers.

For the 2005 release of SQL Server Analysis Services, we started from ground up, rewriting the original (and now aging) code base. We built enterprise infrastructure into the core of the server.

SQL Server 2008 release continues to improve architecture and functionality of Analysis Services. While improving the performance of query execution, it also introduces query language extensions and new management capabilities.

Who Is This Book's Intended Audience?

In this book, we bring you the tools you need to fully exploit Analysis Services and explain the architecture of the system. You'll find all of the coverage of our previous book (just in case you were wondering if you needed to go back and read that one first), including the basic architecture established in Analysis Services 2005, as well as all the improvements introduced in Analysis Services 2008. *Analysis Services Unleashed* gives you a full understanding of multidimensional analysis and the MDX query language. It also exposes all the aspects of designing multidimensional applications and management of the system.

How This Book Is Organized

The book is divided into the following nine parts:

Parts I and II are devoted to a formalized description of the multidimensional model implemented in the new version of the OLAP server. We give you the vocabulary and concepts you'll need to work with this model.

In Part III, we present a detailed discussion of MDX and explanation of the way we use it to query multidimensional data. You'll need a practical grasp of the data model and MDX to take advantage of all the functionality of Analysis Services.

We devote the middle section of the book in Parts IV–VII to the practical aspects of loading and storing data in Analysis Services, as well as methods of optimizing data preparation and data access. In addition, we examine server architecture.

In the last section of the book, Parts VIII–IX, we discuss data access, the architecture of client components, and data protection. In addition, we examine the practical aspects of administering the server and monitoring its activities.

We wish you great success in your work with Analysis Services 2008, and we hope that our humbly offered book is of service to you.

Conventions Used in This Book

Commands, scripts, and anything related to code are presented in a special `monospace` computer typeface. Bold indicates key terms being defined, and italic is used to indicate variables or for emphasis. Great care has been taken to be consistent in letter case, naming, and structure, with the goal of making command and script examples more readable. In addition, you might find instances in which commands or scripts haven't been fully optimized. This lack of optimization is for your benefit, as it makes those code samples more intelligible and follows the practice of writing code for others to read.

Other standards used throughout this book are as follows:

CAUTION

Cautions alert you to actions that should be avoided.

NOTE

Notes give you additional background information about a topic being discussed.

PART I

Introduction to Analysis Services

IN THIS PART

CHAPTER 1

Introduction to OLAP and Its Role in Business Intelligence

IN THIS CHAPTER

- The Multidimensional Data Model

In the past decade, Microsoft SQL Server Analysis Services established itself as one of the leaders in the Business Intelligences systems market. Analysis Services helps managers, employees, customers, and partners to make more informed business decisions by enabling them to analyze information accumulated during a company's day-to-day operations.

Success of Analysis Services and the entire Business Intelligence market was predefined by incredible growth of amounts of data accumulated as a result of everyday functioning of a large number of companies. Today it's hard to imagine a business or an organization that doesn't use an online transaction processing (OLTP) system. OLTP systems provide means to highly efficient execution of a large number of small transactions and reliable access to data stored in the result of the transactions.

The volume of the data stored and processed for one day by an OLTP system could be several gigabytes per day; after a period of time, the total volume of data can reach to the tens and even hundreds of terabytes. Such a large volume of data can be hard to store, but it is a valuable source of information for understanding the way the enterprise functions. This data can prove very helpful for making projections that lead to successful strategic decisions, and for improving everyday decision making.

It's easy to see why analysis of data has become so important to the management of modern enterprises. However, OLTP systems are not well suited to analyzing data. In the past decades, an entire new market has emerged for systems that can provide reliable and fast access for analyzing very large amounts of data: online analytical processing (OLAP).

OLAP enables managers, executives, and analysts to gain insight into data using fast, interactive, and consistent interfaces to a wide variety of possible views of information. For example, with OLAP solution, you can request information about company sales in Europe over the year, then drill down to the sales of computers in September, calculate year-to-date sales or compare revenue figures with those for the same products sold in January, and then see a comparison of TV sets sales in Europe in the same time period.

Because OLAP systems are designed specifically for analysis, they typically don't need to both read and write data. All that is necessary for analysis is reading data. With this emphasis on reading only, OLAP systems enjoy a speed advantage over their OLTP cousins. However, a read-only approach to the database architecture is not the only distinction of the OLAP solution. The following rules distinguish OLAP systems from relational databases:

- **Multidimensional data structures**

  OLAP solutions typically use multidimensional data structures that allow analysts and managers to analyze numeric values from different perspectives, such as time, customers, products, and others.

- **Consistently fast data access**

  Architecture of the system allows constantly fast access to the data. To ensure fast, predictable query times, OLAP solutions typically pre-aggregate data.

- **Intuitive interface**

  Skilled analysts and nontechnical users alike can manipulate and analyze data; they can generate reports without involving their organization's IT department.

- **Complex calculations**

  With multiple dimensions come more complex, cross-dimensional calculations. You might need to calculate the subtotal of sales for the state Washington, for example, to be expressed as a percentage of the whole U.S. sales. Further, this result may be presented as part of a time-series analysis (for instance, current month versus last month, versus a year ago).

The Multidimensional Data Model

The design and development of the multidimensional database—especially Microsoft SQL Server Analysis Services, the system designed and developed by the authors of this book—was inspired by the success of relational databases. If you're already familiar with relational databases, you'll recognize some of the terminology and architecture. But, to understand Analysis Services, you must first understand multidimensional data models, how this model defines the data and processes it, and how the system interacts with other data storing systems, primarily with the relational data model.

The multidimensional data model for Analysis Services consists of three more specific models:

- The conceptual data model
- The application data model
- The physical data model

The Conceptual Data Model

The conceptual data model contains information about how the data is represented and the methods for defining that data. It defines data in terms of the tasks that the business wants to accomplish using the multidimensional database. To define conceptual data model, you use the user specifications for the structure and organization of the data, rules about accessing the data (that is, security rules), and calculation and transformation methods.

In a sense, the conceptual data model serves as a bridge between a business model and the multidimensional data model. The solutions architect is the primary user for the conceptual data model. We use Data Definition Language (DDL) and MDX (Multidimensional Extensions) script for the creation of the conceptual model. You can also use Business Intelligence Development Studio to develop the conceptual data model.

The Application Data Model

The application model defines the data in a format that can be used by the analytical applications that will present data to a user in a way that he can understand and use. The primary user for the application data model is the client application, which exposes the model to the user. The application model is built with the MDX language and XML for Analysis protocol. The chapters of Part 3, "Using MDX to Analyze Data," contain detailed information about MDX and a few of most commonly used client applications. The chapters of Part 7, "Accessing Data in Analysis Services," contain information about protocol used by Analysis Services to communicate with client applications.

The Physical Data Model

As in the arena of relational databases, the physical model defines how the data is stored in physical media:

- **Where it is stored**—What drive (or maybe on the network), what types of files the data is stored in, and so on
- **How it is stored**—Compressed or not, how it's indexed, and so on
- **How the data can be accessed**—Whether it can be cached, where it can be cached, how it is moved into memory, and so on

The database administrator is the primary user for the physical data model. We use XML-based commands for manipulation of data on the physical layer.

Figure 1.1 shows relationships between three parts of multidimensional model.

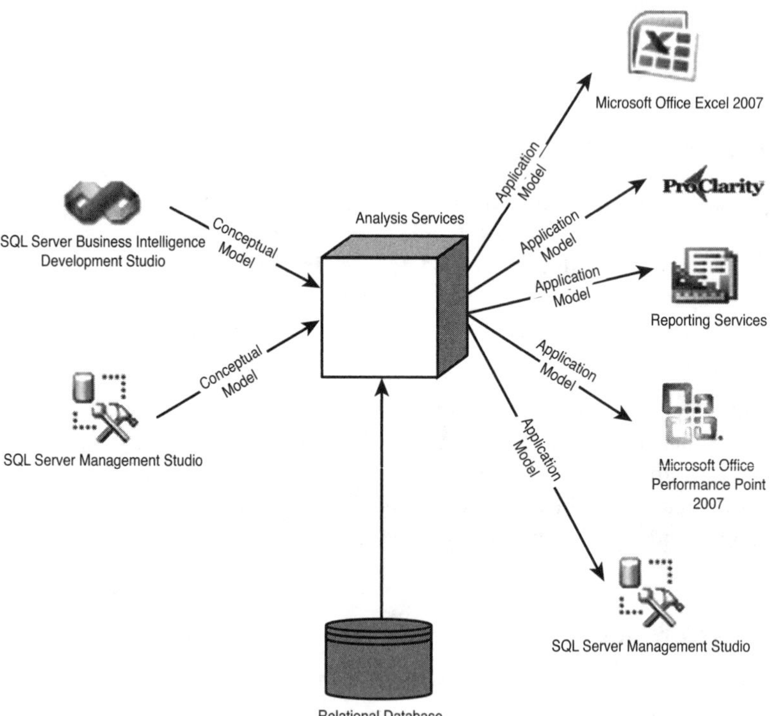

FIGURE 1.1 Submodels of the multidimensional model.

You use SQL Server Business Intelligence Development Studio or SQL Server Management Studio to define a conceptual data model, also known as a Unified Dimensional Model (UDM) or cube. After the conceptual model is defined, you populate it with data by loading/processing the data from the relational database. At this time, you define the physical data model—partitioning scheme of the data, indexing scheme, and so on. The application model of Analysis Services consists of standard data access interfaces. Client applications use those interfaces: XML for Analysis and MDX to communicate with Analysis Services. More than hundred applications available today support the application model of Analysis Services and can work with any Analysis Services cubes.

Unified Dimensional Model

The UDM of Microsoft SQL Server Analysis Services makes it possible for you to set up your system so that different types of client applications can access data from both the relational and the multidimensional databases in your data warehouse, without using separate models for each.

It's been a common industry practice for some time now to build data warehouses that include a relational database for storing data and a multidimensional database for analyzing data. This practice developed because the large volumes of data that multidimensional databases were developed to analyze are typically stored in relational databases. The data would be moved to the multidimensional database for analysis, but relational database would continue to serve as primary storage.

Therefore, it makes sense that the interaction between the stored data and the multidimensional database where it can be analyzed has been an important component of multidimensional database architecture. Our goal for Analysis Services, put simply, is speedy analysis of the most up-to-date data possible.

The speedy and up-to-date parts are what present the challenge. The data in OLTP systems is constantly being updated. But we wouldn't want to pour data directly from an OLTP system into a multidimensional database, because OLTP data is easily polluted by incomplete transactions or incomplete data entered in a transaction. In addition, you don't want your analysis engine to access the OLTP data directly, because that could disrupt work and reduce productivity.

In a data warehouse, OLTP data is typically transformed and stored in a relational database and then loaded into a multidimensional database for analysis. To connect the two databases, you can choose from three methods, each one using a different kind of interaction:

- Relational OLAP (ROLAP), in which no data is stored directly in the multidimensional database. It is loaded from the relational database when it is needed.
- Multidimensional OLAP (MOLAP), in which data is loaded into the multidimensional database and cached there. Future queries are run against the cached data.
- Hybrid OLAP (HOLAP), in which the aggregated data is cached in the multidimensional database. When the need arises for more detailed information, that data is loaded from the relational database.

In earlier versions of Analysis Services, the multidimensional part of the data warehouse was a passive consumer of data from the relational database. The functions of storing data and analyzing data were not only separate, but you had to understand two models—one for accessing a relational database and one for accessing a multidimensional database.

Some client applications would use one model, and others would use the other model. For example, reporting applications traditionally would access the data in a relational database. On the other hand, an analysis application that has to look at the data in many different ways would probably access the data in the multidimensional database, which is designed specifically for that sort of use.

Now, the UDM offers a substantially redefined structure and architecture so that the one model (UDM) serves the purposes of any client application. You no longer have to understand two models; we're providing a unified model. Figure 1.2 shows how many different client applications can use UDM to access data in a variety of different data stores.

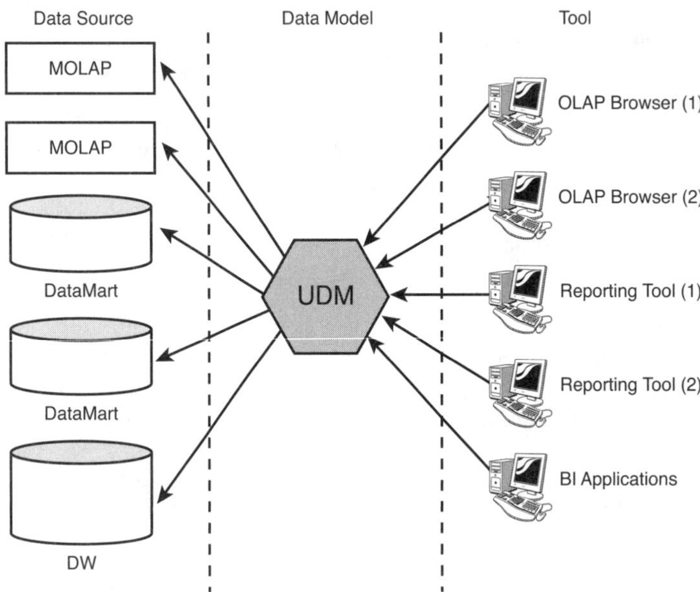

FIGURE 1.2 The UDM provides a unified model for accessing and loading data from varied data sources.

Analysis Services uses *proactive caching* to ensure that the user of the client application is always working with predictable data latency. In essence, proactive caching is a mechanism by which the user can schedule switching from one connection mode (ROLAP, MOLAP, or HOLAP) to another. For example, the user might set his system to switch from MOLAP to ROLAP if the data in the MOLAP system is older than, say, four hours.

With UDM at the center of the multidimensional model, you no longer need to have different methods of data access for different data sources. Before UDM, every system had a number of specialized data stores, each one containing data that was stored there for a limited number of users. Each of these data sources would likely require specific methods of data access for loading data into the multidimensional model. With Analysis Services, all the data of the enterprise is available through the UDM, even if those data sources are located on different types of hardware running different operating systems or different database systems. OLAP now serves as an intermediate system to guarantee effective access to the data.

Basic Concepts

When you start to build a multidimensional model, you think about business entities your organization operates with and about values that you need to analyze. For example, in our fictional organization—a chain of grocery stores known as Food Mart—we operate with warehouses, stores, products, customers, and different currencies, as shown in Figure 1.3. Those business entities became *dimensions* of our multidimensional model. Typically, you want to analyze data in a context of a time periods, and therefore the `Time` dimension is present in almost all multidimensional models. Actual values or facts that you are analyzing, such as sales, costs, and units, are called *measures*.

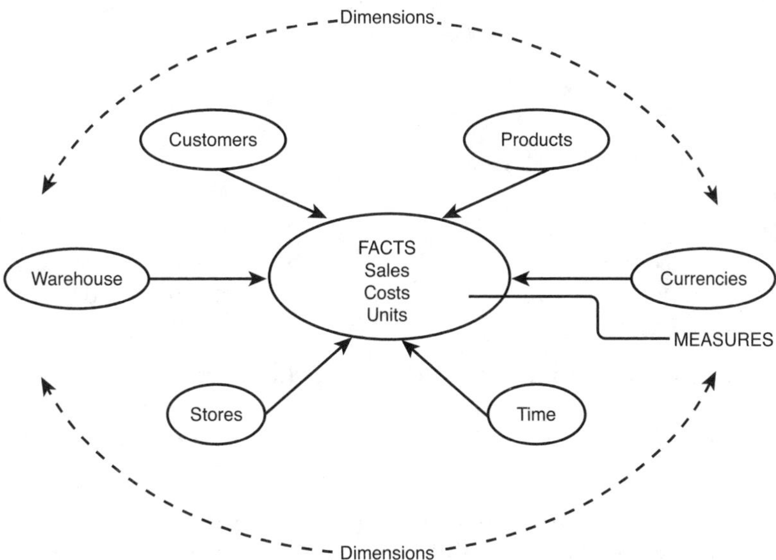

FIGURE 1.3 A multidimensional model consists of dimensions and measures.

Each individual element of the dimension is called a *member*. For example, "Club 1% Milk" is a member of the `Products` dimension, Irina Gorbach is a member of the `Customers` dimension, and January 1997 is a member of the `Time` dimension.

Each business entity usually has multiple characteristics. For instance, a customer can have the following properties: name, gender, city, state, and country. You might look at the products by name, Stock Keeping Unit (SKU), brand, product family, product category, and so on. We call these characteristics of the business entity *dimension attributes*. Figure 1.4 shows dimension attributes.

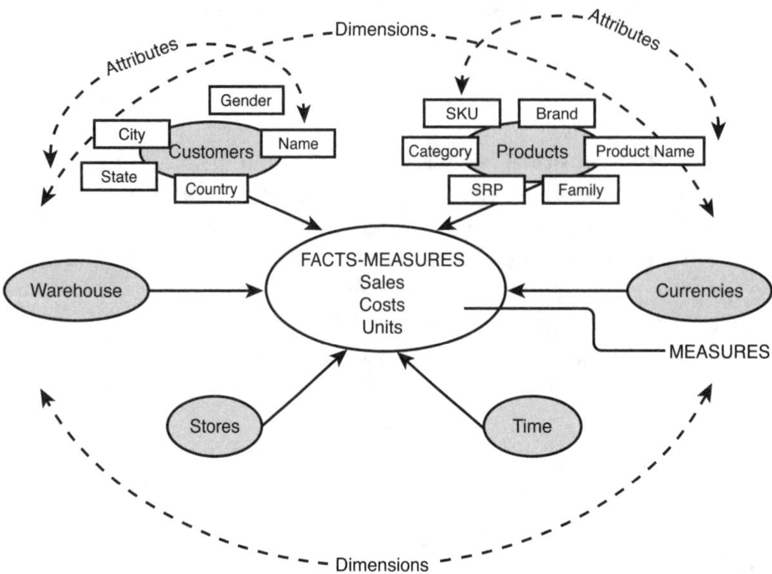

FIGURE 1.4 Each dimension is defined by its attributes.

Dimension attributes are not completely independent from each other. For example, `Year` contains `Quarter`, and `Quarter` contains `Month`. We can say that `Year`, `Quarter`, and `Month` attributes are related to each other.

If members of different attributes have a hierarchical structure, attributes can be organized in a *hierarchy*. For example, you can create the hierarchy `Calendar—Year` > `Quarter` > `Month` within the `Time` dimension, because the year contains quarters and quarters contains months.

After data is loaded in the cube, you can access it with many client applications. Microsoft Excel is one of the most frequently used application. Figure 1.5 shows Excel 2007 exposing data stored in Analysis Services cube.

This Excel spreadsheet demonstrates sales and cost for products in different time periods based on the data stored in the FoodMart 2008 database.

In Chapter 2, "Multidimensional Space," we explain the terms that we use to describe multidimensional space.

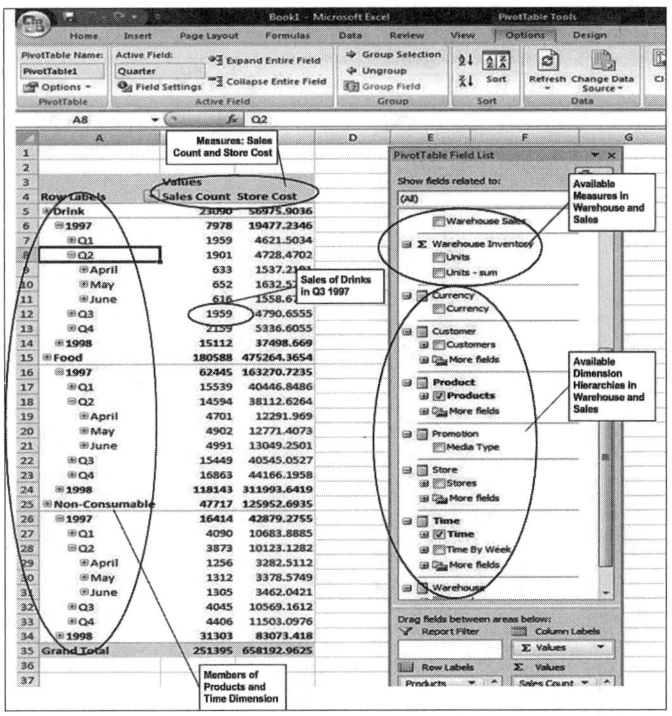

FIGURE 1.5 Accessing data in FoodMart 2008 sample using Excel 2007.

CHAPTER 2

Multidimensional Space

IN THIS CHAPTER

Working with relational databases, we're used to a two-dimensional space—the table, with its records (rows) and fields (columns). We use the term *cube* to describe a multidimensional space, but it's not a cube in the geometrical sense of the word. A geometrical cube has only three dimensions. A multidimensional data space can have any number of dimensions; and those dimensions don't have to be the same (or even similar) size.

One of the most important differences between geometric space and data space is that a geometric line is made up of an infinite number of contiguous points along it, but our multidimensional space is discrete and contains a discrete number of values on each dimension.

Describing Multidimensional Space

We're going to define the terms that we use to describe multidimensional space. To a certain extent, they are meaningful only in relation to each other:

- A *dimension* describes some aspect of the data that the company wants to analyze. For example, your company would have a data with time element in it—the `Time` could become a dimension in your model.
- A *member* corresponds to one point on a dimension. For example, in the `Time` dimension, Monday would be a dimension member.
- A *value* is a unique characteristic of a member. For example, in the `Time` dimension, 5/12/2008 might be the value of the member with the caption "Monday."

- An *attribute* is the full collection of members. For example, all the days of the week would be an attribute of the `Time` dimension.
- The *size*, or *cardinality*, of a dimension is the number of members it contains. For example, a `Time` dimension made up of the days of the week would have a size of 7.

To illustrate, we'll start with a three-dimensional space for the sake of simplicity. In Figure 2.1, we have three dimensions: (1) `Time` in months, (2) `Products` described by name, and (3) `Customers` described by their names. We can use these three dimensions to define a space of the sales of a specific product to specific customers over a specific period of time, measured in months.

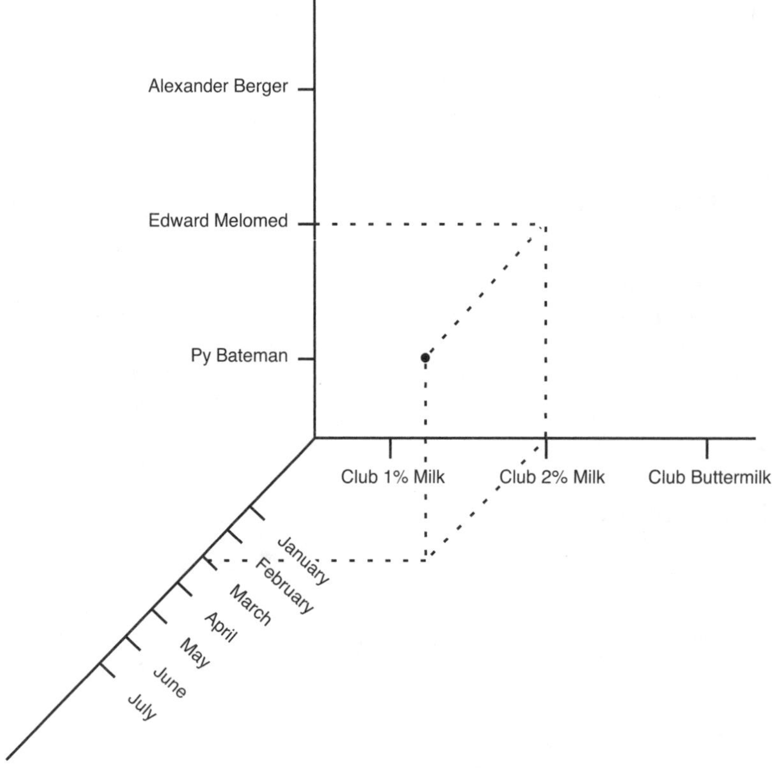

FIGURE 2.1 A three-dimensional data space describes sales of products to customers over a time period.

In Figure 2.1, we have only one sales transaction represented by a point in the data space. If we represent every sales transaction of the product by a point on the multidimensional space, those points, taken together, constitute a "fact space" or "fact data."

It goes without saying that actual sales are much less than the number of sales possible if we were to sell each of our products to all our customers each month of the year. That's the dream of every manager, of course, but in reality it doesn't happen.

The total number of possible points creates a theoretical space. The size of the theoretical space is defined mathematically by multiplying the size of one dimension by the product of the sizes of the other two. In a case where you have a large number of dimensions, our theoretical space can became huge; but no matter how large the space gets, it remains limited because each dimension is distinct and is limited by the distinct number of its members.

The following list defines some more of the common terms we use in describing a multidimensional space:

- A *tuple* is a coordinate in multidimensional space.
- A *slice* is a section of multidimensional space that can be defined by a tuple.

Each point of a geometric space is defined by a set of coordinates, in a three-dimensional space: *x*, *y*, and *z*. Just as a geometric space is defined by a set of coordinates, multidimensional space is also defined by a set of coordinates. This set is called a *tuple*.

For example, one point of the space shown in Figure 2.1 is defined by the tuple ([Club 2% Milk], [Edward Melomed], [March]).

An element on one or more dimensions in a tuple could be replaced with an asterisk (*) indicating a wildcard. In our terminology, that is a way to specify not a single member but all the members of this dimension. By specifying an asterisk in the tuple, we turn the tuple from a single point into a subspace (actually, a normal subspace). This sort of normal subspace is called a *slice*.

You might think of an example of a slice for the sales of all the products in January to all customers as written (*, *, [January]). But for simplicity, the wildcards in the definitions of slice are not written; in our case, it would be simply ([January]). Figure 2.2 shows the slice that contains the sales that occurred during January.

You can think of many other slices, such as the sales of all the products to a specific customer ([Edward Melomed]), the sales of one product to all customers ([Club 2% Milk]), and so on.

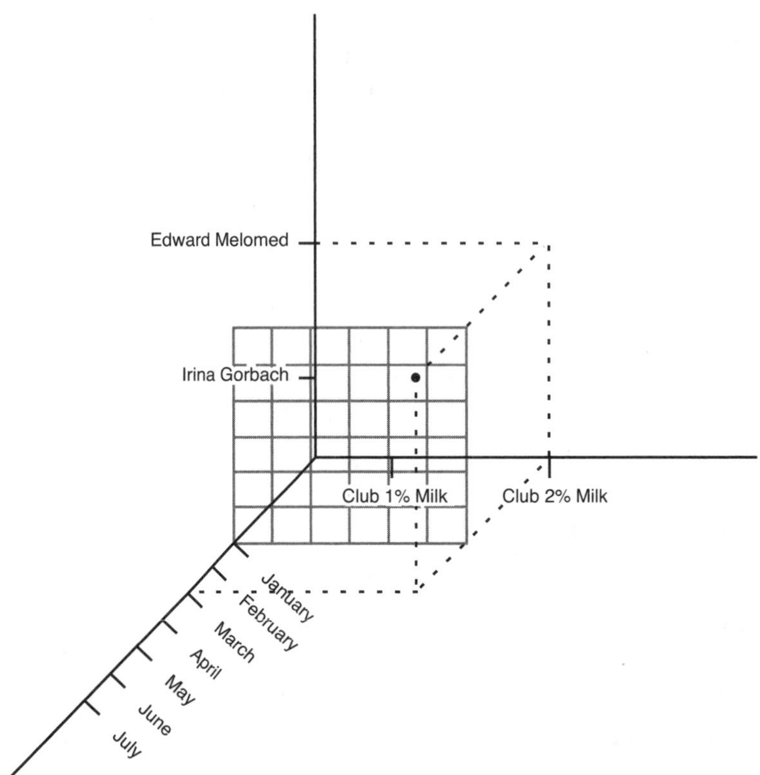

FIGURE 2.2 A slice of the sales from January.

Dimension Attributes

But how would you define the space of sales by quarter rather than by month? As long as you have a single attribute (months) for your `Time` dimension, you would have to manually (or in our imaginations) group the months into quarters. When you're looking at multiple years, your manual grouping starts to be unwieldy.

What you need is some way to visualize the months, quarters, and years (and any other kind of division of time, maybe days) in relation to each other—sort of like a ruler enables us to visualize the various divisions of a foot or a yard, and the inches and standard fractions of inches along the way.

In essence, what you need is additional attributes (quarters, years, and so forth). Now you can use months as your key attribute and relate the other attributes (related attributes) to the months—3 months to a quarter, 12 to a year.

So, back to our example. We want to "see" the individual months in each quarter and year. To do this, we'll add two related attributes to the `Time` dimension (quarter and year) and create a relationship between those related attributes and the key attribute (month). Now we can create a "ruler," like the one in Figure 2.3, for the dimension: year-quarter-month.

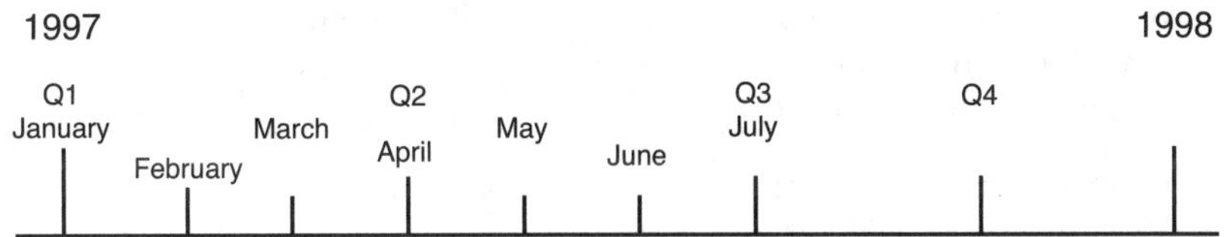

FIGURE 2.3 Related attributes (year, quarter) are calibrated relative to the key attribute (month).

Now we have a hierarchical structure for our "ruler"—a *dimension hierarchy*. The dimension hierarchy contains three hierarchy levels—Years, Quarters, and Months. Each level corresponds to an attribute. If you look at Figure 2.4, which appears a little later, you can see our ruler, with its hierarchical structure, within our multidimensional space.

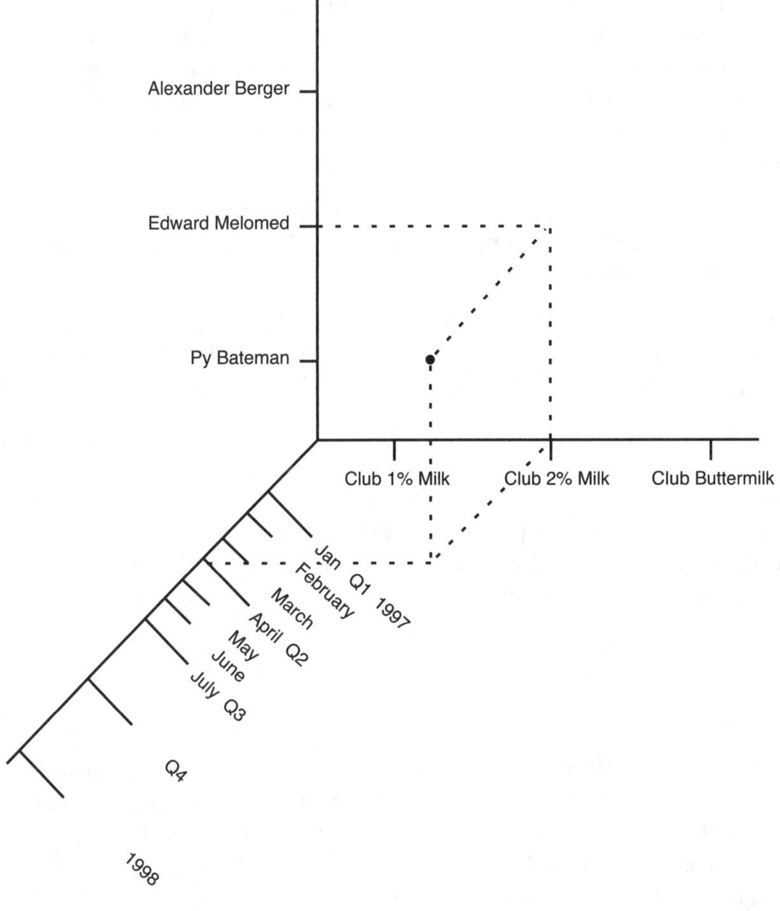

FIGURE 2.4 Related attributes create new points in multidimensional space.

A dimension can have more than one hierarchy. For example, if we count time in days, we could add another attribute: the days of the week. And we could remove the key attribute designation from month and give it to day.

Now we can have two dimension hierarchies: year, quarter, month, day; and year, week, day.

NOTE

We sneaked an additional attribute in there—week. We had to do that because a month doesn't divide nicely into weeks. So, in the second dimension hierarchy, we dropped month and substituted week (by ordinal number).

Cells

With our ruler added to this multidimensional space, we can see (in Figure 2.4) some new positions on the ruler that correspond to the members of the related attributes (quarter, year) that were added. These members, in turn, create a lot of new points in the multidimensional space. However, you don't have any values for those new points because the data from our external source contained only months. You won't have values for those points until (or unless) you calculate them.

At this point, you have a new space—the logical space—as opposed to the fact space, which contains only the points that represent actual sales and the theoretical space that represents all possible sales transactions could happen.

Your cube, then, is made up of the collection of points of both the theoretical (including fact space) and logical spaces (in other words, the "full space" of the multidimensional model). Each point in the cube's space is called a *cell*.

Therefore, a cell in the cube can fall into one of the three spaces. The cell in the fact space is associated with an actual sale of a product to a customer. In Figure 2.5, we can see a fact cell that represents an actual sale: It contains the amount that a customer paid for the product. If the sale wasn't made (that is, a potential sale), our cell is just a theoretical point in the cube (a theoretical cell). We don't have any data in this cell. It's an empty cell with a value of NULL. For the fact cell, where we have the amount that the customer paid, that amount is the cell value.

Measures

The value in a cell is called a *measure*. Figure 2.5 shows the amount the customer paid for the product. To tell the truth, we arbitrarily chose the amount paid as the value for that cell. We could have used some other value that describes the sale—such as the number of items (of that product) the customer bought. As a matter of fact, that's a good idea. We'll just add another measure so that we have two: the amount the customer paid and the quantity of items of the product that she bought.

These measures, taken together, can be seen as a dimension of measures—a measure dimension. Each member of this dimension (a measure) has a set of properties, such as data type, unit of measure, and (this is the most important one) the calculation type for the data aggregation function.

Aggregation Functions

The type of calculation is the link that binds together the theoretical (fact) and logical space of the cube. It is the data aggregation function that enables us to calculate the values of cells in the logical space from the values of the cells in the fact space; we cannot calculate values the based on the empty values in the theoretical space.

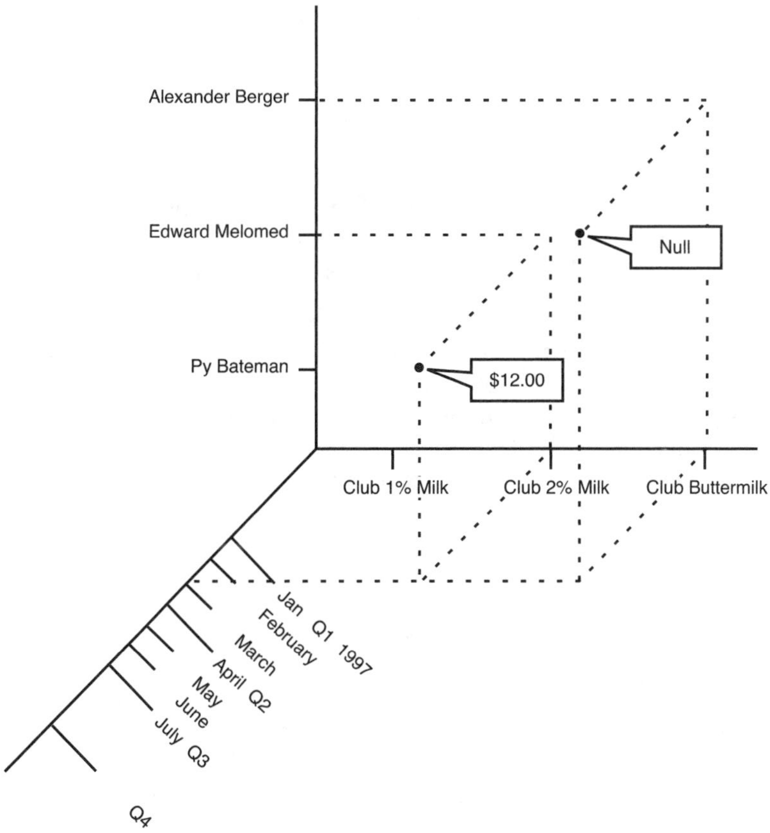

FIGURE 2.5 This cube diagram shows two cells: one with a real value and one with a NULL value.

An aggregation function can be either simple (additive) or complex (semi-additive). The list of additive aggregation functions is pretty limited—the *sum* of the data, the *minimum* and *maximum* values of the data, and a calculation of the *count*, which is really just a variation on the *sum*. All other functions are complex and use complex formulas and algorithms, which we discuss in Chapter 12, "Cube-Based MDX Calculations."

As opposed to geometric space in which the starting point is the point at which all the coordinates equal 0, the starting point for multidimensional space is harder to define. For example, if one of our dimensions is month, we don't have a value of 0 anywhere along the dimension. Therefore, you can define the beginning of multidimensional space by the attribute that unites all the members of the dimension; that attribute contains only one member, All. For simple aggregation function, such as sum, the member All is equivalent to the sum of the values of all the members of the factual space; for complex aggregation functions, All is calculated by the formula associated with the function.

Subcubes

An important concept in the multidimensional data model is a subspace or subcube. A subcube represents a part of the full space of the cube as some multidimensional figure inside the cube. Because the multidimensional space of the cube is discreet and limited, the subcube is also discreet and limited. The slice that we discussed earlier is a case of a subcube in which the boundaries are defined by a single member in the dimension.

The subcube can be either normal or of an arbitrary shape. Subcube consists of the points in the multidimensional space. In a normal subcube, a coordinate that exists on one dimension must be present for every coordinate on the other dimensions among subcube points. An arbitrary shape subcube doesn't have this limitation and can include points with any coordinates. In Figure 2.6, you can see examples of a normal- and an arbitrary-shaped subcube.

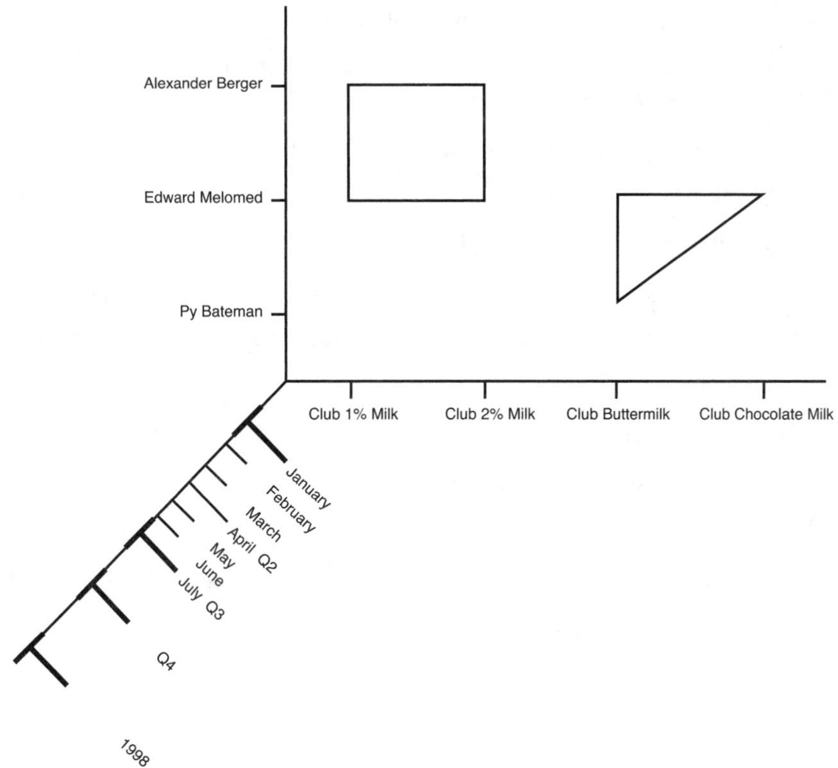
Alexander Berger
Edward Melomed
Py Bateman
Club 1% Milk
Club 2% Milk
Club Buttermilk
Club Chocolate Milk
January
February
March
April
Q2
May
June
July
Q3
Q4
1998

FIGURE 2.6

Describing multidimensional space requires a new vocabulary:

- **Aggregation function**—A function that enables us to calculate the values of cells in the logical space from the values of the cells in the fact space
- **Attribute**—A collection of similar members of a dimension
- **Cell value**—A measure value of a cell
- **Dimension**—An element in the data that the company wants to analyze
- **Dimension hierarchy**—An ordered structure of dimension members
- **Dimension size**—The number of members a dimension contains
- **Measure**—The value in a cell
- **Member**—One point on a dimension
- **Member value**—A unique characteristic of a member
- **Tuple**—A coordinate in multidimensional space
- **Slice**—A section of multidimensional space that can be defined by a tuple
- **Subcube**—A portion of the full space of a cube

CHAPTER 3

Client/Server Architecture and Multidimensional Databases: An Overview

IN THIS CHAPTER

- Two-Tier Architecture
- One-Tier Architecture
- Three-Tier Architecture
- Four-Tier Architecture
- Distributed Systems

The architecture of multidimensional databases in many respects follows the design of relational databases. Similarly to relational databases, Microsoft SQL Server Analysis Services supports a variety of architectures for accessing data:

- Two-tier architecture, in which data is stored on the server and moved to the client in response to a query
- One-tier architecture, in which the data is stored on the same computer as is the client application
- Three-tier architecture, in which an Internet server sits between the database server and the client

NOTE

We've used the term *tier* to describe these architectures. We use this term to describe physical layers—components of each layer are separate applications and can even run on separate machines. If you choose to look at the tiers as logical ones—layers of protocols between components—you would get different numbers of layers (tiers).

- Four-tier architecture, in which data is stored in a relational database, cached in a multidimensional database, and an Internet server facilitates communication between the multidimensional database server and the client

NOTE

You could view a relational online analytical processing (ROLAP) system as a three-tier architecture, too. In that case, OLAP server is middle tier between a client application and data stored in the relational database.

Two-Tier Architecture

In the most common architecture, represented in Figure 3.1, data is stored on the server, and the client application uses queries to access that data. This two-tier architecture is characterized by simplicity and effectiveness because there is a direct connection between the server and the client, with nothing in between.

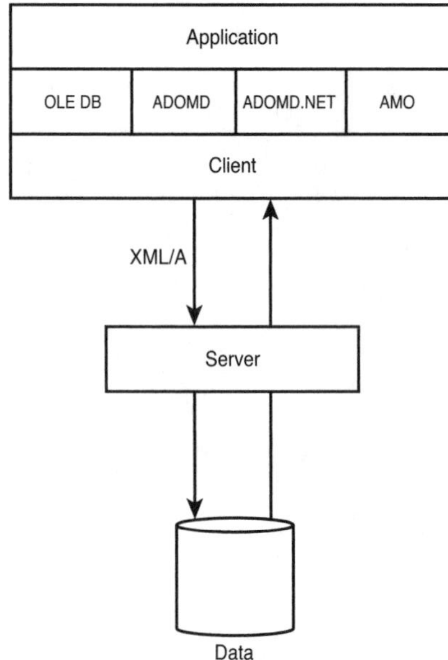

FIGURE 3.1 In this two-tier architecture, data is stored on the server.

Let's look at each separate component in more detail. The server software receives a request from the client. It processes the request and formulates an answer based on the data located on a hard disk or cached in RAM. In our architecture, the client and the server use the XML for Analysis (XML/A) protocol to send and receive data. The client application can use various object models to interact with the client, which in turn uses XML/A to connect to the server. You can find detailed information about connecting the client application to the server in Chapter 31, "Client/Server Architecture and Data Access."

XML/A, as is obvious from the name, is a protocol developed for communication with analytical data providers. It has received wide support in the industry, and has obtained the status of a standard. You can find more information about XML/A in Chapter 32, "XML for Analysis."

The object models we use for administering the multidimensional database are Decision Support Objects (DSO) and Analysis Management Objects (AMO), discussed in Chapter 34, "Analysis Management Objects." For data access, we use OLEDB for OLAP, ADOMD, and ADOMD.NET. You can find more information about these object models in Chapter 31, "Client/Server Architecture and Data Access," and Chapter 33, "ADOMD.NET."

One-Tier Architecture

The simplest architecture (one-tier) is illustrated in Figure 3.2; it's commonly known as a *local cube*. In a local cube, the multidimensional database becomes part of the client application and allows access to multidimensional data located on the hard disk of the client computer.

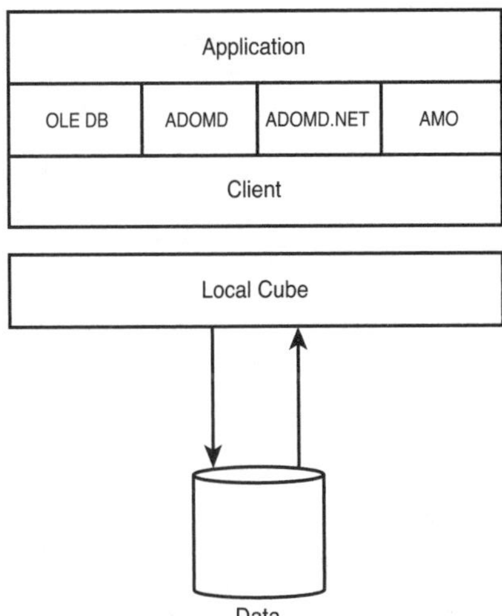

FIGURE 3.2 With a local cube, the client application can access information in the local cube on the client computer.

When you have both the cube and the client application on the same computer, you don't need a network protocol to move data from one to the other. We use XML/A to communicate between the client and the local cube. And the application has the same choice of object models for administering the database as for accessing the cube data.

One drawback to the local cube architecture is that your computer must have enough resources to hold all that data along with the client application, and the power to make the calculations required by the queries to the cube.

A local cube, otherwise known as one-tier architecture, frees the user from the network—a handy arrangement when traveling and unable to connect.

Three-Tier Architecture

Once the Internet gained wide usage, a different architecture to make the most of its advantages was needed. Three-tier architecture, illustrated in Figure 3.3, is the solution that has been established.

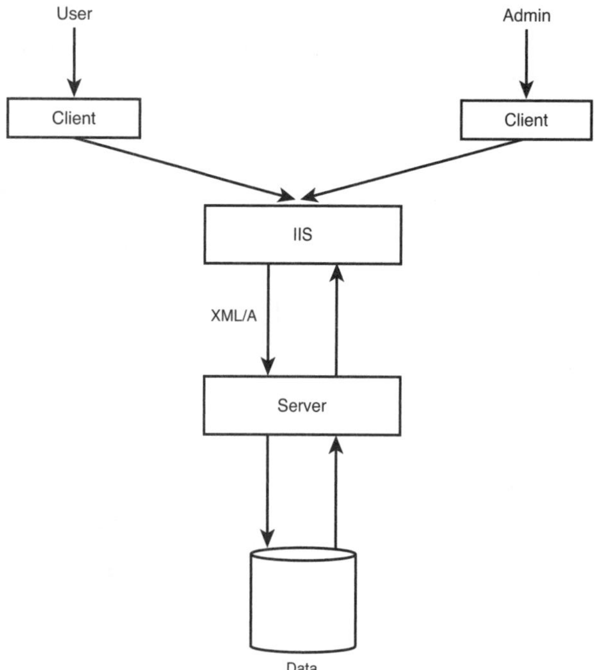

FIGURE 3.3 In three-tier architecture, the Internet Information Services acts as a middle tier between the client and the database server.

With this architecture, the client establishes a connection over HTTP with an Internet server, which then connects to the OLAP server. The OLAP server, usually located on another computer, sends the response data to the Internet server, which prepares the data for client consumption in the form of web pages.

The client application can use the same object models for administering the database and for accessing data as a client application in the two-tier architecture. In addition, a client application can use web pages and HTTP for those purposes.

In a three-tier architecture, an Internet server acts as a middle tier to connect the client application to the OLAP server. Analysis Services uses Microsoft Internet Information Services (IIS) as the Internet server.

Four-Tier Architecture

In the four-tier architecture, illustrated in Figure 3.4, the data is stored in a data warehouse that includes both a relational database (in our case, SQL Server) and a cache of multidimensional data (Analysis Server). After the response data is converted into web page format on the Internet server, the data is returned to the client.

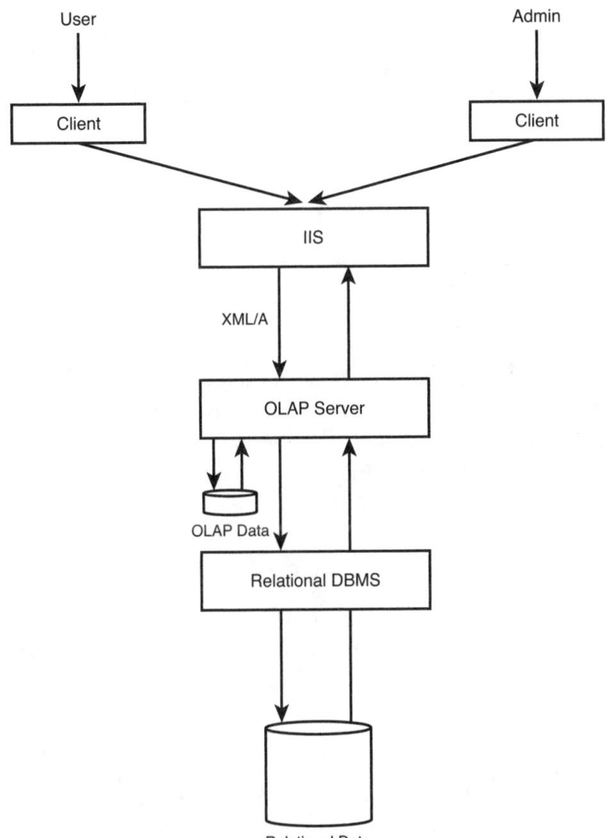

FIGURE 3.4 In this four-tier architecture, data is stored in a data warehouse that consists of a relational database and a multidimensional database.

With the data warehouse, we need some way to connect the relational database and the multidimensional database. In addition, we don't want to have to worry about whether the data needed by the query is in one or the other. Here we find the Unified Dimensional Model (UDM) useful.

Briefly, UDM manages the request for data, taking the needed data from the multidimensional database or moving it from the relational database to the multidimensional. You can find more information about UDM in Chapter 1, "Introduction to OLAP and Its Role in Business Intelligence."

XML/A, the various object models, and HTTP are used in four-tier architecture in the same way they are used in three-tier architecture.

Distributed Systems

These four architecture systems aren't the only ways to build multidimensional database systems. There are a variety of systems for distributed storage of data inside a multidimensional database.

Distributed Storage

The following list describes the distributed storage systems that have been developed for Analysis Services as of now:

- **Remote partitions**—Sections of data are stored on other servers, called *remote servers*, that are connected to the main computer, the *master*. Remote partitions make it possible to work with almost unlimited quantities of data.
- **Linked objects**—A *publisher* server contains multidimensional data objects (cubes and dimensions), which are mirrored on a *subscriber* server. The client application queries the subscriber. The referenced objects on the subscriber server initially contain no data, just a link to the data in the original objects. The subscriber server can make calculations in response to a query, and can cache data obtained from the publisher server. Linked objects make it possible to support an unlimited number of users because calculation power can be distributed among many different servers.

These distributed systems provide the possibility of storing and processing practically unlimited volumes of data. We take a closer look at the architecture of distributed systems in Chapter 25, "Building Scalable Analysis Services Applications."

Thin Client/Thick Client

The variety we find among the different tier systems is just one aspect of the differences we can find in client/server architecture with respect to multidimensional databases. We also find differences in the interaction and distribution of functions between client software and server software.

These variations came about because of two factors. First, the client side today has computational power comparable with the server. This means that the client computer can take on many of the tasks that were previously reserved for the server. The second factor is related to the first. With client computers taking on more of the computational tasks, and data being exchanged over the Internet, customers are concerned with the integrity and security of their systems. In addition, many companies are reluctant to invest in the new software needed to take advantage of the possibilities on the client side.

This dilemma has given rise to two varieties of client/server architecture, known as *thin client* and *thick client*:

- A thin client carries out practically no operations besides sending requests to the server and obtaining and unpacking answers. Thin client architecture is popular with Internet applications, where it can be difficult—not to mention inadvisable—to install new software onto the client computers.
- A thick client is able to not only obtain but also cache and process information. This makes it possible to minimize the amount of communication with the server. Thick client architecture is popular in extranet applications, where the network administrator in the company can install additional software at will.

The client for Analysis Services 2000 is a thick client. But, because of the increasing popularity and use of the Internet in enterprise database systems, the client for later versions of Analysis Services became a thin client. Moving to the thin client architecture makes it possible for you to keep all of your data on the server, so that you don't have to move data around very much to respond to queries. However, you will need more powerful servers to serve the same number of users as you could with Analysis Services 2000.

PART II

Creating Multidimensional Models

IN THIS PART

CHAPTER 4

Conceptual Data Model

IN THIS CHAPTER

The conceptual multidimensional data model is the foundation for multidimensional databases. All the components and architecture of a multidimensional database create, control, and provide access to the data in the model. Because it is simple and flexible, not to mention effective, the multidimensional model has led to widespread adoption of Analysis Services in a short period of time.

Many people look at the multidimensional data model as simply metadata—data that describes the data stored in the relational database. We're going to look at this from a different angle. We see the conceptual model as an independent specification of the data in the multidimensional system. A relational database might be the source of the data or the place where the data is stored. But, the multidimensional database is a completely independent system that can be both the source and the storage place of the data. If the source of the data is external to the multidimensional database, it is defined by the `Data Source` property. Any dependency between multidimensional data and relational data is defined by the `Data Binding` property.

Data Definition Language

We use Data Definition Language (DDL) to define and alter the data model. Extensible Markup Language (XML), which has grown popular among software developers in recent years, turns up in many of the components of our system, including DDL. As the foundation for DDL, XML is easy to use, convenient, and efficient. Throughout this book, we use DDL a lot to describe the data model, so you'll want to be familiar with it. However, we focus our discussion here on the semantic properties of the language. You can look for details of the syntax of DDL in Books Online.

DDL is object oriented. It enables you to define a set of objects that are part of the multidimensional model and to define all the properties necessary to those objects.

You can use Microsoft Business Intelligence Development Studio and SQL Server Management Studio to work with the conceptual model of Analysis Services. Under the hood, those applications generate DDL commands and send them to Analysis Services. However, although you can avoid delving into the details of DDL, we highly recommend you to spend time trying to understand it so that you can take full advantage of the capability to talk directly to the Analysis server in its own language. In this chapter, we introduce you to the object model that defines the conceptual model and discuss the common characteristics of all the objects. In the following chapters, we'll delve deeper into the most important objects of the conceptual model, such as `Dimension`, `Cube`, `Measure Group`, and so on.

Objects in DDL

All the objects in DDL are either major objects or minor objects. *Major objects* are objects that the user can manipulate—independently of their parent objects—to create and change the model. *Minor objects* are children of major objects.

The root object (which is a major one) of the model is `Database` (sometimes called `Catalog`), which allows you to navigate to all the objects of the model.

Major objects must have two unique identifiers: the `ID` and `Name` properties. Minor objects sometimes don't need these properties, because they are always part of a major object. In addition, each object (major or minor) can have a `Description` property that contains text that describes the purpose of the object (useful for the developer who created the object and the user of the application that uses the object). Objects can also have the `Annotation` property, or lists of `Annotations`, that external applications use to display or manipulate their data.

LISTING 4.1 The DDL Definition of the FoodMart Database

```
<Databasexmlns="http://schemas.microsoft.com/analysisservices/2003/engine">
    <ID>FoodMart 2008</ID>
    <Name>FoodMart 2008</Name>
    <CreatedTimestamp>0001-01-01T08:00:00Z</CreatedTimestamp>
    <LastSchemaUpdate>0001-01-01T08:00:00Z</LastSchemaUpdate>
    <LastProcessed>0001-01-01T08:00:00Z</LastProcessed>
    <State>Unprocessed</State>
    <LastUpdate>0001-01-01T08:00:00Z</LastUpdate>
    <DataSourceImpersonationInfo>
        <ImpersonationMode>Default</ImpersonationMode>
        <ImpersonationInfoSecurity>Unchanged</ImpersonationInfoSecurity>
```

```
    </DataSourceImpersonationInfo>
    <Dimensions />
    <Cubes />
    <DataSources />
    <DataSourceViews />
    <Translations />
</Database>
```

You can see in the example presented in Listing 4.1 that the database contains collections of the objects, dimensions, cubes, and so forth. (The ending *s* on `Dimensions`, `Cubes`, and so on denotes a collection.) The `Dimension` and `Cube` objects are major objects and can be changed independently of the `Database` object definition. You can find detailed information about dimensions in Chapter 5, "Dimensions in the Conceptual Model," and about cubes in Chapter 6, "Cubes and Multidimensional Analysis."

Figure 4.1 contains the most important objects of our multidimensional model, with major objects in dark gray. Objects that represent the physical model and objects that represent database security aren't included in the figure. These objects are discussed in later chapters.

In the following sections, we give you an idea of some of the properties that are commonly used in our conceptual model:

- Multilanguage support
- Ways of ordering your data
- Ways to specify default properties

NOTE

When you specify the identifier, name, and translation of an object, you choose from a limited set of characters; in addition, the strings are limited in length. It's important to pay attention to all these limitations, because usually it takes a long time to figure out what's causing an error or strange behavior that is related to errors in the names. Sometimes, the fix of an error like this can require a change in design.

Multilanguage Support

The Analysis Services multidimensional model features multilanguage support, which comes in handy considering the trend toward internationalization and globalization of today's enterprises. That support means that the data warehouse can contain data in multiple languages, which, of course, affects data storage requirements. The object's `Language` (sometimes known as `Locale`) property is the identifier for a specific language; it is used for both the metadata and in the data itself. In the metadata, it defines the language of the object's `Name` property.

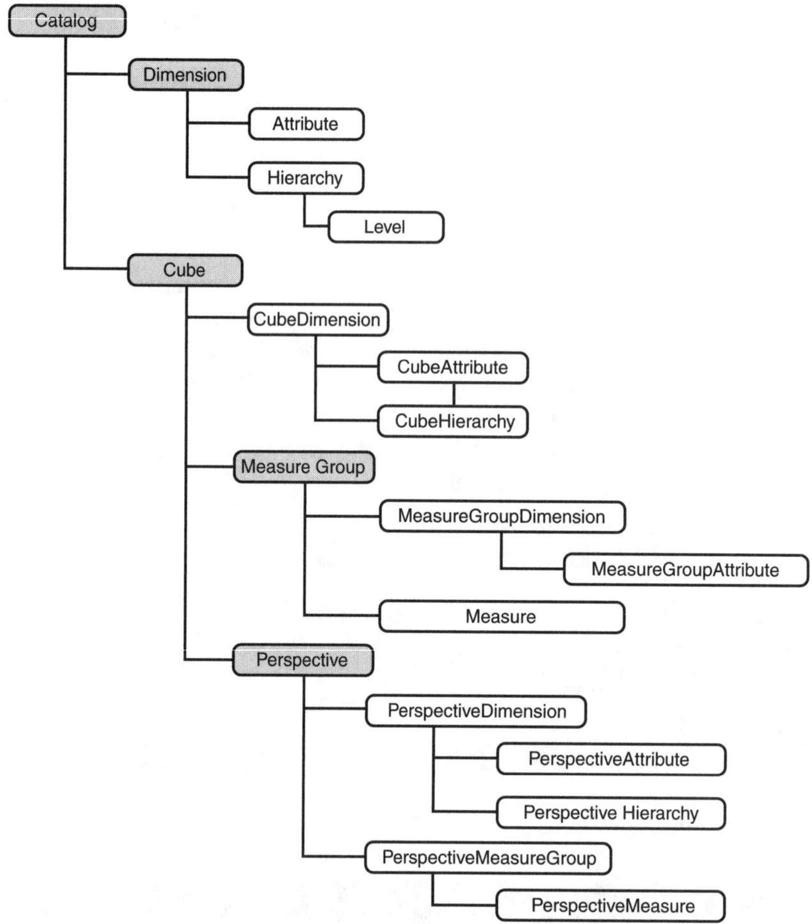

FIGURE 4.1 The major objects of the conceptual model are shown in dark gray.

The `Translation` property of an object enables you to define translation of the object's `Name` into different languages. The `Language` property of the `Translation` defines to which language `Name` is translated.

The `ID` property of the object, once it's specified, can't be changed. The name of the object and the translation of that name can be easily changed, and because of that can't be used for cross-references.

LISTING 4.2 Translating a Database Object Name to Russian

```
<Database xmlns="http://schemas.microsoft.com/analysisservices/2003/engine">
    <ID>FoodMart 2008</ID>
    <Name>FoodMart 2008</Name>
    <Translations>
        <Translation>
```

```
            <Language>1049</Language>
            <Caption>Сеть Продуктовых Магазинов</Caption>
        </Translation>
    </Translations>
</Database>
```

If you specify this translation in DDL definition, the user application will have access to the caption that is specified in the translation, and can use it in place of the name wherever necessary.

Rules of Ordering

The order of object elements is not all that important. When possible, however, Analysis Services preserves the order that you assigned for the elements. But for some objects, Analysis Services assigns a new order, usually based on the alphabet.

If order is based on the alphabet, the order can differ from one language to another. Not only does alphabetic order change from one language to another, but there are rules of ordering, defined by the `Collation` property, that add different bases for ordering. `Collation` and its properties, such as `Ignore Case` or the ignoring of special characters, define different ways of ordering for different languages.

Specifying Default Properties

The DDL language has rules for specifying default properties. These rules specify the values that properties take if they're not explicitly specified in the object definition. Usually if there isn't a specific default value, the server assigns a value. Therefore, it's not always possible to predict what value will be assigned. It also might turn out that in the next version of Analysis Services, the default values will be interpreted differently. It's a good idea to avoid situations where the server would define values for you. However, if you're not interested in the value, you can just go with whatever value the server assigns.

Another rule holds that you don't need to specify a collection of objects if the collection is empty. The server doesn't have default values for empty collections; it assumes that an empty collection doesn't have any objects, and therefore no values. (We would assume that, too.) However, there are some cases in which the server would copy a collection from another object. (For more information about exceptions to these rules, see Chapter 6, "Cubes and Multidimensional Analysis," and Chapter 7, "Measures and Multidimensional Analysis.")

Rules of Inheritance

Analysis Services has two distinct ways of inheriting values from the parent at the time of object's creation:

- Static inheritance
- Dynamic inheritance

Static inheritance means that at the time the object is created any of the values not specified in the object's definition will be explicitly assigned values taken from the parent. For example, if you create a `Dimension` object and omit the `Language` property, one will be created in the new dimension and an assigned value will be copied from the `Database` object. That also means changing parent object properties leads to the new child objects inheriting new values and old objects keeping the old values. Therefore, you might end up in a situation where some of the objects in the collection differ without you taking explicit action.

Dynamic inheritance means the property of the object is not explicitly defined for the object at the time of the creation (if not specified by you). When you are trying to obtain object metadata from the server, the dynamically inherited property will not appear in the object definition. Its value is calculated by the server at the time it requires. For example, if the `ErrorConfiguration` object is not explicitly specified for the `Partition` object at the time of creation, you will discover the `ErrorConfiguration` object missing from the partition definition when you try to query partition metadata. During the partition processing, the server will query parent objects of the partition to obtain values needed to handle errors.

CHAPTER 5

Dimensions in the Conceptual Model

IN THIS CHAPTER

- Dimension Attributes
- Dimension Hierarchies
- Attribute Hierarchies

You define multidimensional space by specifying a set of dimensions. Therefore, the dimension is the central object of the multidimensional model. Many other objects are based on the dimension. In different objects of the model, dimensions are represented in different forms. The basic form of dimension is the `Database` dimension, from which all other dimension forms in the model derive. The `Database` dimension is a major object, and therefore has `Name` and `ID` properties. Other dimensions reference the `Database` dimension and then add properties that distinguish them. For example, a cube uses `Cube` dimension, which references a `Database` dimension.

Listing 5.1 is the Data Definition Language (DDL) that describes the most generic definition of the `Database` dimension. The `Name` property in our sample dimension is `Customer`; the `ID` property is also `Customer`. These two are the only properties defined in our dimension (the `Customer` dimension). In the next sections of this chapter, we slowly introduce other properties of a dimension object.

LISTING 5.1 Use DDL to Define a Basic **`Database`** Dimension

```
<Dimension>
     <ID>Customer</ID>
     <Name>Customer</Name>
     <Annotations />
     <Attributes />
     <Hierarchies />
</Dimension>
```

This definition contains neither a definition of multidimensional space nor a dimension hierarchy. If we want to define a multidimensional space, we must use a collection of attributes to define the coordinates of that space. In the next section, we look at the attribute collection for our sample `Customer` dimension.

Dimension Attributes

The multidimensional model contains a collection of attributes that defines a set of "domains" of a dimension's data; one domain is a dimension attribute. We use the term *domain* as it defined in the relational database theory: a limited list of values (scalars). However, implementations of relational databases essentially ignore this definition. In practice, implementations of the relational data model manipulate columns that will accept any value (of the appropriate type).

In the multidimensional model, *attribute* defines domain—a list of the same type values, which we call key values. All key values of attribute have the same data type. Key is a unique identifier of a dimension member. (For the definition of a dimension member, see Chapter 2, "Multidimensional Space.") For each unique key value, there is a unique dimension member. The difference between the implementation of a domain in the relational and multidimensional data models is shown in Figure 5.1.

Relational Model			*Multidimensional Model*			
Column = "Domain"			*Attribute = "Domain"*			
Column 1	**Column 2**	**Column 3**	**Key**	**Name**	**Translation**	**Property**
Irina	Gorbach	F	01	Gorbach	Gorbach	F
Alexander	Berger	M	02	Berger	Berger	M
Edward	Melomed	M	03	Melomed	Melomed	M
.....	.....	.....	.....	.....	.....	.....
Value N	Value N	Value N	Value N	String N	String N	Value N

FIGURE 5.1 The implementation of a "domain" differs between the relational and the multidimensional models.

As shown in a Figure 5.1, an attribute is an analog of a column in the relational implementation of the domain. However, in addition to the scalar values, the multidimensional model allows the association of an additional set of properties with every dimension member (for example, `Name`, `Caption`, `Value`, and so on).

Listing 5.2 shows the DDL definition of the key attribute of the `Customer` dimension in the FoodMart 2008 database.

LISTING 5.2 DDL Definition for the Key Attribute of the **`Customer`** Dimension

```
<Attribute>
    <ID>Customer</ID>
    <Name>Customer</Name>
    <Usage>Key</Usage>
    <KeyColumns>
        <KeyColumn>
            <DataType>Integer</DataType>
            <Source>
                <TableID>dbo_customer</TableID>
                <ColumnID>customer_id</ColumnID>
            </Source>
        </KeyColumn>
     </KeyColumns>
     <NameColumn>
        <DataType>WChar</DataType>
        <DataSize>151</DataSize>
        <Source>
            <TableID>dbo_customer</TableID>
            <ColumnID>name</ColumnID>
        </Source>
    </NameColumn>
    <AttributeRelationships />
</Attribute>
```

Attribute Properties and Values

A dimension attribute contains a limited list of key values. Each unique key value is associated with a unique member of the dimension. The key is the unique identifier of that dimension member. Dimension members included in an attribute are called attribute members.

In the multidimensional model (as opposed to the relational model), the attribute also contains properties that define different characteristics of the attribute members. All attribute members have the same properties.

Table 5.1 lists the main properties of an attribute member.

TABLE 5.1 Attribute Properties

Name	Description
Type	Defines a type for the attribute. Typically, the Type property is not used in the multidimensional model per se. You can specify it in the multidimensional model so that analytical applications could use it as a property to choose the appropriate user view of the data and allow appropriate access to the member (for example, Time or Account dimensions).
Usage	Defines whether the attribute is the key attribute (used as the key for the dimension), an additional attribute for the dimension, or a parent attribute.
KeyColumn	Defines a source, type, and size of the key value for the attribute member. The key of the attribute is, practically speaking, a unique identifier of a member. The key value type can be either text or numeric. For example, 02052008 can be the key of the member in the Day attribute.
NameColumn	Defines a source for the string used to identify a member by a user. In contrast to a key, the name value has to be text. For example, February 5, 2008 is a name of a member in the Day attribute. The NameColumn property can have the same value as KeyColumn if the KeyColumn type is text (obviously).
ValueColumn	Defines the source of additional value of the member. Usually, the value of the attribute is equivalent to the value of the key (defined by KeyColumn). In some situations, however, they differ. Most often, this happens when the value is defined by something other than the numeric data type, such as a picture or video or sound file. In our example, 36 will be the value of a member, which corresponds to the thirty-sixth day of the year.
OrderBy	Defines whether the order of the members is determined by key or by name.
OrderByAttributeID	Defines a different attribute that determines the order. This is an optional property that works with OrderBy. If this property is defined, Analysis Services will use it to sort members of the current attribute by key or name of the specified attribute. For example, you can sort product by its Stock Keeping Unit (SKU).
MemberNameUnique	Defines whether the name is unique for all the attribute members. Uniqueness of the key is an important requirement for defining an attribute. Attribute names don't have to be unique. However, duplicate names can cause some inconveniences when using the dimension and can affect the performance of name resolution. We recommend using unique names when possible.

TABLE 5.1 Attribute Properties

Name	Description
`Translation`	Defines source of strings translating a member name to different languages. To make the view of a member more accessible in a multicultural organization, for each attribute member you can define a collection of possible `Translations` that specify the language into which the member name will be translated. (The language is defined by the `Language` property.) The `Translation` is not usually used to reference a dimension member; more often, it is used to display the member to the user. The member caption is the translated name if a `Translation` is applied (one caption for each language).
`EstimatedCount`	Defines expected size of an attribute. A count of the members of an attribute can help determine the best internal structure for your data. If you accurately specify a value for this property in the development stage, the system can optimize the use of the attribute and things will go more smoothly in later stages.

Once you've specified these properties for an attribute, you're ready to populate it. Sometimes, populating an attribute with members is a pretty simple task. For example, the `Gender` attribute generally requires only two values: male and female. On the other hand, populating an attribute such as `Customer` can turn out to be a more complex task, because the number of members in the attribute can be very large: tens and even hundreds of millions. See Chapter 21, "Dimension and Partition Processing," for detailed information about loading attribute data.

Relationships Between Attributes

Even though the number of attributes in a dimension usually doesn't vary as widely as the number of members of an attribute, it can reach to the tens and even hundreds. Nonetheless, only one of those attributes can be the key attribute. Additional (related) attributes define different aspects and properties of the key attribute. For example, we can add `Gender` and `Marital Status` attributes to the `Customer` attribute.

Related Attributes

Every attribute has a key, but sometimes the attribute itself is the key of the dimension. Additional attributes in a dimension can be related not only to the key attribute, but to each other. For example, in the `Customer` dimension, suppose we introduce the country and city where the customer lives. The country is a property of the city, so you get two new attributes related to each other. We call these *related attributes*.

Even though dimension attributes can be related to each other or not related, all attributes are related to the key attribute. The relationship to the key can be either direct or indirect, through other attributes.

You have a direct relationship between two attributes if there is no intervening attribute between them. An indirect relationship is a relationship in which there are one or more attributes between the two. The relationship chain can be longer than three attributes, but there has to be an attribute at the end that is directly related to the key.

The collection of attributes creates a single semantic space that defines one member of the key attribute. You can envision this semantic space as a tree of dimension attributes, such as that illustrated in Figure 5.2.

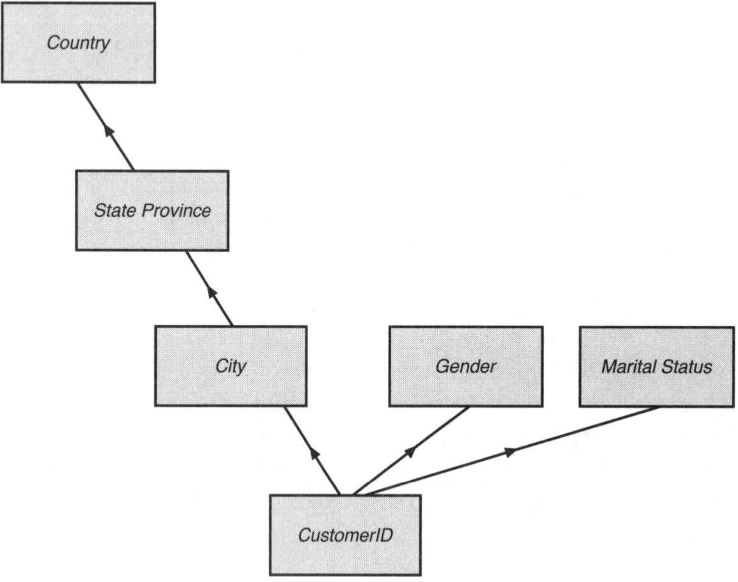

FIGURE 5.2 Tree of dimension attributes.

The key attribute is `Customer ID`, located in the root of the tree of attributes. The attributes `Marital Status`, `Gender`, and `City` directly relate to the key attribute. The `Marital Status` and `Gender` attributes are not related to each other. The connection between them is through `Customer ID`. Therefore, to traverse the tree from attribute `Marital Status` to attribute `Gender`, the direction of traversal will change from "toward" the key attribute to direction "from" the key attribute.

`Attribute City` is directly related to `Customer ID`. Attribute `Country` is directly related to attribute `State Province`, but indirectly related to `Customer ID`. Your eye can follow the line from `Country` to `Customer ID` without changing direction.

Listing 5.3 shows a simple DDL definition of the diagrammed collection of attributes.

LISTING 5.3 DDL Definition of the Attribute Tree

```
<Attributes>
    <Attribute>
```

```
        <ID>Customer</ID>
        <Name>Customer</Name>
        <Usage>Key</Usage>
        <KeyColumns/>
        <AttributeRelationships>
            <AttributeRelationship>
                <AttributeID>City</AttributeID>
                <Name>City</Name>
            </AttributeRelationship>
            <AttributeRelationship>
                <AttributeID>Marital Status</AttributeID>
                <Name>Marital Status</Name>
            </AttributeRelationship>
            <AttributeRelationship>
                <AttributeID>Gender</AttributeID>
                <Name>Gender</Name>
            </AttributeRelationship>
        </AttributeRelationships>
    </Attribute>
    <Attribute>
        <ID>City</ID>
        <Name>City</Name>
        <KeyColumns/>
        <AttributeRelationships>
            <AttributeRelationship>
                <AttributeID>State Province</AttributeID>
                <Name>State Province</Name>
            </AttributeRelationship>
        </AttributeRelationships>
    </Attribute>
    <Attribute>
        <ID>State Province</ID>
        <Name>State Province</Name>
        <KeyColumns/>
        <AttributeRelationships>
            <AttributeRelationship>
                <AttributeID>Country</AttributeID>
                <Name>Country</Name>
            </AttributeRelationship>
        </AttributeRelationships>
    </Attribute>
    <Attribute>
        <ID>Country</ID>
        <Name>Country</Name>
        <KeyColumns />
    </Attribute>
```

```
    < Attribute>
          <ID>Marital Status</ID>
          <Name>Marital Status</Name>
          <KeyColumns />
     </Attribute>
     <Attribute>
          <ID>Gender</ID>
          <Name>Gender</Name>
          <KeyColumns/>
     </Attribute>
</Attributes>
```

To define a dimension, it is not enough to specify a relationship between attributes. Every relationship has multiple properties that specify, for example, the type of the relationship as flexible or rigid, optionally of the relationship as mandatory or optional, cardinality as one to one or one to many, and so on.

NOTE

We provide more detailed information about relationships later in this chapter, in the section "Relationships Between Attributes." This more detailed information will help you formulate the correct definition of relationships so that you can optimize the performance of the dimensional model, and consequently the performance of the system.

Attribute Member Keys

Each member of an attribute is identified by its key; each member key is unique within the attribute. The keys of all the members of an attribute have the same type. As a member is loaded into the collection that makes up the attribute, it receives a unique number, called `Data ID` (mostly used internally).

Simple and Composite Keys

In contrast to the "domain" of the relational model, where the scalar is always a simple value, the members of an attribute in the multidimensional model can have either simple keys or composite keys:

- A *simple key* is defined by a single value of any data type allowed in the multidimensional database.
- A *composite key* is defined by a combination of values of various data types. A composite key, like any key, must be unique for each attribute member.

You need a composite key when you can't rely on the uniqueness of the key to identify a specific member. For example, if you have an attribute (collection) of world cities, to uniquely identify any one city you need to include in the key the country and perhaps even province or state. (There could be a number of cities with the same name located in one country—the United States is notorious for that.) Thus, the composite key.

Now, if you also had an attribute of countries, the value of a country would be present in both attributes (cities and countries). Composite keys, then, lead to duplication of data and consume more resources.

The Unknown Member

In a relational database, you have a value with its own set of rules—`NULL`—that takes the place of an unspecified value. In our implementation of the multidimensional database, the concept of the `Unknown Member` serves a similar purpose: to define a dimension member with an unspecified key. Every attribute has an unknown member, even though it might be inaccessible. Even an empty attribute has one member, the unknown member.

An unknown member has no specified key. It's possible that some other member of the attribute would have a key with the value `NULL`. Such an attribute would have both an unknown member and a member with a `NULL` key value. We talk more about unknown members in Chapter 7, "Measures and Multidimensional Analysis."

Data Specification

To define keys and other data in the multidimensional model, you can use the DDL object `DataItem`. `DataItem` defines the primary properties of multidimensional data such as key, name, and so on. Table 5.2 describes the properties of `DataItem`.

TABLE 5.2 Properties of **`DataItem`**

Name (DDL)	Description
`DataType`	Defines the data type of the item. Data types in multidimensional databases are a subset of the data types supported by relational databases. From version to version of Analysis Services, we've extended the set of data in the multidimensional model to such an extent that it is pretty close to the full set of relational data types. Nonetheless, some data types are still supported by the relational model, but not by the multidimensional model.
`MimeType`	Defines the logical type of binary data: a picture, sound track, video track, the output of an application such as an editor, and so forth.
`Data Size`	Defines size for text or binary data, in characters and bytes, respectively. If you don't specify a size, by default it will equal 255 characters for text data and 255 bytes for binary data.
`Data Format`	Defines the rules of transformation of data from numeric format into text, if such a transformation is required. Analysis Services uses the format types used in the `Format` function of Visual Basic.

TABLE 5.2 Properties of **DataItem**

Name (DDL)	Description
Collation	Defines the rules for comparing strings of text data. Collation determines whether two text values are equal or different from each other, and how they should be ordered. For example, Collation could specify whether to ignore case in determining if two strings of text are the same or different.
NullProcessing	Defines the rules for processing NULL data. NullProcessing can be set to one of five values: If you set it to Preserve, Analysis Services preserves the NULL value. Preserve takes additional resources to store and process NULL data. (We look at the question of the resources required for Preserve in more detail when we discuss the physical data model in Chapter 20, "The Physical Data Model.") If you set it to ZeroOrBlank, Analysis Services converts the NULL value to 0 if the data type is not a string, and to a blank if the data type is a string. If you set it to Unknown Member, the NULL value is associated with an unknown member. If you set it to Error, the NULL value is not allowed and the server will show an error message. If you set it to Automatic, the server will choose the best value, depending on the context.
Trimming	Defines the rules for deleting trailing spaces at the beginning and end of text. You can use Trimming to avoid the repetition of two strings of text that differ only by leading or trailing spaces.
InvalidXmlCharacters	Defines the rules of processing invalid XML characters. This property is useful if you think your users will receive data in XML format. In those cases, you can use InvalidXmlCharacters, with one of three possible values: Preserve, which doesn't change the character; Remove, which removes the characters from the text; or Replace, which replaces each invalid character with a question mark.

Listing 5.4 shows the DDL definition of a composite key, which uses DataItems.

LISTING 5.4 DDL Definition of a Composite Key

```
<KeyColumns>
    <KeyColumn>
        <DataType>WChar</DataType>
        <DataSize>50</DataSize>
        <Source>
```

```
                <TableID>dbo_customer</TableID>
                <ColumnID>city</ColumnID>
            </Source>
        </KeyColumn>
        <KeyColumn>
            <DataType>WChar</DataType>
            <DataSize>50</DataSize>
            <Source>
                <TableID>dbo_customer</TableID>
                <ColumnID>state_province</ColumnID>
            </Source>
        </KeyColumn>
    </KeyColumns>
```


Attribute Member Names

An attribute member's identifier is its name. The attribute member name is used pretty much where you want to reference a specific attribute member. The name of the attribute member can be either unique inside of the attribute or not. However, if the name is unique within an attribute, Analysis Services can support it more efficiently. You can use a property such as the `MemberNameUnique`. Otherwise, the property will come from the key. The `MemberNameUnique` property is uniqueness of the attribute members' names, Analysis Services uses the names of members to generate the member unique name; otherwise, it uses member keys.

We use the `DataItem` object to specify the attribute member name. Unlike the data type for the key, the data type for the member name can only be text or a format that can be converted to text.

When you define a member name, avoid using spaces and special characters; they complicate the use of member names. It's a good idea to avoid long names, too, because they take more resources to store and retrieve and can therefore decrease system performance. Storing the attribute member names can require gigabytes of disk space. Loading the names into memory can be the main cause of a slowdown.

`Collation` is important part of the member name specification. The collation of a name can change whether the name is unique or not. For example, suppose you have some name that uses capital letters whereas another, similar name uses lowercase letters (for instance, DeForge and Deforge). Depending on the `Collation` property value, the system might treat these similar names as either different or the same, resulting in confusion and unpredictable results for the user.

In addition, `Collation` affects the order the members will be sorted in. Sorting is an important aspect of how attribute members are used in the system. Defining the right ordering scheme is not always a simple task. For example, months in the year are usually not sorted by name; it's typical to sort months by the numbers that indicate their place in the year.

In a typical sort order, you can use the key to define the order of the attribute members. If the key is defined by the text names of the months, the typical sort order would begin with August, which wouldn't make sense in most cases. To solve this problem, you create another attribute, related to the original one that contains the numbers that indicate the order the months appear in the year. Then, you order by the key value of that related attribute.

The locale for the attribute member name defines the language of the member. When a certain locale is specified, the attribute member name itself is in the language of that locale. To specify that the name of the attribute member should be translated when it appears in other locales, use the `Translations` property.

Everything we've said about the member attribute name is also true for the `Translations` property, with one exception. Uniqueness of a translation is not defined in the model because the translation is not used to identify the member, but only for displaying the name of the member. When a user works on a client computer with a specific language, the `Language` property enables the server to use the right translation to create a `Member Caption` (used in the application model) in the language of the user.

Relationships Between Attributes

The `Relationship` between attributes in a dimension defines the possible associations that one attribute can have with another. `Relationship` affects all the functions of Analysis Services. It defines the properties of association that the current attribute has with other attributes, including whether an attribute can be accessed through the current attribute.

If one attribute can be accessed through another, that other attribute is treated as a member property of the current attribute. For example, `Age` and `Marital Status` are additional properties for our `Customer` attribute. Table 5.3 describes the properties of `Relationship` that can be used in the conceptual model.

TABLE 5.3 Properties of **`Relationship`**

Property	Description
`RelationshipType`	Defines the rules for modifying the key value of a member of related attribute. This property can be set to one of the two values: `Rigid`: The key value of the related attribute and current attribute are bound together and can't change without a full reprocessing of the dimension. In our example, `Gender` can be defined as a dependent attribute with a rigid relationship, because it won't change in the dimension.

TABLE 5.3 Properties of **Relationship**

Property	Description
	`Flexible`: The key of a dependent attribute, and therefore the whole member of the dependent attribute, can be changed at any time. In our example, the `Marital Status` property is a dependent attribute with a flexible relationship because it will periodically change (unfortunately).
`Cardinality`	Defines the nature of the relationship of the key of related attributes when those members are used as member properties.
	`One-to-One`: There is one (and only one) member of the current attribute that relates to each member of the related attribute. For example, if we were associating the names of months with the numbers that represent their order in the year, we would have a one-to-one relationship.
	`One-to-Many`: One of the members of the related attribute can be used as a property of various members from the current attribute. For example, member `Married` from attribute `Marital Status`, can be applied to many members of `Customer` attribute. One-to-many cardinality is much more frequently used than one-to-one.
`Optionality`	Defines the relationship of sets of members in the related attribute and in the current attribute. You can't set this property through the Dimension Editor; use DDL.
	`Mandatory`: For each member of the related attribute, there is at least one member of the current attribute that references that member. For example, each state has to have at least one city.
	`Optional`: For some of the members of the related attribute, there might not be any member of the current attribute that references that attribute. For example, there are cities that don't have any stores.
`Name and Translations`	When the related attribute is used as a member property of the current attribute, usually the name of the property of the current attribute is the same as the name of the related attribute. For example, when the `Gender` attribute is used as a property of the `Customer` attribute, we say that the `Customer` attribute has a property, `Gender`. However, if we want the property of the `Customer` attribute to be known as `Sex` rather than `Gender`, we define the name in the relationship as "Sex."
`Visibility`	Determines whether the related attribute is accessible to the user as a member property for the current attribute.
	`False`: The related attribute can't be used as a member property of the current attribute.
	`True`: The user can access the related attribute as a member property of the current attribute.

5

In Figure 5.3 you can see a diagram of the `Customer` dimension that shows the relationships of attributes and the properties of those relationships:

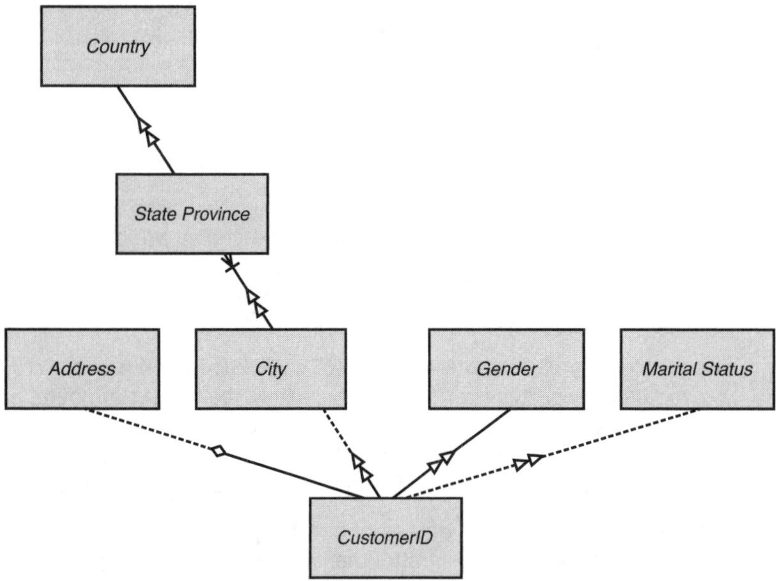

FIGURE 5.3 The `Customer` dimension has different attributes with different types of relationships.

- In terms of `Type`, you can see a `Rigid` relationship, indicated by a solid line, between `Customer ID` and `Gender`.
- A `Flexible` type is indicated by a dotted line. You can see a `Flexible` relationship between `Customer ID` and `Marital Status`.
- In terms of `Cardinality`, `One-to-Many` is indicated by a triangle in the middle of the relationship line. You have a one-to-many relationship for most attribute relationships.
- A `One-to-One` cardinality is indicated by a diamond in the middle of the line. There is only one example of a one-to-one relationship, that between the `Customer ID` and `Address` attributes. (That's true in our FoodMart 2008 database, although in reality you could have two customers who live at the same address.)
- A `Mandatory` relationship is indicated by a *V* sign and the end of a line. You can see a mandatory relationship between the `City` and `State Province` attributes.
- An `Optional` relationship (most of the relationships in Figure 5.3) is indicated by an absence of symbols.

Dimension Hierarchies

The hierarchy, which can be seen as a navigational path, is the primary means of access to the multidimensional model. It consists of attributes arranged in descending (or ascending, depending on the way you look at it) levels, with each level containing attribute members. Efficient use of hierarchies significantly increases the effectiveness of the multidimensional model from the point of view of both the client (the way the user can manipulate the data) and of the server (in making the necessary calculations).

The task of defining a hierarchy is simply to define the hierarchy object itself, and to specify the collection of all the levels and all their properties. Levels have two important properties:

- **`SourceAttributeID`**—Defines the source for the level members. In the level, you can see all the members from the source attribute, along with all their parameters and properties. After the `SourceAttributeID` has defined a member as belonging to a level, the member gains two characteristics:
    - A parent member is a member from the level above, which current member belongs to.
    - Children are members from the next level that belongs to the current member.
- **`HideMemberIf`**—Defines the rules for displaying members for the client application. Some members will be hidden so that not all the members of the source attribute will be apparent in the hierarchy. Use of this property significantly diminishes the effectiveness of the hierarchy and complicates the calculation algorithms. We recommend that you avoid using this parameter.

Types of Hierarchies

The definition of a hierarchy is typically very simple. However, hierarchies can differ from each other, depending on the type of attributes they contain and the relationships between them. Figure 5.4 shows an example of a simple geography-based hierarchy, based on the attributes of our `Customer` dimension.

Natural Hierarchies and Their Levels

In the `Customer` dimension, dependencies exists between attributes. Because country is a dependent attribute of the state, if you know the state, you can unambiguously determine what country it belongs to. The same is true for city and state. Because the state is a related attribute for the city, if you know the city you can unambiguously say what state it belongs to.

In this hierarchy, the presence of a key attribute changes nothing. The entire structure of the hierarchy is determined by the relationships between the attributes that are used as levels in the hierarchy. Such hierarchy is called a *natural hierarchy*. All levels of a natural hierarchy are built from related attributes, and the levels are located in correspondence with the direction of the relationships of attributes. As its name suggests, it is the most effective form of hierarchy. In Analysis Services 2000, this was the only possible type of hierarchy.

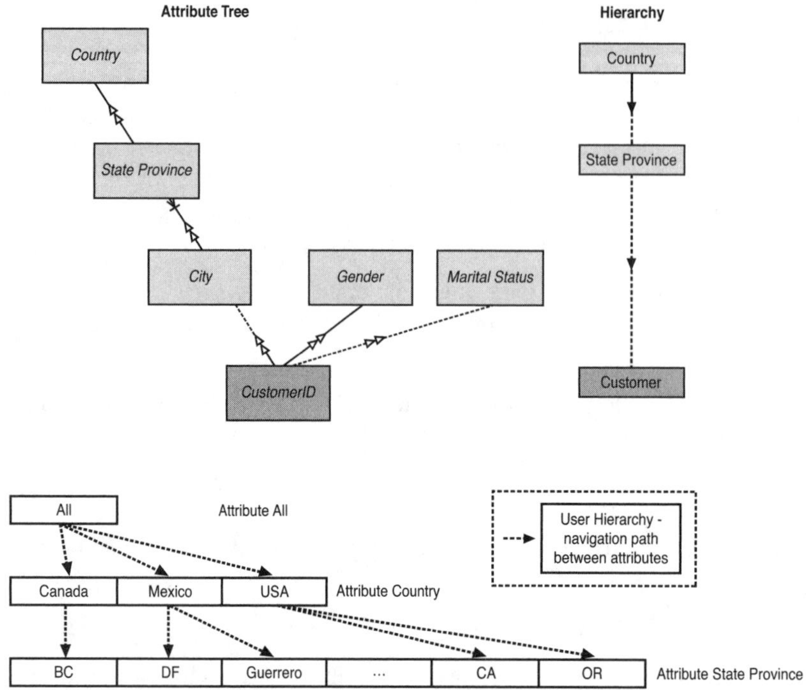

FIGURE 5.4 `Customer` dimension and `Geography` hierarchy.

Analysis Services 2005 introduced a new type of hierarchy, the *unnatural hierarchy*. We'll use an example that has two attributes, `Marital Status` and `Gender`, which are not related to each other. If you used an earlier version of Analysis Services to create a two-level hierarchy that includes these two attributes, you would have to perform a whole series of crafty manipulations with the data. With the current version of Analysis Services, it is just as easy to create this type of hierarchy as it was in earlier versions to create a natural hierarchy.

The unnatural hierarchy differs from the natural hierarchy in the way it defines which members belong to which parents. Whereas the natural hierarchy defines its parent/child relationships by the relationships between members, the unnatural hierarchy defines its parent/child relationships by the relationships of the members to the key attribute.

Let's look at the `Customers` dimension in terms of an unnatural hierarchy. We'll use the attributes `Marital Status` and `Gender`. The key attribute in the dimension is `Customer ID`. Let's say you have two groups of customers that are (1) male and married and (2) male and unmarried. Your hierarchy will contain a member "male" that has two children, "married" and "unmarried." If you add some female members, some married and some unmarried, your hierarchy will change. For unnatural hierarchies, depending on what the key attribute contains, the view of the hierarchy can change.

Another difference between the two types of hierarchies is that the unnatural hierarchy can support many-to-many relationships (as well as one to many) among the members from different levels of the hierarchy. The natural hierarchy, in contrast, can support only a one-to-many relationship. So, in the `Customer` dimension, with an unnatural hierarchy the attribute member with `Marital Status` "married" could have two parents, `Male` and `Female`, as could the attribute member "unmarried."

At first glance, natural and unnatural hierarchies appear to have the same look and same behavior. And they do—in many cases, they do look and behave the same. However, it's best to use natural hierarchy unless you really need an unnatural hierarchy. Because of the types of relationships between attributes, you could see a drop in performance.

NOTE

When you define a dimension, you need to be careful when you're defining relationships between attributes and building hierarchies based on them. You want to avoid unnatural hierarchies and to be careful that, in natural hierarchies, the direction of the level follows the relationships between attributes. Business Intelligence Development Studio 2008 warns you when you create an unnatural hierarchy.

Hierarchy Member Reference

When you use hierarchies in a client application, it's important to know how to reference the hierarchy members. The most general and reliable way is to reference a member through every level of the hierarchy by using the keys. Because each member key is unique within the parent, the full path of the keys is the unique identifier for each hierarchy member.

But using keys isn't always that easy. Sometimes it makes more sense to define a full path using the names of the members. This way is easier, but it doesn't always unambiguously identify a member if the member name isn't unique. Two different members with the same name and same parent would have same path.

Using the full path (either names or keys) to reference members is not always effective. Analysis Services provides the `Unique Name` property, which gives each member of the hierarchy a unique name generated by the system. This `Unique Name` should be considered an internal system identifier; we don't recommend that you to parse or generate unique names in your application.

NOTE

We strongly advise against any attempt to design or to reverse-engineer unique names and the way they are generated. The rules can change from version to version.

In a natural hierarchy, the key of the member is a unique identifier within the level of the hierarchy. In most cases, the system will attempt to use the member key as the member unique name. In an unnatural hierarchy, because it can support a many-to-many relationship, such a member could be used multiple times in the same level for different parents.

In an unnatural hierarchy, therefore, you would get a unique identifier with the combination of the parent's unique name and the key of current member. This is one more difference between natural and unnatural hierarchies, which is essential to understand when you use hierarchies in applications.

All Level and Key Level

An important characteristic of any hierarchy is the presence or absence of the `All` level and the `Key` level. The `All` level is a level that unites all the members of the hierarchy in one member at the top of the hierarchy. Omitting the `All` level can sometimes seem convenient (for example, it doesn't make sense to aggregate currencies), but might make it harder for the system to support the hierarchy. When the `All` level is omitted, the upper level of the hierarchy has a group of members rather than one member. In this case, understanding which member is the default one is not always easy. (For a detailed explanation about default members, see Chapter 10.)

The `Key` level is a level based on the key attribute of the dimension. Including it doesn't change the hierarchy, because internally every hierarchy contains a `Key` level, even though it might not be visible. If you do include the `Key` level in the hierarchy, the user can drill down to all elements of the `Key` level from the previous levels. If the key attribute is large, containing a large number of members, including the `Key` level can cause a burden on the system, and the drill down can even crash the user application.

An additional reason not to include the `Key` level is that the system needs to determine the order of the members in the hierarchy. If the operation to determine the order is performed over many members, it can require significant resources.

We recommend that you do include the `All` level in your hierarchy and do not include a very large `Key` level.

Attribute Hierarchies

If you didn't build a user-defined hierarchy, or when you need to reference a member outside the hierarchy, you can use an attribute hierarchy. Each attribute in the model has an attribute hierarchy. Attribute hierarchy is defined by two levels: the `ALL` level and the level that is based on the source attribute. The name of the attribute hierarchy is the same as the name of the source attribute. If you include an attribute hierarchy, you can reference any member of the attribute without creating user-defined hierarchies. You don't have a specific DDL object called an attribute hierarchy; the attribute properties include a property for the attribute hierarchy.

Attribute hierarchies can seem small. For example, in the hierarchy for the attribute `Gender`, we see only two members: both genders, male and female. However, in reality the hierarchy includes the `Key` level, which for the `Customer` dimension, for example, can contain an enormous number of members.

Building such hierarchies can consume a lot of resources, and if the user uses them, thinking that they're small, an operation can considerably decrease system performance. You can disable attribute hierarchies to avoid this problem, but then the attribute hierarchy would not be created at all. Alternatively, you can define the attribute hierarchy as unordered, in which case the members would not be sorted but would appear in the order defined by the system. Or you can define the attribute hierarchy as not optimized—it will be accessible for browsing, but the performance of browsing such attribute will still be suboptimal because the number of structures required for effective work will not be created.

The following list contains attribute properties that define the behavior of the attribute hierarchy:

- **`IsAggregatable`** determines whether it's possible to aggregate data associated to the attribute members. If data is aggregatable, the system will define an **`ALL`** level above the attribute level. We recommend that you avoid defining an attribute as not aggregatable because that creates a whole series of problems. For example, it's probably necessary to create the `Currency` attribute as nonaggregatable because it doesn't make sense to perform simultaneous operations in dollars and euros. On the other hand, to define the `Year` attribute in the `Time` dimension as not aggregatable isn't logical because it does make sense to use it to sum across all years, even if it is almost never used.
- **`AttributeHierarchyEnabled`** determines the presence or absence of an attribute hierarchy. By default, all attributes have an attribute hierarchy; you can use this property to disable the attribute hierarchy.
- **`AttributeHierarchyOrdered`** defines an attribute hierarchy as unordered. Using this property is helpful if the attribute hierarchy is enabled but not used often, and the order of members doesn't matter.
- **`AttributeHierarchyOptimizedState`** turns off optimization for the hierarchy. This property is useful if the attribute hierarchy is not used often and the user will accept a slowdown in requests that use the hierarchy. Turning off optimization saves resources when you build the hierarchy.
- **`AttributHierarchyVisible`** determines whether the attribute hierarchy is accessible through different discover queries. If you set this parameter so that the hierarchy is not visible, the client application will not be able to determine the presence of the hierarchy, although it will be able to use it.
- **`AttributeHierarchyDisplayFolder`** allows you to enable the application to group hierarchies in folders. You can use it to assign a name to the folder that the attribute hierarchy will be placed in.

When you're designing a cube, you must figure out in detail what attribute hierarchies are necessary, and in what state they're necessary. An excessive number of hierarchies can take up a significant amount of resources during the loading and storing of dimensions. It will create so many choices that the user can be confused.

To make your application effective and efficient, we recommend that you design user hierarchies, which provide the user with a convenient way to access members.

If the applications contain well-designed hierarchies, the system can perform more effectively. A lack of user hierarchies makes it difficult for the server to predict the methods of access to the members, in which case, the system doesn't attempt to optimize anything.

NOTE

If the priorities for the hierarchies aren't determined by the user, the hierarchy that appears first is given first priority in many systems' operations. You should order hierarchies in DDL by their importance and assign first position to the most important hierarchy, one that is used most frequently.

CHAPTER 6

Cubes and Multidimensional Analysis

IN THIS CHAPTER

- Cube Dimensions
- The Dimension Cube
- Perspectives

The main object you use in multidimensional analysis is the cube. As opposed to the geometric cube, our multidimensional cube (hypercube) can have any number of dimensions, and its dimensions aren't necessarily of equal size. It's not really a cube as we understood "cube" from our geometry classes, but we've borrowed the term for multidimensional analysis.

A cube defines a multidimensional space, the data available for analysis, the methods for calculating the data, and restrictions to data access. To define all this, a cube has two main collections: a collection of dimensions that defines the dimensions in our multidimensional space, and a collection of data values (measures) that reside along those dimensions and that we'll analyze. In Chapter 12, "Cube-Based MDX Calculations," we discuss the way cubes define the rules for calculating the values of the cube. In the chapters of Part 8, "Security," we examine the rules that govern access to the data in the cube.

The cube is a major object and accordingly has all the parameters that characterize the major object: `Identifier`, `Name`, `Description`, `Language`, `Collation`, `Annotation`, and a collection of `Translations`. The `Language` and `Collation` parameters of the cube define the language for all the elements that don't have those properties specified.

In the following list, we define the most important parameters of the conceptual model of the cube:

- **`Visible`** determines whether the cube is visible to the user or whether users accesses the cube's data through other objects.

- **Dimensions** defines the dimensionality of the cube, the most important characteristic of a cube. This collection includes all the dimensions except the **Measure** dimension. (We provide more information about the Measure dimension in Chapter 7, "Measures and Multidimensional Analysis.")
- **MeasureGroups** defines the measures in the cube that are accessible for analysis.
- **CubePermissions** defines access to data. (For more information about security architecture, see Chapter 35, "Security Model for Analysis Services.")
- **Perspectives** defines different views of the cube. The **Perspectives** collection enables you to limit the visibility to some elements of the cube and to simplify the model for the user.
- **MDXScripts** defines the methods for using the physical space (see Chapter 2, "Multidimensional Space") to calculate the theoretical space of the cube. The rules and language for building the script are covered in Chapter 12, "Cube-Based MDX Calculations."
- **KPIs** defines a list of objects that support key performance indicators that are available for the client application. We cover the KPIs in Chapter 15, "Key Performance Indicators, Actions, and the **DRILLTHROUGH** Statement."
- **Actions** is a list of objects that enable you to define the actions that must occur in an application when the user accesses specific cells of the cube. We cover actions in Chapter 15.

A cube has a large number of parameters that define the behavior of its elements during its life cycle or that define default parameters for various elements of the physical model. (For information about those parameters, see the chapters in Part 5, "Bringing Data into Analysis Services," and Part 6, "Analysis Server Architecture.")

In Listing 6.1, we show the definition of the Warehouse and Sales cube, without expanding the Dimensions collection and the Measures collection. This definition of the cube from the point of view of the conceptual data model is very simple.

LISTING 6.1 A Cube Definition

```
<Cube xmlns="http://schemas.microsoft.com/analysisservices/2003/engine">
  <ID>FoodMart2008</ID>
  <Name>Warehouse and Sales</Name>
  <Language>1033</Language>
  <Translations>
    <Translation>
      <Language>1049</Language>
      <Caption>Сеть Продуктовых Магазинов</Caption>
    </Translation>
  </Translations>
```

```
  <Dimensions />
  <MeasureGroups />
</Cube>
```

Cube Dimensions

The multidimensional space of a cube is defined by a list of its dimensions, which is a subset of the dimensions in the database. In Listing 6.2, you can see the definition of the `Dimensions` collection for our `Warehouse and Sales` cube.

LISTING 6.2 The **`Dimensions`** Collection for the Cube **`Warehouse and Sales`**

```
<Dimensions>
  <Dimension>
    <ID>Product</ID>
    <Name>Product</Name>
    <DimensionID>Product</DimensionID>
    <Attributes>
      <Attribute>
        <AttributeID>Product</AttributeID>
      </Attribute>
      <Attribute>
        <AttributeID>Brand Name</AttributeID>
      </Attribute>
      <Attribute>
        <AttributeID>SKU</AttributeID>
      </Attribute>
      <Attribute>
        <AttributeID>SRP</AttributeID>
      </Attribute>
      <Attribute>
        <AttributeID>Product Subcategory</AttributeID>
      </Attribute>
      <Attribute>
        <AttributeID>Product Category</AttributeID>
      </Attribute>
      <Attribute>
        <AttributeID>Product Department</AttributeID>
      </Attribute>
      <Attribute>
        <AttributeID>Product Family</AttributeID>
      </Attribute>
    </Attributes>
    <Hierarchies>
```

```
        <Hierarchy>
          <HierarchyID>Hierarchy</HierarchyID>
        </Hierarchy>
      </Hierarchies>
    </Dimension>
    <Dimension>
      <ID>Time</ID>
      <Name>Time</Name>
      <DimensionID>Time By Day</DimensionID>
      <Attributes>
        <Attribute>
          <AttributeID>Time By Day</AttributeID>
        </Attribute>
        <Attribute>
          <AttributeID>The Day</AttributeID>
        </Attribute>
        <Attribute>
          <AttributeID>The Month</AttributeID>
        </Attribute>
        <Attribute>
          <AttributeID>The Year</AttributeID>
        </Attribute>
        <Attribute>
          <AttributeID>Week Of Year</AttributeID>
        </Attribute>
        <Attribute>
          <AttributeID>Quarter</AttributeID>
        </Attribute>
      </Attributes>
      <Hierarchies>
        <Hierarchy>
          <HierarchyID>Hierarchy</HierarchyID>
        </Hierarchy>
        <Hierarchy>
          <HierarchyID>Hierarchy 1</HierarchyID>
        </Hierarchy>
      </Hierarchies>
    </Dimension>
  </Dimensions>
```

In most cases when you define a cube, it's enough to enumerate the database dimensions used in the cube, and you don't need to include any additional information. When you enumerate the database dimensions, all the database dimension objects (attributes and hierarchies) that were available at the time the cube was created are copied to the cube dimensions.

However, sometimes you need to make the availability of objects in the cube different from the availability of the objects in the database. To do this, you can define some parameters of dimension on the cube level. For example, you can hide an attribute by setting its parameters `Enable` or `Visible` to `true`. You can't expand the space. On the cube level, you can only reduce the space defined by the dimensions. It means you cannot enable an attribute or hierarchy in the cube, if it was disabled in a database.

Cube dimensions are minor objects and can be changed only with the cube itself. (You can't send a command that will change only a dimension of a cube; your command must change the whole cube.) In the following list, we define the most important parameters of the conceptual model of the cube dimension:

- **DimensionID** defines the database dimension on which the cube dimension is based. All the parameters of the cube dimension will be the same as those of the database dimension at the time they were included in the cube. If the name of database dimension changes later, that change won't affect the cube dimension.
- **ID** is the identifier of the cube dimension. This identifier can be used for reference by other elements of the cube. (You can find more information on this in Chapter 7.)
- **Name** is the name by which this dimension will be available to the cube user. In most cases, this name is the same as the name of the database dimension, but it can differ if necessary.
- The **Translations** collection defines the translation to different languages of the name of the dimension. If the name of the dimension is the same in the cube as it is in the database, you don't need the **Translations** collection. If you specify a `Translations` collection for the cube, any translation defined for the database dimension is no longer available.
- **HierarchyUniqueNameStyle** defines the rules for creating a unique name for the hierarchy. When the name of the hierarchy is unique across all the dimensions in the cube, you can use that hierarchy name without qualifying it with the dimension name. This makes it possible to use hierarchy-oriented applications that don't reference dimensions.
- **MemberUniqueNameStyle** defines the rules for creating unique names for the members of a hierarchy in a cube. This parameter enables the server to create member unique names according to the full path to the member. We don't recommend using this parameter because the server would have to use a relatively inefficient code path to create the unique names.

NOTE

It's best that you treat the unique name of a member as an internal name, and that you don't base any application that you might write on the rules of unique name generation. The unique name can change as the structure of the model changes, or during an update to another version of Analysis Services. The name can also change when some internal setting that controls the rules for defining unique names changes.

Therefore, we recommend that you avoid building your architecture based on what you know about the unique name structure, because it's internally controlled. Don't try to parse a unique name and don't store data based on the unique name of a member. Use the member key or the fully qualified path (by their names or keys) to the member in the hierarchy.

- The **`Attributes`** collection defines the list of attributes, with parameters, that differ from the attributes in the database dimension. If all the parameters are the same in the cube dimension as they are in the database dimension, this collection remains empty. If you can, avoid filling such a collection; otherwise, there may be some confusion as to why the same dimension behaves differently in different cubes from the same database.
- The **`Hierarchies`** collection defines the list of hierarchies whose parameters differ in the cube dimension from those in the database dimension. If all the parameters are the same in the cube dimension as they are in the database dimension, this collection remains empty. As with the **`Attributes`** collection, avoid filling such a collection, if possible; otherwise, there may be some confusion as to why the same dimension behaves differently in different cubes from the same database.

The collections of attributes and hierarchies of the cube dimension have a great effect on the data model. In addition, they can affect the performance of the system while it's filling the model with data and querying that data.

Cube Dimension Attributes

A cube dimension, by our specifications, contains references to database dimensions. When you create a cube, the database dimensions are copied to the cube along with all the information they contain. When the database dimensions are copied to the cube, the cube gets them as they are at that moment. If you change the dimensions later, those changes won't appear in the cube until you make any change to the cube.

Most of the time, that's all you need. Sometimes, however, there's more information in the database dimension properties than the cube needs. For example, the `Time` dimension often contains attributes for days and hours or for the days of the week. But, the current cube doesn't need those attributes. If we leave all these attributes in the dimension, they are visible to the user and will just make his work more difficult. In addition, supporting those attributes requires considerable system resources. When you define the cube, you can use the following parameters to exclude the attributes the cube doesn't need (or to reduce the resources spent on them):

- **AttributeID** references the ID of the attribute in the database dimension. You can't rename this attribute in the cube. Cube attributes don't have their own IDs or names in the cube; they inherit all the properties of the cube dimension attribute, including translations. However, you can define annotations on the cube attribute.
- **AttributeHierarchyEnable** enables you to turn off the attribute hierarchy in the cube, even if it's turned on in the dimension. When this property is turned off, the attribute is unavailable to the client application, just as if the attribute hierarchy were turned off in the database dimension. You can use this parameter to ensure that additional resources won't be spent to support this attribute in the cube. However, if the attribute is used in other hierarchies in the cube, you can't use this parameter to turn off the attribute hierarchy.
- **AttributeHierarchyVisible** enables you to make the hierarchy attribute invisible to the user. In contrast to the use of the **AttributeHierarchyEnable** parameter, with this parameter the hierarchy is still available to any user who knows how to access it. And the cube will require the same resources to support it as it would for a visible hierarchy.
- **AttributeHierarchyOptimizedState** enables you to turn off some of the resources spent supporting an attribute on the cube (such as turn off building aggregations and indexes for this attribute). From the standpoint of the cube model, nothing changes; but access to data through this attribute will take more time. We recommend that you turn off optimization for any attribute hierarchy that you've defined as invisible. If you turn off the attribute hierarchy rather than making it invisible and not optimized, the server spends fewer resources to support it.

Changing the parameters of attributes can make a big impact on the structure of the model and on the performance of the system. However, use those settings carefully because they change behavior from cube to cube.

Dimension attributes that don't participate in the data definition of the measure group (for a definition of measure groups and granularity, see Chapter 7) will be automatically turned off by the system. This means that the system doesn't have to spend resources to support them. For example, if the `Time` dimension has `Day` and `Hours` attributes, but the data in the cube is stored only by date, the system won't use the `Hours` attribute, and so it won't spend resources to support it. Therefore, you don't need to set the `AttributeHierarchyEnable` property yourself—the system will do this for you automatically.

Cube Dimension Hierarchies

A lot of what we said earlier about dimension attributes, particularly about attribute hierarchies, applies to all the other hierarchies of a cube dimension. The multidimensional model enables you to control the user's access to cube hierarchies and attribute hierarchies. In addition, you can similarly set parameters to limit the system resources spent on supporting cube hierarchies.

The following list describes the parameters of the cube hierarchy. (They're similar to those of attribute hierarchies.)

- **HierarchyID** is a reference to the ID of the dimension hierarchy. You can't rename hierarchies; they inherit properties from the database dimension, including translation. However, you can define annotations.
- **Enabled** enables you to turn on or off the dimension hierarchy in the cube. However, if it's turned off in the database, you can't turn it on in the cube. In addition, if one of the attributes in the cube hierarchy has the attribute hierarchy turned off, you can't turn this hierarchy on in the cube.
- **Visible** enables you to make the hierarchy invisible to users. However, users can access the hierarchy if they know how to call it.
- **OptimizedState** enables you to redefine optimization as it's defined for different attributes, thereby turning off some of the resources used to support the cube hierarchy. Nonetheless, if some other hierarchy optimizes this attribute, this attribute will be optimized.

Role-Playing Dimensions

In the multidimensional model, the same database dimension can play multiple roles. For example, the typical use of a `Time` dimension for a travel application is to store data for the time of arrival and departure. The `Time` dimension can be used twice. In one case, it's used to define departure time, and in another it's used to define arrival time. You can just rename the two `Time` dimensions to `Departure Time` and `Arrival Time`. We show you how to do just that in Listing 6.3.

LISTING 6.3 A Cube with Two **Time** Dimensions

```
<Cube xmlns="http://schemas.microsoft.com/analysisservices/2003/engine">
  <ID>Flight</ID>
  <Name>Flight</Name>
  <Annotations />
  <Language>1033</Language>
  <Translations />
  <Dimensions>
    <Dimension>
      <ID>Departure Time</ID>
      <Name>Departure Time</Name>
      <DimensionID>Time By Day</DimensionID>
    </Dimension>
    <Dimension>
      <ID>Arrival Time</ID>
      <Name>Arrival Time</Name>
      <DimensionID>Time By Day</DimensionID>
    </Dimension>
  </Dimensions>
  <MeasureGroups>
```

```
  </MeasureGroups>
</Cube>
```

You have to give these two versions of the `Time` dimension different IDs and names (`Departure Time` and `Arrival Time`) in the cube so that each is a completely independent dimension, with all the information it contains. Because of this independence, you can change any attribute in one of the dimensions and it won't change in the other.

NOTE

If you use a role-playing dimension in your cube, your hierarchy names are not unique across the cube. Therefore, if you reference an element of the dimension, you have to qualify the hierarchy name by the name of the dimension.

Hierarchy-based applications can't work with role-playing dimensions.

It's efficient to use role-playing dimensions because all the information for both of the dimensions is stored in the database only once. In addition, because each is a completely independent dimension in the cube, with independent management, you can optimize attributes in one differently than you do in the other. For example, you might optimize the `Arrival Time` dimension on the level of hours, and the `Departure Time` dimension on the level of days.

The Dimension Cube

Database dimensions are very important in the conceptual model. But the application model (MDX) recognizes only cube dimensions. In a client application, you can't access information in a database dimension if the dimension isn't included in a cube. Even if it's included in a cube, your application will have access to the data in the database dimension according to permissions specified in the cube.

To make it possible for a client application to gain access to all the information in the database, Analysis Services automatically creates a dimension cube when you create a database dimension. That cube contains only one dimension and no measures. You can use the dimension in the dimension cube to access information that's contained in the database dimension. Just use the same application that you use to gain access to information inside any of the other cubes.

The only difference is that the name of the dimension cube is the name of the dimension preceded by a dollar sign. For example, `$Customers` would be the name of the dimension cube for the `Customer` dimension. Security for the dimension cube is exactly the same as specified for the database dimension. The current version of Analysis Services allows only the database administrator access to the dimension cube.

Perspectives

Analysis Services introduces perspectives to simplify data models that can be used in applications. A cube can contain hundreds of hierarchies and tens of different measures, which are available for analysis by hierarchies. Analysis Services perspectives enable you to define a subset of the objects of the application's model into an independent model. The perspective acts like a window into one area of the cube, one that the application can handle.

A perspective is defined by a name (that you specify) and the objects (that you select) it inherits from a cube. Any object that you don't select are hidden. The objects that are available in the perspective are the following:

- Dimensions (hierarchies and attributes)
- Measure groups (measures)
- KPIs
- Calculated members
- Actions

Perspectives don't slow down the system and don't require additional resources. All their use does is create an additional layer of metadata, which specifies the part of the cube that is visible to the user. No real data is stored in the perspective; the data is retrieved from the original cube.

You use perspectives to control the scope of a cube exposed to users. To the user, a perspective looks like any other cube available for the application. With perspectives, you can reduce clutter and make it possible for different types of users to see different parts of the cube.

You can't use perspectives as a security tool to limit access to cube information. Even though the data the user sees is limited by the perspective, if he knows how, he can access any information in the cube.

A perspective is a major object and has all the properties of major objects: `ID`, `Name`, `Description`, `Translations`, and `Annotations`. A perspective doesn't have its own `Language` or `Collation` properties. It uses these properties of the cube.

To define a perspective, you specify five collections with names similar to the collections in a cube:

- **`Dimensions`** specifies the list of dimensions that are visible in the perspective.
- **`MeasureGroups`** specifies the list of measure groups that are visible in the perspective.
- **`Calculations`** specifies the list of calculations that are visible in the perspective.
- **`KPIs`** specifies the list of key performance indicators available through the perspective.
- **`Actions`** specifies the list of actions available through the perspective.

None of the elements of a collection is derived from the cube. You have to define all the collections when you create a perspective. If you don't define a collection for any type of element (say hierarchy), that element won't be visible in the perspective. If you don't specify an attribute in the perspective, that attribute isn't visible through the perspective.

Listing 6.4 shows a definition of a perspective for `Warehouse and Sales` cube, with only one dimension and one measure visible.

LISTING 6.4 A Perspective for a Cube

```
<Perspectives>
    <Perspective>
        <ID>Perspective</ID>
        <Name>Product Sales</Name>
        <Dimensions>
            <Dimension>
                <CubeDimensionID>Product</CubeDimensionID>
                <Attributes>
                    <Attribute>
                        <AttributeID>Product</AttributeID>
                    </Attribute>
                    <Attribute>
                        <AttributeID>Brand Name</AttributeID>
                    </Attribute>
                    <Attribute>
                        <AttributeID>SKU</AttributeID>
                    </Attribute>
                    <Attribute>
                        <AttributeID>SRP</AttributeID>
                    </Attribute>
                    <Attribute>
                        <AttributeID>Product Subcategory</AttributeID>
                    </Attribute>
                    <Attribute>
                        <AttributeID>Product Category</AttributeID>
                    </Attribute>
                    <Attribute>
                        <AttributeID>Product Department</AttributeID>
                    </Attribute>
                    <Attribute>
                        <AttributeID>Product Family</AttributeID>
                    </Attribute>
                </Attributes>
                <Hierarchies>
                    <Hierarchy>
```

```
                    <HierarchyID>Hierarchy</HierarchyID>
                </Hierarchy>
            </Hierarchies>
        /Dimension>
    </Dimensions>
    <MeasureGroups>
        <MeasureGroup>
            <MeasureGroupID>Sales Fact 1997</MeasureGroupID>
            <Measures>
                <Measure>
                    <MeasureID>Unit Sales</MeasureID>
                </Measure>
            </Measures>
        </MeasureGroup>
    </MeasureGroups>
</Perspective>
</Perspectives>
```

CHAPTER 7

Measures and Multidimensional Analysis

IN THIS CHAPTER

Measures are the values that you are going to analyze; they are united in the measure groups by their relationships to dimensions in the cube. Measures are ultimately the most important semantic part of the cube because they are based on the fact data (sometimes called *facts*) that you're going to analyze. They usually contain numeric metrics that describe the results of business activity. In our `Warehouse and Sales` cube, we have created `Store Sales`, `Unit Sold`, and `Store Sales` measures that enable the analysis of sales in different stores.

Measures define which data is available for analysis, and in what form and by what rules that data can be transformed. The *measure group* defines how the data is bound to the multidimensional space of the cube.

All the measures in a cube constitute the `Measures` dimension. The `Measures` dimension is the simplest dimension in the cube. It has only one attribute—`Measure`—whose members are measures. The `Measure` attribute is not aggregatable and doesn't have the `ALL` member. The `Measure` dimension has just one hierarchy. It exists in every cube and doesn't require definition other than the definitions of the measures.

Measures in a Multidimensional Cube

Measures define the following:

- How and what you will analyze in your model
- The resources that will be used for your analysis
- The precision of analysis that will be available
- The speed with which the data will be loaded into the model and retrieved from it

In Data Definition Language (DDL), a *measure* is a minor object of the model, defined by the major object, the measure group. (We discuss measure groups later in this chapter.) When you edit a measure, the specifications for the whole measure group are sent to Analysis Services.

Making sure that you have the right set of measures in the model and the correct definition for each one is very important for the performance of the system. Table 7.1 describes the measure properties available in the conceptual model.

TABLE 7.1 Measure Properties

Property	Description
`Name`	The name of the measure. The name of a measure should be unique not only in the measure group, but also in the cube. As you would for any other name in the system, avoid using very long strings because they make the system less convenient and slow it down.
`ID`	The unique identifier used to reference the measure. The `ID` defines the key of the measure and, as opposed to the `Name`, can't be changed when you edit the model.
`Description`	A description of the measure.
`Translations`	Defines the translations for the name of the measure and the corresponding member in the `Measure` dimension to languages different from the language of the cube.
`Visible`	Determines whether the measure is visible to the user of the application model. Turn off the `Visible` property when the measure is used only for internal computations.
`Source`	The data specification for the measure (see Chapter 5, "Dimensions in the Conceptual Model"). The `Source` property defines all the information needed for the correct loading of measure data into the model.

TABLE 7.1 Measure Properties

Property	Description
AggregateFunction	Determines how data is calculated for the multidimensional space from the data values of the fact space. The system supports four types of additive aggregations (Sum, Count, Min, and Max), nonadditive DistinctCount and None functions, and six types of semi-additive measures (FirstChild, LastChild, FirstNonEmpty, LastNonEmpty, AverageOfChildren, and ByAccount). (You can find information about semi-additive aggregations in Chapter 13, "Dimension-Based MDX Calculations.")
DataType	For the most part, the Source property defines the data specification for the measure. However, for the Count and DistinctCount aggregation types, you need more to your definition. When you count something in a measure, you need to know the data type for the count. This data type is likely to differ from the type of data used for the items counted. For example, if you're calculating the distinct count of a certain string, the count of strings would have an integer data type.
MeasureExpression	Defines the formula used to calculate the value of the measure, if this value is based on other measures. This formula can reference data from the same measure group or from a different measure group. We cover the MeasureExpression property in Chapter 8, "Advanced Modeling."
DisplayFolder	Determines in which folder the measure should be included when it appears in the user application.
FormatString	Defines the format for displaying the measure data to the end user.
BackColor	Defines the background color used in displaying the data.
ForeColor	Defines the foreground color used in displaying the data.
FontName	Defines the font used in displaying the data.
FontSize	Defines the size of the font used in displaying the data.
FontFlags	Defines characteristics of the fonts used to display the data.

In your applications, you can also apply rules for the data format. For example, you could specify that values of sales over 200 should appear in bold. The client application retrieves the data formatting information through cell properties. For more information about how to extract cell properties, see Chapter 11, "Advanced MDX." For more information about how to define custom formatting, see Chapter 12, "Cube-Based MDX Calculations," and Chapter 13, "Dimension-Based MDX Calculations."

Listing 7.1 shows the definition of a measure in XML. The default value for the `AggregateFunction` property is `SUM`. (It's the one that is most commonly used.) If you use a different aggregation than `SUM`, you must specify it; you don't need to specify `SUM`.

NOTE

Analysis Services has default values for all the measure properties.

LISTING 7.1 A Definition of the **Store Sales** Measure

```
<Measure>
    <ID>Store Sales</ID>
    <Name>Store Sales</Name>
    <Source>
        <DataType>Double</DataType>
        <Source xsi:type="ColumnBinding">
            <TableID>dbo_sales_fact_1997</TableID>
            <ColumnID>store_sales</ColumnID>
        </Source>
    </Source>
</Measure>
```

The `AggregateFunction` and `DataType` measure properties define the behavior of the measure. These two properties are related to each other, so it's a good idea to keep one property in mind when you define the other. Let's look at each aggregation and the data type for it.

SUM

For the `SUM` aggregation, the value of the measure is calculated by adding together the data on the various levels. For example, the sales in our sample model are defined by summing; to determine the sum of sales for this year, we sum the sales made during each quarter of the year.

Any integer data type works for `SUM`, but it's important to pay attention to the size of the data for this type so that you don't get overflow from the summing of large numbers. When you use float numbers, you don't usually get overflow, but performance can suffer and you can lose precision to the point that it affects the results of your analysis. For our `Store Sales` measure, the data type is `Currency`. The data maintains greater precision, and it won't overflow; the `Currency` data type can hold huge numbers, enough to hold the sum of sales in most models.

Avoid using Date/Time types with SUM because the results can be unexpected and hard to understand. You can't use the String data type with SUM aggregation.

MAX and MIN

The MAX and MIN aggregations calculate the minimum and maximum values, respectively, for the measure. For example, if you create the measure Min Units Sold with aggregation function MIN, to calculate its value for the month of December, Analysis Services will find the lowest Min Units Sold value of each day. These two types of aggregation can take the same data types that SUM does. What's different is that these two never lose precision and never overflow. Other data types, such as Date/Time, work better with MAX and MIN than with SUM. You can't add dates and times, but you can easily determine the minimum and maximum (that is, earliest and latest). When it's calculating the maximum or minimum of the values of a measure, the system ignores NULL values for the MAX and MIN aggregations.

You can't use the String data type with MAX and MIN aggregation.

COUNT

The COUNT aggregation calculates the number of records in which the measure value is not NULL. When it comes to the data type of the records you're counting, it doesn't really matter what that data type is. This aggregation function is merely counting the records (so long as they're not NULL). Therefore, 100 records of one data type are equivalent to 100 records of any other data type. When you define the Source property of a measure, it's best not to mess with the data type of the values; just leave it the same as the original data type in the relational table; it won't affect the aggregation result.

You can use the String data type for measure values with COUNT aggregation, unlike with SUM, MIN, and MAX aggregations. It won't cost any more resources because the system stores the number of records with no consideration for their values. When it comes to the data type of the count itself, the integer data types are preferred; choose one that minimizes the chance of overflow.

Our sample cube has a count of sales: Sales Count measure. It doesn't matter that the value of the measure has a Currency data type as defined in the relational database.

DISTINCT COUNT

The DISTINCT COUNT aggregation calculates the number of records with unique values within the measure. For example, you can define DISTINCT_CUSTOMER measure that calculates the number of unique customers your store has had. Consider the fact table shown in Figure 7.1. It has three columns Customer_ID, Product_ID, and Time_ID. The Product_ID and Time_ID columns are used to build Product and Time dimensions. The

Customer_ID column is used as a source of Distinct_Customer measure. To calculate value of this measure, Analysis Services scans over the Customer_ID column and counts the unique customer IDs. In our example, there are two unique customers: 1 and 2.

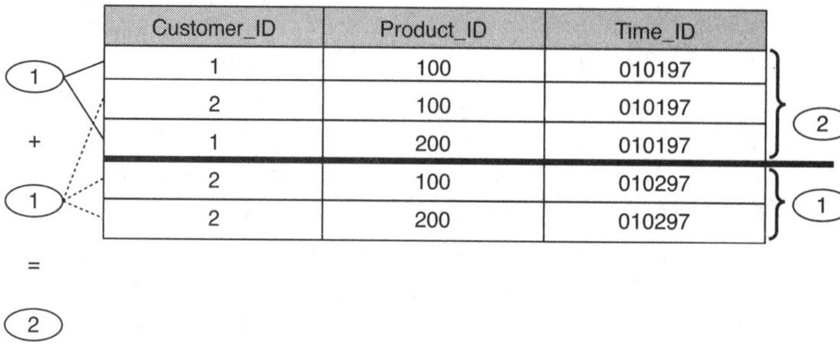

Customer_ID	Product_ID	Time_ID
1	100	010197
2	100	010197
1	200	010197
2	100	010297
2	200	010297

FIGURE 7.1 Fact table with column used to calculate a DISTINCT_COUNT measure.

One of the most important characteristics of the DISTINCT_COUNT measure is that you cannot calculate the value on the top level by summing values on the level below; the DISTINCT_COUNT measure is not aggregatable. In our example, our store has two unique customers, and therefore the value of the measure corresponding to the member full year of 1997 is 2. However, the value of the DISTINCT_CUSTOMER measure for January 1997 is also 2, and for February 1997 is 1 (see Figure 7.2).

	DISTINCT_CUSTOMER
1997	2
Jan 97	2
Feb 97	1

FIGURE 7.2 DISTINCT_CUSTOMER measure by Time dimension.

The value of a measure is stored in the format defined by the data specification in the Source property. The String data type is acceptable for this aggregation function, along with others we've discussed. The rules for comparing string data to determine whether a value is unique within the measure are defined by Collation in the data specification.

With DISTINCT_COUNT aggregation, your cost per record is greater than for other aggregation types because the system has to store the actual value for each record that has a unique value, including string values (which take 2 bytes per character and 6 bytes per string). This cost is multiplied by the number of records because the system has to keep the records for each unique value; that is, the system has not only to keep more in the record, but it also has to keep more records.

If the data specification dictates that NULL values be counted in the measure, the system reports all the records with NULL values as a distinct value. It takes a great deal of resources to store data for a DISTINCT COUNT aggregation, and many resources to access the data.

This can affect the performance of the system, as compared to other aggregation types such as `COUNT`. In a measure group, you can have only one measure with the aggregation function `DISTINCT COUNT`. If you have a measure with a `DISTINCT COUNT` aggregation in a measure group, we recommend that you avoid having a measure with any other aggregation function in the same measure group.

Measure Groups

Measure groups—in other words, fact data—define the fact space of the data in the cube. In many respects, they define the behavior of the physical data model. Facts lie on the border between the physical and conceptual models and define the following:

- What data will be loaded into the system
- How the data will be loaded
- How the data is bound to the conceptual model of the multidimensional cube

NOTE

Don't worry if you're wondering when we decided that measure groups are the same as facts. We introduced you to the term *measure group* first, but it is essentially the same as a fact. Different uses, however, require one term or another. DDL, for example, uses *measure group*.

Measures of the same granularity are united in one measure group (fact). That granularity defines the dimensionality of the fact space and the position of the fact in the attribute tree of each dimension.

Granularity is a characteristic of a measure group that defines its size, complexity, and binding to the cube. In our sample cube `Warehouse and Sales`, we have two facts: One contains data about sales, the other one about the warehouses. Each of these facts has a set of dimensions, which define how the measures of a fact are bound to the cube. The `Warehouse` measure group has `Product`, `Time`, `Store`, and `Warehouse` dimensions. The `Sales` measure group has `Product`, `Time`, `Store`, `Promotion`, and `Customer` dimensions, as shown in Figure 7.3. Each measure group can aggregate data starting from a different level. For example, you can choose to keep daily sales data, but weekly or monthly warehouse information. We go into greater detail about granularity in a later section, "Measure Group Dimensions." Having different measure groups within the same cube allows you to analyze data related to each measure group independently and data shared between the measure groups together in the same query. For example, you can request information about units of a product sold in a store and units ordered from warehouse for this store.

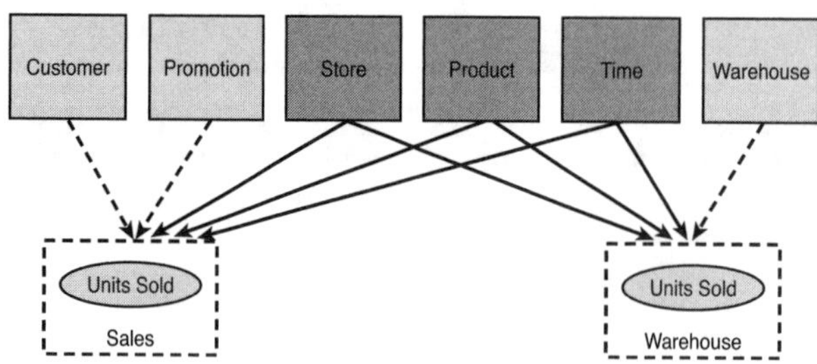

FIGURE 7.3 Cube with two measure groups

In DDL, a measure group (fact) is a major object and, therefore, is defined and edited independently of the other objects in the system. As any other major object, a measure group has `ID`, `Name`, `Description`, `Annotations`, and `Translations` properties. A measure group doesn't have its own language; it takes on the language property of the cube to which it belongs. In addition, a measure group contains time and date stamps that indicate when it was created and loaded with data.

Of the many properties of a measure group, some belong to the physical model: those that define what data is loaded into the cube and how it is stored there. We discuss those properties in Chapter 20, "Physical Data Model." Here, we go into detail about the properties that define the conceptual data model. Table 7.2 describes those properties.

TABLE 7.2 Measure Group Properties

Property	Description
`Type`	The type of measure group, such as `Exchange Rate` or `Inventory`. Analysis Services doesn't use the `Type` property internally, but the property can be passed to the client application for better visualization of the model.
`Measures`	A list of the measures that make up the fact. The fact must contain at least one measure.
`Dimensions`	The collection of dimensions that define the granularity and the binding of the fact to the multidimensional space of the cube. Each dimension can have a different relationship to the fact. We cover those relationships in more detail in Chapter 8.
`IgnoreUnrelatedDimensions`	Defines the behavior of the model when data is retrieved from the measure group by dimensions that are not used in the fact. In this case, there are two possible behaviors: Such dimensions are ignored and data is retrieved using other dimensions; or such dimensions are used, and the data is considered missing for such request.

TABLE 7.2 Measure Group Properties

Property	Description
`EstimatedRows`	On the boundary between the physical and conceptual models. The number of rows the creator of the model estimates that the fact will hold. Data is loaded into the fact by portions, called *partitions*. The number of rows that can be loaded into the fact is unlimited except by the physical limitations of the hardware and the volume of data accumulated by the user. However, if you know the number of the rows that exist in the fact, you can help the system make better decisions when it chooses internal data structures for data storage and algorithms for their processing.

Listing 7.2 is the definition of the measure group `Sales` for our `Warehouse and Sales` cube.

LISTING 7.2 Data Definition Language for a Measure Group

```
<MeasureGroup>
    <ID>Sales</ID>
    <Name>Sales</Name>
    <Measures>
        <Measure>
            <ID>Store Sales</ID>
            <Name>Store Sales</Name>
            <Source>
                <DataType>Double</DataType>
                <Source xsi:type="ColumnBinding">
                    <TableID>dbo_sales_fact_1997</TableID>
                    <ColumnID>store_sales</ColumnID>
                </Source>
            </Source>
        </Measure>
        <Measure>
            <ID>Sales Fact 1997 Count</ID>
            <Name>Sales Count</Name>
            <AggregateFunction>Count</AggregateFunction>
            <Source>
                <DataType>Integer</DataType>
                <DataSize>4</DataSize>
                <Source xsi:type="RowBinding">
                    <TableID>dbo_sales_fact_1997</TableID>
                </Source>
            </Source>
        </Measure>
```

```
    </Measures>
    <Dimensions />
    <Partitions />
</MeasureGroup>
```

This example is not a full example. Some properties are missing from the DDL, such as the definitions of dimensions (to be explained later) and partitions (part of the physical model). In addition, certain properties, such as AggregateFunction, have default values assigned when they are missing from the DDL.

Measure Group Dimensions

A *measure group dimension* is a list of the cube dimensions that belong to the fact (measure group). The data space (dimensionality) for a fact is a subset of data space of the cube, defined by the measure group dimensions (that are a subset of the cube dimensions). If the list of dimensions in the cube is the same as the list of those in the measure group, you could say that the measure group has the same dimensionality as the cube. In that case, all the dimensions in the cube define how the data is loaded into the measure group. However, most cubes have multiple measure groups, and each measure group has its own list of dimensions.

In our example, the Warehouse measure group contains only four cube dimensions: Product, Time, Store, and Warehouse. All the other cube dimensions are unrelated to the Warehouse measure group (or to the measures of the measure group). Unrelated dimensions don't define how the data is loaded into the fact. When users request data using an unrelated dimension in a query, Analysis Services based on the IgnoreUnrelatedDimensions measure group property either returns a NULL value or uses other measure group dimensions to resolve the request. For example, suppose a user requests the value of Units Ordered measure by specifying coordinates on the Time, Product, and Customer dimensions. Whereas Time and Product dimensions are related to the Warehouse measure group, the Customer dimension is not related.

A measure group dimension doesn't have its own name or ID. A measure group dimension is referenced by the ID of the cube dimension. The Annotations property is the only property that a measure group dimension has.

Granularity of a Fact

Each dimension of a measure group defines the rules for loading the fact data for that dimension into that measure group. By default, the system loads data according to the key attribute of the dimension. In our sample, the day defines the precision of the data for our Sales measure group. In this case, we would say that the Date attribute of the Time dimension is the one that defines the granularity (or the depth) of data for the fact.

The attributes that define granularity in each dimension of the measure group, taken together, make up a list called the *measure group granularity*. In our sample, the measure group granularity of the Warehouse measure group is a list that contains the Product,

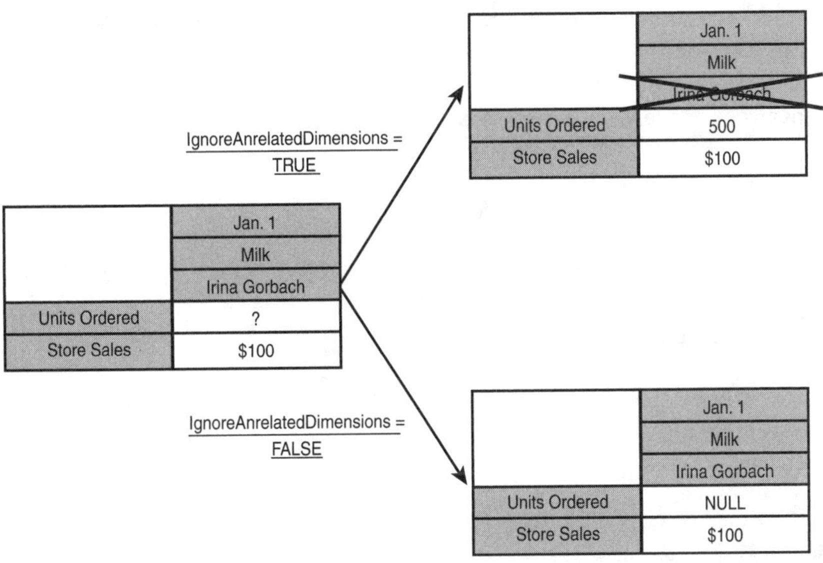

FIGURE 7.4 Using the `IgnoreUnrelatedDimensions` dimensions property.

`Date`, `Store`, and `Warehouse` attributes. The `Units Ordered` measure of the `Warehouse` measure group will be loaded by only those four attributes. Because the `Date` attribute is the granularity of the `Warehouse` measure group, you can't drill down to the hour when a product will arrive at a warehouse or at a store from a warehouse. You can drill down only to the day.

If the granularity of the measure group dimension is the key attribute, you don't have to specify anything else. If not, you have to define a list of attributes for the measure group dimension and to specify which of them is a granularity attribute; otherwise, you'll get an error.

To define a measure group dimension attribute, you specify the `ID` of that attribute in the `Database` dimension, its `Type` property, and its `Annotations` property. To mark an attribute as a granularity attribute, set its `Type` property to `Granularity`. It is theoretically possible to have several granularity attributes for each dimension, but the current version of the system allows only one granularity attribute for each dimension.

When you change a granularity attribute, the volume of data loaded into the measure group changes. In our sample, if we change the granularity attribute of the `Time` dimension from the `Date` attribute to the `Month` attribute, the fact data will be summarized by month. The volume will be 30 times smaller than it would be when using the `Date` attribute as the granularity attribute. After you've specified granularity by month, you can't go back and analyze the data by day.

Now that the `Month` attribute is the granularity attribute, the `Date` is unrelated to the fact, in the same way that a cube dimension that isn't included in a measure group is unrelated. Similar to an unrelated dimension, data won't exist in the measure group for unrelated attributes. If a user requests data by an unrelated dimension or unrelated attribute, the IgnoreUnrelatedDimensions property of the measure group defines the behavior. Listing 7.3 shows an XML definition of the dimensions of our Warehouse measure group.

LISTING 7.3 Dimensions of the **Warehouse** Measure Group

```
<Dimensions>
    <Dimension xsi:type="RegularMeasureGroupDimension">
        <CubeDimensionID>Customer</CubeDimensionID>
        <Attributes>
            <Attribute>
                <AttributeID>Customer</AttributeID>
            <KeyColumns />
                <Type>Granularity</Type>
            </Attribute>
        </Attributes>
    </Dimension>
    <Dimension xsi:type="RegularMeasureGroupDimension">
        <CubeDimensionID>Product</CubeDimensionID>
        <Attributes>
            <Attribute>
                <AttributeID>Product</AttributeID>
                <KeyColumns />
                <Type>Granularity</Type>
            </Attribute>
        </Attributes>
    </Dimension>
    <Dimension xsi:type="RegularMeasureGroupDimension">
        <CubeDimensionID>Store</CubeDimensionID>
        <Attributes>
           <Attribute>
                <AttributeID>Store</AttributeID>
                <KeyColumns />
                <Type>Granularity</Type>
            </Attribute>
        </Attributes>
    </Dimension>
    <Dimension xsi:type="RegularMeasureGroupDimension">
        <CubeDimensionID>Time</CubeDimensionID>
        <Attributes>
            <Attribute>
                <AttributeID>Time By Day</AttributeID>
                <KeyColumns />
                <Type>Granularity</Type>
            </Attribute>
        </Attributes>
```

```
    </Dimension>
</Dimensions>
```

Measure Group Dimension Attributes and Cube Dimension Hierarchies

Take a look at Figure 7.5. Suppose that you change the granularity attribute for the `Customer` dimension in our sample from the `Customer` attribute to the `City` attribute. You'll lose sales data not only for the `Customer` attribute, but also for the `Gender` attribute.

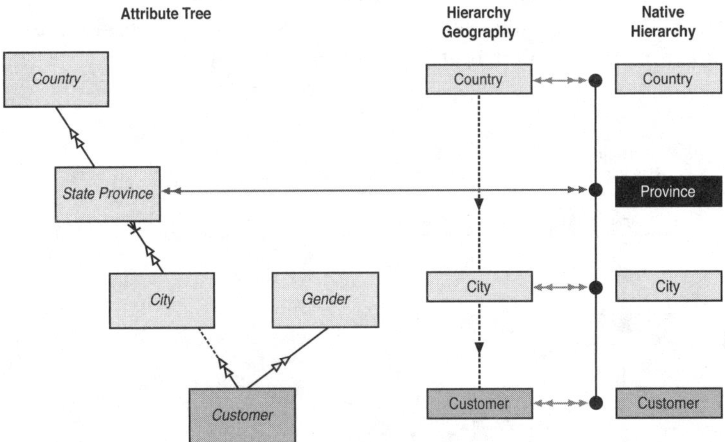

FIGURE 7.5 The key attribute `Customer` is used as the granularity attribute and in the user-defined hierarchy `Geography`.

When the granularity of a measure group changes, it's not easy to figure out which attributes are related and which are unrelated to the measure group. To make a decision, Analysis Services uses dimension hierarchies defined for a cube. By default, when the granularity attribute is the key attribute, any cube dimension hierarchy can be used to analyze measure group data. When an attribute other than the key attribute defines the granularity of a measure group for a dimension, only the hierarchies that pass through this attribute are available for analysis. For a precise definition of which hierarchies and attributes are available for analyzing measures of a measure group, we introduce a new term: native hierarchy. A *native hierarchy* is a foundation for every dimension hierarchy. It includes all the attributes that are included in the dimension hierarchy and any attributes that are part of the uninterrupted path, through attribute relationships, from the top attribute of a hierarchy to the key attribute. If there is no uninterrupted path, the hierarchy is an *unnatural* hierarchy. When it encounters an unnatural hierarchy, Analysis Services divides it into two or more native hierarchies. Analysis Services builds one native hierarchy for each user-defined hierarchy when it processes a database dimension. It uses native hierarchies to make a decision whether an attribute is related to a measure group.

In Figure 7.5, you can see an example of the native hierarchy for the hierarchy `Geography: Country–City–Customer`. The `Country–City–Customer` path doesn't include the `State/Province` attribute, but the native hierarchy includes the `State/Province` attribute to provide an uninterrupted path from the top attribute (`Country`) to the key attribute (`Customer`). Existence of the `State/Province` attribute in the native hierarchy makes the `State/Province` attribute related to the measure group. Therefore, even if you change the granularity attribute for the `Customer` dimension to the `State/Province`, users of the multidimensional model will be able to access the measure group data using the `Geography` hierarchy (`Country` and `State/Province` levels).

You can also have alternative paths from one attribute to the key attribute. Figure 7.6 shows an example of the hierarchy `Time: Year–Quarter–Date`, based on an attribute tree that has an alternative path from the `Date` attribute to the `Year` attribute.

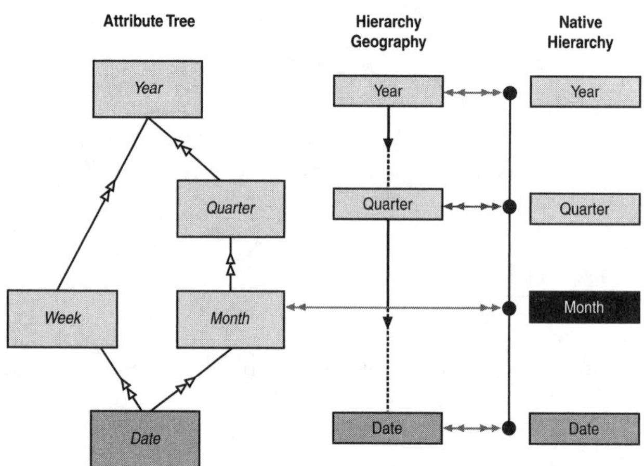

FIGURE 7.6 An alternative path from the `Year` attribute to the `Date` attribute.

The presence of alternative paths can cause ambiguity when Analysis Services builds a native hierarchy. Analysis Services chooses one of the two paths to build the natural hierarchy and can choose the undesired path. If your user-defined hierarchy is between the `Year` and `Date` attributes, Analysis Services can't distinguish between the two alternative paths. To build a native hierarchy, Analysis Services chooses the shortest uninterrupted path to the key attribute. So, to query data in the measure group, you can use only attributes from that path; other attributes will be treated as unrelated. For example, if Analysis Services chooses `Year–Week–Date` attributes for native hierarchy, you won't be able to use this hierarchy if the granularity attribute of the `Time` dimension is `Month` or `Quarter` attributes. This means that if you use `Year`, `Week`, or `Date` attributes in a query, they will be treated as unrelated attributes.

It's a best practice to avoid alternative paths in the attribute tree altogether. If you can't avoid alternative paths, at least avoid ambiguity by defining your hierarchy with attributes that fully define the path for the native hierarchy.

When you change the granularity attribute from one attribute to another, the hierarchies and attributes available for analysis can also change. Only the native hierarchies that pass through the new granularity attribute are available for analysis. On those hierarchies, only the attributes that are above the granularity attribute are related to the measures of the measure group.

Figure 7.7 shows fact data for sales in different countries. When you choose `State/Province` as the granularity attribute of the `Customer` dimension, the only hierarchy available for analysis is the `Geography` hierarchy from the previous example (shown in Figure 7.7; `Country–City–Customer`), and the only attribute that is related to the fact is `Country`, because it's the only attribute from this hierarchy that is above granularity attribute `State/Province`. For the `Time` dimension, the only hierarchy that is accessible in our fact is the `Time` hierarchy (`Year–Quarter–Date`), because we didn't create the hierarchy passing through the `Week` attribute.

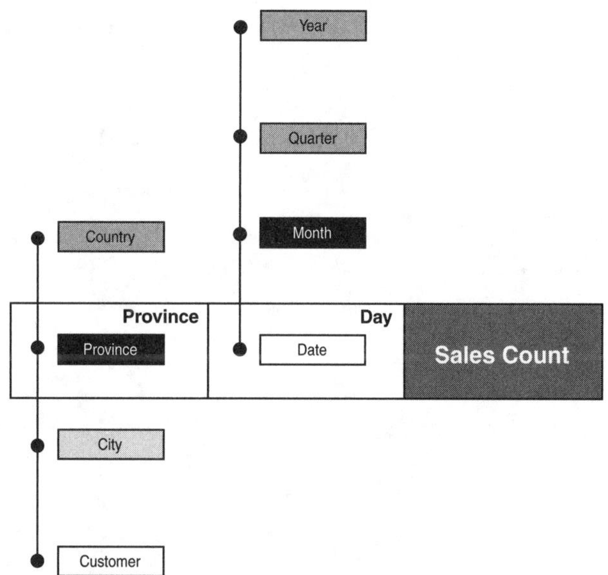

FIGURE 7.7 `Province` and `Date` as granularity attributes.

In Figure 7.7, the `State/Province` attribute is the granularity attribute, but not the key attribute, for the `Customer` dimension. Therefore, members of the `State/Province` attribute are leaf members of the `Customer` measure group dimension. It is into these leaf members that data is loaded. If the `Time` dimension is tied to the fact by the granularity attribute `Date`, even if the `Time` dimension has the `Minute` attribute, the data is loaded to the fact by days and not minutes. The members of the `Date` attribute are leaf members of the `Time` dimension in this case.

CHAPTER 8
Advanced Modeling

IN THIS CHAPTER

- Parent-Child Relationships
- Attribute Discretization
- Indirect Dimensions
- Measure Expressions
- Linked Measure Groups

In the previous chapters, we covered basic aspects of multidimensional modeling. In many cases, it would be enough to build a sophisticated multidimensional model. However, some business problems may require more complex solutions. In this chapter, we discuss advanced functionality of Analysis Services.

Parent-Child Relationships

Often in the data model, a dimension is defined not by multiple attributes and relationship between them but by parent-child relationship inside one attribute. Let's look at an `Employees` dimension as an example. It contains a list of all the employees in an organization. The hierarchy of the organization can be represented by levels of management, where employees of one level report to the employees of the other level. However, in the real-world organizations, structure is not that rigid—the office assistant can report to a vice president, same as the general manager, who has a few levels of reports. The structure of organization is often defined as parent-child, where each employee has a manager. Analysis Services provides parent-child relationship between attributes to enable this functionality.

To define parent-child relationship, you create two attributes: a key attribute that has a list of all the employees, and the parent attribute that contains an ID of the employee's manager, as shown in Figure 8.1. Thus, from relational prospective, the parent attribute provides a self join to the key attribute. For example, for the `Employees` dimension, we define an `Employee` attribute as the key attribute and a `Manager` attribute as parent attribute. The employee ID of the manager references the ID in the `Employee` attribute, because every manager is also an employee of an organization.

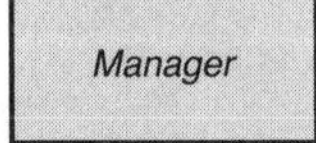

FIGURE 8.1 Parent-child relationship in the `Employees` dimension.

To define an attribute as a parent, use the `Usage` parameter of an attribute. After you create a parent attribute and start to process a dimension, Analysis Services analyzes the structure of relationships between members in key and parent attributes. It detects relationship and recognizes that some members have no parents. Others might have only one parent (ancestor) above them, some might have two ancestors, and so on. At this time, the system creates physical attributes corresponding to each level of the parent-child relationship. The key attribute is divided into a set of attributes, according to their relationships. Each attribute will contain only members that have the same types of relationships with its siblings—and have the same number of ancestors (see Figure 8.2). You can use the Naming template and the Naming Template Translation parameters of the parent attribute to give names to these real attributes.

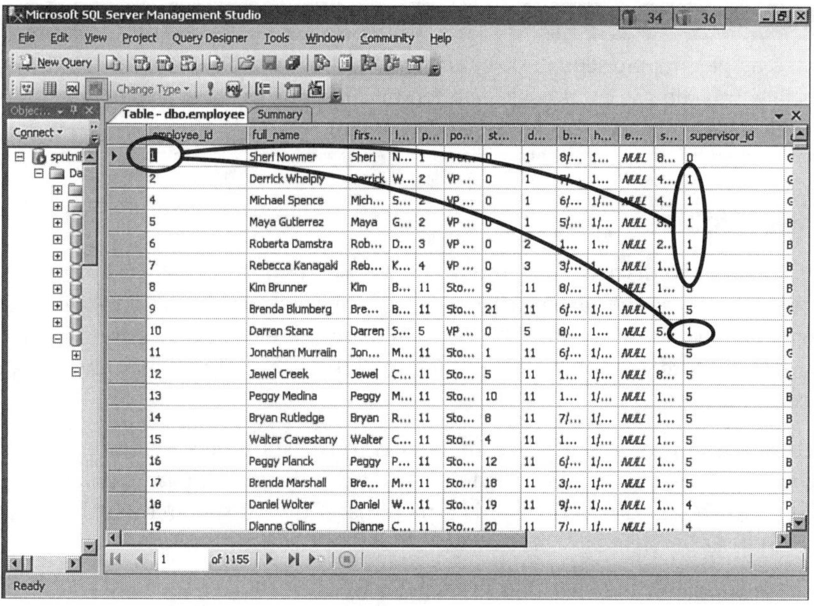

FIGURE 8.2 Levels in parent-child relationship.

The members that belong to each real attribute share some specific characteristic. One layer contains all the employees. The other contains only managers (who are also employees and therefore contained in the `Employee` attribute). Some members (for example, managers) have two roles. In the first role, the member represents an individual employee. In the second role, it represents a manager. In that second role, the member is the parent to some other members—those in the `Employee` attribute.

Analysis Services provides an additional intrinsic property to distinguish these roles: `DataMember`. You can use `DataMember` property in calculations when you need to associate a calculation with the employee role of a manager. For example, you use the `DataMember` property to calculate the full salary of the department, including the salary of the manager.

8

NOTE

Defining attributes as parents provides flexible functionality. However, be careful about using this capability; you can get into trouble with too much flexibility. For example, the number of levels in a hierarchy can change based on the data.

Parent-Child Hierarchies

The last hierarchy we want to discuss is the hierarchy whose definition is based on the `Parent` attribute. (For details about `Parent` attributes, see the section "Parent Attributes" in Chapter 5, "Dimensions in the Conceptual Model.") When you're creating a parent-child hierarchy, the parent attribute goes on top of the regular attribute that will play the role of the child of the parent attribute.

The parent and child attributes form a special hierarchy. In the simplest case, the parent-child hierarchy contains only two attributes: the parent attribute, and the key attribute, which acts as a child attribute. At this time, this type of parent-child hierarchy is the only one supported by Analysis Services.

Figure 8.3 shows an example of a parent-child hierarchy based on our sample `Employee` attribute in the `Employees` dimension. In the figure, we can see the hierarchy built on this attribute in both a diagram and an actual hierarchy from FoodMart.

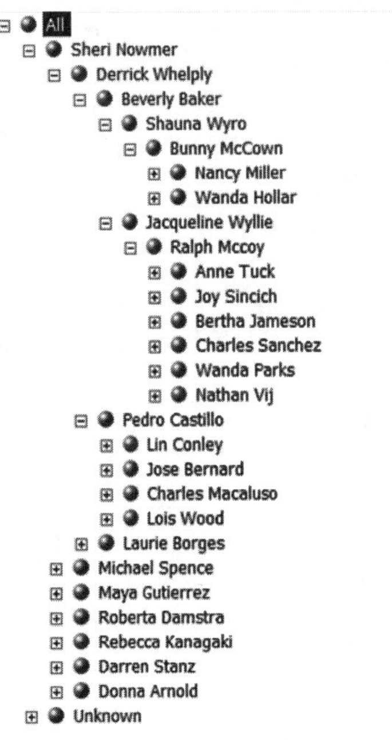

FIGURE 8.3 This hierarchy is based on the `Employees` attribute of the `Employee` dimension.

The definition of a parent-child hierarchy is based on the data that is loaded in the key attribute (as opposed to the typical hierarchy, which isn't dependent on data being present in an attribute).

The hierarchy is built on a collection of attributes within attributes. The key attribute will be divided internally into several attributes, which contain members from the various levels. The hierarchy includes one level for each nested attribute that contains data. If more data is introduced, the number of levels can change. The parent-child hierarchy can be seen as a single hierarchy whose structure is determined by the data that populates it.

There are a couple of important characteristics of the parent-child hierarchy: First, it's unbalanced; and second, it's flexible. It's independent of the parameters set for the relationships of the parent and child attributes.

Members of the key attribute for a parent-child hierarchy can be found on any level of the hierarchy. Data members, which are usually one level below the member for which they represent data, can also appear on any level of a parent-child hierarchy. Members on the lowest level of the hierarchy are the only ones that don't have data members (which would be below them, which would be impossible). Truly speaking, they are data members of themselves.

The parent-child hierarchy is unbalanced because you can't control which member has children and which doesn't, or what level the parent member will be on. To produce a balanced parent-child hierarchy, the user must carefully craft the relationships of the members so that members from the lowest level of the hierarchy are the only ones that don't have children.

In addition, members can change their positions in the hierarchy whenever you update the dimension. This capability makes the hierarchy flexible.

Parent-child hierarchies enable you to create a flexible data structure. However, to construct and maintain a parent-child hierarchy requires considerably more resources from the system. The complexity a parent-child hierarchy introduces into multidimensional cubes can greatly influence the effectiveness of the model and make it difficult for the user to understand the model. We recommend that you avoid using parent-child hierarchies except when they are absolutely necessary.

Attribute Discretization

When we speak of the values of an attribute, we can be talking about two different types. Discrete values are those that have clear boundaries between the values. For example, the `Gender` attribute is typically considered to have only discrete values (that is, male or female). For the majority of attributes, the possible values are naturally discrete.

Contiguous values are those for which no clear boundaries exist, where the values flow along a continuous line. For example, a worker's wage typically falls in a range of possible values. And, the more employees you have, the more possibilities exist in that range. Some sets of contiguous values can be of infinite or a very large number of possibilities. It can be difficult to work efficiently with such a wide range of values.

You can use discretization to make it easier to work with large numbers of possible values. Discretization is the process of creating a limited number of groups of attribute values that are clearly separated by boundaries. You use discretization to group contiguous values into sets of discrete values.

Analysis Services supports several variations of attribute discretization, based on algorithms of various complexity. They all do basically the same thing—group contiguous values into discrete ranges. The different methods specify different ways to group the values. We also support an additional, user-defined discretization method, not available in the Dimension Editor (use Data Definition Language [DDL]). With this method, you can define the groupings for the attribute values.

To have Analysis Services apply discretization to a contiguous attribute, you set two properties:

- `DiscretizationMethod` defines the specific method for discretization.
- `DiscretizationBucketCount` defines the number of groups the values will be placed in.

Analysis Services supports methods of discretization shown in Table 8.1.

TABLE 8.1 Methods of Discretization

Method	Description
`Cluster`	Uses the K-Means algorithm to finds ranges on the input values
`EqualArea`	Specifies that when the distribution of continuous values is plotted as a curve, the areas under the curve covered by each range are equal
`Threshold`	Specifies that when the distribution of continuous values is plotted as a curve, ranges are created based on the inflection points (where gradient changes direction) in their distribution curve
`Automatic`	Chooses the best grouping technique among `EqualArea`, `Cluster`, and `Threshold` methods
`UserDefined`	Specifies that the user can define a custom grouping of the members

Listing 8.1 shows an example of DDL that creates an attribute that will be grouped by customer IDs using a discretization algorithm.

LISTING 8.1 Defining a Discretization Method

```
<Attribute>
    <ID>Customer Id</ID>
    <Name>Customer Id Group</Name>
    <KeyColumns>
        <KeyColumn>
            <DataType>Integer</DataType>
            <Source xsi:type="ColumnBinding">
                <TableID>dbo_customer</TableID>
                <ColumnID>customer_id</ColumnID>
```

```
            </Source>
        </KeyColumn>
    </KeyColumns>
    <NameColumn>
        <DataType>WChar</DataType>
        <Source xsi:type="ColumnBinding">
            <TableID>dbo_customer</TableID>
            <ColumnID>customer_id</ColumnID>
        </Source>
    </NameColumn>
    <DiscretizationMethod>Automatic</DiscretizationMethod>
</Attribute>
```

For a user-defined method, you define the boundaries for every group that you specify. In this process, you have to define the binding of the attribute to the data source. (For more information about attribute bindings, see Chapter 18, "DSVs and Object Bindings.")

When you create attribute groups, it's helpful to give them names that are intuitive for users. Analysis Services has templates that can help generate names for the groups.

You can also use attribute discretization for attributes that are already discrete but that have a large number of values, such as the `CustomerID` attribute in the `Customer` dimension. You can use a discretization method to group these attribute members into groups that are more easily usable for analysis.

Indirect Dimensions

All the measure group dimensions we've discussed so far have been direct. Not only are they direct, they are also regular. Their granularity attributes directly define how data is loaded into the fact. (See the section "Granularity of Fact" in Chapter 7, "Measures and Multidimensional Analysis.")

8

However, Analysis Services supports two types of measure group dimensions:

- **Direct**, which are directly related to the fact
- **Indirect**, which are bound to the fact through other dimensions or measure groups

Indirect dimensions do not define how data is loaded into the fact. Whether you include an indirect dimension in the fact affects only the logical representation of data in the cube. Adding or removing an indirect dimension doesn't require reloading data in the fact. Because you don't have to reload the data into the fact, you can change the number of dimensions you use to analyze the data in the measure group without reloading that data. We have three types of indirect dimensions:

- Referenced dimensions
- Many-to-many dimensions
- Data-mining dimensions (not discussed in this book)

Referenced Dimensions

A dimension is a referenced one if its granularity attribute is in reality an attribute of another dimension. A common example might involve the `Customer` dimension in a measure group in which you need to analyze customer data according to the `Geography` dimension, which contains data about where customers live. Your measure group doesn't contain any geographic data, but the `Customer` dimension contains the ZIP Code of each customer. You can use the `ZIP Code` attribute to bind the customer data to the `Geography` dimension, as long as the `Geography` dimension contains a `ZIP Code` attribute as shown in Figure 8.4. In this case, the `Geography` dimension is a referenced dimension of the `Sales` measure group by the `Customer` dimension.

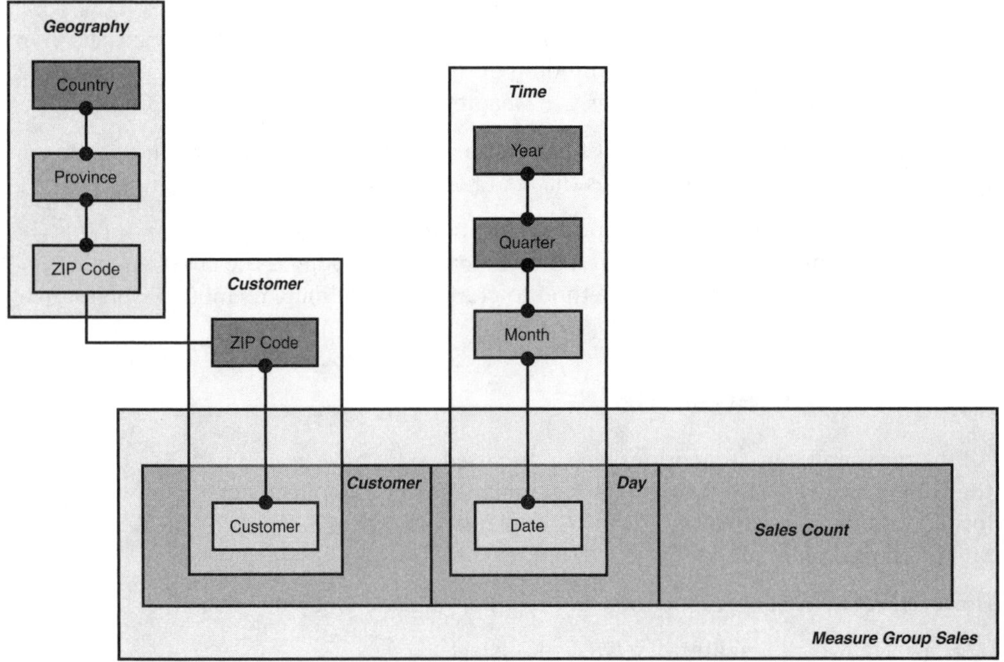

FIGURE 8.4 The `Geography` dimension is a referenced dimension to the `Sales` measure group by the `Customer` dimension.

The most important difference in the definition of a referenced dimension and a regular (direct) dimension is the addition of two properties:

- `IntermediateCubeDimensionID` defines the cube dimension that the referenced dimension can use to bind to the fact data (in our example, the `Customer` dimension).
- `IntermediateGranularityAttributeID` defines an `IntermediateCubeDimension` attribute you can use as a source of data for the granularity attribute (`ZIP Code`) in the intermediate dimension.

These two properties, which distinguish a referenced dimension, make it possible to bind the dimension to the fact even though the granularity attribute is not bound to the fact.

In addition to indirect dimensions that are referenced, there are also direct referenced dimensions. A referenced dimension is one that has a value of `Regular` for its `Materialization` property. In the model, therefore, the data from the intermediate granularity attribute is loaded into the fact, thus extending the fact data. Analysis Services materializes the granularity attribute of the referenced dimension during measure group processing. In our example, the data for the `ZIP Code` attribute is added to the fact, making the `Geography` dimension bound to the fact just like any regular dimension (see Figure 8.5).

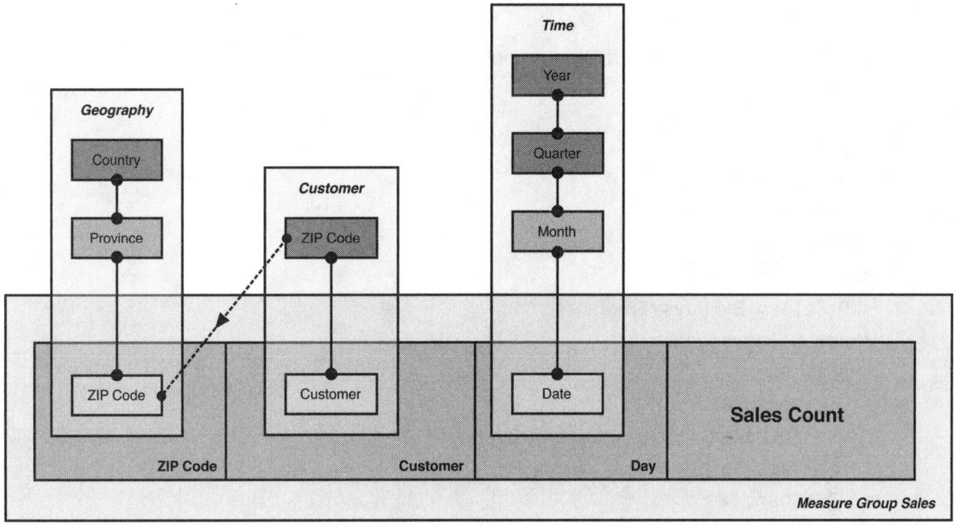

FIGURE 8.5 The `Geography` dimension is a materialized referenced dimension to the `Sales` measure group.

When the value of the `Materialization` property is `Indirect`, data for the `ZIP Code` attribute isn't loaded into the fact. Every time we need data about the geographical location of sales, the system searches the `Customer` dimension and maps the data in the `Geography` dimension to the value of the `ZIP Code` attribute of the `Customer` dimension. Now information about sales can be enriched by the information about country and province where the sale occurred.

In Listing 8.2, we define a referenced dimension from the `HR` cube in our FoodMart 2008 database. The `HR` cube contains data about employees and their salaries. This cube has a `Salary` measure group that contains information about the salaries of employees by time. However, we also want to find data about salaries paid to employees according to the store where they work.

To serve both these needs, the system uses the `Store` dimension as a referenced dimension. The `Employees` dimension has data for each employee describing the store each employee works in. Therefore, the `Employees` dimension serves as the intermediate dimension through which information about the salaries of the employees is bound to information about the stores in which they work. We can now see how much employee salaries cost the company per store.

NOTE

We excluded from our example the parts of the definition that aren't related to the point we're making in this section. For example, we omitted the definitions of the dimensions.

LISTING 8.2 Defining a Referenced Dimension

```
<Cube>
     <ID>HR</ID>
     <Name>HR</Name>
    <Dimensions />
    <MeasureGroups>
          <MeasureGroup>
          <ID>Salary By Day</ID>
          <Name>Salary</Name>
          <Measures>
               <Measure>
               <ID>Salary Paid - Salary By Day</ID>
               <Name>Salary Paid</Name>
               <Source>
                    <DataType>Double</DataType>
                    <Source xsi:type="ColumnBinding">
                    <TableID>salary_by_day</TableID>
                    <ColumnID>salary_paid</ColumnID>
                    </Source>
                </Source>
               </Measure>
          </Measures>
          <StorageMode>Molap</StorageMode>
          <ProcessingMode>Regular</ProcessingMode>
          <Dimensions>
               <Dimension xsi:type="RegularMeasureGroupDimension">
               <CubeDimensionID>Employees</CubeDimensionID>
               <Attributes>
                    <Attribute>
                    <AttributeID>Employee</AttributeID>
                    <KeyColumns>
                <KeyColumn>
```

```
                    <NullProcessing>UnknownMember</NullProcessing>
                         <DataType>Integer</DataType>
                         <Source xsi:type="ColumnBinding">
                              <TableID>salary_by_day</TableID
                              <ColumnID>employee_id</ColumnID>
                         </Source>
                         </KeyColumn>
                    </KeyColumns>
                    <Type>Granularity</Type>
                    </Attribute>
               </Attributes>
          </Dimension>
          <Dimension xsi:type="ReferenceMeasureGroupDimension">
               <CubeDimensionID>Store</CubeDimensionID>
               <Attributes>
                    <Attribute>
                    <AttributeID>Store</AttributeID>
                    <Type>Granularity</Type>
                    </Attribute>
               </Attributes>
     <IntermediateCubeDimensionID>Employees</IntermediateCubeDimensionID>
<IntermediateGranularityAttributeID>StoreId</IntermediateGranularityAttributeID>
               </Dimension>
               </Dimensions>
          </MeasureGroup>
     </MeasureGroups>
</Cube>
```

It's possible to get to a point where you have a chain of referenced dimensions, when a dimension that is bound to the fact through another dimension is itself a referenced dimension, and so on and on. However, you need to be careful about creating loops of referenced dimensions.

NOTE

The creation of chains of indirect referenced dimensions is not supported by Analysis Services.

Indirect referenced dimensions don't define how data is loaded into the fact, making it possible to change a dimension, or change whether the dimension is included in the measure group, without reloading the data. Members of the dimension are resolved at the time of the query, rather than upon loading the data. Even if you completely change the data of the dimension or change the structure of the dimension, the system won't have to reload the data. The system also doesn't index the measure group data by the indirect referenced dimension. Therefore, the performance of queries working with indirect referenced dimensions is worse than the performance of direct referenced or materialized dimensions. On the other hand, if the dimension data changes, it doesn't require a re-indexing of the fact.

Many-to-Many Dimensions

The ability to define many-to-many dimensions significantly enriches modeling capabilities of Analysis Services. Dimension of this type can be bound to fact through the other fact (thus enabling you to overcome a known limitation of multidimensional modeling that prevents assignment of the same data to multiple members of one dimension). Many-to-many dimensions in Analysis Services let you solve multiple business problems (for example, managing a single account with multiple co-owners, making a demographic analysis of sales data where a single customer can belong to multiple demographic groups, revenue allocation between multiple producers, and many others. Let's take a look at an example of a many-to-many dimension based on the FoodMart 2008 database. In this example, we want to analyze the sales of products to customers based on the warehouse availability of these products. In other words, we want to know how fast products currently stored in a certain warehouse are sold (and therefore might need to be requested from the supplier).

In Figure 8.6, we look at the sales of products to customers in our store over a period of time. We define a simple measure group `Sales` with the following dimensions:

- **The `Product` dimension**—Products sold in the store

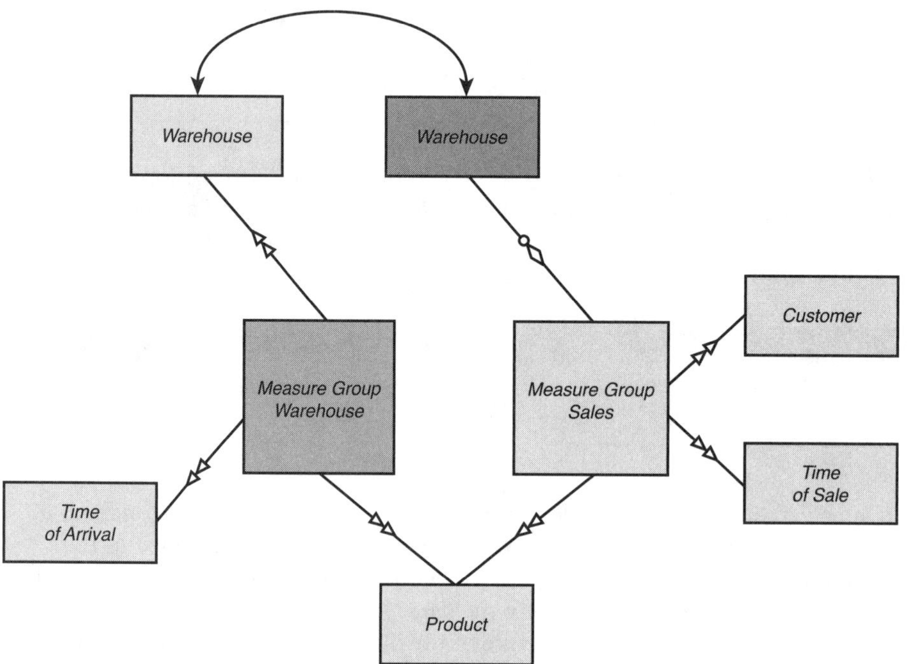

FIGURE 8.6 Relationship between `Warehouse` and `Sales` facts by the `Product` dimension.

- **The `Customer` dimension**—Customers who bought a product
- **The `Time` dimension**—Date of the purchase

The measures available for analysis describe the count of the units of the product bought by customers and the amount paid for the products. This model makes it possible to produce an analysis of the products bought by our customers and a count of those products, and we can analyze all of that based on the date of that purchase. Now, let's assume that we have another fact, `Warehouse`, that contains information about products in the warehouses from which the store gets its products. Therefore, the `Warehouse` fact will also have three dimensions:

- **The `Product` dimension**—Products in the warehouses
- **The `Warehouse` dimension**—Warehouse that contains the products
- **The `Time` dimension**—Date the products arrived at the warehouse

The measure of this fact contains the count of a specific product that was delivered to the warehouse at a specific time.

Because our task is to analyze sales of products by the `Warehouse` dimension, we need to include this dimension in the `Sales` measure group. We can do so by using a many-to-many dimension. All we have to do is define the cube dimension (`Warehouse`) that we want to include in the measure group (`Sales`) as a many-to-many dimension, and then to specify the `Warehouse` measure group through which the `Warehouse` dimension joins with `Sales` data. We call such a measure group an intermediate fact. The intermediate fact, `Warehouse`, is specified by the `MeasureGroupID` property of the dimension definition (see Listing 8.3).

LISTING 8.3 DDL for the **`Warehouse`** Dimension Included in the **`Sales`** Fact as a Many-to-Many Dimension

```
<Dimension xsi:type="ManyToManyMeasureGroupDimension">
    <CubeDimensionID>Warehouse</CubeDimensionID>
    <MeasureGroupID>Warehouse</MeasureGroupID>
</Dimension>
```

Defining the many-to-many dimension is easy; finding out what happens in the system then is not so easy. Let's explore what happens. First, Analysis Services determines a common dimension for both the `Sales` and `Warehouse` facts. Through this dimension, Analysis Services will join two facts together. Analysis Services determines common dimensions by looking for measure group dimensions that have the same value for the `CubeDimensionID` property, and that aren't many-to-many dimensions. In the scenario we're working with, we have two common dimensions: `Product` and `Time`. The `Product` dimension defines this joint between the `Sales` fact and the `Warehouse` fact. However, we don't want to use the `Time` dimension as a common dimension because the time of the purchase and the time of the product's arrival at the warehouse are not related. Therefore, we have to use a role-playing dimension to define two different cube dimensions: `Time of`

Sale and Time of Arrival. Now we have two different dimensions, one to use in each of the facts.

As it turns out, the Product dimension is common to both facts. The Time and Customer dimensions are regular dimensions of the Sales measure group. The Warehouse dimension is a regular dimension of the Warehouse measure group and a many-to-many dimension for the Sales measure group. The dimension that's included as a many-to-many dimension should be present in the intermediate fact (the one the relationship is defined through). The common dimensions have to be either regular or referenced dimensions. Many-to-many dimensions can create complex chains, with facts being related to one fact through many other facts. Analysis Services determines whether there are loops in chains, and lets you know about it by generating an error message.

When you define relationships between measure groups that are defined by a many-to-many dimension, you can end up with common dimensions that have different granularity for different measure groups. If this happens, Analysis Services uses the deepest common granularity for the relationships between the measure groups.

Now let's take a look how Analysis Services generates a response to the query that involves many-to-many dimension. For example, we introduce a question to determine the value of the sales of products delivered by a warehouse. If we ask for the total sales supplied by just one warehouse, Analysis Services iterates the sales by product, selects only records with the products the particular warehouse supplied, and sums the sales of those products.

If you were to ask for the sum of sales for each warehouse, Analysis Services would go through the same process for each warehouse. If you were to then add the sums of the warehouse sales to get the total sales of all warehouses, you would get a strange result. The sum of sales by warehouses will be larger than sales by the stores. Results differ because data from some records is included in the sum multiple times. For example, multiple warehouses can supply the same product, and sales of that product will be applied to sales of all the warehouses. Therefore, the summing (aggregating) of a measure using a many-to-many dimension doesn't follow the rules of aggregation—that is, it's not aggregatable, and not additive.

It's not always easy to interpret the results of a query that uses many-to-many dimensions; in many cases, you can get quite unexpected results. If you look at the result of sales in our FoodMart example by the Warehouse dimension, the results don't make sense. That's because we built only one Time dimension in to the sample. You actually need two Time dimensions for products in relation to warehouses: the time the product arrives at the warehouse, and the time it was sold in a store. If you have only one Time dimension, that dimension is common and is applied to only the sales of products on the day those products arrived at the warehouse. That sales figure would be much less than expected; the data is unusable.

Using many-to-many dimensions for queries requires more system resources, especially when you have many common dimensions and their granularity is at a low level. Resolution of a query under these conditions requires that Analysis Services get all the records of the measure group at a granularity level common to all the common dimensions—and doing so can really eat up your system resources. For more information about query resolution involving many-to-many dimensions, see Chapter 30, "Architecture of Query Execution—Retrieving Data from Storage."

The performance of queries that use many-to-many dimensions is worse than the performance of queries that use regular dimensions. Even if you have not explicitly used a many-to-many dimension in your query, Analysis Services uses the default member from this dimension. (For more information about the default members, see Chapter 5, "Dimensions in the Conceptual Model," and Chapter 10, "MDX Concepts.") There is a way to query a measure group that has a many-to-many dimension without performance degradation: by defining the direct slice for your many-to-many dimension. We explain the concept of the direct slice in the next section, "Measure Expressions."

When it comes to loading data into a measure group and indexing it, many-to-many dimensions work pretty much the same way that indirect referenced dimensions work: The data in the measure group isn't loaded by the dimension, and the measure group isn't indexed by the dimension. Indeed, a many-to-many dimension is an indirect dimension. When an indirect dimension is changed, or added to, or removed from a measure group, the measure group doesn't require reloading and re-indexing. There is no need to reload and re-index your measure group if there is a change in the intermediate measure group that binds the dimension to your measure group.

Measure Expressions

A measure expression is a definition of an arithmetic operation that calculates value of a measure using values of two other measures. Analysis Services allows only two operations between measures: multiplication and division.

The measure expression is a functionality that enables you to provide an effective solution for a small but very common set of problems. For example, corporations that sell in more than one country record sales in the currency of the country where the sale is made. Because the `Sales` fact contains sales in different currencies, it is almost impossible to analyze the sales of the corporation across countries. To solve this problem, you use a measure group that contains the daily conversion rates between currencies. You need to get all the sales into one currency, so choose one currency—exchange currency (sometimes also called pivot currency)—and multiply sales by the conversion rates of your chosen currency. Figure 8.7 shows a diagram of this type of analysis.

In our FoodMart example, you want the `Sales` measure group to save the type of the currency for each sale. The dimension that defines the currency in which the transaction was reported is `Transaction Currency`. The `Transaction Currency` is a role-playing dimension for the `Currency` database dimension. The `Exchange Rate` measure group contains a daily exchange rate between the members of the `Transaction Currency` dimension and members of the `Exchange Currency` dimension, which is a role-playing dimension for the `Currency` database dimension.

The `Exchange Currency` dimension is also included as a many-to-many dimension in the `Sales` measure group. This makes it possible to choose the currency in which you want to see sales analyzed. With this model, all you have to do to get your sales in any currency is

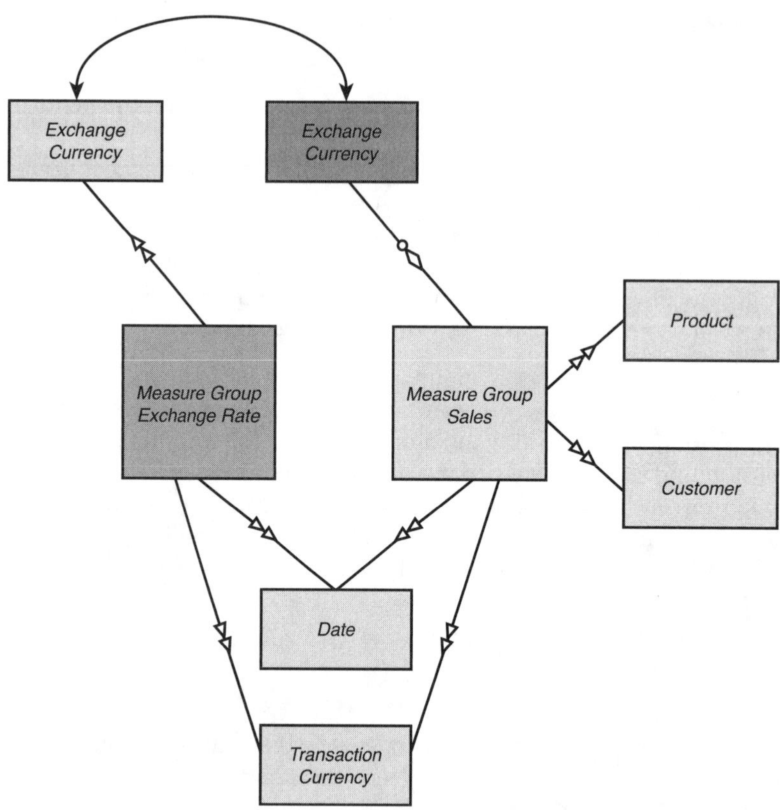

FIGURE 8.7 You can use a measure expression to convert currencies.

define a measure expression for the `Store Sales` measure: the multiplication of the sales from the `Sales` measure group by the exchange rate of the `Exchange Rate` measure group. Listing 8.4 shows the DDL that defines this measure expression.

LISTING 8.4 DDL for Measure Expression

```
<Measure>
    <ID>Sales</ID>
    <Name>Sales</Name>
    <Source>
        <DataType>Double</DataType>
        <Source xsi:type="ColumnBinding">
            <TableID>dbo_sales_fact_1997</TableID>
            <ColumnID>store_sales</ColumnID>
        </Source>
    </Source>
    <MeasureExpression>[Sales]*[Rate]</MeasureExpression>
</Measure>
```

The measures involved in a measure expression can be from one measure group or from several different measure groups. The model uses the same process to resolve a join of two measures as it uses for many-to-many dimension. Here is the process that Analysis Services follows to resolve the join:

1. Creates a list of dimensions that are common to the two measure groups
2. Identifies the deepest common granularity
3. Retrieves the value of the measure
4. Executes the measure expression operation for every record with the common granularity

Everything you read about many-to-many dimensions in the "Many-to-Many Dimensions" section earlier in this chapter is also true for measure expressions that are defined by measures from different facts, with one exception: Executing the operations for a measure expression requires more resources.

You've been using measure expressions to analyze sales in some currency other than dollars: To see the results in a specific currency, you choose the corresponding `Currency` member from the `Currency Exchange` dimension. If, on the other hand, you need to analyze only U.S. sales, you're not interested in an analysis in any other currency; the transaction data is already in U.S. dollars. The process that Analysis Services goes through is to convert the data from dollars to dollars by first multiplying all the records with common granularity by the value 1.0, and then summing the results. Using a measure expression in this case lowers performance without giving any benefits in return.

A better approach to this analysis is to add a direct slice for the `Currency Exchange` dimension. To do this, in addition to regular list of currencies, such as euros, rubles, or dollars, add an artificial member called `SalesCurrency` to the `Currency Exchange` dimension. For this member, define the exchange rate as equal to 1.0, regardless of the `Transaction Currency`. In practice, introducing this new member means that you can analyze sales in the same currency in which they were made.

Now you can set the `DirectSlice` property for the `Currency Exchange` dimension to the member `SalesCurrency`. When a request is made for `SalesCurrency` data from the `Sales` measure group, the data can be used directly without using a measure group expression, and Analysis Services will not apply the join between two measure groups. You can use the `SalesCurrency` member of the `Currency Exchange` dimension to get your results in dollars for U.S. transactions, which results in better performance than you will get if you use a measure expression alone.

Linked Measure Groups

Use a linked measure group when you want to include a measure group from another cube in your cube. That other cube can be in the same database, another database, or even on another computer. (We discuss linked measure groups in detail in Chapter 25, "Building Scalable Analysis Services Applications," where we cover methods of storing data in the physical data model.)

Using a linked measure group to include data from other cubes enables you to widen the information available in a cube. From the standpoint of the model, you don't get any additional capabilities from a linked measure group than you get from a regular measure group. You just simplify access to the data that already exists in the model without the repetition of loading it from the various data sources.

Linked measure groups are similar to virtual cubes in Analysis Services 2000, but they enable a new capability: to change the dimensionality of the measure group by including indirect dimensions in the measure group (that is, many-to-many dimensions, referenced dimensions, and data-mining dimensions).

Linked measure groups give new ways of defining different data models based on the models of other cubes. Because of this, the linked measure group is an important element of both the physical model and the conceptual model.

CHAPTER 9

Multidimensional Models and Business Intelligence Development Studio

IN THIS CHAPTER

- Creating a Data Source
- Designing a Data Source View
- Designing a Dimension
- Designing a Cube
- Configuring and Deploying a Project So That You Can Browse the Cube

Analysis Services includes SQL Server Business Intelligence Development Studio (BI Dev Studio), which provides a user interface for developing multidimensional models. We are going to use it to work through an example from our sample database FoodMart 2008 to show you the structure of the model and the objects it contains. Along with the walkthrough, we show you how to use the BI Dev Studio wizards to create new objects for your model.

You can find the FoodMart 2008 sample database on the Internet at http://www.samspublishing.com and http://www.e-tservice.com/downloads.html. Those of you who are familiar with Analysis Services 2000 know about the FoodMart 2000 sample database. FoodMart 2008 is to some degree based on the earlier database, but it has been changed to take advantage of the flexibility and power of Analysis Services 2008.

Here's what we will do with BI Dev Studio and FoodMart 2008 in this chapter:

- Create a data source
- Create a data source view
- Create a dimension
- Modify your dimension
- Create your cube
- Modify your cube
- Build cube perspectives

- Define translations for your cube
- Deploy your cube

To start your hands-on exploration of building a multidimensional model with BI Dev Studio, you will open a sample project. Download the new FoodMart 2008 sample database at http://www.e-tservice.com/downloads.html and restore it into one of the folders on your computer. Then, navigate to that folder.

Creating a Data Source

The first task of creating your multidimensional model is to create a data source. The data source is an object that defines the way that Analysis Services connects to the relational database or other sources.

Creating a New Data Source

You will use the Data Source Wizard to create your data source object. First, you will choose a data connection. If you are following along with the FoodMart 2008 sample project, you can use the data connection that appears by default. Or you can define a new data connection.

Launching the Data Source Wizard

1. Right-click the Data Sources node in the Solution Explorer of BI Dev Studio and select New Data Source from the menu that appears.
2. The Data Source Wizard appears; it goes without saying that you can skip the Welcome page.
3. On the Select How to Define the Connection page, you can select an existing connection under Data Connections.

To define a new connection instead of using an existing one, click New on the Select How to Define the Connection page of the wizard. Doing so lands you in the Connection Manager, where you will define that new connection. (There really isn't much defining going on if you are using an existing connection.)

NOTE

We cannot give you details about what to do in the Connection Manager, because the user interface looks different depending on the type of data source you are connecting to.

When you are done with the Connection Manager, you will find yourself back in the Data Source Wizard, on the same page you were on before you were whisked away to the

Connection Manager. Now you are ready to join the ranks of the people who selected an existing data connection.

Defining the Credential Analysis Services Will Use to Connect

Now that we are all back together, we are going to move on to the Impersonation Information page. Here's where you are going to specify the credentials that Analysis Services will use to connect to the relational database (in our sample, FoodMart 2008 SQL Server database). For detailed information about specifying these credentials, see Chapter 18, "DSVs and Object Bindings."

On the Completing the Wizard page, you give your data connection a name. And you are done—for now.

Modifying an Existing Data Source

There will likely come a time when you need to modify the data source that you created. Analysis Services provides a tool for that: the Data Source Designer. You use the Data Source Designer to change the properties of your data source object.

You open the Data Source Designer from BI Dev Studio. Right-click `FoodMart 2008.ds`, and then click View Designer from the menu that appears.

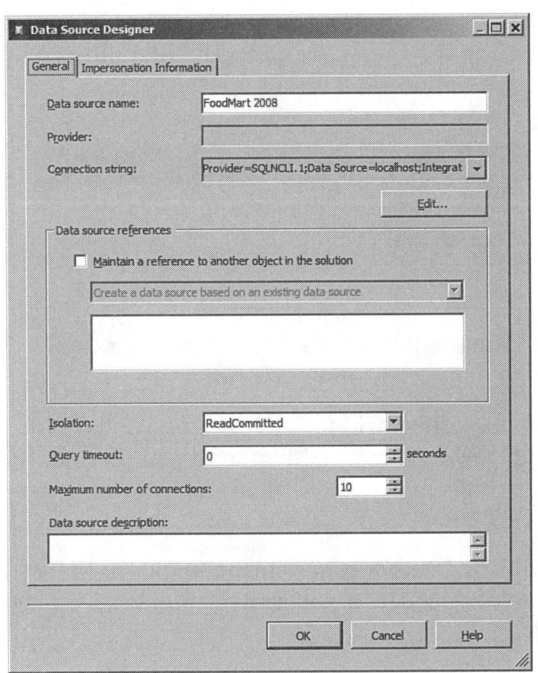

FIGURE 9.1 Use the Data Source Designer to edit your data source properties.

NOTE

You will find `Food Mart 2008.ds` in the Solution Explorer, under Data Sources.

The most common editing task is to change the connection string. The connection string specifies the server that contains the relational database that Analysis Services connects to. It also defines the client object model that the Analysis Services uses for that connection (for example, SQL Native Client, ADO.NET).

To modify the connection string, click the Edit button that is just below it. Doing so takes you to the Connection Manager, where you can make your modifications.

You will find more information about using the Data Source Designer to modify other properties of your data source, including the properties that appear on the Impersonation Information tab, in Chapter 35, "Security Model for Analysis Services."

Modifying a DDL File

So far, we have been working in the BI Dev Studio user interface. For every object in your project, BI Dev Studio creates a file (sometimes more than one) containing the Data Definition Language (DDL) definition of the object. In the process of deployment, BI Dev Studio validates all the objects, compiles one command to create or modify all the objects your project needs, and then sends the command to the server.

You can use Notepad to view all the DDL files in your project and change them yourself. However, BI Dev Studio provides a user interface you can use to edit a DDL definition of an object in an XML editor.

To View a DDL Definition

In the Solution Explorer, right-click the file `FoodMart 2008.ds` (the data source for our sample database). From the resulting menu, select View Code.

In Figure 9.2, you see the DDL definition of the FoodMart 2008 data source, `FoodMart 2008.ds`.

You can modify the DDL definition for an object directly in the XML editor. We have to admit, developers are more comfortable with this style of work than most people. And, we hope they are happy to find that they can directly change the DDL definition (the source code) for an object.

The XML editor is the same editor you find in SQL Server Management Studio. As in most XML editors, the XML tags and elements are color-coded. If you mistype or misplace a tag or parts of it, the color automatically changes.

The work you do in the XML editor is mirrored in the BI Dev Studio user interface. So, if you use the XML editor to modify the DDL definition of an object, save it, and later open

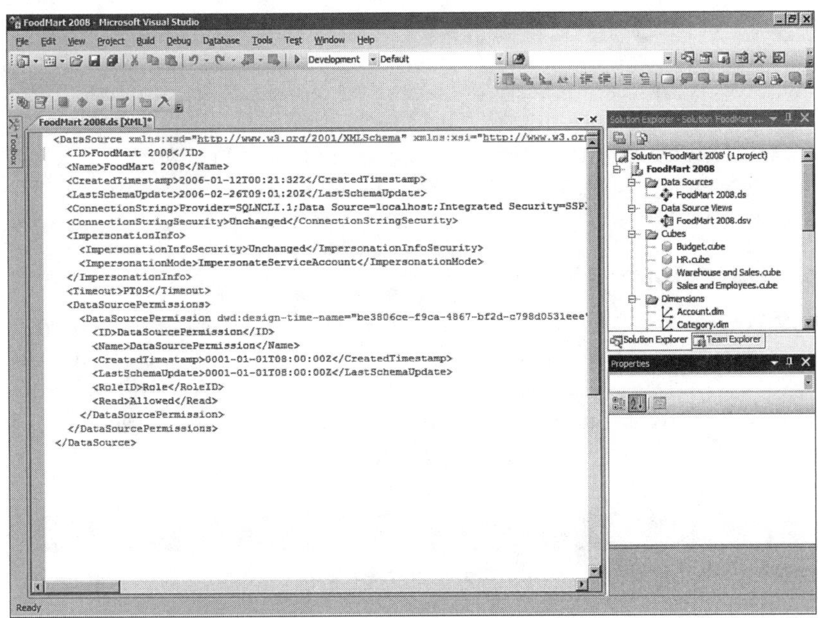

FIGURE 9.2 You can view the DDL definition of an object in BI Dev Studio.

your object (let's say it is a dimension object) in the Dimension Designer, you will see the modifications you made earlier in the XML editor.

Often, an easier approach is to use the XML editor rather than the BI Dev Studio user interface. For example, you cannot change the ID of a dimension in the dimension editor. It is possible that the dimension could be used in more than one cube. In that case, changing the ID of the dimension requires going through all the cubes in the database to determine which cubes the dimension is used in, and then changing the ID of the dimension in all those. But, the DDL definition of the entire database, including all the objects, is a much better vehicle for this sort of change. You can simply do a search and replace and change the dimension ID wherever it occurs.

In our sample FoodMart 2008 data source, shown in Figure 9.2, you can easily modify the name of the server that your data source points to. All you do is change the content of the `<ConnectionString>` element.

Any time you are having a hard time finding a property of some object among all the other properties, you can switch to the DDL definition of the object. Then, you can easily search for the property and modify it directly in the DDL definition.

Throughout this book, we give you lots of examples of DDL definitions. Now with the View Code option, you can look directly at the DDL definition of one of your own objects in the XML editor, and you can make the changes you want.

Designing a Data Source View

A Data Source View (DSV) is an Analysis Services object that represents an abstraction level on top of a relational database schema. (For detailed information about DSVs, see Chapter 18.) You might create a DSV that includes only the tables and relationships relevant to your multidimensional model. You can also create named queries and calculated columns in the DSV so that you can extend the relational schema.

Creating a New Data Source View

To create a new DSV, you use the Data Source View Wizard. When you are in the wizard, you have to choose a data source. If you need to create a new data source, you can do that from the Data Source View Wizard—the Data Source View Wizard takes you into the Data Source Wizard and then returns you to where you came from. (Yes, you are going in circles. Do not ask.)

NOTE

You can also start with the Data Source View Wizard to create a new data source and then create a DSV for it.

Launch the Data Source View Wizard

1. In the Solution Explorer, right-click the Data Source Views node to launch the Data Source View Wizard. Breeze through the Welcome page as usual.
2. On the Select a Data Source page, under Relational Data Sources, select the data source you want to use a DSV for, and then click Next. If you need to create a new data source, click New Data Source; doing so takes you to the Data Source Wizard. Complete the Data Source Wizard. (You can find the steps for this in the preceding section.) When you finish the Data Source Wizard, it sends you back to Select a Data Source page of the Data Source View Wizard. Select your new data source and click Next.
3. If the Data Source View cannot find relationships between tables in the relational database, go to the Name Matching page, where you will find options for creating logical relationships by matching columns in the relational database.
4. On the Select Tables and Views page, the available tables and views are listed under Available Objects. There is another list under Included Objects, blank in the beginning, of the tables or views included in your DSV. Between the two lists are two arrows, one pointing left and one pointing right. To add tables or views from the Available Objects list to the Included Objects list, click the arrow that points to the right.

   You can see the Select Tables and Views page in Figure 9.3.

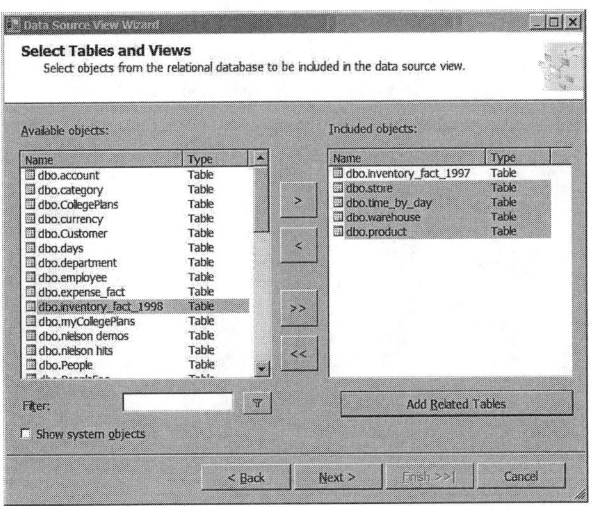

FIGURE 9.3 Use the arrows to move tables from one column to the other.

5. On the Completing the Wizard page, you can name your DSV.

You can make your life easier if the first table you add is the one you want to use as a fact table. Use the arrow to add that table to your DSV. Then, click the Add Related Tables button. The related dimension tables will appear in the Included Objects list. If you want to also include tables that are related to the dimension tables, click the Add Related Tables button again. Now tables are added to the list under Included Objects.

Modifying a DSV

We are going to use FoodMart 2008 to demonstrate how to modify a DSV. Our DSV is a pretty simple one; it includes only about 20 tables. But, some DSVs can get much more complex, especially when your multidimensional model is created on top of a relational schema with a lot, maybe hundreds, of tables and relationships.

To work with the FoodMart 2008 DSV in the DSV Designer, start in BI Dev Studio. In the Solution Explorer, right-click `FoodMart 2008.dsv`. From the menu that appears, select View Designer. Figure 9.4 shows you what you will see as BI Dev Studio shifts to its DSV Designer. The DSV Designer consists of multiple UI elements described in Table 9.1.

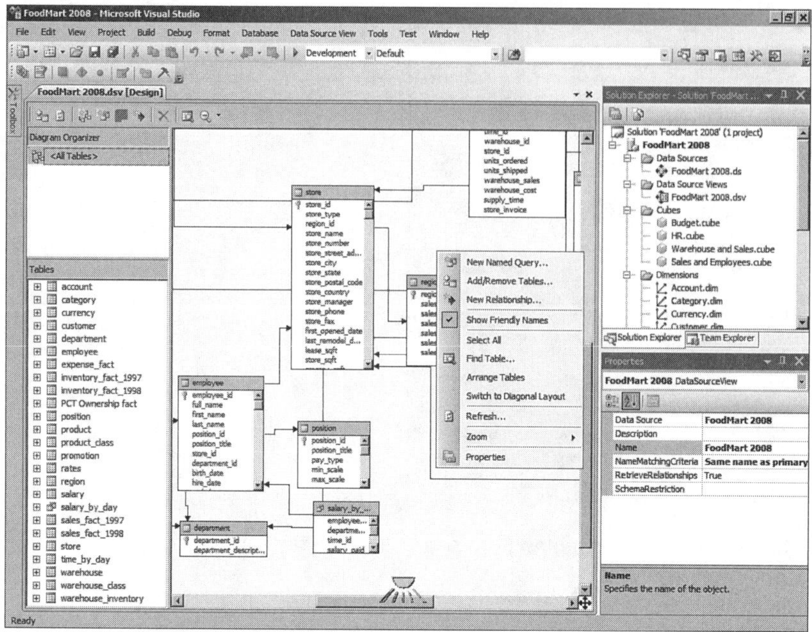

FIGURE 9.4 You can modify the properties of your DSV in the DSV Designer of BI Dev Studio.

TABLE 9.1 The DSV Designer User Interface

UI Space	Description
Center pane	Tables and the relationships between them. For each table, the table columns are listed.
Left pane	By default, the Diagram Organizer contains an All Tables diagram—one that contains all the tables in the DSV. To create a new diagram, right-click anywhere in the Diagram Organizer space. From the menu that appears, select the type of diagram you want to create.
	Under Tables is a list of all the tables that are included in your DSV. Expand a table node to see all the columns in the table. Click a column to show the column's properties in the Properties pane.
Properties pane	Beneath the Solution Explorer on the right, the Properties pane contains the properties of one column of the table that is expanded in the tables.

You can use the DSV Designer to refine your DSV, as follows:

- You can drag and drop to rearrange tables and relationships.
- You can delete tables from the DSV by selecting them and pressing the Delete key.
- You can add tables to the DSV by right-clicking anywhere in the center pane and selecting Add/Remove Tables from the resulting menu.

- You can use that same menu to create a named query that will appear as a new table in the DSV. (Select New Named Query.)
- To create a new named calculation, which will appear as a new column in a table, right-click the table and select New Named Calculation from the resulting menu.

Editing a Named Calculation

You can edit the properties of a named calculation in the Edit Named Calculation dialog box. You can reach that dialog box by double-clicking the column that represents the named calculation. The dialog box already contains values for each property; you can change any or all of them.

In Figure 9.5, you can see the Edit Named Calculation dialog box that displays when you double-click the `WeekOfYear` column in the `time_by_day` table.

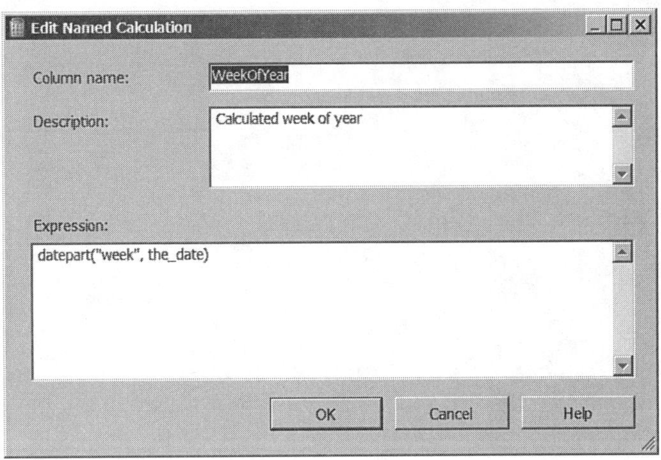

FIGURE 9.5 Use the Edit Named Calculation dialog box to change the properties of a named calculation.

9

Designing a Dimension

After you have created your DSV, you are ready to start creating the dimensions for your multidimensional model. For details about dimensions, see Chapter 5, "Dimensions in the Conceptual Model."

Creating a Dimension

Review the names of the dimensional tables before you start designing your dimensions.

You use the Dimension Wizard to create your dimensions.

Launch the Dimension Wizard

1. In the Solution Explorer of BI Dev Studio, right-click the Dimensions node.
2. From the menu that appears, select New Dimension. Bypass the Welcome page of the wizard.

---

1. On the Select Creation Method page, select Use an Existing Table, as shown in Figure 9.6.

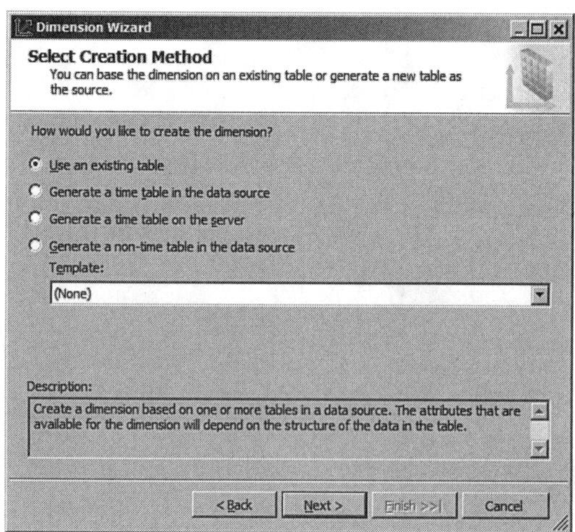

FIGURE 9.6 Select the Build Dimension Using a Data Source option on the Select Build Method page.

2. On the Specify Source Information page, under Data Source View, select a DSV to base your dimension. Choose a main table for your dimension (from the Main Table drop-down list). Under Key Columns, you will see a key column suggested for you by BI Dev studio based on the key of the relational table. You can change that column or add more columns if you would like a key attribute of your dimension to be based on the composite key.

   You can change the member name column for your key attribute in the Name column drop-down list.

   When you have everything as you like it, click Next.
3. If the Dimension Wizard detects that one or more tables are related to the selected dimension table, your next page will be the Select Related Tables page, where you

can select additional tables. When you have selected your tables, click Next. (This page will not appear if there is only one possible dimension table in your DSV.)

4. On the Select Dimension Attributes page, you can see the attributes that Analysis Services suggests in the Attribute Name column. (That column contains all the attributes found in the dimension tables.) You can reject the suggestions and substitute your own, and you can change the names of the attributes, as shown in Figure 9.7.

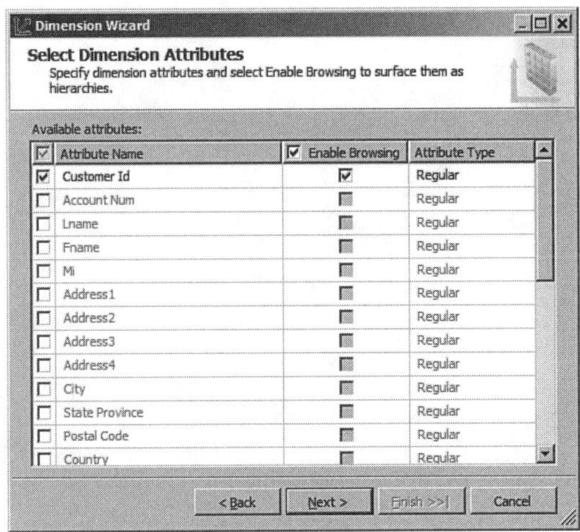

FIGURE 9.7 Select the dimension attributes on the Select Dimension Attributes page.

In the Attribute Key Column, you will find the key column for the attribute. If you select a key column, you will enable a drop-down list from which you can change the column.

In the Attribute Name Column, you will find the name column for the attribute. Just like with the key column, you can select a new column.

When satisfied with all your selections and changes, click Next.

5. On the Completing the Wizard page, you can review the dimension structure and name your dimension. After you click Finish, the Dimension Editor appears with your new dimension.

In Analysis Services 2008, the Dimension Wizard has been greatly simplified. It does not suggest that you choose the dimension type or that you start building hierarchies. You will use Dimension Editor to finish your dimension design.

Modifying an Existing Dimension

Now we are going to use the Dimension Editor in BI Dev Studio to modify the `Customer` dimension. Double-click the `Customer` dimension in the Solution Explorer, and the Dimension Editor will open, with the Dimension Structure tab showing, as shown in Figure 9.8.

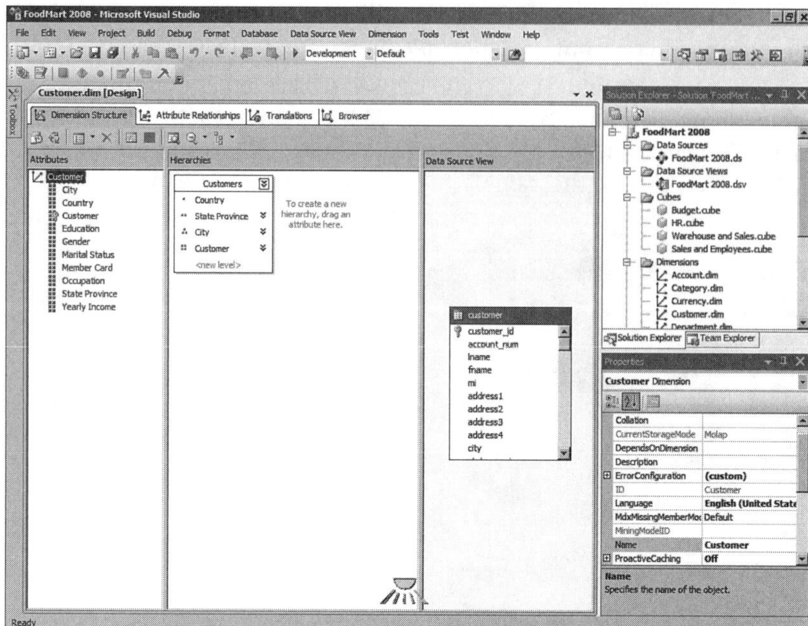

FIGURE 9.8 Start with the Dimension Structure tab in the Dimension Editor.

- The left pane contains the name of the dimension with a list of the all the attributes for the dimension. Select the dimension to see its properties in the Properties pane. Select an attribute to see its properties there.
- The Hierarchies and Levels pane contains the user-defined hierarchies, each one in a table with the names of its levels.
- The Data Source View pane, on the right, contains the dimension tables with their columns.

Working with Attributes

You can create a new attribute on the Dimension Structure tab by dragging a column from a table in the Data Source View pane to the Attributes pane. You can modify an existing attribute on the Dimension Structure tab by selecting an attribute in the Attributes pane; its properties appear in the Properties pane in the lower-right corner. You can change the properties there.

When you create a dimension in the Dimension Wizard, you do not have the opportunity to define the relationships between the dimension attributes. We strongly recommend that you define the relationships between the attributes in your dimension before you use it in the cube. Figure 9.9 shows the Attribute Relationship tab of the Dimension Editor as it appears when you are working on defining relationships. Attribute Relationship tab is new in Analysis Services 2008. It shows you the relationship chains and enables you to easily create attribute relationships.

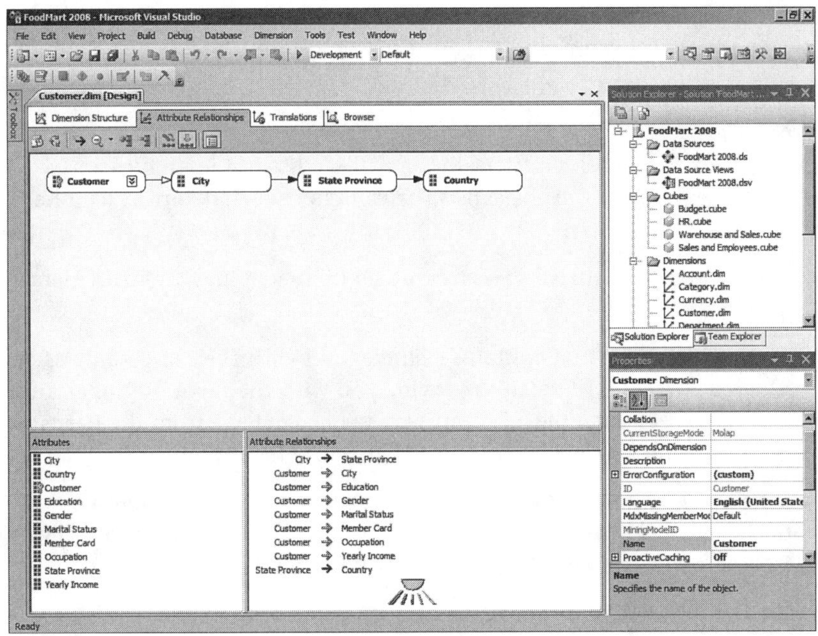

FIGURE 9.9 Define attribute relationships in the Dimension Editor.

To create a new attribute relationship object, in the Attribute Relationship tab drag one attribute on top of another. The attribute that you want to drag to another should be the "more granular" (in other words, the attribute that will appear higher in the level hierarchy). For example, drag the `City` attribute on top of `State Province` attribute to create a relationship.

By default, Analysis Services creates the `RelationshipType` property as `Flexible`. You can see a relationship's properties in the Properties pane if you select the relationship in the main pane. Change the property to `Rigid` if you are sure that the members of the `City` attribute are not going move to another state. Specifying a `Rigid` relationship guarantees that an aggregation based on attributes with rigid relationships will not get dropped after an incremental update of the dimension.

If you made a mistake and dragged a wrong attribute and created an unwanted relationship, you have an option to delete an attribute relationship by selecting an arrow in a flow chart diagram in the main drawing pane or by selecting a relationship in the Attribute Relationship pane in the lower middle.

In many cases, as in our example, you want the `Name` column and the `Key` column to be different. We have already done this for the `Customer` attribute in the `Customer` dimension. Here's how we did it:

1. Select the `Customer` attribute.

2. In the Properties pane, scroll down to the Source. In the drop-down box of the `NameColumns` property, select (new) and choose a new column in the Object Binding dialog box.

Working with Hierarchies

When an end user connects to the server, typically he will see list of hierarchies and a list of the levels in each hierarchy. From these lists, he can choose what sort of data he wants to view.

There are two types of hierarchy in Analysis Services: attribute hierarchies and user hierarchies.

An attribute hierarchy is a hierarchy that contains a single level with the same name as the attribute it is based on. Attribute hierarchies provide you with the flexibility to arrange a report in a number of ways. For example, you can place a `Gender` level from the `Gender` attribute hierarchy on top of the `Age` level from the `Age` attribute hierarchy.

You are going to pay a price for this flexibility. If the only hierarchies you have in your dimension are attribute hierarchies, you need to define ways to drill down from one level to another. Otherwise, the performance of your system will be significantly degraded.

For the attributes that are not queried often, we recommend that you set the `AttributeHierarchyOptimizedState` property to `NotOptimized`.

To Hide an Attribute Hierarchy from the End User

1. Select the attribute in the Attributes pane of the Dimension Editor.
2. In the Properties pane, change the attribute property `AttributeHierarchyVisible` to `False`.

User hierarchies are the hierarchies you create in your dimension by dragging and dropping attributes into the Hierarchies and Levels pane in the Dimension Editor. (You can accomplish the same thing by editing the DDL.) Go back to Figure 9.8 to see the `Customer` dimension with a single hierarchy (`Customers`). The hierarchy contains levels, which we created by dragging attributes into the hierarchy.

There are two types of user hierarchies: natural hierarchies and unnatural hierarchies. See Chapter 5, "Dimensions in the Conceptual Model," for details about natural and unnatural hierarchies.

In a natural hierarchy, every attribute is related to its parent attribute in the hierarchy. An attribute relationship object points to the parent of an attribute. In our example of the `Customers` hierarchy in Figure 9.9, you see the `City` attribute is related to the `State Province` attribute.

Although unnatural hierarchies give you a great deal of flexibility, they lead to poor performance. It is always better to create natural hierarchies in your dimensions.

Working with Translations

Analysis Services offers powerful multilingual support for multidimensional models. You can define translations for every visible caption in your dimensions and in your cubes. You use the Translations tab in the Dimension Designer to define translations.

We will turn once again to our FoodMart 2008 sample. Click the Translations tab in the Dimension Designer and you should see (in Figure 9.10) the way we have initially defined our translations.

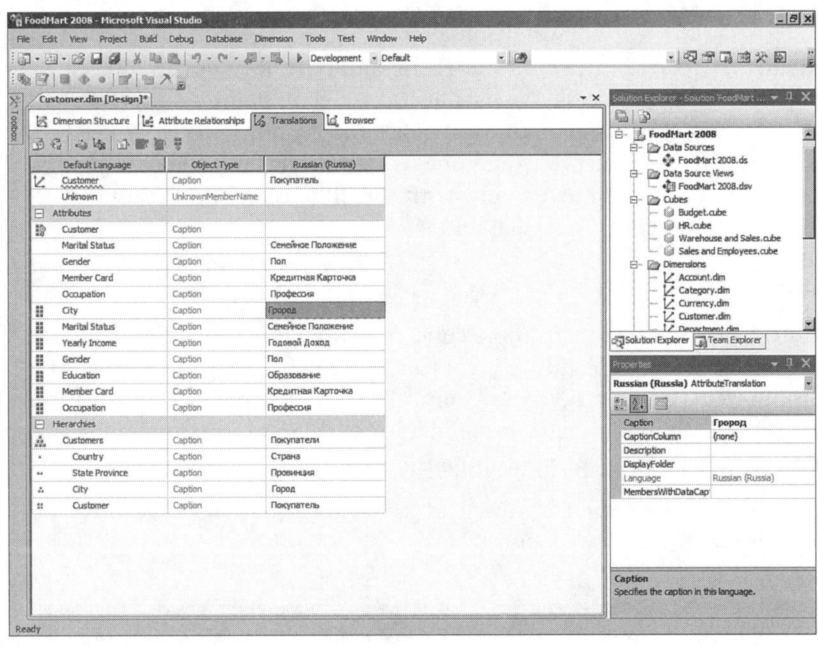

FIGURE 9.10 Define translations for your dimension on the Translations tab.

For FoodMart 2008, we have defined a Russian translation for the `Customer` dimension. All the authors speak Russian, so that was our first choice. In the Properties pane, you can see the locale identifier for the translation selected for the `City` attribute: `1049`. That is the identifier for Russian. You would get the same value for `Translation` for any of the attributes of the `Customer` dimension.

When your users browse the cube and see the `City` attribute in Russian, they probably want to see the name of each city also in Russian. They want to see not only the `City` attribute caption translated to Russian, but also all the members for the `City` attribute translated to Russian. To accomplish this, you specify that the `CaptionColumn` property points to the column in the relational database that contains the Russian translations of each of the member cities.

Using the Browser Tab

Click the Browser tab to browse your dimension. When you open the Browser tab, you will see one of the hierarchies of your dimension. At the top of the screen is a text box titled Hierarchy, with a drop-down list of the hierarchies in your dimension. Another text box (Language) contains a drop-down list of languages. This drop-down list is likely to contain more languages than you have defined for your dimension. Select a language to view the hierarchy in the selected language.

Designing a Cube

A cube is the fundamental object of the multidimensional model. It is a major object, one that defines the data that you can access. We have just worked on defining dimensions because dimensions play a major role in defining a cube. You do not necessarily need to design your dimensions before you define your cube; you can start with the cube. For our purposes, however, we are going to design a cube with the dimensions we already have. For detailed information about cubes, see Chapter 6.

Creating a Cube

You can use the Cube Wizard to design a simple cube, including dimensions, if you have not already created them. As handy as it is to create an entire cube using just a single wizard, it is something we recommend only for simple models. If you are using advanced dimensions (for example, a dimension with more than one table), we recommend that you use the Dimension Wizard to create your dimensions before you create your cube.

We are going to show you how to create a cube, and will assume that you have already created the dimensions you need for your cube.

Launch the Cube Wizard

1. In the Solution Explorer of BI Dev Studio, right-click the Cubes node.
2. From the resulting menu, select New Cube.

When the Cube Wizard appears, you can—as usual—speed on through the Welcome page. Then, you get down to the business of creating your cube:

1. On the Select Creation Method page, for our purposes go ahead and accept the defaults.
2. On the Select Measure Group Tables page, select the DSV you used to create your dimensions from the drop-down box.

   In the Measure Group Tables pane, you see the list of all tables in your DSV. In the beginning, none of the tables are designated to be a measure group tables. Click the

Suggest button for BI Dev Studio to suggest measure group tables, as shown in Figure 9.11.

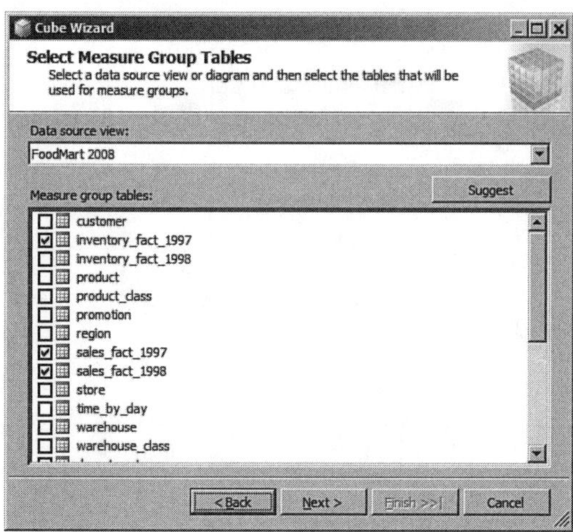

FIGURE 9.11 Select measure group tables for your cube.

3. On the Select Measures page, under Measures, you will see the available measure groups and measures. (Measure groups are first-class objects in the tree view.) You can change the names of the measure groups and measures. Just select one, press F2, and enter the name you want.

   When you have finished your changes, click Next.
4. On the Select Existing Dimensions page, you select the existing database dimension you want to be included in your cube.
5. On the Select New Dimensions page, you see tree view of new dimensions that BI Dev Studio suggests you create. Under dimension nodes, you see the tree of the attributes. Click the check boxes to deselect the dimensions\attributes you do not want to be included. When you have finished your changes, click Next.
6. On the Completing the Wizard page, you can preview the cube. If you want, you can change the cube's name in the Cube Name text box. For our purposes, name your cube **MySampleCube** and click Finish.

Modifying a Cube

The `MySampleCube` you have created has a structure similar to that of the `Warehouse and Sales` cube in our sample FoodMart 2008 database. We will use the Cube Designer in BI Dev Studio to examine the structure of `MySampleCube`.

To open `MySampleCube` in BI Dev Studio, right-click the file in the Solution Explorer and select View Designer from the resulting menu.

On the Cube Structure tab of the Cube Designer, you will see a diagram of your cube, as shown in Figure 9.12.

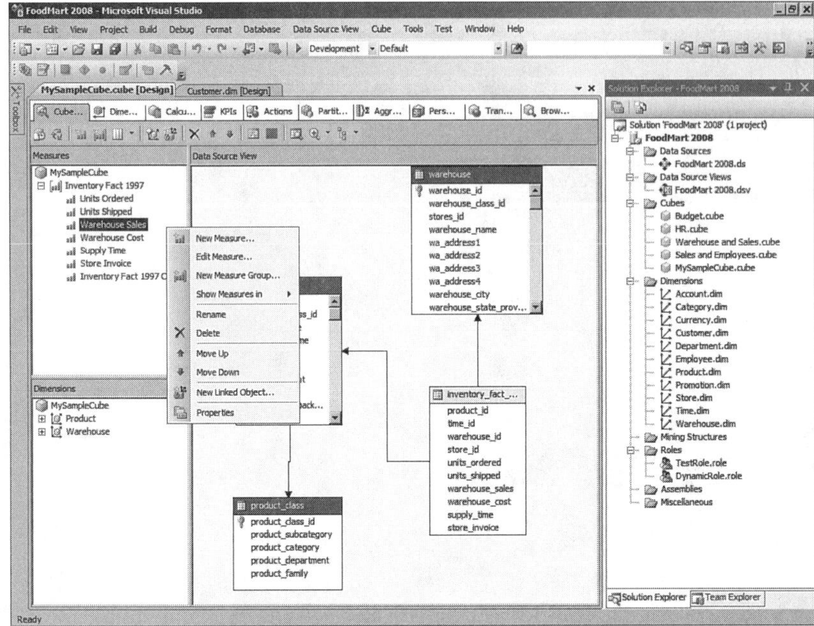

FIGURE 9.12 You can see a diagram of `MySampleCube` on the Cube Structures tab of the Cube Designer.

Working with Measures and Measure Groups

All of your measure groups and measures are listed in the Measures pane. (See Chapter 7, "Measures and Multidimensional Analysis," for more information.)

You can click a measure group or a measure to see its properties in the Properties pane. You can drag and drop columns from Data Source View pane, which shows all the tables that your cube is based on.

Right-click anywhere in the Data Source View pane. On the resulting menu, select Show Tables. The tables that you see listed in the Show Tables dialog box are the tables from your DSV that are not included in the diagram. You can select one or more of these tables to include them in the diagram.

Right-click anywhere in the Measures pane (see Figure 9.12). From the resulting menu, you can do the following:

- Create a new measure or measure group
- Delete a measure or measure group
- Rearrange order of the measures or measure groups
- Create a new linked object

Working with Linked Objects

You use linked objects to reuse an object (dimension or measure group) that resides in a different database, perhaps on a different server. You can link only dimensions from different databases. The linked object points to the object you want to reuse.

For more information about linked objects, see Chapter 25, "Building Scalable Analysis Services Applications."

Launch the Linked Object Wizard

1. On the Cube Structure tab, right-click anywhere in the Measures pane.
2. From the resulting menu, select New Linked Object.

When the Linked Object Wizard appears, you can, as usual, speed on through the Welcome page. Then, you get down to the business of creating your linked object:

1. On the Select a Data Source page, under Analysis Services Data Sources, a list of available Analysis Services data sources appears. You can select a data source from the list or click New Data Source.

NOTE

An Analysis Services data source is the data source pointing to another instance of Analysis Services and not to the relational database.

---

2. The Data Source Wizard appears on top of your Linked Object Wizard.
3. On the Select How to Define the Connection page, select an existing connection under Data Connections that points to another instance of Analysis Services that contains the objects you want to link to. Click Next.
4. On the Impersonation Information page, select Use the Service Account, and click Next.
5. On the Completing the Wizard page, click Finish.
6. Back in the Linked Object Wizard, on the Select a Data Source page, select your newly created Analysis Services data source, and then click Next.
7. If you connected to an instance of Analysis Services that holds another copy of the FoodMart 2008 database, on the Select Objects page you should see something like Figure 9.13. Here you can select measure groups and dimensions to link to. (If you select only one measure group, make sure that you also select some of the dimensions belonging to it.)

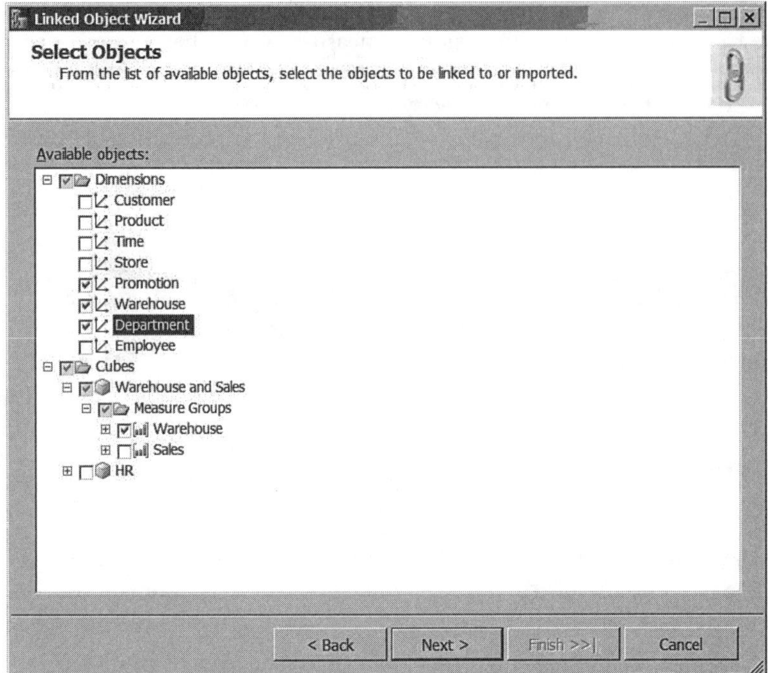

FIGURE 9.13 Select the objects you want to link to.

8. On the Completing the Wizard page, review the names of the new linked dimensions and measure groups. If the Linked Object Wizard detects that you already have an object with the same name as one of your linked objects, it renames the linked object to avoid duplication. Click Cancel to avoid creating extra objects in the FoodMart 2008 sample database.

Defining Cube Dimension Usage

The role of a dimension in a cube is defined by its relationship to a measure group. We are going to move now to the Dimension Usage tab of the cube editor to review those relationships in the `Warehouse and Sales` cube from the FoodMart 2008 sample database.

The Dimension Usage tab will look like the one depicted in Figure 9.14. It displays a grid that contains a column for each measure group and a row for each dimension. The intersections of the rows and columns show the names of the granularity attributes. For example, the intersection of `Product` dimension and `Warehouse` measure group shows that the granularity attribute is `Product`.

Click the `Product` granularity attribute, and the Define Relationship dialog box appears, as shown in Figure 9.15.

In the Define Relationship dialog box, you can see how a dimension is related to a measure group. The dialog box displays the granularity attribute, the dimension table, and measure group table.

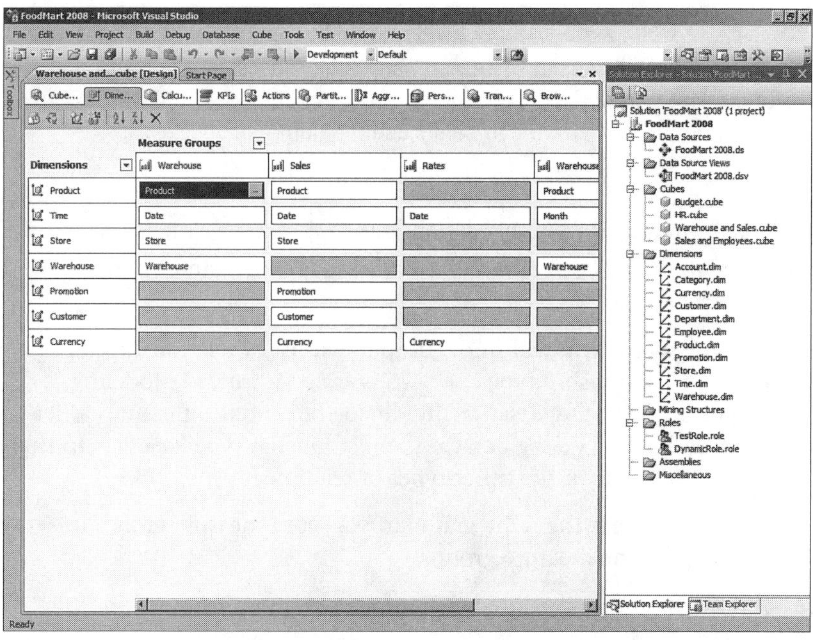

FIGURE 9.14 Review the relationships of dimensions and measure groups.

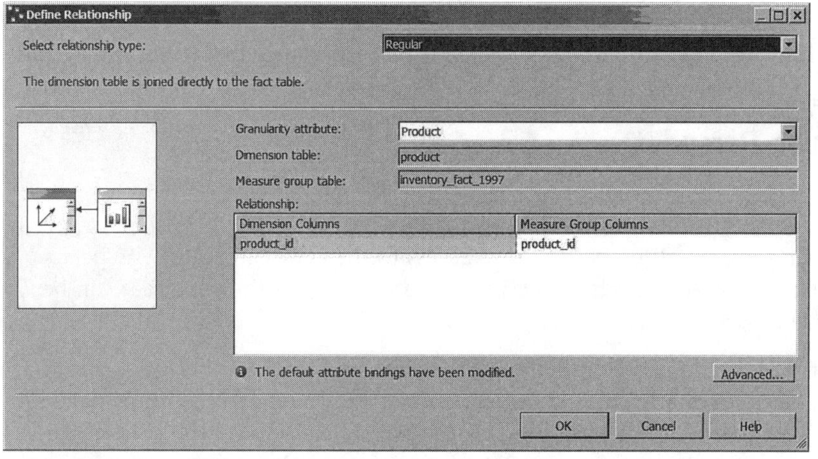

FIGURE 9.15 You can review the relationship between the measure group and the dimension.

Under Relationship, you will find two columns: Dimension Columns and Measure Group Columns. Under Dimension Columns, you will see the name of the key column of the `Product` attribute: `product_id`. Under Measure Group Columns, you will see the name of the column in the `inventory_fact_1997` table (the measure group table): `product_id`.

NOTE

Because the measure group could consist of several partitions, you will see only the name of the table of the first partition. But, the rest of the partitions need to have the same columns as the first partition, so we can safely use the name: `product_id`.

Our `Product` granularity attribute is based on a single key column. If a granularity attribute is based on more than one key column, you must map every dimension key column to a measure group column.

In the Select Relationship type box, you will find a drop-down list of relationship types. (For more information about relationship types, see Chapter 8, "Advanced Modeling.") Depending on your selection, the Define Relationship dialog box looks different. Earlier we described the Define Relationship dialog box for the relationship type `Regular`. In the following list, we briefly define some of the other types of relationships:

- **`Fact`**—The `Fact` dimension has the same granularity as your measure group; it is based on the same table as the measure group.
- **`Referenced`**—A dimension that is related to the measure group through another dimension.
- **`Many-to-many`**—For a many-to-many dimension, you need only specify the name of the intermediate measure group. (For more information about many-to-many relationships, see Chapter 8.)
- **`Data mining`**—A dimension that is built on top of the source dimension using the mining model.

Building a Cube Perspective

A cube perspective is similar in concept to a view in relational databases. There is a difference, however: A perspective in Analysis Services 2008 does not make it possible to specify security for the perspective—all users that have access to the cube can see all the perspectives in the cube. In essence, a cube perspective is another view of the cube that can be presented to the end user.

Suppose that you want to build a complex cube that involves lots of dimensions and that every dimension has a lot of attributes and hierarchies. And, the measure groups have lots of measures. Such a cube would be hard for a user to navigate. To make the cube easier to navigate and browse, you can create a perspective in your cube that shows customers only the information they are interested in.

To create a cube perspective, we will use the Perspectives tab in the Cube Designer. Right-click anywhere in the Perspectives tab and select New Perspective from the resulting menu.

The essence of designing a perspective is to select the measure groups and measures that will be included in the perspective. You also select the hierarchies and attributes that will be visible to the user. You can do all this on the Perspectives tab, shown in Figure 9.16.

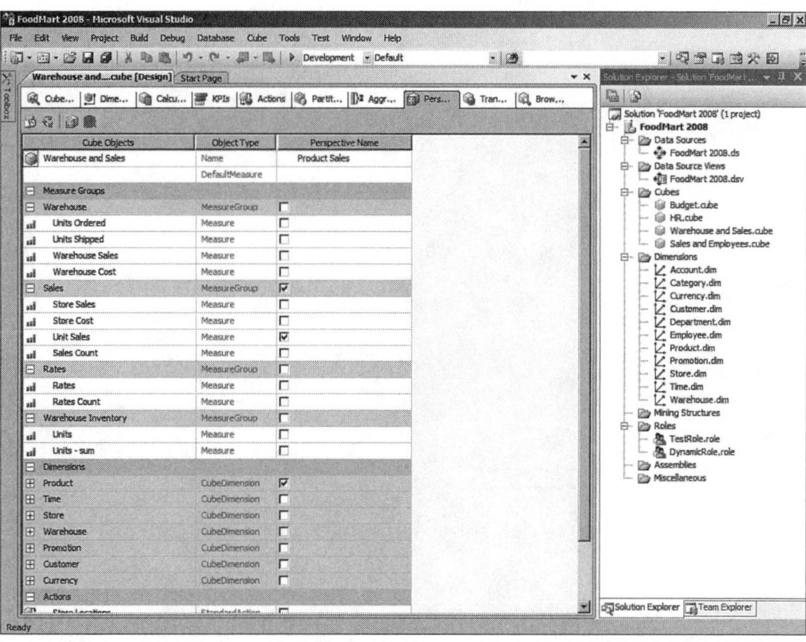

FIGURE 9.16 Select the objects you want your user to see in your perspective.

In the Cube Objects column, you can see the measure groups (those are highlighted), measures, dimensions, hierarchies, and attributes available for your perspective. In the Perspective Name column, just click the ones you want to include.

After you have created your perspective, name it in the Perspective Name column. Our sample perspective is named `Product Sales`. To the user, it will look just like another cube, very much the same way the regular cubes in Analysis Services 2000 were visible to the end user.

Defining Cube Translations

Earlier in this chapter, we have described how to define translations for dimensions in your database. Now we are going to turn our attention to defining translations for your cube.

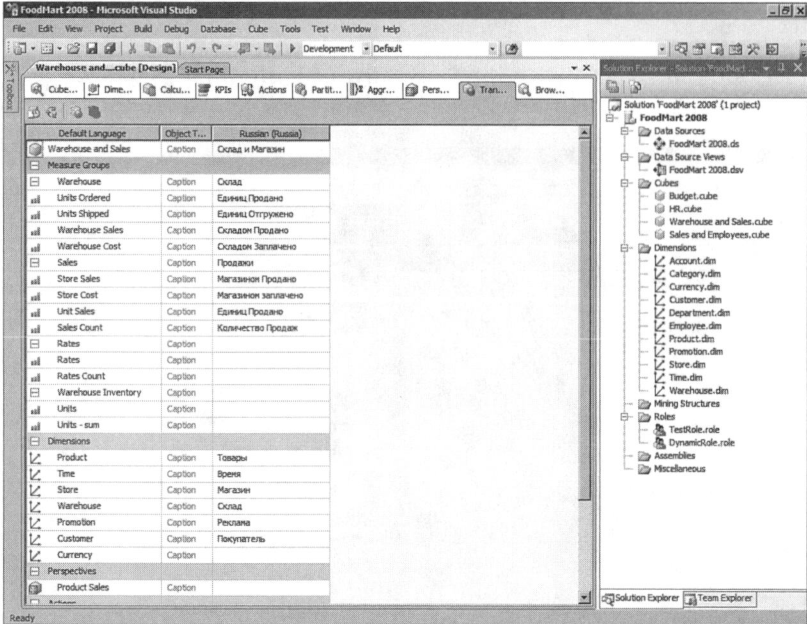

FIGURE 9.17 Use the Translations tab to define translations for your cube.

You define object captions in different languages for your cube objects. To do this, you create a translation for each language. Figure 9.17 shows the Translations tab in the Cube Designer.

In Figure 9.17, you can see a Russian translation defined for the `Warehouse and Sales` cube. When you want to create a new translation, you will use the Translations tab:

1. Right-click anywhere in the Translations tab space.
2. From the resulting menu, select New Translation.
3. In the Select Language dialog box, select the language you want from the very long list of available languages.
4. In the column headed by the name of the language, type the caption for the individual objects.

If you have not specified a caption for a certain object in this new language, the server uses the default object name. Go back and look at Figure 9.17, and you will see that we did not create a translation for the `Product Sales` perspective. There is nothing in the cell in the Russian column, but the server will supply one.

Configuring and Deploying a Project So That You Can Browse the Cube

After you have created a cube—data source, DSV, and dimensions—you will be almost ready to deploy your project to the Analysis Services. First, you configure the project to determine how the BI Dev Studio will build and deploy the project. Then, after you deploy the project, you can browse your cubes and verify that the numbers you expect are correct.

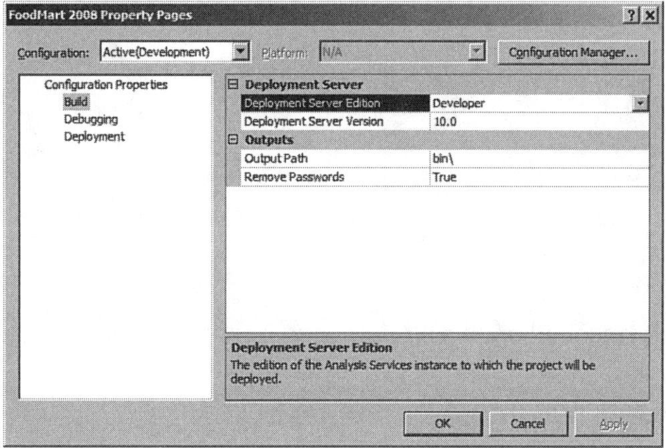

FIGURE 9.18 Use this dialog box to change the properties of the project.

Configuring a Project

To configure your project for deployment, you use the *ProjectName* Property Pages dialog box. Right-click the project name in the Solution Explorer. From the resulting menu, select Properties. For our sample database. you would see the FoodMart 2008 Property Pages dialog box, as shown in Figure 9.18.

Under Configuration in the navigation pane, select one of the three options available: Build, Debugging, and Deployment.

The Build Option

For our FoodMart 2008 sample shown in Figure 9.18, Build is the selection you see.

In the Results pane, you see the Deployment Server Edition property. The edition we used for our sample FoodMart 2008 is the Developer edition. Other possible values are Enterprise, Evaluation, and Standard. Because some Analysis Services features are not avail-

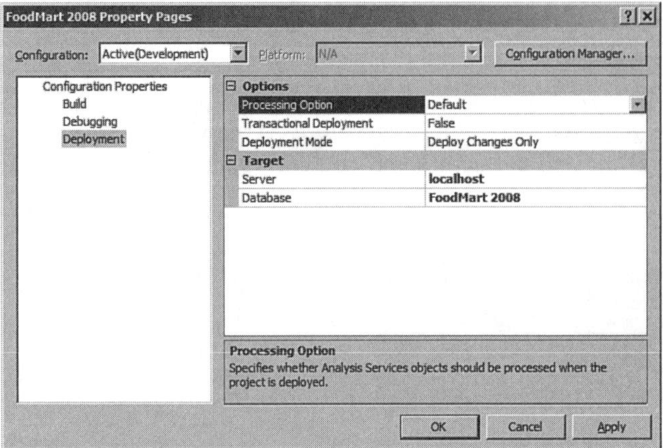

FIGURE 9.19 Review and change your deployment options.

able in certain editions, your deployment attempt can result in an error reporting that the feature is not supported.

Be sure to set your project Deployment Server Edition and Deployment Server Version properties to the edition and version of the instance of Analysis Services you are deploying the project to.

The Deployment Option

If you select Deployment, you will see deployment options in the *ProjectName* Property Pages dialog box (see Figure 9.19).

Under Options, click the value shown for Deployment Mode. The choices—Deploy All and Deploy Changes Only—instruct BI Dev Studio to compare the state of the project and the state of the live database residing on the Analysis Server and either (1) deploy all the objects in the project or (2) deploy only the changes that were made.

Under Options, click the value for Processing Option. Then, click the arrow to see the drop-down list: Default, Do Not Process, and Full. If you do not want your database to be processed right after it has been created or modified, select Do Not Process.

NOTE

The processing operation can take a long time if there is a lot of data to be read and processed by Analysis Server. If that is the case for your solution, we recommend that you modify your project settings so that deployment of your solution will be processed at a later time.

Transactional deployment specifies whether commands sent in the deployment script should be treated as a single transaction.

The `Server` and `Database` properties (under Target) specify which server and which database to connect to.

Deploying a Project

When you have all your settings specified, you are ready to deploy your project. Right-click the database name in the Solution Explorer of BI Dev Studio. From the resulting menu, select Deploy. From here, BI Dev Studio takes over.

First, BI Dev Studio builds the solution, verifying that all the objects and their relationships are defined correctly. If BI Dev Studio detects any errors, those errors and their descriptions appear in the lower part of the screen in the error pane.

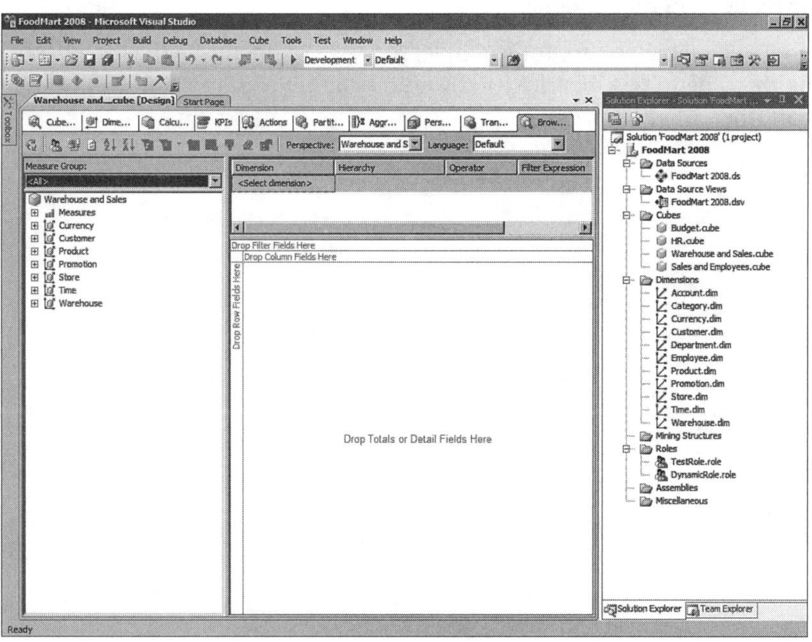

FIGURE 9.20 Use the Browser tab to browse your cube.

Once you have a successful build, BI Dev Studio creates a deployment script and sends it to the Analysis Server. By default, the script contains a `Create` statement and a processing command instructing Analysis Server to create the database on the server and process it.

Browsing a Cube

After your project has been deployed and your cube has been processed, you are ready to browse your cubes. You can use the Browser tab of the Cube Designer to browse the cube you have created or editing.

Figure 9.20 shows the `Warehouse and Sales` cube on the Browser tab.

You can see the cube measures, hierarchies, and levels in the navigation pane. From there, you drag and drop them onto the Office Web Components (OWC) control embedded in the Results pane. In the OWC, you can arrange the fields in any way you want to browse the results of the pane.

Above the OWC is an area where you can define filter conditions:

- The Perspectives drop-down list in the toolbox enables you to switch from one perspective to another.
- The Language drop-down list enables you to change languages so that you can test translations you defined for the cube.

The icons in the toolbox enable you to, for example, process your cube, change the user currently browsing the cube to test security roles, and reestablish a connection if it is lost for one reason or another.

PART III

Using MDX to Analyze Data

IN THIS PART

CHAPTER 10
MDX Concepts

IN THIS CHAPTER

- The SELECT Statement
- Query Execution Context
- Set Algebra and Basic Set Operations
- MDX Functions
- Referencing Objects in MDX and Using Unique Names

In previous chapters, we have discussed how multidimensional databases are designed, but not how they are used. In the next few chapters, we discuss how the data stored in Analysis Services can be retrieved and the different ways this data can be calculated and analyzed.

Among modern database systems, the most popular way of accessing data is to query it. A query defines the data that the user wants to see, but doesn't define the steps and algorithms that have to be performed to retrieve the data.

Structured Query Language (SQL) is one of the most popular query languages used to retrieve relational data. However, it was not designed to work with the rich data model supported by multidimensional databases. To access data stored in Online Analytical Processing (OLAP) systems, Microsoft invented Multidimensional Expressions (MDX). Currently, MDX is an industry standard, and a number of leading OLAP servers support it. It is also widely used in numerous client applications that enable the user to view and analyze multidimensional data.

You can use MDX not only to query data but also to define server-side calculations, advanced security settings, actions, key performance indicators (KPIs), and so on. So, even if you are not planning to write a client application that will generate MDX statements, you might find MDX useful to define security and program Analysis Services.

If you want to practice writing MDX statements, you can use SQL Server Management Studio (SSMS). The samples that we provide in this chapter were created in SSMS.

The SELECT Statement

The syntax of MDX was designed with SQL as a prototype. But new concepts and semantics were introduced to make it more intuitive to query multidimensional data. Similar to SQL, MDX is a text query language. As with SQL, the most important statement is the statement for retrieving data: the SELECT statement. The SELECT statement poses a question about the data and returns the answer. That answer is a new multidimensional space. Like SQL, SELECT in MDX has the three main clauses SELECT, FROM, and WHERE. (To be completely accurate, the SELECT statement in MDX has more than three clauses, but we talk about the others in Chapter 12, "Cube-Based MDX Calculations.")

- The SELECT clause defines a multidimensional space that will be the result of the query.
- The FROM clause defines the source of the data, which can be either the name of the cube containing the data, name of a dimension cube (dimension name preceded by the $ sign), or another query. (We discuss these more advanced queries in Chapter 11, "Advanced MDX.")
- The WHERE clause specifies rules for limiting the results of the query to a subspace of the data. The process of limiting the results is called *slicing*. In Analysis Services 2008, the slicing can occur not just on a single plane, but in more complex figures. These more complex cases are presented in Chapter 11. The WHERE clause is optional and can be omitted from the query.

Here is a simple MDX SELECT statement:

```
SELECT <definition of the resulting multidimensional space> FROM <source subspace>
WHERE <limiting the results to subspace>
```

The SELECT Clause

The result of a relational query is a two-dimensional table. The result of an MDX query is a multidimensional subcube; it can contain many dimensions. To differentiate the dimensions in the original cube from dimensions in the subcube that results from the query, we call a dimension in the multidimensional result an *axis*.

When you create a multidimensional query, you should list the axes that will be populated with the results. Theoretically, no limitations apply as to the number of axes that you can request with an MDX query. In the real world, however, the number of axes is limited by the number of dimensions in the multidimensional model; by the physical limitations of the computer; and most important, by the capabilities of the user interface to display the results in a format that is understandable to humans. For example, SSMS supports only two axes. The authors of this book have never seen a query containing more than three axes, but that doesn't mean that you can't invent a new user interface that can use sound or smell to represent the data on the fourth and fifth axes.

You use an ON clause to list the axes in a SELECT statement. The axes are separated from each other by a comma (,). The syntax is as follows:

```
SELECT <content of the axis> ON axis(0),
<content of the axis> ON axis(1),
<content of the axis> ON axis(2)
...
<content of the axis> ON axis(n),
from <cube_name>
```

There are various ways to name an axis. The most generic one is to put the axis number in parentheses following the word *axis*: `ON Axis(0)` or `ON Axis(1)`. To simplify the typing of your MDX statement, you can omit `Axis` and the parentheses and just write the number corresponding to the axis: `ON 0` or `ON 1`.

The most commonly used axes have names and can be referenced by their names. Axis number 0 is called `columns`, axis number 1 is `rows`, and axis number 2 is `pages`. This is the most common way to specify an axis; frequently the query will look like Listing 10.1.

LISTING 10.1 Using the Names of Axes

```
SELECT <content of the axis> ON COLUMNS,
<content of the axis> ON ROWS,
<content of the axis> ON PAGES
from <cube_name>
```

Defining Coordinates in Multidimensional Space

Now that we know how to define an axis in an MDX query, we can review the information that should be supplied as an axis definition. In SQL, you use a `SELECT` clause to define the column layout of the resulting table. In MDX, you use a `SELECT` clause to define the axis layout of the resulting multidimensional space. Each axis is defined by the coordinates of the multidimensional space, which are the members that we are projecting along the axis.

Internally in Analysis Services, members are created on the dimension attribute; in MDX, you navigate to a member only through a navigation path—hierarchy. In Chapter 5, "Dimensions in the Conceptual Model," we explained two kinds of hierarchy: the user-defined hierarchy and the attribute hierarchy.

You can use either a user-defined hierarchy or an attribute hierarchy (as long as it's set in the model as enabled) to define the coordinates of a multidimensional space. However, each member that can be accessed through the user hierarchy can also be accessed through the attribute hierarchy. Internally, the system uses members of the attribute hierarchy to define the space. If the user has specified a member using a user-defined hierarchy, the system projects that member onto the attribute hierarchy. (For more information about the rules for this process, see Chapter 11.)

Each point in a multidimensional space is defined by a collection of coordinates—a *tuple*—where each coordinate corresponds to a dimension member. You define a tuple by enclosing a comma-delimited list of members in parentheses. For example, a simple tuple that contains two members would be `([1997], [USA])`. The simplest (but not the best) way to reference a member in MDX is to enclose its name in square brackets. (We talk about better ways to reference a member later in this chapter.)

Each member of the tuple belongs to a different hierarchy; you can't create a tuple that has more than one member coming from the same hierarchy. Each tuple has two properties: *dimensionality*—a list of the dimension hierarchies that this tuple represents—and the actual members contained in the tuple. For example, dimensionality of the tuple `([1997],[USA])` is `Time.Year` and `Store.Countries`, and the member values are `1997` and `USA`.

Tuples that have the same dimensionality can be united in a *set*. As the name implies, an MDX set is a set in the mathematical sense—a collection of objects. Therefore, all the laws defined by set algebra apply to MDX sets.

The simplest way to define a set is to explicitly list its tuples between braces. For example, a set containing two tuples can be represented in the following way:

```
{([1997],[USA]), ([1998],[USA])}
```

To return to our discussion about specifying axes: You can define a multidimensional space that you need to retrieve from the cube by projecting a set on an axis.

NOTE

In Analysis Services 2005 and Analysis Services 2008, sets that reference the same dimension can be projected on different axes, but they have to reference different hierarchies.

Let's take a look at an example of a simple request. In this example, we use a very simple cube, shown in Figure 10.1.

This cube has three dimensions (`Stores`, `Products`, and `Time`) and a measure dimension with three measures (`Store Sales`, `Store Cost`, and `Units Sold`). We placed the `Time` dimension along the x-axis, the `Store` dimension along the y-axis, and the `Products` dimension along the z-axis.

Next, we analyze the products in the Food and Drink product families, sold over some period of time; let's say from the beginning of 1997 to the end of 1998 in all the counties where FoodMart Enterprises has stores. We project the `Time` dimension and `Products` dimension on the `Columns` axis and measures on the `Rows` axis. As a result, we get a two-dimensional space, shown in Figure 10.2.

Listing 10.2 demonstrates how you write such a projection in MDX.

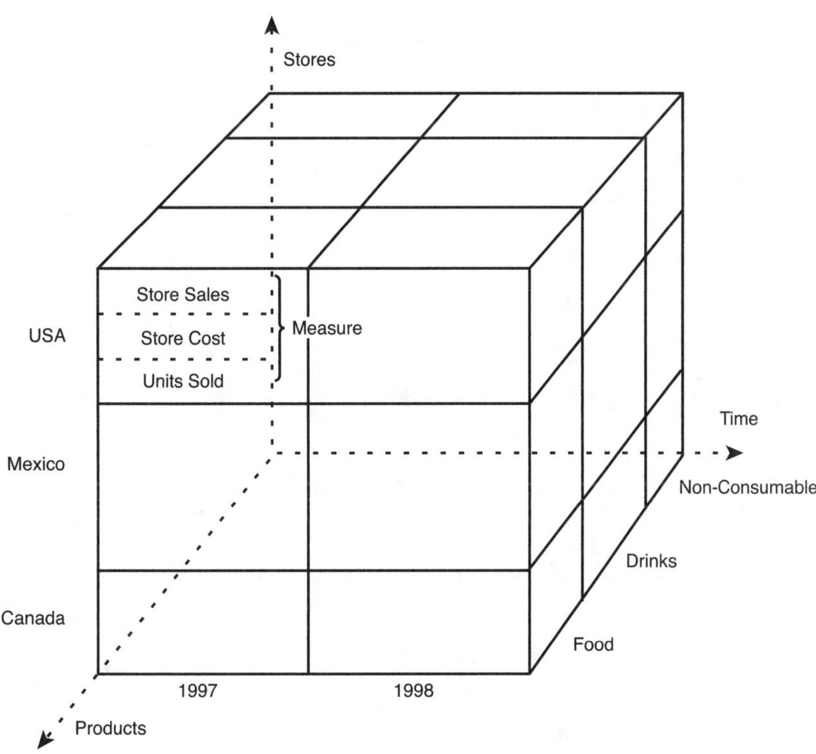

FIGURE 10.1 A simple three-dimensional cube contains dimensions on three axes.

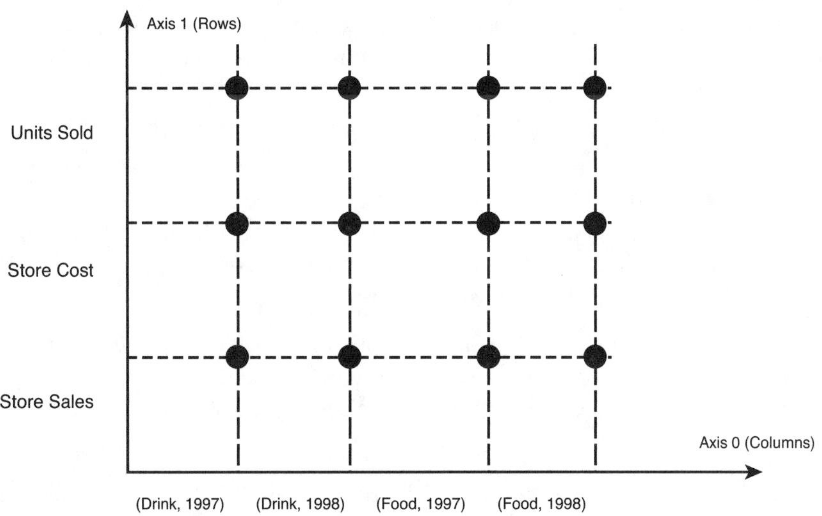

FIGURE 10.2 The projection of dimension members on two axes produces a two-dimensional space.

LISTING 10.2 Dimension Members Are Projected on Two Axes

```
SELECT
{([Drink],[1997]),([Drink],[1998]),([Food], [1997]),([Food], [1998])} ON COLUMNS,
{[Measures].[Store Sales],[Measures].[Store Cost], [Measures].[Unit Sales]} ON ROWS
FROM [Warehouse and Sales]
```

If we execute this query in the MDX query editor of SSMS, we get the results arranged in a grid, shown in Figure 10.3.

	Drink	Drink	Food	Food
	1997	1998	1997	1998
Store Sales	48836.2100000001	93742.1600000003	409035.59	778135.800000001
Store Cost	19747702346	37498.6690000001	163270.7235	311993.641900003
Unit Sales	24597	46954	191940	365923

FIGURE 10.3 The results of our query appear in this grid.

Default Members and the WHERE Clause

Each cell in a multidimensional space is defined by all the attributes (or attribute hierarchies) in the cube. Some of the attributes are specified in a `SELECT` clause and define the shape of the resulting multidimensional space. But what happens when the cube has more attributes than the ones that we projected on the axes in Figure 10.1? How can those missing coordinates be defined?

Look back at Figures 10.1 and 10.2. Figure 10.1 represents the multidimensional space where data is stored, and Figure 10.2 represents the multidimensional space that is the result of the query. Now let's pick up one of the resulting cells (for example, `Store Sales`, `Drink`, `1997`) and see how the system assigned coordinates that can be used to retrieve the data from the cube.

You can see in Figure 10.4 that the cell coordinates are based on the attributes of all the dimensions in the cube: `Store`, `Product`, `Time`, and `Measures`. The coordinates on three of those dimensions were defined by the `SELECT` statement and are shaded in the figure. The fourth dimension, `Stores`, was left undefined by the query.

When the cube has more attributes than the number of attributes that are projected on the axes, the system creates an axis, called the *slicer axis*, which contains all the other attributes. The slicer axis is made up of one member from each of those attributes; those members are called *default members*.

In the design phase, you can choose a specific member as the default member for the attribute, by setting the `DefaultMember` property of either the `Dimension` attribute or the `Perspective` attribute. For example, you might decide that the default member of the `Currency` attribute should be the U.S. dollar. If you don't specify a default member in the model, however, the system chooses default members automatically.

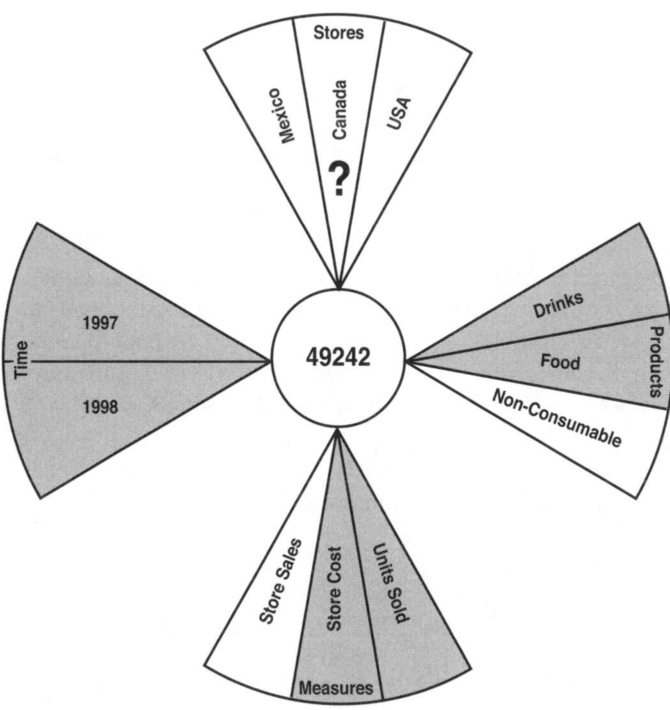

FIGURE 10.4 The coordinates of the cell are based on the attributes of the dimensions in the cube.

Usually, if the attribute is aggregatable (the attribute hierarchy has an `ALL` level), the member `ALL` is used as the default member. This arrangement makes sense because a user typically wants to see aggregated values unless she didn't explicitly specify a coordinate in her query. For example, if user explicitly did not specified `Stores` dimension in the query, Analysis Services uses member `ALL`, and the result value will be total costs in all the stores.

If attribute cannot be aggregated, Analysis Services chooses any member from this attribute—usually it's the first member of an attribute—but the rules are a little bit more complicated, because the system tries to choose a member other than `Unknown`, hidden, or secure.

The notion of the default member is an important one. Analysis Services uses default members every time the MDX query hasn't specified a coordinate from particular attribute. When you write your query, it's important to know which member is the default member. To find out which member is the default member, you can use either `Schema Rowset` or the MDX function `Hierarchy.DefaultMember`. (Even though we're looking for a member of an attribute, MDX works through the hierarchy.) Here's an example of the MDX function:

```
SELECT [Store].[Stores].DefaultMember ON COLUMNS FROM [Warehouse and Sales]
```

Figure 10.5 illustrates the result of this query.

10

FIGURE 10.5 The default member of the `Stores` hierarchy of the `Store` dimension appears as a result of the query.

You can specify in the query the exact member (a slice) or a set of members (a subcube) you want to slice the data by. To limit the results to a particular slice or subcube, you can specify the slice or subcube in a `WHERE` clause. In the preceding example, instead of using the default member of the `Store` dimension, we could have specified a `Country` attribute or any other attribute of the `Store` dimension we want to see the data for, as we do in Listing 10.3.

LISTING 10.3 Using a **WHERE** Clause to Slice the Result by Country

```
SELECT
{([Drink],[1997]),([Drink],[1998]),([Food],[1997]),([Food],[1998])} ON COLUMNS,
{[Measures].[Store Sales],[Measures].[Store Cost],[Measures].[Unit Sales]} ON ROWS
FROM [Warehouse and Sales] WHERE [Store].[Stores].[Store Country].[Mexico]
```

Figure 10.6 shows the result of the query in the preceding listing.

	Drink	Drink	Food	Food
	1997	1998	1997	1998
Store Sales	(null)	36890.3099999999	(null)	311041.43
Store Cost	(null)	14724.0922	(null)	124871.303100001
Unit Sales	(null)	18483	(null)	146642

FIGURE 10.6 The query with the **WHERE** clause results in this data.

NOTE

Analysis Services 2000 supports only a single tuple in a `WHERE` clause. But Analysis Services 2005 and Analysis Services 2008 support a set of tuples in a `WHERE` clause. (See Chapter 11 for details about sets in the `WHERE` clause.)

It's not mandatory that you have a `WHERE` clause in your query.

The WHERE clauses in SQL and MDX are conceptually different. A SQL WHERE clause is used to restrict the rows that are returned as a result of the query; it's there to condition the result. On the other hand, an MDX WHERE clause is used to define a slice of the cube. It's mainly designed to clarify the coordinates for the dimension attributes that weren't specified in the SELECT clause.

Now that we're talking about the differences between the WHERE clause in MDX and SQL, we need to mention one similarity introduced in Analysis Services 2005: The WHERE clause in MDX can also serve to restrict the tuples that are returned by the query. But we are getting a bit ahead of ourselves. We talk about this capability of the MDX query in the section "Existing and Nonexisting Tuples, Auto-Exist" in Chapter 11.

Query Execution Context

Now that we've covered how you create an MDX query, we move on to what happens on the server when Analysis Services receives the query. Analysis Services first iterates over the members of the sets along each axis.

NOTE

Those members are returned to the client application, and the client application usually displays them as labels on a grid, or maybe labels along the axes of a chart.

Analysis Services then calculates the cell value for the intersection of the coordinates from each axis. The coordinate in which context the value is calculated is called the *current* coordinate.

In a simple case where there is only one tuple in the WHERE clause, Analysis Services creates the current coordinate using one member from each attribute of each of the dimensions in the cube. If there is a set in the WHERE clause, the current coordinate is a more complex data structure: a subcube. (For a discussion of such complex cases, see the section "Sets in a Where Clause" in Chapter 11.)

The current coordinate is built from the members of the attributes that were used in the WHERE clause and from members of the attributes corresponding to the current iteration over each axis. For attributes that have been referenced neither on the axes nor in the WHERE clause, Analysis Services uses the default members. In Listing 10.5, we look under the hood as Analysis Services calculates a single cell of a simple query.

LISTING 10.5 Calculating a Cell in a Simple Query

```
SELECT {([Customer].[Customers].[Country].&[USA])} ON COLUMNS,
       {([Product].[Products].[Product
Family].[Drink],[Time].[Time].[Year].[1998])} ON ROWS
FROM [Warehouse and Sales]
WHERE [Measures].[Unit Sales]
```

As we go along, we explain what Analysis Services does along the way as it populates the current coordinate.

1. The current coordinate is populated with the default members of all the attribute hierarchies. Internally it looks like this:

```
(Measures.DefaultMember,
Customer.City.All, Customer.Country.All, Customer.All, Customer.Education.All,
➥Customer.Gender.All,...
Product.Brand.All, Product.Product.All, Product.Category.All, Product.
➥Department.All, Product.Family.All,...
Time.Date.All, Time.Day.All, Time.Month.All, Time.Quorter.All, Time.Week.All,
➥Time.Year.All,...
Store.Store.All, Store.Store City.All, Store.Store Country.All, Store.Store
➥Manager.All,...
   )
```

2. The current coordinate is overwritten with the members used in the `WHERE` clause:

```
([Measures].[Unit Sales],
Customer.City.All, Customer.Country.All, Customer.All, Customer.Education.All,
➥Customer.Gender.All,...
Product.Brand.All, Product.Product.All, Product.Category.All, Product.
➥Department.All, Product.Family.All,...
Time.Date.All, Time.Day.All, Time.Month.All, Time.Quorter.All, Time.Week.All,
➥Time.Year.All,
Store.Store.All, Store.Store City.All, Store.Store Country.All, Store.Store
➥Manager.All,...
   )
```

3. The current coordinate is overwritten with the members used in the `Columns` and `Rows` axis:

```
([Measures].[Unit Sales],
Customer.City.All, Customer.Country.USA, Customer.All, Customer.Education.All,
➥Customer.Gender.All,...
Product.Brand.All, Product.Product.All, Product.Category.All, Product.
➥Department.All, [Product].[Product Family].[Drink],...
➥Time.Date.All, Time.Day.All, Time.Month.All, Time.Quorter.All, Time.Week.All,
Time.Year.1998,...
Store.Store.All, Store.Store City.All, Store.Store Country.All, Store.Store
➥Manager.All,...
   )
```

4. The value of the first cell produced by this query is calculated from the coordinates produced by step 3.

In many cases, it's useful to reference the current coordinate in an MDX expression. For this, MDX provides the `<hierarchy>.CurrentMember` function. This function returns a projection of the current coordinate onto a particular hierarchy.

NOTE

The `CurrentMember` function returns a member. So, in the case where your `WHERE` clause contains more than one member from the attribute that the hierarchy corresponds to, the `CurrentMember` function returns an error.

Set Algebra and Basic Set Operations

In the earlier discussion about the multidimensional coordinate system and ways of defining the coordinates of multidimensional space, we stated—although not in these exact words—that you can define a multidimensional space by projecting a set on an axis. In this section, we discuss set algebra in greater detail and how it is used in MDX.

Three set algebra operations and two basic set operations enable you to construct new MDX sets from existing ones:

- `Union`
- `Intersect`
- `Except`
- `CrossJoin`
- `Extract`

Union

`Union` combines two or more sets of the same dimensionality into one set, as shown in Figure 10.7. The resulting set contains all the tuples from each of the sets. If a tuple exists in both of the original sets, it is added to the new (`Union`) set just once—the duplicate tuple is not added. This operation is equivalent to the addition operator.

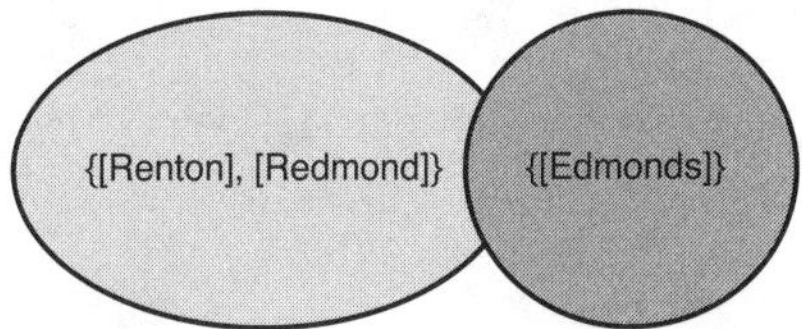

FIGURE 10.7 These two sets have been united using the `Union` operation.

10

The code that produces this result is as follows:

```
SELECT Union({[Renton],[Redmond]},{[Edmonds]}) ON COLUMNS
FROM [Warehouse and Sales]
```

Which returns the following set:

```
{Renton, Redmond, Edmonds}
```

Because Union is the equivalent of an addition operation, you can also use a + operator to create a union of sets:

```
SELECT {[Renton],[Redmond]}+{[Edmonds]} ON COLUMNS FROM [Warehouse and Sales]
```

MDX supports one more syntax for the Union operation using curly braces, but that operation is not exactly equivalent to the Union function or to the + operator. When two sets that are united by curly braces have duplicated tuples, the resulting set retains the duplicates. For example

```
SELECT {{[Renton],[Redmond],[Edmonds]},{[Edmonds]}} ON COLUMNS
FROM [Warehouse and Sales]
```

Returns the following set:

```
{Renton, Redmond, Edmonds, Edmonds}
```

Intersect

Intersect constructs a new set by determining which tuples the two sets have in common, as shown in Figure 10.8.

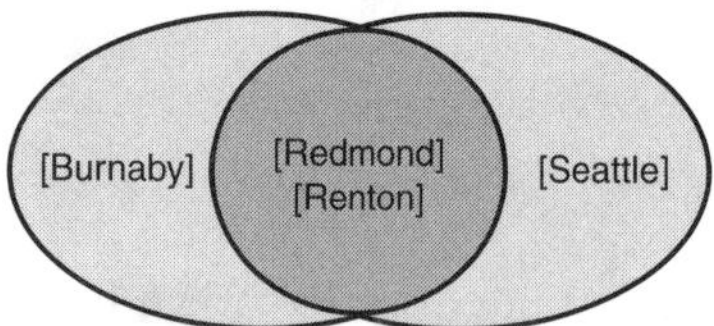

FIGURE 10.8 The intersection of two sets constitutes a new set with the tuples that the two original sets have in common.

For example, the following code

```
SELECT INTERSECT({[Burnaby], [Redmond], [Renton]}, {[Redmond], [Renton],[Everett]})
➥ON COLUMNS FROM [Warehouse and Sales]
```

Returns the following set:

```
{Redmond, Renton}
```

Except

Except finds the differences between two sets, as shown in Figure 10.9. This operation constructs a new set that contains elements that are members of one set, but not members of the other. This operation is equivalent to the subtraction operator (-).

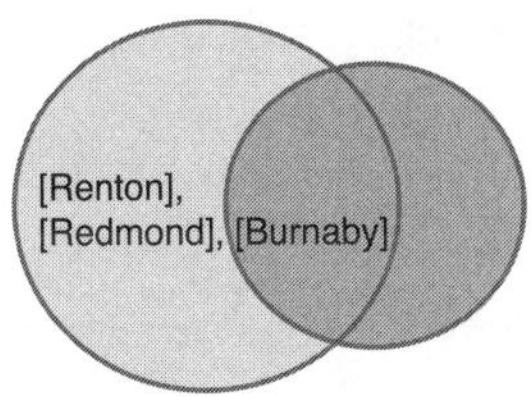

FIGURE 10.9 After an Except operation, a new set that contains elements that are members of one set, but not members of the other, is constructed.

For example

```
SELECT Except({[Renton],[Redmond],[Burnaby]},{[Burnaby]}) on COLUMNS FROM
➥[Warehouse and Sales]
```

Returns the following set:

```
{Renton, Redmond}
```

Because Except is equivalent to the subtraction operator (-), MDX provides an alternative syntax for this operation. The following query, an example of that alternative syntax, returns the same results as the previous one:

```
SELECT {[Renton],[Redmond],[Burnaby]}-{[Burnaby]} ON COLUMNS FROM [Warehouse
➥and Sales]
```

CrossJoin

CrossJoin is one of the most often used operations of MDX. It generates a set that contains all the possible combinations of two (or more) sets, as shown in Figure 10.10.

	[1997]	[1998]
[USA]	([1997],[USA])	([1998],[USA])
[Canada]	([1997],[Canada])	([1998],[Canada])
[Mexico]	([1997],[Mexico])	([1998],[Mexico])

FIGURE 10.10 Using CrossJoin on two sets results in a set that contains a combination of the two.

This function is typically used to project members from different hierarchies on the same axis. CrossJoin is equivalent to the multiplication operation. For example

```
SELECT CROSSJOIN({[1997],[1998]},{[USA],[CANADA], [MEXICO]}) ON COLUMNS FROM
➥[Warehouse and Sales]
```

Results in the following set:

```
{([1997],[USA]),([1997],[Canada]),([1997],[Mexico]),
([1998],[USA]),([1998],[Canada]),([1998],[Mexico])}
```

And the following

```
SELECT {[1997],[1998]}*{[USA],[CANADA],[MEXICO]} ON COLUMNS FROM [Warehouse and
➥Sales]
```

Results in the same set.

NOTE

In Analysis Services 2000, there was one small difference between these two syntaxes: The `CrossJoin` function was limited to working with two sets, whereas the * operator functioned like a `CrossJoin` with as many sets as your system permits. This limitation was lifted in Analysis Services 2005; the `CrossJoin` function now can take any number of sets.

Extract

`Extract` creates a set that contains only tuples of a specific hierarchy from the set as specified by the hierarchy expression in the second argument of the `Extract` function. This operation is the opposite of `CrossJoin`.

For example

```
SELECT Extract(CROSSJOIN({[1997],[1998]},{[USA],[CANADA], [MEXICO]}),
➥[Time].[Time]) ON COLUMNS FROM [Warehouse and Sales]
```

Results in the following set:

```
{[1997],[1998]}
```

MDX Functions

You can create new sets by performing certain set algebra operations on existing sets, but you must have some original sets to start with. If you had to enumerate tuples to create a set, you would be forced into a process that would be highly inconvenient, not to mention not optimal, and, more than that, not scalable.

To enable you to avoid such pain, MDX provides a rich set of functions so that you can create set objects that you can use to operate with sets. In addition to functions for working with sets, MDX provides functions that operate with other multidimensional objects such as dimensions, hierarchies, levels, members, tuples, and scalars. (A *scalar* is a constant value, such as a number or a string.)

You can use MDX functions to construct MDX fragments, also known as MDX expressions. In this chapter, we explain how to use MDX functions and take a look at a few of the most basic and important functions in MDX.

If you look at things from a syntactical point of view, you can divide MDX functions into two groups: methods and properties. There's no important difference between those groups, except their syntax.

Methods have the following syntax:

```
<function_name>([<parameter>[,<parameter>...]])
```

For example

```
CROSSJOIN({[1997],[1998]},{[USA],[CANADA], [MEXICO]})
```

Properties have the following syntax:

```
<object_name>.<property_name>[(<parameter>[,<parameter>...]])
```

For example

```
[Time].[Time].DefaultMember
```

Both kinds of MDX functions return MDX values of one of the following types: `Dimension`, `Hierarchy`, `Level`, `Member`, `Tuple`, `Set`, and `Scalar`. These values can be passed as parameters to other MDX functions.

For example, the `CrossJoin` function produces a set that we pass as a parameter to the `Extract` function:

```
EXTRACT(CROSSJOIN({[1997],[1998]},{[USA],[CANADA],[MEXICO]}),
[Time].[Time])
```

Now that we've covered how MDX functions can be written and used, let's take a look at the most commonly used functions and lay a foundation for understanding more complex ones.

Functions for Navigating Hierarchies

Multidimensional data stored in Analysis Services is often traversed using navigation paths that are defined by hierarchies. Members in the hierarchies are usually displayed as a tree. In Figure 10.11, you can see the user-defined hierarchy `Stores` of the `Store` dimension.

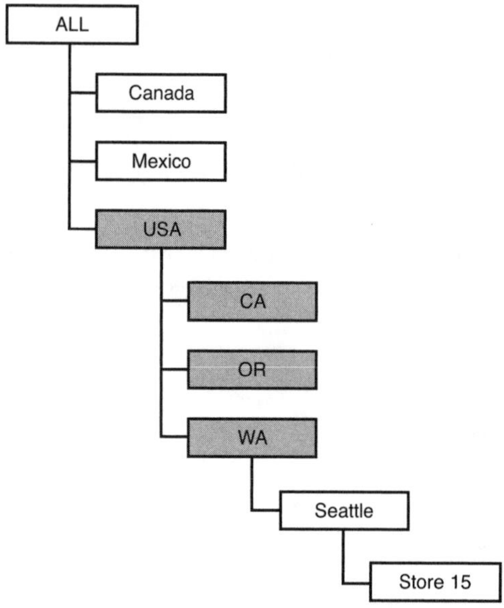

FIGURE 10.11 The Stores hierarchy appears as a tree.

In this hierarchy, the member ALL is the parent of the members on the next level of the hierarchy: Canada, Mexico, and USA. The states CA, OR, and WA are children of USA, and so on. The states CA, OR, and WA are also descendants of the member ALL, and ALL is an ancestor of the members that represent the states.

What we just said in English can be expressed in MDX using hierarchy navigation functions:

```
<member>.Children, <member>.Parent, <level>.Members, <hierarchy>.members,
➥Descendants and Ancestors
```

Let's use our tree of members of the Stores hierarchy to see how you can use the .Children function. In this example, we call this function on the member USA:

```
SELECT [USA].Children ON COLUMNS FROM [Warehouse and Sales]
```

It returns a set that contains all the children of the member USA—that is, the states—as shown in Figure 10.12.

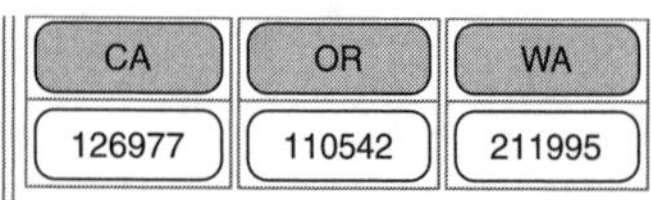

CA	OR	WA
126977	110542	211995

FIGURE 10.12 The function .Children produces a set of members that are children of the current member.

The `Descendants` function is a little bit more complex, but it is more flexible and easier to use. We can call it to get the children of the children of members all the way down to the bottom of the hierarchy (leaves).

For example, if we need to analyze the sales of the stores located in different U.S. cities, we would write the following query:

```
SELECT DESCENDANTS([USA],[Store City]) ON COLUMNS
FROM [Warehouse and Sales]
```

This query returns the set shown in Figure 10.13.

HQ	Store 6	Store 7	Store 24	Store 14	Store 11	Store 13	Store 2	Store 3	Store 15	Store 16	Store 17	Store 22	Store 23
(null)	22804	53074	47305	3794	38579	71963	4686	32810	58816	18948	69888	4658	22189

FIGURE 10.13 The function **Descendants** returns a set of members that are descendants of the member on a particular level of the hierarchy.

To view the leaf members that are descendants of the member `USA`, we would write the following query:

```
SELECT DESCENDANTS([Store].[Stores].[Store Country].[USA], , LEAVES) on COLUMNS
FROM [Warehouse and Sales]
```

That query returns the set of leaf members shown in Figure 10.14.

HQ	Store 6	Store 7	Store 24	Store 14	Store 11	Store 13	Store 2	Store 3	Store 15	Store 16	Store 17	Store 22	Store 23
(null)	22804	53074	47305	3794	38579	71963	4686	32810	58816	18948	69888	4658	22189

FIGURE 10.14 Using LEAVES keyword in descendants function.

MDX supports many more functions that fall under the category of hierarchy navigation functions, such as `.FirstChild` and `.LastChild`, functions for operating on siblings, and so on. We don't discuss all MDX functions here (if we did, this book would be far too heavy to read), but you can find the syntax of those functions in Books Online.

The Function for Filtering Sets

To solve a business problem, you often need to extract from the set tuples that meet certain criteria. For this, you can use the MDX function `Filter`. `Filter` takes two parameters: a set and an MDX expression that evaluates to a Boolean. A `Filter` function evaluates the Boolean expression against each tuple in the set and produces a set that contains tuples from the original set for which the Boolean expression evaluated to true. For example, if we want to see the stores where the sales in 1998 dropped compared to 1997, we write the following expression:


```
Filter( [Store].[Stores].[Store].members, ( [Unit Sales], [1998]) < ( [Unit
➥Sales], [1997])).
```

Or, we can put this expression into a `SELECT` statement and execute it in the SSMS. Figure 10.15 shows the results.

	Store 7	Store 24	Store 14	Store 11	Store 13	Store 2	Store 3	Store 23
1997	25663	25635	2117	26079	41580	2237	24576	11491
1998	24061	24222	2027	25266	35346	1984	24069	9710

FIGURE 10.15 The `Filter` function returns the set of stores that have been less profitable in 1998 than in 1997.

```
SELECT
Filter([Store].[Stores].[Store].members,
([Unit Sales],[1998]) < ([Unit Sales],[1997])) ON COLUMNS,
{[1997],[1998]} ON ROWS FROM [Warehouse and Sales] WHERE [Unit Sales]
```

In MDX, it is not only the cell values that are calculated in the query context; all MDX expressions are calculated in the query context, too. To execute a `Filter` function, we have to evaluate a filter expression: `([Unit Sales],[1998]) < ([Unit Sales],[1997])`. This expression contains only attributes from the `Measure` and `Time` dimensions. All the other attributes are obtained by the steps described in the section "Query Execution Context." Analysis Services first applies the default members of all the attributes to the current coordinate, and then it overwrites the attributes referenced in the `WHERE` clause. Then Analysis Services overwrites the attributes from the expression and, finally, it overwrites the attributes in the filtering set. Let's use another example to show which attributes are used during different stages of `Filter` function execution. Let's assume that we need to analyze the sales by store in the year 1997, and filter out the stores that sold more than 1,000 items, as in Listing 10.6.

LISTING 10.6 A **`Filter`** Expression Affects the Current Coordinate

```
SELECT Filter( [Store].[Store].[Store Country].members,
➥[Measures].[Unit Sales].Value >1000) ON COLUMNS
➥FROM [Warehouse and Sales] WHERE ([Time].[Time].[Year].[1997])
```

In this query, we filter the stores by the measure `Unit Sales`. Our FoodMart stores were first created in the United States; so, in 1997, all sales occurred only in the United States. But in 1998, products were sold in all three countries. If the `Filter` expression were calculated in the context of the expression rather than the context of the entire query, we would get all three countries: the United States, Mexico, and Canada. (The default member of the `Time` dimension is the member `ALL`.) In this query, however, we get only one county—USA—because the current context for the execution of the expression includes members specified in the `WHERE` clause (see Figure 10.16).

To look a little deeper into this case, we can ask, "What would happen if the attributes used in the filter expression were the same as the attributes used in the `WHERE` clause?" Let's say that the query has a `Measure` dimension in both the `WHERE` clause and the filter

USA
227238

FIGURE 10.16 The WHERE clause affects the calculation of the filter expression and result of the `Filter` function.

expression. When Analysis Services executes the filter expression, it would use the `Unit Sales` measure; but to calculate the cell values, it would use the `Store Sales` measure (see Figure 10.17).

```
SELECT Filter( [Store].[Store].[Store Country].members,
[Measures].[Unit Sales].Value >1000) ON COLUMNS FROM [Warehouse and Sales]
WHERE ([Time].[Time].[Year].[1997],[Measures].[Store Sales])
```

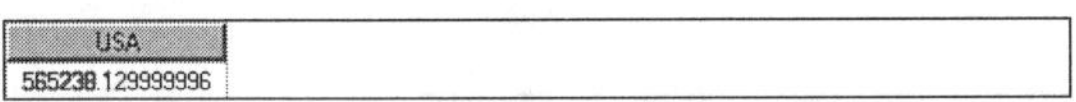

USA
565238.129999996

FIGURE 10.17 When the same attribute is used in the WHERE clause and in the filter expression, the `Filter` function is calculated using the attribute specified in the filter expression, but the cell value is calculated using the attribute specified in the WHERE clause.

NOTE

The rules we just discussed are true for all MDX expressions, not just for the `Filter` function.

Functions for Ordering Data

When you're analyzing data, you quite often need to see it in some particular order associated with the data values. For example, perhaps you want to see the stores that are performing well first and lower-performing stores last. The `Order` function sorts the tuples in the set according to the value of the expression you provide as a parameter. For example, if we are ordering stores according to the values of the `Store Sales` measure, we can write the following MDX statement:

```
SELECT Order( [Store].[Stores].[Store].members, [Measures].[Store Sales], BDESC) ON
➥COLUMNS FROM [Warehouse and Sales]
```

That statement returns the set shown in Figure 10.18.

Store 13	Store 17	Store 15	Store 11	Store 24	Store 7	Store 16	Store 3	Store 6	Store 8	Store 12	Store 19	Store 21	Store 10	St
71963	69888	58816	38579	47305	53074	18948	32810	22804	8153	5191	25061	26060	23902	2

FIGURE 10.18 When you pass the BDESC keyword to the `Order` function, it returns a set of members sorted in descending order.

10

In this statement, we specified that we want our set to be sorted in descending order. And we ignored the hierarchical order of the set; that is, we broke the hierarchy.

Here's an example where it helps to use the hierarchical order. Suppose we need to analyze store performance, but we want to do this in context of the country where the store is located. Therefore, we won't just sort the stores by comparing them to other stores; first, we order the values for the countries where the stores located. Then, we order the states, and then the cities, and after all that, the stores. Now we can compare the value of the sales in one store to the sales in other stores in the same city.

Here's a simpler example that demonstrates how the `Order` function can be used on a smaller set that contains countries and states of the `Store` dimension. In this example, we use a user-defined hierarchy `Stores` shown in Figure 10.11. By passing the keyword `DESC` to the `Order` function, we tell the system to keep the hierarchical order defined by the user-defined hierarchy when it orders the members of the set, as shown in Figure 10.19.

USA	WA	CA	OR	Mexico	Zacatecas	DF	Yucatan	Veracruz	Guerrero	Jalisco	Canada	BC	Unknown	Un
449514	211995	126977	110542	141052	42258	37591	8153	23902	26865	2283	36300	36300	(null)	(

FIGURE 10.19 When you pass the **DESC** keyword to the `Order` function, it takes into account the hierarchical order of the set and return a set of members sorted in descending order.

```
SELECT Order({[Store].[Stores].[Store Country].members,
              [Store].[Stores].[Store State].members},
 [Measures].[Store Sales], DESC) ON COLUMNS
FROM [Warehouse and Sales]
```

The results of this query show that the most sales occurred in the United States, and among the states in the United States, Washington had the biggest sales, followed by the stores in California and then in Oregon.

Referencing Objects in MDX and Using Unique Names

You can choose from various ways to specify `Dimension`, `Hierarchy`, `Level`, and `Member` names in an MDX statement:

- By name
- By qualified name
- By unique name

By Name

Examples in earlier sections have referenced members and other MDX objects by their names. Although this is the simplest syntax for writing an MDX statement by hand (without involving software that generates MDX), it has its drawbacks.

To resolve a member that is referenced by its name, Analysis Services has to iterate over all the dimensions and all their hierarchies, looking for the member with that name. This activity uses a lot of resources, especially when some of the dimension members are stored in a relational database (a ROLAP dimension). In addition, referencing the object by name can also cause ambiguous results in some circumstances (for example, when there are members with the same name in different dimensions, such as `USA` in both the `Customer` and `Product` dimensions).

By Qualified Name

Another way to identify a dimension, hierarchy, level, or member is to use a qualified name:

- For a dimension, this method is almost equivalent to identifying it by name. The only requirement is that the name is surrounded by brackets (`[` and `]`). For example:

  ```
  [Time]
  ```

- For a hierarchy, a qualified name is the qualified name of the dimension separated from the name of the hierarchy with a period (`.`). For example:

  ```
  [Time].[Time]
  ```

- For a level, a qualified name is the qualified name of the hierarchy concatenated with a period (`.`) and the name of the level. For example:

  ```
  [Time].[Time].[Year]
  ```

- For a member, a qualified name is the qualified name of the level or hierarchy followed by the names of all the parents of the current member and the name of the current member. For example:

  ```
  [Time].[Time].[1998].[Q1].[January]
  ```

Referencing objects by qualified names is the oldest way of referencing objects, and is somewhat faster than referencing object by names. It works quite well for dimensions, hierarchies, and levels, but it has many drawbacks for specifying a member.

If a qualified name is created by concatenating the names of the member's parents, the name becomes immobile. It becomes outdated if the member is moved from one parent to another. Think about a customer in the `Customers` hierarchy: That customer could move to a different city, and the name of the member that represents it would be invalidated.

By Unique Name

The third (and, in our view, the correct) way of referencing an object is to use its unique name. Analysis Services assigns a unique name to every dimension, hierarchy, level, and member. The client application that generates MDX or programmer who writes an MDX query can retrieve the unique name of the object using a schema rowset or from the results of another MDX request.

10

In the current version of Analysis Services, the unique name of a member is usually generated based on the member key, but there are quite complicated rules for the unique name generation. We aren't going to provide those rules in this book for a reason. The OLE DB for OLAP specification is quite strict about one rule: An MDX writer should never generate a unique name himself; a unique name should be retrieved from the server.

This rule is imposed not only because the generation of a unique name is a complex task, but because the providers that support MDX can have different algorithms for generating unique names. In addition, those algorithms change from version to version. If you want your application to work with the next and previous versions of Analysis Services and not to break in the corner cases, you should be extra careful not to generate unique names in your application.

CHAPTER 11
Advanced MDX

IN THIS CHAPTER

- Using Member and Cell Properties in MDX Queries
- Dealing with Nulls
- Type Conversions Between MDX Objects
- Strong Relationships
- Sets in a WHERE Clause
- SubSelect and Subcubes

In Chapter 10, "MDX Concepts," we covered working with simple Multidimensional Expressions (MDX) queries. MDX is a complex language. To help you take advantage of its power, we're going to explore advanced MDX capabilities. You can use the technologies discussed here to make it easier to get information from your multidimensional database, understand the information as you retrieve from it, and structure the information that you receive.

Using Member and Cell Properties in MDX Queries

In addition to values of members and cells, the SELECT statement returns properties associated with cells and members. By default, all you can retrieve with the simple MDX queries that we covered in Chapter 10 is a basic set of properties. We're going to use member properties and cell properties to retrieve extended information about the multidimensional data.

Member Properties

For every dimension member in the system, there are properties that characterize this member (for example, the name of the member, its key, its unique name, and a caption translated to a certain language). There are two kinds of member properties:

- **Intrinsic member properties** are available for any member, regardless of the structure of multidimensional model and content of the data. You don't have to define them in the model. Examples of intrinsic properties include MEMBER_NAME, MEMBER_UNIQUE_NAME, MEMBER_CAPTION, PARENT_UNIQUE_NAME, and many others. You can find a full list of intrinsic properties in SQL Server Books Online.

- **Custom member properties** are defined by relationships between attributes in the multidimensional model. All dimension attributes that are related to each other make up a set of the custom member properties. In our FoodMart example, Store Manager, Store Sqft, and Store Type are custom member properties for all members of the Store attribute. (For more information, see Chapter 5, "Dimensions in the Conceptual Model.")

In Analysis Services 2000, you had to define all member properties when creating a multidimensional model. In Analysis Services 2005 and Analysis Services 2008, member properties are implicitly created when you define dimension attributes and the relationships between them, but they can be modified by a designer of multidimensional model if needed.

There are two different ways of using an MDX query to request a member property. In the following query, we use a DIMENSION PROPERTIES clause of an axis specification to get the name of the manager of Store 1:

```
SELECT [Store 1] DIMENSION PROPERTIES [Store].[Store].[Store Manager]
        ON COLUMNS FROM [Warehouse and Sales]
```

This query, in addition to standard properties such as MEMBER_NAME, MEMBER_UNIQUE_NAME, and so on retrieves the Store Manager property for all the members you specified in the axis specification. You can use this syntax if, for example, you want to display member properties in the user interface, maybe as an additional column to a report. You can see member properties in SQL Server Management Studio by double-clicking the member name, as shown in Figure 11.1.

Another way to retrieve member properties is to use the MDX Properties function. This function is called on the member and takes a string containing the name of member property. One way you might use this function is to order a set of members by a property. For example, the following query orders the set of all stores by the store size:

```
SELECT
{[Measures].[Store Cost]} ON COLUMNS,
Order( [Store].[Store].[Store].members,
store.store.currentmember.Properties("Store Sqft")) ON ROWS FROM [Warehouse and
Sales]
```

Cell Properties

Just like the dimension member has member properties associated with it, each cell has cell properties associated with it. Analysis Services supports only intrinsic cell properties, unlike the member properties for which both intrinsic and custom properties are supported. The designer of the multidimensional model can't create custom cell properties.

All MDX SELECT statements return a default set of cell properties:

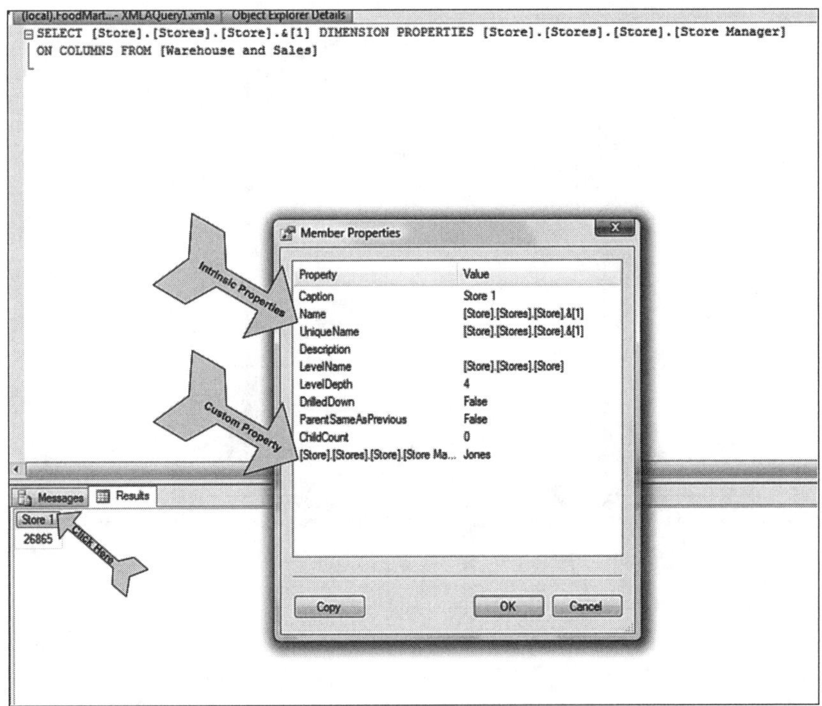

FIGURE 11.1 Custom and intrinsic member properties.

- **CELL_ORDINAL**—The ordinal number of the cell in the resultset
- **VALUE**—The value of the cell
- **FORMATTED_VALUE**—The string that represents the value of the cell, with special formatting applied to it

When you write an MDX query, you can list other properties that you want to retrieve as part of the query response. You can use the CELL PROPERTIES clause in the SELECT statement to specify those properties. In the following query, we request the name of the font that the client application can use to display the cell value and the string that Analysis Services uses to format the value:

```
SELECT Measures.Members on COLUMNS FROM [Warehouse and Sales]
CELL PROPERTIES VALUE, FORMATTED_VALUE, FONT_NAME, FORMAT_STRING
```

Figure 11.2 shows the results of this query.

CAUTION

There is a small, but important, difference between cell properties and member properties:

- If a DIMENSION PROPERTIES clause is present in a query, all standard member properties are retrieved by the query.

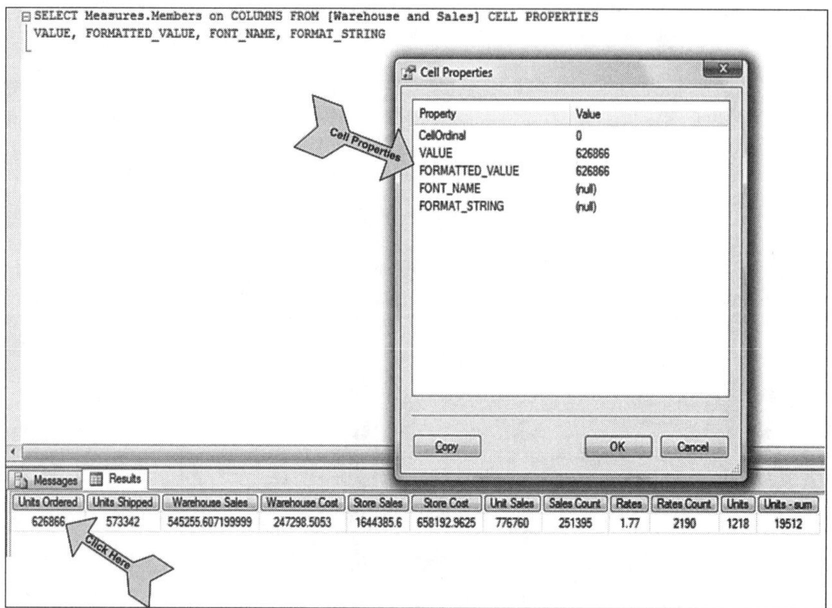

FIGURE 11.2 Cell properties.

▶If a CELL PROPERTIES clause is present in a query, only the properties you specified in the clause are returned in the result.

This means that if you have included a CELL PROPERTIES clause, the VALUE property won't be returned unless you explicitly specify it in the CELL PROPERTIES clause.

Most cell properties are used to enable client applications to provide "smart" formatting and coloring of the cell display. For example, FORMAT_STRING and FORMATTED_VALUE are intended to enable custom formatting of values, such as putting a dollar sign ($) before a value that represents currency. This formatting is controlled by rules defined by the OLE DB for OLAP specification.

NOTE

On the MSDN website, you can find various documentation about how the formatting works, at http://msdn.microsoft.com/en-us/library/aa262745.aspx. You can find out how formatting works in the OLE DB for OLAP specification (content of FORMAT_STRING topic) at http://msdn.microsoft.com/en-us/library/ms146084.aspx.

The FORE_COLOR and BACK_COLOR properties were designed to enable the client application to draw the attention of the user to particular patterns in the data. For example, you could enable the application to display profits in green and losses in red in a financial report.

You can use other cell properties to enable a client application to take advantage of some of the advanced features of Analysis Services. For example, you can use the ACTION_TYPE property to retrieve information about an action associated with the cell. (For more information about actions, see Chapter 15, "Key Performance Indicators, Actions, and the DrillThrough Statement.")

Dealing with Nulls

In MDX, you define the resulting multidimensional space using dimension members. In practice, it's quite possible that an MDX query would reference a member that doesn't exist in the cube or a cell value that is empty. In scenarios such as that, you have to deal with null values and null members.

Null Members, Null Tuples, and Empty Sets

When you write an MDX expression or an MDX query, you might specify a coordinate using a member that lies outside of the boundaries of the cube. There are different scenarios in which this might happen (for example, a query that requests the parent of a member at the top level). To work with such scenarios, Analysis Services uses the concepts of the null member and the null tuple:

- Analysis Services uses a null member to reference a coordinate that is outside the cube space.
- If a tuple contains at least one null member, it's called a *null tuple.*

In some cases, null members and null tuples are allowed; in others, they are not. For example, some MDX functions return an error if a null member or tuple is passed as a parameter, such as <null_member>.Dimension; others don't return an error: IsAncestor(<null_member>,<member>).

If a set contains only null tuples, it's called an *empty set.* If a set contains both regular and null tuples, only regular tuples are returned to the user. For example, the following query returns just one tuple, shown in Figure 11.3:

```
SELECT {[All], [All].Parent} ON COLUMNS FROM [Warehouse and Sales]
```

FIGURE 11.3 Only regular tuples are returned to the user.

Let's take a look at some scenarios in which null members, null tuples, and empty sets might occur.

Missing Member Mode

In Analysis Services 2000, referencing a member by a name that doesn't correspond to any member in the cube produces an error. But Analysis Services 2005 introduces a new feature, Missing Member mode, to deal with situations such as these:

- When you write an MDX query, you might mistakenly specify a member that doesn't exist in the cube.
- In an even more common scenario, a client application might save queries that reference certain members, but those members no longer exist after the cube is reprocessed.

Missing Member mode allows an MDX query or expression to reference members that do not exist in the cube. Those members are converted internally to null members and are treated by the system as any other null member. The behavior of Analysis Services when Missing Member mode is turned on is close to the behavior of SQL Server. For example, if we want to select some of the customers of our FoodMart stores, we could write the following SQL query:

```
SELECT   lname   FROM   dbo.customer WHERE lname = 'Berger' or lname='Gorbach'
```

There is no customer named Gorbach in the database, so this query would return only the rows for Berger. It would not return an error.

In a similar MDX query, the absence of Gorbach in the database would trigger an error in Analysis Services 2000, but not in later versions of Analysis Services with Missing Member mode turned on. The following MDX query returns a single member, Berger:

```
SELECT {[Customer].[Alexander Berger],[Customer].[Irina Gorbach]} ON
        COLUMNS FROM [Warehouse and Sales]
```

Figure 11.4 shows the result of this query, where only Alexander Berger is listed.

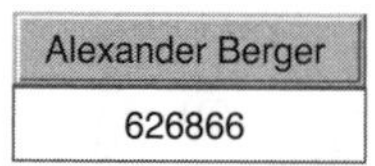

FIGURE 11.4 The system converts a member that does exist to a null.

Missing Member mode was designed to support reporting applications that store queries against cubes with some dimensions that change frequently. Certain dimensions are more flexible than others when it comes to changes in data. For example, a customer dimension probably changes a lot, but a time dimension is pretty stable.

So, it makes sense to allow and disallow Missing Member mode per dimension. To make this possible, the dimension has an `MdxMissingMemberMode` property, which can be set to `Error` or `IgnoreError`. By default, the missing member mode is set to `IgnoreError`.

However, because Missing Member mode is specified per dimension, you'll get an error if you misspell the name of a dimension.

Missing Member mode is automatically turned off when you specify an expression for dimension security, key performance indicators, actions, or cube calculation (all features that we haven't talked about yet, but promise to in future chapters). It would cause quite a mess if a typo in the dimension security definition caused dimension security to be ignored.

A client application can use the `MdxMissingMemberMode` connection string property to turn off Missing Member mode. For example, if an application allows user input a text of an MDX expression and needs to generate an error when a user misspells a member name, the application would turn off the feature.

Existing and Nonexisting Tuples, Auto-Exist

Previously, we said that the space of the cube can be defined by the members of the attribute hierarchies. In reality, however, actual space of the cube is smaller. There are combinations of members from different attribute hierarchies that just don't exist in the dimension table or in the cube. For example, because Nina Metz is female, we have a record `Nina Metz, F` in the `Customer` dimension table. Therefore, the tuple `([Customer].[Gender].&[F], [Nina Metz])` exists in the `Customer` dimension. But, the tuple `([Customer].[Gender].&[M], [Nina Metz])` doesn't exist. So, we have an existing tuple and a nonexisting tuple.

It is possible to reference a tuple that doesn't exist in the cube, but it will resolve to a null tuple internally. For example, the following query returns an empty result because the tuple `([Customer].[Gender].&[M], [Nina Metz])` doesn't exist:

```
SELECT {([Customer].[Gender].&[M], [Nina Metz]) } on COLUMNS FROM [Warehouse and
Sales]
```

The result of executing an MDX expression can't be a nonexisting tuple. Therefore, the system internally removes nonexisting tuples from the set in an operation we call *auto-exist*. You can see the results of the system employing auto-exist in the execution of the following `CrossJoin` function. If the sets participating in the `CrossJoin` function belong to the same dimension, the tuples that don't exist are removed. For example, if we take a set with two customers—Nina Metz (female) and David Wall (male)—and use `CrossJoin` to combine it with a set containing a single member, `[Customer].[Gender].&[M]`, the resulting set won't contain the full `CrossJoin (Nina Metz, M), (David Wall, M)`, but only the single tuple `(David Wall, M)`:

```
SELECT { [Nina Metz], [David Wall] } * [Customer].[Gender].&[M] on COLUMNS
FROM  [Warehouse and Sales]
WHERE [Measures].[Unit Sales]
```

Figure 11.5 shows the results of this query.

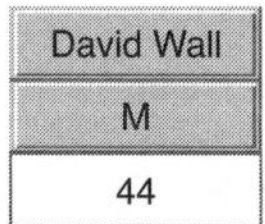

FIGURE 11.5 Analysis Services converts a nonexisting tuple to a null tuple.

In Analysis Services, you can place members of the same dimension, but of different hierarchies, on different axes. In the following query, we have a cell referenced by tuples on different axes and the crossjoin of those tuples doesn't exist:

```
SELECT { [Nina Metz], [David Wall] } ON COLUMNS, [Customer].[Gender].&[M]
ON ROWS FROM [Warehouse and Sales] WHERE [Measures].[Unit Sales]
```

Contrary to what you might expect, Analysis Services doesn't remove the cell referenced by the tuple—`([Nina Metz], [Customer].[Gender].&[M])`—from the resultset, but the cell produced by that combination of tuples will be a nonexisting cell. A nonexisting cell is not just an empty cell; it can't be written back to and you can't define a calculation on the nonexisting cell.

Let's look at an example of a query that produces nonexisting cells. If we place an existing set of two customers—`Nina Metz` and `David Wall`—on one axis and a set that contains the member `[Customer].[Gender].&[M]` on the other axis, the result of the query will be two cells. But the cell produced by the intersection of `Nina Metz` and `Gender Male` is a nonexisting cell. You can see this result in Figure 11.6.

Analysis Services doesn't perform auto-exist between the sets of the axes. But, it does perform auto-exist on the sets projected on the axes with the set projected on the `WHERE` clause. For example, if we put the same set—`{[Nina Metz], [David Wall]}`—on the axis

	Nina Metz	David Wall
M	(null)	44

FIGURE 11.6 The cell produced by the intersection of `Nina Metz` and `Gender Male` is a nonexisting cell.

but [Customer].[Gender].&[M] on the WHERE clause, the tuple [Nina Metz] will be removed from the set projected on the COLUMNS axis:

```
SELECT { [Nina Metz], [David Wall] } ON COLUMNS
FROM [Warehouse and Sales] WHERE ([Measures].[Unit Sales],[Customer].[Gender].&[M])
```

Figure 11.7 shows the results of this query.

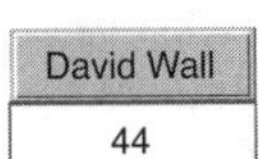

David Wall
44

FIGURE 11.7 Analysis Services applies auto-exist between the sets used on each axis and a set used in a WHERE clause.

You don't have to rely on the system's auto-exist operation to find out which members exist with each other: You can use the MDX function Exists, which was introduced in Analysis Services 2005. Exists takes two sets as parameters and returns a set of tuples from the first set that exist with one or more tuples from the second set:

```
SELECT Exists({[Nina Metz], [David Wall]}, [Customer].[Gender].&[M]) ON COLUMNS
FROM [Warehouse and Sales] WHERE [Measures].[Unit Sales]
```

For example, to retrieve a set of occupations of customers who have a graduate degree, you could write the following query:

```
SELECT Exists([Customer].[Occupation].members
[Customer].[Education].&[Graduate Degree])} on COLUMNS
FROM [Warehouse and Sales]
```

Figure 11.8 shows the results of this query.

All	Management	Professional
626866	626866	626866

FIGURE 11.8 Results of the Exists function.

Nulls and Empty Cells

The logical space of a cube that can be addressed from an MDX query is large. It includes combinations of all the members of all the hierarchies, regardless of whether any data for those combinations exists.

For example, our FoodMart enterprise started its operations in the United States and then extended its operations to Canada and Mexico. Therefore, in 1997, there were sales only in U.S. stores, so there would be no data in the multidimensional space about sales in Canadian and Mexican stores. Suppose that you send the following MDX query to get information about the store sales in 1997 and the occupations of the customer who shopped in those stores, and compare that information across countries where there are stores:

```
SELECT    [Customer].[Occupation].[Occupation].members ON COLUMNS,
          [Store].[Stores].[Store Country].members ON ROWS
FROM [Warehouse and Sales] where ([Measures].[Store Sales],[Time].[Time].[Year].[1997])
```

When you look at the results, shown in Figure 11.9, you see a lot of empty cells. There are many scenarios in which you would like to remove the coordinate (tuple) that would result in empty cells at the intersection of coordinates on the other axes. In Figure 11.9, such tuples and cells appear in gray.

	Clerical	Management	Manual	Professional	Skilled Manual
Canada	(null)	(null)	(null)	(null)	(null)
Mexico	(null)	(null)	(null)	(null)	(null)
USA	8791.30999999999	82377.5699999999	138457	186109.690000001	149502.560000001
Unknown	(null)	(null)	(null)	(null)	(null)

FIGURE 11.9 The results of the query contain empty cells.

To remove coordinates such as those from the resulting multidimensional space, you can use the NON EMPTY operator. Let's see what happens when we rewrite the preceding query using a NON EMPTY operator:

```
SELECT    [Customer].[Occupation].[Occupation].members ON COLUMNS,
          NON EMPTY [Store].[Stores].[Store Country].members ON ROWS
FROM [Warehouse and Sales]
WHERE ([Measures].[Store Sales],[Time].[Time].[Year].[1997])
```

You can see the results (only the cells that contain data) of our new query in Figure 11.10.

	Clerical	Management	Manual	Professional	Skilled Manual
USA	8791.30999999999	82377.5699999999	138457	186109.690000001	149502.560000001

FIGURE 11.10 Results of the query with the NON EMPTY operator.

However, even if you use the NON EMPTY operator, your query results can contain empty cells because NON EMPTY removes tuples for which *all* the cells are empty. If we were talking about two-dimensional space, the preceding sentence would go something like this: Your query results can contain empty cells because `NON EMPTY` removes only columns or rows in which *all* the cells are empty.

Now let's modify our query. We want to see the occupations of customers across products, according to the years in our time dimension (1997 and 1998). We are going to get some empty cells, but the `NON EMPTY` operator will not remove the tuples Canada and Mexico that correspond to those empty cells because the tuple `(Canada, Clerical, 1997)` is empty, but the tuple `(Canada, Clerical, 1998)` is not:

```
SELECT [Customer].[Occupation].[Occupation].members * Time.Time.Year.members
➥ON COLUMNS,
NON EMPTY [Store].[Stores].[Store Country].members ON ROWS
FROM [Warehouse and Sales] WHERE ([Measures].[Store Sales])
```

The results of this query, in Figure 11.11, show some null (empty) cells.

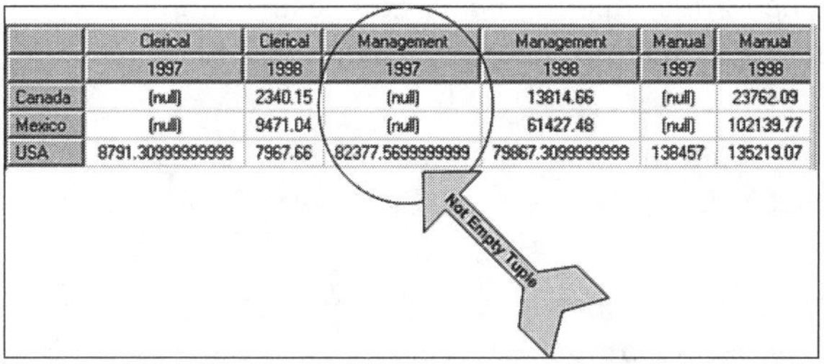

	Clerical	Clerical	Management	Management	Manual	Manual
	1997	1998	1997	1998	1997	1998
Canada	(null)	2340.15	(null)	13814.66	(null)	23762.09
Mexico	(null)	9471.04	(null)	61427.48	(null)	102139.77
USA	8791.30999999999	7967.66	82377.5699999999	79867.3099999999	138457	135219.07

Not Empty Tuple

FIGURE 11.11 A query with a `NON EMPTY` operator can return a resultset that contains empty cells.

Using the `NON EMPTY` operator to remove empty cells is one of the most often used features of MDX. We (the developers of Analysis Services) tried our best to make the execution of this operator as fast as possible, but under certain conditions using the `NON EMPTY` operator can take a substantial amount of time and memory.

The `NON EMPTY` operator operates on the top level of the query. Therefore, the sets defining the axes are generated first, and then the tuples leading to empty cells are removed. There are many scenarios in which an application's performance would greatly benefit if the empty tuples were removed earlier in the query execution logic.

If an MDX query uses a `Filter` function to filter a very large set based on an expression that contains a tuple value and the space of the cube is very sparse, it is much more productive to remove all the tuples that produce the empty cells before performing the filtering. MDX provides the `NonEmpty` function that allows the removal of such tuples from the set.

For example, suppose that you need to filter all the customers with all the stores where they shop. (This would produce a pretty big set.) Now imagine that you want to filter out the customers who bought more than 10 products in each store. To do this, you can write an MDX query:

```
SELECT Filter([Customer].[Customers].[Customer].members *
[Store].[Stores].[Store Country].members, [Measures].[Unit Sales] >10) ON COLUMNS
FROM [Warehouse and Sales] WHERE [Measures].[Unit Sales]
```

You can easily use the NonEmpty function to optimize this query so that it will remove the empty tuples before the set is filtered:

```
SELECT Filter(NonEmpty([Customer].[Customers].[Customer].members *
[Store].[Stores].[Store Country].[Canada],
[Measures].[Unit Sales]), [Measures].[Unit Sales] >10) ON COLUMNS
FROM [Warehouse and Sales] WHERE [Measures].[Unit Sales]
```

NOTE

The NonEmpty function in Analysis Services 2005 replaces NonEmptyCrossjoin from earlier versions because in some advanced scenarios, NonEmptyCrossjoin returns unexpected results.

For example, NonEmptyCrossjoin doesn't work with calculated members or other cube calculations. (You'll find information about those in Chapter 12, "Cube-Based MDX Calculations.")

If you have been using the NonEmptyCrossjoin function in your MDX expressions, we strongly recommend that you replace it with NonEmpty.

At first glance, the NonEmpty function and the NON EMPTY operator seem to be the same thing, but they are executed in different contexts. Queries that might look similar can produce different results. Let's take a look at two queries, one using NonEmpty and another using NON EMPTY:

```
SELECT    [Time].[Time].[Year].[1997] ON COLUMNS,
          NonEmpty  ([Store].[Stores].[Store Country].members) ON ROWS
FROM [Warehouse and Sales]
```

and

```
SELECT    [Time].[Time].[Year].[1997] ON COLUMNS,
          NON EMPTY [Store].[Stores].[Store Country].members ON ROWS
FROM [Warehouse and Sales]
```

The difference between these two is just one space—the one between *non* and *empty*—but those queries return different results. You can see both of those results a little later on, in Figures 11.12 and 11.13.

	1997
Canada	(null)
Mexico	(null)
USA	227238

FIGURE 11.12 The `NonEmpty` function produces null values for Canada and Mexico.

If we analyze the context in which the two algorithms are applied, we can see the rationale for each. The `NonEmpty` function is evaluated when the set that is placed against the `ROWS` axis is evaluated. This evaluation is done independently of an evaluation of the set that is placed against the `COLUMNS` axis. In our query, the set of the `ROWS` axis references only the `Store` dimension, not the `Time` dimension. So, `the NonEmpty` function is evaluated in the context of the default member `ALL` of the `Time` dimension. Therefore, the `NonEmpty` function is calculated for the values of total sales in each country. The values are not empty for both Canada and Mexico.

Therefore, the tuples for Canada and Mexico are not removed from the set after the `NonEmpty` function is applied. When the actual cell values are calculated, however, they are calculated for the intersection of the `COLUMNS` and `ROWS` axes. The current coordinate of the `Time` dimension, therefore, is the year 1997 (where we have no data for either Canada or Mexico), and thus we end up with null values, as you can see in Figure 11.12.

On the other hand, the `NON EMPTY` operator takes into consideration the tuples from all the axes. Therefore, when the `NON EMPTY` algorithm is applied, the results are calculated in the context of the year 1997, for which we have no data for Canada and Mexico. So, the `NON EMPTY` algorithm removes the tuples Canada and Mexico from the results, as you can see in Figure 11.13.

	1997
USA	227238

FIGURE 11.13 The `Non Empty` operator removes Canada and Mexico from the results.

Type Conversions Between MDX Objects

MDX in Analysis Services 2000 is strongly typed. If a function or expression is defined to accept an object of a particular type, you have to explicitly convert the object to that type (if such a conversion is possible, of course) before you can pass it to the function or expression. Let's take a look at the syntax of a `SELECT` statement:

```
SELECT <set> ON COLUMNS, <set> on ROWS FROM <cube> WHERE <set>
```

In Analysis Services 2000, you can't write a query with a single tuple where a set was expected. You have to explicitly convert the tuple to a set:

```
SELECT {[Promotion].[Media Type].[Bulk Mail]} ON COLUMNS FROM [Warehouse and Sales]
```

This limitation is lifted in Analysis Services 2005, which supports implicit type conversion. You can rewrite the preceding query to pass a member to the axis definition expression:

```
SELECT [Promotion].[Media Type].[Bulk Mail] ON COLUMNS FROM [Warehouse and Sales]
```

Of course, this particular improvement might not seem like a big deal, but this simplification lifts a burden from the MDX programmer. Now you don't have to remember to enclose an expression in curly braces to convert a member to a set, nor do you have to enclose an expression in parentheses to convert a member to a tuple.

Not all types of objects can be converted to the objects of another type. There are special rules for type conversion. Figure 11.14 shows what types of objects can be converted to which other types of objects and the rules that govern those conversions. In the diagram, a circle denotes a type and an arrow denotes a conversion rule.

Most of the type conversion rules can be deduced using a common sense. For example, a tuple can always be converted to a set that contains that tuple; analogously, a member can be converted to a tuple that contains the member.

However, some conversion rules, such as those that were invented in an effort to bring the syntax of MDX and SQL closer together, are a bit more complicated. The conversion of a level to a set allows you to write MDX queries in a way that mimics column specifications in SQL. For example, if you needed to use an SQL query to list all the stores, you would write the following:

```
SELECT  store_name FROM store
```

In MDX, the same query would look like this:

```
SELECT  [Store].[Store].[Store].Members ON COLUMNS FROM [$Store]
```

The type conversion rule allows you to skip `.Members` so that it looks like you put only an attribute name on the axis specification. Now you can write an MDX query that looks more like the SQL query:

```
SELECT [Store].[Store].[Store] ON COLUMNS FROM [$Store]
```

Strong Relationships

In the "Query Execution Context" section in the preceding chapter, you can find a discussion about the logic used to generate the current coordinate. The *current coordinate* is a tuple that consists of members corresponding to each attribute in the cube. The current coordinate is generated in the following process starting with the default members for

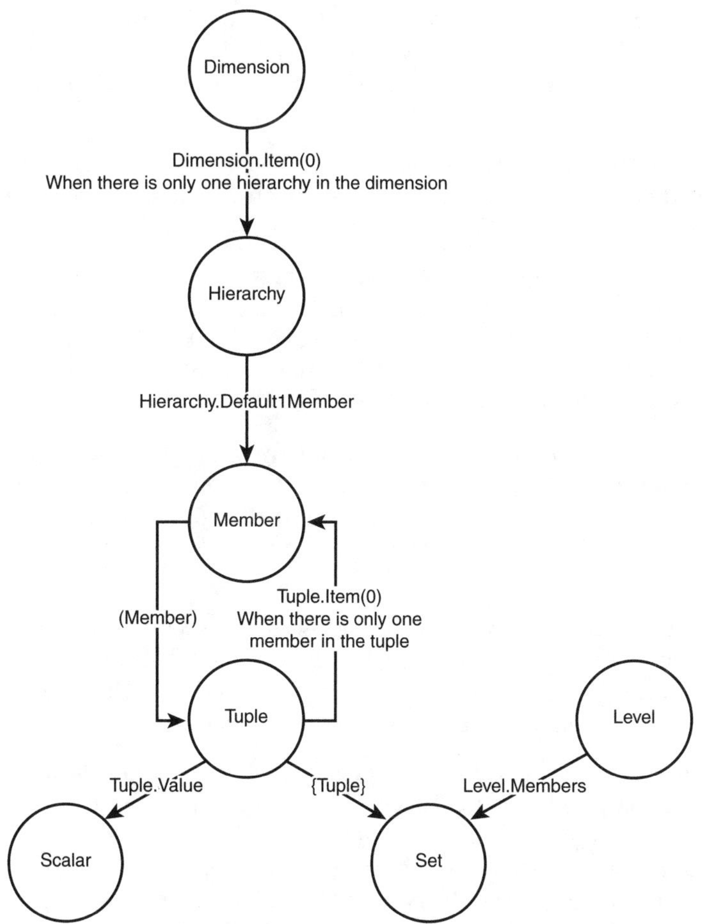

FIGURE 11.14 Objects of certain types can be implicitly converted to other types.

each attribute: The default members are overwritten by the members of attributes specified in the WHERE clause, and then those members are overwritten by members of attributes from each axis. When we say *overwritten,* we mean that the member corresponding to the attribute is changed. In reality, the process is a little more complicated. Let's take a look at this complexity in the following query:

```
SELECT [Time].[Year].CurrentMember ON COLUMNS FROM [Warehouse and Sales]
WHERE [Time].[Time].[Quarter].&[Q1]&[1998]
```

Our cube has three members of the Year attribute: ALL, 1997, and 1998. Assume that you wrote this query and, when you put a slice on the Quarter attribute, you meant Q1 of 1998. But, if Analysis Services blindly follows the rules defined in Chapter 10, you would end up with this as the current coordinate:

```
(..., Time.Year.ALL, Time.Quarter.Q1, Time.Month.ALL,..)
```

The current coordinate of the Year attribute hierarchy would be ALL, and the preceding query would return the member ALL. But, this is not what you really wanted; you meant to request the member 1998. To prevent such errors, Analysis Services applies an algorithm called *strong relationships*.

You'll have an easier time understanding the strong relationships algorithm if you go back and review attribute relationships, covered in Chapter 5. In an attribute relationship, there is one value of the related attribute for each unique value of an attribute.

For example, for each unique value of the Quarter attribute, there is a corresponding unique value of the Year attribute; and for each unique value of the Day attribute, there is a unique value of the Month attribute. Therefore, Day relates to Month, Month relates to Quarter, and Quarter relates to Year. So, we can say that Quarter is a *related attribute* to the Month attribute and is a *relating attribute* to the Year attribute.

You can think of these relationships as similar to a native hierarchy that is automatically created for you. In Analysis Services 2000, which has hierarchy-based architecture, it's not possible to change the current coordinate for quarter without also changing it for the year. By implementing the strong relationships algorithm, we are trying to achieve the same behavior.

When you create a current coordinate with strong relationships, Analysis Services changes not only the value of the attribute specified in the query or expression but also its related and relating attributes. In our example, not only is the Quarter attribute overwritten, but also the Year, Month, Day, and any other attributes related to the Quarter attribute.

When an attribute is overwritten because it is a related or relating attribute, an *implicit overwrite* occurs. In general, implicit overwrite occurs according to the following rules:

- The attribute related to the current one (on top of the current one) is overwritten with the related value. For example, when the current attribute—Quarter—is overwritten with the value Q1, 1998, the Year attribute is overwritten with 1998.
- The attributes relating to the current one (below the current one) are overwritten with the member ALL.

However, when an attribute is overwritten as a result of an implicit overwrite, its own related and relating attributes are not overwritten. For example, if, in the Time dimension the attribute Quarter is overwritten, all the attributes above it are overwritten with their related values (Year is overwritten with the member 1998), and all the attributes below it are overwritten with the member ALL. But after the attribute Year is implicitly overwritten, its relating attribute, Week, is not overwritten. Figure 11.15 demonstrates these rules.

If we finally execute the MDX query that we started with at the beginning of this section

```
SELECT [Time].[Year].CurrentMember ON COLUMNS FROM [Warehouse and Sales]
WHERE [Time].[Time].[Quarter].&[Q1]&[1998]
```

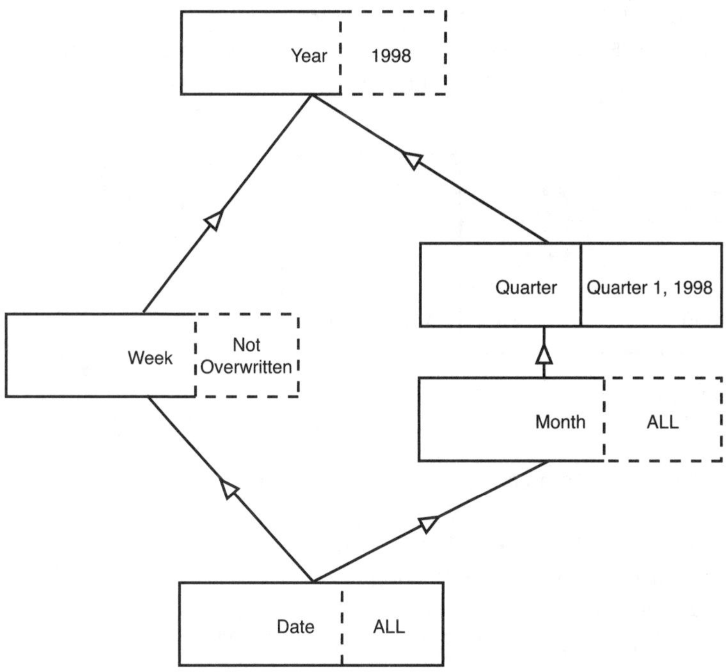

FIGURE 11.15 The rules of the strong relationships algorithm.

we'll get the result we expected—the value of the current member of the `Year` attribute is `1998`, shown in Figure 11.16. The `Year` attribute has been overwritten and now appears as `1998`.

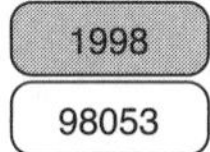

FIGURE 11.16 The `Year` attribute has been overwritten.

Sets in a WHERE Clause

So far, all our examples contained one tuple in a `WHERE` clause—we were slicing the cube in only one layer. Starting from Analysis Services 2005, you can request data sliced by two or more members. You can specify almost any set expression in the `WHERE` clause.

We'll start with a relatively simple example: Our slice contains an `OR` condition between members of the same attribute. You need to analyze the units ordered by warehouses located in different countries over a time period. You aren't interested in the total orders of all possible products, just products in the Drink and Food categories. To accomplish this, you specify a set expression `{[Product].[Products].[Product Family].[Drink], [Product].[Products].[Product Family].[Food]}` in the `WHERE` clause. In the result, you'll get cells that contain aggregated values as you can see in Figure 11.17.

	Canada	Mexico	USA
1997	Food + Drink	Food + Drink	Food + Drink
1998	Food + Drink	Food + Drink	Food + Drink

FIGURE 11.17 A set in a WHERE clause.

The following MDX query enables us to meet the goals we set earlier:

```
SELECT { [Warehouse].[Warehouses].[Country].&[Canada],
         [Warehouse].[Warehouses].[Country].&[Mexico],
         [Warehouse].[Warehouses].[Country].&[USA] }              ON COLUMNS,
        {[Time].[Time].[Year].[1997], [Time].[Time].[Year].[1998]} ON ROWS
FROM    [Warehouse and Sales]
WHERE   {[Product].[Products].[Product Family].[Drink],
        [Product].[Products].[Product Family].[Food] }
```

Figure 11.18 shows the same table that you saw in Figure 11.17, with the values filled in.

	Canada	Mexico	USA
1997	(null)	(null)	185891
1998	29341	114642	180502

FIGURE 11.18 The results of executing the query with a set in the WHERE clause.

NOTE

When it calculates the values of the cells, Analysis Services uses an aggregation formula that corresponds to the measure. In our example, the default measure is `Units Ordered`, whose aggregation function is `SUM`, so the values of the products in the Food family were added to the values of those in the Drink family.

In the example, we used only one attribute in the `WHERE` clause—`Product Family`—but we did that just for the sake of simplicity. The same logic we used in that example could easily be extended to a case in which we have a crossjoin of members from two or more attributes. Internally, it would still be a normal subcube. (For a definition of a normal subcube, see the "Subcubes" section in Chapter 2, "Multidimensional Space.") Let's move the Time attribute to the WHERE clause. Now our query reads like this:

```
SELECT { [Warehouse].[Warehouses].[Country].&[Canada],
         [Warehouse].[Warehouses].[Country].&[Mexico],
         [Warehouse].[Warehouses].[Country].&[USA] } ON COLUMNS
FROM   [Warehouse and Sales]
WHERE  {{[Product].[Products].[Product Family].[Drink],
        [Product].[Products].[Product Family].[Food] } *
        {[Time].[Time].[Year]. [1997], [Time].[Time].[Year].[1998]} }
```

Figure 11.19 shows the results of this query.

Canada	Mexico	USA
29341	114642	366393

FIGURE 11.19 This query with a crossjoin of two sets in WHERE clause.

NOTE

One limitation applies to the types of sets that can be placed in a WHERE clause: You cannot use more than one measure in a WHERE clause. That's understandable because the aggregation of values that result from a query sliced by two wouldn't make sense.

Analysis Services doesn't limit you to the use of "pure" crossjoins in a WHERE clause; you can also use an arbitrary set. Internally, it would be resolved to an arbitrary subcube. (For a definition of an arbitrary subcube, see the "Subcubes" section in Chapter 2.) The following query is an example of a WHERE clause with an arbitrary set:

```
SELECT { [Warehouse].[Warehouses].[Country].&[Canada],
         [Warehouse].[Warehouses].[Country].&[Mexico],
         [Warehouse].[Warehouses].[Country].&[USA]   } ON COLUMNS
FROM   [Warehouse and Sales]
WHERE  {([Product].[Products].[Product Family].[Drink], [Time].[Time].[Year].[1997]),
        ([Product].[Products].[Product Family].[Food] , [Time].[Time].[Year].[1998]) }
```

Figure 11.20 shows the results of this query.

Canada	Mexico	USA
26249	99747	182957

FIGURE 11.20 These are the results of a query execution with an arbitrary set in the WHERE clause.

Execution of a query that includes a set in the WHERE clause is naturally more expensive than execution of a query that contains a single tuple. But, executing a query that contains an arbitrary set triggers a quite advanced algorithm. So, it can bring some performance penalties. In most cases, we advise that you rewrite the query to put a normalized set in the WHERE clause.

SubSelect and Subcubes

A basic MDX query retrieves data from the multidimensional space of a whole cube. However, sometimes it's very useful first to limit the multidimensional space according to certain rules, create a subspace—a subcube—and then execute a query to retrieve data from the subcube. An example of an application that takes advantage of the subcube feature is a cube browser in the Business Intelligence Development Studio. With this browser, a user can filter out part of a cube to create a subcube. She would choose a subset of various dimension members, and then browse the data within the subset. What makes this possible is that, behind the scenes, the browser creates a subcube from the dimension members. The browser can then use Office web components to generate the same sort of queries to browse the subcube in the same way it would browse the whole cube.

We illustrate the concept of a subcube with the simple cube shown in Figure 11.21. It has three dimensions—Store, Product, and Time—and a measure dimension with three measures: Store Sales, Store Cost, and Unit Sales. We can create a subcube that has members corresponding to the year 1998 and contains only stores located in the United States. We have shaded the space of the subcube so that you can see that the subcube has the same structure as the original cube, except that it's been carved out of the original cube.

When we analyze the products in the Food and Drink product families that were sold over period of time in all the stores, we will get the results shown in Figure 11.22. The results contain only data for the members that exist in our subcube.

To make it possible to query subcubes, Analysis Services supports two new MDX constructs: SubSelect and CREATE SUBCUBE. In reality, both are parts of the same functionality—creating a subcube and executing a query in the context of this subcube. SubSelect enables you to write a single query that contains definitions of both axes and a subcube.

You use a standalone MDX statement (CREATE SUBCUBE) to create a subcube. This statement creates a subcube definition in context of which all subsequent queries will be executed until a DROP SUBCUBE statement is issued. So, the difference between SubSelect and a subcube is just the lifetime of the subcube definition.

In the following example, we write a CREATE SUBCUBE statement that creates the subcube illustrated in Figure 11.21:

```
CREATE SUBCUBE [Warehouse and Sales] as SELECT
{[Store].[Stores].[Store Country].[USA] } ON COLUMNS,
{ [Time].[Time].[1998] } ON ROWS FROM
 [Warehouse and Sales]
```

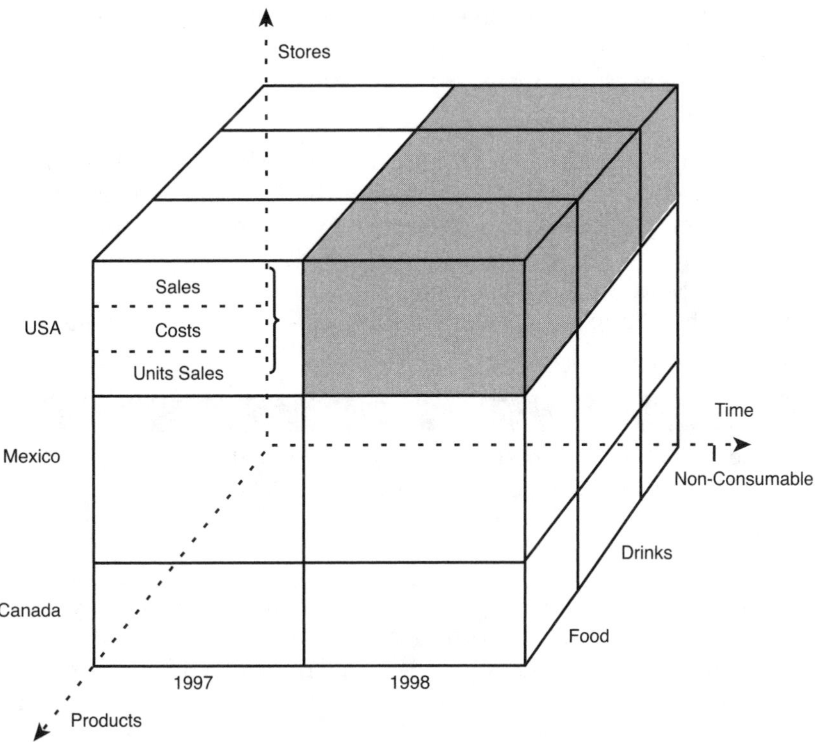

FIGURE 11.21 This subcube has the same dimensionality as the original cube, but some portions of the multidimensional space are cut out.

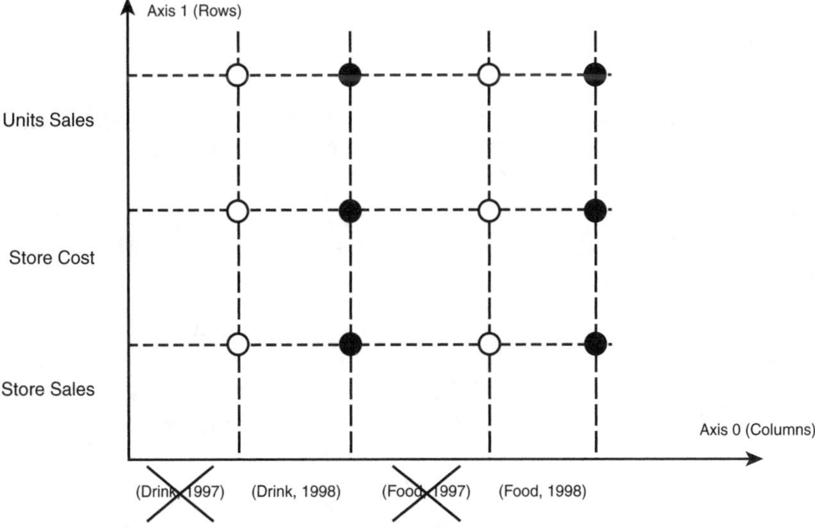

FIGURE 11.22 The results of the query issued against a subcube contain only coordinates that correspond to members in the subcube.

As you can see, we are defining a subcube using the SELECT statement. The designers of Analysis Services chose to use SELECT statements to define subcubes because any SELECT statement results in a multidimensional space. That multidimensional space is a subspace of the original cube—a subcube.

However, the definition of the axes used in such a SELECT statement is a little different. In a regular SELECT statement, it's usually the axes that define the shape of the resulting multidimensional space. However, shape of the subcube is exactly the same as the shape (but smaller) of the original cube. We would get the same result if we rewrote the CREATE SUBCUBE statement and projected the Time dimension against the COLUMNS axis and the Store dimension against the ROWS axis (or even if we projected both of these dimensions against the same axis).

NOTE

Even though a subcube definition has almost the same syntax as a SELECT statement, there are some syntactical limitations. For example, a subcube definition can't have WITH and NON EMPTY clauses.

After a subcube is created, the result of any query issued against it will contain only members that exist in the subcube. So, if we write an MDX query to analyze the products in different product families that were sold over some period of time in different stores, we'll get results, as shown in Figure 11.23, and they will contain only information about sales that happened in 1998 in U.S. stores:

```
SELECT  [Store].[Stores].[Store Country].members ON COLUMNS,
        [Time].[Time].[Year].members ON ROWS FROM [Warehouse and Sales]
```

	USA
1998	222276

FIGURE 11.23 When our query is executed in the context of the subcube, only products sold in the United States in 1998 (tuples that exist in the subcube) are returned to the user.

The SubSelect construct is very similar to the CREATE SUBCUBE statement. The only difference is the lifetime of the subcube. Analogous to the CREATE SUBCUBE statement, the SubSelect construct also uses a SELECT statement to create a subcube.

A FROM clause contains information about the source of data to be queried (a cube or a subcube). If the source of data is a subcube, the FROM clause needs some sort of language construct to define that subcube, and that would be a nested SELECT statement—a SubSelect clause. The following is a Backus Naur Form (BNF) of a query with a SubSelect clause:

```
WITH <with clause> SELECT <select clause> FROM [NON VISUAL](<subcube>)
WHERE <where clause>
```

If we need to define a subcube only for the lifetime of a single query, we can use SubSelect to write an MDX statement. This query produces exactly the same results as a SELECT statement sent against a subcube created by a `CREATE SUBCUBE` statement. (You can see those results in Figure 11.23.)

```
SELECT  [Store].[Stores].[Store Country].members ON COLUMNS,
        [Time].[Time].[Year].members ON ROWS FROM
        ( SELECT {[Store].[Stores].[Store Country].[USA] } ON COLUMNS,
                 { [Time].[Time].[1998] } ON ROWS FROM [Warehouse and Sales])
```

NOTE

Analysis Services enables you to create multiple subcubes and nested SubSelects. Each subsequent subcube is executed on the top of the previous one.

So far, we have been a little vague about the meaning of "only members that exist with the subcube are returned." What it really means is that auto-exist operation is performed on the sets that are projected on each axis using sets in a subcube as a filter set. (Check the "Existing and Nonexisting Tuples, Auto-Exist" section earlier in this chapter for information about exist and auto-exist.)

So, our preceding example is equivalent to the following MDX query:

```
SELECT Exists([Store].[Stores].[Store Country].members, ([Store].[Stores].
      [Store Country].[USA],[Time].[Time].[1998])  ) ON COLUMNS,
      Exists( [Time].[Time].[Year].members,
       ([Store].[Stores].[Store Country]. [USA],[Time].[Time].[1998])  ) ON ROWS
       FROM [Warehouse and Sales]
```

The results of a query that uses an `Exists` function is equivalent to the query against a subcube, which is shown in Figure 11.24.

	USA
January	19823
February	17345
March	16814
April	17116
May	19136
June	18810
July	16781
August	15812
September	19252
October	23907
November	19163
December	18317

FIGURE 11.24 The results of the query contain tuples for the months of the year 1998.

Auto-exist means that not only members that are actually present in the subcube definition will be returned, but also any members that exist together in the dimensional table. So, if we modify the preceding query to drill down into the months rather than the years, we will get data for the months of 1998. That modified query follows:

```
SELECT [Store].[Stores].[Store Country].members ON COLUMNS,
       [Time].[Time].[Month].members ON ROWS FROM
       ( SELECT {[Store].[Stores].[Store Country].[USA] } ON COLUMNS,
                { [Time].[Time].[1998] } ON ROWS FROM [Warehouse and Sales])
```

Figure 11.24 shows the results of this query.

Although the results of a query executed in the context of a subcube never contain tuples that don't exist in the subcube, tuples that don't exist in the subcube can be referenced in the query. The following query demonstrates this concept:

```
CREATE SUBCUBE [Warehouse and Sales] as SELECT
{[Store].[Stores].[Store Country].[USA] } ON COLUMNS,
{ [Time].[Time].[1998] } ON ROWS FROM [Warehouse and Sales]
```

We have created a subcube that restricts our multidimensional space to the data in the 1998 year period, but we need to filter out certain stores to restrict the results to the stores in which sales in the current year (1998) have grown compared to the preceding year (1997):

```
SELECT Filter([Store].[Stores].[Store].members,
([Measures].[Store Sales],[Time].[Time].[Year].[1998]) >
([Measures].[Store Sales],[Time].[Time].[Year].[1997])) ON COLUMNS,
[Time].[Time].[Year].members ON ROWS
FROM [Warehouse and Sales] WHERE [Measures].[Store Sales]
```

Because the year 1997 doesn't exist in the subcube, we need to go outside the boundaries of the subcube to calculate the MDX expression used in the `Filter` expression. When we execute the preceding query, it produces the results shown in Figure 11.25.

	Store 6	Store 15	Store 16	Store 17	Store 22
1998	47843.9199999999	56579.46	54984.9399999998	75219.1299999999	4847.95

FIGURE 11.25 Tuples outside of the boundaries of the subcube can be used in MDX expressions when the query executed in the context of the subcube.

Neither `CREATE SUBCUBE` nor SubSelect changes a current coordinate. (We introduced the concept of the current coordinate in Chapter 10.) For example, if we create a subcube that contains only the member `1998` and we issue the following query containing the `[Time].[Time].currentmember` expression, the query will return the member `ALL` as the current member of the Time dimension, even though that member 1998 has been used to create a subcube. You can see the results of this query in Figure 11.26.

```
SELECT [Time].[Time].currentmember ON COLUMNS FROM
(SELECT [Time].[Time].[Year].[1998] ON COLUMNS FROM [Warehouse and Sales])
```

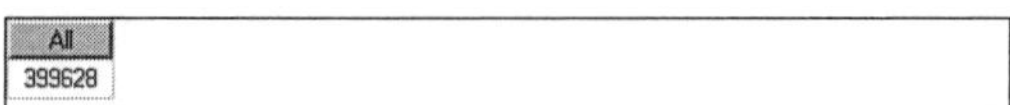

FIGURE 11.26 The current coordinate on the Time dimension is the member ALL even though the subcube restricts the space to the year 1998.

If the query or MDX expression uses a .CurrentMember function or relies on the default member, it's important to know which member is actually the current coordinate.

A default member always should exist with a subcube. If a current default member doesn't exist with the subcube, Analysis Services will assign a new one. If the attribute is aggregatable, the member ALL becomes the new default member for that attribute. If the attribute is nonaggregatable, the default member is the first member that exists in the subcube.

So, for example, if we have restricted the number of measures by issuing a SubSelect, the default member of the Measure dimension will be the first measure that exists with the subcube. The results of the following query are shown in Figure 11.27.

```
SELECT Measures.defaultmember ON COLUMNS FROM
(SELECT {[Measures].[Store Sales], [Measures].[Unit Sales] } ON COLUMNS FROM [Ware-
house and Sales])
```

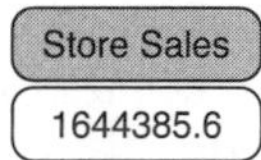

FIGURE 11.27 Because a default member doesn't exist with the subcube, a new one (Unit Sales) has been assigned by the system.

Applying Visual Totals

So far, we have been talking about what happens with the tuples that are returned as a result of a query when that query is executed in the context of the subcube. But there's more to it than that: Creating a subcube can affect not only the set of tuples, but also the values of the cells. Creating a subcube can affect how Analysis Services calculates the total—aggregated values. Let's take the `Time` hierarchy of the `Time` dimension as an example. Look at Figure 11.28 for an illustration.

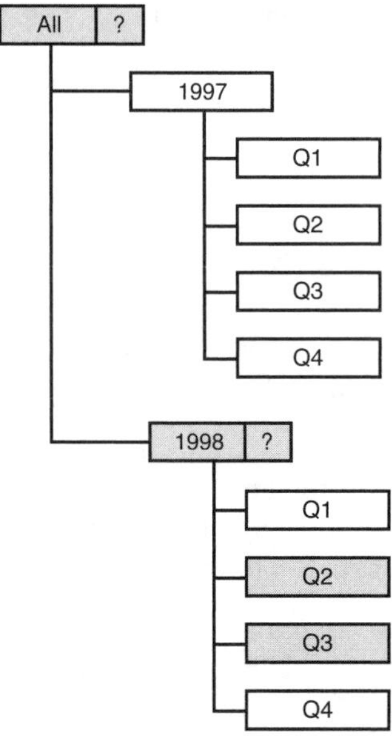

FIGURE 11.28 The `Time` hierarchy appears as a tree.

As shown in Figure 11.28, the `Time` hierarchy has the member `ALL` on the top level. On the next level—`Year`—there are two members: `1997` and `1998`. On the third level—`Quarters`—there are eight members, and so on down the tree. If we query `Sales Counts` for 1997, Analysis Services will return an aggregated value of all the children of the member `1997` (that is, the quarters of the year). The same applies to the year 1998.

The cell value for the coordinate at the top of the tree—the member `ALL`—will have an aggregated value of the years 1997 and 1998. So far, so good. Let's look at a query that is executed in the context of a subcube that restricts our space to just two members on the third level—`Q2` and `Q3` of the year `1998`.

By default, when Analysis Services calculates the value of the top-level cell, it aggregates the values of the cells that correspond to the child members that exist with a subcube. So, in our example, Analysis Services would aggregate the values of `Q2` and `Q3`. Visually, the total values seem correct. You'd never know that there were two quarters left out. This behavior of the system is called *visual totals*.

There are many applications of visual totals. For example, it is used when dimension security is turned on. Or a client application can use a `VisualTotals` MDX function to achieve visual totals behavior. (If you're familiar with Analysis Services 2000, the concept of visual totals is not new.)

Let's go back to our query that we want to execute in the context of a subcube that restricts our space to just two members on the third level—Q2 and Q3 of the years 1998. You can see the result of our query in Figure 11.29. The result has a visual totals value for the members 1998 and ALL:

```
SELECT {[Time].[Time].[All], [Time].[Time].[Year].members,
[Time].[Time].[Quarter].members} ON COLUMNS FROM
(SELECT {[Time].[Time].[Quarter].&[Q2]&[1998],[Time].[Time].[Quarter].&[Q3]&[1998]}
ON COLUMNS FROM [Warehouse and Sales])
WHERE [Measures].[Unit Sales]
```

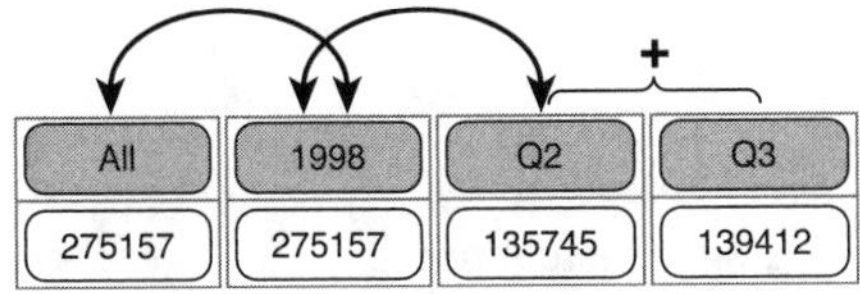

FIGURE 11.29 The cells for the members 1998 and ALL show visual totals of Q2 and Q3.

When designing Analysis Services 2005, we thought that applying visual totals on SubSelects produces the most natural results—results you want to see for your query when it is executed in a context of a SubSelect. However, practice showed that often customers want to see those values without applying visual totals. For example, you want to minimize size of your result and see sales values only for Q2 and Q3, but you still need to see actual value of sales in the whole year. To provide this functionality, Analysis Services 2008 supports NON VISUAL keyword for SubSelects and subcube expression, which turns off visual total behavior. For example, we can add the NON VISUAL keyword to our preceding query and it will return value for member All and 1998 as the sum of all of their children, as shown in Figure 11.30.

```
SELECT {[Time].[Time].[All], [Time].[Time].[Year].members,
[Time].[Time].[Quarter].members} ON COLUMNS FROM
NON VISUAL (SELECT
{[Time].[Time].[Quarter].&[Q2]&[1998],[Time].[Time].[Quarter].&[Q3]&[1998]}
 ON COLUMNS FROM [Warehouse and Sales])
WHERE [Measures].[Unit Sales]
```

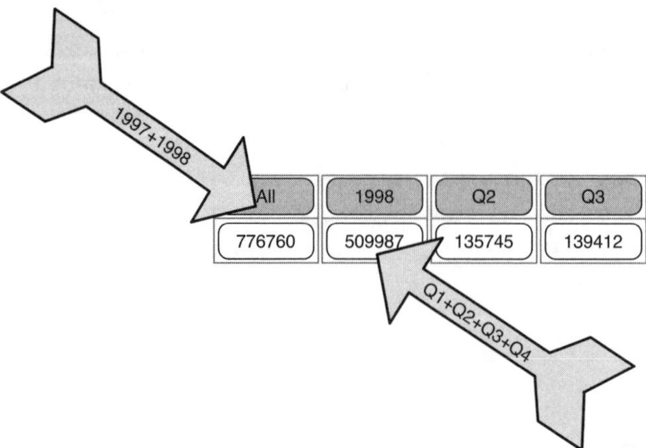

FIGURE 11.30 The cells for the members **1998** and **ALL** show actual totals.

CHAPTER 12

Cube-Based MDX Calculations

IN THIS CHAPTER

- MDX Scripts
- Calculated Members
- Assignments
- Named Sets
- Order of Execution for Cube Calculations

When we discussed calculations of cell values and Multidimensional Expressions (MDX) in the Chapter 11, "Advanced MDX," we assumed that those values derive from the fact data. Indeed, in simple cubes, the data for the lowest granularity (leaf cells) is equivalent to the physical data—fact data. And data for higher granularity—aggregated values—is calculated using an aggregate function associated with a measure.

Usually, this function is an additive formula such as `SUM`, `MIN`, `MAX`, or `COUNT`, but it can be one of the more complex built-in aggregate functions (semi-additive measures) that Analysis Services supports. (We introduce semi-additive measures in Chapter 13, "Dimension-Based MDX Calculations.") Figure 12.1 shows how fact data can be aggregated using a simple `SUM` formula.

In addition to those built-in formulas, Analysis Services enables designers and MDX developers to define their own calculation formulas (MDX calculations).

To understand the concept of MDX calculations, imagine an Excel spreadsheet in which each cell contains either a value or a formula. Similarly, in a multidimensional cube's cell, you can have either a value derived from fact data or a custom formula for the calculation of the value. Figure 12.2 illustrates the use of both additive `SUM` formulas and custom MDX calculations (shown in the figure as `=Formula`).

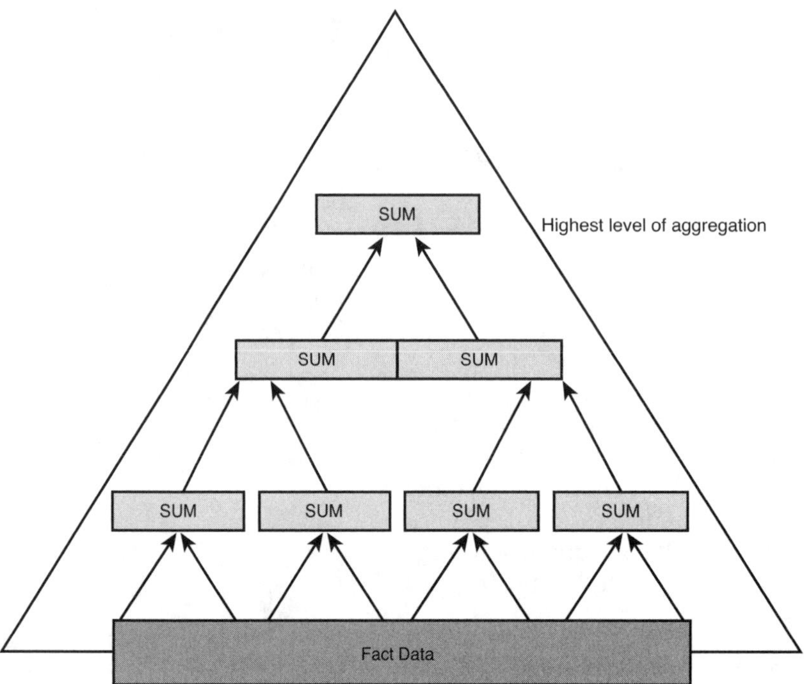

FIGURE 12.1 Fact data is aggregated using a SUM formula.

Analysis Services supports a number of different kinds of calculations and different ways to specify the formula:

- Calculated members extend a multidimensional space and enable a designer to create new logical coordinates in the space and assign formulas to the newly created coordinates.
- Assignments, known in Analysis Services 2000 as *calculated cells,* overwrite the values of cells with formulas, which Analysis Services uses to calculate the new cell values.
- Named sets enable you to create a set expressions associated with a name (alias) that you can use later in other MDX expressions.
- Dimension-based calculations enable you to associate a simple operator (unary operator) or a more complex MDX formula (custom member formula) with an individual member of a dimension attribute. For more information, see Chapter 13.
- Semi-additive measures are built-in Analysis Services `Aggregate Function` properties of a measure, which specify that certain formulas are used to aggregate values along the `Time` dimension, whereas other dimensions are aggregated using other formulas. For more information, see Chapter 13.

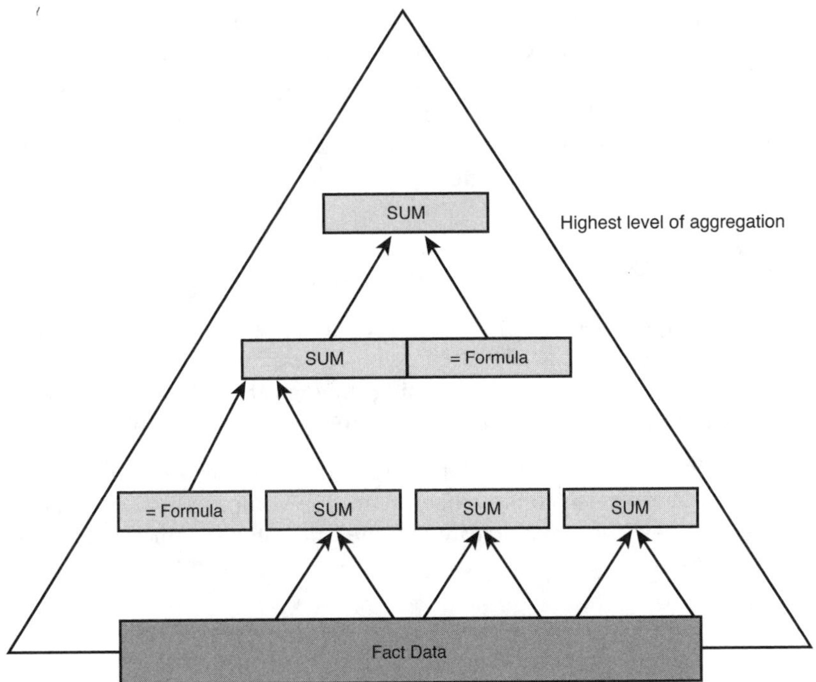

FIGURE 12.2 Custom formulas (MDX calculations) are assigned to cells of a cube.

MDX Scripts

Starting from Analysis Services 2005, the way you define and store calculations inside the cube is vastly improved and simplified. All cube-based calculations are stored in the same location: an MDX script. Having a single location for the majority of calculations simplifies development; it improves visibility and simplifies maintenance of dependencies between calculations.

You can use Data Definition Language (DDL) or Business Intelligence Development Studio (BI Dev Studio) to create an MDX script. Semicolons separate the commands in a script. The script might look like the code in a procedural language, but it is indeed MDX, a declarative language. That is, MDX commands declare calculations; after those calculations are declared, they are always in effect. When Analysis Services loads the cube, it loads the MDX script as part of the cube. The MDX commands evaluate in the order in which they appear in the script.

NOTE

In Analysis Services 2000, commands that create cell calculations execute according to the properties `SOLVE_ORDER` and `CALCULATION_PASS_NUMBER`. In later versions of Analysis Services, the order that the commands appear in the script replaces `SOLVE_ORDER` and `CALCULATION_PASS_NUMBER`.

MDX scripts can contain different kinds of commands, depending on the type of calculations under creation. An MDX script can create calculated members, named sets, and assignments. In contrast, a cube does not contain the definitions of dimension calculations such as unary operators or custom member formulas; they are instead part of the dimension definition. Now let's look at how different kinds of Analysis Services calculations work and how they interact with each other.

Calculated Members

One of the most common ways to specify a formula for calculating a cell value is to create a calculated member. When you define a calculated member, you extend the dimension by one more coordinate—a member—thereby extending the logical multidimensional space, too. MDX queries and other MDX expressions can then use that new member.

The value for the cell specified by the calculated member is not retrieved from the fact data; the formula specified in the calculated member definition computes it at runtime. In Figure 12.3, you can see the new coordinate created by the calculated member. It appears as the shaded column in the table.

	Time.1997	Time.1998	Time.CalculatedMember
Product.Drink	18991	31652	Formula
Product.Food	167439	294481	Formula
Product.Non-Consumable	40808	73495	Formula

FIGURE 12.3 The new cells associated with the new coordinate are shaded in this table.

Calculated members are not additive. That is, if you create a calculated member on a level lower than the top level, the value for its parent is aggregated from that parent's children. However, the aggregation does not use the calculated member itself.

For example, assume that you have a simple cube with one measure and one hierarchy. The hierarchy has three "real" members: `memberA=1` and `memberB=2`, and the member `ALL`. The member `ALL`, which equals `3`, is the sum of `memberA` and `memberB`. When you create a calculated member, `memberC=5`, as a child of the member `ALL`, the value of the cell corresponding to the member `ALL` doesn't change. It remains the sum of the real members `memberA` and `memberB` (that is, `3`).

Defining Calculated Members

There are three ways to create calculated members, and they differ only in the lifetime of the member:

- A calculated member created using the `WITH` clause of a `SELECT` statement is available in the scope of the current query execution.
- A calculated member created using the `CREATE MEMBER` statement is available in the scope of a session. It is generally available to subsequent queries from the same user. For more information about sessions, see Chapter 32, "XML for Analysis."
- A calculated member defined in an MDX script is available to all users of the cube.

Let's look at a simple example: You want to write an expression that returns not only values for `Store Sales` and `Store Cost`, but also the profit from those sales. To that end, you define a *calculated measure* (a calculated member on a measure dimension) `[Profit] = [Store Cost] - [Store Sales]`.

To create the calculated member, follow the steps listed here in BI Dev Studio. By doing so, the calculated member will be available for use by all the users of the cube.

1. In BI Dev Studio, open the FoodMart 2008 project.
2. In the Solution Explorer, double-click the `Warehouse and Sales` cube to open the cube editor.
3. On the Calculations tab, right-click anywhere in the Script Organizer, and choose New Calculated Member from the contextual menu.
4. Type the name of your calculated member—**`Profit`**—in the Name text box.

NOTE

Because a calculated member is a new dimension member, it's created as member one of the dimension hierarchies. When you create the calculated member, you need to specify a hierarchy to which calculated member belongs. You can also specify the member that should be its parent or you can omit the parent. If you omit the parent, the system will create the calculated member on the top level of the hierarchy.

5. Specify `Measures` as the parent hierarchy.

6. In the Expression box, enter the MDX expression to define the formula associated with this calculated member, as shown in Figure 12.4.

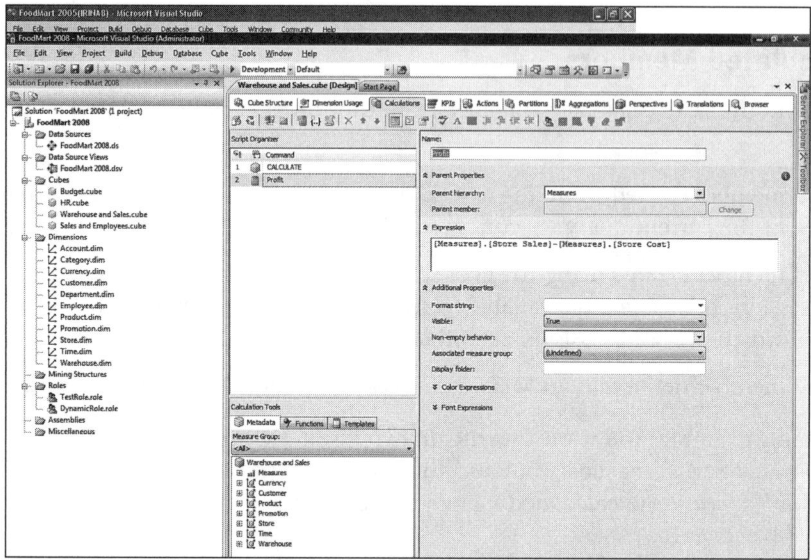

FIGURE 12.4 Create a calculated member in BI Dev Studio.

In addition to the formula of the calculated member, you can specify additional cell properties such as `Format String`, `Color Expressions`, `Font Expressions`, and so on.

If you were creating a calculated member that would be a percentage of sales in the first quarter, you could select the `Percent` property from the Format String drop-down list. The value calculated using the calculated member would then appear as a percentage.

On the server, you use the MDX statement `CREATE MEMBER` to create calculated members. If you use the user interface, BI Dev Studio generates this MDX statement for you:

```
CREATE MEMBER CURRENTCUBE.[MEASURES].Profit
 AS [Measures].[Store Sales]-[Measures].[Store Cost], Visible=1
```

If you want to see and modify the `CREATE MEMBER` statement that BI Dev Studio generated for you, click the Script View toolbar button so that you can work with the `CREATE MEMBER` statement in text format. If you want to write your own `CREATE MEMBER` statement, use the following syntax:

```
CREATE MEMBER [<cube_name>.][<path to the parent member or name of
 the hierarchy>].[name of the member] AS
<formula for calculated member>
[, <CalcProperty_Identifier>=<PropertyExpression>]
```

Because of the effort to simplify MDX, Analysis Services allows you to omit the hierarchy name in the calculated member definition. If the name of the hierarchy is not present in the name of the calculated member under creation, Analysis Services uses the `Measure` hierarchy. For example, the following `CREATE MEMBER` statement omits the name of the hierarchy:

```
CREATE MEMBER [Warehouse and Sales].Profit AS [Store Sales]-[Store Cost]
```


In addition to the `CREATE MEMBER` statement syntax supported by all versions of Analysis Services, starting from Analysis Services 2005, system support the following way to create calculated members:

```
CREATE [HIDDEN] [<parent>.]<name> = <expression>
```

The following statement creates the same calculated member used in the earlier example:

```
CREATE Profit = [Store Sales]-[Store Cost];
```

The difference between these two syntaxes is the calculation pass on which the calculated member is created. `CREATE MEMBER` syntax creates calculated member on calculation pass 1—on the same pass as on which the `Calculate` statement is executed. `CREATE` syntax creates a calculated member on the calculated pass corresponding to its location in the MDX script. For information about passes, see the "Order of Execution for Cube Calculations" section later in this chapter.

After creating and storing a calculated member in the cube, you can use it in queries. For example, you can reference the calculated member `Profit` in the following `SELECT` statement:

```
SELECT {[Measures].[Store Sales], [Measures].[Store Cost], [Measures].[Profit]}
ON COLUMNS FROM [Warehouse and Sales]
```

When Analysis Services calculates the cell value, it executes the formula defined for the calculated member. Figure 12.5 shows the result of the query.

Store Sales	Store Cost	Profit
1644385.6	658192.962500003	986192.637499992

FIGURE 12.5 The query results in a value for FoodMart's profit.

NOTE

If a query uses a calculated member that is stored in the cube, after calculating its formula, the calculated value can be stored in the calculation cache. Subsequent queries will not have to recompute the formula because Analysis Services will retrieve the value from the cache. (See Chapter 29, "Architecture of Query Execution—Calculating MDX Expressions," for more information.)

The CREATE MEMBER statement is intended not only to be used to define calculated members stored in the cube; it can also be issued from a client application to create a calculated member in a session. The calculated member is available only to queries issued from the same user during the same session. These calculated members are *session-scope* calculated members.

You can use the DROP MEMBER statement to remove a calculated member from a session. After the DROP MEMBER statement executes, the calculated member is no longer available:

```
DROP MEMBER [Warehouse and Sales].Profit
```

To define a calculated member in the scope of a query, MDX provides the WITH clause. The WITH clause precedes the SELECT clause in the statement, creating a section for the definition of calculated members (and other calculations that we will introduce later in this chapter) in the query:

```
WITH MEMBER <calculated member> AS <calculated member formula>
SELECT <definition of the resulting multidimensional space>
FROM <source sub_space> WHERE <limiting the results to sub_space>
```

The WITH clause is very similar to the CREATE MEMBER statement, except it is not a standalone statement, but is part of the SELECT statement. For example, you can create the Profit calculated member with the following query:

```
WITH MEMBER Measures.Profit AS [Measures].[Store Sales]-[Measures].[Store Cost]
SELECT Measures.Profit ON COLUMNS FROM [Warehouse and Sales]
```

Common customer scenarios create a calculated member on the Measure dimension. However, other scenarios have to create a calculated member on some other dimension. For example, you can create a calculated member on the Time dimension to aggregate values for the first and second quarters of a year:

```
WITH MEMBER [Time].[Time].[Year].[1998].[FirstHalfYear] AS
 [Time].[Time].[Quarter].&[Q1]&[1998]+[Time].[Time].[Quarter].&[Q2]&[1998]
SELECT {[Time].[Time].[Year].[1998].[FirstHalfYear]} ON COLUMNS
FROM [Warehouse and Sales]
```

NOTE

To achieve better performance in Analysis Services 2005, we recommended you to use NON EMPTY BEHAVIOR property as often as possible. Analysis Services 2008 detects NON EMPTY behavior automatically and optimizes appropriate MDX calculations. Therefore, when working with Analysis Services 2008, we recommend removing this property and letting the system choose the optimal execution plan.

NON EMPTY BEHAVIOR Property

One of the most often misused properties assigned to a calculated member, or any other type of calculation, is NON_EMPTY_BEHAVIOR. NON_EMPTY_BEHAVIOR is an optimization hint that enables Analysis Services to improve the performance of MDX queries. There are two distinct ways Analysis Services uses the NON_EMPTY_BEHAVIOR property:

- During execution of the NON EMPTY operator or NonEmpty function
- During the calculation of cell values

Because the NonEmpty function and the NON EMPTY operator eliminate tuples associated with empty cells, their execution can take a long time when performed on large and sparse multidimensional space. To optimize execution, Analysis Services does not iterate over and calculate each cell (empty or nonempty), but sends a request to the storage engine subsystem, which returns only non-null records. For more information about architecture of query execution, see Chapter 29.

This approach works well when a subspace referenced in an MDX query covers data derived from fact data that is stored in the storage engine subsystem. However, this approach cannot be used when there is a calculated member, another type of calculation, or cell security defined on at least one of the cells. This is where NON_EMPTY_BEHAVIOR comes in handy.

The NON_EMPTY_BEHAVIOR property of a calculated member tells the system that the calculated member is NULL or not NULL in the same cases in which a real member or a set of real members is NULL or not NULL. For example, suppose that you create the Measures.X as Measures.[Unit Sales]*1.1 calculated member. If Unit Sales is NULL when you multiply it by any constant, the calculated member will also be NULL, and vice versa. Therefore, when you create the calculated member *X,* you can assign it a NON_EMPTY_BEHAVIOR property:

```
CREATE MEMBER [warehouse and sales].Measures.x AS
 [Measures].[Unit Sales]*1.1,
 NON_EMPTY_BEHAVIOR =[Measures].[Unit Sales]
```

You can specify more than one real member as the value of a NON_EMPTY_BEHAVIOR property. For another example, suppose that you create another simple calculated member: Measures.Profit = [Measures].[Store Sales]-[Measures].[Store Cost]. Profit is

NULL only when both Store Sales and Store Cost are NULL. Therefore, you can assign the {[Measures].[Store Sales], [Measures.[Store Cost]} set as the NON_EMPTY_BEHAVIOR property for this calculated member.

Unfortunately, when the NON_EMPTY_BEHAVIOR property contains more than one member, Analysis Services cannot use it while calculating cell values. Therefore, we recommend that you use a single member in the NON_EMPTY_BEHAVIOR property if possible. For example, if the Store Cost measure and the Store Sales measure belong to a single measure group, their NON_EMPTY_BEHAVIOR will usually be the same. Therefore, instead of assigning a set that contains two members to the NON_EMPTY_BEHAVIOR property, you can assign a single member—for example, [Measures].[Store Sales].

NOTE

Even though the NON_EMPTY_BEHAVIOR property is very powerful and can speed up your query by an order of magnitude, be extremely careful when you use it. If you specify the NON_EMPTY_BEHAVIOR property for a calculated member that does not always behave in the same way as a real member, your query will produce unexpected results.

Analysis Services also uses the NON_EMPTY_BEHAVIOR property during the calculation of cell values. If Analysis Services could detect that the cells with complex MDX expressions assigned to them are empty when it calculates the results of an MDX query, it could skip the calculation of those complex expressions and dramatically reduce the time of query execution.

Assignments

Although calculated members extend the multidimensional space, Analysis Services provides an assignment operator that you can use to overwrite the values of the existing cells of the cube. You can assign a special formula, defined as an MDX expression, to a cell or to a group of cells—a *subcube*.

The major difference between calculated members and cell calculations is the way that the calculations affect aggregation behavior. Calculated members do not affect aggregations and do not change the value of the cell referenced by the parent member. On the other hand, if you use an assignment operator to change the value of a cell that corresponds to a child member, the value that corresponds to its parent does change.

One example of a business use for assignment operators is in budgeting applications. For example, assume that you plan to open new stores in Canada and want to predict the sales you would get if the number of stores in Canada were to be five times fewer than in the United States (see Figure 12.6). (We are taking a somewhat simplified approach and assuming that our Canadian customers are going to love our FoodMart stores every bit as much as our United States customers do.)

	Store Sales
Store.Canada	(Store.USA)/5
Store.Mexico	NULL
Store.USA	565238,12999

FIGURE 12.6 Assignment of an MDX expression to a subcube.

Analysis Services 2000 created cell calculations using the `CREATE CELL CALCULATION` statement or the `WITH CELL CALCULATION` clause of the `SELECT` statement. Although those language constructs are still available in Analysis Services to support legacy applications, we recommend using the assignment operator syntax.

Assignment Operator

The simplest way to define a cell calculation is to use an assignment operator. The assignment operator has the following syntax:

```
<sub_cube_expression> = <mdx formula>
```

To the left of the equal sign of the assignment operator, you specify the scope of the assignment—the subspace of the cube to which the calculation applies. To the right side, you specify the MDX expression.

To define a subcube, you specify a `CrossJoin` set built from one or more sets. Each of the sets internally decomposes into sets—each of which contains the members of a single attribute.

As with other MDX expressions, you can use the members of a user-defined hierarchy or an attribute hierarchy to define *`sub_cube_expression`*. You can also use an MDX expression that evaluates to a set.

Not all kinds of sets can decompose into sets that contain members from a single attribute. Analysis Services supports the following kinds of sets as part of scope definition:

- A set that contains a single tuple
- A set that contains all the members of a hierarchy
- A set that contains all the members of a level
- A set that contains a collection of members from a single natural hierarchy—a hierarchy whose levels are built from related attributes, and whose levels are located in

the same order as the relationships of attributes (see Chapter 5, "Dimensions in the Conceptual Model")

- A set that contains the descendants of a member
- A set that contains the leaf members of a hierarchy

You do not have to list all the attributes explicitly in a *sub_cube_expression*. You can use asterisk (*) to replace an attribute and to indicate that the subcube contains all the members of this attribute. In addition, you can use an asterisk as a *sub_cube_expression* to indicate that all the members of the cube belong to this subcube.

NOTE

We use the same term—*subcube*—to refer to the subspace used by both the assignment operator and the CREATE SUBCUBE statement. However, the way you define a subcube in assignment operator differs from the way you define a subcube in the CREATE SUBCUBE statement. Beyond their names, there is no relation between two features. You cannot use a subcube created by a CREATE SUBCUBE statement in an assignment operator and vice versa. In addition, the subcubes function in different ways after creation.

When you define a *sub_cube_expression*, you normally use the simplified syntax of the CrossJoin function. Place the list of sets inside brackets and use commas to separate the sets.

The following is an example of the syntax of an assignment operator that you might use in your effort to budget sales in Canada:

```
([Time].[Time].[Year].[1997],[Measures].[Store Sales],
[Store].[Stores].[Store Country].[Canada]) =
([Store].[Stores].[Store Country].[USA])/5
```

The subcube doesn't have to be represented as a single tuple—we used one for the sake of simplicity in the preceding example. However, the shape of the subcube cannot be arbitrary. For example, the following assignment operator returns an error:

```
{([Time].[Time].[Year].[1997],[Measures].[Store Sales],
 [Store].[Stores].[Store Country].[Canada]),( [Time].[Time].[Year].[1998],
 [Measures].[Store Sales], [Store].[Stores].[Store Country].[Mexico])} =
([Store].[Stores].[Store Country].[USA])/5
```

NOTE

For the definition of an arbitrarily shaped subcube, refer to the "Subcubes" section in Chapter 2, "Multidimensional Space."

As with calculated members, you can define assignments that will be available in the scope of the current query, of the current session, or of the cube. Assignments created for the entire cube are stored in an MDX script; this sort of assignment is the most commonly used type.

To create an assignment operator for use in the scope of the cube, follow the steps listed here in BI Dev Studio:

1. In BI Dev Studio, open the FoodMart 2008 project.
2. In the Solution Explorer, double-click the `Warehouse and Sales` cube to open the cube editor.
3. On the Calculations tab, right-click anywhere in the Script Organizer, and choose New Script from the contextual menu.
4. In the right pane of the Calculations tab, type the assignment operator or copy and paste the code from earlier in this section, as shown in Figure 12.7.

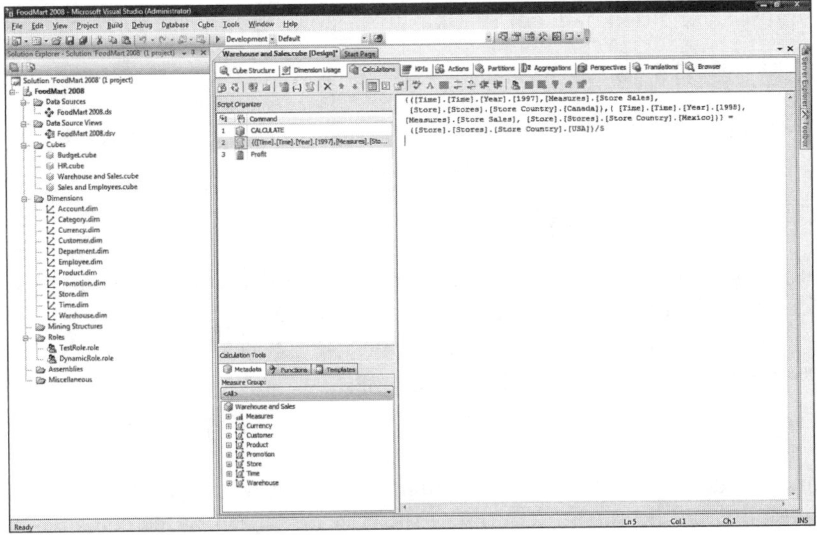

FIGURE 12.7 You use the Calculations tab to define an assignment operator.

After you deploy the MDX script that contains the assignment operator, the formula specified in the assignment operator calculates the cell values in the subcube:

```
SELECT [Measures].[Store Sales] ON COLUMNS,
[Store].[Stores].[Store Country].members ON ROWS
FROM [Warehouse and Sales]
WHERE ([Time].[Time].[Year].[1997])
```

The results of these calculations appear in a grid in SQL Server Management Studio, as shown in Figure 12.8. Store Sales in Canada is 113047, calculated by the assignment operator as one-fifth the value of Store Sales for the United States.

	Store Sales
Canada	113047.625999999
Mexico	(null)
USA	565238.129999996
Unknown	(null)

FIGURE 12.8 The results of the MDX query show sales numbers for Canada, calculated by the assignment operator.

You might want to assign a value to a subcube based on some condition. For example, perhaps you want to have the value of a cell overwritten only if its original value is NULL. To do this, you can use a condition operator that has the following syntax:

```
IF <expression> THEN <assignment operator> END IF
```

We recommend that you avoid using conditions because their use can have negative impact on performance, particularly on the speed at which queries execute.

Specifying a Calculation Property

You can use an assignment operator to define not only the formula that Analysis Services uses to calculate cell values, but also to define formulas that assign cell properties to cells and the calculation rules and optimization hints that Analysis Services can use in calculating cell values. Use the following syntax to specify cell properties:

```
[<calculation property name>(<subcube definition>) = <mdx formula>]
```

For example, to assign a dollar sign to cells that contain store sales, you can specify the following assignment operator in the MDX script of the Warehouse and Sales cube:

```
FORMAT_STRING(([Measures].[Store Sales]))='currency'
```

After applying the script to the cube, executing the following MDX query in Microsoft SQL Server Management Studio returns values for Store Sales with the dollar sign:

```
SELECT measures.members on COLUMNS FROM [Warehouse and Sales]
```

The result of this query, illustrated in Figure 12.9, shows the application of the FORMAT_STRING property to the cells associated with the Store Sales measure.

Units Ordered	Units Shipped	Warehouse Sales	Warehouse Cost	Store Sales	Store Cost	Unit Sales	Sales Count
626866	573342	545255.6072	247298.5053	$1,644,385.60	658192.962500003	776760	251395

FIGURE 12.9 A dollar sign is prepended to the `Store Sales` values.

Scope Statements

When writing complex calculations, you might need to break them down into separate statements; when defining a subcube for an assignment operator, you might need multiple steps. To help with this, MDX designers introduced one more language construct: `Scope`. The `Scope` statement enables you to specify the subcube in which subsequent statements will execute; it enables you to target calculations to a subcube.

A `Scope` statement is useful if you need to create multiple assignment operators that will affect partially overlapping subcubes. In the previous example, you predicted the sales in new stores in Canada. If you want to predict the sales in new stores in Mexico, too, and you opened a different number of stores in Canada than in Mexico, you need to use different allocation formulas: for Canada, `Sales` as `USA/5` (20% of United States sales) and for Mexico, `Sales` as `USA/2` (50% of United States sales). You would use the following assignment operators:

```
( [Time].[Time].[Year].[1997],[Measures].[Store Sales],
 [Store].[Stores].[Store Country].[Canada]) =
( [Store].[Stores].[Store Country].[USA])/5;
 [Time].[Year].[1997],[Measures].[Store Sales],
 [Store].[Stores].[Store Country].[Mexico]) =
( [Store].[Stores].[Store Country].[USA])/2;
```

However, these operators contain a lot of repeated information. You can make them simpler by rewriting them using the `Scope` statement:

```
Scope ([Time].[Time].[Year].[1997],[Measures].[Store Sales]);
([Store].[Stores].[Store Country].[Canada]) =
([Store].[Stores].[Store Country].[USA])/5;
([Store].[Stores].[Store Country].[Mexico]) =
([Store].[Stores].[Store Country].[USA])/2;
End Scope;
```

NOTE

The Scope statement is static: It is evaluated just once—when the script is loaded in the cube—and is not reevaluated for each query. We highly recommend using the power of the Scope operator and putting the more computation-intensive expressions in the Scope operator or in the *<sub_cube_expression>* of the assignment operator rather than in the rightmost part of the assignment.

When you define an assignment operator inside of a Scope statement, you can use the This operator to assign an expression to the whole subcube defined by the Scope statement.

Nested Scope Statements

You can define a Scope statement inside another Scope statement to create nested Scope statements. (Conceptually, this is true even for an initial Scope statement created inside the scope of a whole cube.) A nested Scope statement inherits some of the attributes from a parent Scope statement. The rules of inheritance are somewhat similar to the rules of coordinate overwrites and of strong relationships (see Chapters 10, "MDX Concepts," and 11, "Advanced MDX"). Both sets of inheritance rules depend on the relationships between attributes, but differences between the rules exist and are worth discussing. (For a deeper discussion about attribute relationships, see Chapter 5, "Dimensions in the Conceptual Model.")

- If a subcube definition of a nested Scope statement explicitly specifies an attribute, it overwrites the subcube's coordinate that corresponds to that attribute. For example, if you have the following Scope statements, the Country attribute USA changes to Canada, and the subcube that corresponds to stores in Canada takes on the value 1:

```
Scope ([Store].[Stores].[Store Country].[USA]);
       Scope ([Store].[Stores].[Store Country].[Canada]);
          //The scope is on [Store].[Stores].[Store Country].[Canada]
          This = 1;
     End Scope;
End Scope;
```

- An attribute specified by a nested Scope statement does not overwrite its related (on top of the current one) attribute. This is the primary difference with rules for coordinate overwrites.

  For example, the following Scope statements, in which the parent statement has a slice on the Country attribute and the nested Scope statement has a slice on the State attribute, do not overwrite the attribute Country, which is related to the State attribute. They assign the value 1 to the subcube that corresponds to the CrossJoin([Store].[Stores].[Store Country].[USA], [Store].[Stores].[Store State].[WA]) set.

```
Scope ([Store].[Stores].[Store Country].[USA]);
     Scope([Store].[Store State].[WA]);
          //Scope is on ([Store].[Stores].[Store Country].[USA],
          // [Store].[Stores].[Store State].[WA]);
          This = 1;
     End Scope;
End Scope;
```


- An attribute specified by a nested Scope statement overwrites its relating attribute with the member ALL. (The *relating* attribute is the one below the current attribute.)

  For example, in the following Scope statements, the parent Scope statement has a slice on the State attribute and the nested Scope statement has a slice on the Country attribute. The statements overwrite the State attribute, which is relating to Country, and assign the value 1 to the subcube that corresponds to USA and not to Washington:

```
Scope([Store].[Store State].[WA]);
     Scope ([Store].[Stores].[Store Country].[USA]);
          //scope is on ([Store].[Stores].[Store Country].[USA],
          // ([Store].[Store State].[(All)]);
          This = 1;
     End Scope;
End Scope;
```

- If the member ALL is not specified for an attribute in the nested Scope statement, but the parent Scope statement has a member ALL for the attribute related to the current one, the member ALL is removed from the subcube. The following two examples demonstrate this rule:

```
Scope ([Store].[Store Country].Members);
     Scope([Store].[Store State].[Store State].Members);
          // Nested scope requested all members from level Store State of the
          // hierarchy Store State (not including member ALL)
          //The parent scope requested all members from the hierarchy Store
➥Country,
          // including member ALL.
          //Now the member ALL is removed from the Store Country and scope is
➥on
          // ([Store].[Store Country].[Store Country].Members,
          //([Store].[Store State].[Store State].Members)
           This = 1;
     End Scope;
End Scope;
```

In this example, the nested Scope statement affects the attributes specified by the parent Scope statement by removing the member ALL from the subcube:

```
Scope ([Store].[Store Country].[All]);
     Scope([Store].[Store State].[Store State].Members);
         // Nested scope requested all members from level Store State of the
         // hierarchy Store State (not including member ALL)
         //The parent scope requested the member ALL from the hierarchy
➥Store Country,
         //Now the member ALL is removed from the Store Country and scope is
➥on
         // ([Store].[Store Country].[Store Country].Members,
         //([Store].[Store State].[Store State].Members)
          This = 1;
     End Scope;
End Scope;
```

Root and Leaves Functions

To simplify the definitions of subcubes used in assignment operators and in Scope statements, Analysis Services supports some helper functions, such as Leaves and Root. These functions enable you to specify a subcube on the top or bottom of a cube.

The Root Function

The Root function evaluates to a subcube that contains a cell or a group of cells on the top of the cube. In other words, the function produces a subcube defined by a tuple, or multiple tuples, that have members from all the attribute hierarchies in the cube or dimension, depending on the parameter of the function. The tuple would contain the member ALL for aggregatable attributes or all members from the top level for nonaggregatable attributes.

The Root function has the following syntax:

```
Root([<dimension>])
```

You can use the Root function in two ways. The one we recommend is to use the function in an MDX script as part of the Scope statement and assignment operators to specify the subcube. This approach comes in handy when you want to do top-to-bottom allocations and have to assign some value to the cells at the top of the cube.

The second way of using the Root function is as part of an MDX expression. When an MDX expression calls the Root function, the function returns a Tuple object rather than a subcube. That Tuple object contains as many members as there are attribute hierarchies in the cube or dimension.

Calling a `Root` function from an MDX expression is useful when you need to calculate the percentage of a total. For example, to calculate the sales in your store as a percentage of the sales in all stores, you can write the following MDX expression:

```
([Store].[Stores].[Store Country].[Canada].&[BC].&[Vancouver].&[19],
 [Measures].[Store Sales])/(Root([Store]),[Measures].[Store Sales])
```

The Leaves Function

The `Leaves` function returns a subcube that contains cells associated with leaf members of the specified dimension or with leaf members of all the dimensions in a cube (depending on the parameter of the function).

The `Leaves` function has the following syntax:

```
Leaves([<dimension>])
```

There are many scenarios in which it is useful to assign a calculation to the leaf members of a dimension. Let's look at one of them. The FoodMart 2008 database contains international data. Imagine that the values of sales in the stores in the database are in the currency in which the transactions occurred. If the store is in the United States, the currency is U.S. dollars; for stores in Mexico, the currency is Mexican pesos; and for sales in Canada, the currency is Canadian dollars. However, when you analyze the sales in different stores and compare sales in different countries, you do not want to compare pesos to dollars.

To solve this problem, you can write an MDX script that converts all the sale values to U.S. dollars so that your user sees the values of the sales as if the transactions were actually in U.S. dollars. You do not have to multiply sales by rate on all levels of the cube; you need multiply them only on leaves, and Analysis Services aggregates the values for upper levels. Because rates changes only by time and currency (not by product, store, or customer), it is enough that you assign the multiplication operator on the leaves of the `Time` dimension and the leaves of the `Currency` dimension:

```
CALCULATE;
Scope(leaves(time),leaves(currency), measures.[store sales]);
    this = measures.[store sales]*[Measures].[Rates];
End Scope;
```

Now when you execute a query that retrieves store sales for stores in different countries, you will see that because the conversion rate from USD to USD is `1`, the values for sales in the United States didn't change compared to the result of the same query executed without the preceding MDX script. However, the values for sales in Mexico and Canada do change; they convert to U.S. dollars:

```
SELECT measures.[store sales] ON COLUMNS,
     [Store].[Stores].[Store Country].members ON ROWS
FROM [warehouse and sales]
```

Figure 12.10 shows the results of this query.

	Store Sales
Canada	65690.4582
Mexico	43029.359
USA	1116046.55
Unknown	(null)

FIGURE 12.10 The results of the query shows the sales of stores in U.S. dollars.

NOTE

We do not recommend assigning a calculation to the leaf members of a cube. That operation causes a recalculation of the values of the whole cube, and that can kill the performance of the query.

Calculated Cells

If you use assignment operators and `Scope` statements in an MDX script, you can do almost everything that calculated cells in Analysis Services 2000 could do—and much more. However, the functionality available through assignment operators lacks some minor capabilities of calculated cells. For example, when you use an assignment operator, you cannot explicitly change the solve order or pass of the calculations. (You will read more about passes later in this chapter.) If you absolutely have to change pass or solve order, or if you have a cube that was migrated from Analysis Services 2000, use calculated cells rather than assignment operators and `Scope` statements.

You would also use calculated cell syntax to define cell calculation in the scope of a query because `Scope` statements and assignment operators work only in the context of a cube or a session. To specify a calculated cell in the scope of a query, you can use the `WITH` clause, which is already familiar to you from the earlier section on calculated members. See Table 12.1 for detailed descriptions of `WITH` clause components.

TABLE 12.1 Components of the **WITH** Clause for Creating Calculated Cells

Clause	Description
`FOR`	Defines the subcube to which the calculation applies.
`AS`	Defines the formula to calculate the cell value.
`CONDITION`	Further restricts the subcube to which the calculated cells apply. This expression should evaluate to a Boolean value. If the condition expression evaluates to `TRUE` during the calculation of the cell value, the cell will have the calculation formula specified by the `AS` clause applied.

The combination of the calculation subcube and the calculated cells condition is the *calculation scope*:

```
WITH CELL CALCULATION <calculation name> FOR '<subcube definition>'
 AS '<calculation formula>' [<conditions>]
 SELECT <definition of the resulting multidimensional space>
 FROM <source subspace>
 WHERE <limiting the results to subspace>
```


For example, we could have used the following query from our earlier example to display sales in U.S. currency rather than the original Canadian dollars and Mexican pesos:

```
WITH CELL CALCULATION
 CurrencyConversion FOR '(leaves(time),leaves(currency), measures.[store sales])'
 AS measures.[store sales]*[Measures].[Rates]
SELECT measures.[store sales] ON COLUMNS,
 [Store].[Stores].[Store Country].members ON ROWS
FROM [Warehouse and Sales]
```

Because you want to use calculated cells only in pretty exotic situations, we won't go into further detail about calculated cells.

Named Sets

To simplify complex MDX expressions or to improve the performance of some queries, you can extract the definition of some sets into a separate named set expression. Similar to calculated member, you can define a named set in different scopes. The scope in which you define a named set affects its lifetime:

- A named set defined in an MDX script as part of a cube is available to all the queries run against the cube.
- A named set defined on a session is available to subsequent queries from the same user during the same session.
- A named set defined as part of a query is available only in the context of this current query.

Use the `WITH` clause to define a named set as part of a query (as you do for a calculated member):

```
WITH [DYNAMIC¦STATIC] SET <named set> AS <named set formula>
SELECT <definition of the resulting multidimensional space>
FROM <source subspace>
WHERE <limiting the results to subspace>
```

For example, you can define the `TopCustomers` named set with the following code:

```
WITH SET TopCustomers AS
```

```
'TopCount([Customer].[Customers].[Customer].members,5, [Measures].[Sales Count])'
SELECT TopCustomers ON COLUMNS
FROM [Warehouse and Sales] WHERE [Measures].[Sales Count]
```

You can use the following MDX `CREATE SET` statement to define a named set on a session:

```
CREATE [DYNAMIC¦STATIC] SET [<cube_name>.][name of the set] AS < named set formula >]
```

Therefore, you could define the `TopCustomers` named set from the earlier example on the session with the following statement:

```
CREATE SET [Warehouse and Sales].TopCustomers AS '
TopCount([Customer].[Customers].[Customer].members,5, [Measures].[Sales Count])'
```

When you no longer need a named set, you can use the `DROP SET` statement to remove the named set from the session:

```
DROP SET [Warehouse and Sales].TopCustomers
```

As in other kinds of calculations, you can define a named set as part of an MDX script and it will be available from any query against the cube. To create a named set for use in the scope of the cube, you can use the user interface provided by BI Dev Studio:

1. In BI Dev Studio, open the FoodMart 2008 project.
2. In the Solution Explorer, double-click the `Warehouse and Sales` cube to open the cube editor.
3. On the Calculations tab, right-click anywhere in the Script Organizer, and choose New Named Set from the contextual menu.
4. Specify the name of the set in the Name box and the formula associated with the set in the Expression box.

After you define a named set, you can use it in subsequent queries. For example, you can reference the `TopCustomers` named set in the following `SELECT` statement:

```
SELECT TopCustomers ON COLUMNS FROM [Warehouse and Sales]
```

NOTE

Named sets in Analysis Services 2005 are static: They are parsed and resolved just once. Analysis Services 2008 supports both static and dynamic named sets.

Static Name Sets

A static named set is resolved either when the `CREATE SET` statement is executed or, if the named set was defined with a `WITH` clause, right after the `WHERE` clause is resolved. When a query references a static named set, the named set is not resolved again in the context of the current coordinate.

Let's go a little deeper. Assume that you want to count the customers that made more than 10 purchases every month. Write the following query:

```
WITH
 MEMBER Measures.x AS 'count(Filter([Customer].[Customers].[Customer].members,
 (Time.Time.Currentmember,[Measures].[Sales Count])>10))'
SELECT Measures.x ON COLUMNS,
[Time].[Time].[Month] ON ROWS FROM [Warehouse and Sales]
```


The values that result from this query are different for each month because when the `Filter` function executes inside the cell value, the current coordinate of the `Time` dimension is set to a particular month. Figure 12.11 shows the results of this query.

	x
January	87
February	96
March	115
April	80
May	78
June	86
July	126
August	82
September	68
October	73
November	126
December	128
January	348
February	332
March	332
April	316
May	315
June	321
July	332
August	309
September	354
October	307
November	378
December	449

FIGURE 12.11 The `Filter` function takes the current member of the `Time` dimension into consideration.

If you modify this query to use a named set and move the `Filter` function into the named set expression, it will be evaluated at the beginning of the query in the context of the default member of the `Time` dimension—member `ALL`:

```
WITH
 SET FilterSet as Filter([Customer].[Customers].[Customer].members,
 (Time.Time.currentmember,[Measures].[Sales Count])>10)
MEMBER Measures.x AS 'COUNT(FilterSet)'
SELECT Measures.x ON COLUMNS,
 [Time].[Time].[Month] ON ROWS
FROM [Warehouse and Sales]
```

Figure 12.12 shows the results of this query.

	x
January	6219
February	6219
March	6219
April	6219
May	6219
June	6219
July	6219
August	6219
September	6219
October	6219
November	6219
December	6219

FIGURE 12.12 The value for each cell contains the same value because they were calculated in the context of the member ALL.

However, static named sets can sometimes improve performance. Suppose that you want to know the aggregated value of purchases by your best customers in the United States every day. Write the following expression:

```
WITH
MEMBER Measures.BestSales as 'AGGREGATE(TopCount(
Descendants([Customer].[Customers].[Country].&[USA],, LEAVES), 5,
 [Measures].[Sales Count] ),[Measures].[Sales Count])'
SELECT Measures.BestSales ON COLUMNS,
[Time].[Time].[Date].members ON ROWS FROM [Warehouse and Sales]
```

After executing this query, Analysis Services repeatedly calculates the `Descendants` set for each cell. However, the result of the `Descendants` function in this case is static—it always contains stores in the United States. Therefore, if you move the `Descendants` function into the named set, Analysis Services calculates its value just once, when the named set resolved. The following query executes almost twice as quickly as the previous one:

```
WITH
SET USADescendants AS Descendants([Customer].[Customers].[Country].&[USA],,
LEAVES) member Measures.x AS 'AGGREGATE(TopCount(USADescendants, 5,
 [Measures].[Sales Count] ),[Measures].[Sales Count])'
SELECT Measures.x ON COLUMNS,
[Time].[Time].[Date].members ON ROWS FROM [Warehouse and Sales]
```

We did not move the `TopCount` function into the named set because doing so would affect the results of the query.

Dynamic Named Sets

Analysis Services 2008 supports dynamic named sets, in addition to the static named sets supported by earlier versions. Analysis Services now enables you to create a named set on a session or in MDX script of a cube and revaluate it in context of each query that references it. In a sense, dynamic named sets created with a `CREATE SET` statement behave the same way as named sets created in a query do—it uses sets or tuples specified in a `WHERE` clause and a SubSelect of a query. To demonstrate the difference between dynamic and static sets, let's take on the following example:

1. Create a static named set for finding our best customers, using the following expression:

```
CREATE SET [Warehouse and Sales].TopCustomers AS
   'TopCount([Customer].[Customers].[Customer].members,5, [Measures].[Sales
   Count])'
```

2. Execute query that should return the best customers in year 1997:

```
SELECT TopCustomers ON COLUMNS
FROM [Warehouse and Sales] WHERE
   ([Time].[Time].[Year].[1997],[Measures].[Sales Count])
```

Figure 12.13 shows the results of this query. Because our named set is static, this query returns the best customers in a context of the default member—member `ALL` of time dimension and doesn't take our `WHERE` clause into consideration.

Dawn Laner	Ida Rodriguez	Mary Francis Benigar	James Horvat	George Todero
104	125	146	127	123

FIGURE 12.13 Static named set doesn't take `WHERE` clause of a query into consideration.

Now let's use dynamic named set rather than a static one:

1. Create a dynamic named set for finding our best customers, using the following expression:

```
CREATE DYNAMIC SET [Warehouse and Sales].DynamicTopCustomers AS
    'TopCount([Customer].[Customers].[Customer].members,5, [Measures].[Sales
    Count])'
```

2. Execute query that should return the best customers in year 1997:

```
SELECT DynamicTopCustomers ON COLUMNS
FROM [Warehouse and Sales] WHERE
    ([Time].[Time].[Year].[1997],[Measures].[Sales Count])
```

3. Figure 12.14 shows the results of this query. Because our named set is dynamic, this query returns the best customers in a context of the `WHERE` clause—member 1997 of `Time` dimension.

Mary Francis Benigar	James Horvat	Jack Zucconi	Ida Rodriguez	Beradette Marschang
146	127	126	125	123

FIGURE 12.14 Analysis Services executes dynamic named set in context of the WHERE clause.

4. You can also check that the result displayed in Figure 12.14 indeed shows the best customers of 1997 by executing following query:

```
SELECT TopCount([Customer].[Customers].[Customer].members,5,
[Measures].[Sales Count]) ON COLUMNS
FROM [Warehouse and Sales] WHERE
    ([Time].[Time].[Year].[1997],[Measures].[Sales Count])
```

NOTE

Dynamic named sets are evaluated in a context of `WHERE` clause and SubSelect of every query, but they are not evaluated in a context of every cell.

To reinforce this point, we modify a named set used in a query corresponding to Figure 12.12. We create a dynamic named set that contains a filter set and then use it in a query:

```
CREATE DYNAMIC
 SET [Warehouse and Sales].FilterSet AS
Filter([Customer].[Customers].[Customer].members,
 (Time.Time.CurrentMember,[Measures].[Sales Count])>10)
WITH MEMBER Measures.x AS 'COUNT(FilterSet)'
SELECT Measures.x ON COLUMNS,
```

```
[Time].[Time].[Month] ON ROWS
FROM [Warehouse and Sales]
```

After executing this query, we get the same result (shown in Figure 12.12) we had before with a static set. A filter set uses the default member of the `Time` dimension (member `All`), and not the current member (the current month that corresponds to each individual cell).

Order of Execution for Cube Calculations

To get the results you expect from cube calculation, you must pay attention to the order Analysis Services uses to calculate a cell value when more than one calculation (assignment operator or calculated member) applies to the cell. Cube data is loaded into Analysis Services in multiple stages, called *passes*. First (at pass 0), the cube's logical space is not calculated. Only leaf members are loaded from the fact data; the values of nonleaf cells are null. After fact data is loaded (at pass 0.5), Analysis Services loads the values of the cells associated with measures that have one of the following aggregate functions: `SUM`, `COUNT`, `MIN`, `MAX`, and `DISTINCT COUNT`. At this stage, cells associated with semi-additive measures are not populated and dimension and cube calculations are not applied.

Analysis Services populates the logical space of the cube when it executes the `Calculate` command. The `Calculate` command usually is the first command encountered in an MDX script, but if a cube does not have an MDX script, Analysis Services generates a `Calculate` command.

NOTE

When a cube has an MDX script, it should have a `Calculate` command that populates the nonleaf cells with data.

The `Calculate` command has very simple syntax:

```
Calculate;
```

When we use the word *populate*, we do not mean that every cell of the cube is calculated. The cell values and other cell properties will be calculated when the query requests a specific cell (unless retrieved from the cache). *Populate* means that all the data structures are prepared and when the client application eventually requests the cell, the structures will be ready.

During execution of the `Calculate` command, the cells associated with semi-additive measures are populated; unary operators and custom member formulas are applied. For information about semi-additive measures, unary operators, and custom member formulas, see Chapter 13.

Each operator in an MDX script, including the `Calculate` command, creates a new pass. We will show how passes work in a simple cube with a single dimension, `D1`, which has four members: `ALL`, `M1`, `M2`, and `M3`. The cube contains the following MDX script:

```
Calculate;
M1=1;
(M1,M2)=2;
```

When the cube is loaded, Analysis Services processes the script and creates a pass for each statement in it, as shown in Figure 12.15.

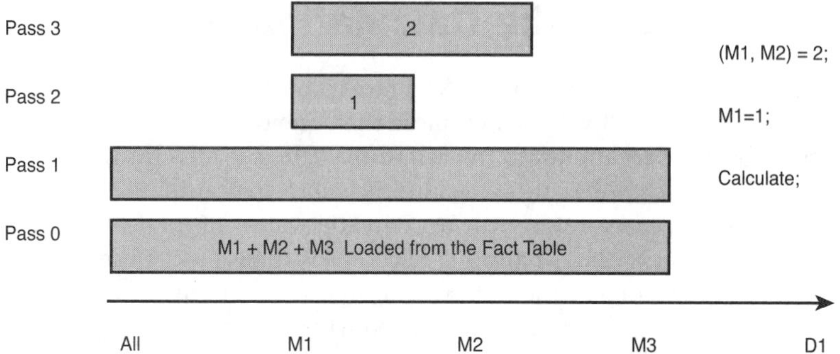

FIGURE 12.15 Analysis Services creates a pass for each statement in the MDX script.

When a cell of a cube is calculated, the order in which calculations are applied depends on the type of calculations used to calculate the cell. If only cube calculations cover a cell, Analysis Services uses the "highest pass wins" rule.

A calculation *covers* a cell if the calculation is explicitly specified for a subcube or if the calculation is specified for a descendant of the cell (because to calculate the value of that cell, Analysis Services must aggregate values of its descendants). So, in our example, the calculation on pass 2—`(M1, M2)=2;`—covers not only the cells associated with members `M1` and `M2`, but also those associated with their ancestor: the member `ALL`.

The Highest Pass Wins

Cube calculations are applied to a cell starting from the highest pass (the "highest pass wins" rule). In the preceding example, if you query a cell associated with `M1`, the query will return `2` because the highest pass available for that coordinate assigned the value `2` to the cell. For a cell associated with M3, the highest pass is pass 1, so a query will return a fact data value.

If you use legacy `Create Cell Calculation` syntax or you create a calculated member using `Create Member` syntax, you can explicitly specify the pass on which you want to create your calculation. If you do this, however, more than one calculation might end up on the same pass, and Analysis Services would have to choose which calculation should take precedence over the other. It will use the `SOLVE_ORDER` property, if you specified one for your calculation. If even the `SOLVE_ORDER` properties for the two calculations are the same, Analysis Services first uses the calculation created before the other (see Figure 12.16).

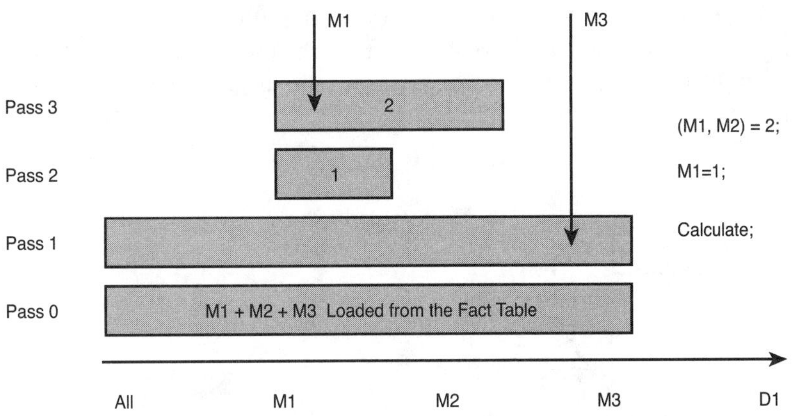

FIGURE 12.16 Cell values are calculated starting from the highest pass available.

Analysis Services provides a robust and powerful way to use MDX scripts to create and store calculations. We do not recommend that you use legacy functionality and play with passes unless you are sure that you want to change the order in which you call the calculations.

There are side effects to the "highest pass wins" rule, but there are ways to achieve the behavior you want. The following script provides an example:

```
M1=1;
M2=M1;
M1=2;
```

If you are used to programming in any programming language, you probably expect for the cell associated with the member `M1` to have the value `2` and the cell associated with `M2` to equal `1`. However, that is not what happens. Figure 12.17 demonstrates the steps Analysis Services takes to retrieve both cells.

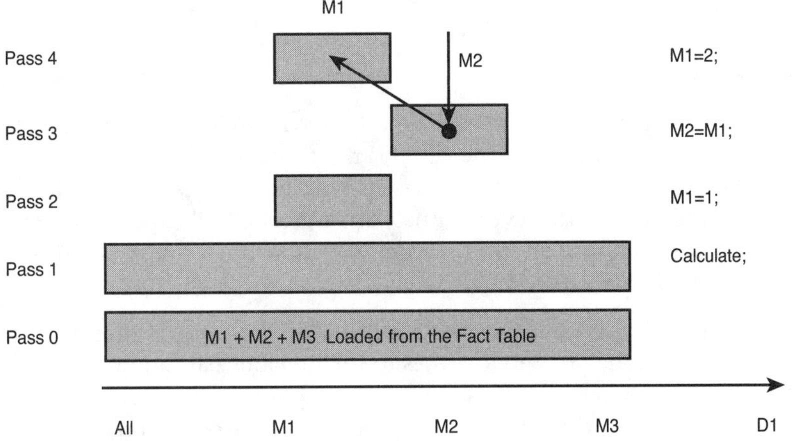

FIGURE 12.17 The value of M2 equals the value of M1 on the highest pass.

You can avoid this result by using a FREEZE statement. A FREEZE statement pins cells to their current values. Changes to other cells have no effect on the pinned cells. Therefore, you can change the script to include a FREEZE statement and the diagram of the calculation of the cell value for M2 changes, as shown in Figure 12.18.

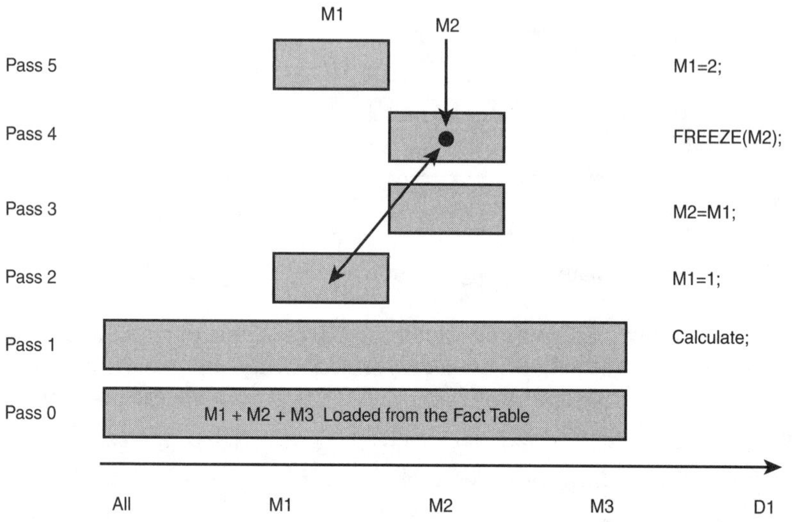

FIGURE 12.18 The value of M2 equals the value of M1 on the pass before the FREEZE statement.

```
M1=1;
M2=M1;
FREEZE(M2);
M1=2;
```

Recursion Resolution

The expression associated with a calculation often depends on the value of itself (recursion)—for example, when the expressions on the left and right sides of an assignment operator involve the same cell (M1 = M1*2). This expression means that the value of the cell associated with M1 should double. However, if Analysis Services blindly applies the "highest pass wins" rule, it will run into an infinite loop. A recursion resolution algorithm makes it possible to avoid such undesired effects.

The algorithm is simple: Analysis Services calculates a cell starting from the highest pass. If there is a recursion on this pass, Analysis Services goes to the previous pass and tries to evaluate an expression on it. If the previous pass also has a recursion, the operation repeats until it encounters a pass in which there is no recursion. If the operation encounters a circular reference, it raises an error.

Let's look at how the algorithm works on a simple script:

```
Calculate;
M1=1;
M1=M1*2;
```

To calculate the value of the cell associated with the M1 member, the expression on pass 3—M1=M1*2;—is evaluated first. The expression recursively calls M1. Instead of trying to evaluate M1 on the highest pass, Analysis Services moves to pass 2—the previous pass covering space for M1—and tries to evaluate the expression M1=1;. Because that expression is not recursive, the result of the evaluation on pass 2 propagates to pass 3, where it is used to calculate M1*2. Therefore, the resulting value for this cell is (1*2) or, in other words, 2, as shown in Figure 12.19.

Recursion happens not only when an expression explicitly uses the value of itself. Recursion also occurs in a more subtle case: when the value for a descendant depends on the value of its ancestor. One of the common cases of this scenario occurs in the distribution of a budget between different departments of an organization. Consider the following script as an example:

```
Calculate;
{M1, M2, M3} = ALL/3;
```

When a user requests the value associated with one of the members—let's say M2—Analysis Services tries to retrieve the value of the ALL member on pass 1. It calculates the value of the ALL member as an aggregation of its descendants; therefore, Analysis Services needs the value of M2. At this stage, we get a recursion. (We are already inside the calculation of the value for M2.) Therefore, the recursion resolution algorithm decreases the pass number to pass 1, and Analysis Services calculates the value for M2, which happens to be the value loaded from the fact table. As a result, it calculates the value for the ALL member as an aggregation of the fact data. The value divides equally among all the descendants. Figure 12.20 shows the steps that the recursion resolution algorithm went through to resolve the value for M2. Solid lines indicate steps that it actually performed; dashed lines indicate steps that it might have happened, but did not because of recursion resolution.

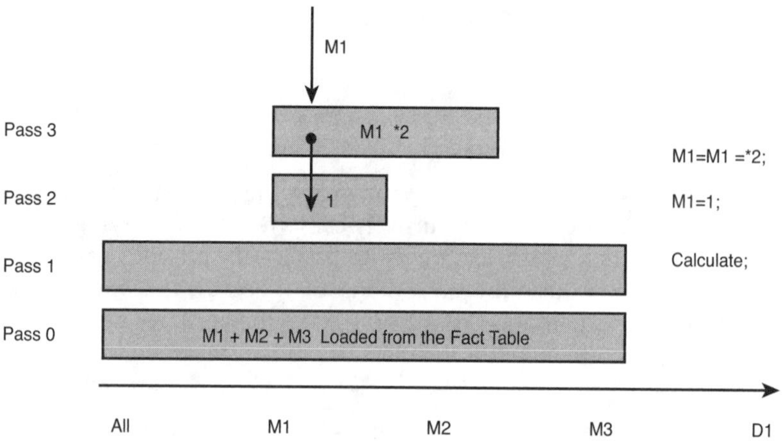

FIGURE 12.19 Analysis Services uses a recursion resolution algorithm to calculate the value of a cell associated with the M1 member.

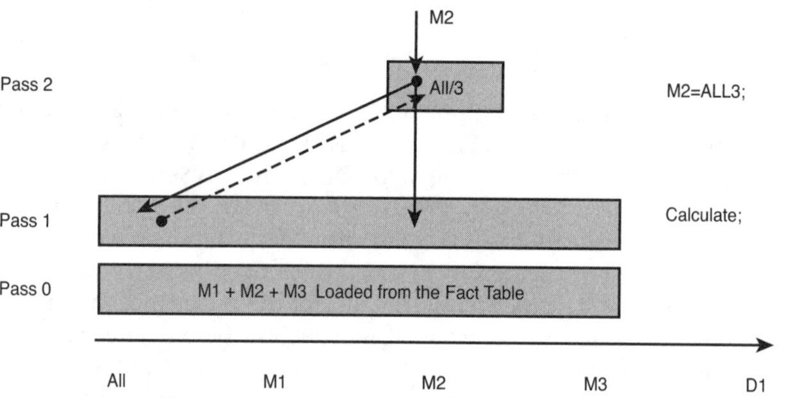

FIGURE 12.20 The recursion resolution algorithm uses the value of M2 on pass 2 to calculate an aggregated value for the ALL member.

CHAPTER 13

Dimension-Based MDX Calculations

IN THIS CHAPTER

- Unary Operators
- Custom Member Formulas
- Semi-Additive Measures
- Order of Execution for Dimension Calculations

Assignment operators, calculated members, and named sets—cube-based calculations discussed in Chapter 12, "Cube-Based MDX Calculations"—provide a powerful mechanism, MDX scripts, for specifying various kinds of custom formulas to calculate data. However, sometimes it is better to base your definition of calculations on dimension members—perhaps by assigning a different formula to each dimension member.

If a dimension has many members, you would have to create as many formulas in the script as there are dimension members. In addition, if a formula applies to a dimension (which could be included in various cubes) and not to the cube, using a cube-based calculation would require that you replicate the calculation in all the cubes in which the dimension is used.

Three features of Analysis Services enable you to specify the calculation of data as part of the dimension definition. Those features enable you to place MDX formulas or rules for data computation in the same place where the dimension data is stored—in the dimension:

- Unary operators
- Custom member formulas
- Semi-additive measures

Unary Operators

When a custom calculation is not specified, the default behavior of Analysis Services is to use the formula defined by the measure's aggregate functions, starting from the highest granularities (lower levels of the dimensions) to produce total values for the lowest granularities (top levels of the dimensions). However, there are dimensions for which typical summing, counting, and finding the minimum or maximum are just not enough. A good example of such a dimension is an `Account` dimension, which has members such as `Assets`, `Liabilities`, and `Net Income`. The rules of aggregation for these members differ from those of simple summing. For example, you do not add assets and liabilities.

One of the ways to get around this dilemma is to specify unary operators on a dimension, one unary operator for each dimension member. The unary operator defines the arithmetic operator to apply to the value of the member when rolling it up to produce the aggregated value. Analysis Services supports seven unary operators. Table 13.1 describes each one.

TABLE 13.1 Unary Operators Supported by Analysis Services

Unary Operator	Description
+	Adds the value of the member to the aggregate value.
-	Subtracts the value of the member from the aggregate value.
*	Multiplies the value of the member by the aggregate value.
/	The aggregate value divided by the value of the member.
~	Ignores the value of the member in the aggregation.
`<<Factor>>`	Multiplies the value by the factor and adds the result to the aggregate values. (`Factor` is any numeric value.)
	An empty unary operator is equivalent to the + operator.

To create a unary operator in a dimension, you typically add a column to the dimension table in the relational database. Each row corresponds to a dimension member; the value of that row in the unary operator column contains a specific unary operator for that member.

After you create an unary operator column, you specify the `UnaryOperatorColumn` property of the attribute to which you assign the unary operator. You can do this in SQL Server Business Intelligence Development Studio (BI Dev Studio) or by manually issuing a Data Definition Language (DDL) statement.

NOTE

For a parent-child dimension—and parent-child is the type of the dimension in which unary operators are mostly used—you specify unary operators on the parent attribute.

To apply unary operators to the `Account` dimension of the FoodMart 2008 database, follow these steps:

1. In BI Dev Studio, open the FoodMart 2008 project.
2. In the Solution Explorer, double-click the `Account.dim` dimension to open the dimension editor.
3. Right-click the `Accounts` attribute (the parent attribute of the `Account` dimension) in the Attributes pane, and choose Properties from the contextual menu.
4. In the property pane, select the `UnaryOperatorColumn` property and set it to the `account.account_rollup` column.

If you browse the `Account` dimension, you will see a hierarchy of members with unary operators, as shown in Figure 13.1.

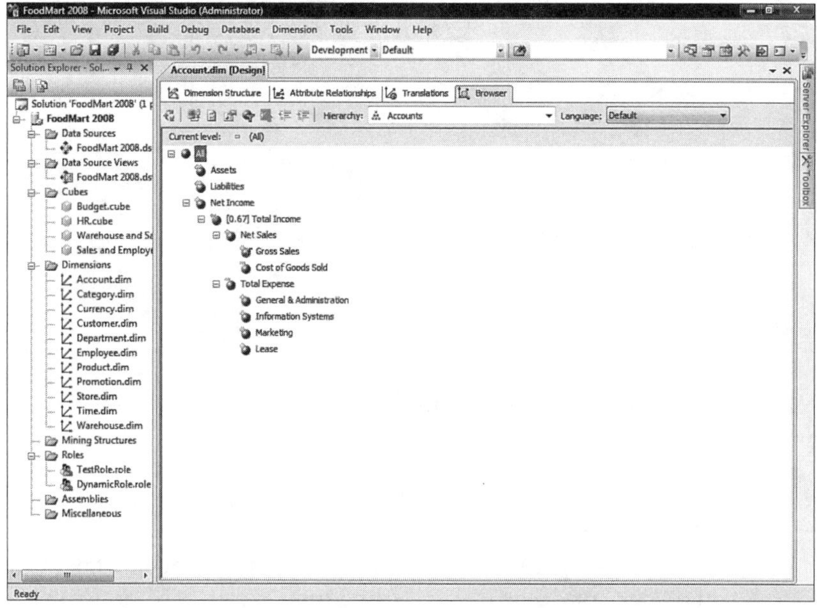

FIGURE 13.1 Icons indicating the unary operators appear next to the dimension members.

Now browse the `Budget` cube that contains the `Account` dimension, by following these steps:

1. Right-click the `Budget` cube in the Solution Explorer to open the cube browser, and choose Browse from the contextual menu.
2. Drag the `Amount` measure and drop it in the data area of the browser.
3. Drag the `Account` dimension and drop it in the rows area.
4. Drill down into the `Account` dimension.

In Figure 13.2, you can see that Total Expense equals General & Administration plus Information Systems plus Marketing plus Lease. Similarly, the Net Sales equals Gross Sales minus Cost of Goods Sold.

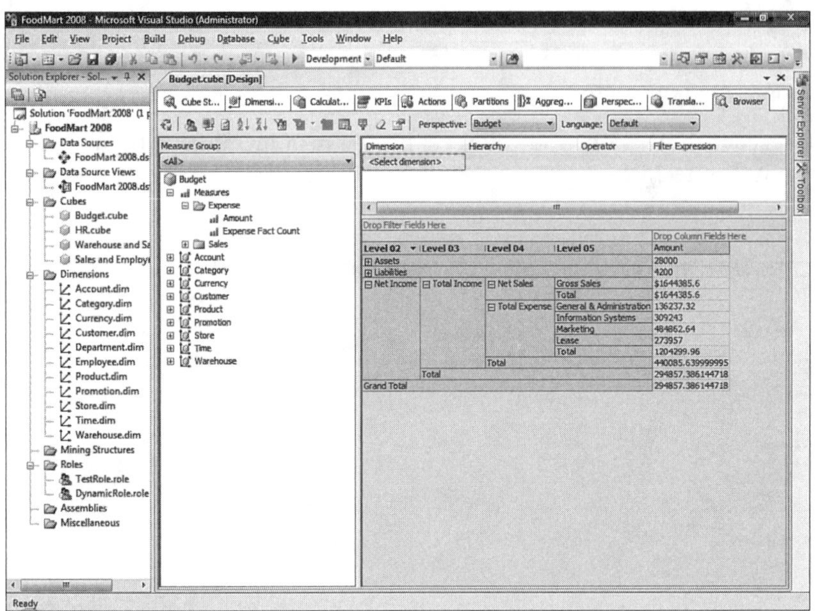

FIGURE 13.2 Browse the data of the `Budget` cube to see the rollup of accounts in the `Account` dimension.

The unary operators +, -, *, /, and ~ are supported in Analysis Services 2000. However, `Factor` is a unary operator, introduced in Analysis Services 2005. Here is an example of the `Factor` unary operator at work: Suppose that FoodMart has to pay an income tax of 33%. You would calculate the taxable income by subtracting total expenses from net sales. Then, you would multiply the result by a factor of .33 to calculate the tax. To calculate income after taxes, you then subtract the tax from the taxable income. In other words, you would use the following formula to calculate net income:

> Net Income = (Net Sales – Total Expense) – (Net Sales – Total Expense) * 0.33 = (Net Sales – Total Expense) * 0.67.

To do all this, add one more record to the `Account` table in the relational FoodMart `2008` database—that record corresponds to the `Total Income` member, which has associated with it the factor `0.67` (1 – 0.33). As a result of this factor unary operator, Analysis Services multiplies the value of the `Total Income` member by 0.67, and then adds the result to the aggregated value of the other siblings (zero, in our case, because `Total Income` is the only child of `Net Income`).

Look again at Figure 13.2 to see the values associated with the `Total Income` and `Net Income` members, which have the income tax included in their calculation.

Custom Member Formulas

When you define how to aggregate the values of members, you might have to do more than to specify a trivial operator. You might have to use a more complex formula that demands operators other than the simple add, subtract, or multiply—or even factor. In such cases, you typically create one more column in the relational dimension table and assign an MDX expression—a custom member formula—to members of the dimension.

To create a custom member formula in a dimension, you follow a process similar to the one you use to create unary operators. You add a column to the dimension table in the relational database. Each row corresponds to a dimension member; the value of that row in the custom member formula column contains an MDX expression for that member. (When you do not need an expression specified for that member, you can leave a `NULL` value in the column.)

After you create your custom member formula column, you specify the `CustomRollupColumn` property of the attribute to which you assign the custom member formula. You can do this in BI Dev Studio or by manually issuing a DDL statement.

NOTE

For a parent-child dimension—and parent-child is the type of the dimension where custom member formulas are mostly used—you specify the `CustomRollupColumn` property on the parent attribute.

For example, in the FoodMart `Account` dimension, the value of `Gross Sales` does not come from the `Budget` cube. However, it does exist in our Unified Dimensional Model (UDM)—in the `Store Sales` measure of the `Sales` measure group of the `Warehouse and Sales` cube. When you are working in the `Budget` cube, you can retrieve this information either by linking to the `Sales` measure group (for information about linked measure groups, see Chapter 25, "Building Scalable Analysis Services Applications") or by using the `LookupCube` MDX function.

Even though the `LookupCube` MDX function is probably easier to understand, linked measure groups yield better performance, and they fit better into the UDM. The UDM brings all the information that your organization needs into one unit, so you can use the same data in different cubes without replicating it. Therefore, we are going to have you use the second approach and create a linked measure group, `Sales`, in the `Budget` cube.

Now that information about sales is accessible in the `Budget` cube, you can assign the simple MDX formula (`[Measures].[Store Sales], [Account].[Accounts].[All]`) to the `Gross Sales` member. In Figure 13.3, you can see this formula in the table row that contains `Gross Sales`.

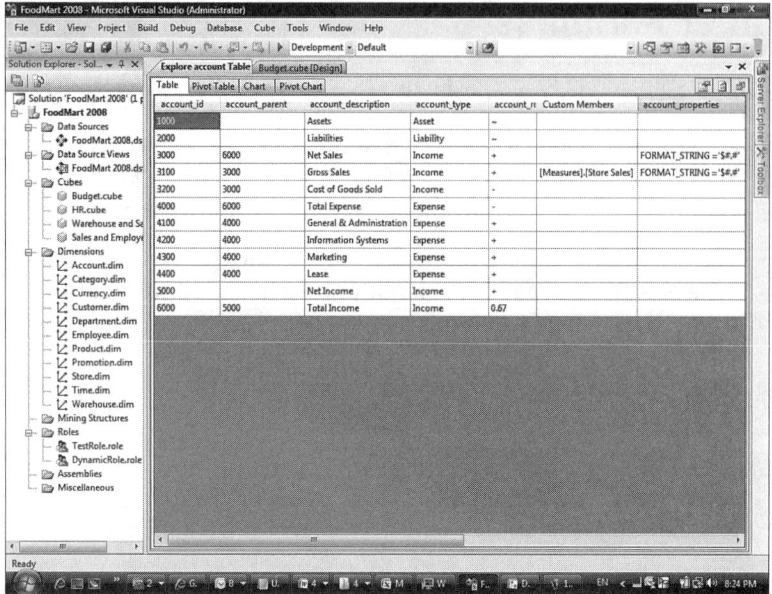

FIGURE 13.3 The formula `[Measures].[Store Sales]` appears in the same row as the `Gross Sales` member.

If you go back to Figure 13.2, which shows the results of browsing the cube, you can see that the value of `Gross Sales` corresponds to the total sales of all the stores in the FoodMart enterprise.

Using custom member formulas enables you to not only change how values are aggregated for particular dimension member, but you can also change the properties of cells associated with a member using custom member properties.

To create a custom member property in a dimension, you follow a process similar to the one you use for creating custom member formulas. You add a column to the dimension table in the relational database. Each row corresponds to a dimension member; the value of that row in the custom member property column contains the name of a valid cell property (for more discussion of cell properties, refer to Chapter 11, "Advanced MDX") and the value of such property, using the following syntax:

```
<property identifier> = '<property value>' [, <property identifier> =
 '<property value>'...]
```

After you create a column for your custom member property, you specify the `CustomRollupPropertiesColumn` property of the dimension attribute to which you assign the custom member property. If you have a parent-child dimension, you set the `CustomRollupPropertiesColumn` property on the parent attribute—in FoodMart 2008, that would be the `Accounts` attribute for the `Account` dimension.

In the FoodMart 2008 sample, we created an `account_properties` column in the `accounts` table and we assigned the `FORMAT_STRING` property to two accounts: `Net Sales` and `Gross`

Sales. Analysis Services uses the FORMAT_STRING property to format net sales and gross sales in U.S. dollars.

Analysis Services can now use custom properties when you query the data. In Microsoft SQL Server Management Studio, issue the following query to retrieve the Amount measure for each account:

```
SELECT [Measures].[Amount] ON COLUMNS,
[Account].[Accounts].members ON ROWS
 FROM [Budget]
```

You can see the result of this query in Figure 13.4.

	Amount
All	294857.386144718
Assets	672000
Liabilities	100800
Net Income	294857.386144718
Total Income	440085.639999994
Net Sales	$1644385.6
Gross Sales	$1644385.6
Cost of Goods Sold	(null)
Total Expense	1204299.96
General & Administrati...	136237.32
Information Systems	309243
Marketing	484862.64
Lease	273957

FIGURE 13.4 The FORMAT_STRING custom property has been applied to format net sales and gross sales in U.S. dollars.

Semi-Additive Measures

In a cube that doesn't have calculations defined, data for the highest granularity (leaf cells) is equivalent to the physical data—the fact data. You use the Aggregation Function property of the Measure object to calculate aggregated values. To aggregate values, Analysis Services 2000 supports only measures with additive functions such as SUM, MIN, MAX, COUNT, and nonadditive DISTINCT_COUNT. Analysis Services 2005 extended the list of aggregation functions to support measures with semi-additive and nonadditive aggregation functions. With semi-additive measures, you can aggregate the values of a cube by summing the cells associated with child members along most dimensions and use nonadditive aggregation functions to aggregate members along the Time dimension.

Look at this example of a semi-additive measure: For each month the employees of your warehouse do inventory, a column in the fact table contains the number of products found in inventory. To the `Warehouse and Sales` sample cube, we added a new measure group, `Warehouse Inventory`, to demonstrate such a scenario. The `Warehouse Inventory` measure group has the following dimensions: `Time` (with granularity on months), `Product`, `Warehouse`, and one measure, `Units`.

If you assign a `SUM` aggregation function to the `Units` measure, the aggregated value for the members on the `Product` dimension calculates correctly because you sum the values of all the products in a product family to calculate the number of products in that product family. However, you would not get a correct result if you were to sum the number of products in monthly inventories to get the value for products counted in the year-end inventory.

To compare yearly inventories, a manager looks at the results of the inventory taken at the end of the last month of the year. Because of this practice, the measure `Units` is additive, along all the dimensions except the `Time` dimension. It is a semi-additive measure.

Analysis Services supports seven types of semi-additive aggregation functions for measures, as described in Table 13.2.

TABLE 13.2 Semi-Additive Aggregation Functions

Aggregation Function	Description
`None`	No aggregation is performed on any dimension; data values equal the values in the leaf cells.
`FirstChild`	Uses the `SUM` aggregation function for any dimensions except the `Time` dimension. The aggregated value along the `Time` dimension is the value for the first descendant of the member on the granularity attribute.
`LastChild`	Uses the `SUM` aggregation function for any dimension except the `Time` dimension. The aggregated value along the `Time` dimension is the value for the last descendant of the member on the granularity attribute.
`FirstNonEmpty`	Uses the `SUM` aggregation function for any dimension except the `Time` dimension. The aggregated value along the `Time` dimension is the value for the first descendant of the member on the granularity attribute that is not `NULL`.
`LastNonEmpty`	Uses the `SUM` aggregation function for any dimension except the `Time` dimension. The aggregated value along the `Time` dimension is the value for the last descendant of the time dimension that is not `NULL`. Our inventory example uses this aggregation function for the measure `Units` so that the values associated with a specific year are the same as the values for the last month of that year. If no inventory count took place in the last month, the value for the previous month is used.

TABLE 13.2 Semi-Additive Aggregation Functions

Aggregation Function	Description
`AverageOfChildren`	Uses the `SUM` aggregation function for any dimension except the `Time` dimension. The aggregated value along the `Time` dimension is the average of all the descendants of the member on the granularity attribute.
`ByAccount`	Uses the `SUM` aggregation function for any dimension except the `Time` dimension. The aggregated value along the `Time` dimension depends on the current member of the `Account` dimension (more about this aggregation function later in this chapter).

In our sample, we assigned the aggregation function `LastNonEmpty` to measure `Units`. The following query requests the number of products that belong to the Oysters product subcategory for all the months and quarters of the year 1997, and the year 1997 itself.

You can see the results of this query in Figure 13.5.

```
SELECT
DESCENDANTS([Time].[Time].[Year].[1997],[Time].[Time].[Date],
BEFORE_AND_AFTER) ON COLUMNS,
[Product].[Products].[Product Subcategory].[Oysters] ON ROWS
FROM [Warehouse and Sales] WHERE [Measures].[Units]
```

	1997	Q1	January	February	March	Q2	April	May	June	Q3	July	August	September	Q4	October	November	December
Oysters	40	(null)	(null)	(null)	(null)	0	0	(null)	(null)	22	22	(null)	(null)	40	40	(null)	(null)

FIGURE 13.5 The value for `Units` on the shelves in 1997 is the same as `Units` in October and Quarter 4.

Because the aggregation function of measure `Units` is `LastNonEmpty`, the value associated with `Units` in 1997 is equal to the value of the `Units` in the fourth quarter—the last nonempty child of member 1997. The value associated with `Units` in the fourth quarter is the same as that for last month of the fourth quarter that has a value—October.

`ByAccount` Aggregation Function

Sometimes business rules demand an algorithm for aggregating values along the `Time` dimension that is more complicated than a single aggregation function assigned to a measure. The `Budget` cube in our FoodMart 2008 sample database has an `Account` dimension and the `Amount` measure. For calculating annual income, it makes perfect sense to sum the income values from each quarter. However, it does not make sense to sum assets (such as land, equipment, and so on) or liabilities across quarters. You would use a different aggregation function to calculate assets and liabilities than you would to calculate income.

Follow these steps to assign different aggregation functions to different accounts:

1. Assign the `ByAccount` aggregation function to the `Amount` measure.
2. Map each member of an account dimension to a specific account type. Analysis Services recognizes any dimension as an account dimension if the dimension type is `Account`. To do this mapping, you follow these steps:
   A. Add a column to the dimension table in the relational database. Each row of the column corresponds to member of the `Account` dimension and has an account type associated with a member. In general, the account type can be any word or any string expression that makes sense to your organization; for example, it could be `Income`, `Expense`, `Asset`, or `Liability`.
   B. Create a new attribute `AccountType` of type `AccountType`, in the `Account` dimension based on the new column. This attributed is related to the key attribute of the `Account` dimension such that there is a one to one relationship between members of the `Account` attribute and `AccountType` attribute.
3. In the `Account` collection property of the `Database` object, define the mapping between account types (defined by the `AccountType` attribute) and aggregation functions as described next.

Because different companies have different rules for aggregating different accounts, and different companies also have their own naming systems for different account types, Analysis Services enables you to define custom mapping between account types and aggregation functions. You can create this mapping either by issuing a DDL request that alters the database or by using BI Dev Studio. Listing 13.1 shows a portion of the DDL that defines the mapping between account types and aggregation functions.

LISTING 13.1 Account Type Mapping

```
<Accounts>
    <Account>
        <AccountType>Balance</AccountType>
        <AggregationFunction>LastNonEmpty</AggregationFunction>
         <Aliases>
            <Alias>Balance</Alias>
         </Aliases>
    </Account>
    <Account>
         <AccountType>Asset</AccountType>
         <AggregationFunction>LastNonEmpty</AggregationFunction>
         <Aliases>
              <Alias>Asset</Alias>
         </Aliases>
     </Account>
</Accounts>
```

You can use BI Dev Studio to create the mapping between account type and aggregation function: Right-click FoodMart 2008 and choose Edit Database from the contextual menu. The database editor, shown in Figure 13.6, appears. You can use the editor to modify account type mapping. Analysis Services uses the value in the Alias column to map from the account type specified in the `Account Type` attribute to the measure's aggregation function.

You can also use the Account Time Intelligence Wizard to simplify the process of associating different aggregation functions to different accounts, by following these steps:

1. In the Solution Explorer, right-click the `Budget` cube and select Add Business Intelligence from the contextual menu.
2. Proceed to the Choose Enhancement page of the wizard and select Define Account Intelligence.
3. On the next page, choose your account dimension—`Account`.
4. Map the account types specified in the relational account table to the built-in account types.
5. Map the built-in account types to the types specified by the members of the `Account Type` attribute.

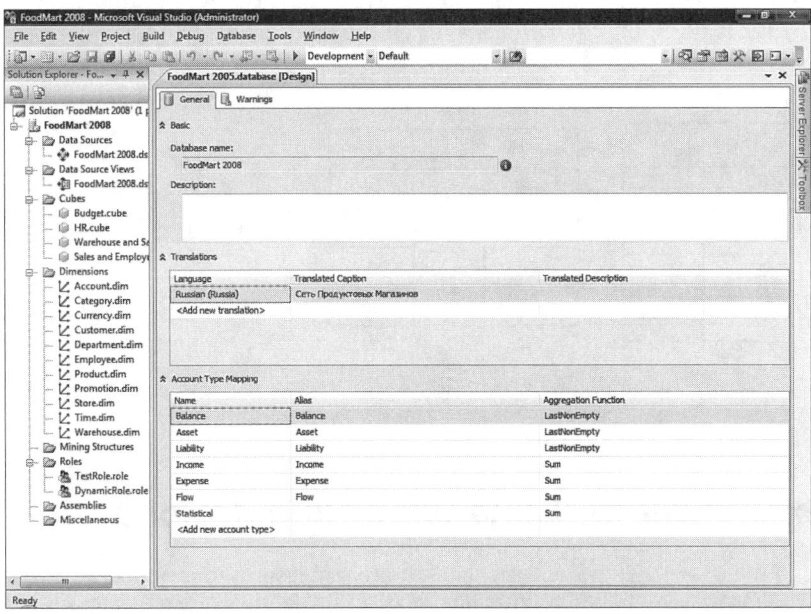

FIGURE 13.6 Use BI Dev Studio to define the mapping between aggregation function and account types.

When a cell based on the measure with the aggregation function ByAccount is calculated, Analysis Services, under the covers, finds the Account dimension (the dimension marked as being of type Account) among the cube dimensions. It retrieves the Account Type attribute for the current member, finds an account that has an Alias that is equivalent to the Account Type, and then maps it to an aggregation function.

Analysis Services generates an error if it cannot find a dimension of type Account among the cube's dimensions, or an attribute of the type AccountType on the Account dimension. If Analysis Services cannot find an element in the Accounts collection in the database that has an Alias that corresponds to an Account Type found in the Account Type attribute, or if the Accounts collection is not defined, Analysis Services assigns the SUM aggregate function to the measure. In Figure 13.7, you can see the process of mapping an aggregate function to the account type of the current member of the Account dimension.

Now that you have set up account intelligence for your Budget cube, execute the following query:

```
SELECT DESCENDANTS([Time].[Time].[Year].[1997],[Time].[Time].[Month], BEFORE)
 ON COLUMNS, [Account].[Accounts].members on ROWS from [Budget]
 WHERE [Measures].[Amount]
```

In the results of the query, shown in Figure 13.8, you can see that value associated with Amount in 1997 for Assets is equal to the Amount of Assets in Quarter 4, and the value for Net Income in 1997 is the sum of Net Income for all the quarters of the year.

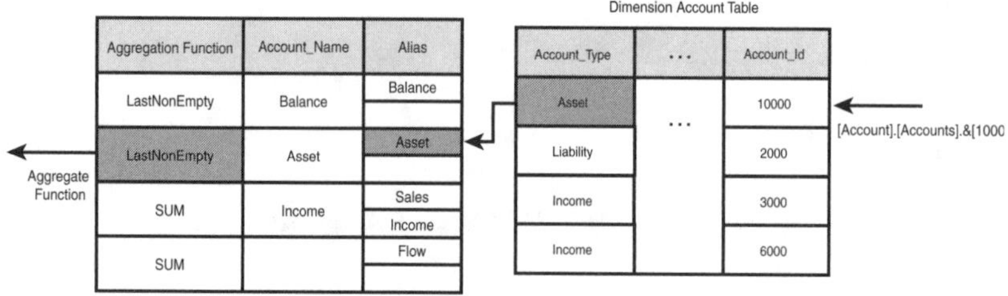

FIGURE 13.7 The current member on the Account dimension is mapped to an aggregation function.

Order of Execution for Dimension Calculations

During execution of the Calculate statement, semi-additive measures, unary operators, and custom member formulas are loaded. This means that all the dimension calculations are created in the same pass as the Calculate statement—pass one, in most cases.

The "highest pass wins" rule is applied when calculating a cell using only cube calculations—cell assignment operators and calculated members. (For more information about the "highest pass wins" rule, see Chapter 12.) However, when at least one dimension calculation covers the cell, a different rule applies: This time, the rule is the "closest wins."

	1997	Q1	Q2	Q3	Q4
All	267166.318954955	65706.0842366998	61041.4905205078	66056.1592454197	74362.5849523277
Assets	28000	28000	28000	28000	28000
Liabilities	4200	4200	4200	4200	4200
Net Income	267166.318954955	65706.0842366998	61041.4905205078	66056.1592454197	74362.5849523277
Total Income	398755.690000002	98068.7800000007	91106.700000001	98591.2800000004	110988.93
Net Sales	$565238.1	$139628.4	$132666.3	$140271.9	$152671.6
Gross Sales	$565238.1	$139628.4	$132666.3	$140271.9	$152671.6
Cost of Goods Sold	(null)	(null)	(null)	(null)	(null)
Total Expense	166482.44	41559.57	41559.57	41680.61	41682.69
General & Administrati...	22246.08	5561.52	5561.52	5561.52	5561.52
Information Systems	44713.8	11178.45	11178.45	11178.45	11178.45
Marketing	66860.96	16654.2	16654.2	16775.24	16777.32
Lease	32661.6	8165.4	8165.4	8165.4	8165.4

FIGURE 13.8 The results of the query show data for all accounts for 1997.

A cell is covered by a dimension calculation when the cell or one of its descendants is associated with either a semi-additive measure or a member has a nontrivial unary operator (anything other than the + operator), or has not-`NULL` custom member formula.

The Closest Wins

With the "closest wins" rule, the order of execution of calculations depends on the distance between the current cell and the cell for which you created the calculation.

We will examine the "closest wins" rule on the same simple cube we have been working with in previous chapters. It has just one dimension—the `Time` dimension, which has two attributes: `Year` and `Quarter`. Each attribute has the members shown in Figure 13.9. In this cube, values are aggregated, starting with members of granularity attribute (at the fact level) `Quarter` to members on the `Year` attribute, and eventually to the member `ALL`.

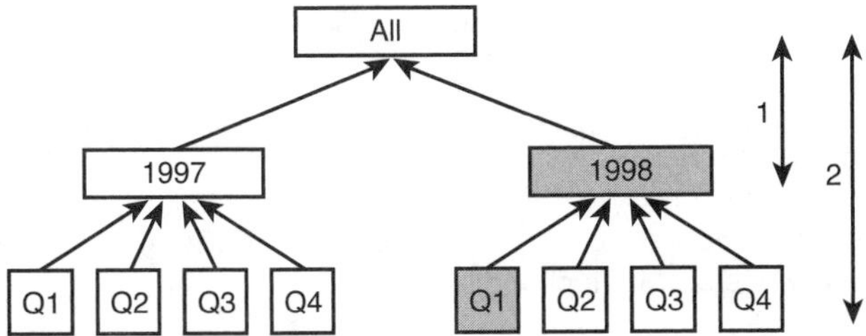

FIGURE 13.9 The distance between member ALL and Q1 is 2, and between member ALL and 1998 is 1.

The distance between `1998` and `ALL` is 1; the distance between `Q1` and `ALL` is 2. Therefore, if you assign one calculation on `1998` and another calculation on `Q1` (the order does not matter), when you query the value associated with the member `ALL`, Analysis Services uses the calculation assigned to member `1998`.

To make our example a little more complex, we added one more dimension to the cube: the `Account` dimension. It has the members `ALL`, `Income`, and `Expense`. There are unary operators (+ and -) assigned to this dimension, as shown in Figure 13.10.

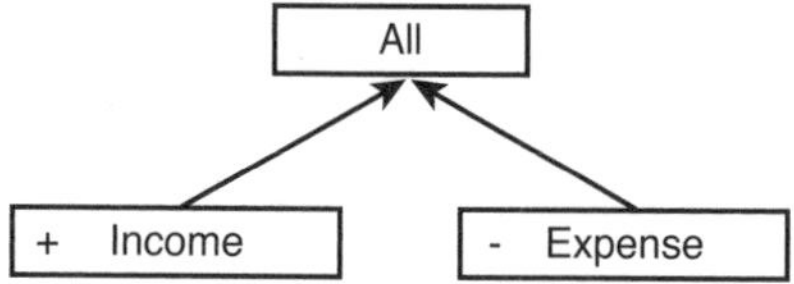

FIGURE 13.10 Unary operators are assigned to the members `Income` and `Expense`.

	All Time	1997	1998
All Accounts	3	1	2
+Income	12	4	8
-Expense	9	3	6

FIGURE 13.11 The aggregated values are calculated with unary operators.

The `Calculate` statement aggregates the fact data as shown in Figure 13.11. (We dropped the `Quarter` attribute for the sake of simplicity.)

If we create the following script in this cube, we will get the result shown in Figure 13.12:

```
Calculate;
(Account.Income, Time.1998)=5;
```

	All Time	1997	1998
All Accounts	0	1	-1
+Income	9	4	5
-Expense	9	3	6

FIGURE 13.12 The assignment operator is applied to the cell (`Account.Income, Time.1998`), but for other cells the unary operator is applied.

When you request the value for the tuple (Account.Income, Time.1998), the assignment operator (Account.Income, Time.1998)=5; wins because it was applied on a specific cell: (Account.Income, Time.1998). The distance from this calculation to the cell currently being queried is 0. There is no other calculation covering this cell because we defined the unary operator for the aggregated value—All Accounts—and not on each member itself. For values associated with the tuple (All Time, All Accounts), the unary operator wins because the distance from it to the cell is 0.

NOTE

Be careful with cubes in which dimension calculations coexist with cube calculations; pay close attention to evaluation rules.

Now we change the script a little and assign a value to the tuple (All Accounts, 1998). This changes the way the cube aggregates, as shown in Figure 13.13:

```
Calculate;
(Account.All Accounts, Time.1998)=5;
```

For the cell (All Accounts, All Time), the distance to the assignment operator is 1, and to the unary operator the distance is 0, because the unary operator is defined on the member ALL Accounts. Therefore, the unary operator wins, and Analysis Services ignores the assignment operator.

If more than one calculation is the same distance from the current cell, then and only then are passes considered. Therefore, if a cell calculation applies at a cell that has the same

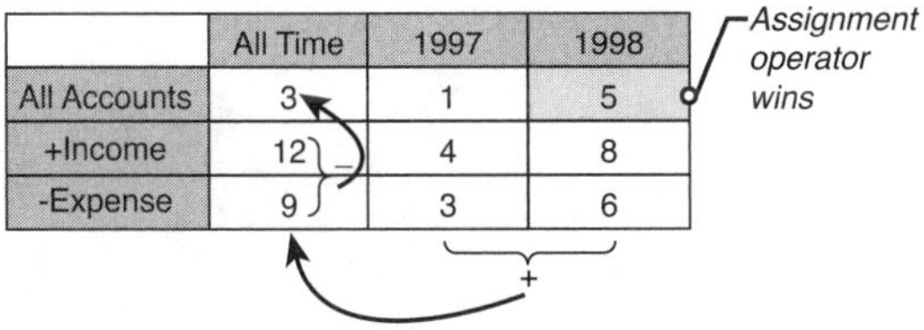

	All Time	1997	1998
All Accounts	3	1	5
+Income	12	4	8
-Expense	9	3	6

FIGURE 13.13 The assignment operator wins over the unary operator for cell with the tuple (All Accounts, 1998).

distance from a cell as does a unary operator, the cell calculation wins (because it usually is created on a pass higher than 1, where the `Calculate` statement usually executes).

There can be more than one calculation on the same pass if you explicitly specify a pass for a calculated cell or calculated member or if there is more than one dimension with unary operators or custom rollups; the `SOLVE_ORDER` property would be used. A calculation with the highest `SOLVE_ORDER` property takes precedence over a calculation with a lower one. By default, Analysis Services assigns a `SOLVE_ORDER` property and passes as shown in Table 13.3.

TABLE 13.3 Default Solve Order and Passes for Different Types of Calculations

Calculation Type	Default Solve Order	Default Pass
Assignment operator	0	Position in the script
Calculated cell	0	1 or explicitly specified
Calculated member	0	1
Unary operator	–5119	`Calculate` statement
Custom member formula	–5119	`Calculate` statement
Custom member property	–5119	`Calculate` statement
Semi-additive measure	–5631	`Calculate` statement

NOTE

When more than one dimension has unary operators or custom member formulas, the order of dimensions and hierarchies in the definition of the cube is important.

CHAPTER 14

Extending MDX with Stored Procedures

IN THIS CHAPTER

- Creating Stored Procedures
- Calling Stored Procedures from MDX
- Security Model
- Server Object Model
- Calling Back into Stored Procedures
- Using Default Libraries

You can use the Multidimensional Expressions (MDX)-based scripting language to define custom calculations inside a cube or in a dimension. MDX, MDX scripts, and dimension-based calculations provide powerful mechanisms to meet the requirements of many applications. (For more information about MDX, see Chapter 10, "MDX Concepts," Chapter 11, "Advanced MDX," Chapter 12, "Cube-Based MDX Calculations," and Chapter 13, "Dimension-Based MDX Calculations.")

There are scenarios, however, in which the tasks you have to solve are computationally complex or require getting data from sources outside the multidimensional model. For example, you might use web services application programming interfaces (APIs) to retrieve data from the Internet. To support such scenarios, Analysis Services integrates its multidimensional engine with common language runtime to enable you to use any common language runtime-supported procedural language to write stored procedures.

Analysis Services 2000 supports Component Object Model (COM)-based user-defined functions to extend the already rich set of MDX functions. Analysis Services 2005 and 2008 also support COM-based extensions to provide support to legacy applications, and extend the idea of user-defined functions far beyond Analysis Services 2000 functionality. Analysis Services provides an object model that models the MDX language for use by programmers writing procedural code. Analysis Services enables programmers to achieve tight integration between the implementation of stored procedures and the context in which the query that calls a stored procedure executes. (For more information about query context, see Chapter 26, "Server Architecture and

Command Execution.") Analysis Services 2008 extends stored procedures functionality by enabling calling back into stored procedures when certain events on the server occur. You can use the process shown in Figure 14.1 to create, publish, and use stored procedures.

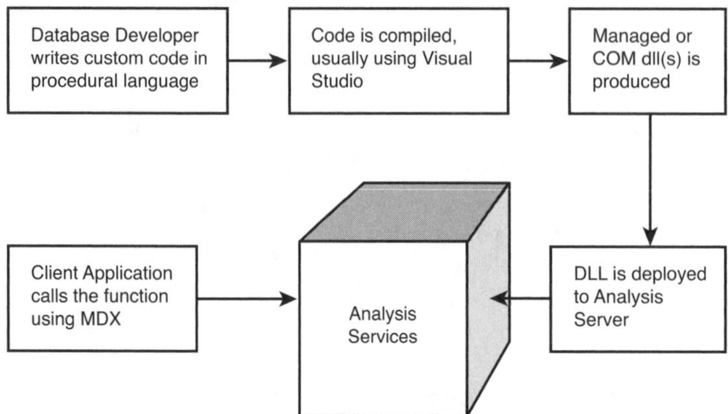

FIGURE 14.1 You use this process to create and use stored procedures and user-defined functions.

As you can see, you start by authoring stored procedures. You can use a common language runtime language such as C#, Visual Basic .NET, C++, or even COBOL to create a library. In addition, you can write your library in languages that support COM automation, such as C++, Visual Basic, Delphi, and others.

You then compile the code and deploy it in units called assemblies. An assembly is a compiled module that contains both metadata and code. The term *assembly* usually refers to managed code. In Analysis Services, we use it to refer to libraries written in managed code or in native code.

In its simplest form, an assembly is a dynamic link library (DLL) in which all the functionality is self-contained. In a more complex form, an assembly could comprise multiple DLLs and resource files and might depend on other assemblies. Analysis Services can load and host assemblies. Native code compiles into COM libraries that contain or reference a type library. That type library contains metadata about the classes, interfaces, and functions that the library implements.

After writing and compiling the code for your stored procedure, you deploy the resulting DLL to Analysis Services. When you are done, client applications and MDX expressions can call the functions that the assembly implements.

Creating Stored Procedures

The first step in creating a stored procedure (illustrated in Figure 14.1) is to write your code in a procedural language and compile it into a binary file—an assembly.

Before you can use an assembly, you have to deploy it to Analysis Services. You can use either the Data Definition Language (DDL) command `<Create Assembly>` or the Analysis Management Objects (AMO) model to deploy your assembly. (See Chapter 34, "Analysis Management Objects," for more information about AMO.) You can also use the tools shipped with Analysis Services: SQL Server Management Studio and Business Intelligence Development Studio (BI Dev Studio). These tools use AMO under the covers to create the DDL and send it to Analysis Services. When the DDL executes, it creates the assembly object on the server.

An `Assembly` object is a major object. In the current release, Analysis Services supports only server- and database-based assemblies. Each assembly is available to all users of a system or users of any cube in a database.

As do most other metadata objects, the `Assembly` object has `Name`, `ID`, `Description`, and other properties. However, the way of creating and storing an `Assembly` on the server depends on the type of the assembly; a difference exists between common language runtime and COM assemblies. Properties of the `Assembly` object also vary for different types of the `Assembly` object. Analysis Services internally has two different `Assembly` objects: `ClrAssembly` and `ComAssembly`.

Creating Common Language Runtime Assemblies

An assembly usually is created on a development computer and then moved to a server computer. It is quite common for a service account, under which the server runs, not to have access to the directory where an assembly is located on the development computer and vice versa. Therefore, we decided not to rely on using file APIs to copy files, but to embed the binary representation of the files into the DDL request.

When a client application deploys an `Assembly` object, it should detect all files that are part of the assembly, read those files, and write the bytes into the DDL request. This might seem like a cumbersome process, but you do not need to do it manually if you are using AMO, which will do the job for you. (SQL Server Management Studio and BI Dev Studio use AMO to deploy assemblies; so if you use a user interface, you don't need to deploy dependencies manually.) Under the covers, AMO analyzes the root DLL of the assembly, determines the list of files the assembly depends on, filters out the system assemblies already installed on the server by the .NET Framework, and transfers the remaining files to the server. For example, if your assembly `A` depends on the assembly `System.Data` and the assembly `B` (written by you), AMO packs assemblies `A` and `B` into the DDL request. Optionally, you can embed the bits of the files that contain debug information (PDB files) in the request.

When Analysis Services receives a request to create or alter an assembly, it decodes the binary representation of each file and creates files that are stored in a data directory of

Analysis Services, together with the metadata of the `Assembly` object. Table 14.1 describes the main properties of the `ClrAssembly` object.

TABLE 14.1 ClrAssembly Properties

Name	Description
`System`	The current version of Analysis Services contains three system assemblies: the `System Data Mining` assembly, the `VBAMDX` assembly used to support Visual Basic for Applications functions in MDX expressions, and the `ExcelMDX` assembly used to support Excel worksheet functions in MDX expressions.
`PermissionSet`	Defines a set of permissions to enforce code access security. You can find information about code access security later in this chapter.
`ImpersonationInfo`	Defines a set of properties that outline the security impersonation method that Analysis Services uses when it executes a stored procedure. You can find information about impersonation later in this chapter.
`Files`	A list of properties related to the files of assemblies, dependent assemblies, and debugging files. Each `Files` property has the following properties: ▶ **`Name`**: The name of the file. ▶ **`Type`**: Specifies whether the file is `Main` (the root DLL of the assembly), `Dependent` (other DLLs of the assembly or dependent assemblies), or `Debug` (PDB files for debugging an assembly). ▶ **`Data`**: Data blocks that contain a binary representation of a file. The data is encoded in base64 binary.

Listing 14.1 shows a simple C# common language runtime library that extracts the last name from a person's full name.

LISTING 14.1 Stored Procedure That Extracts the Last Name from a Full Name

```
using System;


namespace SimpleStoredProcedure
{
    public class SampleClass
    {
        public string x()
        {
            return null;
```

```
        }
        public static string GetLastName(string fullName)
        {
            string[] names = fullName.Split(' ');
            if (names.Length <= 0)
                return fullName;
            else
                return names[names.Length - 1];
        }
    }
}
```

After you have written the code and compiled it into a .NET assembly, you can deploy it to a server. You can either issue a DDL request similar to the one in Listing 14.2 (we removed some of the data blocks to make the listing smaller), or you can use BI Dev Studio or SQL Server Management Studio.

14

NOTE

Listing 14.2 contains lines of binary data.

LISTING 14.2 DDL Request to Create an Assembly

```
<Create AllowOverwrite="true"
xmlns="http://schemas.microsoft.com/analysisservices/2003/engine">
     <ObjectDefinition>
     <Assembly xsi:type="ClrAssembly"
xmlns:xsd="http://www.w3.org/2001/XMLSchema"
xmlns:xsi="http://www.w3.org/2001/XMLSchema-instance">
          <ID>SimpleStoredProcedure</ID>
          <Name>SimpleStoredProcedure</Name>
          <Description/>
          <ImpersonationInfo>
               <ImpersonationMode>Default</ImpersonationMode>
          </ImpersonationInfo>
          <Files>
               <File>
                    <Name>SimpleStoredProcedure.dll</Name>
                    <Type>Main</Type>
                    <Data>
                    <Block>TVqQAAMAAAAEAAAA//8AALgAAAAAAAAAQAAAAAAAAAA
➥AAAAAAAAAAAAAAAAAAAAAAAAAAAAAAAAAAAgAAAAA4fug4AtAnNIbgBTM0hVGhpcyBw
➥cm9ncmFtIGNhbm5vdCBiZSBydW4gaW4gRE9TIG1vZGUuDQ0KJAAAAAAAAABQRQAATAEDAP
➥JOJ0QAAAAAAAAAAOAADiELAQgAABAAAAAgAAAAAAAAbicAAAAgAAAAQAAAAABAAAAgAAAA
```

```
➥EAAABAAAAAAAAAAAEAAAAAAAAAAACAAAAAEAAAAAAAAAAMAAAQAABAAABAAAAAAEAAAEAAAAA
➥AAABAAAAAAAAAAAAAAABwnAABPAAAAAEAAAJgDAAAAAAAAAAAAAAAAAAAAAAAAAAGAAAAwA
➥AACEJgAAHAAAAAAAAAAAAAAAAAAAAAAAAAAAAAAAAAAAAAAAAAAAAAAAAAAAAAAAAAAAAIA
➥AACAAAAAAAAAAAAAAAACCAAAEgAAAAAAAAAAAAAAC50ZXh0AAAAdAcAAAAgAAAAEAAAABAA
➥AAAAAAAAAAAAAAAAACAAAGAucnNyYwAAAJgDAAAAQAAAABAAAAAgAAAAAAAAAAAAAAAAA
➥BAAABALnJlbG9jAAAMAAAAAGAAAAAQAAAAMAAAAAAAAAAAAAAAAAAAAQAAAQgAAAAAAAAAA
➥AAAAAAAAAAAAAAAAAAAAAAAAAAAAAAAAAAAAAAAAAAAAAAAAAAAAAAAAAAAAAAAAAAAAAAAAAAAA
➥AAAAAAAAAAAAAAAAAAAAAAAAAAAAAAAAAAAAAAAAAAAAAAAAAAAAAAAAAAAAAAAAAAAAAAAAAAAA
➥AAAAAAAAAAAAAAAAAAAAAAAAAAAAAAAAAAAAAAAAAAAAAAAAAAAAAAAAAAAAAAAAAA==</Block>

                  </Data>
                </File>
                <File>
                  <Name>SimpleStoredProcedure.pdb</Name>
                  <Type>Debug</Type>
                  <Data>
<Block>TWljcm9zb2Z0IEMvQysrIE1TRiA3LjAwDQoaRFMAAAAAAgAAAQAAABcAAAB0AAA
➥AAAAAABYAAAAAAAAAAAAAAAAAAAAAAAAAAAAAAAAAAAAAAAAAAAAAAAAAAAAAAAAAAAAAAAAAAAA
➥AAAAAAAAAAAAAAAAAAAAAAAAAAAAAAAAAAAAAAAAAAAAAAAAAAAAAAAAAAAAAAAAAAAAAAAAAAAA
➥AAAAAAAAAAAAAAAAAAAAAAAAAAAAAAAAAAAAAAAAAAAAAAAAAAAAAAAAAAAAAAAAAAAAAAAAAAAA
➥AAAAAAAAAAAAAAAAAAAAAAAAAAAAAAAAAAAAAAAAAAAAAAAAAAAAAAAAAAAAAAAAAAAAAAAAAAAA
➥AAAAAAAAAAAAAAAAAAAAAAAAAAAAAAAAAAAAAAAAAAAAAAAAAAAAAAAAAAAAAAAAACIBIz//////
➥////////////////////////////////////////////////////////////////////////////
➥////////////////////////////////////////////////////////////////////////////
➥////////////////////////////////////////////////////////////////////////////
➥////////////////////////////////////////////////////////////////////////////
➥////////////////////////////////////////////////////////////////////////////
➥////////////////////////////////////////////////////////////////////////////
➥////////////////////////////////////////////////////////////////////////////
➥////////////////////////////////////////////////////////////////////////////
➥////////////////////////////////////////////////////////////////////////////
➥/////////////////////////////////////////////w==</Block>

                  </Data>
                </File>
              </Files>
              <PermissionSet>Safe</PermissionSet>
            </Assembly>
          </ObjectDefinition>
        </Create>
```

You can use SQL Server Management Studio to deploy an assembly by following these steps:

1. Compile the code in Listing 14.1 into the `SimpleStoredProcedure.dll` file using a C# compiler.

2. Connect to your Analysis Services server.
3. In Object Explorer, expand the list of databases and navigate to the FoodMart 2008 database.
4. Right-click the Assemblies node, and choose New Assembly from the resulting menu.
5. In the Register Database Assembly dialog box, select `SimpleStoredProcedure.dll` as the filename of the assembly.
6. SQL Server Management Studio produces a name of the assembly that is, by default, the same as the name of the file. You can change it; but in this example, we keep the default name as shown in Figure 14.2.

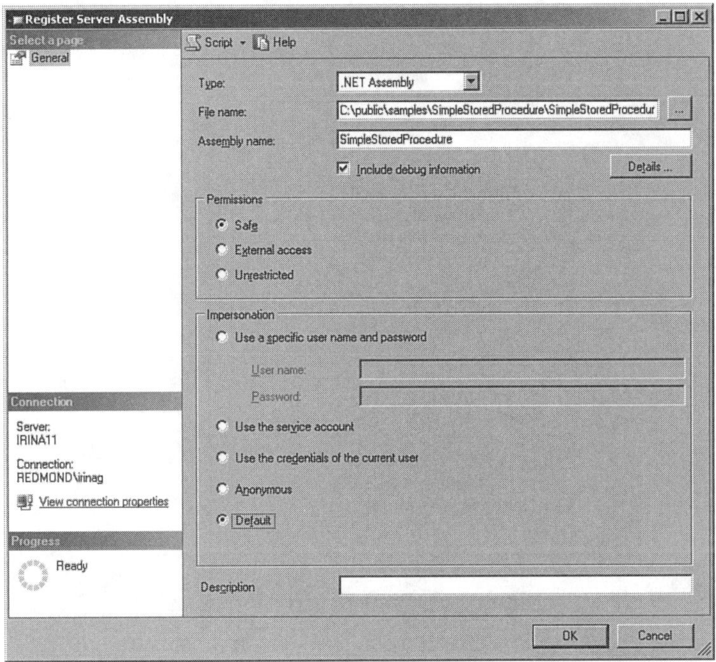

FIGURE 14.2 You can use SQL Server Management Studio to deploy the assembly to a server.

7. Keep the default values of the remaining properties, `Permissions` and `Impersonation`, and click OK.

NOTE

In the current release of Analysis Services, you cannot register common language runtime assemblies on local cubes, only on the server.

Using Application Domains to Sandbox Common Language Runtime Assemblies

Recent versions of Windows operating systems use process boundaries to isolate applications running on the same computer. There is no protection of the process from DLLs running inside the process. The .NET Framework introduces a layer of protection, the application domain, which enables multiple "applications" to run within the same process. Multiple application domains can run in the same process with a level of isolation that typically exists in separate processes. If an unhandled exception occurs in an application domain, it does not affect the code running in another application domain.

Because an assembly can contain unreliable code that could jeopardize the whole server, Analysis Services creates an application domain for each `Assembly` object and marshals all calls to it, as shown in Figure 14.3.

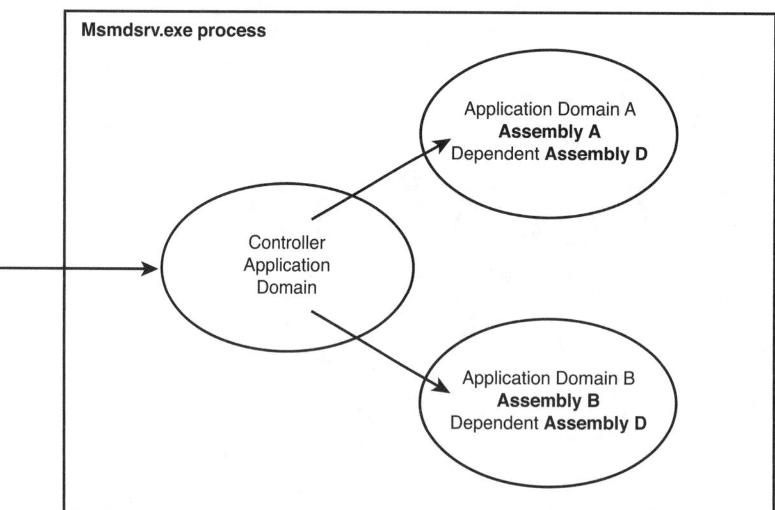

FIGURE 14.3 Each common language runtime stored procedure runs in a separate application domain.

Multiple application domains have both an upside and a downside. Obviously, they help the system to stay stable, allow the enforcement of different security settings per assembly (discussed in more detail later in this chapter), and enable the unloading of assemblies from memory when they are no longer needed.

The drawback is also obvious: Each call to a stored procedure requires marshaling across application domain boundaries. Even though the cost of such marshaling is much less than marshaling between processes, it can be noticeable, especially when calling a stored procedure frequently (for example, to execute a value for each cell of the request).

Creating COM Assemblies

COM assemblies are automation libraries. Any programming language that supports automation interfaces, such as Visual Basic or C++, can implement them. Analysis Services calls the functions in a COM assembly through the `IDispatch` interface.

It is not enough to copy the file to the computer to make a COM library available for use by any application; you have to register it in the system registry. Therefore, we decided that COM assemblies cannot be copied to the server computer as part of the execution of `Create` or `Alter` DDL requests. If Analysis Services only copied a file and did not register it with the system Registry, COM interfaces would not work. If Analysis Services were to register a COM library in a Registry, we would end up in DLL hell.

Therefore, before using any COM library in Analysis Services, the server administrator must copy it to the server computer and use the `regsvr32.exe` application to register it in the system Registry. After installing the DLL on the server computer, you can register the COM library with Analysis Services by issuing `Create` or `Alter` Assembly DDL commands. The properties of a COM assembly, shown in Table 14.2, differ from those of a common language runtime assembly.

TABLE 14.2 **`ComAssembly`** Properties

Name	Description
`Source`	Specifies either the `ProgID` of a COM object or the path to a COM type library (TLB, DLL, EXE). If you specify a `ProgID`, the server uses the system Registry to get to the type library.
`ImpersonationInfo`	Defines a set of properties that describe the security impersonation that Analysis Services uses when it executes a stored procedure.

Analysis Services accesses COM assemblies through automation interfaces exposed by the library. Just like any automation library, a COM assembly must have a type library embedded in the library or in a separate file. There is no requirement that any special interfaces implemented by an assembly for Analysis Services to use stored procedures. Nevertheless, to allow late binding, Analysis Services requires that all functions intended for use with Analysis Services be implemented in the `IDispatch` interface.

NOTE

By design, COM assemblies are less secure than common language runtime assemblies are. If you are implementing a new stored procedure, we suggest that you write it in managed code and deploy it to the server as a common language runtime assembly. Support for COM assemblies is turned off by default; you can enable it by setting the server configuration property `ComUdfEnabled` to `1`. You can use a COM assembly when porting existing user-defined functions written for Analysis Services 2000.

Calling Stored Procedures from MDX

After registering an assembly with Analysis Services, you can call it from MDX expressions and queries. Because stored procedures extend native MDX functions, you can use them in any expression that allows an MDX function with the same return type. For example, if you call a stored procedure from the axis definition of the `SELECT` statement, it should return a `Set` object or another MDX object that you can convert to a `Set` object, such as a `Member` or `Tuple`. (For the rules of type conversions, see Chapter 11.) You can see an example in the following query:

```
SELECT MyUserDefinedFunctionAsSet() ON COLUMNS from MyCube
```

NOTE

If the stored procedure returns a numeric or string expression, the axis definition clause of a `SELECT` statement cannot use it.

A stored procedure that does not return a value (the return type is `void`) cannot be used as part of an MDX expression or `SELECT` statement. You can use it only from a `CALL` statement (provided by Analysis Services). For example, you can write a stored procedure that performs a file copy operation and call it with the following expression:

```
CALL CopyFile("sourcefile.txt", "destfile.txt")
```

The `CALL` statement executes outside the context of an MDX query. It is useful for performing administrative tasks, rather than retrieving data. Like a stored procedure that does not return any values, a `CALL` statement can execute stored procedures that return a `DataSet` object or an object that implements the `IDataReader` interface. In both cases, Analysis Services uses the serialization interfaces of the .NET Framework to serialize the value returned from the stored procedure.

Stored procedures can be referenced from MDX by name (with some limitations explained later in this chapter) or by qualified name. If you deploy more than one assembly, it is possible you could end up with more than one function with the same name, and that can cause ambiguity.

NOTE

To avoid ambiguity, we strongly recommend using the qualified names of stored procedures. As a bonus, if you use qualified names, you get faster name resolution.

The qualified name of a stored procedure consists of three components (assembly name, class name or interface name, and method name) separated by either a period (.) or an exclamation mark (!). Table 14.3 describes these components. Some components of a qualified name are optional, whereas others are not.

TABLE 14.3 Components of a Stored Procedure's Qualified Name

Name	Description
`AssemblyName`	The name of the `Assembly` object as created during deployment of the assembly to Analysis Services. This component is mandatory for common language runtime assemblies, and optional for COM assemblies.
`ClassName` (for Common Language Runtime assemblies)	The full or partially qualified name of the class that implements the stored procedure. A class name usually includes a namespace separated from the name of the class by a period (.).
`InterfaceName` (for COM assemblies)	The name of the interface to which the stored procedure belongs. Do not confuse an interface name with a class name; a single class can implement multiple interfaces. When creating a COM assembly in Visual Basic, the interface name is the name of the class preceded by an underscore (_).
`MethodName`	The name of the method—function, procedure, or property—being invoked.

14

You can use the following MDX request to invoke the stored procedure that extracts the last name from a full name (as shown in Listing 14.1). The request references the stored procedure by its qualified name.

```
with member measures.CustomerLastName as
'SimpleStoredProcedure.SimpleStoredProcedure.SampleClass.GetLastName
([Customer].[Customers].CurrentMember.Name)'
SELECT
Measures.CustomerLastName ON COLUMNS,
[Customer].[Customers].[Customer].members.Item(0) ON ROWS
FROM [warehouse and sales]
```

In this example, we specified the full name of a stored procedure. If you know that your stored procedure has a unique name across the assembly, you can skip some components of the qualified name and issue this simpler request:

```
with member measures.CustomerLastName as
'SimpleStoredProcedure.GetLastName
([Customer].[Customers].CurrentMember.Name)'
SELECT
```

```
Measures.CustomerLastName ON COLUMNS,
[Customer].[Customers].[Customer].members.Item(0) ON ROWS
FROM [warehouse and sales]
```

Security Model

Analysis Services is a server application that serves the requests of hundreds and thousands of users. Therefore, it has to run in a stable state for long periods. Because assemblies deployed on the server contain unknown code (that is, unknown to developers of Analysis Services), a poorly written or malicious assembly could cause a malfunction of the system. To prevent this, Analysis Services provides three layers of security:

- Role-based security
- Code access security
- User-based security

Role-Based Security

Role-based security allows the system to grant access to certain objects based on the role the user plays. (For more information about role-based security, see Chapter 35, "Security Model for Analysis Services.")

Because an assembly contains code not shipped with Analysis Services and potentially comes from an untrusted source, only the system administrator can deploy an assembly to Analysis Services. Even a database administrator does not have permission to deploy an assembly. Although that can be inconvenient, it is better to be safe than sorry. When sharing Analysis Services among multiple database publishers, this protection makes it impossible for one database administrator to deploy an assembly that would jeopardize the work of the whole server.

However, there is no restriction on invoking an assembly. Therefore, any user can issue a query that executes code in an assembly, as long as she has access to the database or server to which the assembly belongs.

Code Access Security

One of the most important features of the .NET Framework is code access security. It enables administrators not only to restrict the users that access the system, but also to prevent code from performing certain operations. For example, you can configure the system so that it will not allow code from untrusted sources to work with the file system or to make network calls.

Analysis Services uses the `PermissionSet` property of a `ClrAssembly` object to provide code-based security for common language runtime assemblies. The `PermissionSet` property specifies the actions that the assembly can perform. You can specify one of three settings for the `PermissionSet` property: `Safe`, `External_Access`, or `Unrestricted`. Table 14.4 describes these settings in more detail.

TABLE 14.4 Settings of the **PermissionSet** Property

Name	Description
`Safe`	Allows a stored procedure to execute a simple computation, but does not give access to protected resources, such as the network or files.
`External_Access`	Allows a stored procedure to perform computations. Makes it possible to carry out the following actions on external resources: ▶ Read and write environment variables. ▶ Assert and stop a stack walk on a given permission. ▶ Provide serialization services. ▶ Read system Registry settings. ▶ Access domain name system (DNS) servers on the network. ▶ Connect to HTTP Internet resources. (There is no right to accept HTTP connections.) ▶ Use sockets to connect to a transport address. ▶ Read and write files in the file system. ▶ Read and write to the operating system's event log. ▶ Use the SQLClient ADO.NET-managed provider to connect to SQL Server.
`Unrestricted`	The least secure setting; no restrictions are applied. With this setting applied, any code (even unverifiable) can execute. Grant this permission set with the utmost care.

14

User-Based Security

When a stored procedure accesses resources that are outside an Analysis Services process, such as a file system or network resources, the credentials it uses to access those resources can make an important difference to the security of your system. When you configure your security settings, it is a good idea to ask yourself questions about the resources your stored procedures need access to and about who can access them. For example, if a server runs under an account that has access to files stored on the hard drive but the user that calls a stored procedure does not have access, you can configure your system so that the stored procedure executes under the server's credential. In this way, the stored procedure can have access to the files.

You can use the `ImpersonationInfo` property of an `Assembly` object to specify the security account under which Analysis Services executes the stored procedure. Just before invoking the stored procedure, Analysis Services impersonates the thread with the credentials of the account specified in the `ImpersonationInfo` property. After the stored procedure executes, the impersonation reverts to the original account. Figure 14.4 shows a diagram of this process.

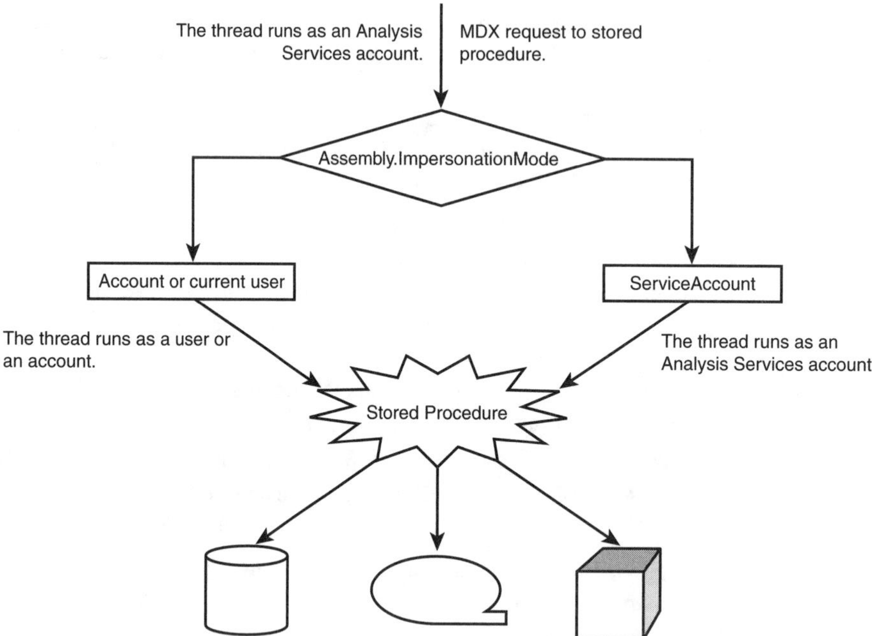

FIGURE 14.4 Before invoking the stored procedure, Analysis Services impersonates a thread to run under a specified account.

Table 14.5 describes the settings of the `ImpersonationInfo` property.

TABLE 14.5 Settings of the **`ImpersonationInfo`** Property

Name	Description
`ImpersonationMode`	Specifies the account the server should impersonate before the server calls a method in an assembly. The values for the `ImpersonationMode` property include the following: ▶ `Impersonate ServiceAccount` — Analysis Services calls the code in the stored procedure with the credentials of the account under which the Analysis Services server started.

TABLE 14.5 Settings of the **ImpersonationInfo** Property

Name	Description	
	▶ `ImpersonateAccount`	Analysis Services calls the code in the stored procedure with the credentials specified in the `Account` property of the `ImpersonationInfo` object.
	▶ `Impersonate CurrentUser`	Analysis Services calls the code in the stored procedure with the credentials of the user that executes the query that invokes the stored procedure.
	▶ `Default`	In the current version of Analysis Services, the default setting for this property is `Impersonate CurrentUser`.
`Account`	The name of the user account to use for impersonation when the `ImpersonationMode` property is set to `ImpersonateAccount`.	
`Password`	The password for the account specified in the `Account` property. Analysis Services never stores passwords in clear text; it encrypts the `Password` property. Analysis Services will not return the `Password` of an assembly object to the user.	

14

Server Object Model

Analysis Services not only enables you to extend the MDX language and publish assemblies that operate over generic data types such as numeric or string values, but it also provides a powerful mechanism that exposes Analysis Services objects to stored procedures written in procedural languages. This mechanism enables you to use procedural and object-oriented code to program multidimensional databases. You can also integrate the code of a stored procedure with the context of the MDX query calling it. Analysis Services provides an object model—ADOMDServer or server object model—that enables this functionality by exposing Analysis Services objects as managed objects that you can use inside your stored procedure.

The server object model is an assembly shipped with Analysis Services that provides a set of classes similar to the client object model—ADOMD.NET (for information, see Chapter 33, "ADOMD.NET"). However, despite their similarity, the server and client object models are independent entities, with some overlapping classes and other classes implemented in just one model. Only the stored procedure that is running inside Analysis Services can call the server object model; no other application can invoke it. Three groups of objects are provided by the ADOMDServer object model:

- **Metadata objects**—Cubes, dimensions, hierarchies, levels, members, key performance indicators (KPIs), and named sets

- **MDX objects**—`Set`, `Tuple`, `Member`, `Expression`, and others
- **Helper objects**—`SetBuilder`, `TupleBuilder`, and others

The diagram in Figure 14.5 shows the hierarchy of all the objects exposed through the server object model. We limited the diagram to the objects related to the online analytical processing (OLAP) server, and we omitted data-mining objects because they are outside the scope of this book.

The Analysis Services process comprises two sections of code: native and managed. The native code implements most of the server subsystems. On the other hand, managed code hosts the common language runtime assemblies and stored procedures. All the objects of the ADOMDServer object model are thin managed wrappers over their corresponding native objects. When you call a method on an object from your stored procedure, the call marshals from managed code to native code and delegates to the native object. You can see this process illustrated in Figure 14.6.

NOTE

The server object model is available only to common language runtime assemblies and stored procedures written in managed code.

Operations on Metadata Objects

The root of the object model is the `Context` object. It is one of the most important objects in the object model because it enables you to bind the query execution context with the managed code of the stored procedure. The `Context` object provides static methods that allow a stored procedure to perceive the current context of the query that invokes it. The `Context` object also enables you to navigate metadata objects, starting with the cube collection.

Because the current version of Analysis Services allows you to use only one cube in the `SELECT` statement, the collection of cubes exposed from the `Context` object always contains only one cube: the cube queried by the current request. You also can access this cube from the `CurrentCube` property of the `Context` object.

The properties and methods that you can use in stored procedures to operate with collections are the same as for most of the ADOMDServer collections.

Each of the collections in ADOMDServer implements the `IEnumerable` and `ICollection` interfaces (as shown in Figure 14.7) and all the methods and properties supported by those interfaces.

`Count`

`Count` returns the number of elements in the collection.

`Item`

`Item` (`indexer` in C#) provides access to the elements of a collection. Most ADOMDServer collections provide two overloads for this method: by index and by name. For example, in C#, this code expresses access to the elements of a collection:

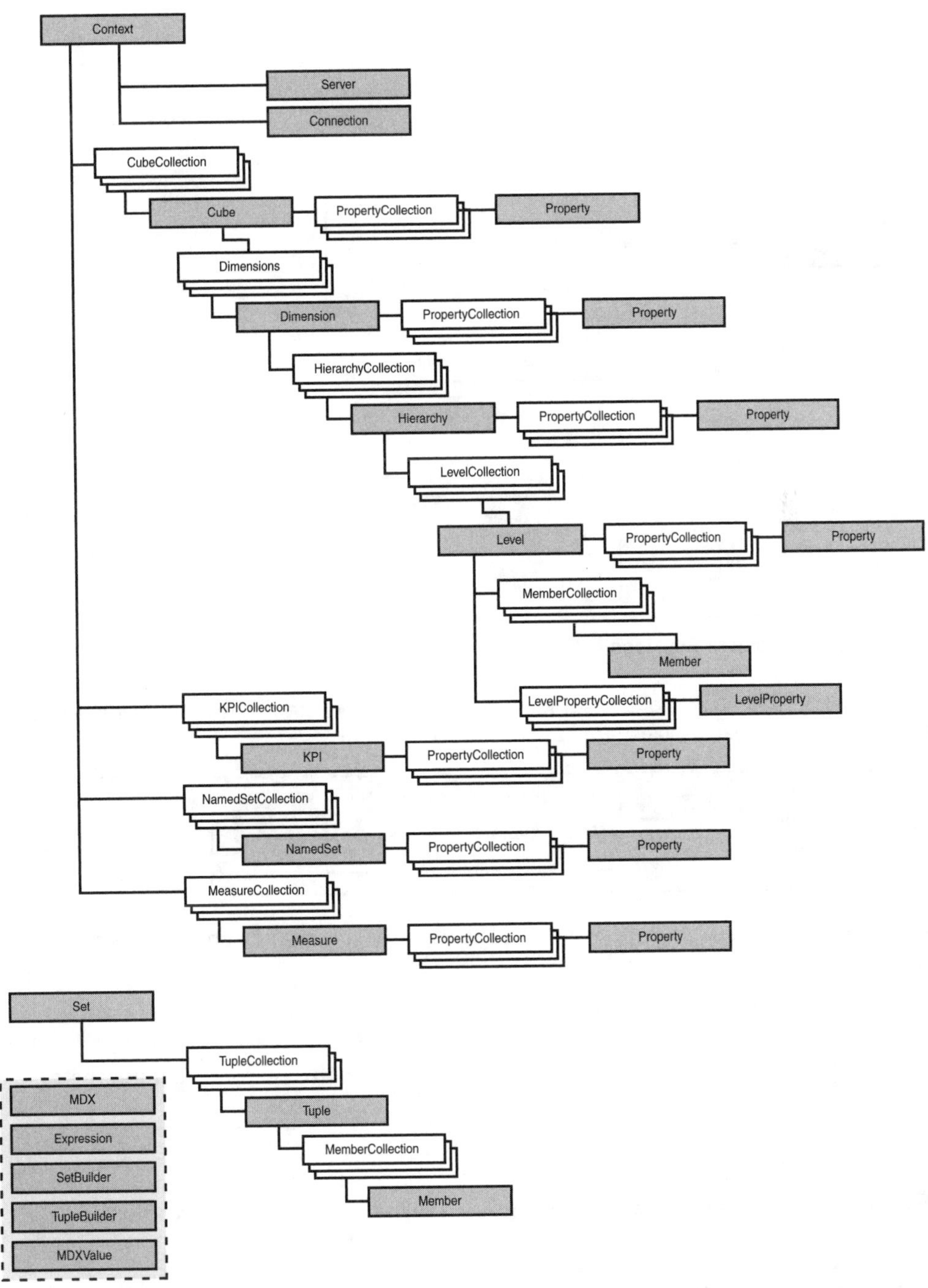

FIGURE 14.5 This hierarchy of objects is supported by the ADOMDServer object model.

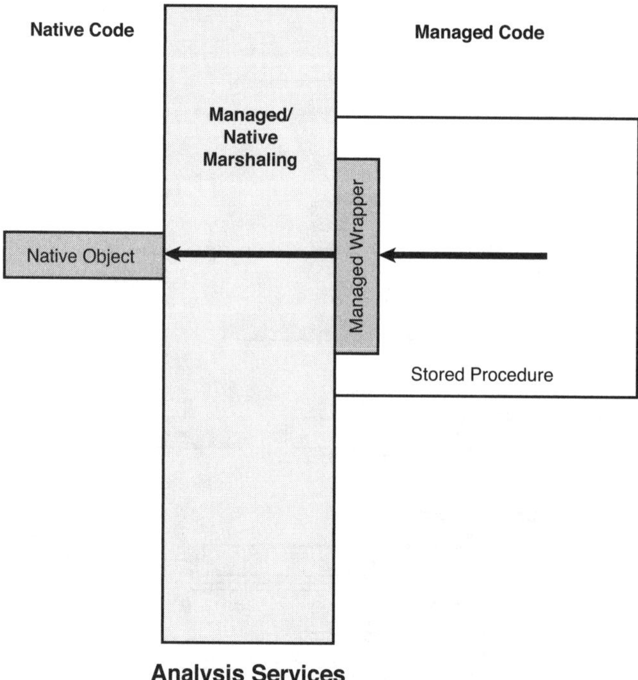

FIGURE 14.6 The objects of the ADOMDServer object model are thin managed wrappers over their corresponding native objects.

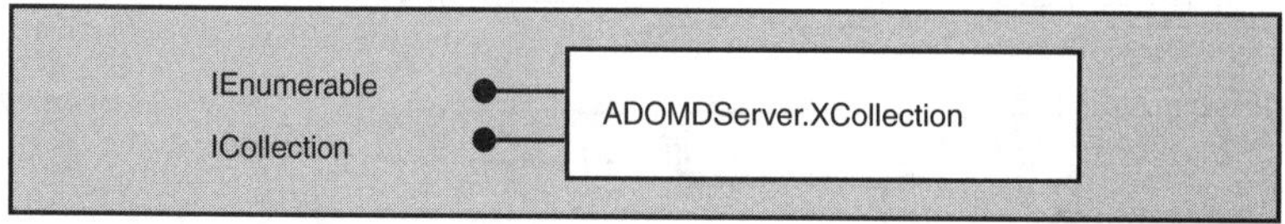

FIGURE 14.7 All ADOMDServer collections implement `IEnumerable` and `ICollection` interfaces.

```
Dimension dim = cube.Dimensions[0];
```

That call returns the first element of the collection. Alternatively, you could use the following:

```
Dimension dim = cube.Dimensions["Customer"];
```

That call returns an element of a collection with the name `Customer`. Note that it uses a name rather than a unique name.

NOTE

Access to an element of a collection by index is more efficient than access by name. If you have the opportunity, use the first method overload.

If no element with that name exists in the collection, or if an index oversteps the bounds of a collection, Analysis Services throws an exception. Because exception handling always slows down the system, use these methods only if you know that an element exists in the collection.

Find

`Find` returns the specified element of the collection. Unlike `Item`, it does not throw an exception, but returns `null` if the object does not exist in the collection. For example

```
Dimension dim = cube.Dimensions.Find("Customer");
```

returns an object with the name `Customer`, but

```
Dimension dim = cube.Dimensions.Find("foo");
```

returns `null`.

GetEnumerator

`GetEnumerator` returns an `Enumerator` object, which our code uses for the iteration of a collection. Let's look at a small piece of code that iterates the collection:

```
// Get an Enumerator object
IEnumerator enumerator = Context.CurrentCube.Dimensions.GetEnumerator();
➥Dimension dim;
//Iterate the elements of the collection through the end of the collection
➥while(enumerator.MoveNext())
{
     dim = enumerator.Current;
}
```

C# and VB .NET provide special keywords for the iteration of collections: `foreach` (C#) and `for each` (VB .NET):

```
foreach(Dimension dim in Context.CurrentCube.Dimensions)
{
...
}
```

You can't create a metadata object in a stored procedure—metadata objects don't have public constructors. You can either navigate to it from the `Context` object or get it as a parameter passed from an MDX expression.

Operations on MDX Objects

`Member`, `Tuple`, `Set`, `Expression`, `MDX`, and `MDXValue` belong to the MDX Objects category of the objects in the server object model. `Member`, `Tuple`, and `Set` objects are managed wrappers on top of the native MDX objects with the same name.

The `MDX` object provides a way for you to use MDX functions directly from the managed code; it has static functions with names similar to MDX functions. Unfortunately, we could not implement all the functions. However, if the function you need is not in the supported set, you can write your own MDX expression as a string, pass it to the `Expression` object, and call its `Calculate` method.

You can also use the `Expression` object to pass an MDX expression into a stored procedure. For example, if you use a stored procedure to implement a special filter, you can define the signature of the function as `public Set SpecialFilter(Set set, Expression exp)`. When you call this function from MDX, you can pass any MDX expression as the second parameter, as follows:

```
SELECT MyClass.SpecialFilter([Time].[Year].members, Measures.Sales > 0 )
ON COLUMNS FROM [Warehouse and Sales]
```

The `Expression.Calculate` method and MDX functions provide the `MDXValue` object as a return type. `MDXValue` provides type conversion between other objects. For example, if you call the `Calculate` function over an expression that evaluates to a set, `Calculate` returns `MDXValue`. You can then call the `MDXValue.ToSet` function to convert the `MDXValue` to a `Set` object.

You usually work with MDX objects of the object model through the input parameters and return values of the stored procedure. However, you can also use `TupleBuilder` and `SetBuilder` objects to build new `Tuple` and `Set` objects. Follow the example in Listing 14.3: a stored procedure that filters a set by a regular expression passed by the user. This stored procedure takes two parameters—a `Set` and a `string`—and returns another `Set` object to the MDX query.

LISTING 14.3 A Stored Procedure That Filters a Set by a Regular Expression

```
// Filter the set by the regular expression passed to the function
➥public Set FilterByRegEx(Set inputSet, string stringRegEx)
{
    //Parse regular expression
    Regex rx = new Regex(stringRegEx);
    SetBuilder setBuilder = new SetBuilder();
    foreach (Tuple tuple in inputSet.Tuples)
    {
        if (rx.IsMatch(tuple.Members[0].Caption))
            setBuilder.Add(tuple);
    }
    return setBuilder.ToSet();
}
```

The `FilterByRegEx` function uses a string passed from the caller to initialize the .NET Framework `Regex` class, which works with regular expressions. Then, the function iterates over all the tuples in the original set. For each tuple, it checks whether the caption of the first member of the tuple matches the conditions specified by the regular expression. (For the sake of simplicity, we assume that the set contains members from only one hierarchy.) A class designed for efficient set creation—`SetBuilder`—adds tuples that match the conditions to the new set.

To compile the code in Listing 14.3, you need to add a reference to the server object model library, which is listed between .NET libraries as `Microsoft.AnalysisServices.AdomdServer`. If it's not listed, you can browse to find `Microsoft SQL Server\MSSQL.2\OLAP\bin\msmgdsrv.dll`. After you compile the code and deploy the compiled assembly to the server, you can write MDX queries that filter a set by any regular expression you or your user provide. You can use the following query to retrieve the set of all 1% milk products available through the FoodMart enterprise. Figure 14.8 shows the results.

```
SELECT StoredProcedureOM.StoredProcedureOM.SetOperations.FilterByRegEx
( DESCENDANTS([Product].[Products].[Product Category].[Dairy].children,
[Product].[Products].[Product]) , "(1%.+Milk)¦(Milk.+1%)") ON COLUMNS
FROM [Warehouse and Sales]
```

Booker 1% Milk	Carlson 1% Milk	Club 1% Milk	Even Better 1% Milk	Gorilla 1% Milk
212	259	448	360	493

FIGURE 14.8 The query returns a list of products that have 1% and Milk in their names.

Calling Back into Stored Procedures

Analysis Services 2008 extends stored procedure functionality by enabling the server to call back into a stored procedure while certain events occur. The callback functionality addresses various business problems. For example, one problem that developers of multidimensional solutions face is that they need to provide information personalized for different users. In our FoodMart enterprise, different departments have different goals. Employees responsible for food sales need to see metrics specific for goals of their department, whereas employees responsible for drink sales need completely different metrics.

The callback functionality is built on top of the managed stored procedure. It enables developers to personalize the Unified Dimensional Model (UDM) by plugging in custom functionality into the model and instantiating the custom code when certain system events occur. Let's walk through the process of creating and executing personalized extensions. Suppose we need to create a cube where each employee can see his own set of calculated members. To enable this scenario, the developer writes a managed assembly and deploys it to the server. Using server object model, the developer writes code that validates the current user and creates a calculated member relevant to this user. When a user starts a new session, Analysis Services invokes the assembly, executes it, and creates a calculated member on the session, as shown in Figure 14.9.

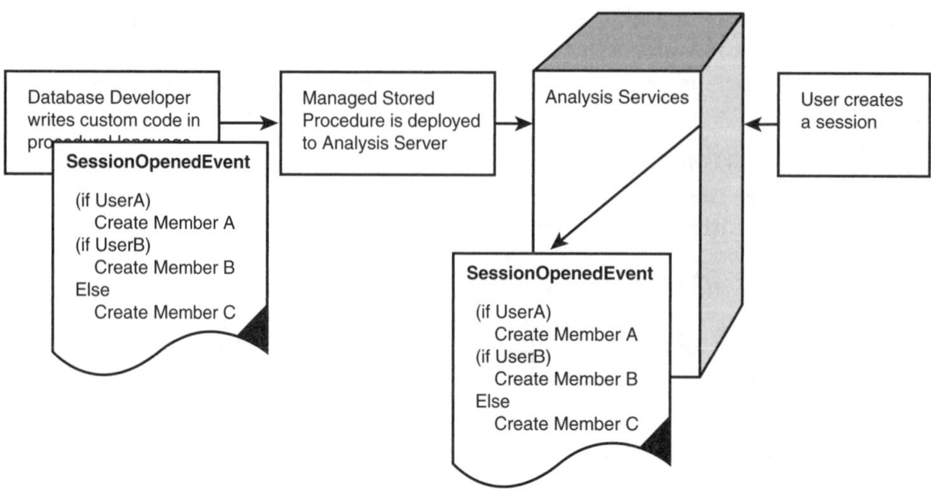

FIGURE 14.9 Process to create a stored procedure with a callback.

In Analysis Services 2008, stored procedures can subscribe to the four events shown in Table 14.6. Your code can subscribe to events using mechanism of events and delegates provided by .NET Framework.

TABLE 14.6 Callback Plug-In Events

Name	Description	Demand
`SessionOpened`	A new user session is created on the server.	`Context.Server.SessionOpened`
`SessionClosing`	User's session is about to be closed.	`Context.Server.SessionClosing`
`CubeOpened`	First time a cube is queried by a session.	`Context.CurrentConnection.CubeOpened`
`CubeClosing`	No more queries will be served for this cube on the session.	`Context.CurrentConnection.CubeClosing`

To tell Analysis Services which class contains callbacks, you can use the custom attribute `[PluginAttribute]`. Analysis Services 2008 extends the server object model interface with new functions, which you can use to specify a callback function that the server calls on a certain events. Listing 14.4 shows an example of a library that implements a personalization plug-in.

LISTING 14.4 Stored Procedure That Implements a Plug-In

```
namespace PasTestPlugIn
```

```
{
    [PlugInAttribute]
    public class PlugIn
    {
        public PlugIn()
        {
            Context.Server.SessionOpened += new EventHandler(this.SessionOpened);
            Context.Server.SessionClosing += new EventHandler(this.SessionClosing);
        }
        void SessionOpened(object sender, EventArgs e)
        {
            PlugInSession session = new PlugInSession(); // This one will subscribe
➥to the events.
        }

        void SessionClosing(object sender, EventArgs e)
        {
        }
}
   public class PlugInSession
    {
        public PlugInSession()
        {
            Context.CurrentConnection.CubeOpened += new EventHandler(CubeOpened);
            Context.CurrentConnection.CubeClosing += new EventHandler(CubeClosing);
        }

        public void CubeOpened(object sender, EventArgs e)
        {
            string serverName = Context.Server.Name;

            if (Context.CurrentDatabaseName == "Foodmart 2008")
            {
                CubeDef cube = Context.CurrentCube;
                System.Security.Principal.GenericIdentity userIdentity =
                       Context.CurrentConnection.User;
                if (userIdentity.Name == "redmond\\irinag")
                     CreateCalcMembersForIrina(cube);
                if (userIdentity.Name == "redmond\\edwardm")
                     CreateCalcMembersForEdward(cube);
                if (userIdentity.Name == "redmond\\sashab")
                     CreateCalcMembersForSasha(cube);
            }
        }
        public void CreateCalcMembersForIrina (CubeDef cube)
                {
```

14

```
                    string cubeName = cube.Name;

                    AdomdCommand command = new AdomdCommand();
                    command.CommandText = "create member [" + cubeName + "].
➥[measures].[test measure] as 1, " +
                        "caption='Test Measure', display_folder='Test Measures'";
                    command.ExecuteNonQuery();
                }
            }
}
```

Using Default Libraries

Analysis Services uses stored procedure technology to extend the number of built-in MDX functions. It automatically registers two powerful libraries: the Visual Basic for Applications library and the Microsoft Excel worksheet library. We should reveal that there is also a third library—System—that contains system data-mining stored procedures we do not discuss in this book.

Analysis Services ships with the `msmdvbanet.dll` common language runtime assembly, which automatically deploys to the server the first time Analysis Services starts. This assembly duplicates the functions provided by Microsoft Visual Basic for Applications Expression Services that Analysis Services 2000 supports. We ported this code in C# because the 64-bit platform does not support VBA Expression Services.

The Excel worksheet library provides a rich set of statistical functions. This library is part of the Excel installation. Because installing Analysis Services does not install Excel, calls to Excel's functions succeed only after you install Excel on the server.

Like any other stored procedure, you can reference the Excel and VBA functions by name or by qualified name. You should use the prefix `VBA!` or `Excel!` before the name of the function to speed name resolution and to avoid ambiguity. For example, you can use the Visual Basic function `Left` to filter a set of customers whose names starts with the letter *A*. The following query returns the results shown in Figure 14.10.

```
SELECT Filter([Customer].[Customers].[Customer].members,
VBA!Left([Customer].[Customers].currentmember.Name,1)='A') ON COLUMNS
FROM [Warehouse and Sales]
```

Alexandra Wellington	Ana Quick	Anastacio Butcher	Ann Pearce	Amanda Thomas	Amy Soldani	Andrew Fahlenkamp	Ann Evans	Ann Hass
62866	626866	626866	626866	626866	626866	626866	626866	626866

FIGURE 14.10 The query returns customers whose names start with the letter A.

CHAPTER 15

Key Performance Indicators, Actions, and the DRILLTHROUGH Statement

IN THIS CHAPTER

- Key Performance Indicators
- Actions
- Drillthrough

To help decision makers with their jobs, modern business intelligence applications have to provide capabilities beyond the mere browsing of data. Custom vertical solutions are often built on top of analytical server applications to assist managers in monitoring the health of an organization. Other applications enable workers to perform operations derived from the data stored in the analytical server.

Analysis Services makes it possible for you to integrate business practices with the data on which those practices are based. You can store the business logic necessary for advanced client capabilities on the server. Your users can take advantage of those capabilities by using generic client applications, such as Microsoft Excel.

Some of the advanced functionality that enables you to do these things includes key performance indicators (KPIs), which you can use to integrate business metrics into a data warehousing solution. With other functionality (actions), your applications can enable end users to act on decisions they make when they're browsing data stored in a multidimensional database. In addition, your users can drill deeper into data with the drillthrough functionality of Analysis Services.

Key Performance Indicators

One of the ways modern business estimate the health of an enterprise is by measuring its progress toward predefined goals using key performance indicators. *KPIs* are customizable business metrics that present an organization's status and trends toward achieving predefined goals in an easily understandable format. After a business defines its mission or objectives, KPIs can be defined to measure its progress toward those objectives.

In general, each KPI has a target value and an actual value. The target value represents a quantitative goal considered critical to the success of a business or organization. The goals of organizations can vary widely for different types of businesses, because their aims are often dissimilar. For example, a business might have KPIs concerning sales, net profit, and debt ratio, whereas a school might define a KPI relating to graduation rate, and a database administrator might define a KPI relating to the speed with which requests are processed. To determine the health of the business, the actual values are compared to the target values. KPIs are advantageous in that they provide a clear description of organizational goals, and distill large amounts of data to a single value that can be used by upper management to monitor business performance and progress toward organizational benchmarks.

Analysis Services enables you to create KPI objects and store them on the server. It also provides a generic interface for client applications to access KPIs. Through that interface, a generic client application such as Microsoft Excel, which does not know anything about a particular business logic, can interact with and display KPI data.

KPIs can be rolled into a *scorecard*—a group of KPIs—that shows the overall health of the business, where each KPI is a metric of one aspect of business growth.

Defining KPIs

In Analysis Services 2008, there are two ways to create KPIs, and they differ only by the lifetime of the KPI object:

- A KPI defined as part of the cube's metadata and available to all users of the cube. Both Analysis Services 2005 and 2008 support this method of KPI definition.
- A KPI created using the `CREATE KPI` statement is available in the scope of a session. It is generally available to subsequent queries from the same user. For more information about sessions, see Chapter 32, "XML for Analysis." Session-based KPIs are introduced in Analysis Services 2008.

When creating a KPI, you define a collection of MDX expressions that are used to evaluate the current value of a metric, the status of this metric, its trend, and its growth. For example, KPI value can be growth of sales in the current time period comparing to the sales in the previous period, goal can be a desirable percent of growth for a time period, status typically shows whether growth during the current time period larger than expected, and finally trend evaluates the progress toward the goal over time (see Figure 15.1).

Cube-Based KPIs

KPIs defined as part of the cube can be produced in Analysis Services either by using Business Intelligence Development Studio (BI Dev Studio) or by issuing a `<Create>` or `<Alter>` Data Definition Language (DDL) request to the server.

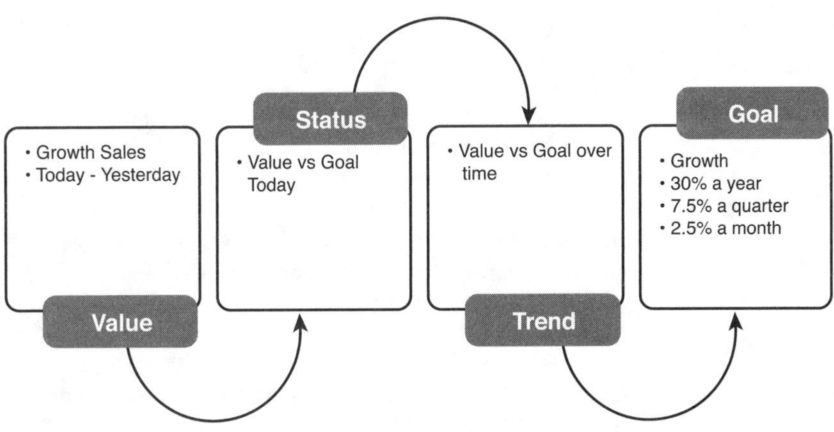

FIGURE 15.1 KPI metrics for Growth in Sales.

A `KPI` is a minor object defined by the `Cube` major object, and can be edited when the whole cube is edited. As with most metadata objects, a `KPI` object has `Name`, `ID`, `Description`, `Translations`, `DisplayFolder`, and `Annotations` properties. Table 15.1 describes the main properties of a `KPI` object.

TABLE 15.1 **`KPI`** Object Properties

Name	Description
`Value`	Defines an MDX expression that returns the actual value of the KPI. You can use a `Value` expression to specify the total amount of sales or revenue or a ratio of growth.
`Goal`	Defines an MDX expression that returns the goal of the KPI, such as the percentage of satisfied customers.
`Status`	Defines an MDX expression that returns a value expressing the relation of the KPI to the goal. `Status` is often normalized to an expression that returns a value between -1 and 1 indicating the success or failure of a KPI.
`StatusGraphic`	Specifies a graphical representation of status to provide easy visualization of the KPI. The value of this property is a string that maps to a set of bitmaps.
`Trend`	Defines an MDX expression that returns the trend of the KPI over time. The trend is often normalized to an expression returning values between -1 and 1, indicating a downward trend, an upward trend, or something in between.

TABLE 15.1 **KPI** Object Properties

Name	Description
TrendGraphic	Specifies a graphical representation of a trend to provide easy visualization of the KPI. The value of this property is a string that maps to a bitmap.
ParentKpiID	Enables a hierarchical organization of KPIs. For example, you could define a Customer Scorecard KPI to have the children Customer Satisfaction and Customer Retention.
Weight	Defines an MDX expression that assigns a relative importance of the current KPI to its parent.
AssociatedMeasureGroupID	Defines a measure group associated with this KPI, which is used to specify dimensionality of the KPI. This property is optional. If it is not specified, the KPI will have the dimensionality of all the measure groups in the cube.
CurrentTimeMember	An MDX expression that defines the current member of the Time dimension that is relevant for the KPI. If this property is not specified, the default member of the Time dimension will be used.

Now that you know what properties the KPI object has, you can create a sample KPI that enables a manager of your enterprise to monitor growth in sales. This KPI monitors the ratio between the sales counts in the current period to those of the previous period.

To do this, you can use the MDX expression in Listing 15.1 to create the value of the KPI. This expression calculates the ratio between the sales in the current time period and the sales in the previous time period. Because it doesn't make sense to compare the sales for the member ALL, the expression returns NA for the member ALL.

LISTING 15.1 MDX Expression for the Value of a KPI

```
Case
    When [Time].[Time].CurrentMember.Level.Ordinal = 0 Then "NA"
    When IsEmpty ( ( [Time].[Time].PrevMember,
            [Measures].[Sales Count] ) ) Then Null
    Else ( [Measures].[Sales Count] -
         ( [Time].[Time].PrevMember, [Measures].[Sales Count] ) )
         / ( [Time].[Time].PrevMember, [Measures].[Sales Count])
End
```

Now you have to define the goal that the enterprise strives to achieve, by specifying the MDX expression in Listing 15.2.

LISTING 15.2 MDX Expression for a KPI Goal

```
Case
     When [Time].[Time].CurrentMember.Level Is [Time].[Time].[Year] Then .30
     When [Time].[Time].CurrentMember.Level Is [Time].[Time].[Quarter] Then .075
     When [Time].[Time].CurrentMember.Level Is [Time].[Time].[Month]  Then .025
     When [Time].[Time].CurrentMember.Level Is [Time].[Time].[Date]  Then .0008
     Else "NA"
End
```

To calculate the status, compare `Value` and `Goal` using the expression in Listing 15.3.

LISTING 15.3 MDX Expression for KPI Status

```
Case
     When KpiValue("Growth in Sales" ) >= KpiGoal ( "Growth in Sales" ) Then 1
     When KpiValue("Growth in Sales" ) >= .90 * KpiGoal("Growth in Sales") And
     KpiValue("Growth in Sales") < KpiGoal ("Growth in Sales") Then 0
     Else -1
End
```

You are finally ready to define the trend (see Listing 15.4).

LISTING 15.4 MDX Expression for a KPI Trend

```
Case
     When [Time].[Time].CurrentMember.Level is [Time].[Time].[(All)] Then 0
     When KpiValue("Growth in Sales") -
          (KpiValue("Growth in Sales"), ParallelPeriod ([Time].[Time].[Year], 1,
           [Time].[Time].CurrentMember)) /
          (KpiValue("Growth in Sales"), ParallelPeriod ([Time].[Time].[Year], 1,
           [Time].[Time].CurrentMember)) <=.02 Then 0
     When KpiValue("Growth in Sales") - (KpiValue("Growth in Sales"),
          ParallelPeriod ([Time].[Time].[Year], 1, [Time].[Time].CurrentMember ))/
        (KpiValue("Growth in Sales"), ParallelPeriod([Time].[Time].[Year], 1, [Time].
         [Time].CurrentMember ) ) >.02 Then 1
     Else -1
End
```

Now you create a `KPI` object using the user interface provided by BI Dev Studio by following these steps:

1. In BI Dev Studio, open the FoodMart 2008 project.
2. In the Solution Explorer, double-click the `Warehouse and Sales` cube to open the cube editor.
3. On the KPI tab, right-click anywhere in the KPI Organizer and choose New KPI from the resulting menu.
4. Type the name of your KPI—**`Growth in Sales`**—in the Name text box.
5. Because this KPI analyzes data about sales, which is stored in the `Sales` measure group, choose Sales from the Associated Measure Group drop-down list to associate the KPI with the `Sales` measure group.
6. Copy and paste the `Value`, `Goal`, `Status`, and `Trend` MDX expressions into the corresponding boxes of the KPI tab. Then, select the graphics to associate with the `Status` and `Trend` indicators.

The KPI you created is a standalone KPI. Because the KPI isn't part of the scorecard, you don't specify the `ParentKpiID` and `Weight` properties. Nor do you have to specify the `CurrentTimeMember` property, but it's always a good idea to provide a detailed `Description` property. Figure 15.2 shows the KPI tab filled out with the information given earlier.

When you deploy FoodMart 2008 project to the server, BI Dev Studio sends the DDL to the server, which then alters the cube and saves the `KPI` object. Listing 15.5 shows the portion of DDL related to the creation of the KPI.

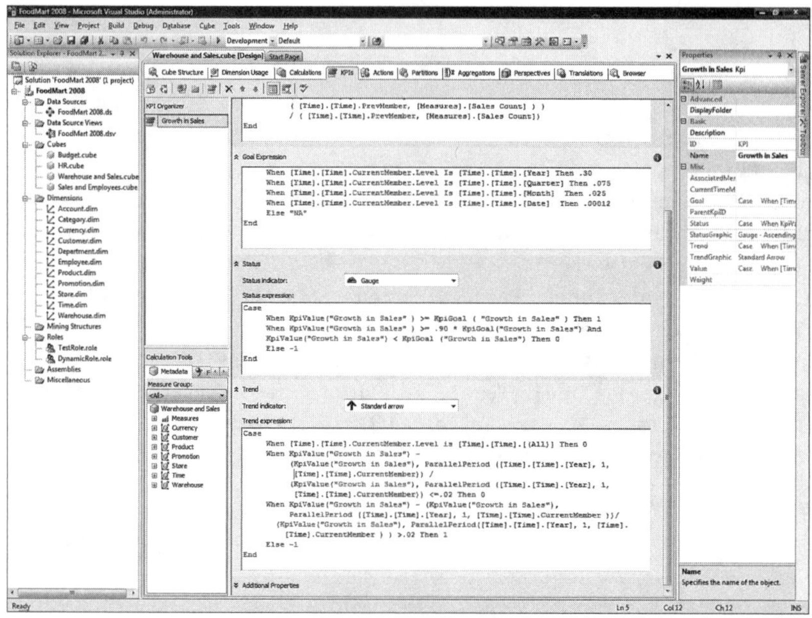

FIGURE 15.2 You can use BI Dev Studio to create a KPI.

LISTING 15.5 DDL Request for Creating a KPI

```
<Kpis>
  <Kpi>
      <ID>KPI</ID>
      <Name>Growth in Sales</Name>
      <Description>The ratio between the sales count in the current period to
       ➥that of the ratio between the sales count in the current period to that of
      ➥the previous period</Description>
      <Value>
        Case When [Time].[Time].CurrentMember.Level.Ordinal = 0 Then   "NA"
             When IsEmpty ( ( [Time].[Time].PrevMember, [Measures].[Sales Count] ) )
                   Then Null
             Else ( [Measures].[Sales Count] - ( [Time].[Time].PrevMember,
             [Measures].[Sales Count] ) ) / ( [Time].[Time].PrevMember, [Measures].
             [Sales Count])
        End
      </Value>
      <DisplayFolder/>
      <AssociatedMeasureGroupID>Sales Fact</AssociatedMeasureGroupID>
      <Goal>
        Case
         When [Time].[Time].CurrentMember.Level Is [Time].[Time].[Year] Then .30
         When [Time].[Time].CurrentMember.Level Is [Time].[Time].[Quarter] Then .075
         When [Time].[Time].CurrentMember.Level Is [Time].[Time].[Month] Then .025
         When [Time].[Time].CurrentMember.Level Is [Time].[Time].[Date] Then .012
         Else "NA"
       End
      </Goal>
      <Status>
         Case When KpiValue("Growth in Sales" ) >= [KpiGoal ( "Growth in Sales" )
                                                                         Then 1
         When KpiValue("Growth in Sales" ) >= .90 * KpiGoal("Growth in Sales") And
              KpiValue("Growth in Sales") < KpiGoal ("Growth in Sales") Then 0
        Else -1
       End
     </Status>
     <Trend>
       Case
        When [Time].[Time].CurrentMember.Level is [Time].[Time].[(All)] Then 0
        When //VBA!Abs ( KpiValue("Growth in Sales") - (
                       KpiValue("Growth in Sales"),
             ParallelPeriod ([Time].[Time].[Year], 1, [Time].[Time].CurrentMember)) /
             (KpiValue("Growth in Sales"), ParallelPeriod ([Time].[Time].[Year], 1,
                       [Time].[Time].CurrentMember)) // ) <=.02 Then 0
```

15

```
         When KpiValue("Growth in Sales") - (KpiValue("Growth in Sales"),
              ParallelPeriod ([Time].[Time]. [Year], 1,
              [Time].[Time].CurrentMember ))/(KpiValue("Growth in Sales"),
        ParallelPeriod([Time].[Time].[Year], 1, [Time].[Time].CurrentMember ) ) >.02
            Then 1
        Else -1
       End
       </Trend>
       <StatusGraphic>Gauge - Ascending</StatusGraphic>
       <TrendGraphic>Standard Arrow</TrendGraphic>
       <Weight />
       <ParentKpiID />
       <CurrentTimeMember/>
   </Kpi>
</Kpis>
```

During the deployment of a `KPI` object, under the covers Analysis Services analyzes the expressions associated with the `Value`, `Goal`, `Status`, `Trend`, and `Weight` properties and creates hidden calculated members on the `Measure` dimension associated with each property. If an expression just references a calculated measure, Analysis Services uses the existing calculated measure and won't create a new one. For example, if your expression for the `Value` property refers to the calculated measure `MyKPIValue` that you have already created in an MDX script, Analysis Services won't create a new calculated measure for the value expression, but will instead use the existing `MyKPIValue` calculated measure.

Session-Based KPIs

To allow you to create KPIs on your own machine, which you won't have to deploy to the server, Analysis Services 2008 supports session-based KPIs. Session-based KPIs are similar to session-based calculated members. They are created by a `CREATE` KPI statement and can be deleted by a `DROP` KPI statement.

A `CREATE` KPI statement has the following syntax:

```
CREATE MEMBER [<cube_name>.][<KPI name] AS <KPI Value>[,<Property
➥Name>=<Property_Value>]
```

In this statement, you specify cube name and name of the KPI you create. As *`KPI Value`*, you can specify MDX expression that returns the actual value of the metric. In the `CREATE` KPI statement, you can also specify one or more of optional properties. The properties are similar to ones you use to create a `KPI` object on the server (see Table 15.1). Properties that have slightly different names are described in Table 15.2.

Listing 15.6 shows example of KPI being created by CREATE KPI statement.

TABLE 15.2 Properties Supported by **CREATE** KPI Statements

Name	Description
`Status_Graphic`	Specifies a graphical representation of status to provide easy visualization of the KPI. The value of this property is a string that maps to a set of bitmaps.
`Trend_Graphic`	Specifies a graphical representation of a trend to provide easy visualization of the KPI. The value of this property is a string that maps to a bitmap.
`Parent_KPI`	Enables a hierarchical organization of KPIs. For example, you could define a `Customer Scorecard` KPI to have the children `Customer Satisfaction` and `Customer Retention`.
`Associated_Measure_Group`	Defines a measure group associated with this KPI, which is used to specify dimensionality of the KPI. This property is optional. If it is not specified, the KPI will have the dimensionality of all the measure groups in the cube.
`Current_Time_Member`	An MDX expression that defines the current member of the `Time` dimension that is relevant for the KPI. If this property is not specified, the default member of the `Time` dimension is used.

LISTING 15.6 CREATE KPI Statement

```
Create KPI [Warehouse and Sales].[Growth in Sales] as
   Case
     When [Time].[Time].CurrentMember.Level.Ordinal = 0
       Then   "NA"
     When
      IsEmpty ( ( [Time].[Time].PrevMember, [Measures].[Sales Count] ) ) Then Null
     Else ( [Measures].[Sales Count] - ( [Time].[Time].PrevMember,
        [Measures].[Sales Count] ) ) / ( [Time].[Time].PrevMember, [Measures].
        [Sales Count]) End,
     GOAL=
       Case
```

```
        When [Time].[Time].CurrentMember.Level Is [Time].[Time].[Year] Then .30
        When [Time].[Time].CurrentMember.Level Is [Time].[Time].[Quarter] Then .075
        When [Time].[Time].CurrentMember.Level Is [Time].[Time].[Month] Then .025
        When [Time].[Time].CurrentMember.Level Is [Time].[Time].[Date] Then .0008
        Else "NA" End,
    STATUS=
       Case
        When
         KpiValue("Growth in Sales On Session" ) >=  KpiGoal( "Growth in Sales" )
➥Then 1
        When KpiValue("Growth in Sales On Session" ) >= .90 *
             KpiGoal("Growth in Sales") And KpiValue("Growth in Sales") <
             KpiGoal ("Growth in Sales") Then 0
        Else -1 End,
   TREND=
      Case
        When [Time].[Time].CurrentMember.Level is [Time].[Time].[(All)] Then 0
        When //VBA!Abs ( KpiValue("Growth in Sales") -
            (KpiValue("Growth in Sales"),
            ParallelPeriod ([Time].[Time].[Year], 1, [Time].[Time].CurrentMember)) /
            (KpiValue("Growth in Sales"),
          ParallelPeriod ([Time].[Time].[Year], 1, [Time].[Time].CurrentMember) )
➥=.02
             Then 0
         When KpiValue("Growth in Sales") - (KpiValue("Growth in Salesn"),
           ParallelPeriod ([Time].[Time].[Year], 1, [Time].[Time].CurrentMember ))/
            (KpiValue("Growth in Sales On Session"),
            ParallelPeriod([Time].[Time].[Year], 1, [Time].[Time].CurrentMember ) )
➥>.02
            Then 1
            Else -1
      End,
   STATUS_GRAPHIC='Gauge - Ascending',
   TREND_GRAPHIC='Standard Arrow'
```

Discovering and Querying KPIs

After a KPI object is deployed on the server or created on a session, client applications can take advantage of it. Analysis Services provides standard interfaces that allow any generic application to retrieve a KPI and show it to the end user without knowing what kind of data is being analyzed.

A client application performs a few simple steps to retrieve KPI data, as shown in Figure 15.3.

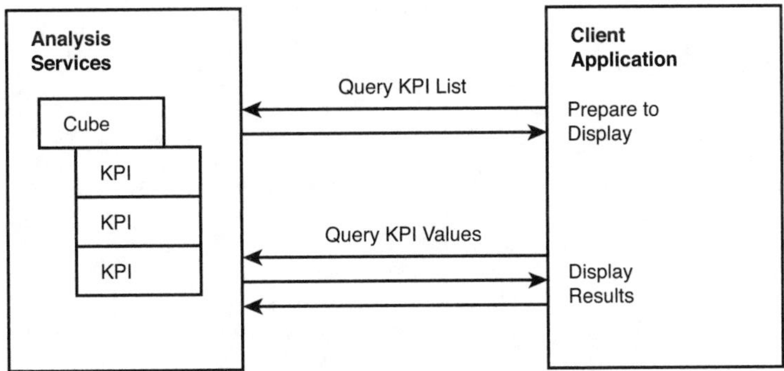

FIGURE 15.3 Steps to retrieve KPI data.

To retrieve KPI data, first the client application retrieves the list of KPIs available on the server/session. To do this, it issues a schema rowset request for `MDSCHEMA_KPIS`. This schema's rowset has a list of columns that repeat the properties of the `KPI` object. The schema rowset is used to enumerate the names of available KPIs and to retrieve the KPI properties, such as `StatusGraphic` and `TrendGraphic`. Other columns of the schema's rowset, such as `Value`, `Goal`, `Trend`, `Status`, and `Weight`, contain the names of the calculated measures associated with `Value`, `Goal`, `Status`, `Trend`, and `Weight` expressions, respectively.

Although the client application can use those names to generate an MDX query for the actual values of those calculated members, we recommend a simpler way to access values associated with KPI expressions. Client applications can use the helper MDX functions provided by Analysis Services—`KPIGoal`, `KPIStatus`, `KPITrend`, `KPIValue`, `KPIWeight`, and `KPICurrentTimeMember`—to access the values of the KPI properties. For example, a client application could issue the simple MDX request shown in Listing 15.7.

LISTING 15.7 An MDX Statement That Requests KPI Property Values

```
SELECT
     {KPIValue("Growth in Sales"), KPIGoal("Growth in Sales"),
     KPIStatus("Growth in Sales"),KPITrend("Growth in Sales")}
     ON COLUMNS,
     Store.Store.members on ROWS
FROM [warehouse and sales]
WHERE [Time].[Time].[Year].[1998]
```

This request returns the results shown in Figure 15.4.

Messages | Results

	Growth in Sales Value	Growth in Sales Goal	Growth in Sales Status	Growth in Sales Trend
All	0.895021707336734	0.3	1	1
HQ	(null)	0.3	-1	0
Store 1	(null)	0.3	-1	0
Store 10	(null)	0.3	-1	0
Store 11	-2.92836398838335E-02	0.3	-1	0
Store 12	(null)	0.3	-1	0
Store 13	-0.153892260433056	0.3	-1	0
Store 14	-4.30188679245283E-02	0.3	-1	0
Store 15	6.59879336349925E-02	0.3	-1	1
Store 16	0.117209679599838	0.3	-1	1
Store 17	6.52718168812589E-03	0.3	-1	0
Store 18	(null)	0.3	-1	0
Store 19	(null)	0.3	-1	0
Store 2	-0.121739130434783	0.3	-1	0
Store 20	(null)	0.3	-1	0
Store 21	(null)	0.3	-1	0
Store 22	8.96191187453323E-03	0.3	-1	0
Store 23	-0.156078860898138	0.3	-1	0
Store 24	-5.65781346510192E-02	0.3	-1	0
Store 3	-2.60284408329101E-02	0.3	-1	0
Store 4	(null)	0.3	-1	0
Store 5	(null)	0.3	-1	0
Store 6	6.94057226705796E-02	0.3	-1	1
Store 7	-6.85999756305593E-02	0.3	-1	0
Store 8	(null)	0.3	-1	0
Store 9	(null)	0.3	-1	0
Unknown	(null)	0.3	-1	0

FIGURE 15.4 Results of MDX request with the values of KPI properties.

Finally, the client application has to map the graphic properties returned by the schema rowset, such as `KPI_STATUS_GRAPHIC` and `KPI_TREND_GRAPHIC`, to the actual image that it displays. Analysis Services includes a set of images that you can use to display the status and trends of KPIs. The images are located in the `C:\Program Files\Microsoft Visual Studio 9.0\Common7\IDE\PrivateAssemblies\DataWarehouseDesigner\KPIsBrowserPage\Images` directory. Of course, you don't have to use those files; you can use your own graphics files.

Actions

Actions are another feature that allows tighter integration between analytical systems and vertical applications. Actions enable you to create a tightly integrated system that not only discovers trends in data and enables managers to make decisions based on those discoveries, but they also make it possible for the end user to act on the manager's decisions. For example, suppose that a user browses an inventory cube and discovers a low level in the inventory of a certain product. He can use actions to trigger a supply chain system procurement order for the product.

Analysis Services enables you to create objects associated with actions and store them on the server. It also provides a generic interface that client applications can use to access actions. In this way, it provides an automated means for software (such as Microsoft Excel) that doesn't know anything about a certain business application to execute an operation associated with actions.

Let's look at one of the common scenarios in which you might use actions. A user uses an application (for example, Microsoft Excel) to browse marketing data. He right-clicks a customer's name and Excel requests the list of actions associated with the member of the `Customer` dimension. The list might look like this:

- Show Customer Details Form
- Send Email to Customer
- Add Customer to Mailing List
- Mark Customer for Later Treatment

When the user selects Show Customer Details Form, Excel determines that this is a URL action and launches Internet Explorer to show a page that contains the customer details form. This page is part of the company's customer relations management system, and it contains detailed information about the customer.

Analysis Services doesn't have any information about the meaning of an action, nor does it execute actions; it merely provides the information that the client application needs to execute an action. Even a client application that is completely generic can use actions. The actions mechanism provides a standard way for any client application to trigger an action. However, if you are writing a client application for your IT organization and design a cube, you can have proprietary actions to trigger custom functionality.

15

Defining Actions

You can use BI Dev Studio to create a DDL request, or you can issue one. `Action` is a minor object defined by the `Cube` major object; it can be edited only when the entire cube is edited. As do many other objects, an `Action` object has `Name`, `ID`, `Description`, `Translations`, and `Annotations` properties.

All actions are context sensitive; that is, they can apply to specific hierarchies, levels, attributes, members, and cells, or to an entire cube. Different members or cells can offer different actions even if they are in the same cube or dimension. Three buckets of properties define an action:

- Properties that define the scope or target of the action (`Target Object`, `TargetType`, and `Condition`). These are described in more detail in Table 15.3.
- Properties that define the action itself (`Action Type` and `Expression`).
- Additional properties that define an action and provide miscellaneous information about it.

TABLE 15.3 Properties That Define the Scope of an Action

Name	Description
`Condition`	Enables restriction of the scope to which an action applies. This property can contain any MDX expression that resolves to a Boolean `TRUE` or `FALSE` value.
`Target`	Defines the object to which the action is attached.
`TargetType`	Defines the type of the object to which the action is attached. An action can be attached to `cube`, `dimension`, and `level` objects; a member; or all members of an attribute, level, or hierarchy. An action can also be assigned to a cell or group of cells.

Table 15.4 describes the properties that define the operations that a client application must accomplish to act on an action.

Table 15.5 describes some of the properties that specify how the action is presented to the user and provide additional information about the action to the client application.

TABLE 15.4 Properties That Define the Function of an Action

Name	Description
`Expression`	An MDX expression that Analysis Services evaluates to a string. A client application uses this string to perform an action. The client application passes this string to another application or to a module, depending on the type of action. This property is available for all action types except `Report` and `Drillthrough`. For example, expression can contain an URL, which an application can pass to Internet Explorer.
`Type`	Defines the type of the action and operation that the client application should perform with the string that results from evaluation of the `Expression` property. Analysis Services supports the following nine actions: `URL`, `HTML`, `CommandLine`, `Dataset`, `Rowset`, `Statement`, `Proprietary`, `Drillthrough`, and `Report`. ▶ `URL` — The content of the `Expression` property evaluates to a URL that can be passed to an Internet browser. ▶ `HTML` — The content of the `Expression` property evaluates to a string that contains HTML script. Save the sting to a file and use an Internet browser to render it. ▶ `Statement` — The content of the `Expression` property evaluates to a string that contains an MDX, DMX (Data Mining Extensions), or SQL (Structured Query Language) statement. It can be executed using an OLE DB provider, ADO.NET, ADOMD.NET, or XML for Analysis.

TABLE 15.4 Properties That Define the Function of an Action

Name	Description	
	▶ `Dataset`	The content of the `Expression` property evaluates to a string that contains an MDX statement. It can be executed using an Analysis Services OLE DB provider, ADOMD.NET, or XML for Analysis. The result of the execution of such a statement should be in multidi-
	▶ `Rowset`	The content of the `Expression` property evaluates to a string that contains an MDX, DMX, or SQL statement. It can be executed using an OLE DB provider, ADO.NET, ADOMD.NET, or XML for Analysis. The result of the execution of such a statement should be in
	▶ `CommandLine`	The content of the `Expression` property evaluates to a string that contains a command that can be executed in a command prompt.
	▶ `Proprietary`	A custom client application that owns both the cube and the client user interface can use the string returned by the action to execute a specific operation.
	▶ `Report`	Indicates that the `Action` object defines the parameters needed to build a URL that can be passed to SQL Server Reporting Services to generate a report. The returned action string is a URL that can be passed to an Internet browser that can invoke a report. The `MDSCHEMA_ACTIONS` schema rowset (discussed later in this chapter) returns the content of an `ACTION_TYPE` column as a URL so that legacy client applications can take full advantage of this type of action.
	▶ `Drillthrough`	Indicates that the `Action` object defines the parameters needed to build a `DRILLTHROUGH` statement that can be passed to any client component capable of query execution (similar to the action of the `ROWSET` type). The `MDSCHEMA_ACTIONS` schema rowset returns the content of an `ACTION_TYPE` column as a `ROWSET`. `Drillthrough` actions are always defined on cells.

Two action types deserve special attention: `Report` and `Drillthrough`. These action types are based on the other types `URL` and `Rowset`. They're helper types that provide infrastructure

TABLE 15.5 Additional Properties That Define an Action

Name	Description
Application	Defines the name of the application that the client application uses to invoke the action (for example, Internet Explorer).
Caption	Defines the string to be displayed by the client application during the enumeration of actions. The content of this property can be either an MDX expression that evaluates to a string (in this case, the CaptionIsMDX property should be set to TRUE) or a string. Use the Translations property of the Action object to provide a translation of the Caption to another language.
CaptionIsMDX	Set this property to TRUE if the content of the Caption property is an MDX expression.
Invocation	Used by a client application to help determine when an action should be invoked. Actions are usually invoked when a user performs some interaction with a client application. Specify INTERACTIVE as the value of the Invocation property.

for generating DRILLTHROUGH statements and a URL in a format that Reporting Services understands. When you define a Drillthrough action, you must specify the additional properties described in the "Drillthrough" section later in this chapter. Properties of Report action objects are described in Table 15.6.

Now you'll create a sample Action object that displays a map with the location of a store pinned on it using the MSN Map service available on the Internet. The FoodMart 2008

TABLE 15.6 Properties of Report Action Objects

Name	Description
Path	A virtual directory in Internet Information Services (IIS) where Reporting Services is referenced.
ReportFormatParameters	A list of additional parameters required by the report to customize the formatting of the report. The difference between ReportParameters and ReportFormatParameters is minimal: The Value property of ReportFormatParameters is a scalar string, not an MDX expression. For more information about report parameters, see Books Online articles for SQL Server Reporting Services.

`ReportParameters`	A list of parameters defined by the report designer and required by the report. Each parameter has two properties: `Name` and `Value`. The `Value` property can be an MDX expression that Analysis Services evaluates into a string and concatenates with `ServerName`, `Path`, and `Name`, and with other report parameters. Because the resulting string will eventually be passed to an Internet browser as a URL, it should be properly encoded. It's a good practice to wrap the `Value` property of the report parameter into the `UrlEscapeFragment` function, provided by Analysis Services. For more information about report parameters, see Books Online articles for SQL Server Reporting Services.
`ReportServer`	The name of the computer on which Reporting Services is running.

database doesn't store the street locations of the stores, so the example displays only the city where the store is located.

1. In BI Dev Studio, open the FoodMart 2008 project.
2. In the Solution Explorer, double-click the `Warehouse and Sales` cube to open the cube editor.
3. On the Actions tab, right-click anywhere in the Action Organizer and choose New Action from the resulting menu.
4. Type the name of your action—**`Store Locations`**—in the Name text box.
5. To associate your action with each store, choose Attribute Members as the `TargetType` for your action and the `[Store].[Store City]` attribute hierarchy for your target.
6. Type the following MDX expression in the Condition text box_FIRST:

   ```
   NOT([Store].[Store Country].Currentmember  IS [Store].[Store
   Country].[Mexico])
   ```

   With this expression, you specify that the action covers only the stores located in the United States and Canada, as if the MSN Map service didn't support maps for Mexico. (In reality, the service does support maps for Mexico, but we're demonstrating setting conditions here.)
7. In the Action Type box, select URL and write an MDX expression that generates a URL that the client application can feed to the MSN Map service.

   The URL begins with a prefix that consists of a domain name and a page name. The prefix is followed by a number of parameters that define the location (or locations) that will appear on the map. Listing 15.8 shows the expression to use.

LISTING 15.8 Expression for the Store Locations Action

```
"http://maps.msn.com/home.aspx?plce1=" +
// The name of the current city
[Store].[Store City].CurrentMember.Name + "," +
// Append state-province name
[Store].[Store State].CurrentMember.Name + "," +
// Append country name
[Store].[Store Country].CurrentMember.Name
```

Set the following properties: `Invocation` as `Interactive`, `Application` as `Internet Explorer`, `Description` as "This action displays a map with the location of a store pinned on it," `Caption Is MDX` as True, and `Caption` as the following MDX expression:

```
"View Map for " + [Store].[Store City].CurrentMember.Member_Caption
```

Figure 15.5 shows the Actions tab with the information already entered.

After you save your work in BI Dev Studio and deploy the project, the DDL is sent to the server, where it alters the cube and saves the created `Action` object. Listing 15.9 shows a portion of the DDL that creates the `Action` object.

LISTING 15.9 DDL That Creates an **`Action`** Object

```
<Actions>
     <Action xsi:type="StandardAction">
          <ID>Action</ID>
          <Name>Store Locations</Name>
          <Description>This action displays a map with the location of a store
                      pinned on it</Description>
          <Application>"Internet Explorer"</Application>
          <Caption>"View Map for " +
                   [Store].[Store City].CurrentMember.Member_Caption</Caption>
          <CaptionIsMdx>true</CaptionIsMdx>
          <Condition>NOT([Store].[Store Country].Currentmember IS
                  [Store].[Store Country].[Mexico])</Condition>
          <Expression>"http://maps.msn.com/home.aspx?plce1=" +
          // The name of the current city
         [Store].[Store City].CurrentMember.Name + "," +
         // Append state-province name
          [Store].[Store State].CurrentMember.Name + "," +
          // Append country name
          [Store].[Store Country].CurrentMember.Name</Expression>
          <Target>[Store].[Store City]</Target>
          <TargetType>AttributeMembers</TargetType>
```

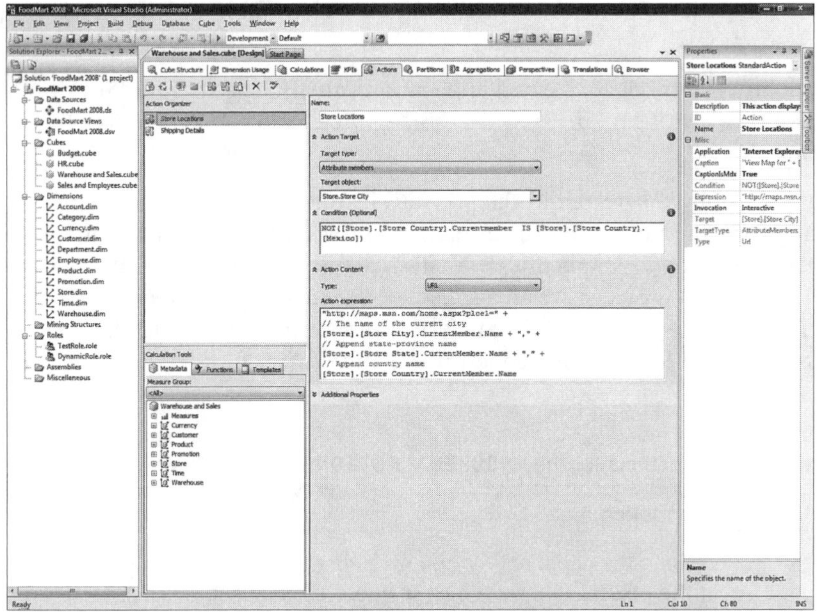

FIGURE 15.5 You can use BI Dev Studio to create an `Action` object.

```
            <Type>Url</Type>
            <Invocation>Interactive</Invocation>
        </Action>
</Actions>
```


Discovering Actions

When an `Action` object is deployed on the server, client applications can take advantage of it to retrieve actions and execute them using the standard interface provided by Analysis Services.

To discover which actions are assigned to a particular object, a client application issues a schema rowset request for `MDSCHEMA_ACTIONS`. The difference between an `Actions` schema rowset and many other schema rowsets supported by Analysis Services is that `MDSCHEMA_ACTIONS` never retrieves the full list of actions defined on the cube or database. It returns only valid actions that are available in the current context. Therefore, to retrieve information about actions, a client application must pass parameters (also called restrictions) to schema rowset that define an object for which action is called. Table 15.7 describes these mandatory restrictions.

In addition to mandatory restrictions, a client application can also specify other restrictions that limit the list of actions returned by Analysis Services. Table 15.8 describes these optional restrictions.

Now you retrieve the action you created in the previous listing—the action that displays the locations of the stores on a map. To execute a schema rowset request, the client application can use client components shipped with Analysis Services such as ADOMD.NET or the Analysis Services OLE DB provider. It can also issue a `Discover` XML/A request. (For more information, see Chapter 32, "XML for Analysis," and Chapter 33, "ADOMD.NET.") You're going to issue an XML/A `Discover` request using Microsoft SQL Server Management Studio.

TABLE 15.7 Mandatory Restrictions for the **MDSCHEMA_ACTIONS** Schema Rowset

Name	Description	
COORDINATE	Defines the coordinate in the multidimensional space or the name of the object, either of which is interpreted by Analysis Services based on the `COORDINATE_TYPE` restriction.	
COORDINATE_TYPE	Corresponds to the `TargetType` property of the `Action` object; specifies the type of object for which the client application requests the list of actions. Analysis Services supports the following list of coordinate types:	
	▶ MDACTION_COORDINATE_CUBE	`MDSCHEMA_ACTIONS` retrieves the actions defined on the `Cube` object—actions with `Cube TargetType`. It does not return actions specified for dimensions, levels, members, or cells of the cube.
	▶ MDACTION_COORDINATE_DIMENSION	`MDSCHEMA_ACTIONS` retrieves the actions defined on the dimension object specified in the `COORDINATE` restriction. It does not return actions specified for levels, members, or cells of the dimension.
	▶ MDACTION_COORDINATE_LEVEL	`MDSCHEMA_ACTIONS` retrieves the actions defined on the level object specified in the `COORDINATE` restriction. It does not return actions specified for any members or cells of the level.

	▶ MDACTION_COORDINATE_MEMBER — MDSCHEMA_ACTIONS retrieves the actions defined on the member object specified in the COORDINATE restriction.
	▶ MDACTION_COORDINATE_CELL — MDSCHEMA_ACTIONS interprets the COORDINATE restriction as a subcube specification and retrieves all the actions applicable to the cell specified by the subcube.
CUBE_NAME	The name of the cube in whose context all other restrictions are resolved.

TABLE 15.8 Optional Restrictions for the **MDSCHEMA_ACTIONS** Schema Rowset

Name	Description
ACTION_NAME	The name of the action.
ACTION_TYPE	The type of the action. If the client application supports only actions of specific types, it might provide the type in ACTION_TYPE restriction. If client application doesn't provide this restriction, Analysis Services by default returns actions of all types except Proprietary.
CATALOG_NAME	The name of the database. If this restriction is not specified, the default database will be used. If this restriction specifies a database other than the default, Analysis Services will return an empty result.
INVOCATION	Type of invocation. The current version of Analysis Services supports only actions of INTERACTIVE invocation type.

LISTING 15.10 XML/A Discover Request That Retrieves the List of Actions

```
<Envelope xmlns = "http://schemas.xmlsoap.org/soap/envelope/">
     <Body>
          <Discover xmlns = "urn:schemas-microsoft-com:xml-analysis">
               <RequestType>MDSCHEMA_ACTIONS</RequestType>
               <Restrictions>
                    <RestrictionList>
                         <CATALOG_NAME>FoodMart 2008</CATALOG_NAME>
                         <CUBE_NAME>Warehouse And Sales</CUBE_NAME>
                         <COORDINATE>
                             [Store].[Stores].[Store City].[Victoria]
                         </COORDINATE>
                         <COORDINATE_TYPE>4</COORDINATE_TYPE>
                    </RestrictionList>
               </Restrictions>
               <Properties>
                    <PropertyList>
                         <Catalog>FoodMart 2008</Catalog>
                    </PropertyList>
```

```
            </Properties>
        </Discover>
    </Body>
</Envelope>
```

This request returns the following XML that represents the rowset in XML/A format:


```
<soap:Envelope xmlns:soap="http://schemas.xmlsoap.org/soap/envelope/">
    <soap:Body>
        <DiscoverResponse xmlns="urn:schemas-microsoft-com:xml-analysis">
            <return>
                <xsd:complexType name="row">
                    <xsd:sequence>
                        <xsd:element sql:field="CATALOG_NAME"
              name="CATALOG_NAME" type="xsd:string" minOccurs="0" />
                        <xsd:element sql:field="SCHEMA_NAME" name=
              "SCHEMA_NAME" type="xsd:string" minOccurs="0" />
                        <xsd:element sql:field="CUBE_NAME" name=
              "CUBE_NAME" type="xsd:string" minOccurs="0" />
                        <xsd:element sql:field="ACTION_NAME" name=
              "ACTION_NAME" type="xsd:string" minOccurs="0" />
                        <xsd:element sql:field="ACTION_TYPE" name=
              "ACTION_TYPE" type="xsd:int" minOccurs="0" />
                        <xsd:element sql:field="COORDINATE" name=
              "COORDINATE" type="xsd:string" minOccurs="0" />
                        <xsd:element sql:field="COORDINATE_TYPE" name=
              "COORDINATE_TYPE" type="xsd:int" minOccurs="0" />
                        <xsd:element sql:field="ACTION_CAPTION" name=
              "ACTION_CAPTION" type="xsd:string" minOccurs="0" />
                       <xsd:element sql:field="DESCRIPTION" name=
              "DESCRIPTION" type="xsd:string" minOccurs="0" />
                        <xsd:element sql:field="CONTENT" name=
              "CONTENT" type="xsd:string" minOccurs="0" />
                        <xsd:element sql:field="APPLICATION" name=
             "APPLICATION" type="xsd:string" minOccurs="0" />
                        <xsd:element sql:field="INVOCATION" name=
             "INVOCATION" type="xsd:int" minOccurs="0" />
                    </xsd:sequence>
                </xsd:complexType>
            </xsd:schema>
            <row>
                <CATALOG_NAME>FoodMart 2008</CATALOG_NAME>
                <CUBE_NAME>Warehouse and Sales</CUBE_NAME>
                <ACTION_NAME>Store Locations</ACTION_NAME>
```

```
                    <ACTION_TYPE>1</ACTION_TYPE>
                    <COORDINATE>
                        [Store].[Stores].[Store City].[Victoria]
                    </COORDINATE>
                     <COORDINATE_TYPE>4</COORDINATE_TYPE>
                     <ACTION_CAPTION>View Map for Victoria</ACTION_CAPTION>
                    <DESCRIPTION>This action displays a map with the location
                                 of a store pinned on it</DESCRIPTION>
                    <CONTENT>
                          http://maps.msn.com/home.aspx?plce1=Victoria,BC,Canada
                    </CONTENT>
                    <APPLICATION>"Internet Explorer"</APPLICATION>
                    <INVOCATION>1</INVOCATION>
             </row>
         </root>
    </return>
</DiscoverResponse>
 </soap:Body>
</soap:Envelope>
```

15

Now the client application can use the string returned to it in the `CONTENT` column of the rowset

```
http://maps.msn.com/home.aspx?plce1=Augusta,Georgia,United States&amp;regn1=0
```

and pass it to Internet Explorer or another Internet browser.

If you don't want to mess with writing XML to test the actions that you create, you can use the cube browser in BI Dev Studio, as follows:

1. Open the FoodMart 2008 project.
2. In the Solution Explorer, double-click the `Warehouse and Sales` cube.
3. In the cube editor, select the Browse tab and drag the `Store City` hierarchy onto the browsing control.
4. Click a city (for example, Seattle), and then right-click.
5. On the resulting menu, choose View Map for Seattle (see Figure 15.6), and you can now browse the action's results in Internet Explorer.

Drillthrough

When they browse analytical data stored in Analysis Services, users usually work with aggregated values. They usually start to analyze the data from the top, and drill down when they discover something interesting in the data. In some situations, a user would want to see the individual transactions that contributed to the cube's aggregated data. For example, a user who is browsing inventory data collected in a warehouse might drill down to the information about units that have been ordered for the warehouse and shipped from warehouse to stores. In other situations, a user might need to see the individual transactions that contributed to the sales completed at a store during a specific month or even a day. The operation that enables a user to drill down to a lower level of detail is called, as you might guess, *drillthrough*.

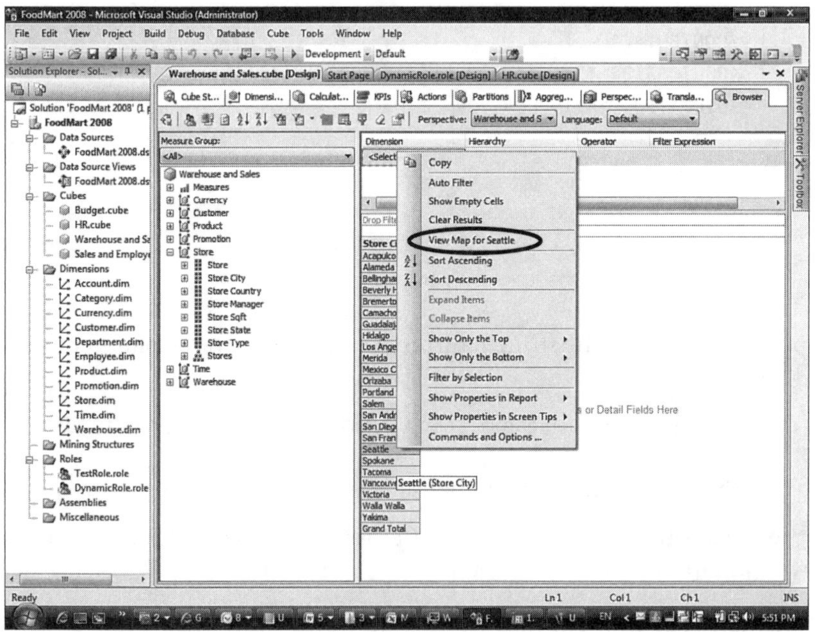

FIGURE 15.6 You can use BI Dev Studio to browse an action.

Although drillthrough is supported in Analysis Services 2000; the operation has been significantly redesigned for Analysis Services 2005 and Analysis Services 2008 continue to support 2005 model. In Analysis Services 2000, drillthrough queries the relational database that the multidimensional database was built from. It then retrieves one or more recordsets that corresponds to the fact data associated with a cell in the multidimensional space. Analysis Services 2000 allows client applications to get columns of relational tables that are not part of the multidimensional model. For example, if a phone number of a customer is not built in to a cube, the drillthrough request could get a rowset that contains the phone numbers of customers.

That approach doesn't fit very well into the Unified Dimensional Model (UDM). The idea behind UDM is that the multidimensional model should be rich enough to contain all the information that client applications need. Therefore, if a phone number of a customer is important for the functionality of the system, it should be built in to the UDM as an attribute of the `Customer` dimension.

The main difference between drillthrough in Analysis Services 2000 and 2008 is that in Analysis Services 2008, drillthrough returns data from the bottom level of the cube, and columns returned by drillthrough should be part of the cube schema.

DRILLTHROUGH Statement

A client application uses a `DRILLTHROUGH` statement to invoke a drillthrough operation. The statement has the following syntax:

```
DRILLTHROUGH [MAXROWS Integer_Expression] <MDX SELECT statement>
             [RETURN Column_Expression [, Column_Expression ...]]
```

You specify the cell for the drillthrough operation by a `SELECT` statement. The list of columns to be retrieved is specified in a `RETURN` clause.

15

NOTE

Drillthrough in Analysis Services 2008 has the same limitation as in previous versions: It can be executed on only a single cell. An error will be returned if a `DRILLTHROUGH` statement contains a `SELECT` statement that returns more than one cell.

You can use the `RETURN` clause to specify the subset of columns that you want your `DRILLTHROUGH` statement to return.

A *column* is an object that is not typical to a multidimensional request. Drillthrough columns are dimension attributes or cube measures. You can specify a column with the following format: `[<domain name>.][<table name>].[<column_name>]`. For a dimension attribute, the `<domain name>` is the name of a cube; for a measure, it's the measure group that this measure belongs to. To distinguish a dimension name from the name of a measure group or a cube, `<table name>` is the name of the dimension preceded by a dollar sign ($), and `<column name>` is the name of the attribute or measure.

For example, the `DRILLTHROUGH` statement in Listing 15.11 returns a rowset that contains the products that were shipped from the FoodMart warehouses on a specific date and the stores they were shipped to.

LISTING 15.11 **DRILLTHROUGH** Request

```
DRILLTHROUGH MAXROWS 15
SELECT ([Time].[Time By Week].[Year].[1997].&[4]&[1997].&[385])
ON COLUMNS
FROM [Warehouse and Sales]
 RETURN [$product].[product], [$store].[store], Key([$store].[store]),
[$Measures].[Units Shipped]
```

Let's take a look at the results of this query, shown in Figure 15.7.

Fields in the columns corresponding to the `Units Shipped` measure contain actual values of that measure for lower details of the data. Fields corresponding to the `Dimension` attribute contain the member name of the member on the lower granularity being queried.

If you want to request properties of an attribute other than `Name`, you can use a helper function as you did to retrieve the `Key` value of the stores in the example. Analysis Services supports the following helper functions: `Key`, `Name`, `MemberValue`, `Caption`, `UniqueName`, `CustomRollup`, `CustomRollupProperties`, and `UnaryOperators`.

[$Product].[Product]	[$Store].[Store]	[$Store].[Store]	[Warehouse].[Units Shipped]
Fast Apple Fruit Roll	Store 14	14	2
High Top Garlic	Store 14	14	70
Red Wing Copper Cleaner	Store 14	14	47
Horatio Chocolate Donuts	Store 14	14	41
PigTail Orange Popsicles	Store 14	14	20
Better Fancy Canned Anchovies	Store 14	14	17
Big Time Waffles	Store 14	14	14
Hilltop Multi-Symptom Cold Remedy	Store 14	14	37
Big Time Frozen Chicken Thighs	Store 14	14	45
Walrus Light Beer	Store 14	14	70

FIGURE 15.7 Rowset with all the products shipped on specified date.

`DRILLTHROUGH` internally retrieves detailed data from a `Measure Group` object. Therefore, the `RETURN` clause can contain only the measures and attributes that belong to the same measure group—the target measure group. A target measure group is defined by the measures specified in the `RETURN` clause of the `DRILLTHROUGH` statement and not by coordinates of the cell on the `Measure` dimension.

Our designers decided to have target measure groups specified in RETURN clauses to support drill-across scenarios. For example, imagine that a user is browsing the data stored in one measure group. That measure group has a high level of detail and stores data aggregated from some point. Perhaps it doesn't have records for each sales transaction that occurred during the day; the sales are aggregated daily. If the user found something interesting, she would probably want to see the individual transactions that contributed to a sale.

To make it possible for her to see those individual transactions, you issue a drillthrough request. Because the data retrievable by a DRILLTHROUGH statement must be stored in a cube (in either relational online analytical processing [ROLAP] or multidimensional online analytical processing [MOLAP] form), you can add low granularity data into your existing measure group to bring more data into Analysis Services. Or, you could create another measure group—one that would probably be based on a ROLAP partition—and a dimension that has granularity on a lower level of details. (Individual transactions could be stored in this measure group.) With this approach, the data that is used most often by analytical applications (aggregated data) is stored separately from rarely used data (drillthrough data).

When Analysis Services receives a drillthrough request, it analyzes the columns specified in the RETURN clause. It then uses those columns to identify the target measure group and maps the cube coordinates specified in the SELECT statement to the coordinates in the target measure group.

Defining DRILLTHROUGH Columns in a Cube

Because a RETURN clause is optional for a DRILLTHROUGH statement, you don't have to define one in a client application. The columns that the application is to retrieve by the DRILLTHROUGH statement can come from the cube definition.

In a cube, columns for a drillthrough query are defined by Drillthrough actions, which were previously discussed in this chapter. A cube designer can create a Drillthrough action and mark it as the default. When Analysis Services processes a DRILLTHROUGH statement with no RETURN clause, it internally requests MDSCHEMA_ACTIONS and retrieves the default action targeted on the current coordinate (the coordinate specified in the inner SELECT statement). It then retrieves the action string from the CONTENT column and appends that string to the original DRILLTHROUGH statement.

You can have multiple default Drillthrough actions in a cube, but they have to cover different portions of the cube. For example, it's a common practice to create a default action for each measure group by using a MeasureGroupMeasures MDX function to specify a target property of the action.

In addition to the standard properties of an `Action` object, a `Drillthrough Action` object has two additional properties, as described in Table 15.9.

TABLE 15.9 Properties of **`Drillthrough`** Actions

Name	Description
`Column`	Defines an array of columns to be used in the `RETURN` clause of the `DRILLTHROUGH` statement. This property is defined as a metadata `Binding` object of a dimension attribute or a measure. (For information about bindings, refer to Chapter 18, "DSVs and Object Bindings.")
`DEFAULT`	Defines a `Drillthrough` action as the default action. If the action is defined as the default, the columns it specifies will be appended to any `DRILLTHROUGH` statement without a `RETURN` clause.

Let's use BI Dev Studio to create a default `Drillthrough` action that targets to the `Warehouse` measure group and returns the columns `Product`, `Store`, and `Unit Shipped`:

1. In BI Dev Studio, open the FoodMart 2008 project.
2. In the Solution Explorer, double-click the `Warehouse and Sales` cube to open the cube editor.
3. On the Actions tab, right-click anywhere in the Action Organizer and choose New Drillthrough Action from the resulting menu.
4. Type the name of your action—**`Shipping Details`**—in the Name text box.
5. Choose `Warehouse` as an action target; `TargetType CELLS` will be automatically assigned to this action by BI Studio.
6. Assign columns to the action by choosing appropriate attributes `Store` and `Products`, and measure `Units Shipped` in the drillthrough columns editor. (You don't need to specify any conditions.)
7. Set these additional properties: Default as True, Maximum Rows as 15, Description as Details of the Shipping, Caption Is MDX as False, and Caption as Shipping Details, as shown in Figure 15.8.

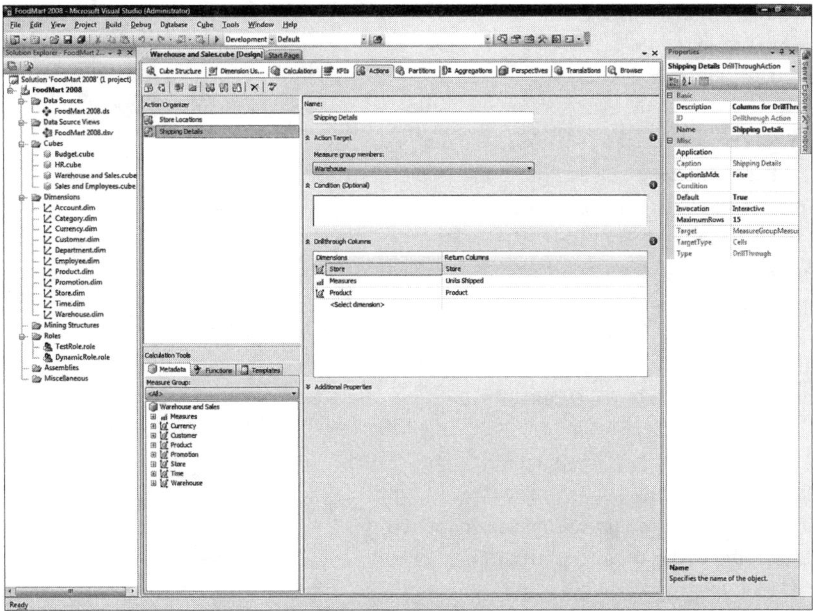

FIGURE 15.8 A `Drillthrough` action is created using BI Dev Studio.

You don't need to generate attribute and measure bindings to define the columns of the `Drillthrough` action because BI Dev Studio does this for you. However, if you manually generate the DDL definition for the `Drillthrough` action, it will have the format shown in Listing 15.12.

LISTING 15.12 DDL Definition for a **`Drillthrough`** Action

```
<Action xsi:type="DrillThroughAction">
    <ID>Drillthrough Action</ID>
    <Name>Shipping Details</Name>
    <Description>Columns for Drillthrough query to get details of the
        ➥shipping</Description>
    <Application />
    <Caption>Shipping Details</Caption>
    <CaptionIsMdx>false</CaptionIsMdx>
    <Condition />
    <Target>MeasureGroupMeasures("Warehouse")</Target>
    <TargetType>Cells</TargetType>
    <Type>Drillthrough</Type>
```

```
        <Invocation>Interactive</Invocation>
        <Default>true</Default>
        <MaximumRows>15</MaximumRows>
        <Columns>
            <Column xsi:type="CubeAttributeBinding">
            <CubeID>FoodMart2008</CubeID>
            <CubeDimensionID>Store</CubeDimensionID>
            <AttributeID>Store</AttributeID>
            <Type>All</Type>
        <Ordinal>0</Ordinal>
        </Column>
        <Column xsi:type="MeasureBinding">
            <MeasureID>Units Shipped</MeasureID>
        </Column>
        <Column xsi:type="CubeAttributeBinding">
            <CubeID>FoodMart2008</CubeID>
            <CubeDimensionID>Product</CubeDimensionID>
            <AttributeID>Product</AttributeID>
            <Type>All</Type>
            <Ordinal>0</Ordinal>
        </Column>
        </Columns>
    </Action>
</Actions>
```

A client application doesn't need to generate a `DRILLTHROUGH` statement to take advantage of drillthrough functionality. Even a generic client application that doesn't have information about the data stored in the cube can use drillthrough if the cube designer created `Drillthrough` actions in the cube. A client application can query `MDSCHEMA_ACTIONS` to retrieve a string containing an already-generated statement. For more information about using `MDSCHEMA_ACTIONS`, refer to the "Discovering Actions" section earlier in this chapter. You can also use the cube browser to test your `Drillthrough` action by clicking the cell and then right-clicking the cell value.

CHAPTER 16

Writing Data into Analysis Services

IN THIS CHAPTER

- Using the UPDATE CUBE Statement to Write Data into Cube Cells
- Updatable and Non-Updatable Cells
- Lifetime of the Update
- Enabling Writeback
- Converting a Writeback Partition to a Regular Partition
- Other Ways to Perform Writeback

Typically, you can retrieve data stored in Analysis Services and use it to solve different business problems. However, for some business problems, you might need to either enter new data or change existing data within Analysis Services. For example, you might want to see how increasing of the sales of a particular product would affect total sales, or what would happen to profitability if you increased the web advertising budget by 5% and cut the telemarketing budget by 10%. Analysis Services supports two modes of writing data into a cube: temporary writeback (also known as what-if analysis) and permanent writeback.

Temporary writeback enables you to play with numbers retrieved from Analysis Services—you can interactively change the data in the cells of a cube, and then immediately view what impact such a change would have on the rest of the cells. With temporary writeback, your changes exist only in the writeback cache. The changes are not available to other users, and Analysis Services discards them when the session ends.

Permanent writeback enables you to save results of your experiments on the server and share your findings with other users. Analysis Services saves the changes in the writeback cache to a special partition, and makes them available after the session ends. Figure 16.1 shows the difference between temporary and permanent writeback.

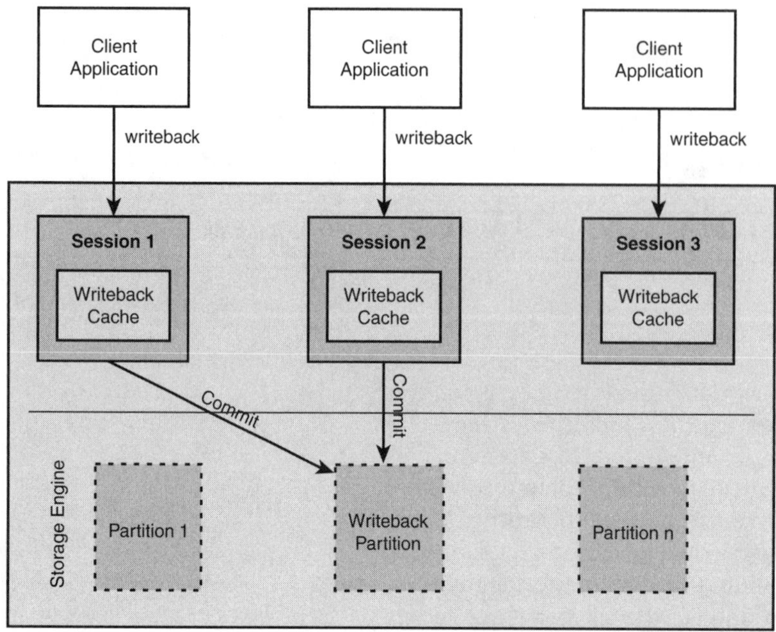

FIGURE 16.1 With temporary writeback, your changes are not available to other users, but you can commit them and save results of your experiments to the server.

Using the UPDATE CUBE Statement to Write Data into Cube Cells

You can use the UPDATE_CUBE MDX (Multidimensional Expressions) statement to write data to any cell in the cube that aggregates to its parent by using the SUM aggregation function. The UPDATE CUBE statement has the following syntax:

```
UPDATE CUBE <cube_name>
     SET
          <cell_update>[, <cell_update>...]
         [<allocation_specification>
<cell update> ::= <tuple>.VALUE = <numeric_expression>
<allocation_specification> ::=
     USE_EQUAL_ALLOCATION ¦
     USE_EQUAL_INCREMENT ¦
     USE_WEIGHTED_ALLOCATION [BY <weight_value_expression>]  ¦
     USE_WEIGHTED_INCREMENT [BY <weight_value_expression>] ]
```

Let's examine how the UPDATE CUBE statement works by issuing a query that writes to a leaf member of the Time dimension:

```
UPDATE CUBE [Warehouse and Sales]
```

```
SET
    ([Time].[Time].[Date].[1998-12-02 00:00:00] ) = 1000
```

Under the covers, this statement updates the writeback cache, the memory that contains the updated values for a session. Internally, the writeback cache doesn't contain a single, updated value for the cell corresponding to the specified tuple, but instead has two values: the original value and the delta—the difference between the original value and the new value specified by the `UPDATE CUBE` statement. When your query requests a new value, Analysis Services first retrieves the original value, and then retrieves the delta value from the writeback cache and adds it to the original value, as shown in Figure 16.2.

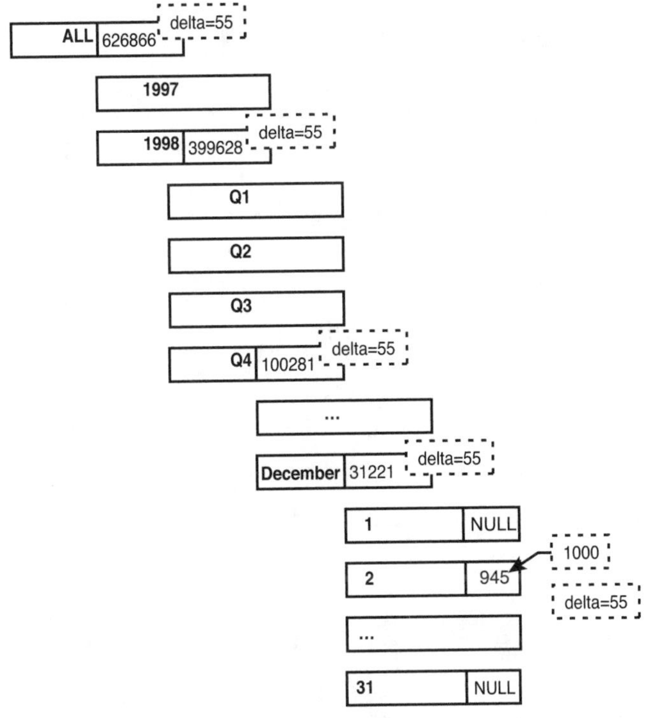

FIGURE 16.2 The value for an updated cell is calculated as a sum of the original value and the delta value.

If a user requests a parent of the updated cell, its value is not recomputed from the lower level by summing all the children, but is instead calculated by adding the delta—calculated when the `UPDATE CUBE` statement was executed—to the original value of the cell retrieved from storage. In the preceding example, you set the value of cell that corresponds to the units ordered on December 2, 1998 to `1000`. When Analysis Services executes the `UPDATE CUBE` statement, it calculates the delta value, `55`, by subtracting the original value, `945`, from the new value, `1000`. Now if you query the value for units ordered in Quarter 4 of 1998, Analysis Services doesn't sum up the units ordered for each

16

day of that quarter, but instead retrieves the pre-aggregated value stored for Quarter 4 of 1998, `100281`, and adds the delta value to it to get the updated value, `100336`.

Here's another example: The following query executes on a new connection in SQL Server Management Studio. The query requests a grand total of all ordered units, units ordered on December 2, 1998, units ordered in December 1998, units ordered during the fourth quarter of 1998, and units ordered in 1998:

```
SELECT {[Time].[Time].[All], [Time].[Time].[Year].[1998],
 [Time].[Time]. [Quarter].&[Q4]&[1998], [Time].[Time].[Month].&[12]&[1998],
[Time].[Time].[Date].[1998-12-02 00:00:00]} ON COLUMNS
FROM [Warehouse and Sales]
```

The query returns the result shown in Figure 16.3.

All	1998	Q4	December	1998-12-02 00:00:00
626866	399628	100281	31221	945

FIGURE 16.3 Units ordered during different time periods based on the data stored in the cube.

Now we issue the `UPDATE CUBE` statement described earlier and set the units ordered on December 2, 1998 to `1000`:

```
UPDATE CUBE [Warehouse and Sales]
     SET
         ([Time].[Time].[Date].[1998-12-02 00:00:00] ) = 1000
```

After submitting cube update, issue the original query again. You'll notice that all the values have increased by 55, as shown in Figure 16.4.

All	1998	Q4	December	1998-12-02 00:00:00
626921	399683	100336	31276	1000

FIGURE 16.4 Units ordered during different time periods based on the data updated by the `UPDATE CUBE` statement.

The `UPDATE CUBE` statement enables you to write to almost any cell of the cube. However, when you update a cell other than a leaf cell for a measure group, Analysis Services divides the new value between the children of the nonleaf cell and inserts a delta value into the writeback cache for each affected child.

For example, update the cell corresponding to the units of Ebony Mandarin Oranges ordered in the Treehouse Distribution warehouse during December of 1998, and set its value to `40000` by issuing the following `UPDATE CUBE` statement:

```
UPDATE CUBE [Warehouse and Sales]
```

```
SET
      ([Time].[Time].[Month].&[12]&[1998],
       [Warehouse].[Warehouses].[Warehouse].&[13],
       [Product].[Products].[Product].&[826]) = 40000
```

Then, run the following query, which shows you the values for the units of Ebony Mandarin Oranges ordered in the Treehouse Distribution warehouse during 1998, during the fourth quarter of 1998, during December 1998, and on December 3, 1998. As displayed in Figure 16.5, the value for December 3, 1998 is now equal to 40000 divided by 31 because December 1998 has 31 child cells:

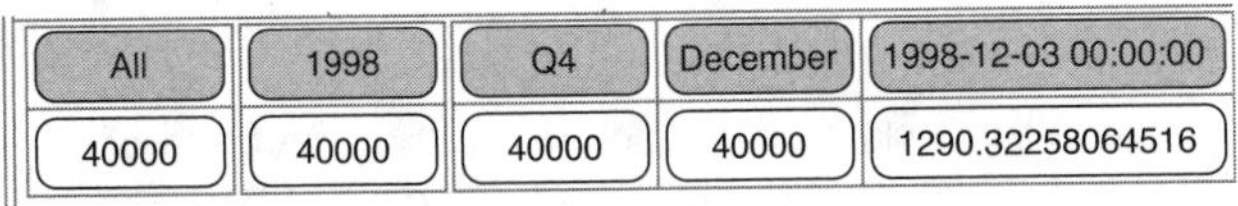

All	1998	Q4	December	1998-12-03 00:00:00
40000	40000	40000	40000	1290.32258064516

FIGURE 16.5 Values for cells corresponding to the levels lower than a cell being updated are calculated by dividing the new value by the number of children.

```
SELECT {[Time].[Time].[All], [Time].[Time].[Year].[1998],
        [Time].[Time].[Quarter].&[Q4]&[1998],
        [Time].[Time].[Month].&[12]&[1998],
        [Time].[Time].[Date].[1998-12-03 00:00:00]} ON COLUMNS
FROM [Warehouse and Sales]
WHERE ( [Measures].[Units Ordered],
[Warehouse].[Warehouses].[Warehouse]. &[13],
[Product].[Products].[Product].&[826] )
```


By default, Analysis Services divides the new value equally among the children of a cell. You can include the `allocation_specification` clause of the `UPDATE CUBE` statement to specify the formula by which you want to distribute the updated value. Analysis Service supports four types of allocations, as shown in Table 16.1.

TABLE 16.1 Allocation Methods

Method	Description
USE_EQUAL_ALLOCATION	The new value assigned to the parent cell is divided equally between the children of the parent cell (the default allocation). Analysis Services uses the following formula: Child_Value = New_Parent_Value / Number Of Descendants

USE_EQUAL_INCREMENT	The value in each child cell is incremented by the delta of the new value assigned to the parent cell divided by the number of child cells. Analysis Services uses the following formula: Child_Value = Old_Child_Value + (New_Parent_Value-Old_Parent_Value) / Number of Descendants
USE_WEIGHTED_ALLOCATION	The new value assigned to the parent cell is divided between children cells according to the weight specified by the `Weight_Value_Expression` clause. `Weight_Value_Expression` should evaluate to a numeric value between `0` and `1`. Analysis Services uses the following formula: Child_Value = New_Parent_Value * Weight
USE_WEIGHTED_INCREMENT	The value in each child cell is incremented by the delta of the new value assigned to the parent cell divided between children cells according to the weight specified by the `Weight_Value_Expression` clause. `Weight_Value_Expression` should evaluate to a numeric value between `0` and `1`. Analysis Services uses the following formula: Child_Value = Old_Child_Value + (New_Parent_Value - Old_Parent_Value) * Weight

NOTE

When you specify a tuple expression in an `UPDATE CUBE` statement, you can use a partial tuple specification (in which you don't explicitly specify all the attributes needed to identify the tuple). If you use a partial tuple specification, the default member from any dimension not explicitly included is used to "complete" the tuple.

If you use a partial tuple specification, keep in mind that the `ALL` member is typically used as the default member for most dimensions. For example, your `UPDATE CUBE` statement updates a cell on the top of some dimensions. This means that the update will be distributed between all the leaf cells associated with each dimension not explicitly included. Such an update might affect a huge number of cells and take a lot of time and resources. Doing updates in a more controlled fashion, by explicitly specifying the tuple for the cell to be updated, is strongly recommended.

The syntax of the `UPDATE_CUBE` statement enables you to update more than one cell at a time. You can batch multiple cell updates into a single `UPDATE_CUBE` statement to save time on the command round trip. Analysis Services executes each update within the statement sequentially in the order updates appear in the statement. For example, in the following `UPDATE_CUBE` statement, Analysis Services first performs an update to the cell defined by `([Time].[Time].[Month].&[12]&[1998], [Warehouse].[Warehouses].[Warehouse].&[13], [Product].[Products].[Product].&[826])`, performs allocations down to all the leaf cells, and only then starts to perform an update of cells associated with the `([Time].[Time].[Month].&[12]&[1998], [Store].[Stores].[Store].&[15], [Product].[Products].[Product].&[826])` tuple:

```
UPDATE CUBE [Warehouse and Sales]
    SET
        ([Time].[Time].[Month].&[12]&[1998],
         [Warehouse].[Warehouses].[Warehouse].&[13],
         [Product].[Products].[Product].&[826]) = 1000,

        ([Time].[Time].[Month].&[12]&[1998],
         [Store].[Stores].[Store].&[15],
         [Product].[Products].[Product].&[826]) = 3000
```

In our example, the `UPDATE CUBE` statement updates leaf cell `([Time].[Time].[Month].&[12]&[1998], [Warehouse].[Warehouses].[Warehouse].&[13], [Store].[Stores].[Store].&[15], [Product].[Products].[Product].&[826])` twice—the first time by assigning it the value `1000/26` (1,000 divided by number of stores) and the second time by assigning it the value `3000/25` (3,000 divided by number of warehouses), as shown in Figure 16.6.

To check the value of this cell after the update, execute the following query:

```
SELECT {[Time].[Time].[Year].[1998] } ON COLUMNS,
                ([Warehouse].[Warehouses].[Warehouse].&[13],
[Store].[Stores].[Store].&[15])  on ROWS
FROM [Warehouse and Sales]
WHERE ( [Measures].[Units Ordered], [Product].[Products].[Product].&[826] )
```

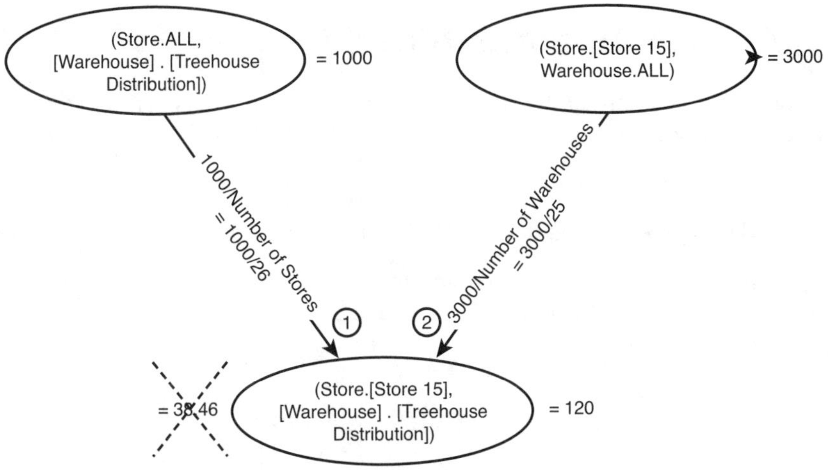

FIGURE 16.6 Order of updates within the UPDATE_CUBE statement.

Figure 16.7 shows the result of the query execution.

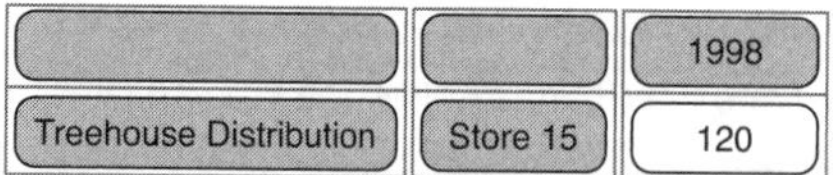

		1998
Treehouse Distribution	Store 15	120

FIGURE 16.7 Last update within the UPDATE_CUBE statement wins.

When a single UPDATE CUBE statement contains multiple update clauses, Analysis Services performs updates sequentially because execution of the first update can affect the result of the subsequent updates. This consideration is important when the same cells are updated by both updates (cell ([Warehouse].[Warehouses].[Warehouse].&[13], [Store].[Stores].[Store].&[15]) in our example). However, when both updates are independent from each other, Analysis Services can optimize the performance of the update by choosing a better execution plan. To optimize the scenario where updates within UPDATE CUBE statement update different set of cells, Analysis Services 2008 introduces a new connection string property Update Isolation Level. When this property is set to 1 (isolated), Analysis Services improves the performance by evaluating each update in parallel without any consideration for the others. With the Update Isolation Level property set to 0 or 2 (default behavior, not isolated), Analysis Services performs updates sequentially.

NOTE

Although setting Update Isolation Level property to isolated can improve performance of the update, we recommend that you do it with utmost care. You should use this property when you are certain that updates are independent from each other; otherwise, the writeback operation can lead to unexpected results.

Updatable and Non-Updatable Cells

The UPDATE CUBE statement enables you to update almost any cell in a cube. However, there are exceptions. The following cells cannot be updated:

- Cells based on calculated members.
- Measures aggregated by any aggregation function other than Sum.
- Cells protected from a user by cell security. For more information about cell security, see Chapter 37, "Securing Cell Values."

- Tuples that don't exist in a measure group (in cubes that contain more than one measure group). In such cases, the `UPDATE CUBE` statement returns an error even when the `IgnoreUnrelatedDimension` property is turned on. For example, you cannot update a cell referenced by the tuple (`[Customer].[Customer].[CustomerName].[Alexander Berger], Measures.[Units Ordered]`) because the `Units Ordered` measure belongs to the `Warehouse` measure group, but the `Customer` dimension is not included in the `Warehouse` measure group.
- Cells associated with members in indirect dimensions such as referenced, many to many, and data mining. For more information about dimension types, see Chapter 8, "Advanced Modeling."

NOTE

Client applications can determine whether a cell is updatable before executing an `UPDATE CUBE` statement by using the `UPDATABLE` cell property. For more information about how to use cell properties, see Chapter 11, "Advanced MDX." If you are writing a client application that performs either temporary or permanent writeback, you can add this property to the request and allow or disallow update capabilities to users of your application.

The value of the `UPDATABLE` cell property is a bitmask whose value is positive if a cell is updatable and negative if a cell cannot be updated. In addition to the success or failure information, the property value contains bits corresponding to the causes of the failure. You can find all possible values of this property in SQL Server Books Online.

Lifetime of the Update

As mentioned earlier, the main difference between permanent and temporary writeback is the persistence and availability of the changes. With permanent writeback, updates are stored on the server; with temporary writeback, changes are available only on the current session to the user that issued an update.

Typically, the `UPDATE CUBE` statement executes inside a transaction. A transaction starts by a `BEGIN TRANSACTION` statement, one or more `UPDATE CUBE` statements execute, and then either a `ROLLBACK TRANSACTION` statement executes to roll back and discard the changes or the `COMMIT TRANSACTION` statement executes to commit and store the changes on the server.

In addition to such explicit transactions initiated by a client request, Analysis Services supports implicit transactions. In other words, if you have not explicitly started a transaction by using a `BEGIN TRANSACTION` statement before sending an `UPDATE CUBE` statement, Analysis Services implicitly starts a transaction for you. The changes from an `UPDATE CUBE` statement called in an implicit transaction are available only on your session and aren't stored on the server unless you explicitly execute a `COMMIT TRANSACTION` statement to save your changes on the server. If you delete a session before committing the implicit transaction, Analysis Services automatically rolls back your changes.

Writeback data is permanently stored on Analysis Services in a special partition, called the *writeback partition*. This partition contains the delta values for each cell changed using an `UPDATE CUBE` statement. When you issue a `COMMIT TRANSACTION` statement, Analysis Services stores the delta values for updated cells in this partition.

When calculating the results of an MDX query, Analysis Services queries and aggregates the results from all relevant partitions to return cell values. Analysis Services treats the writeback partition as any other partition on the server, and when changes are made they automatically become effective and visible to all users for that cube. This architecture allows the server to answer any query immediately after a writeback is committed without the need to recalculate the cube or its aggregations.

Immediately after a permanent writeback has been committed to the server, it should become visible to all the users of the cube, including users who might have already used temporary writebacks. Therefore, before it can commit the transaction, Analysis Services needs to perform the operations shown in Figure 16.8:

1. Move delta values from the writeback cache into the writeback partition.
2. Delete the writeback cache on the session that committed the transaction.
3. Iterate over other sessions that have a writeback cache and recalculate the delta values for cells that are already in the cache by subtracting the delta value stored in the writeback partition from the delta value stored in the writeback caches of the other sessions.

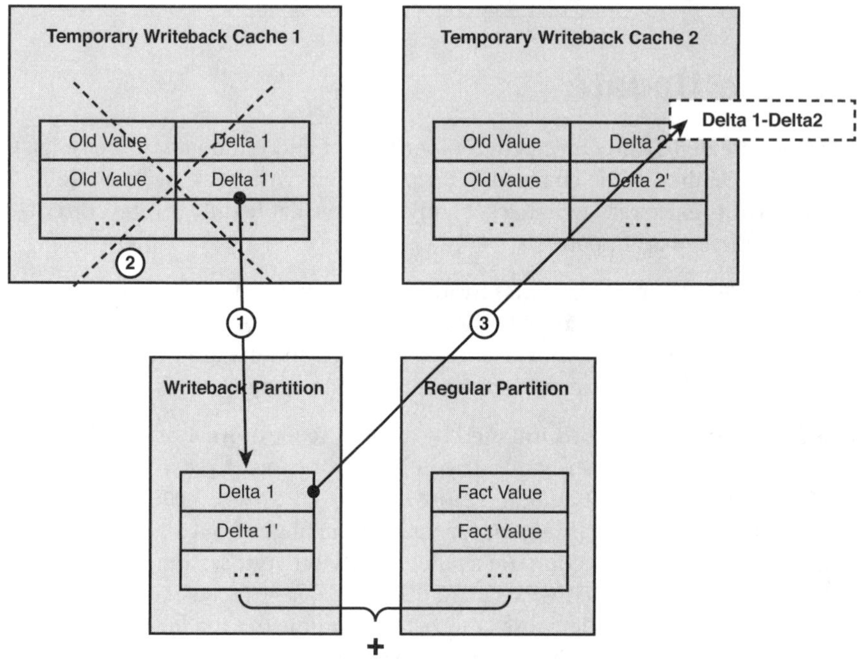

FIGURE 16.8 Operations that Analysis Services performs after the user commits an update.

If many clients perform temporary writebacks on a single cube and one of them commits changes to the server, it might take a considerable amount of time to conclude the operation because the server has to update the writeback caches of all other affected sessions. In addition, Analysis Services has to clean caches (discussed in Chapter 29, "Architecture of Query Execution—Calculating MDX Expressions") because the data stored there becomes invalid.

Analysis Services 2008 enables you to store writeback data in multidimensional online analytical processing (MOLAP) partitions in addition to relational online analytical processing (ROLAP) writeback partitions supported by earlier versions of Analysis Services. For more information about partition types, see Chapter 20, "Physical Data Model." In both cases, the writeback partition is based on a relational table, called a *writeback table*. During execution of the `COMMIT TRANSACTION` statement, Analysis Services stores the delta values for updated cells in this table. In case of the ROLAP writeback partition, Analysis Services doesn't need to perform additional operations during the commit stage. However, in case of the MOLAP writeback partition, in addition to storing data in the relational table, Analysis Services processes data from the writeback cache and writes it into MOLAP partition. (For more information about processing the MOLAP partition, see Chapter 21, "Dimension and Partition Processing.")

Because Analysis Services needs to process the MOLAP partition while executing the `COMMIT TRANSACTION` statement, it takes longer to commit transactions to the MOLAP writeback partition. However, storing writeback data in the MOLAP partition rather than the ROLAP partition improves performance of queries that use writeback data, because reading data from MOLAP partitions is much more efficient than reading data from the ROLAP partition. In addition to this obvious optimization, storing writeback data in MOLAP partition improves performance of the `UPDATE CUBE` statement. During execution of each `UPDATE CUBE` statement, Analysis Services retrieves delta values stored in the writeback partition and uses those values to calculate new deltas. Therefore, keeping writeback data in MOLAP partition speeds up process of reading the data from the writeback partition and results in faster execution of the `UPDATE CUBE` operation.

Enabling Writeback

For writeback operations to succeed, you must enable writeback capabilities on the measure group to which you are writing the data. To enable writeback, you have to perform the following steps in BI Dev Studio:

1. In BI Dev Studio, open the FoodMart 2008 project.
2. In the Solution Explorer, double-click the `Warehouse and Sales` cube to open the cube editor.
3. On the Partitions tab, expand the list of partitions for the measure group you are writing to (in this example, we write into the `Warehouse` measure group), right-click anywhere in the Partition Organizer, and then choose Writeback Settings from the contextual menu, as shown in Figure 16.9.

4. In the Enable Writeback - Warehouse dialog, choose the data source and name of the writeback table Analysis Services should use to store delta values.
5. Choose the storage mode for the writeback partition as either ROLAP or MOLAP, and then click OK.
6. When you process the affected measure group, Analysis Services connects to the specified data source, creates the writeback table, and defines the partition that contains writeback values.

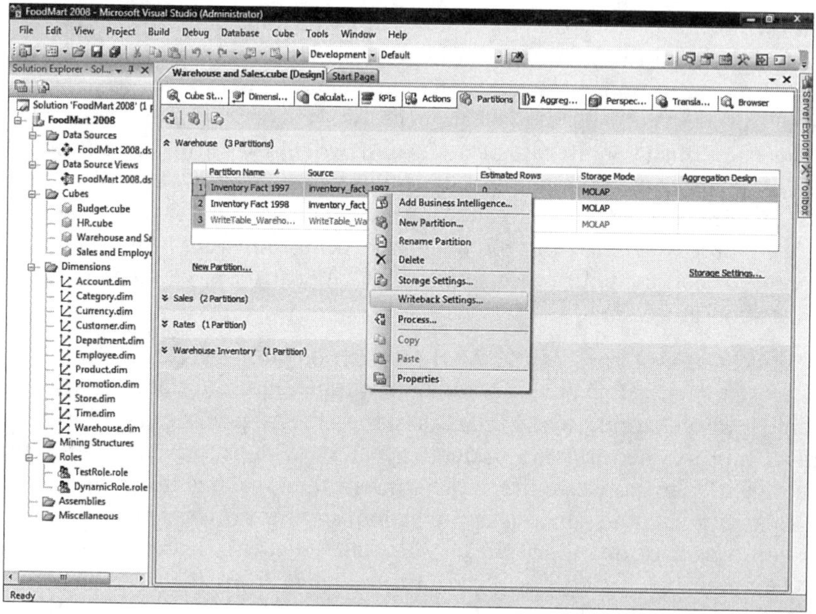

FIGURE 16.9 To enable a writeback, right-click the Partition Organizer and choose Writeback Settings.

In addition to the columns that contain the delta values of updated values and the identifiers of updated members, the writeback table contains two columns, `MS_AUDIT_TIME` and `MS_AUDIT_USER`, which enable you to audit any changes committed to the cube. You can query the values of these columns and find out which user updated the cell values.

NOTE

Analysis Services doesn't allow you to create a writeback partition in a measure group that contains at least one measure with an aggregate function other than `SUM`.

You can also delete a writeback partition and disable permanent writeback functionality on a measure group by completing the following steps in BI Dev Studio:

1. In BI Dev Studio, open the FoodMart 2008 project.
2. In the Solution Explorer, double-click the `Warehouse and Sales` cube to open the cube editor.
3. On the Partitions tab, expand the list of partitions for the measure group you are writing to (in this example, we write into the `Warehouse` measure group), right-click anywhere in the Partition Organizer, and then choose Writeback Settings from the contextual menu.
4. In the Disable Writeback - Write Table_Warehouse dialog, click OK; writeback data will become inaccessible.

You can also use SQL Server Management Studio to enable and disable permanent writeback on your measure group.

NOTE

Even if permanent writeback functionality is disabled, you can still perform temporary writeback operations.

Converting a Writeback Partition to a Regular Partition

After changes done by an `UPDATE CUBE` statement are committed to the writeback partition, if it is absolutely necessary, you can edit the relational table that contains writeback data, removing records or changes made at a certain time. When you are sure that you want to keep the changes stored in a writeback partition permanently, you can convert the writeback partition to a regular partition using SQL Server Management Studio as follows:

1. Connect to the FoodMart 2008 database.
2. In the Object Explorer, drill down to the `Warehouse and Sales` cube, the `Warehouse` measure group, and right-click the writeback partition.
3. Choose Convert to Partition from the resulting menu.
4. In the Convert to Partition for Measure Group Warehouse dialog, enter the new name of the partition, choose to process a partition, and click OK.

This partition then becomes a regular partition, and writeback is disabled. As a result, you'll have to perform the preceding steps again to enable writeback to the server.

Other Ways to Perform Writeback

In addition to the `UPDATE CUBE` statement discussed earlier in this chapter, you can use the `IRowsetChange` OLE DB interface to provide writeback capabilities. Using an OLE DB provider to update cell values is not a new functionality. This method of updating cell data in the cube has been available in all versions of Analysis Services and documented in the OLE DB for OLAP specification. Because it's a well-documented and established method for updating cell data, we won't spend too much time discussing it here.

If you write your application in native code using Visual Basic or another language that supports OLE automation, you might use ADO MD to update the cube through a `CellSet object`. The `CellSet` object in ADO MD enables you to not only read cell data but also write it. ADO MD has also been available for a while and is also well documented.

Unfortunately, the `CellSet` object included with ADOMD.NET object model doesn't provide the capability to write cell data. However, you can execute `UPDATE CUBE` statements to update cell values.

PART IV

Creating a Data Warehouse

IN THIS PART

CHAPTER 17

Loading Data from a Relational Database

IN THIS CHAPTER

When you have defined all your dimensions and measure groups, you are ready to populate your model with data. In this chapter, we discuss how Analysis Services loads data from a relational database; in other words, how it determines where data for a multidimensional object comes from. We also examine how Analysis Services accesses relational databases.

Loading Data

Analysis Services loads data into its multidimensional stores by issuing SQL queries to relational databases and processing the response. To determine where relational data is located and which flavor of the SQL language to use, Analysis Services uses three types of objects: `DataSource`, `DataSourceView`, and `Binding`:

- `DataSource` objects define the physical location of relational data. Typically, the object contains a connection string that Analysis Services uses to establish a connection to the relational database.
- `DataSourceView` objects define the logical layout of the relational tables and columns used to populate the multidimensional data model. The object defines data types of the columns, and enables you to specify additional joins between tables.
- `Binding` objects define which tables or columns defined in `DataSourceView` or directly in relational database Analysis Services should use to populate multidimensional object.

Figure 17.1 shows how Analysis Services uses those objects to populate a partition with data. Analysis Services locates a partition `Binding` object associated with the partition to find out which relational table contains the data, and then it iterates over every measure and granularity attribute in the measure group to find information about which relational columns it needs.

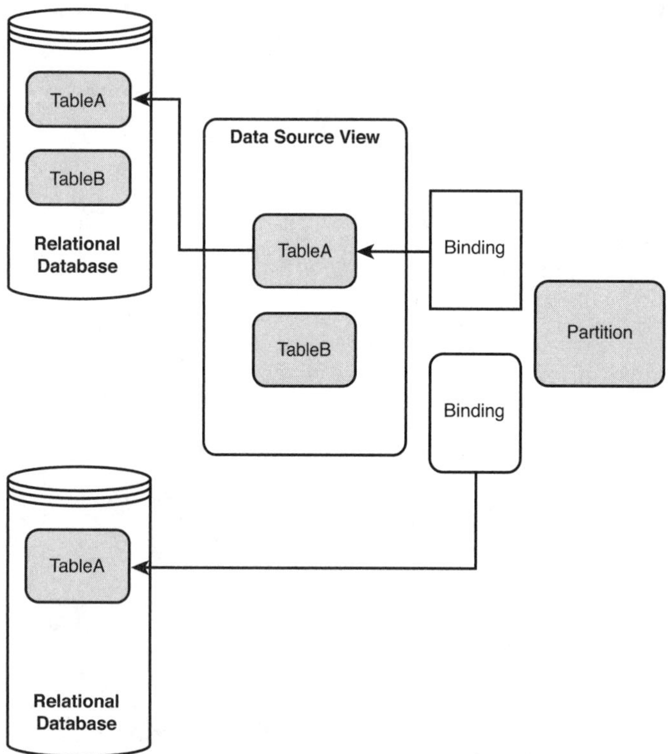

FIGURE 17.1 Binding between multidimensional objects and source of data.

Typically, a binding does not reference relational tables directly. Analysis Services provides a layer of abstraction between the multidimensional object and the relational database—the *Data Source View* (DSV).

The bindings for the partition reference a table object in the DSV, which in turn maps to a table, view, or query in Microsoft SQL Server (or other supported relational engine). After Analysis Services determines what data it needs for the processing operation, it builds an abstract query that lists all the tables and columns of the relational database.

Analysis Services builds the abstract internal query by using an abstract internal Extensible Markup Language (XML) definition. It then translates the query to one with semantics specific to the data source. (For example, a query for SQL Server needs different quote identifiers than a query intended for an Oracle database.) Figure 17.2 diagrams this process.

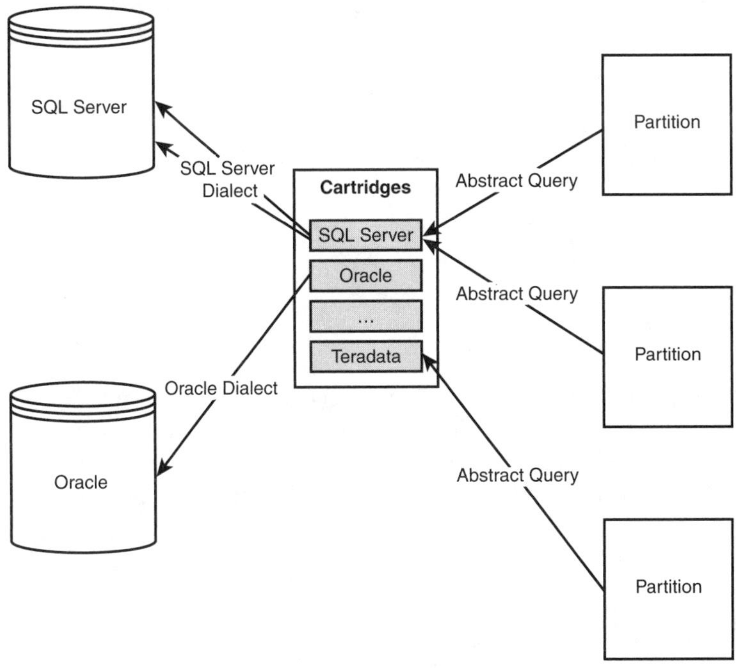

FIGURE 17.2 The internal query is translated to a query with provider-specific semantics.

In Figure 17.2, you can see the process of transforming the abstract query to one that the data source can read. Analysis Services uses XML to build the internal query based on the partition's binding and the DSV. To transform the query to the SQL format, Analysis Services uses an XSL (Extensible Stylesheet Language) transformation (cartridge). The specific cartridges are stored as files in the `cartridges` folder located in the installation directory, under the `bin` folder. If you look in that folder, you will find a file named `sql70.xsl`. That is the cartridge used to transform an abstract internal XML query into a query in syntax of SQL Server 7.0.

NOTE

If you are using an OLE DB or .NET provider that is not on the list of the supported providers, Analysis Services will try to use the `sql2000.xsl` cartridge. A query to an unknown provider issues in the SQL Server 2000 format.

After all this, Analysis Services passes the query to the specific client library responsible for establishing a connection to the external database. Such a library, for example, could be the OLE DB provider for SQL Server or the Oracle OLE DB provider. The `DataSource` object keeps the information that specifies which client library to use and the connection string properties for establishing a connection.

Analysis Services 2008 supports reading data from the following:

- SQL Server 7.0, 2000, 2005, 2008
- Microsoft Access
- Oracle
- Teradata
- DB2
- Sybase
- Informix

Analysis Services supports OLE DB providers and .NET managed providers. If you create a data source object in Business Intelligence Development Studio (BI Dev Studio; discussed in Chapter 9, "Multidimensional Models and Business Intelligence Development Studio"), you can select the appropriate provider in the Connection Manager dialog box of the Data Source editor.

Data Source Objects

A *data source object* is the Analysis Services object that defines where the data comes from. It defines which client library is loaded, and it defines the connection string for establishing the connection. It also defines the credentials for establishing the connection. In short, the data source object defines all the things necessary for establishing a connection to a source of data.

`DataSource` is a major object; it has `ID` and `Name` properties. You can create and edit the `DataSource` object independently from other objects. The most important information defined by the `DataSource` object is `ConnectionString`. It defines properties that the client library (OLEDB or ADO.NET provider) uses to establish a connection to the source of data. The `ConnectionString` property defines the name of the provider (the client library used to establish the connection), the name of the server that contains the database, the name of the database, and others.

Data Source Object Properties

Table 17.1 describes the properties of a data source object.

Listing 17.1 shows sample DDL (Data Definition Language) for a data source object that establishes a connection to a local SQL Server located on the local computer, using FoodMart 2008 as the database.

TABLE 17.1 **DataSource** Properties

Name	Description
ConnectionString	The connection string to be passed to the client library. The value of the Provider property of the connection string specifies the name of the provider. The specification of the OLE DB or managed provider defines the remaining connection string properties.
ManagedProvider	The name of the .NET managed provider used to establish the connection. Analysis Services 2008 supports only SQL Server (System.Data.SqlClient) and Oracle (System.Data.OracleClient) providers.
Timeout	The time after which the attempt to establish a connection will be aborted. If the timeout defined in the server configuration property DatabaseConnectionPoolConnectTimeout is smaller than the timeout defined in the DataSource object, the timeout defined in the server configuration will be used. If the value of the Timeout property is 0 (default value), or not defined, Analysis Services uses the value of the DatabaseConnectionPoolConnectTimeout property.
MaxActiveConnections	The maximum number of active connections that can be established to a current data source. The default value is 10. If Analysis Services needs to create more connections, additional requests will wait for existing connections to complete their work. This property is provided to prevent Analysis Services from generating huge simultaneous load on a relational database, which can cause performance degradation during data load. Use a negative value to specify that there is no limit to the number of connections.
Isolation	The locking mode used when establishing a connection to the relational database. The default value for this property is ReadCommitted. If you specify Snapshot, you can achieve higher transaction concurrency in a relational database, but you pay a price in performance. To decide on the best value for the Isolation property, it is best to check the documentation for the relational database.

LISTING 17.1 DDL That Defines a Data Source Object

```
<DataSource>
    <ID>FoodMart2008</ID>
    <Name>FoodMart 2008</Name>
    <ConnectionString>Provider= SQLNCLI.1; Data Source=localhost; Integrated
    Security=SSPI; Initial Catalog=FoodMart2008</ConnectionString>
</DataSource>
```

Data Source Security

When Analysis Services establishes a connection to external data sources, it is important to control the user account under which it establishes this connection. Establishing connections in Analysis Services 2000 is always under Analysis Services account credentials. There are pros and cons to this approach. It's easy for a database administrator to set the security settings of a relational database—permission is required for only a single account. However, this approach lacks flexibility. Establishing all connections under one account means that a single account must have access to all data across all databases.

Starting from Analysis Services 2005, a database administrator can configure different credentials under which connections to different relational databases are established. You use the `ImpersonationInfo` object (which is part of the data source object) to define those credentials. The properties of the `ImpersonationInfo` object define the credentials that Analysis Services uses to establish a connection. Listing 17.2 is the DDL for an `ImpersonationInfo` object in a data source.

LISTING 17.2 DDL That Defines an **`ImpersonationInfo`** Object

```
<ImpersonationInfo>
    <ImpersonationMode>ImpersonateAccount</ImpersonationMode>
    <Account>MyUser</Account>
    <Password>AAAAAA</Password>
</ImpersonationInfo>
```

Table 17.2 describes the properties of the `ImpersonationInfo` object.

TABLE 17.2 **ImpersonationInfo** Properties

Name	Description
ImpersonationMode	Defines the way the data source is impersonated. Values for the ImpersonationMode property include the following: ▶ **Default**—The ImpersonationMode property inherits its value from the DataSourceImpersonationInfo object of the database parent object. If the ImpersonationMode property for the database is also set to Default, the established connection will be under the service account credentials. ▶ **ImpersonateAccount**—Specifies that the connection will be established with the credentials specified in the Account and Password properties of the ImpersonationInfo object. ▶ **ImpersonateCurrentUser**—Specifies the use of the credentials of the current user; used only to run data mining queries. ▶ **ImpersonateServiceAccount**—Establishes the connection with the credentials of the account under which the Analysis Services server started.
Account	Defines the name of the user account to use for impersonation.
Password	Defines the password for the account specified in the Account property.

The DataSourceImpersonationInfo property of a Database object has exactly the same structure as the ImpersonationInfo object. Its only purpose is to serve as a default for data sources with ImpersonationMode set to Default. If the database administrator needs to have the same security settings for all the data sources defined within a database, he can use the DataSourceImpersonationInfo property of the database.

Additional Security Considerations

Up to now, we have been looking at the ways that enable you to define how Analysis Services impersonates the account under which it establishes a connection to a relational database. Those account credentials are important only if the relational database is set up to use Windows authentication. That is the recommended way to set up SQL Server databases.

In many cases, however, the relational database is set up so that the connection credentials provided are simply the Username and Password properties of the connection string. Then the account used for connection impersonation needs only minimal privileges. Therefore, you might consider running Analysis Services under a low-privileged account that is local to the computer involved.

Storing Private Information

Analysis Services developers realize that parts of the data source object, such as the Password and ConnectionString properties, are likely to contain information that is sensitive and private. Storing such information in clear text in memory and on the disk in the metadata files can be a security risk.

To store sensitive information safely and securely, Analysis Services encrypts the `Password` and `ConnectionString` properties. Analysis Services will not return the `Password` of the data source object to the user. When you script a data source object in SQL Server Management Studio, you discover that Analysis Services does not return the `Password` property. The same applies to the `Password` property of the `ConnectionString` property. Analysis Services always tries to parse the value of the `ConnectionString` property and strip any password from it. BI Dev Studio stores the DDL for data sources in `.ds` files in the project folder, but it does not store passwords in those files. If you look in a `.ds` file, you will see the `ImpersonationInfoSecurity` property in place of the password:

```
<ImpersonationInfoSecurity>PasswordRemoved</ImpersonationInfoSecurity>
```

That property indicates that BI Dev Studio removed the password when it saved the project files. Therefore, when you open such projects in BI Dev Studio and deploy the database to the server, BI Dev Studio might prompt you for a password.

Connection Timeouts

Data source definitions include the capability to define a *timeout*—the amount of time that the server waits for an activity to occur in response to some sort of request. Two types of timeout are associated with connections to external data sources: connection timeouts and request timeouts.

A *connection timeout* is the amount of time that Analysis Services waits for the establishment of a successful connection before it reports an error. For example, when you request a connection to a SQL Server relational database, how long should you expect to wait for Analysis Services to indicate that the database is not available at this time?

The Analysis Services `DatabaseConnectionPoolConnectTimeout` property defines the length of the connection timeout. It is set to 60 seconds by default. You can use the connection string's `ConnectTimeout` property to set it to a lesser value for a particular data source.

The `ExternalCommandTimeout` server configuration property determines the length of the query timeout. It is set to 3,600 seconds (1 hour) by default. To set it to a lesser value, specify that value for the `Timeout` property on your data source object.

Connection Pooling

Analysis Services does not create a connection object every time it has to connect to the same relational database. It keeps existing connection objects in a pool and tries to find a matching connection every time there is a new request for a connection. (See Figure 17.3 for an illustration of this practice.) Requests for data might come frequently. Creating a connection is quite expensive from a performance point of view, and doing so might take a toll on the overall performance of the system.

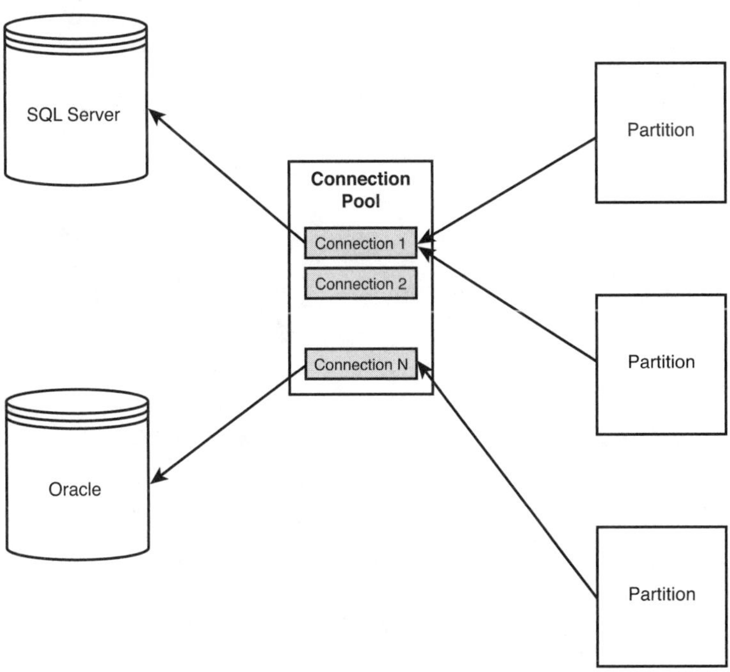

FIGURE 17.3 Connection pooling.

The `DatabaseConnectionPoolMax` server property determines the number of connections kept in the connection pool by Analysis Services. The default value is `50`.

CHAPTER 18

DSVs and Object Bindings

IN THIS CHAPTER

- DSV Objects
- Object Bindings

To populate a multidimensional object with data, you have to specify the way the object maps to the relational schema. For example, to populate a dimensional attribute with data, you must define how the dimension member's names and keys map to columns in the relational database table. You start the mapping by defining a *Data Source View* (DSV)—the Analysis Services object that defines a layer of abstraction on top of the relational database.

DSV Objects

In Analysis Services 2000, you don't have an abstraction layer; that is, no specific object provides a view of the relational database schema. And you might think that you should be able to look directly at relational objects without a layer of abstraction. However, as designers worked on several releases of the multidimensional database, they realized that defining multidimensional objects on top of a relational database requires an abstraction layer. A relational data warehouse schema can get complicated, and its structure can get messy. Multidimensional databases, on the other hand, require pretty clean structures. Hence the need for a layer of abstraction, for a DSV that defines a view to the relational database schema.

To illustrate how problematic it can be to deal directly with a relational schema, let's take as our example a user who, while she designs a cube, realizes that no relationship between a fact and a dimension table is defined in the relational database. She would have to go back to the relational database and create that relationship. Perhaps she would later try to create a dimensional attribute and realize that she has to create a username from two columns in the relational database: First Name and Last Name. She would have to go back to the relational database design tools again. In fact, she might have to go back again and again if she needs to create new views, new calculated columns, and so on. The relational database schema would require many tweaks before she could get it mapped into a structure of attributes and measures in a cube.

Nothing much is more tedious to an application designer than the iterative nature of a process like going back and forth between relational schema design tools and multidimensional object design tools. To make matters worse, sometimes the person designing the cube in Analysis Services has no access to the relational database so that he can make the necessary tweaks.

If you're not yet convinced that you'll need the abstraction later, think about the problem of change management. Let's say that you used Analysis Services to build a cube. It has been deployed and working for a while. Now you want to point your cube to another version of the relational database, perhaps because someone created a new version that contains more data. But, the relational schema has been changed slightly. Now the cube can't process simply because a table or a column name has changed. If your dimensions have hundreds of attributes, a scenario such as this could be a nightmare.

You can use a DSV object to deal with all these problems. A DSV enables you to create a view of a relational database schema inside a multidimensional model. You can create tables, columns, relationships, calculated columns, and named queries that map to the real tables and columns in your relational database. In Business Intelligence Development Studio (BI Dev Studio), a DSV looks just like a relational schema, with tables, columns, and relationships. Listing 18.1 is an example of a DSV.

LISTING 18.1 The Definition of a **Foodmart2008** Data Source View

```
<DataSourceView>
  <ID>Foodmart2008</ID>
  <Name>Foodmart2008</Name>
  <Annotations>
  </Annotations>
    <xs:schema id="Foodmart2008 ....
      <xs:element name="Foodmart2008
       <xs:complexType>
          <xs:choice minOccurs="0" maxOccurs="unbounded">
            <xs:element name="dbo_currency"
              <xs:complexType>
                <xs:sequence>
                  <xs:element name="currency_id"msprop:FriendlyName="currency_id"
➥msprop:DbColumnName="currency_id" msprop:design-time-name="a6b6df3d-0cd1-443e-
➥942c-13c765410175" type="xs:int" minOccurs="0" />
```

```
                <xs:element name="date" msprop:FriendlyName="date"
➥msprop:DbColumnName="date" msprop:design-time-name="2b44ca8c-b80e-480f-a173-
➥5a0490542908" type="xs:dateTime" minOccurs="0" />
                <xs:element name="currency" msprop:FriendlyName="currency"
➥msprop:DbColumnName="currency" msprop:design-time-name="e48ef4a5-7feb-4fbc-9023-
➥5b0da75ab054" minOccurs="0">
                  <xs:simpleType>
                    <xs:restriction base="xs:string">
                      <xs:maxLength value="15" />
                    </xs:restriction>
                  </xs:simpleType>
....
....
</DataSourceView>
```

In the sample DSV, the Data Definition Language (DDL) contains a single table, `dbo_currency`, with three columns: `currency_id`, `date`, and `currency`. The data type for `currency_id` is `int`; for `date`, the data type is `dateTime`; and for `currency`, it is `string` with a length of 15.

The DDL definition of a DSV built with BI Dev Studio usually contains a big Annotations section. The Extensible Markup Language (XML) in the Annotations section of a DSV is used by BI Dev Studio to draw the DSV on the design surface of its DSV editor.

DDL uses a `DataSet` object provided by ADO.NET to store the DSV with its tables, columns, and their relationships. Even the DDL for a DSV with just a single table and single column is quite large. With tens of tables and hundreds of columns, a DSV object can grow really big, really fast. We recommend BI Dev Studio for designing and updating your DSV. As an alternative, you can write a simple application using Analysis Management Objects (AMO; see Chapter 34, "Analysis Management Objects") and ADO.NET to load the DSV schema into a `DataSet` object and then operate with a collection of `DataTable` objects.

NOTE

You'll find a very useful Refresh menu item on the contextual menu of the DSV design surface. Refresh enables you to keep your DSV current with the relational database. The DSV editor detects tables that exist in the DSV but are missing from the relational database. You can review the list of tables and columns that have changed in the relational database before they are removed from the DSV.

Named Queries and Named Calculations

To extend DSV functionality, you can create *named queries*—objects that are similar to views in a relational database. While processing data, Analysis Services uses named queries the same way it uses regular tables in a DSV, but under the hood named queries are built on top of the result of an SQL query, in much the same way that views in a relational database are defined.

A *named calculation* enables you to define a column in a DSV table that is the result of a calculation or expression based on other columns in the same table. Named calculations and named queries give you greater flexibility and help to solve the problems involved in mapping relational tables to multidimensional objects.

Listing 18.2 shows a portion of a DSV containing a named calculation that sets `Count` to `1` for every row in the table. The named calculation is added to the DSV fragment containing the `dbo_currency` table shown in Listing 18.1.

LISTING 18.2 A Named Calculation in a DSV

```
<xs:schema id="Foodmart2008 ....
    <xs:element name="Foodmart2008
    <xs:complexType>
        <xs:choice minOccurs="0" maxOccurs="unbounded">
        <xs:element name="dbo_currency"
            <xs:complexType>
                <xs:sequence>
                    <xs:element name="currency_id" msprop:FriendlyName=
➥"currency_id" msprop:DbColumnName="currency_id" msprop:design-time-name="a6b6df3d-
➥0cd1-443e-942c-13c765410175" type="xs:int" minOccurs="0" />
                   <xs:element name="date" msprop:FriendlyName="date"
➥msprop:DbColumnName="date" msprop:design-time-name="2b44ca8c-b80e-480f-a173-
➥5a0490542908" type="xs:dateTime" minOccurs="0" />
                    <xs:element name="currency" msprop:FriendlyName="currency"
➥msprop:DbColumnName="currency" msprop:design-time-name="e48ef4a5-7feb-4fbc-9023-
➥5b0da75ab054" minOccurs="0">
                   <xs:simpleType>
                       <xs:restriction base="xs:string">
                           <xs:maxLength value="15" />
                       </xs:restriction>
                   </xs:simpleType>
                <xs:element name="Count" msdata:ReadOnly="true" msprop:design-
➥time-name="444d9cec-9df3-4186-9c6a-01697e361075" msprop:DbColumnName="Count"
➥msprop:ComputedColumnExpression="1" msprop:Description="" msprop:IsLogical="True"
➥type="xs:int" />
. . .
```

Named calculations and named queries are powerful features. They provide the ability to load data into multidimensional objects that does not exist in the relational tables. For example, instead of creating a calculated measure, you can create a named calculation and build a real measure using it. With these approach, data is stored within a multidimensional model and is not calculated during query execution, you improve performance of the system by building aggregations using this measure, and so on. However, size of the cube will grow, too, because named calculation is executed only one time—during the processing—and results are stored in a cube.

Object Bindings

To populate dimensions and cubes with data, you need to map them to relational data source or its view—DSV. You can map multidimensional objects to relational objects with *binding objects*; for example, a binding to a column is specified in a `ColumnBinding` object.

When you create a partition object, you don't have to specify a column for every measure. All you have to do is specify the table on which the partition is based. When you create a partition, you specify `TableBindings`.

Analysis Services supports several types of bindings, the most frequently used types are as follows:

- **`ColumnBinding`**—Allows a multidimensional object to be bound to a single column of a table
- **`RowBinding`**—Allows a multidimensional object to be bound to a row in a table
- **`DsvTableBinding` and `TableBinding`**—Allow a multidimensional object to be mapped to a table in DSV or in a relational datasource
- **`QueryBinding`**—Allows a multidimensional object to be mapped to a SQL query that will return a result in a tabular format

Column Bindings

`ColumnBinding` enables you to map columns of the relational table to the dimension attributes, granularity attributes of partitions, and measures of a multidimensional model. Figure 18.1 shows a diagram of attribute and measure binding to the DSV tables.

In Figure 18.1, the member `Name` column and member `Key` column of `Customer` attribute are bound to the columns in the `Customer` DSV table, and the `Sales` measure is bound to the `StoreSales` column of the `Sales fact` table.

Listing 18.3 shows how to specify a binding to a column in the DDL definition of an object.

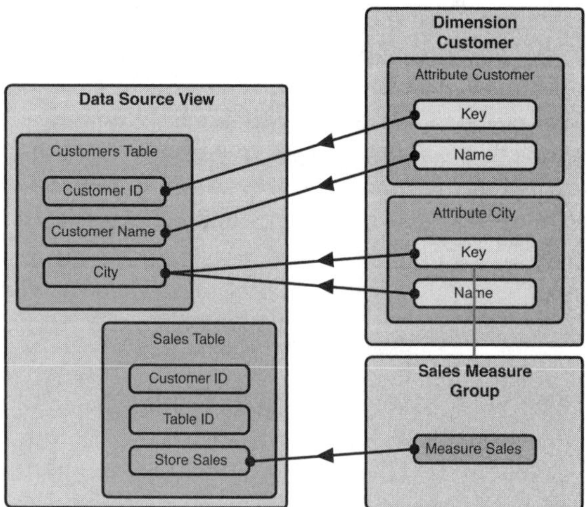

FIGURE 18.1 Multidimensional objects are bound to DSV columns and tables.

LISTING 18.3 An Attribute Key Column Binding

```
<Attribute>
     <AttributeID>Customer</AttributeID>
         <KeyColumns>
             <KeyColumn>
                  <DataType>Integer</DataType>
                  <Source xsi:type="ColumnBinding>
                       <TableID>dbo_customer</TableID>
                       <ColumnID>customer_id</ColumnID>
                  </Source>
             </KeyColumn>
         </KeyColumns>
     <Type>Granularity</Type>
</Attribute>
```

The `<Source>` element defines the binding object: It binds the multidimensional object to the relational one. In the listing, you can see in the `<Source>` element that a `<TableID>` element points to the DSV table, and the `<ColumnID>` element points to a column in that table.

In Listing 18.4, you can see that a measure binding is defined in the same way as an attribute binding.

LISTING 18.4 The DDL That Defines a Measure Binding

```
<Measure>
  <Name>Store Sales</Name>
  <ID>Store Sales</ID>
  <Description />
```

```
  <AggregateFunction>Sum</AggregateFunction>
  <DataType>Double</DataType>
  <Visible>true</Visible>
  <Source>
    <DataType>Double</DataType>
    <DataSize>0</DataSize>
    <NullProcessing>Automatic</NullProcessing>
    <Collation />
    <Format />
    <Source xsi:type="ColumnBinding">
      <TableID>dbo_sales_fact_1997</TableID>
      <ColumnID>store_sales</ColumnID>
    </Source>
  </Source>
  <Translations/>
</Measure>
```

In the listing, the measure is based on the `store_sales` column in the `dbl_sales_fact_1997` DSV table.

Row Bindings

`RowBinding` enables you to map rows of the relational table to objects of the multidimensional model. Typically, you use row binding to map relational table with measures that have the aggregation function `COUNT`. To calculate values of such measures, Analysis Services doesn't need to perform `SUM` (or other calculation) on the field values stored in the relational table; it just needs to calculate the number of records. For example, to calculate the value of the `Sales Count` measure for the year 1997, Analysis Services has to add the number of records corresponding to months of that year.

Listing 18.5 shows how to specify a binding to rows in the DDL definition of an object.

LISTING 18.5 Row Binding

```
<Measure>
  <Name>Sales Count</Name>
  <ID>Sales Count</ID>
  <Description />
  <AggregateFunction>Count</AggregateFunction>
  <DataType>Integer</DataType>
  <Visible>true</Visible>
  <Source>
    <DataType>Integer</DataType>
    <DataSize>4</DataSize>
    <NullProcessing>Automatic</NullProcessing>
    <Collation />
    <Format />
    <Source xsi:type="RowBinding">
      <TableID>dbo_sales_fact_1997</TableID>
```

```
    </Source>
  </Source>
  <Translations/>
</Measure>
```

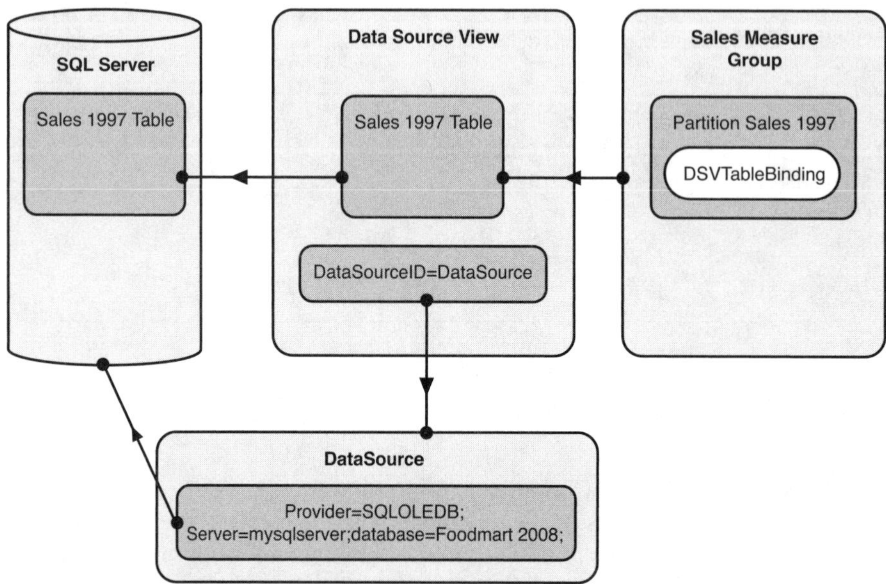

FIGURE 18.2 The partition is bound to a relational table through a DSV table.

Tabular Bindings

Tabular binding defines the mapping between a multidimensional object and a relational table. Typically, you use tabular bindings to map a partition to a relational source of data. Analysis Services supports two types of tabular bindings: `DsvTableBinding` maps an object to a DSV table, and `TableBinding` maps a multidimensional object directly to a table in the relational database.

`DsvTableBinding` has two properties: `DataSourceViewID` and `TableID`, which allow Analysis Services to map partition to a table. Figure 18.2 shows how Analysis Services can locate a relational table (source of data to be loaded into the partition).

Analysis Services uses `DsvTableBinding` associated with a partition. Using the `DataSourceViewID` property, Analysis Services locates the corresponding `DataSourceView` object; and using a `TableID` property, it finds the corresponding DSV table. Then, the table is used to determine columns and joins for SQL query generation. Because each DSV (or even each table in a DSV) has a `DataSource` associated with it, Analysis Services uses the `DataSourceID` property to find the corresponding `DataSource` object and uses it to establish a connection to the relational source of data.

Listing 18.6 shows the DDL definition of binding a partition to a DSV table.

LISTING 18.6 **DSVTableBinding**

```
<Partition>
    <ID>Sales Fact 1997</ID>
    <Name>Sales Fact 1997</Name>
    <State>Unprocessed</State>
    <Source xsi:type="DsvTableBinding">
      <DataSourceViewID>FoodMart 2008</DataSourceViewID>
      <TableID>dbo_sales_fact_1997</TableID>
    </Source>
    <StorageMode>Molap</StorageMode>
    <CurrentStorageMode>Molap</CurrentStorageMode>
    <ProcessingMode>Regular</ProcessingMode>
</Partition>
```

All partitions in a measure group have the same structure: Their structure is defined by granularity attributes and measures in the measure group. When a measure group has many partitions, it becomes impractical to create a table in DSV for each partition. In addition to the `DSVTableBinding`, Analysis Services supports `TableBinding`, which allows mapping of a multidimensional object, such as partition, to a relational table. `TableBinding` supports the following properties: `DataSourceID`, `DbTableName`, and `DbSchemaName`. Figure 18.3 shows the way Analysis Services uses `TableBinding` to load data from a relational engine into a partition.

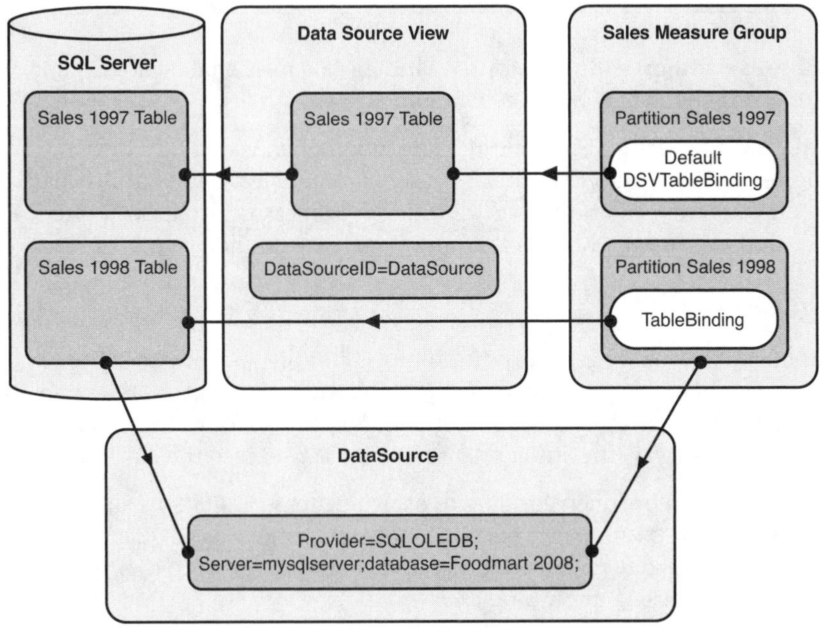

FIGURE 18.3 Partition is bound to relational table.

18

Analysis Services uses a `TableBinding` associated with a partition and a default `DSVTableBinding` associated with a measure group. Using the `DSVTableBinding` property, Analysis Services locates the corresponding `DataSourceView` object and DSV table to determine columns and joins for SQL query generation. Using `TableBinding`, Analysis Services determines the `DataSource` object and name of the actual relational table. It then uses the `DataSource` object to establish a connection to the relational database and `DbTableName` property to construct a `FROM` clause of SQL query to bring data from relational database. Listing 18.7 shows an example of binding to a relational table in the DDL definition of a partition.

LISTING 18.7 A DDL Partition Definition with Table Binding

```
<Partition>
    <ID>Sales Fact 1998</ID>
    <Name>Sales Fact 1998</Name>
    <State>Unprocessed</State>
    <Source xsi:type="TableBinding">
      <DataSourceID>FoodMart 2008</DataSourceID >
      <DbTableName>sales_fact_1998</DbTableName>
      <DbSchemaName>dbo</DbSchemaName>
    </Source>
    <StorageMode>Molap</StorageMode>
    <CurrentStorageMode>Molap</CurrentStorageMode>
    <ProcessingMode>Regular</ProcessingMode>
</Partition>
```

In this listing, you see a partition definition with a binding to a relational database table that you connect to using the FoodMart 2008 data source.

In Analysis Services, the first partition in your measure group often uses a DSV binding because you would use BI Dev Studio to create a measure group object and your first partition. However, when you create additional partitions for your measure group, you often use a table binding so that you can keep the DSV clean and easy to understand.

Query Bindings

Table binding, although it allows for a level of flexibility, is still pretty restrictive. The problem is that the relational table must have the same column names as the DSV table used to define measures in the measure group. Furthermore, you cannot restrict data coming from the table in any way; the entire relational table is read into the partition.

With Analysis Services, you can use query binding to overcome these limitations and provide for ultimate flexibility. *Query binding* enables you to specify an exact SQL query for your partition to use to retrieve data from a relational database. Listing 18.8 shows an example of a partition defined using query binding.

LISTING 18.8 A Partition Defined with Query Binding

```
<Partition>
    <ID>sales_fact_dec_1998</ID>
    <Name>sales_fact_dec_1998</Name>
    <State>Unprocessed</State>
    <Source xsi:type="QueryBinding">
        <DataSourceID>FoodMart 2008</DataSourceID >
        <QueryDefinition>
             SELECT
             [dbo].[sales_fact_dec_1998].[product_id],
             [dbo].[sales_fact_dec_1998].[time_id],
             [dbo].[sales_fact_dec_1998].[customer_id],
             [dbo].[sales_fact_dec_1998].[promotion_id],
             [dbo].sales_fact_dec_1998].[store_id],
             [dbo].[sales_fact_dec_1998].[store_sales],
             [dbo].[sales_fact_dec_1998].[store_cost],
             [dbo].[sales_fact_dec_1998].[unit_sales]
            FROM [dbo].[sales_fact_dec_1998]
            WHERE [dbo].[sales_fact_dec_1998].[time_id]=373</QueryDefinition>
    </Source>
</Partition>
```

In this example, you can see that the partition is defined on top of a SQL query that pulls data from the `sales_fact_dec_1998` table. You can modify the `WHERE` condition to restrict the data for your partition to a specific range of rows.

NOTE

During data processing, Analysis Services enables you to specify additional data binding information—out-of-line bindings. You can provide `DataSource`, `DataSourceView`, or `Binding` objects as part of the `Process` or `Batch` commands. (For more information about the commands, see Chapter 26, "Server Architecture and Command Execution.") Out-of-line bindings override bindings specified as part of the metadata and apply only while Analysis Services executes the command.

CHAPTER 19

Multidimensional Models and Relational Database Schemas

IN THIS CHAPTER

- Relational Schemas for Data Warehouses
- Building Relational Schemas from the Multidimensional Model

The design of relational database schemas of online transaction processing (OLTP) systems sustains multiple updates to the system. Tables, columns, and indexes perform the update operations with maximum efficiency. On the other hand, the report function of data warehouses and multidimensional models benefits from different schema types.

Although Analysis Services provides powerful tools (bindings, Data Source Views [DSV], and so on) for dealing with almost any possible relational schema, building multidimensional models on top of the very complex relational schemas common to OLTP systems is usually not a good solution for reporting purposes. The schemas tend to be extremely complex because, in many cases, they contain modifications to adjust for requirements not taken into account at the time of the original schema's design. OLTP systems are often plagued with data inconsistencies that have to be resolved before data is ready to be loaded into a multidimensional model. Also, indexes of OLTP systems are typically optimized for fast update and concurrent access, whereas loading data into multidimensional models requires indexes of a different type.

Relational Schemas for Data Warehouses

Star and snowflake schemas are the most commonly used relational schemas in data warehouses. A star schema joins a single table that contains facts to the dimension tables through foreign key–primary key relationships. A snowflake schema also joins the dimensional tables to the fact table, but there is no single table for a dimension. Dimension tables are broken into a smaller set of tables joined, in a chain, to the fact table.

The relational schema you choose for your data warehouse depends largely on the way your application collects and works with data. Although there are advantages and disadvantages in choosing one schema over the other in a relational database environment, we concentrate on the advantages and disadvantages of working with the multidimensional model.

The question of what constitutes the optimal schema for a data warehouse is still open. You might find advantages to using star schemas to build your data warehouse. On the other hand, you might choose snowflake schemas, or you might combine the two types. Which schema is right for you depends on how large your data is, how familiar you are with your data, and how clean your procedures for populating your data warehouse are. The following lists contain the advantages and disadvantages of the two schemas:

Advantages

- The dimension is easier to model because a single table is the basis for the entire dimension.
- It is easier to perform incremental updates to the dimension. For the `ProcessAdd` processing command, you need to specify only a single table, or a query based on a single table that contains all the new dimension members you want to see in your dimension.

Disadvantages

- It is harder to detect relationships between attributes at design time because you need to figure out the relationship based on the data in a table and not based on the relationship between tables. For example, to determine when a single product belongs to only one product category, you must run a separate SQL query.
- Processing the dimension is slower because a single attribute member can appear multiple times in a table, and therefore Analysis Services will have to perform additional lookup for an attribute member in a dimension. For example, while processing the `Customer` dimension, Analysis Services will encounter member `WA` as many times as the number of customers in Washington state.
- The relational schema does not enforce quality of data, and therefore there is a higher probability of referential integrity problems. For example, a typo in the name of a state can cause multiple members of the same state to appear in a dimension.

The advantages and disadvantages of snowflake schemas in multidimensional design are as follows:

Advantages

- It is easy and intuitive to design the correct structure for a dimension. It is easier to create natural hierarchies with the Analysis Services Dimension Wizard. After you define the natural hierarchies and the relationships between attributes, you can define a useful set of aggregations for your cube. Given that, you will see improved performance in your cube.

- Processing the dimension is faster because Analysis Services processes each attribute independently from others and sends a query for data required by the attribute. This data often belongs to a single table, which is smaller than a single, large (non-normalized) table.
- The relational schema enforces quality of data, and therefore there is a smaller probability of referential integrity problems.
- Smaller data warehouse size because records for attribute members are stored just once.

Disadvantages

- Relational schema is relatively more complex.
- It is harder to perform incremental updates to the dimension. The `ProcessAdd` command becomes more complex because you need to specify separate DSV in out-of-line binding of the command.

Optimizing Relational Schemas

Relational schemas used in a data warehouse differ from schemas used in OLPT systems. The pattern of their access also differs, and therefore you need to create different sets of indexes.

Microsoft SQL Server provides an easy-to-use and powerful tool: Database Engine Tuning Advisor. The purpose of this tool to help you to create a set of data structures (such as different types of indexes, partitions, and others) to increase query performance of relational databases.

Before we discuss the Database Engine Tuning Advisor tool, it is useful to go over reasoning and tradeoffs associated with creating indexes for relational database objects.

First of all, you can create several types of indexes in relational databases. You can read the "Index Design Basics" topic in the SQL Server Books Online to get a better idea about how indexes affect relational database performance. As a gross generalization, one of the major benefits of creating an index for a relational database table is the increase in performance of `SELECT` relational queries. These are the same type of queries Analysis Services sends to the relational database to retrieve the data during the processing operation.

In many cases, the disadvantage of having an index is that it slows down table updates. `INSERT`, `UPDATE`, `DELETE`, and `MERGE` statements become slower because the relational engine has to adjust all indexes as data in the table changes.

One of the strategies you can implement to work around this problem is to create a new set of tables each time you push updates from the OLTP system into your data warehouse or use the partitioned tables functionality of SQL Server. As the second step of your update, you need to build indexes for these tables.

Another solution is to drop indexes for your databases before updating data warehouse tables and then rebuild indexes afterward.

One of the hardest problems in tuning relational database performance is coming up with a set of indexes best suited to the workload for your tables.

Fortunately, SQL Server provides the Database Engine Tuning Advisor, which enables you to analyze specific query workload and suggests indexes to help optimize query performance.

For example, let's run the Database Engine Tuning Advisor to optimize the performance of relational tables in the FoodMart 2008 relational database for the types of queries Analysis Server sends during processing.

To prepare, you need to capture a trace containing a workload of relational queries Analysis Services generates, as follows:

1. Start SQL Server Profiler. Create a new trace. Connect to your relational database holding the FoodMart 2008 database. Then, on the TraceProperties page, select the TSQL_Replay template and click the Run button to start tracing your SQL Server.
2. Open SQL Management Studio. Connect to Analysis Services and fully process the FoodMart 2008 multidimensional database.
3. When Analysis Services completes processing of your multidimensional database, stop the trace in the SQL Server Profiler. Save your trace to a file. We saved the trace to c:\tmp\ProcessingTrace.trc file.

After you have captured queries in a trace file, you are ready to start using the Tuning Advisor:

4. Open the Database Engine Tuning Advisor either from the Start menu or from Tools menu in SQL Server Management Studio or SQL Server Profiler.
5. When you are in the Database Engine Tuning Advisor, connect to your SQL Server relational database. You will see a new session opened for you, and you will see a list of the database on your server, similar to that shown in Figure 19.1.
6. In the Workload text box, specify the name of the trace file you used to capture the query load, and select FoodMart 2008 as the Database for Workload Analysis.
7. In the Select Databases and Tables to Tune list, select FoodMart 2008, as shown in Figure 19.1. At this point, you are ready to start analyzing your query workload.
8. Click the Start Analysis button to start analyzing your query workload.

A progress window will display. In about a minute, depending on the speed of your relational database server, you will see results of analysis similar to that shown in Figure 19.2. The Database Engine Tuning Advisor can make various recommendations. In our example, it recommended to create quite a few new indexes (as shown in the Index Recommendations list).

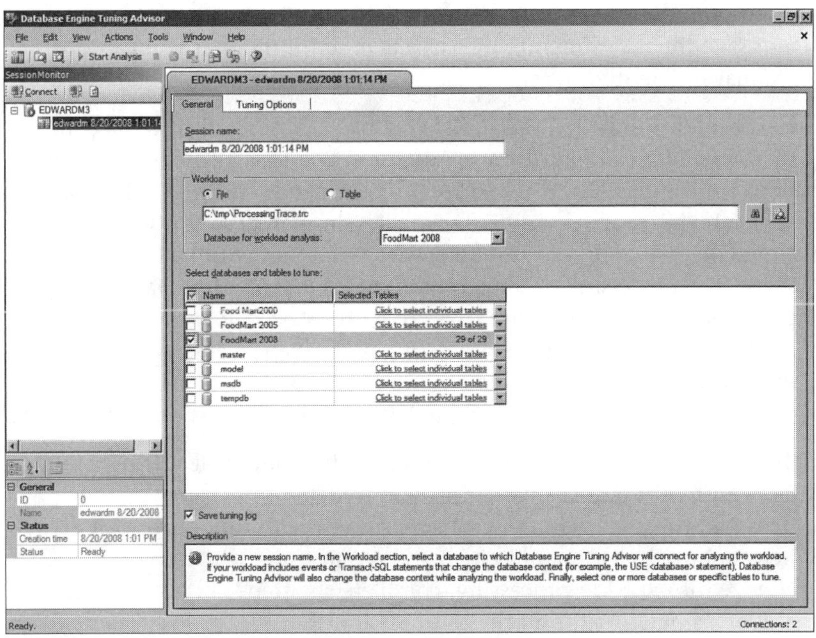

FIGURE 19.1 Launch the Database Engine Tuning Advisor.

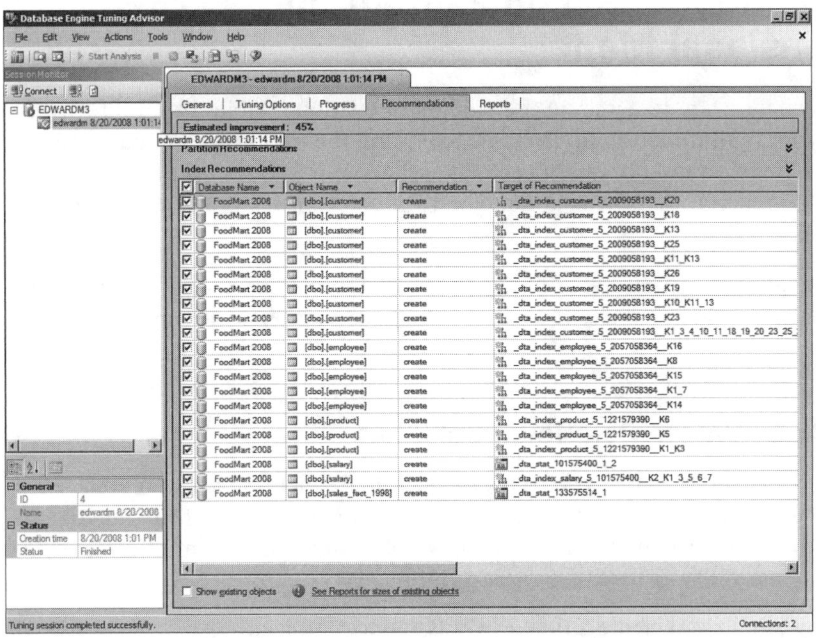

FIGURE 19.2 Database Engine Tuning Advisor recommendations.

You can either apply recommendations immediately (via Actions > Apply Recommendations) or save the recommendations as a SQL script file that you can open later in SQL Server Management Studio.

Before you create recommended indexes, we suggest you take a closer look at the recommendations made by the Database Engine Tuning Advisor. If you look at the list of recommendations (also shown in Figure 19.2), you can see it recommends creating additional indexes for `customer`, `employee`, `product`, and `salary` tables. In many cases, not all the proposed indexes should be created. In our example, we chose to process the entire FoodMart 2008 database, but processing of some multidimensional objects is fast already. When choosing indexes, give preference to the tables that are associated with multidimensional objects for which you want to optimize processing performance. For example, if you want to optimize processing of the `Customer` dimension, you should create indexes for the customer table, whereas processing of the `Product` dimension might be fast enough already.

In some cases, Analysis Services might need to query more than one table during a processing operation, so it might become harder for you to determine exactly which indexes you need. To avoid the guesswork, you can capture trace during processing of a particular multidimensional object. For example, if you are not sure which indexes you should create to optimize for partition processing, complete the steps outlined previously, but choose processing of a single partition only.

Building Relational Schemas from the Multidimensional Model

Analysis Services enables you to generate the schema of relational tables based directly on the structure of your multidimensional database. Defining the multidimensional model first and then designing your data warehouse makes it easier to model your business rules for real-life reporting. If you follow this order, you can base your relational schema on the structure of your model.

You can rely on the wizards in Business Intelligence Development Studio, or you can use one of the templates provided by Analysis Services to bypass some of the steps in the Cube Wizard.

Using Wizards to Create Relational Schemas

The wizards of BI Dev Studio enable you to create relational schemas based on your multidimensional model. They enable you to start designing your cube without first having relational tables to support it. The following steps enable you to create a multidimensional model and to generate a relational schema based on it:

1. Open BI Dev Studio and create a new Analysis Services project.
2. Create a new data source object that points to the relational database that the schema will be generated in. (See Chapter 9, "Multidimensional Models and Business Intelligence Development Studio," for instructions on creating data sources.)

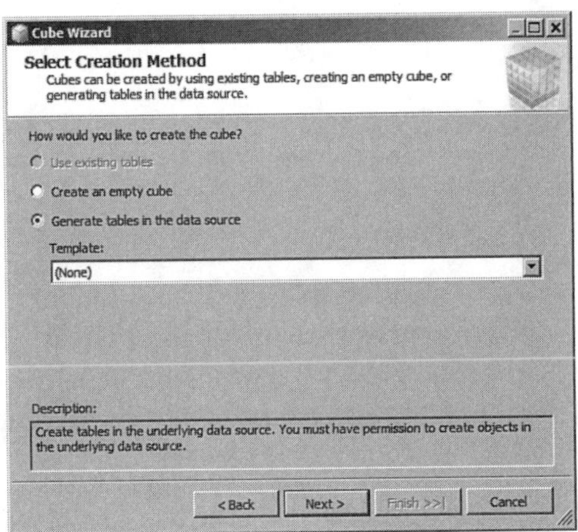

FIGURE 19.3 Launch the Cube Wizard from the Solution Explorer.

3. Right-click the Cubes node in the Solution Explorer to launch the Cube Wizard, as shown in Figure 19.3.
4. On the Select Build Methods page, select the Generate tables in the data source option. Then click the Next button.
5. Create two measures (`store_sales` and `store_cost`) and a measure group (`Sales`). Choose the `Integer` data type and `Sum` aggregate function for your measures. Then, click the Next button.
6. Create four new dimensions—`Product`, `Customer`, `Store`, and `Promotion`—to use in the `Sales` measure group (see Figures 19.4 and 19.5). Clear the `Time` dimension check box, and then click the Next button. On the next page, associate all your dimensions with the `Sales` measure group.

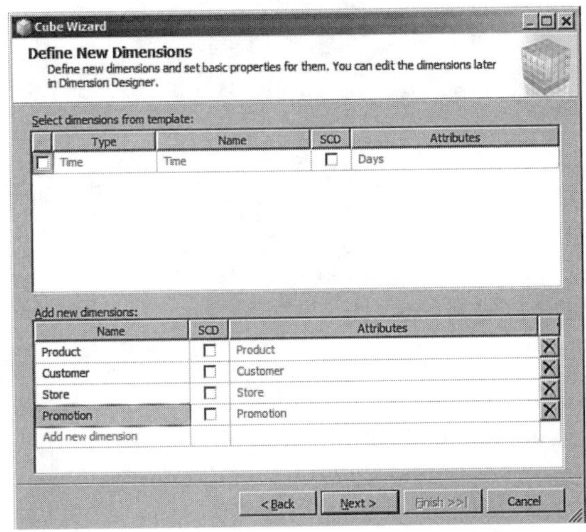

FIGURE 19.4 Use the Cube Wizard to create new dimensions.

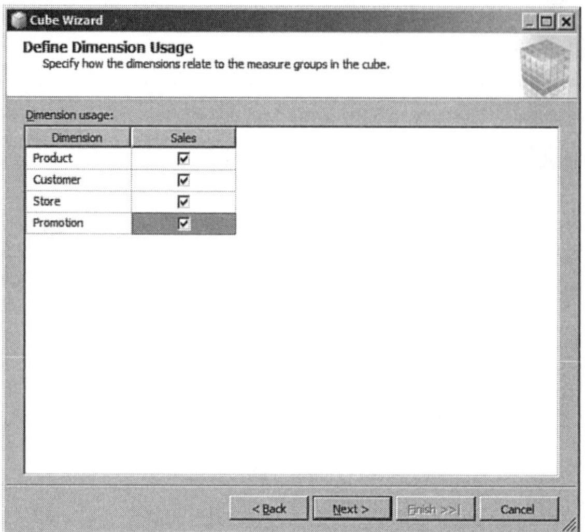

FIGURE 19.5 Select all four dimensions for use in the `Sales` measure group.

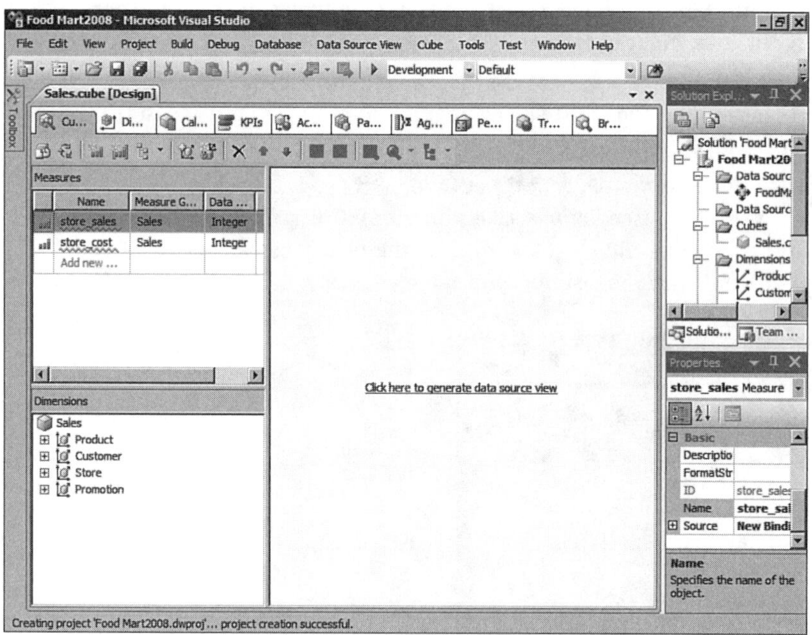

FIGURE 19.6 The `Sales` cube appears in the cube editor.

7. After you name your cube (`Sales`), you are finished with the Cube Wizard. You will see that the `Sales` cube opens in the cube editor and that the four dimensions you created appear in the Solution Explorer (see Figure 19.6).

If you don't want to use the BI Dev Studio wizards, you can use the cube editor to add new measures or new measure groups. Similarly, you can use the dimension editor to add new dimension attributes to your dimensions and to create hierarchies and define relationships between your attributes. You can see an example of the `Product` dimension in Figure 19.7.

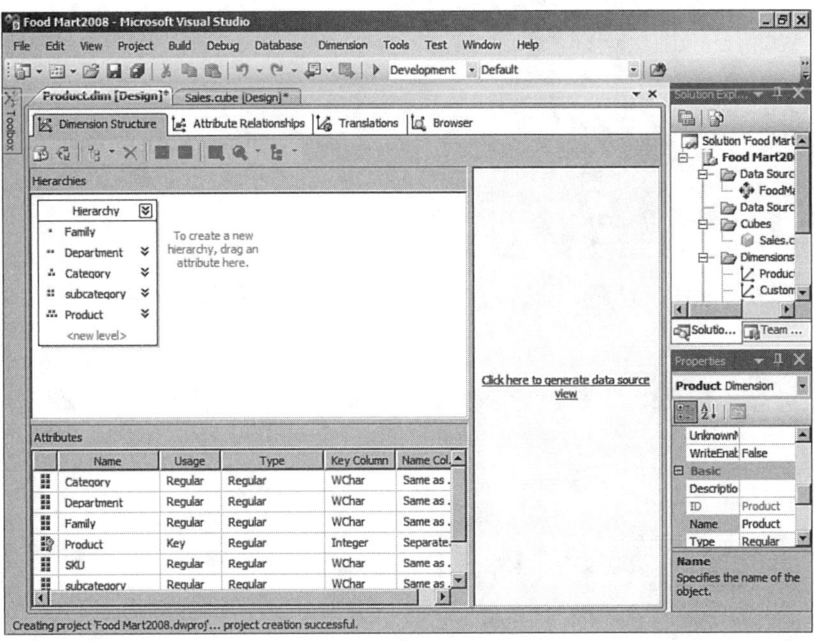

FIGURE 19.7 You can use the dimension editor to add attributes to the `Product` dimension.

8. Click the Click Here to Generate Data Source View link to launch the Schema Generation Wizard. Skip the Welcome page.
9. On the Specify the Target page, name your new data source view. Then, click the Next button.
10. On the Subject Area Database Schema Options page, you can choose the different features you want to create or enforce for the new relational database schema you are about to create (see Figure 19.8). On the Specify Naming Convention page, you can choose prefixes to be used by the Schema Generation Wizard to create tables.
11. In the Schema Generation Progress dialog, you can see the progress of the schema as it generates. After the schema generates, expand the Updating Subject Area Database Completed node and the Tables node (see Figure 19.9).

    In the Schema Generation Progress dialog box, you can see all the SQL statements that the Schema Generation Wizard sent to the relational database to generate tables and keys.

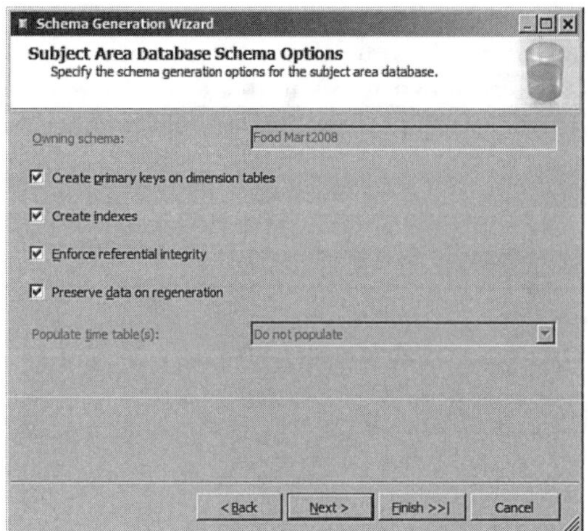

FIGURE 19.8 Choose features for your relational schema.

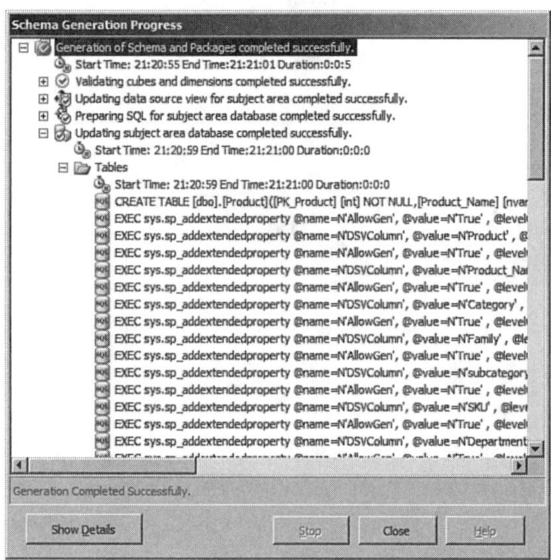

FIGURE 19.9 Click Updating Subject Area Database Completed Successfully.

12. Switch to the cube editor and look at the Data Source View pane, which shows the structure of the relational schema that the Schema Generation Wizard created (see Figure 19.10).

In the star schema shown in Figure 19.10, a table in the relational database represents each dimension. You can also see the primary key–foreign key relationships that the wizard created to enforce referential integrity.

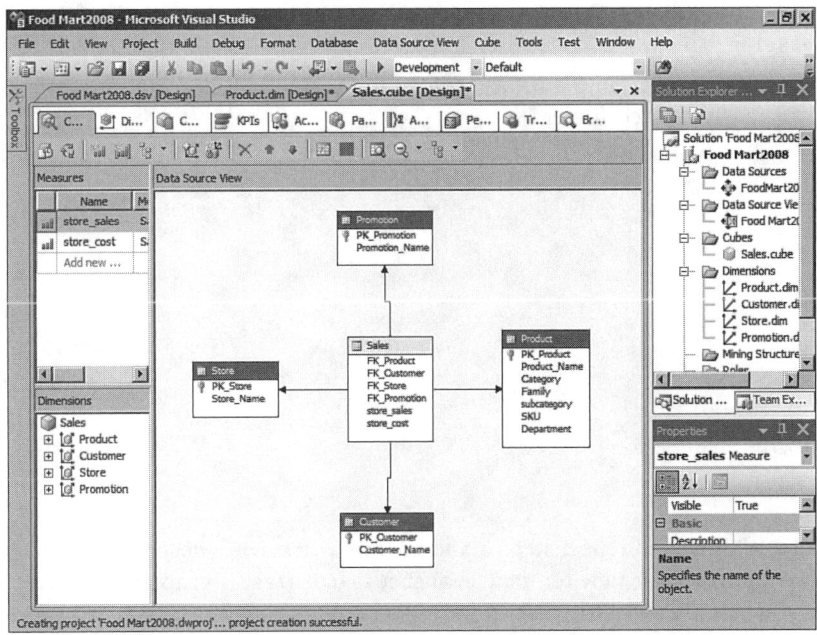

FIGURE 19.10 The Schema Generation Wizard created a star schema.

Using Templates to Create Relational Schemas

You have now created a database schema by creating a cube first. However, it can be tedious to create an entire cube. Analysis Services provides a way for you to create new cubes, dimensions, and the relational schema supporting them based on templates provided by Analysis Services. (You can also create your own templates.) When you are creating several cubes and data warehouses that are similar in structure, the templates come in handy.

The following steps take you through the processes of using a template, and of building your own:

1. First, launch the Cube Wizard.
2. On the second page of the wizard (shown in Figure 19.3 earlier), choose the Build Cube Without a Data Source option.

   To use an existing template to build your cube, click the Use a Cube Template check box and choose the template you want. The default templates provided by Analysis Services are Adventure Works Enterprise Edition and Adventure Works Standard Edition.

   The following steps take you through the process of creating your own template.
3. Navigate to the `Program files\Microsoft SQL Server\100\Tools\Templates\olap\1033\Cube Templates` folder. A folder within the `Cube Templates` folder represents

each of the default templates. Create a new folder here and name it `WarehouseAndSales`.

4. Open your `Food Mart 2008` sample project folder and copy the following files from there into your newly created folder:
   - `Warehouse and Sales.cube`
   - `Customer.dim`
   - `Product.dim`
   - `Promotion.dim`
   - `Store.dim`
   - `Time.dim`
   - `Warehouse.dim`
   - `Currency.dim`
5. Close the Cube Wizard, and repeat steps 1 and 2. Now when you select the Use a Cube Template option, your new template, `WarehouseAndSales`, is visible in the list of templates you can use. Select it.

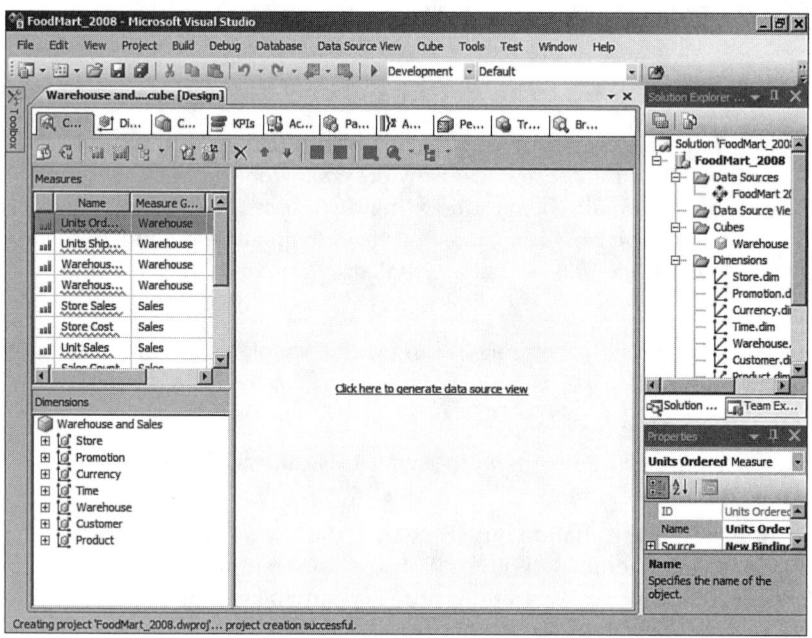

FIGURE 19.11 The cube editor contains measures and dimensions of the `Warehouse and Sales` cube.

6. As you go through the rest of the wizard pages (as shown earlier in Figures 19.4, 19.5, and 19.6), you see that each of them is populated with measures and attributes from the `Warehouse and Sales` cube that you copied from the Food Mart 2008 project.
7. After you complete the wizard, the cube editor appears, as shown in Figure 19.11.
8. Click the Click Here to Generate Data Source View link to launch the Schema Generation Wizard.
9. In the Schema Generation Wizard, you go through exactly the same steps you did in the earlier procedure (see Figures 19.8 and 19.9). At the end of the process, you will see the Data Source View and relational schema that the Schema Generation Wizard built for you.

NOTE

At first, you might see error messages when creating a new schema for the `Warehouse and Sales` cube. That is because our sample `Warehouse and Sales` cube requires you to add a new `Role` object to the database and modify the existing cube perspective to include at least one of the dimensions. After you add the `Role` object, you should see the DSV and relational schema generated for you.

PART V

Bringing Data into Analysis Services

IN THIS PART

CHAPTER 20

The Physical Data Model

IN THIS CHAPTER

The physical data model defines the structure and format of the data as physically stored by Analysis Services. Essentially, the physical model describes how the objects defined by the conceptual model, such as dimensions and partitions, are stored in memory or on a disk, and what data structures Analysis Services uses to support them.

The physical model also defines how data is loaded into Analysis Services from underlying data sources, such as relational databases, and which operations Analysis Services performs to process and convert the data into a multidimensional format.

The physical data model is heavily based on the conceptual data model. After you have defined objects of the conceptual model, in many cases Analysis Services doesn't need any additional information to make decisions about the data structures and forms of storage that it needs to define the physical data model. For example, Analysis Services creates the physical model for dimensions based only on the definitions for those dimensions in its conceptual model. However, you must create additional objects for cubes—partitions and aggregations—that define how the cube's data is physically stored.

In this chapter, we discuss the data structures that Analysis Services uses to store the data physically in memory and on disk. We start with the internal structures that Analysis Services uses to store the data. Then, we discuss how those structures are used to physically model dimension and cube data. Internal data structures are not key part of understanding physical multidimensional model. However, knowing those structures can help you to understand inner workings of the system and make the right decisions while designing and tuning your multidimensional models.

Internal Components for Storing Data

Analysis Services has a scalable architecture that enables it to store data in memory and in the file system, providing fast access to the data for different server subsystems. The key component that serves as a foundation to all the storage systems is a data store structure.

Data Store Structure

To store all kinds of tabular information in memory, Analysis Services uses a data structure called a data store. A data store is very similar to a relational database table—the data in a data store is divided into columns. The columns support various numeric data types, ranging from 1 to 8 bytes in size. Data stores also support string data types, but Analysis Services has a special mechanism to handle strings, as described later in this chapter.

Analysis Services organizes data by records—each column is represented by a field in a record. Each record contains the set of data for all fields. All the records in the data store contain the same number of fields. A field can also be marked as nullable, which means that the field can contain `NULL` values. Analysis Services adds one bit to the end of the record for each nullable field, and uses this bit to indicate that the field contains a `NULL` value. To support null bits, Analysis Services adds a number of bytes to the end of the record equal to the number of nullable columns divided by eight.

The records are grouped into pages, which can be one of three sizes: 64KB, 8KB, or 1KB. Records cannot cross the boundary of a page: If a record doesn't fit into the remaining space on a page, it moves to the next page, potentially leaving part of the page unused. Correspondingly, a record cannot be larger than the size of a single page. Figure 20.1 shows the structure of a store and store pages.

To save memory, Analysis Services doesn't allocate the full-page size for the last page of a data store. Instead, it allocates only the memory necessary to store the data located on that page. This means Analysis Services has two types of pages in a data store: regular pages, which are allocated from the page pool using `PageAllocator` (for more information about `PageAllocator`, see Chapter 27, "Memory Management"); and the last page, which is smaller than a regular page, and allocated from the heap.

You can easily calculate the size of a record and amount of memory needed to store it. The size of a record is the sum of all its fields, in bytes, plus the number of bytes equal to the number of nullable columns, divided by eight. Analysis Services automatically determines optimal size of a page based on the size of the records.

File Store Structure

To provide the scalability required by the large amount of data present in advanced data warehouses, Analysis Services stores data in a data structure called a file store. A file store is bound to a file, and not limited by the memory available on the system. Only pages

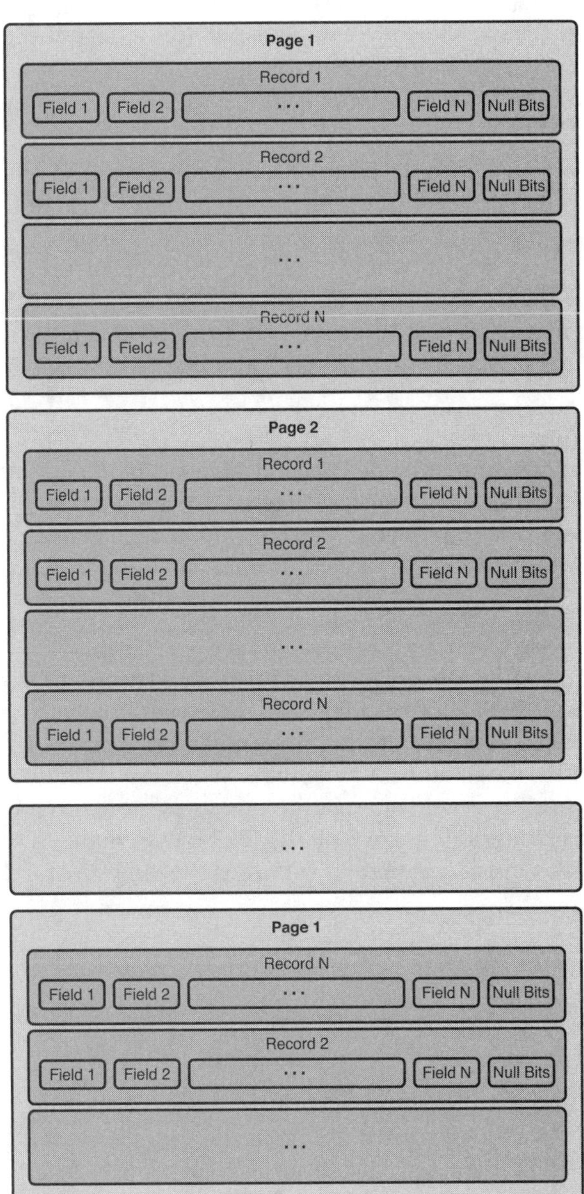

FIGURE 20.1 Data in a store is stored in constant-sized records and divided into pages.

that Analysis Services is currently using are loaded into memory; it swaps the rest of the pages to the file and loads them only when needed. For more information about memory management, see Chapter 27.

The structure of the records and pages stored in a file store is the same as in a data store. There is only one difference between a file store and a data store: A file store has metadata information appended to the end of the file, which enables Analysis Services to load the data store from a file into memory.

Bit Store Structure

For cases in which Analysis Services needs to store only 1 bit per record, it uses a special data structure, called a bit store. A bit store enables Analysis Services to optimize its access to small and frequently used data. Analysis Services writes the records one after another, disregarding byte alignment, so that they occupy the whole page. You can calculate the number of records per page by dividing the page size, in bytes, by eight. Using a bit store when the page size is large and the number of records is small enough ensures that all records are stored on a single page, which drastically increases data access speed.

String Store Structure

When Analysis Services performs operations on multidimensional data, it's very important that the data be stored in records with fixed sizes. However, strings usually don't have a fixed size, and multidimensional operations are typically executed on numeric, not string, data. Therefore, Analysis Services stores string data in a different format and location from data using other data types.

Analysis Services creates an additional store, called a string store, to save text. Therefore, Analysis Services usually creates two stores: a main store for numeric data and a string store for text data. Although Analysis Services supports strings of all data types—such as `char`, `nchar`, and `varchar`—all string data types are internally converted and stored as Unicode strings. A main store can be either a data store or a file store. When the main store is a file store, the string store is also a file store. The page size in a string store is typically larger than that in the main store because strings are typically longer than numbers. Each null-terminated string has at least 8 bytes allocated to it, with the following structure:

- **Bytes 1 to 2**—The original data type of the string
- **Bytes 3 to 6**—The size, in bytes, of the string
- **Bytes 7 to n – 2**—The string data
- **Bytes n – 1 to n**—The Unicode `NULL` character, which terminates the string

The strings are stored in the string store consecutively. The main store represents a string as a 4-byte field that contains the offset location of the string data in the string store. In other words, Analysis Services requires 12 additional bytes to store a single string: 4 bytes to store the position in the string store, 4 bytes to store the size of the string, 2 bytes to store the type of the string, and 2 bytes to store the string's `NULL` terminator character. Therefore, storing strings in Analysis Services—especially short strings—is expensive and lowers the performance of the system. You can see how Analysis Services stores strings in Figure 20.2.

When a store contains string data, the server stores a collation property for each string column in the metadata portion of the data store. The `Collation` property defines how Analysis Services compares strings to each other when it performs comparison or ordering operations.

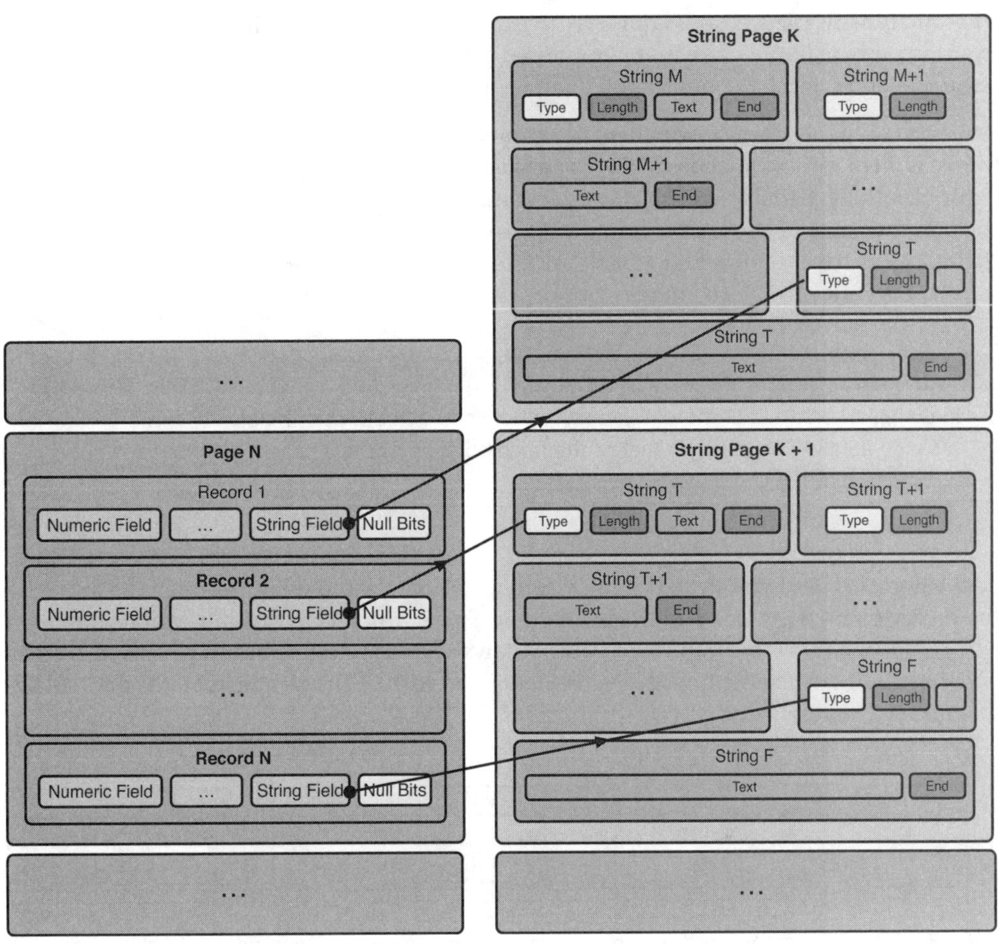

FIGURE 20.2 Analysis Services stores text data in a data structure called a string store.

Compressed Store Structure

Analysis Services can store data in the data store in a compressed format. In that case, the fields of the store typically use fewer bytes than the number of bytes required to store an uncompressed value of a given data type. In reality, the amount of memory required is measured in bits rather than bytes because the fields are packed together and the bits for these fields are stored consecutively, disregarding byte alignment.

When Analysis Services creates a compressed store, it marks some fields of the records as key fields and the other fields as data fields so that the record is divided in two parts: the key part of the record (which contains key fields), and the data part of the record (which contains data fields). Keys are separated from data in a compressed store to make building of indexes more efficient.

Analysis Services analyzes the data to be stored in the compressed store and determines whether it can compress a field and, if so, the ratio of compression it can achieve. Fields that Analysis Services cannot compress are stored separately from the compressed fields, starting on byte boundaries after compressed fields. Key and data parts have the same structure and typically contain both compressed and uncompressed fields.

When Analysis Services decides how many bits it needs to store a field, it analyzes the range of field values (including NULL values) and figures out the number of bits needed to store all values of the field. This means that Analysis Services includes the null bit of a field in the value of the field it compresses, and therefore null value of the compressed field doesn't have to be stored separately. After compression, the record will still have null bits, but only for the fields that are not compressed.

NOTE

If, during its analysis of the data, Analysis Services detects that the size of a compressed field will be close to that of the uncompressed field, Analysis Services will not compress that field.

Uncompressed fields are stored in the record after compressed ones, starting on the boundary of a byte. As a result, there could be a gap, which contains unused bits, between the compressed and uncompressed fields. Analysis Services takes advantage of this gap to store the null bits for the uncompressed fields. Figure 20.3 shows a diagram of the compressed store.

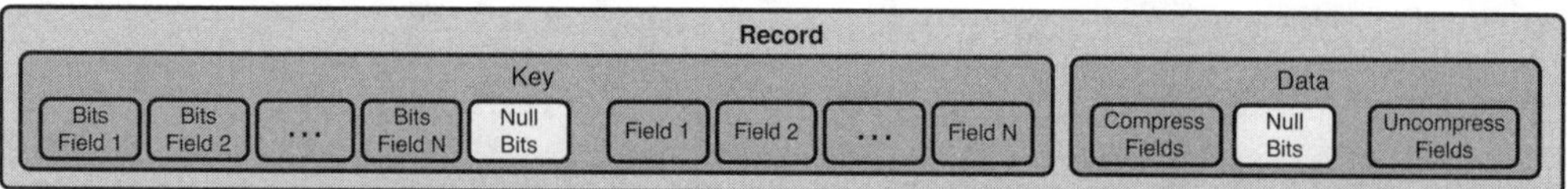

FIGURE 20.3 A compressed record contains compressed and uncompressed fields, divided into key and data sections. Null bits are stored between compressed and uncompressed fields.

The size of the field is defined based on the range of values contained in a field. Because Analysis Services uses a complex compression algorithm, it's hard to predict in advance the size of the record after compression; it can be many times smaller than an uncompressed record. The compression algorithm keeps the size of all the records constant and enables direct access to any record by its ordinal position.

Even though to use the compressed data Analysis Services has to decompress it first, the performance loss caused by decompression is compensated by the performance gained by loading less data from the disk.

Hash Index of a Store

To enable fast access to the data stored in a compressed store by the key value, Analysis Services creates a hash table. The hash table enables fast searching for the ordinal position of a record with a given key. The key of the store is a subset of the fields of the record; the fields that make up a key are stored separately from the data fields. The capability to store the key fields separately from the data fields enables fast computation of the hash function for the key and fast comparison of keys for different records. Therefore, Analysis Services can compare key values in their compressed state without decompression.

The hash table is stored in a separate store. The type used for the main store defines the type of store used for a hash table: If the main store is a file store, the hash table is stored in a file store, too. The page size of the hash store is the same as the page size of the main store.

Data Structure of a Dimension

The dimension is a central component of the multidimensional model. Many other components are based on the dimension. Each dimension consists of members, organized into attributes and hierarchies. The collection of attributes creates a single semantic space, referred to as an attribute tree. For more information about dimensions, dimension attributes, and dimension members, see Chapter 5, "Dimensions in the Conceptual Model." The sections that follow examine how Analysis Services stores data for the dimension and what data structures it uses to organize the data.

Data Structures of the Attributes

The most important components of the dimension are attributes. Attributes define what data is loaded into Analysis Services. The number and size of the attributes define the volume of data that Analysis Services loads into the dimension. You can view all other elements of a dimension data structure as indexes on its attributes. For example, a hierarchy is an index that provides a hierarchical view of the dimension members.

Now let's look at the internal components that Analysis Services uses to build the physical model of attributes.

Key Store

The main data structure of an attribute is a store of keys for attribute members, often referred to simply as attribute keys. Analysis Services stores the attribute keys in a file store and builds a hash index for it—this store is called a key store.

The key store contains only attribute keys; it does not contain any other information. In cases in which the attribute has a simple key, the store has just one field. When an attribute has a composite key, the store has one field per component of the composite key. For more information about simple and composite keys, see Chapter 5. For example, the `Date` attribute of the `Time` dimension has a simple key based on the `time_id` column; therefore, the key store has only one column, which contains `time_id` values. In contrast, the `Month` attribute has a composite key based on the `month_of_year` and `the_year` columns, so the key store has two columns.

The hash table built on the key store allows Analysis Services to look up records in the key store by key values. Analysis Services uses all the fields of a record in the key store to define an index into the hash table; therefore, all the fields are key fields and key store

20

doesn't have any data fields. When a key of an attribute contains strings, the key store has a reference to the string store associated with it, and Analysis Services uses this reference to define an index into the hash table. For example, for the `Month` attribute, Analysis Services builds a hash table that, for January 1998, returns the ordinal position of the record of the key store that contains the member corresponding to January 1998. Figure 20.4 shows the most general schema for storage of attribute keys.

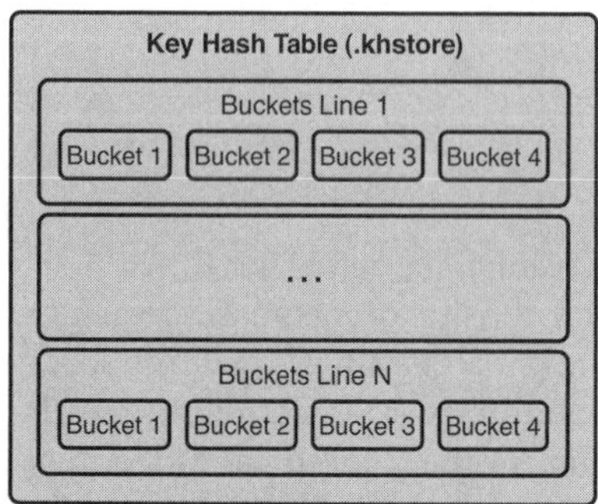

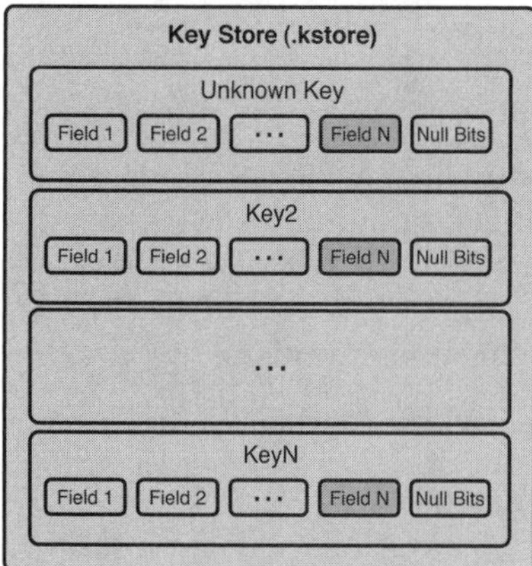

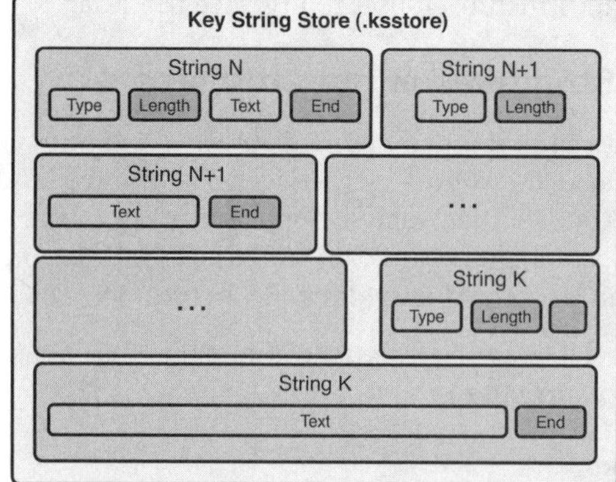

FIGURE 20.4 To store an attribute key, Analysis Services uses a key store, a key string store, and a key hash table.

In the most general case, attribute keys are contained in three stores: a key store, a string store, and a hash store. When you look in the data directory of the server's file system and then in the directory for a dimension, you will find the following files (`<attribute ID>` represents the identifier of the attribute):

- A key store file named `<attribute ID>.kstore`
- A hash store file named `<attribute ID>.khstore`
- A string store file named `<attribute ID>.ksstore`

A string store is optional and is present in the data directory only if an attribute has at least one string key.

The key store contains only unique keys because an attribute can have only unique keys; each record of the key store corresponds to a unique key. When a key is loaded for an attribute, it gets a unique internal identifier, a 4-byte integer representing its ordinal position in the key store. This identifier, called the `DataID`, is a very important element of the system—think of it as a surrogate key for the attribute's member and for its main index. (Unlike SQL Server, however, Analysis Services doesn't store this surrogate key in the record.) Access to the attribute data by the `DataID` is the most efficient way to access a member because it enables direct access to the record. A hash table enables fast searching for `DataID` by member key.

NOTE

DataID is an internal surrogate key for an attribute member.

The data type of the key defines the performance of operations involving attribute keys. Composite keys that contain strings are the least optimal because they require many fields in the key store and an additional string store. Calculation of the hash function of such a key is a complex operation, and the comparison operation of such keys is expensive. The most efficient scheme is to use numeric data types as keys. You should try to avoid using nullable fields as attribute keys because they require additional bits for storage and complicate comparison operations. Therefore, we recommend that you use the most effective key—a non-nullable integer key. If you cannot use an integer key, you should use, in order of preference, a 4-byte numeric field or an 8-byte numeric field.

NOTE

A simple (noncomposite) non-nullable integer key is the most efficient type of key for attributes.

Each attribute contains a special member called an `Unknown` member. For more information about the `Unknown` member, see Chapter 5. The `Unknown` member is not associated with any key, so it can't be found in the hash table of the key store. This member always occupies the first record in the key store; therefore, the key store is never empty and always contains at least one member. Every attribute has an `Unknown` member, even if you have specified in the attribute's definition that you don't want to have an `Unknown` member. For cases in which the user does not want the `Unknown` member, Analysis Services hides it, but data structures of the attribute still contain the `Unknown` member.

Property Store

Each attribute member has intrinsic properties associated with it, such as `Name`, `Caption` (used for translation names to different languages), and values of the functions for dimension calculations, such as custom member formulas and unary operators. All these properties are stored in the property store. In most cases, intrinsic properties are strings—therefore, the property store typically contains string fields. The key to this store is the name of the attribute member. The member name is used to build the hash index, similar to how the hash index is built for keys. The property store itself contains little or no data because most of the data is stored in the string store.

The schema of the property store is similar to that of the key store, in which `<attribute ID>` represents the identifier of the attribute:

- A main store file named `<attribute ID>.astore`
- A hash store file named `<attribute ID>.ahstore`
- A string store file named `<attribute ID>.asstore`

The maximum size of the string store cannot exceed 8GB; therefore, the size of all strings should not exceed 8GB. You should try to avoid using long strings as member names because doing so leads to spending a large amount of resources and slowing name resolution during the query. The size of the `Caption` doesn't greatly affect the performance of the system, but storing it and sending it to the client still takes resources.

When Analysis Services needs to find a member by its name, it uses the hash table of member names. Unlike keys, members can have nonunique names; therefore, the hash table can contain duplicate names. When looking for a member with a certain name, Analysis Services usually takes the first member with that name from the hash table, but which member it picks is not predictable—you should try to have unique names. The key store and the property store are separated from each other to increase productivity of searches by key or by name; the search will be done only on the part of the information that is currently needed. For example, when Analysis Services searches by keys, it doesn't need the property store and can swap it out of memory.

Deleted Member Store

Analysis Services never deletes a member—it marks the member as deleted, but it doesn't physically remove that member from the key store. To store information about deleted attribute members, each attribute supports a special deleted member store. The deleted member store is a bit store because it uses only 1 bit for each member to mark it as deleted. A file with the `.hstore` extension contains the data for this store.

When a member is deleted, all the information about it, except its keys, is deleted from the dimension—but the record in all the stores for a member with this `DataID` is preserved. The key and `DataID` for the deleted member are still reserved. All the data values associated with the deleted member remain in the cube, but now the value of that member is added to the `Unknown` member of the attribute related to the current one. For example, if you delete member `Store 12` in the `Store` attribute, its value is added to the value of the `Unknown` member for the `City` attribute, which is related to the `Store` attribute. If an attribute has more than one related attribute, the value of the deleted member is added to the `Unknown` members of all related attributes. For example, the value of `Store 12` is also added to the `Unknown` member of the `Store Manager` attribute.

When a new member with the same key as the deleted member is added, the deleted member is recovered, the flag that marked it as deleted is turned off, and the data for this member is recovered. Even when the member has a new name, or perhaps a different parent, its DataID is the same as the DataID of the previously deleted member because DataID is an ordinal of the record that contains the key. This can cause some confusion, so you should try to avoid restoring deleted members when possible.

There is no way to remove records of deleted members from the store. If the application deletes and adds a large number of unique members, the size of the attribute can grow, even when there aren't many valid members in the attribute. The only way to get rid of all the deleted members is to fully reprocess the dimension, which requires you to reprocess all the cubes that use this dimension (if the dimension is a regular dimension and not indirect—referenced or many-to-many). For more information about indirect dimensions, see Chapter 8, "Advanced Modeling."

Unary Operator Store

A member can have unary operators associated with it. For more information about unary operators, see Chapter 13, "Dimension-Based MDX Calculations." If an attribute can be aggregated using unary operator expressions, it has a separate data structure, called a unary operator store. A unary operator store is a bit store that contains information for each member of the attribute indicating whether a member has a unary operator associated with it. A file with the .ustore extension contains the data for this store.

The information stored in the unary operator store is separated from other properties to improve calculation performance. The designers of Analysis Services made this decision in the hope that the content of this store would remain small, and would therefore always be loaded into memory. The unary operator store doesn't keep the values of unary operators, which are stored in the property store.

BLOB Store

Analysis Services supports a special kind of member property, named Value. You can set the value of this member property to be the same as the key of the member, or you can base it on data stored in a different column of the source table. This member property is often used to associate columns that have the binary large object (BLOB) data type with the member. BLOB columns are typically used to contain video files, pictures, sound files, and other large binary objects. Because this data is large and rarely used, BLOB data is stored in a separate store so that the sheer volume of this kind of data doesn't interfere with other work. Analysis Services encodes and stores BLOB data as a string.

The following files support the BLOB store, in which <attribute ID> represents the identifier of the attribute:

- A main store file that holds 4-byte offset references to the string store, named <attribute ID>.bstore
- A string store file that contains the string representations of the BLOB values, named <attribute ID>.bsstore

Attribute Relationships

A dimension contains not only attributes, but also relationships between the attributes. For more information about attribute relationships, see Chapter 5. For each member of the attribute, it is important to identify and map the relationships between the member and members from related attributes associated with the current attribute member. Members with such relationships are referred to as related.

To store attribute relationships, Analysis Services creates an efficient data structure—map store—that maps the `DataID` of each member of the current attribute to the `DataIDs` of its related members. However, mapping dimension members to their related members is not the only task that can benefit from using map store. Analysis Services uses the map store to save relationships between the measures in each measure group and the `DataID` of members in the appropriate granularity attributes as part of measure group storage.

Before we can discuss how attribute relationships are stored in a map store, we must take a detailed look at the structure of the map store itself.

Map Store

The structure of a map store is very close to the structure of a compressed store, but has a number of important differences. First, the data stored in the map store is divided into segments. Each segment contains 64K (65,536) records.

Analysis Services compresses the data stored in the map store per segment. Because you do not know the size of any record stored in the map store in advance, you cannot calculate the size of a segment. All records in a given segment have the same size, but because they are compressed and the compression rate differs for each segment, the size of a record can vary from segment to segment.

Each segment is divided into pages, and each page contains 256 records. A page of a segment is not the same as a page in a compressed store, which is determined by the memory required by the page and not by the number of records it stores. Pages are grouped into blocks; by default, each block contains 16 pages, and each segment contains 16 blocks. Therefore, the following formula represents the division of data inside of a segment: 16 pages × 16 blocks × 256 records = 65,536 records. You can use a different distribution to change the division of data within segments; doing so increases the number of records that fit into a segment. For example, you can use one of the following distributions:

- 64 pages × 64 blocks × 256 records = 1,048,576 (1M) records
- 32 pages × 32 blocks × 1024 (1K) records = 1,048,576 (1M) records

You can use the `MapFormatMask` configuration property to change the number of records that fit into a segment. However, the Analysis Services development team conducted a number of experiments and found that the default value (16 pages × 16 blocks × 256 records) is the most optimal setting on a 32-bit platform. We recommend that you use the default value. Figure 20.5 shows the structure of a segment. The structure of a record in the map store is the same as the structure of a record in a compressed store. The difference is in how the data is compressed: The entire store is compressed as a single unit in a compressed store, whereas each segment is individually compressed in a map store.

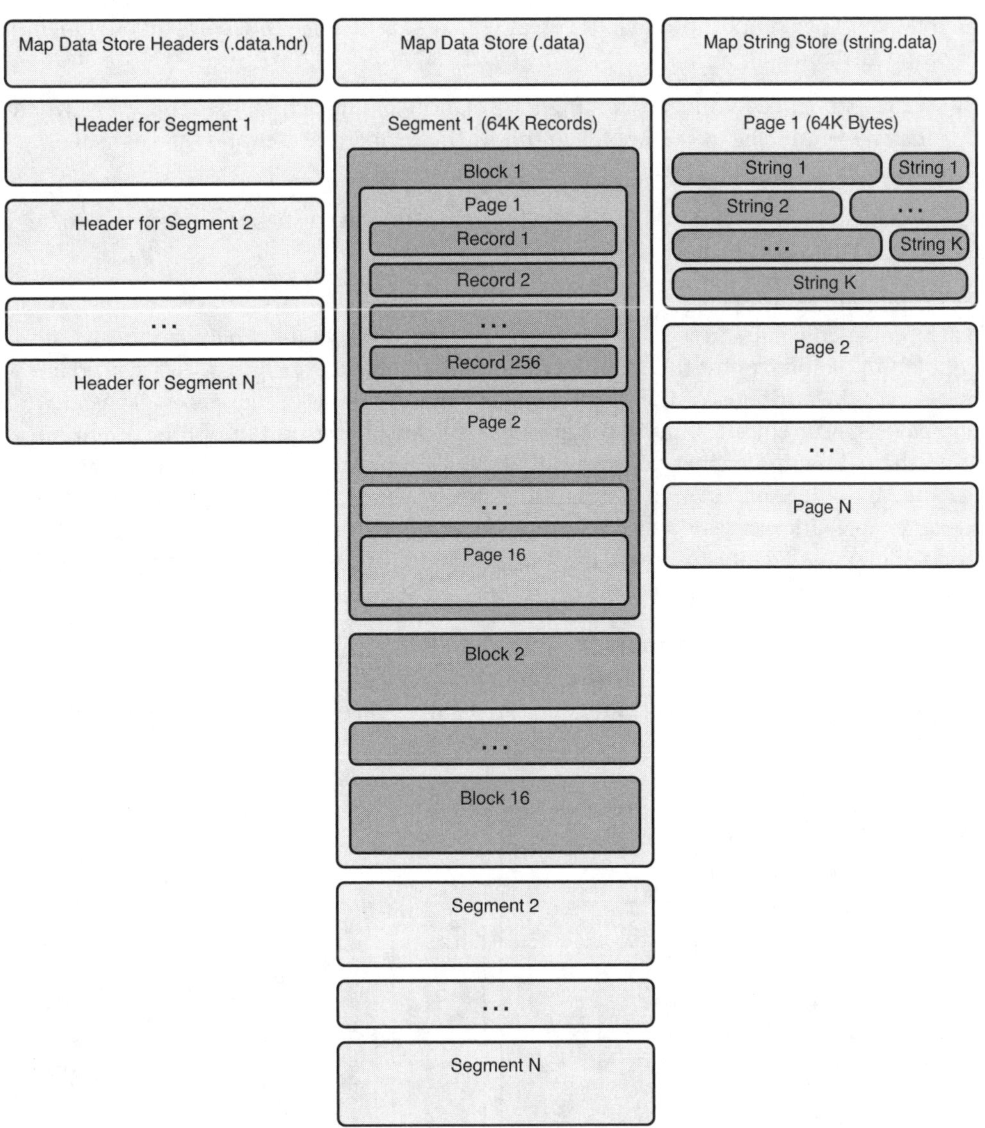

FIGURE 20.5 Map store is stored in three data structures: the map data store headers, the map data store, and the map string store.

Map Stores for Related Attributes

Attribute relationships are stored in the map store. Each record in this store corresponds to the `DataID` of an attribute member; each column in the store corresponds to an attribute related to the current attribute. Because all the fields contain `DataIDs` for the related members, all the fields of the map store are 4-byte integer values, compressed on a per-segment basis. The number of records in the map store is equivalent to the number of members in the current attribute, and the ordinal position of the record is the same as the `DataID` of the current member.

The following files support the map store, in which `<attribute ID>` represents the identifier of the attribute:

- A map store header file, containing information about each segment—such as where it starts within the map store file and how the segment is compressed—named `<attribute ID>.data.hdr`
- A map store file, containing the data for each segment in the map store, named `<attribute ID>.data`

Indexes for Related Attributes

To achieve an efficient access to a member by its related attributes, Analysis Service builds a set of bitmask indexes for the map store containing related attributes. Analysis Services iterates over the attributes of the dimension, and builds bitmask indexes for all the attributes above the current attribute in the attribute tree (attributes on top of the current one, within the natural hierarchies built on this attribute). For example, for the `Customer` attribute, Analysis Services builds bitmask indexes by the `State` and `City` attributes. These indexes enable efficient search of the customers that live in a particular city or state. The bitmask index has architecture similar to indexes used for data stored in the cube, which is discussed later in this chapter.

Overview of Attribute Data Structures

Now that we have discussed all the individual data structures used to store data for an attribute, we can put all the pieces together in a single diagram. Figure 20.6 shows the full schema of an attribute.

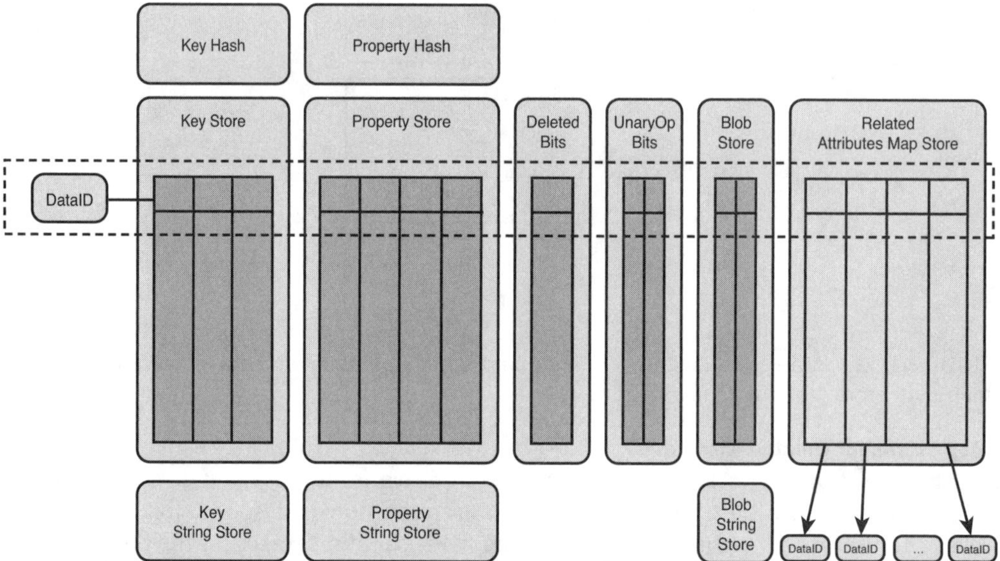

FIGURE 20.6 An attribute's data is stored in multiple data structures: key store, property store, bits for deleted members, store for unary operators, blob store, and map store. Records of all the stores are associated by each member's `DataID`.

An attribute's data is stored in multiple data structures, such as the key store, property store, deleted member store, unary operator store, BLOB store, and a map store containing attribute relationships. Across all the stores for an attribute, each record represents a particular attribute member and the record's ordinal position is the `DataID` value for that attribute member.

All attributes in a dimension are directly or indirectly related to each other, and such relationships define an attribute tree (as discussed in Chapter 5). For example, in the `Customer` dimension, the `City` and `Gender` attributes are related to the `Customer` attribute, and the `State` attribute is related to the `City` attribute. Figure 20.7 shows the schema of the attribute tree of the `Customer` dimension.

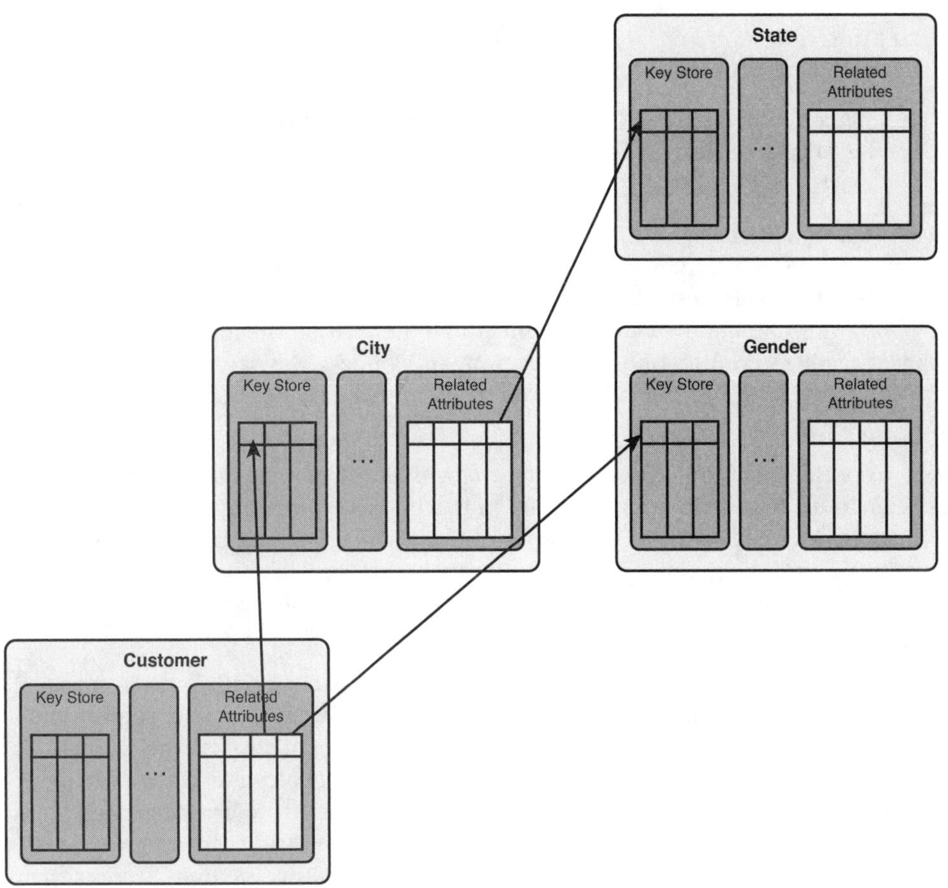

FIGURE 20.7 All attributes in a dimension are directly or indirectly related to each other and create an attribute tree.

In other words, using the terminology for relational data models, the dimension is a fully normalized snowflake schema, the tables of which are joined with each other by the virtual key—the ordinal position of the row.

Data Structures of Hierarchies

Users access data stored in Analysis Services by the navigation paths called hierarchies. To achieve fast access to the members of the dimension through hierarchies, Analysis Services builds special data structures. These data structures are built for each level of the natural hierarchy (as discussed in Chapter 5). Unnatural hierarchies are first broken down into natural hierarchies, and then the data structures are built for those natural hierarchies. Each level of a hierarchy has three data structures, in which `<level ID>` represents the identifier of a level:

- A structure store, a compressed store that contains information about the children and parents of level members, named `<level ID>.lstore`
- A set store, a compressed store that contains information about all ancestors of each level member, named `<level ID>.sstore`
- An order store, a compressed store that contains the position of each member on a level by `DataID`, named `<level ID>.ostore`

Structure Store of a Hierarchy

As its name implies, a hierarchy enables you to access data in a hierarchical view. Each hierarchy contains levels, and each level has references to members. This means that the most important information about the member in a hierarchy is the level index (information about member's position on the level among its siblings), the parent of the member, and the children of the member. All this data is stored in a data structure called a structure store.

The records of the structure store correspond to members of the level. However, the members are ordered not according to their `DataID`, but according to their level index. The structure store has three columns: the level index of the member's parent, the level index of its first child, and the number of children for that member. Therefore, Analysis Services can easily retrieve the level index of the member's parent and the level indexes of its children. Figure 20.8 shows a diagram of a structure store.

The position of the member in a level—the level index—depends on the settings specified in the definition of the attribute from which this level is built. For example, you can order members by their names or keys. However, the ordering is hierarchical, so the ordinal position of the member is determined first by the ordinal of its parent and then by the position of the member among its siblings. Analysis Services starts to order members from the top level of the hierarchy, and because members of this level don't have parents, it orders the members in it by comparing the members to each other. Analysis Services then moves recursively to lower levels of the hierarchy and orders members on those levels, taking into consideration the ordinal of the parents.

Figure 20.9 shows an example that uses hierarchical ordering. Members of all the levels of the hierarchies are supposed to be ordered by their names. But, because they also are ordered according to the position of the parent, the ordinal of the member correspond-

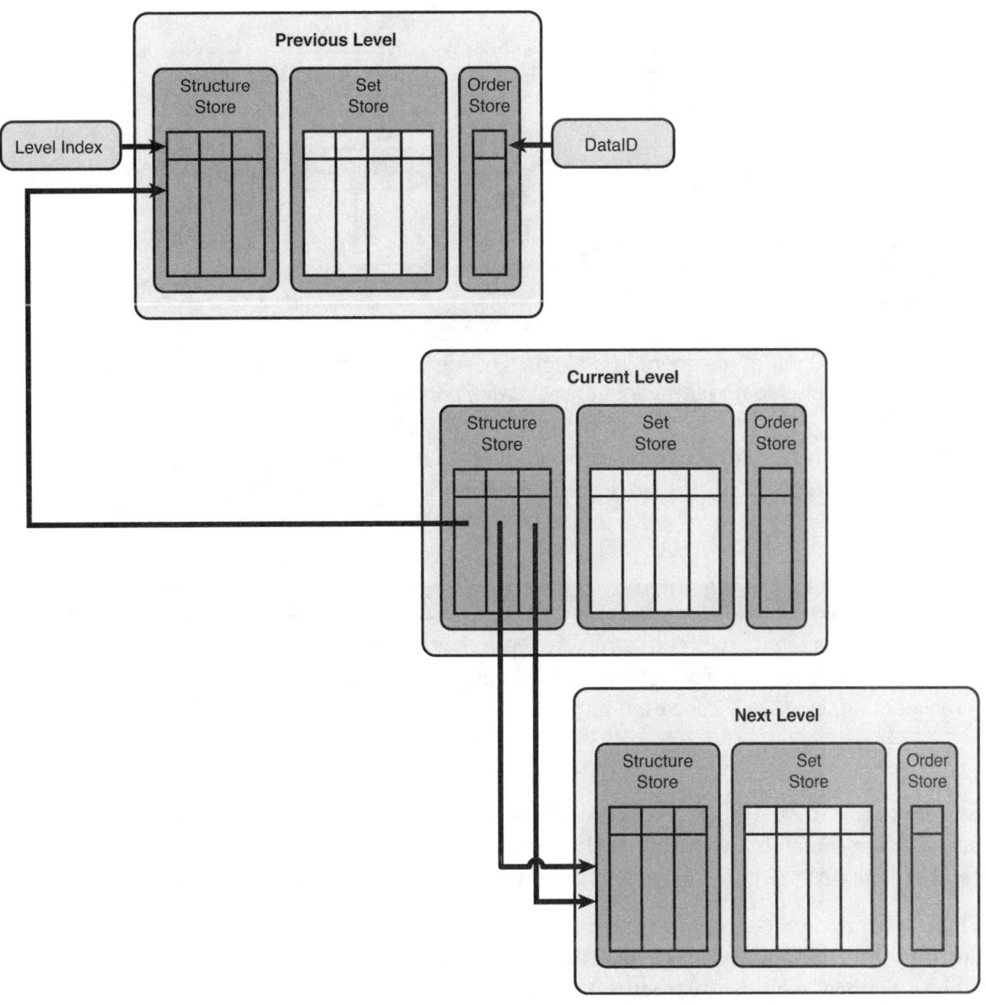

FIGURE 20.8 A structure store contains information about a member's position on the level (among its siblings), the parent of the member, and the children of the member.

ing to customer Py is 4 and Sasha is 3, despite the fact that in alphabetic order it should be opposite.

Set Store of a Hierarchy

To achieve fast mapping from a member in a hierarchy to its position in the attribute, Analysis Services uses a data structure called a set store. For each member of the level, the set store contains the `DataID` of the member and all the ancestors of that member (except for the `ALL` member). Therefore, the set store has as many columns as the member has ancestors, and a column that contains the number of levels between the current level and top of the hierarchy (not including the `(All)` level).

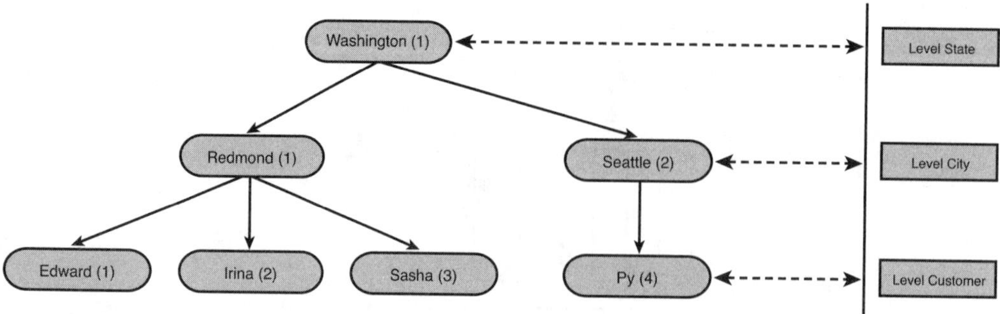

FIGURE 20.9 Order of members in a hierarchy depends not only on a position of the member in an attribute, but also on the ordinal of member's parent.

Each record of the set store can be translated to a data structure called the path, which contains the `DataID`s of all the ancestors of a member and the `DataID` of the member itself.

NOTE

The path is very important data structure. Paths are widely used in Analysis Services architecture—a large number of internal APIs operate with paths and many internal requests are eventually converted to paths.

Let's look at how Analysis Services builds the path of the member. For example, you have the `Customer` hierarchy with the levels `State-City Customer`, and this hierarchy has the members shown in Figure 20.10. Each member has a `DataID` assigned to it.

When Analysis Services builds a set store for the `Customer` level, it enumerates `DataIDs` starting from the top level—`State`—and finishing on the current level. For member `Py`, Analysis Services would construct the path (1, 1, 3), and for member `Edward`, (1, 2, 4).

As you can see, the set store enables efficient access to the `DataID` of a member and any of its ancestors by the level index of the member on a given level.

Order Store of a Hierarchy

Sometimes Analysis Services needs to locate a member in the hierarchy by its `DataID`. To enable quick linking between attribute members and level members, Analysis Services uses an order store. The order store has only one column, which contains the level index of each member.

Decoding Table

Analysis Services often has to find out the `DataID` values of members from higher levels of the hierarchy by the `DataID` of a member from the lower level of the same hierarchy. This process is called decoding. To efficiently perform decoding, Analysis Services builds a special data structure—a decoding table—during dimension processing.

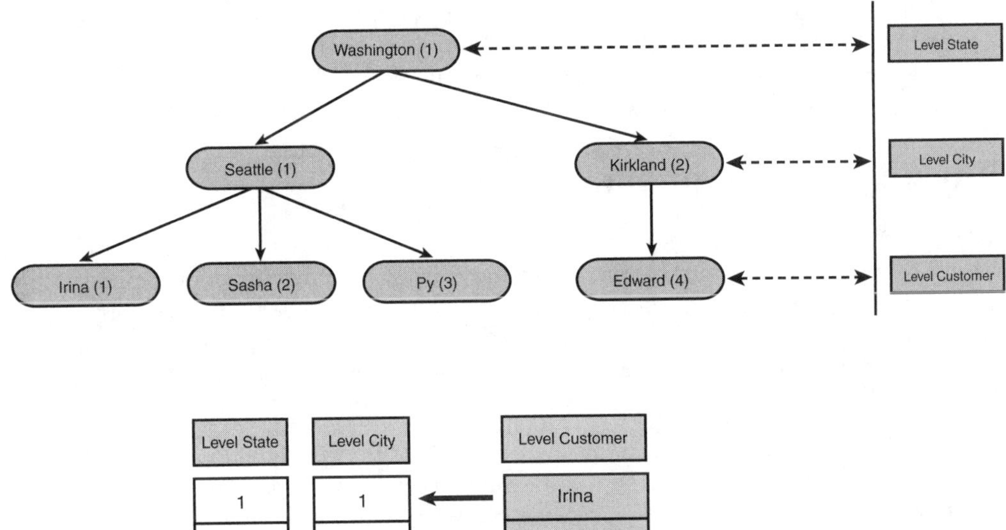

Level State	Level City	Level Customer
1	1	Irina
1	1	Sasha
1	1	Py
1	2	Edward

FIGURE 20.10 Analysis Services builds the path to the member by enumerating the `DataIDs` of its ancestors.

Analysis Services uses the decoding table on different phases of server work (for example, when processing cubes, building indexes, building aggregations, executing queries, and performing other operations). Performance of the server depends heavily on the performance of the decoding operation, especially when decoding is carried out during query execution.

A decoding table is a compressed store, kept in a file named `<level ID>.dstore`, where `<level ID>` represents the identifier of the level. The structure of the decoding table is almost the same as the structure of the set store for a level. Similar to the structure of the hierarchy, a decoding table contains columns with the `DataIDs` of the member's ancestors. However, a number of differences exist between the decoding table and set store of the level:

- Records in a decoding table are ordered not by level index, but by `DataID`. Therefore, the decoding table uses the same order as the keys of the attribute that defines the level.
- There is no need to store the `DataID` of the member because it's already known by the ordinal of the record (which is the `DataID` of the member) in the decoding table. Therefore, the decoding table contains only the `DataID` values of ancestors for the current member.
- The decoding table is built for the levels of native hierarchies. For more information about native hierarchies, see Chapter 7, "Measures and Multidimensional Analysis."

Native hierarchies are very important elements because they define which decoding tables Analysis Services builds and, therefore, which relationships between members are created in the server as decoding tables. All relationships not included in the decoding table are ignored, and data defined by these relationships is not accessible.

Physical Model of the Cube

As opposed to the physical model of the dimension, the physical model of the cube cannot be built without additional information provided by the designer of the multidimensional cube. By itself, the `Cube` object doesn't store data and doesn't have a physical model—it contains only metadata and calculations. Physically, all data for a cube is actually stored in the dimensions and measure groups or facts associated with the cube, as discussed in Chapter 7.

Each measure group can be divided into partitions. A partition defines a portion of the fact data loaded into a measure group. A measure group can have multiple partitions. A partition can contain any number of records, but we recommend that you design partitions that contain between 5 and 20 million records. You can use the Data Definition Language (DDL) to define partitions for a measure group.

Defining a Partition Using DDL

A partition is a major object that you can create independent of the cube or measure group. Similar to other major objects, a partition has `Name`, `ID`, `Description`, and `Annotations` properties. However, a partition doesn't have its own `Collation` or `Language` properties, and instead inherits those properties from the `Cube` object. Many properties of the cube and measure group objects are not used when Analysis Services works with cubes and measure groups themselves, but uses them in children objects—partitions. For example, if you want the partitions of a measure group to have the same `StorageMode` property value, you can specify the value of this property on the measure group and by default, all partitions for that measure group will inherit that property value. You can also explicitly specify different `StorageMode` property values for each partition. Table 20.1 contains descriptions of the most important properties of the partition object.

TABLE 20.1 Partition Properties

Property	Description
`AggregationDesignID`	Defines the identifier of the `AggregationDesign` object used by the partition. For more information about aggregation design, see Chapter 23, "Aggregation Design and Usage-Based Optimization."
`AggregationPrefix`	Defines the prefix used for table names that contain the aggregation data of relational online analytical processing (ROLAP) partitions.

TABLE 20.1 Partition Properties

Property	Description
CreatedTimestamp	Represents the date and time when Analysis Services created the partition.
ErrorConfiguration	Defines the error-handling rules used during processing of the partition. For more information about error configurations, see Chapter 21, "Dimension and Partition Processing."
EstimatedSize	Defines the amount of data, in bytes, which you expect to be loaded into the partition. This property helps Analysis Services determine the best strategy to use during partition processing.
EstimatedRows	Defines the number of records that you expect to be loaded into a partition. Similar to the EstimatedSize property, this property helps Analysis Services determine the best strategy to use during partition processing.
LastSchemaUpdate	Represents the date and time at which the partition was last updated.
LastProcessed	Represents the date and time at which Analysis Services last successfully processed the partition.
ProactiveCaching	Defines the automatic reprocessing rules for the partition when data changes in the underlying data source. For more information about proactive caching, see Chapter 24, "Proactive Caching and Real-Time Updates."
ProcessingMode	Defines the method used to load the partition with data. You can load data and build indexes at the same time, or you can choose to load data, but not build indexes, during partition processing. Indexes can be built lazily when Analysis Services finds an appropriate time. We recommend that you avoid lazy processing: Using it makes it difficult to predict when indexes will be constructed and when Analysis Services will efficiently use the partition.
ProcessingPriority	Defines the priority of building indexes for this partition, relative to other partitions, during lazy processing.
RemoteDatasourceID	Defines the identifier for the Datasource object used by the remote partition. Remote partitions enable you to place partitions on a different server, providing unlimited extension of the volume of stored data. (We discuss remote partitions later in this chapter.)

TABLE 20.1 Partition Properties

Property	Description
`Slice`	Defines what data is loaded into the partition. This is one of the most important properties of the partition because Analysis Services uses `Slice` to quickly determine whether data requested by the user is located in the current partition. While building indexes for multidimensional online analytical processing (MOLAP) and HOLAP partitions, Analysis Services can automatically detect and validate the slice. Therefore, for this type of partitions, you can choose not to explicitly define the slice if indexes are built. However, we strongly recommend that you explicitly specify a slice. This property provides additional validation on the processing stages.
`Source`	Defines the binding to the underlying data source. (For more information about bindings, see Chapter 17, "Loading Data from a Relational Database.")
`State`	Represents the state of the partition. The partition can be `Processed` (filled with data and ready to provide answers to query requests) or `Unprocessed` (partition doesn't have data and will be ignored by Analysis Services during the execution of a query).
`StorageMode`	Represents the type of storage for the partition. Analysis Services supports the MOLAP, ROLAP, and hybrid online analytical processing (HOLAP) storage modes. For more information about different storage modes, see Chapter 1, "Introduction to OLAP and Its Role in Business Intelligence." Although Analysis Services provides the best overall performance with MOLAP storage, you can use ROLAP or HOLAP storage modes if you want to save disk space, reduce processing time, or manage data latency.
`StorageLocation`	Represents the location on the disk where Analysis Services stores data for the partition. By default, data for the partition is stored in the data directory of the server; you should use this property only when it's absolutely necessary to store partition data in a specific location. When you store partition data separately, it complicates maintenance of the server—especially with operations such as backup and restore.
`Type`	Represents the type of the partition. A partition can be one of two types: `Data` (contains regular data loaded from relational database) or `Writeback` (contains data updated by the user). For more information about `Writeback`, see Chapter 16, "Writing Data into Analysis Services." Each measure group can have only one `Writeback` partition.

Listing 20.1 shows an example of the definition for a partition that represents sales in December of 1998.

LISTING 20.1 Definition of the Partition for December 1998

```
<Partition>
    <ID>Sales Fact Dec 1998</ID>
    <Name>Sales Fact Dec 1998</Name>
    <CreatedTimestamp>0001-01-01T00:00:00Z</CreatedTimestamp>
    <LastSchemaUpdate>0001-01-01T00:00:00Z</LastSchemaUpdate>
    <LastProcessed>0001-01-01T00:00:00Z</LastProcessed>
    <State>Unprocessed</State>
    <Source xsi:type="DsvTableBinding">
        <DataSourceViewID>Food Mart2000</DataSourceViewID>
        <TableID>dbo_sales_fact_dec_1998</TableID>
    </Source>
    <StorageMode>Molap</StorageMode>
    <CurrentStorageMode>Molap</CurrentStorageMode>
    <ProcessingMode>Regular</ProcessingMode>
</Partition>
```

Physical Model of the Partition

Analysis Services uses several data structures to store partition data and to enable fast access to this data during query execution:

- Slices, which enable fast detection of partitions that contain requested data
- Map stores, which contains the data loaded from the relational source
- Indexes built by the server for fast access to the data
- Aggregations, which enable fast access to the aggregated data (data that contains totals)
- Aggregation indexes, which enable fast access to the data stored in aggregations

Partition Slice

Analysis Services uses the partition slice to decide quickly whether the partition holds the data requested by the user. Typically, the user defines the partition slice. A partition slice is defined by specifying a MDX expression that resolves to a single tuple. (For more information about tuples, refer to Chapter 10, "MDX Concepts.") For example, if the partition contains only data about sales in December 1998, you can use the following MDX expression to define the partition slice: `[Time].[Time].[Month].&[12]&[1998]`. Note that you can specify the slice that has only one member per attribute; so, for example, you cannot define a slice that will have both `December` and `November` members. However, you can slice by members of multiple attributes; for example, you can slice the data by `December` and `Seattle`.

To exclude partitions that don't contain data requested by the user during the query, Analysis Services builds a special data structure called a subcube, which represents the multidimensional space occupied by the data of the partition. To check whether requested data exists in the partition, Analysis Services then determines whether the subcube represented by the partition intersects with the subcube represented by the query request.

When Analysis Services builds indexes for the partition, it analyzes the slice defined by a user and then redefines the slice for each attribute by detecting sequential range of `DataID`s of members that have data in the partition. For example, if a partition contains data from January to March, Analysis Services detects the range of members from the `Month` attribute as `[1:3]`.

If the starting and ending point of the detected range correspond to the same member, Analysis Services uses this member to define the partition slice. If there is more than one member in the detected range, the range cannot be used as a slice (because a partition slice must always resolve to a single tuple), but the range can still be used when creating a query plan for partition scanning. For more information about query plans, see Chapter 30, "Architecture of Query Execution—Retrieving Data from Storage."

Partition Data

Data for the partition is loaded from the underlying data source. We discuss how Analysis Services processes the data in Chapter 21, "Dimension and Partition Processing," but in this chapter, we describe the data structures that Analysis Services uses to contain the data after processing. Partitions are stored in the map store, described earlier in this chapter. Analysis Services uses the map store data structure to store both the attribute relationships for a dimension and the data for a partition. The main difference between a map store containing attribute relationships and a map store containing partition data is that the record structure of a map store containing partition data contains both the key (the `DataID` of the members corresponding to the granularity attribute) and the data values of the measures contained in the partition. Actually, we called the `DataID` property `DataID` because it associates data stored in the measure group with members of the dimension corresponding to this data.

Values for the measures in the partition are stored in the format appropriate to their data type. Because it is possible for a measure to contain `NULL` values, Analysis Services has to store a null bit if the corresponding measure is marked as nullable (`NullProcessing` property is set to Preserve). When the partition data is stored on the disk, records in the map store are not divided on key and data fields, and all fields are stored as data fields. This enables Analysis Services to reduce the number of unused bits that would otherwise be required to align the boundaries of the key and the data. However, when the map store is loaded into memory, the keys (DataIDs of granularity attributes) are separated from the data (measure values).

Because data in the partition is stored in the map store, it is divided into segments. Segments are divided into blocks, and blocks into pages, as described earlier in this chapter. When you design your model, we recommend that a single partition contain 5 to 20 million records, so the map store for the partition would have 100 to 400 data segments.

The following files support the map store, in which <version> represents the current version of partition data:

- A map store header file, containing information about each segment (such as where it starts within the map store file and how the segment is compressed), named <version>.fact.data.hdr
- A map store file, containing the data for each segment in the map store, named <version>.fact,data
- A string store file, containing string data for the map store, named <version>.fact.string.data

Decoding Partition Attributes

To enable fast access to the data values stored in a partition by their coordinates—attribute members—Analysis Services builds indexes. Indexes are built for the attributes related to the data contained in this partition. An attribute is related to a measure group when it belongs to the dimension that is included in a measure group and is located above the granularity attribute of the measure group in the attribute tree. For more information about related attributes, see Chapter 7.

So, before it can build indexes, Analysis Services has to first decode attributes for which it needs to build the indexes from all the granularity attributes included in the measure group. To do this, Analysis Services iterates through the dimensions related to the measure group and finds the decoding table that enables the server to decode the maximum number of attributes from the granularity attribute. If one decoding table doesn't cover all the needed attributes, Analysis Services will use more than one decoding table.

After Analysis Services finds a decoding table it can use, it extracts the DataID of the granularity attribute from the partition record and uses this DataID to find the DataIDs of members from the attributes related to the granularity attribute. For example, when Analysis Services builds indexes for the partition of the Sales measure group from our Warehouse and Sales cube, it takes the DataID of the member from the Date attribute and uses one of the decoding tables from the Time dimension to decode members on Month, Quarter, and Year attributes.

Figure 20.11 shows the schema of decoding the `Month`, `Quarter`, and `Year` attributes from the `Date` granularity attribute of a partition record for the `Sales` measure group from the `Warehouse and Sales` cube.

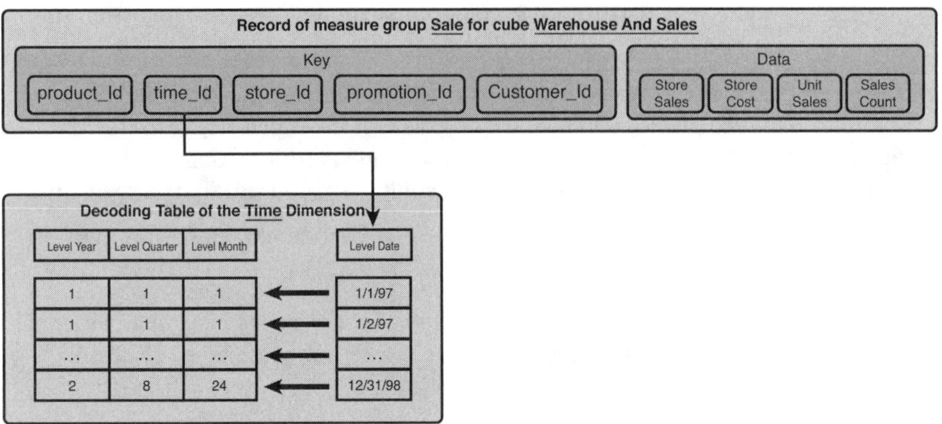

FIGURE 20.11 To build indexes for our sample partition in the `Sales` measure group, Analysis Services decodes `Month`, `Quarter`, and `Year` attributes from the `Date` granularity attribute.

NOTE

Indexing by attributes can require many system resources during the process of building indexes because the process requires all relevant decoding tables to be loaded in memory.

Building the Indexes

Analysis Services builds indexes for attributes that meet all the conditions:

- Related to the granularity attributes of the dimensions in the measure group.
- Marked as browsable in the definition of the attribute. In other words, the `AttributeHierarchyEnabled` property of the attribute is set to `TRUE`.
- Marked as optimized in the definition of the attribute. In other words, the `AttributeHierarchyOptimizedState` property of the attribute is set to `FullyOptimized`.

A partition index is a data structure that, for each member of the attributes related to the measure group, contains information about the pages of the segments, which in turn contain data associated with a given member. A partition index is built for each segment of the partition and contains a two-level bitmap. The bitmap contains information about which pages of the segment contain data corresponding to a certain attribute member. The first bitmap of the index—the block map—contains information about blocks of the segment, which in turn contains records associated with data of this member. The second bitmap—the page map—contains information about pages of the block that contain records associated with data of this member. Figure 20.12 shows an index for the member `December, 1997`.

In our example, look at the structure of the index for one of the segments. The first element of the index is a 16-bit mask, the block map, that contains bits corresponding to each block of the segment (each segment has 16 blocks). For blocks that contain at least one page with data for December 1997, the bit is turned on. If a bit in the block map is turned on for a member, Analysis Services builds one more bitmask, the page map, for this block. A page map is also a 16-bit mask that contains bits for each page of the block. (Each block has 16 pages.) The page map has bits turned on for pages that contain data for December 1997 and bits turned off for pages that don't contain data. In our example, shown in Figure 20.12, only the first and the last blocks contain data for December 1997. The first block has eight pages that contain data.

This way the bitmap index is a simple binary data structure that could, in theory, have from 2 bytes (when there is no data in a segment for the current member) to 34 bytes (when all the blocks contain at least one page with corresponding data). However, Analysis Services doesn't store a bitmap index for a member that doesn't contain data on the segment; it's not possible to have a bitmap index with only 2 bytes. Therefore, the bitmap index can have from 4 bytes (when only one block contains data for the current member) to 34 bytes.

Analysis Services builds a bitmap index for each attribute member represented in a segment. Because each segment has up to 65,536 records, it cannot have bitmap indexes for more than 64K members of the attribute. In this worst-case scenario, each attribute in the segment is used in one page and therefore has a 4-byte bitmask (2 bytes for the block map and 2 bytes for the page map). This means that the index of that segment for members of a single attribute would contain 262,144 bytes (65,536 members × 4 bytes for the bitmask). This is, however, the worst-case scenario. Generally speaking, the index is much smaller.

The following files support the partition index, in which `<attribute ID>` represents the identifier of the attribute:

- A map store header file, containing the list of members that have data in each segment of the map store file and the position of the bitmap indexes for each member contained in a segment, named `<attribute ID>.fact.map.hdr`
- A map store file, containing the bitmap indexes for members, named `<attribute ID>.fact.map`

20

NOTE

For very small partitions, Analysis Services doesn't build indexes, aggregations, or slices. The minimum size of a partition or aggregation required by Analysis Services to build indexes is specified in the server configuration property `IndexBuildThreshold`.

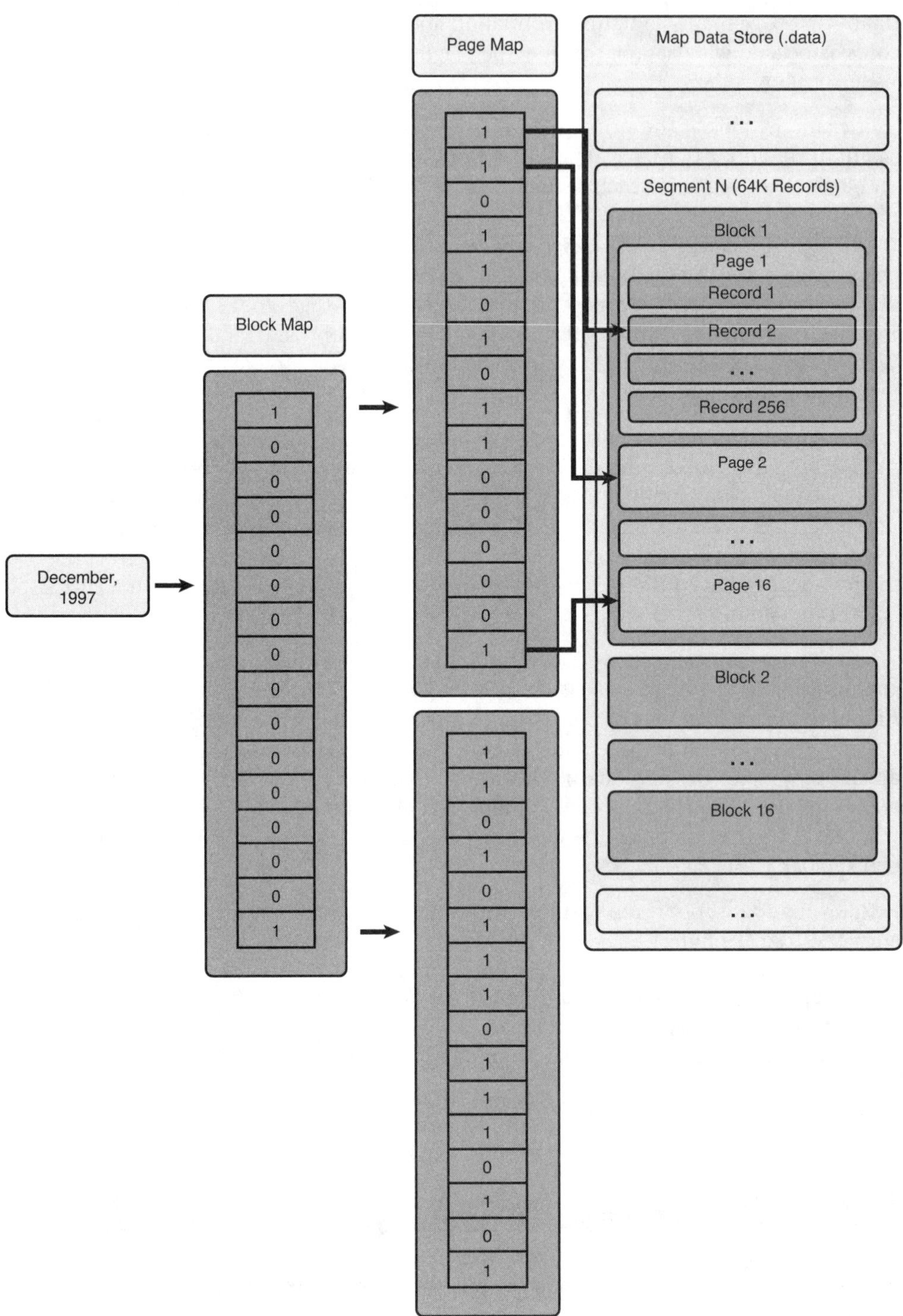

FIGURE 20.12 A partition index is a two-level bitmap that contains information about which partition pages contain data corresponding to the `December, 1997` member.

Aggregations and Aggregation Indexes

Analysis Services can build an aggregation and aggregation index for each partition. For more information about aggregations, see Chapter 23. An aggregation is data summed up, or aggregated, for attributes of a higher level in the attribute tree. For example, you can design an aggregation that contains sales data not by days, but by months. This aggregation is no different from a partition using the `Month` granularity attribute rather than the `Date` granularity attribute. In both cases, Analysis Services builds the same data structures. Similar to the partition index, Analysis Services also builds an index for attributes related to data in the aggregation.

Data is stored in aggregations in the same data structures used to store data for a partition. However, different files are used to store aggregations because Analysis Services separates rigid and flexible aggregations for performance reasons. The following files support aggregations and aggregation indexes, in which `<attribute ID>` represents the identifier of the attribute:

- A map store header file for all the rigid aggregations, which stores information about each segment, such as where it starts within the map store file and how the segment is compressed, named `agg.rigid.data.hdr`
- A map store file for all the rigid aggregations, containing the data for each segment in the map store, named `agg.rigid.data`
- A map store header file for rigid aggregation indexes, which stores the list of members that have data in each segment of the map store file and the position of the bitmap indexes for each member contained in a segment, named `<attribute ID>.agg.rigid.map.hdr`
- A map store file for rigid aggregation indexes, containing the bitmap indexes for members, named `<attribute ID>.agg.rigid.map`
- A map store header file for all the flexible aggregations, which stores information about each segment, such as where it starts within the map store file and how the segment is compressed, named `agg.flex.data.hdr`
- A map store file for all the flexible aggregations, containing the data for each segment in the map store, named `agg.flex.data`
- A map store header file for flexible aggregation indexes, which stores the list of members that have data in each segment of the map store file and the position of the bitmap indexes for each member contained in a segment, named `<attribute ID>.agg.flex.map.hdr`
- A map store file for flexible aggregation indexes, containing the bitmap indexes for members, named `<attribute ID>.agg.flex.map`

For more information about rigid and flexible aggregations, see Chapter 23.

NOTE

Flexible aggregations can be changed during an incremental update of the dimension. For more information about incremental updates, see Chapter 21. Therefore, aggregations stored in the map store file for flexible aggregations (`<attribute ID>.agg.flex`) must be rebuilt after an incremental update of any dimension related to the measure group data. Although aggregations for rigid dimensions are not rebuilt, the partition indexes and aggregation indexes for both rigid and flexible aggregations are also rebuilt.

File Containing Partition Metadata

After Analysis Services completes building a partition, including its indexes and aggregations, the server creates a file that contains all the information about the partition. This file, called a partition metadata file, holds information about the slice, partition indexes, aggregations, and aggregation indexes. This file also contains the position of each aggregation in the files that store aggregation data.

Existence of the partition metadata file on the disk means that the partition was successfully created and processed, and data stored in it can be used for query execution. The partition metadata file is called `info.<version>.xml`, in which `<version>` represents the current version number of the partition.

Remote Partitions

Analysis Services supports the capability to create remote partitions—partitions that are located on another Analysis Services server—to enable solutions to scale out. For more information about remote partitions, see Chapter 25, "Building Scalable Analysis Services Applications."

When Analysis Services builds a remote partition, it first creates the cube, measure group, and dimensions required to support the remote partition on the remote machine. Analysis Services sends all dimension data to the remote machine, and then sends a request to the remote machine to build the remote partition. The server sending the request is usually referred to as the master, and the remote server is referred to as the remote. This way, all the partition data structures will be stored on the remote server.

After partition data structures are built, the remote server sends a copy of the partition metadata file to the master server. When a query request is received by the master server, the server can determine which remote servers, if any, should participate in executing the response of that query without communicating with each remote server. Only when the master server determines that it needs data from the remote server does it send a request to the remote database. The remote database retrieves necessary data and sends the response to the master server, which then integrates data retrieved from all the partitions (local and remote) and returns the response to the user.

Overview of Cube Data Structures

Now that we have discussed all the data structures used to store the data in the cube, let's look at a general overview of the physical model of a cube.

Each cube contains measure groups that contain data with different granularity and dimensionality. Each measure group is divided into partitions that contain part of the measure group data. The partition slice defines what portion of data is stored in a partition. Fact data is stored as partition data. For data stored in a partition, Analysis Services builds indexes. For each partition, you can design aggregations that contain pre-aggregated partition data for higher levels of granularity than the fact data. Analysis Services can also build indexes for aggregations. After a partition is built, Analysis Services creates a metadata file that holds information about that partition. Figure 20.13 shows this entire schema.

When Analysis Services gets a request to retrieve data, it detects what measure groups contain necessary data and iterates over the partitions for those measure groups. Using the partition slice, Analysis Services determines whether the partition contains requested data. If the partition does contain requested data, Analysis Services scans the partition, using indexes and aggregations, and retrieves the requested data.

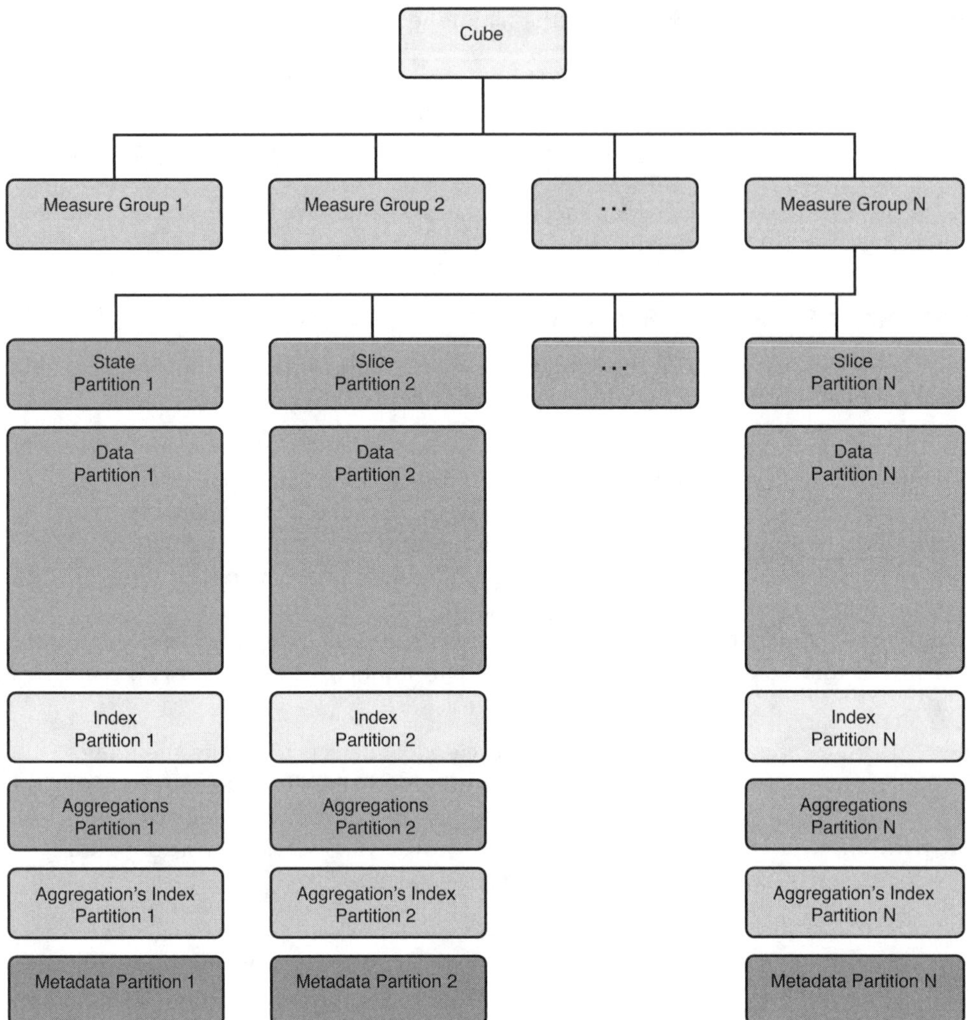

FIGURE 20.13 The general schema of cube data structures.

CHAPTER 21

Dimension and Partition Processing

IN THIS CHAPTER

Analysis Services enables you to access data only after you create a multidimensional model and populate it with data. Processing is the operation of loading data from a source into Analysis Services.

Many objects exist in Analysis Services, but only dimensions and partitions physically store data; processing any object boils down to loading data into dimensions and partitions. For instance, when Analysis Services processes a cube, it actually processes all the partitions in all the measure groups of this cube. If the cube contains unprocessed dimensions, Analysis Services processes these dimensions, too.

Dimension Processing

The processing of dimensions is the first and most important stage of loading data into the multidimensional model. Dimension processing consists of three main phases: attribute processing, hierarchy building, and index building.

Attribute Processing

The first and most important part of dimension processing is the processing of dimension attributes. Attribute processing takes the majority of the time and resources during dimension processing. Analysis Services designers put a lot of effort in to optimize performance and minimize resource usage during attribute processing. As a result, when possible, Analysis Services processes attributes in parallel; even different phases of processing of an attribute are done in parallel.

Attribute Processing Plan

To achieve better processing performance, Analysis Services analyzes the conceptual model of the dimension to detect attribute relationships. Based on the attribute relationships, it builds a processing plan that defines the order of attributes to be processed. Analysis Services builds a tree of attribute dependencies.

At first, Analysis Services schedules attributes that don't have any other attributes related to them—leaf attributes. Then it recursively moves to the attributes for which all their related attributes are already scheduled. Scheduling ends at the root—the dimension's key attribute.

In Figure 21.1, you can see an example of such a relationship tree for the `Customer` dimension in the FoodMart 2008 sample database. Processing of dimension attributes starts from the top and proceeds down the tree. In our example, Analysis Services first schedules processing of the `Country`, `Gender`, and `Marital Status` attributes—these attributes don't have any related attributes. Next, Analysis Services schedules processing of the `State Province` attribute, and then the `City` attribute. At last, Analysis Services schedules the processing of the key attribute for the `Customer` dimension—the `Customer` attribute.

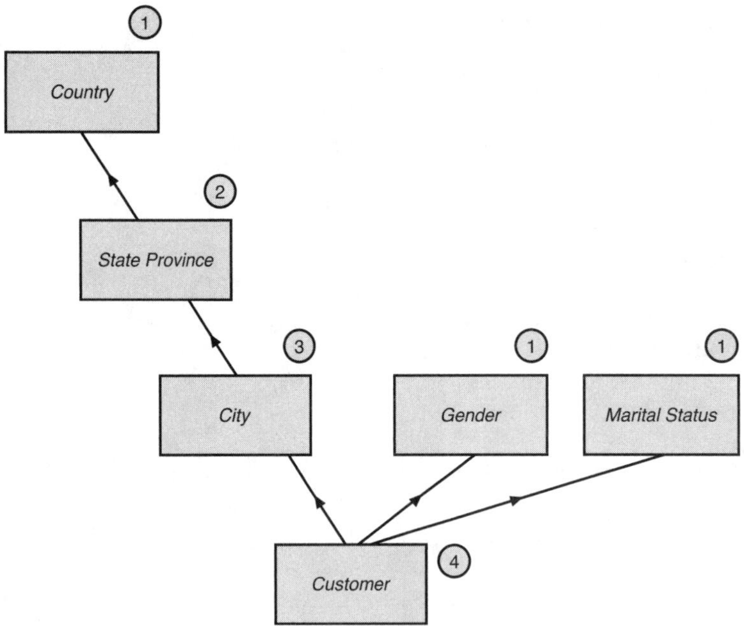

FIGURE 21.1 Scheduling processing of the attributes in the `Customer` dimension.

If, in your dimension, you were to have all attributes related to the key attribute, the processing of a dimension would happen in only two stages: First, Analysis Services would processes all nonkey attributes, and then it would process the key attribute. This loading method is the least effective method of processing attributes. To process an attribute efficiently, Analysis Services requires all its related attributes to be loaded in memory. Therefore, during processing of the key attribute, all its related attributes—all other attributes of the dimension—have to be loaded in memory. If a server doesn't have enough resources, this can cause severe degradation in performance, or even cause Analysis Services to run out of memory and raise an error.

Execution of Processing Plan

The processing of each attribute is done in three parallel tasks: reading the data from the source, processing this data, and writing the data into attribute data structures. Therefore, to process an attribute, Analysis Services creates a tree of processing jobs in which each job is responsible for the completion of one of these tasks. In addition to those three jobs, Analysis Services creates a job that groups all three tasks and is responsible for the processing of an attribute. This job is grouped with similar jobs for other attributes to form a tree of jobs responsible for the processing all attributes in a dimension. Analysis Services uses a subsystem called the Job Coordinator to control and coordinate the execution of the jobs.

Some jobs cannot start before other jobs finish. Analysis Services adds dependencies between the jobs to prevent certain jobs from executing before the jobs on which they depend are finished. Job dependencies enable Analysis Services to execute processing of the dimension attributes according to the processing plan.

To process an attribute, Analysis Services first estimates the amount of memory it needs and tries to allocate the memory required for attribute processing. If Analysis Services cannot allocate the estimated amount of memory for attribute processing, it returns an error to the user. You can configure Analysis Services to ignore this error and let it proceed with attribute processing by using the `MemoryLimitErrorEnabled` server configuration property. In that case, however, execution tasks could "starve" because of a lack of resources, forcing Analysis Services to block or terminate them. For more information about memory allocation, see Chapter 27, "Memory Management."

In the next step, Analysis Services tries to obtain the threads that are required to process an attribute from the thread pool. If it can't obtain enough threads for attribute processing, Analysis Services blocks the processing until the required number of threads becomes available. To start the attribute-processing task, Analysis Services needs three threads at once: one for reading data, one for processing data, and one for writing data.

NOTE

Threads that can be used for processing are kept in the processing thread pool. When the processing job that requested a thread finishes, the thread returns to the thread pool.

Figure 21.2 shows the major execution steps that happen during attribute processing.

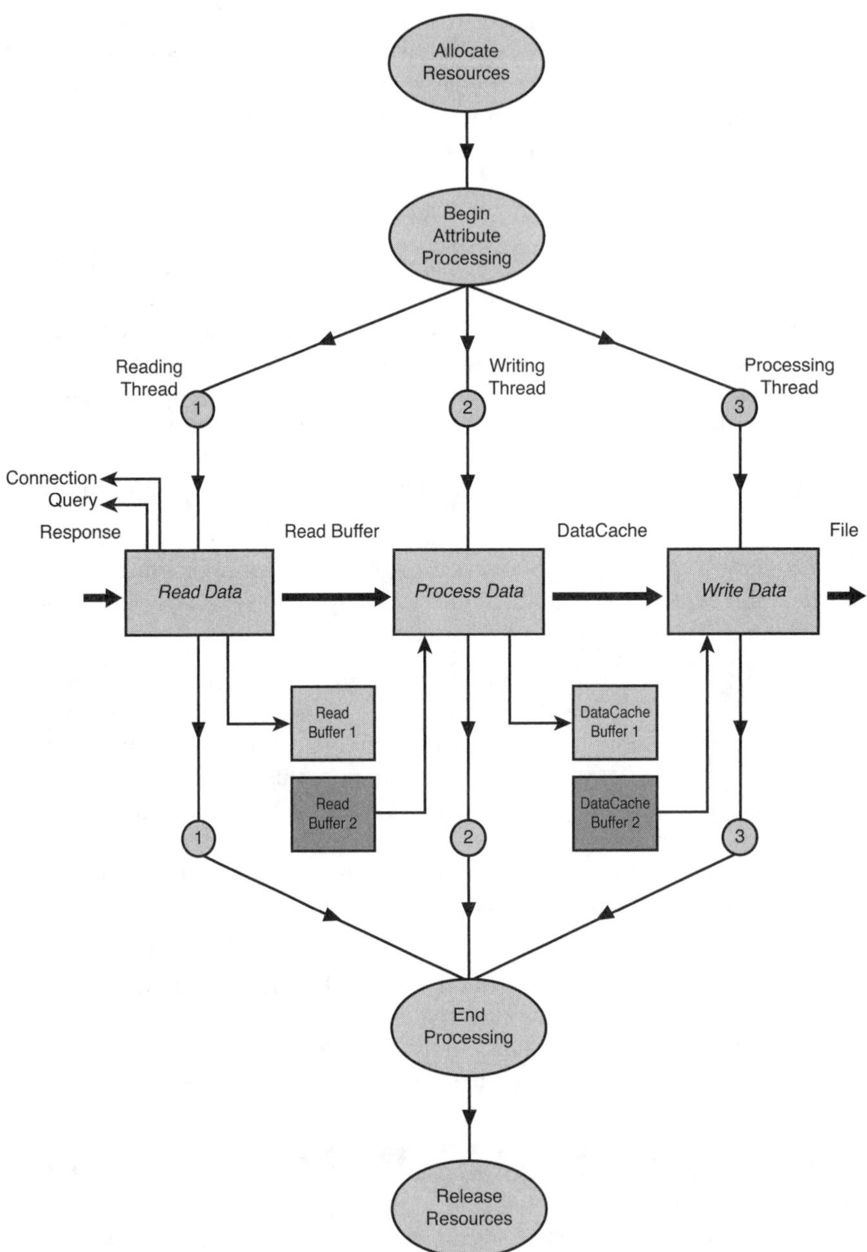

FIGURE 21.2 To process an attribute, Analysis Services first allocates the resources, and then starts threads for reading data, processing data, writing data.

All three threads start execution at once. However, in the beginning, only the Read Data thread is active. Process Data and Write Data threads are blocked and are in the sleep state, waiting for the Read Data thread to read the first chunk of data from the data source.

NOTE

The most general and commonly used form of dimension processing is loading data from relational sources. Therefore, this chapter concentrates on that case.

Read Data Job Analysis Services starts to read data by establishing a connection to the relational database. Connection objects are kept in the connection pool. The number of simultaneous connections is limited by the total number of connection objects in the connection pool, which is controlled by the `DatabaseConnectionPoolMax` server configuration property. The number of connections is also limited by the `MaxActiveConnections` property of the `DataSource` object used during attribute processing. If the processing task cannot obtain a connection object, it waits until a connection becomes available or until the connection timeout expires.

NOTE

Opening too many connections might result in an overload of the relational database. Having too few connections available for processing can cause processing tasks to become blocked.

When a connection is established, Analysis Services constructs and sends a SQL query based on the attribute structure and attribute column bindings. After the query is sent to the relational database, the Read Data thread waits for the query results to come back.

As the results of SQL query execution become available, the Read Data job starts populating one of the two memory buffers with data to be passed to the Process Data thread. As soon as one of the buffers becomes full, it is passed to the Process Data thread, and the Read Data job then populates the second buffer with data.

A read buffer is a file store that can be loaded into memory or swapped to disk. You can control the size of a read buffer by changing the `BufferMemoryLimit` server configuration property. Changing this property affects the performance of reading data from the relational database; but without experimenting, it's hard to give a recommendation as to what size of buffer is optimal for your multidimensional model.

While populating the read buffer with data from the relational database, the Read Data job trims spaces from the strings. The decision as to which space to trim is based on the `Trimming` property of the source column of the attribute. By default, the `Trimming` property is set to `Right`, meaning that the Read Data job will remove all trailing spaces from the strings.

When Analysis Services reads data from a relational database, it uses data types provided by the `Binding` objects to bind to relational data. If the data type of a field in the `Binding` object differs from the real data type of the relational column, the data can get truncated. Analysis Services detects this case and, by default, returns an error to the user. You can configure Analysis Services to ignore this type of error by setting the `IgnoreDataTruncation` server configuration property.

NOTE

You can configure Analysis Services to issue a single SQL query to relational database to process all dimension attributes. This mode is useful if your dimension has many attributes, and the same dimensional table is the basis for most of them. To enable this mode, you can use the `EnableTableGrouping` server configuration property. However, we recommend that you experiment before using this property in production: On large dimensions, setting this property inappropriately can cause degradation in performance.

Process Data Job After Analysis Services fills the first read buffer, it passes the buffer to the Process Data thread. The main task of the processing thread is to convert data from the relational database format to the internal Analysis Services format. During this phase, Analysis Services creates and populates the main attribute data structures, such as the key store, properties store, and so on. For more information about data structures, see Chapter 20, "The Physical Data Model."

During the first stage of processing, the Process Data thread reads records from the read buffer and, for each record, retrieves the value from the columns that contain the key or keys of the attribute. The Process Data thread uses a hash table of the key store to detect whether a key already exists. If the key doesn't exist, it is added to the key store. If the key already exists, Analysis Services can either ignore the record with the duplicate key or report an error and stop attribute processing. By default, Analysis Services ignores duplicate keys during attribute processing. We recommend changing the configuration settings of the processing command so that Analysis Services reports the error. Ignoring duplicate keys simply hides problems with the relational database.

During the second stage, the Process Data thread creates data structures for storing member names, translations, BLOBs (binary large objects), and custom member formulas.

During the third stage, the Process Data thread looks up members related to the current member in the related attributes. This lookup is required to build the Related Attribute Map data structure. To look up related members, the Process Data thread has to obtain the keys of all related attributes. The Process Data thread reads the fields that contain the keys of related attributes from the buffer record and tries to match them in the key store hash table of the related attribute. To perform related attribute key matching, Analysis Services has to load the key hash tables for all related attributes in memory. Having many attributes related to a single attribute might strain memory resources. You should look at the design of your dimensions and make sure to build efficient attribute relationships that don't resolve in many attributes related to a single attribute.

After the Process Data job finds the keys for all related attributes, it then reads and stores their `DataIDs` in the process buffer. If Analysis Services cannot find a related attribute key, it must decide whether to proceed and ignore the missing key, or report the missing key as an error and stop processing. By default, Analysis Services ignores the fact that it didn't find a related attribute key and proceeds with processing. We recommend that you change the processing command options to report such errors (we discuss processing options later in this chapter) so that you can validate the correctness of your data. Ignoring errors affects processing performance, too, because every error causes Analysis Services to execute an additional code path.

When the process buffer becomes full, Analysis Services passes it to the last stage of the attribute processing: the Write Data job. Then, it starts to fill the second process buffer as shown in Figure 21.2. If the second process buffer is still in use by the Write Data thread, the Process Data thread becomes blocked. The minimum size of the process buffer is 64K (65,536) records.

Write Data Job The last stage of attribute processing is the Write Data stage. By this time, Analysis Services has already created and saved the key store, property store, BLOB store, and unary operator store. In this stage, it needs to create a related attributes map store that contains information about attributes related to the current one. For more information about attribute data structures, see Chapter 20.

The Write Data thread performs three main operations:

- Analyzes the data in the process buffer
- Calculates the compression ratio and compresses the data
- Writes the compressed data to disk

The Write Data stage is typically a "light" process in that it doesn't require many system resources. However, if you have many related attributes and the related attributes map store becomes large, Analysis Services might spend noticeable amount of time in the Write Data stage of attribute processing.

Finishing Attribute Processing

The last stage of attribute processing is checking the consistency of processed data and saving the attribute metadata file. The attribute metadata file has the extension `.info.N.xml`, where `N` stands for the version number of the attribute. The appearance of this file in the data folder usually indicates that the processing for that attribute is complete.

During this stage, Analysis Services builds the hash table of the property store and verifies that names of all members in the attribute are unique. If the definition of the attribute requires all member names to be unique and Analysis Services detects duplicate names, it produces an error and terminates processing.

Hierarchy Processing

To achieve fast access to the members of the dimension through hierarchies, Analysis Services builds special data structures. To process dimension hierarchies, Analysis Services creates a Process Hierarchies job, which is marked as dependent on the job responsible for processing attributes. Analysis Services starts a Process Hierarchies job only after all attributes are processed. The processing of a hierarchy doesn't depend on the processing of other hierarchies; therefore, Analysis Services processes hierarchies in parallel. The Process

Hierarchies job creates another set of jobs to process each hierarchy. Each job then tries to obtain a thread from the thread pool, estimates the memory required for its execution, and requests that amount from the Memory Manager. If sufficient resources are available for its execution, the Process Hierarchies job starts processing a hierarchy.

Analysis Services uses file stores for hierarchy data structures. For more information about hierarchy data structures, see Chapter 20. The data in those stores is automatically saved to disk, so Analysis Services doesn't need to have another thread that writes the data to disk.

Hierarchy processing can become a costly operation in terms of memory and processor time. Typically, ordering the members in the hierarchy according to the sort order you defined on the attributes requires the largest chunk of time. For large attributes, we recommend that you disable ordering of members by setting the `AttributeHierarchyOrdered` property of dimension attribute to `FALSE`.

Building Decoding Tables

To enable Analysis Services to look up the `DataID` values of members from higher levels of the hierarchy by the `DataID` of a member from the lower level of the same hierarchy quickly, it builds a data structure called a decoding table. Analysis Services can start building decoding tables only after all attributes are processed. Similar to hierarchy processing, building decoding tables is a single-threaded operation. To build decoding tables, Analysis Services creates a Build Decoding Tables job and creates a dependency on the Process Attributes job. Analysis Services starts to build decoding tables from the top level of the hierarchy and progresses down to the key level.

The processing of decoding tables typically does not require a lot of server resources. A decoding table is a compressed file store, so Analysis Services doesn't need to perform any additional compression and simply saves the decoding table after building it.

Building Indexes

The last data structure that Analysis Service builds for a dimension is a set of bitmask indexes for the map store containing related attributes. Analysis Services builds indexes independently for each attribute; but before it can build indexes, decoding tables should be available. To build attribute indexes, Analysis Services creates a Build Indexes job and creates a dependency on the Build Decoding Table job.

The Build Indexes job creates another set of jobs to build indexes for each attribute. Then each job tries to obtain a thread from the thread pool, estimates the memory required for its execution, and requests that amount from the Memory Manager. If sufficient resources are available, the Build Indexes job starts execution.

NOTE

The Build Indexes job has to load decoding tables for all related attributes into memory. This can cause the allocation of a large amount of memory. If not enough memory is available, Analysis Services might generate an error and terminate processing of the entire dimension. To avoid this error, you can disable indexes on some rarely used attributes by setting the `AttributeHierarchyOptimizedState` property value to `NonOptimized`. (You can get more information about this property in Chapter 5, "Dimensions in the Conceptual Model.")

To build indexes, the Build Indexes job generates an internal request to the dimension. This request has to retrieve `DataIDs` for all attribute members directly or indirectly related to members of the current attribute. Analysis Services doesn't request related attributes that don't have to be optimized. When Analysis Services processes this request, it loads decoding tables to decode `DataIDs` for related attributes. The request then creates a new job that decodes data stored in the first segment of the map store and writes decoded `DataIDs` into a process buffer.

After Analysis Services fills the process buffer, it builds a temporary data structure that accumulates information about the pages of the map store in which the members of a segment are located. When all the members of a segment are processed, Analysis Services then builds an index for that segment.

Analysis Services creates a new job for each segment sequentially. Each subsequent job starts only after Analysis Services knows the size and offset of the resulting index file established during the previous job.

Schema of Dimension Processing

Now that we have discussed all the individual stages for dimension processing, let's pull it all together and see what happens on the Analysis Services while it processes the dimension. Figure 21.3 demonstrates the jobs (and their dependencies) that Analysis Services executes during dimension processing.

Analysis Services create the Process Dimension job responsible for processing the whole `Customer` dimension. This job spans the Process Attributes job, the Process Hierarchies job, the Build Decoding Tables job, and the Build Indexes job. Each of these jobs cannot start before the previous job completes, so Analysis Services defines dependencies between those jobs, which Figure 21.3 shows as arrows. There are complex dependencies between attribute processing jobs because Analysis Services process attributes in the order defined by the attribute tree. All other jobs involved in processing have simple dependencies between them.

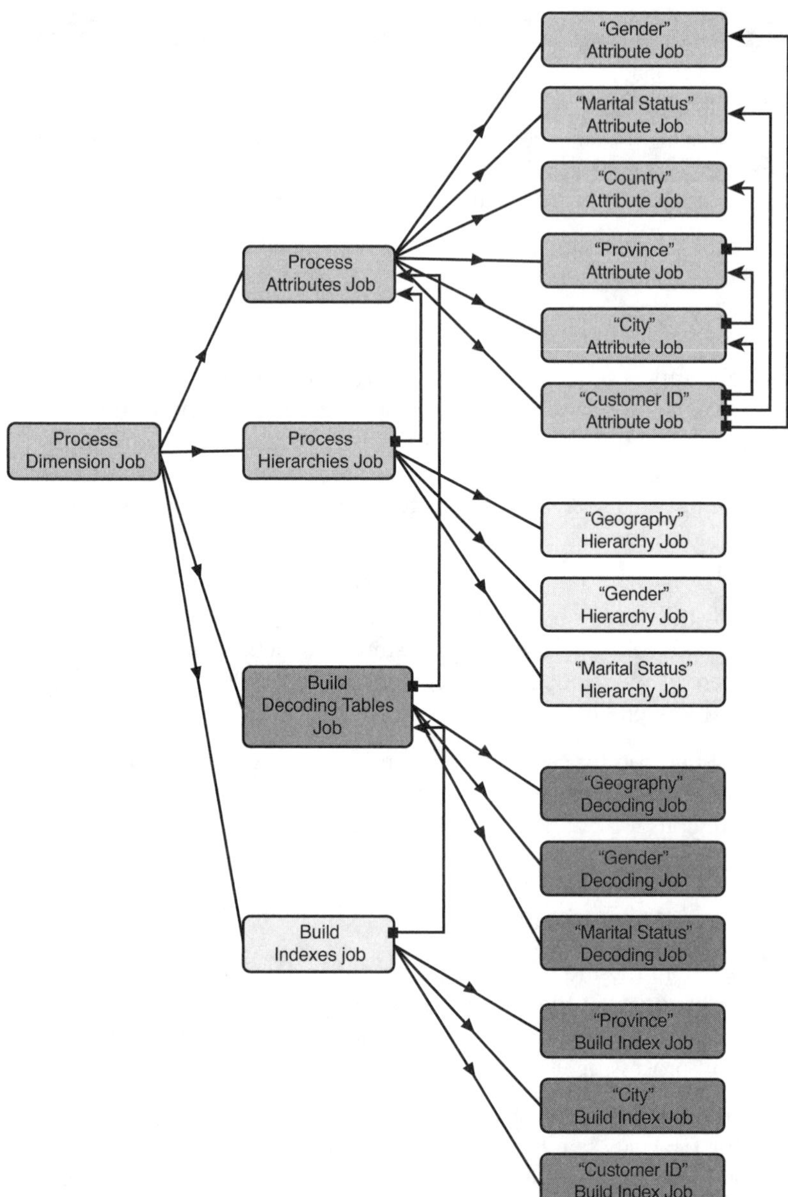

FIGURE 21.3 Analysis Services creates jobs and the dependencies between them to process the `Customer` dimension.

Dimension Processing Options

You process a dimension using one of three processing options: full processing (`FullProcess`), incremental processing (`ProcessAdd`), and updating (`ProcessUpdate`).

Full Dimension Processing

Fully processing a dimension (the `ProcessFull` processing option) causes it to drop all data structures associated with that dimension. New data is loaded into the dimension from the dimension tables and all dimension structures are rebuilt. Analysis Services assigns a new metadata version to the dimension. Data in the partitions of all measure groups that include this dimension as a regular dimension is deleted—you must reprocess these partitions.

Incremental Dimension Processing

Incremental processing is typically the most efficient way to update a dimension. You can only add new members to a dimension during incremental processing (the `ProcessAdd` processing option). The existing members in the dimension retain their `DataID` values, and new members added during incremental processing receive new `DataID` values. You can make the process operation load data from the original relational table or view that contains both old and new members, or you can specify a new table or view that contains only new members. If you use a table that contains both new and old members, Analysis Services updates the properties of existing members (except the `DataID` values and the `DataID` values of related attributes) and adds new members to the dimension. During incremental processing, Analysis Services must rebuild quite a few data structures. It has to rebuild hierarchies because adding new members to the dimension can change the order of members and decoding tables. However, the situation is different for indexes. Analysis Services tries to save processing time by rebuilding indexes only for segments that contain new members (in other words, the last segments of the attributes).

The biggest advantage of using the `ProcessAdd` option is that partitions and partition aggregations are not invalidated. No additional cube data structures are required to be rebuilt because the `DataID` values of existing members used in the fact data, and any existing relationships between such members, remain the same. The new members added to the dimension don't have fact data associated with them in the partitions yet, so adding the new members does not invalidate the existing fact data.

Updating Dimension Processing

When you specify the `ProcessUpdate` processing option, Analysis Services changes the data in the dimension according to changes of the data in the relational data source. This processing option differs from the `ProcessAdd` option because Analysis Services requires that the relational table or view must contain all the members, both old and new, to be included in the dimension. Any member not found in the relational table or view is considered deleted.

While updating a dimension, you can modify any property of a member. Because of this operation, relationships between members can change and dimension members can appear under a different parent in a hierarchy. For instance, if customer `Sasha Berger` moved from Bellevue to Redmond, the `City` related attribute would change to `Redmond`. This is possible if the attribute relationship is defined as `Flexible`. If the attribute relationship is defined as `Rigid`, Analysis Services reports an error when it detects such a change.

From a performance standpoint, the `ProcessUpdate` option is the most expensive of the three dimension processing options. Sometimes, it is even less efficient than the `ProcessFull` option. In many cases, the data structures of the dimension can become less efficient. Updating a dimension causes the partition indexes and the flexible aggregations associated with that dimension to become invalid, requiring you to rebuild them. For more information about flexible aggregations, see Chapter 23, "Aggregation Design and Usage-Based Optimization."

You can specify the `ProcessAffectedObjects` option in your processing command so that Analysis Services rebuilds all such affected flexible aggregations and partition indexes within the same transaction in which it processes the dimension. If you don't specify the `ProcessAffectedObjects` option, Analysis Services starts rebuilding missing data structures using the `LazyProcessing` mechanism (if you enable the `LazyProcessing` option on the partition). It might take a considerable amount of time, however, for the `LazyProcessing` thread to rebuild indexes and aggregations. Users might see a drop in performance while aggregations and indexes are lazily rebuilt.

NOTE

We recommend that you use the `ProcessUpdate` processing option only when you need to make changes to related attribute members. If you have to use this processing option, try to minimize the number of flexible relationships in your dimension.

Processing ROLAP Dimensions

Analysis Services allows you to use the ROLAP (relational online analytical processing) storage mode for dimensions. For such dimensions, Analysis Services doesn't load data from a relational database during processing. The dimension data is stored in a relational database, and Analysis Services retrieves this data from that relational database during query time instead. To answer a query involving a ROLAP dimension, Analysis Services performs operations similar to that of MOLAP (multidimensional online analytical processing) dimension processing. The following steps show what operations Analysis Services performs during query execution:

1. When Analysis Services needs to retrieve data from a ROLAP dimension, it generates an internal request to the dimension.
2. Analysis Services checks the dimension cache and, if data is available in that cache, the data is returned to the caller—the formula engine subsystem.
3. If data is not present in the dimension cache, Analysis Services generates a SQL query optimized to retrieve the minimum required data.
4. After retrieving the result from the relational engine, Analysis Services uses it to perform the `ProcessAdd` operation.
5. During the `ProcessAdd` operation, Analysis Services builds or updates all dimension data structures.
6. After updating the dimension, Analysis Services creates a datacache with the result of the internal request and registers it in the dimension cache.

ROLAP dimensions are designed for scenarios in which Analysis Services had to deal with large dimension sizes. In most cases with the scalable MOLAP dimension architecture, it's not so crucial to use ROLAP dimensions. You need to build a ROLAP dimension only if your dimension is extremely large (containing hundreds of millions of members).

Processing Parent-Child Dimensions

Having a parent-child relationship between attributes in a dimension changes the way that dimension is processed, compared with the way in which a regular dimension is processed. When Analysis Services processes the key attribute of a parent-child dimension, it scans the data retrieved from the relational database twice. During the first scan, Analysis Services processes the key attribute as it would process any other attribute. It builds all regular data structures, such as the key store, the properties store, the BLOB store, and so on, but it doesn't create the related attribute map store. By building the key store, Analysis Services defines the `DataID` for each member of the key attribute.

During the second scan of the retrieved data, Analysis Services resolves the `DataID` for related attributes, including the parent attribute. The members of the parent attribute are actually members of the key attribute. For example, in the `Employee` dimension, the manager is also an employee in the same dimension; therefore, the member associated with the manager has the same `DataID` in the parent attribute as in the key attribute.

There is an interesting aspect to how Analysis Services treats data errors during processing of the parent-child dimension. If, during dimension processing, Analysis Services can't resolve a member of the related attribute because it doesn't exist in the key attribute, it handles this error according to the error configuration properties. If the error configuration is set to `DiscardRecord`, Analysis Services cannot delete this record, so it stops processing the parent-child dimension.

Analysis Services builds the parent-child hierarchy in a different way from how it builds a regular hierarchy. You define a parent-child hierarchy in the conceptual model by specifying two attributes: parent and key. However, Analysis Services builds the levels of the parent-child hierarchy automatically. For each member of the key attribute, Analysis Services iterates over all parent members directly or indirectly related to it, and calculates the number of levels between the current member and the root (the member that doesn't have a parent). Then Analysis Services finds the maximum number of levels and builds an artificial attribute for each level in the parent-child hierarchy.

Because you can add new members to the parent-child dimension during incremental processing (`ProcessAdd`) and updating (`ProcessUpdate`), the number of levels in a parent-child hierarchy might change. This also means that the number of artificial attributes for the dimension will change, too. Because this causes a structural change to the dimension, Analysis Services invalidates the indexes for the current dimension, and the indexes of all partitions built on this dimension. Analysis Services also has to clean all the caches because the data in the caches is now stale. We recommend keeping changes to the parent-child dimension to a minimum, especially any changes that might change the number of levels within the parent-child hierarchy.

Cube Processing

Analysis Services stores the data of the cube in partitions. When you process the cube, you load data into all its partitions. Partitions can have one of three storage modes:

- **ROLAP**—Analysis Services doesn't read any data from the relational database during processing. It only checks the consistency of the partition's metadata.
- **MOLAP**—Analysis Services loads data, and builds indexes and aggregations.
- **HOLAP (hybrid online analytical processing)**—Analysis Services performs all operations done for the ROLAP partition and builds MOLAP aggregations.

Each partition can be processed independently; therefore, you can process partitions in parallel. When you process a database, a cube, or a measure group, Analysis Services schedules the processing of all the partitions contained by those objects. Based on the resources of the system, Analysis Services attempts to schedule partition processing in parallel. Analysis Services processes a partition in two stages, as shown in Figure 21.4.

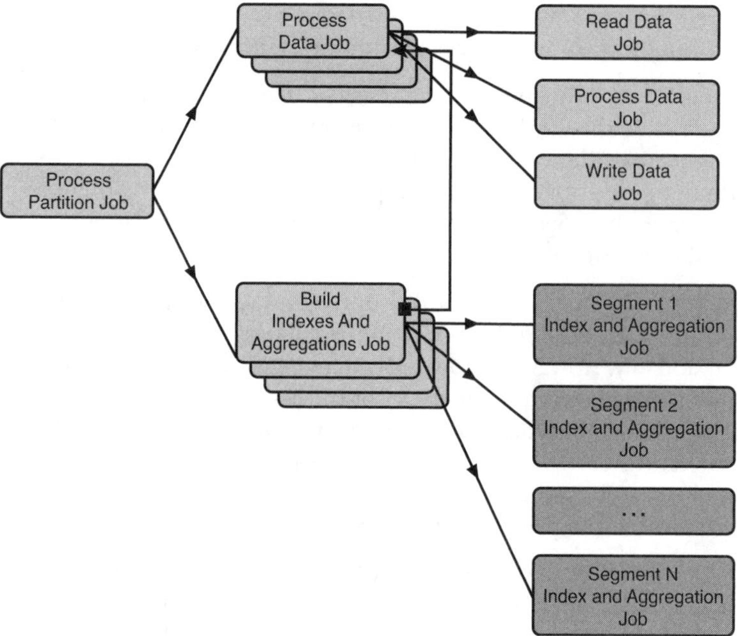

FIGURE 21.4 Analysis Services processes a partition in two stages.

- **Process Data**—Reads data and stores it in the partition files
- **Process Indexes and Aggregations**—Builds indexes and aggregations

Data Processing

Processing partition data follows the same path used when processing dimension attributes, as described earlier (see Figure 21.2). To process data, Analysis Services creates three jobs: the Read Data job, the Process Data job, and the Write Data job.

Before it starts reading data from the relational database, Analysis Services calculates the resources required to process the partition. It then calculates the amount of memory needed during processing and retrieves the necessary threads from the thread pool.

Read Data Job

The Read Data job retrieves a connection object from the connection pool and uses it to connect to the relational database. The number of concurrent connections supported by a relational database is a limited resource. If many processing operations are executing in parallel, the Read Data job might not obtain a connection object immediately; it goes into a sleep state, and waits for a connection object to become available.

After establishing a connection to the relational database, Analysis Services sends a query to populate a partition. The query contains columns for all the measures and columns for all granularity attributes on the measure group. For more information about granularity attributes, refer to Chapter 7, "Measures and Multidimensional Analysis."

Similar to the process used to read dimension data, the Read Data job then fills up the read buffer and passes it to the Process Data job.

Process Data Job

The Process Data job receives the read buffer filled by the Read Data job, similar to the process operation performed during attribute processing. The Process Data job iterates over the records in the read buffer and, for each field that contains a key value of the granularity attribute, looks up the `DataID` in the key hash table of the dimension attribute. It also aggregates measure values from the records that use the same set of keys as the granularity attributes.

To look up `DataIDs` in a dimension, the Process Data job loads key hash tables into memory for all attributes used in the measure group. If your measure group has many large dimensions, Analysis Services can consume large portions of memory during partition processing. If memory is limited, Analysis Services processes a partition in several passes (referred to as multipass processing). During multipass processing, Analysis Services groups several attributes and scans the data for every group to decode keys into `DataIDs`.

If, during processing, Analysis Services encounters several records with the same combination of dimension attribute keys, such records are aggregated according to the measure's aggregate function. Only a single, summary record is saved. However, Analysis Services aggregates values for such records with duplicate key sets only inside the current process buffer. If multiple buffers have such records, the values won't be aggregated during processing and will be aggregated only during query execution. To eliminate as many records with duplicate key sets as possible to improve the efficiency of the system,

Analysis Services defines the size of the process buffer as 1M (1,024 × 1,024) records. If the amount of memory available on the system is not sufficient to allocate a buffer for 1M records, Analysis Services uses a smaller buffer. If your system has enough memory, you can change the configuration of Analysis Services and make the size of the process buffer larger by setting the `BufferRecordLimit` server configuration property.

NOTE

When processing a partition in a measure group that contains a measure with the `DISTINCT_COUNT` aggregate function, Analysis Services requests that the data from the relational database be sorted according to the `DISTINCT_COUNT` measure. With the `DISTINCT_COUNT` aggregate function, Analysis Services aggregates records that have the same value of the `DISTINCT_COUNT` measure (and the same set of keys) and, because records are sorted by value, all records that can be aggregated typically will be close to each other. Therefore, a large process buffer is unnecessary in this case. Analysis Services uses a 64K records buffer to process a partition containing a `DISTINCT_COUNT` measure.

During partition processing, the same errors can occur that were encountered during dimension processing, which was discussed earlier in this chapter. You can use the `ErrorConfiguration` object to control how Analysis Services treats errors. The single difference is that, during partition processing, the keys are not required to be unique, and the `KeyDuplicate` error cannot occur.

The result of the Process Data job is a process buffer. After Analysis Services fills the process buffer, it passes the buffer to the Write Data job.

Write Data Job

The Write Data job performs three operations:

- Analysis Services sorts the data inside the process buffer to cluster and prepare data for compression and building indexes.
- Analysis Services divides data records into segments of 64K (65,536) records, analyzes them, calculates the compression ratio, and then compresses the records. Analysis Services can typically produce the greatest level of compression on integer values, whereas floating-point values have the lowest ratio of compression. We recommend that you use integer or currency data types for measures to speed up partition processing. In addition, compression of the data that uses the double data type can lead to a loss of precision when stored in Analysis Services. The compression algorithm could possibly lose a single digit in the fifteenth place of a double-precision floating-point number. Although you can turn off the `DeepCompressValue` server

configuration property to ensure that Analysis Services won't lose precision, using this property can make compression less efficient. Compression of data stored in Analysis Services is important; in many cases, it can reduce the data to a tenth of its original size. Compression not only saves disk space, but also improves query performance because less data has to be retrieved from the various data stores.

- In the last stage of processing, Analysis Services saves the compressed data segments and segment header to disk, into the partition map store.

NOTE

For `DISTINCT_COUNT` measures, Analysis Services automatically turns off the `DeepCompressValue` server configuration property because losing precision in data for `DISTINCT_COUNT` measures can lead to incorrect results.

Building Aggregations and Indexes

The process of building indexes for a partition is similar to that of building indexes for dimension attributes, as discussed earlier in this chapter. However, there are a number of differences. The main difference is that Analysis Services builds partition indexes together with aggregations.

To build partition indexes, Analysis Services creates the Build Index job. It tries to obtain a thread from the thread pool, estimates the memory required for its execution, and requests that amount from the Memory Manager. If sufficient resources are available, the Build Indexes job starts execution.

The Build Indexes job generates an internal request to the partition. This request has to retrieve `DataIDs` for all attribute members directly or indirectly related to members of the granularity attributes for all the dimensions for which it needs to build indexes (that is, attributes related to granularity attributes, except attributes that were marked as not optimized—where the `AttributeHierarchyOptimized` property is set to `NotOptimized` in the cube attribute). In addition, Analysis Services needs to decode `DataIDs` for attributes used in aggregations. To decode `DataIDs`, Analysis Services loads decoding tables for all these attributes, so the resources required to build partition indexes can be much larger than what is required to build dimension indexes.

Analysis Services builds indexes and aggregations by segments, as shown in Figure 21.5. It creates a new job for each segment sequentially. For each member of each attribute, Analysis Services detects the page of the partition map store where the data is stored and accumulates this information in the internal data structure. When information about the whole segment is accumulated, Analysis Services writes it to the index header file.

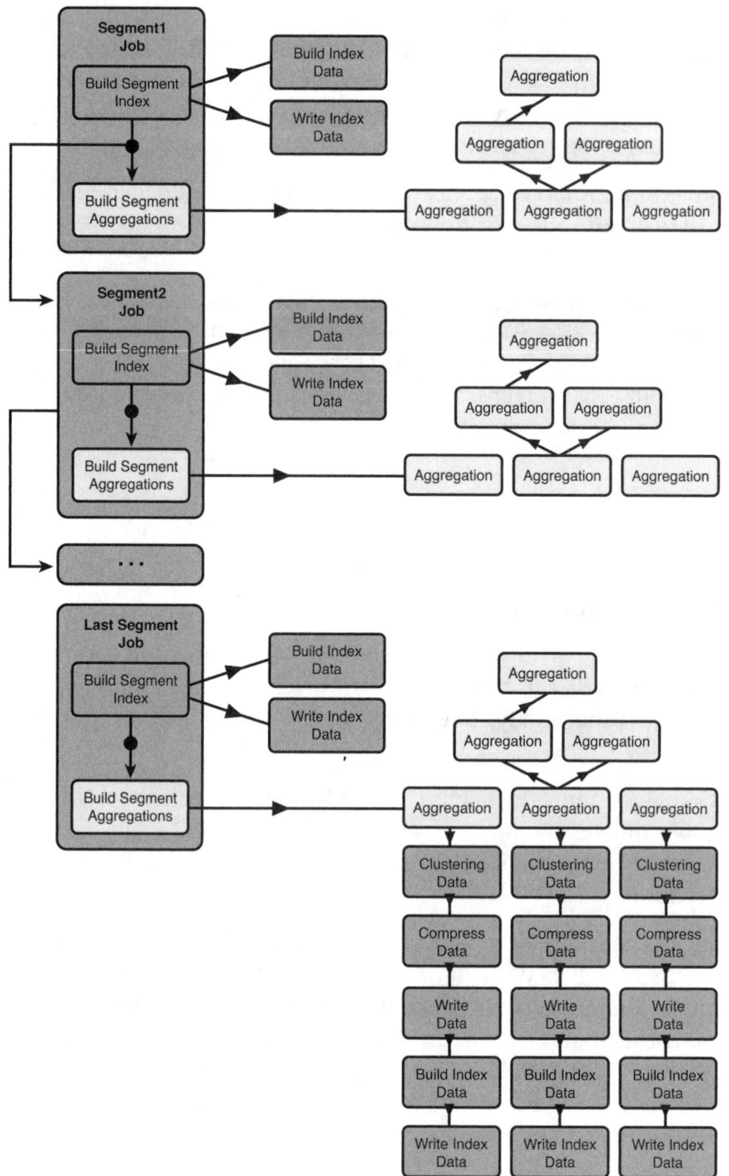

FIGURE 21.5 The process of building partition indexes and aggregations.

After Analysis Services determines the size and offset in the resulting index file, it starts the job for the next segment. In the meanwhile, the current job starts processing aggregations for the segment.

Analysis Services builds aggregations in parallel for several segments. Aggregations have the same data structures as partitions, and aggregation processing goes through the same stages as partition processing.

To build an aggregation, Analysis Services tries to allocate all buffers required for aggregation processing in memory. If the partition is large and has large aggregations, however, the system might not have enough memory. In that case, Analysis Services saves the intermediate results obtained while building aggregations into temporary files. At the end, when Analysis Services completes building aggregations for all partition segments, it merges all the temporary files to create a full set of aggregations.

If possible, try to avoid this situation because saving intermediate results to disk significantly slows down the processing. You can try one of the following:

- Increase the amount of memory available for Analysis Services during processing of partitions.
- Process fewer partitions in parallel.
- Define smaller partitions. We recommend a partition size containing between 5 and 20 million records.
- Design fewer aggregations for your partition.

NOTE

Aggregations with `DISTINCT_COUNT` measures can be large because they have to hold all the distinct values for that measure. When designing aggregations for your partition, try to include an attribute that is logically associated with the `DISTINCT_COUNT` measure. For example, if you have a `DISTINCT_COUNT` measure to count unique customers and a dimension attribute named `Customer Group`, we recommend including the `Customer Group` attribute into all aggregations because it will not change the number of records referenced within the aggregation.

After Analysis Services completes building aggregations for all segments, it sorts the aggregation data to cluster it, divides the aggregation data into the segments, compresses the aggregation data, and writes the data to disk. At the end, Analysis Services also builds indexes for aggregations.

Cube Processing Options

You can use several processing options to process your cube, measure group, and partition: `ProcessFull`, `ProcessData`, `ProcessIndex`, `ProcessClearIndexes`, `ProcessAdd`, and `ProcessClear`. (For more information about how to define the processing options, see Chapter 26, "Server Architecture and Command Execution.")

- `ProcessFull` deletes existing partition data, indexes, and aggregations and fully reprocesses a partition.
- `ProcessData` deletes existing partition data, indexes, and aggregations and loads only data in a partition.
- `ProcessIndex` builds indexes and aggregations for a partition.
- `ProcessClearIndexes` deletes partition indexes and aggregations.
- `ProcessAdd` incrementally updates a partition by adding new data to it.
- `ProcessClear` deletes partition data, indexes, and aggregations.

Therefore, the `ProcessFull` option could be seen as three consecutive commands: `ProcessClear`, `ProcessData`, and `ProcessIndex`.

Loading Data into a Partition

The `ProcessData` option enables you to organize and schedule processing of your data. Because building indexes and aggregations might require large amount of memory, you can separate loading of data into partitions from building indexes and aggregations.

We recommend configuring the `BufferMemoryLimit` server configuration property to maximize the number of partitions you can process in parallel. The processing performance in many cases depends on the speed at which relational database can supply data to Analysis Services. You can use the SQL Server Profiler application to see the SQL queries Analysis Services generates during partition processing and try to optimize your relational database for such requests by building additional indexes. Use SQL Server Database Engine Tuning Advisor for that. Also, `Join` clauses have a large effect on SQL query execution. You can avoid joins by redesigning your conceptual model or changing the binding to the relational data source.

To process a partition, Analysis Services typically utilizes two CPUs. Because partition-processing threads are often waiting (to receive the next portion of data from the network or during I/O operations), you can schedule parallel processing of more partitions than enabled by number of your CPUs. Therefore, if you have four processors in your machine, you can start processing two or more partitions in parallel to utilize your machine. On the other hand, you shouldn't start too many parallel operations. Doing so will cause a situation in which processing operations are spending too much time fighting for shared resources.

Based on empirical data at the time this book was written, if you can process 50K records in a second, you can consider your processing performance as good. If you can load 100K records per second, you can consider your processing performance optimized.

We recommend parallel processing of partitions from the same measure group, and serializing the processing of partitions from different measure groups. Partition processing requires Analysis Services to load hash and decoding tables for the granularity attributes. Different measure groups have different granularity attributes, and Analysis Services could consume a great deal of memory and might have to swap hash and decoding tables to disk while processing in parallel partitions from different measure groups.

Building aggregations and indexes for HOLAP partitions is an expensive operation because to build aggregations, partition data should be loaded into Analysis Services. Even though a HOLAP partition doesn't store processed data (because the storage of the partition itself is ROLAP), it needs data to build indexes and aggregations. Therefore, for HOLAP partitions, the `ProcessData` operation loads data, builds aggregations and indexes, and then disposes of the data. We've found that HOLAP partitions require a lot of management overhead as compared to MOLAP partitions, and have few benefits.

Building Aggregations and Indexes

Analysis Services builds aggregations and indexes when you issue the process command with the `ProcessFull`, `ProcessAdd`, or `ProcessIndex` option. In addition, Analysis Services can build indexes and aggregations as part of its lazy processing.

Lazy processing enables you to process only partition data using the `ProcessData` processing option to enable your users to see data in the partition right away and to postpone building of indexes and aggregations until a later time. Later on, Analysis Services automatically starts building indexes and aggregations for your partition in the background. When it completes these operations, your users will see improved performance.

Analysis Services has a lazy processing thread that periodically wakes up and iterates over all the partitions on the server to decide which indexes and aggregations are missing. Analysis Services starts lazy processing according to the priority specified by the `ProcessingPriority` property of the `Partition` object. The lazy processing thread analyzes CPU utilization and starts to build indexes and aggregations for more partitions to maximize utilization of the CPU.

Analysis Services processes indexes by internally issuing the `Process` command with the `ProcessIndex` option. If during the lazy processing operation you issue any Data Definition Language (DDL) command that affects the partition, Analysis Services cancels the lazy processing. To enable lazy processing, use the Analysis Services server configuration properties shown in Table 21.1.

TABLE 21.1 Lazy Processing Properties

Name	Description
`OLAP\LazyProcessing\Enabled`	A Boolean property that controls whether lazy processing is enabled
`OLAP\LazyProcessing\MaxCPUUsage`	The percentage of the machine's CPU to dedicate to background lazy processing
`OLAP\LazyProcessing\MaxObjectsInParallel`	The maximum number of partitions to process in parallel by lazy processing
`OLAP\LazyProcessing\SleepIntervalSecs`	The number of seconds that the lazy processing thread sleeps between iterations over partitions

The lazy processing mechanism has disadvantages; the main one is that you cannot predict when Analysis Services will finish building indexes and aggregations, so you don't know when users will get improved query performance for your cube. We recommend that you use the `ProcessIndex` processing option to build aggregations and indexes for your partitions. However, there is one exception: When a user performs a `ProcessUpdate` of a dimension that has flexible attribute relationships, Analysis Services deletes all flexible aggregations for all the partitions where changed attribute is used. You have an option to rebuild all aggregations and indexes as part of a dimension `ProcessUpdate` command by using the `ProcessAffectedObjects` processing command option. In that case, an update of the dimension might take a long time. You might decide to let Analysis Services update your dimension and rebuild indexes in the lazy manner.

If you distribute partitions to different machine using the remote-partition capabilities of Analysis Services, you can improve the performance of building indexes and aggregations. Because each machine builds indexes and aggregation independently, it can use more system resources.

To fine-tune the building of aggregations and indexes, you can divide this process into two stages. Build indexes of the partition before defining an aggregation design for it. (See Chapter 23 for more about aggregations and aggregation design.) Issue an `Alter` command to add the aggregation design to your partitions and process the indexes and aggregations again. This time Analysis Services builds only aggregations for your partitions and doesn't rebuild indexes.

You can add additional aggregations to your `AggregationDesign` object and build indexes and aggregations again. In that case, Analysis Services doesn't rebuild all existing aggregations; it builds only new aggregations for your partition.

NOTE

Analysis Services doesn't build aggregations and indexes for small partitions (partitions smaller than 4,096 records). It also doesn't build indexes for small aggregations. You can change this setting by using the `IndexBuildThreshold` server configuration property.

Incremental Updating Partitions

To update your partition incrementally, you can use the `ProcessAdd` processing option. Analysis Services internally implements the `ProcessAdd` operation in two stages. In the first stage, it creates a new partition and processes it with new data. In the second stage, Analysis Services merges the new partition into an existing one using the merge operation.

If we were to look at the larger problem of updating a cube with new data, we would see three main solutions:

- Incrementally update existing partitions in your cube
- Fully reprocess partitions pointing to a table that contains old and new data
- Create a new partition that contains new data

Each of the solutions has both pros and cons. Use an incremental update of a partition if you need to update it often with small amounts of data. After incremental processing, performance of partition slightly degrades because, after merging, the records with duplicate key set end up in different segments and are not aggregated. You should fully reprocess your partition when you see a drop in the performance of query execution.

NOTE

With an incremental update of partition data, Analysis Services cleans all caches of the measure group. Therefore, if you incrementally update your partition too often, you will cause degradation of query performance.

If you have a partition that you have to update often, consider using a remote-partition mechanism, which will help you isolate changes to caches. If a remote partition is updated, Analysis Services cleans the cache on the remote server and on the master server, but all other remote servers keep their caches.

Creating a new partition solves the problems of performance degradation that can happen after an incremental partition update, and doesn't require the long time that a full partition process would. Nevertheless, it can lead your measure group to contain too many partitions. We don't recommend using this method if you often update your cube with small amounts of data.

When designing your application, consider every option and decide which one best suits you. In addition, consider using combinations of update strategies. For example, you could incrementally update one partition every hour, but once a day you could fully process the partition, and once a week you could create a new partition to hold the preceding week's data.

Merging Partitions

Analysis Services enables you to merge two or more partitions in the same measure group into a single one. Internally, Analysis Services uses a merge of partitions during incremental update of partitions. Listing 21.1 shows the DDL for a partition merge, where `Target` is the partition in which you accumulate data and `Source` is the partition from which data merges into the `Target`.

LISTING 21.1 Syntax of the **`MergePartitions`** Command

```
<MergePartitions>
     <Sources>
          <Source>object_reference</Source>
     </Sources>
```

```
    <Target>object_reference</Target>
</MergePartitions >
```

Analysis Services merges partition in several steps. In the first stage, Analysis Services copies the data segments from all partitions into the `Target` partition. Analysis Services copies data from partial segments (segments that have fewer than 64K records) into a separate buffer and creates new segments based on the data in this buffer. In this way, Analysis Services avoids segmentation and fragmentation of data in partitions. Still, the order of data differs from the order of records you would get if you processed the partition using the `ProcessFull` option, because the data is not clustered together.

In the next stage, Analysis Services decides whether to merge partition aggregations. If partitions have the same aggregation design and aggregation exist in every `Source` partition, Analysis Services starts merging aggregation data segments. If a `Source` partition is missing some aggregations, the `Target` partition won't have those aggregations either.

After it completes merging aggregations, Analysis Services tries to merge partition indexes. Only if all source partitions have indexes does Analysis Services merge them. Otherwise, it rebuilds all the indexes for the `Target` partition. The same logic applies for the aggregation indexes—only if they exist in all `Source` partitions does Analysis Services merge aggregation indexes.

NOTE

Analysis Services keeps data in the segments sorted according to the DISTINCT_COUNT measure. As a result, during a merge, Analysis Services merges records from all partitions for the measure group containing `DISTINCT_COUNT` measure according to the sort order. This causes rebuilding of all data segments of the new partition; therefore, the merge operation rebuilds aggregations and indexes of such partitions.

After the `Merge` command finishes, your partition might not have all aggregations and indexes built, so you can send the `Process` command with the `ProcessIndex` option to build missing aggregations and indexes. If you have enabled lazy processing, Analysis Services builds missing indexes and aggregations for you in the background.

Progress Reporting and Error Configuration

While processing objects, Analysis Services produces progress reports. It generates the progress reports as the trace events that enable you to see the stage of processing currently executing. You can use the SQL Server Profiler application to subscribe to the

Progress Report events. (See Chapter 38, "Using Trace to Monitor and Audit Analysis Services," for more information about using Profiler.) The Processing dialog in Business Intelligence Development Studio and in SQL Server Management Studio also listens to the trace events and presents you with information about the progress of your processing operation. For instance, the Read Data thread generates a Progress Report Current event for every 1,000 records it reads from a relational database.

Each progress report also contains information about processing errors. Processing errors are a special category of error. They often indicate inconsistencies and referential integrity problems with your relational data. In many cases, you would like to collect a log of all the errors that happened during processing so that you can go back to the relational database and fix them.

Analysis Services provides you with the option to specify what kind of processing errors you would like to see in the progress report. It also enables you to collect processing errors in a separate log file. For that, you use the ErrorConfiguration object that can be specified for your Dimension, Cube, Measure Group, and Partition objects.

If the ErrorConfiguration object is specified for the parent object, it is used as the default for children objects if you don't explicitly override it in the child object definition.

NOTE

The defaults for missing values in the ErrorConfiguration object are not obtained from the parent object. You can create an empty ErrorConfiguration object for your partition to override values of the measure group's ErrorConfiguration object.

You can also specify ErrorConfiguration as part of your Process command. This definition overrides the ErrorConfiguration objects defined in the metadata. (For more information about Analysis Services commands, see Chapter 26.) An example of defining an ErrorConfiguration object is shown in Listing 21.2.

LISTING 21.2 DDL of **ErrorConfiguration** Object

```
<ErrorConfiguration>
    <KeyErrorLimit>0</KeyErrorLimit>
    <KeyErrorLogFile>c:\tmp\process.log</KeyErrorLogFile>
    <KeyNotFound>ReportAndStop</KeyNotFound>
    <KeyDuplicate>ReportAndStop</KeyDuplicate>
    <NullKeyConvertedToUnknown>ReportAndStop</NullKeyConvertedToUnknown>
    <NullKeyNotAllowed>ReportAndStop</NullKeyNotAllowed>
</ErrorConfiguration>
```

`ErrorConfiguration` Properties

All the properties of the `ErrorConfiguration` object are described in Table 21.2.

TABLE 21.2 **`ErrorConfiguration`** Properties

Name	Description
`KeyErrorLogFile`	Name of the file that Analysis Services uses to log all processing errors. If not specified, Analysis Services doesn't create the file. If you specify only the name of the file without the path, you will see your file created in the Log folder. (The Log folder is specified by the `LogDir` Analysis Services server configuration property.) The default value of the `KeyErrorLogFile` is `empty`.
`KeyErrorLimit`	Number of errors allowed before Analysis Services performs the action defined by `KeyErrorLimitAction`. It can either stop the processing operation or stop logging errors. If the number of errors encountered by Analysis Services has not reached the value specified by `KeyErrorLimit`, the processing completes successfully, and reports the warning about errors encountered during processing. For example, if you set this property to `100` and during processing you encounter 50 errors, you will see that your processing has completed successfully. The response to the `Process` command doesn't have error information, but the errors are written into the error log file and processing dialog reports them. The default value of this property is `0`.
`KeyErrorLimitAction`	Defines what action Analysis Services takes after `KeyErrorLimit` has been reached. Possible values are `StopProcessing` (Analysis Services terminates the processing operation) and `StopLogging` (Analysis Services stops logging errors but continues the processing operation). The default value is `StopProcessing`.
KeyErrorAction	Defines what action Analysis Services performs with the key for which the error occurred. You can select one of two values: `DiscardRecord` or `ConvertToUnknown`. With `DiscardRecord`, Analysis Services discards the record with an invalid key. This can lead to a loss of data. With `ConvertToUnknown`, the record with the invalid key is counted toward the `Unknown` member. The default value is `ConvertToUnknown`.

TABLE 21.2 **ErrorConfiguration** Properties

Name	Description
KeyNotFound	Defines the action that Analysis Services takes if it doesn't find a key of the attribute in the key store (for instance, if Analysis Services processes the Customers attribute in the Customer dimension and cannot find a city for the current customer in the keys hash table of the City attribute). You can select one of the values defined in Table 21.3. The default value to this property is ReportAndContinue.
KeyDuplicate	Defines the action that Analysis Services needs to take if it finds duplicate attribute keys during attribute processing. You can select one of the values defined in Table 21.3. We recommend setting this property to ReportAndStop to catch all inconsistencies in the relational data. The default value of this property is IgnoreError.
NullKeyNotAllowed	Defines the action that Analysis Services takes if it finds a null value in the key field and the key is marked as Error in the value of the attribute's NullProcessing property. You can select one of the values defined in Table 21.3.
NullKeyConvertedToUnknown	Defines the action that Analysis Services takes if it finds a null value in the key field and key is marked as ConvertToUnknown in the value of the attribute's NullProcessing property. (For more information about the NullProcessing property, see Chapter 6, "Cubes and Multidimensional Analysis.") You can select one of the values defined in Table 21.3. The default value of this property is ReportAndContinue.

There are three actions that you can set for KeyNotFound, KeyDuplicate, NullKeyNotAllowed, and NullKeyConvertedToUnknown. You can see descriptions of those values in Table 21.3.

TABLE 21.3 Actions on **KeyNotFound**, **KeyDuplicate**, **NullKeyNotAllowed**, and **NullKeyConvertedToUnknown** Errors

Value	Description
IgnoreError	The error is ignored and processing continues.
ReportAndContinue	The error is counted toward KeyErrorLimit and processing continues.
ReportAndStop	The error causes Analysis Services to stop processing.

Figure 21.6 demonstrates how Analysis Services treats errors occurring during the processing operations, depending on the settings in the `ErrorConfiguration` object.

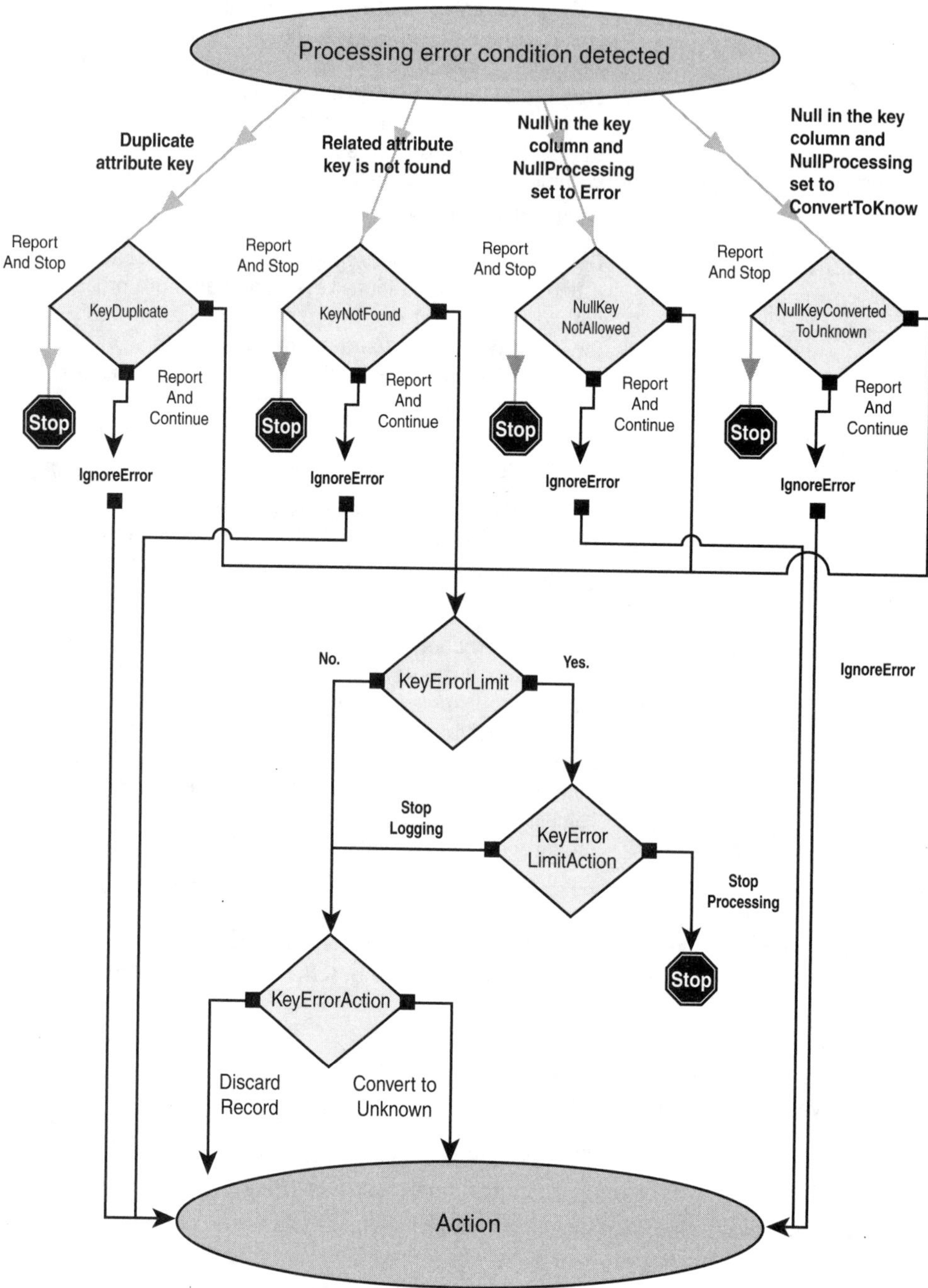

FIGURE 21.6 A scheme of how processing errors are handled.

Logging processing errors is a costly operation. You should log errors only while designing your application. After you have worked through all your issues and referential integrity problems with relational data, you can configure your processing to stop logging on key errors.

Processing Error Handling

While processing Analysis Services objects, you can receive any number of errors not related to data. You encounter errors while connecting to a relational database, errors finding tables or columns in a relational database, timeout errors waiting for a relational database to respond, Analysis Services can run out of memory, and so on.

Every processing thread can encounter an error independent of others. It raises a flag and informs other threads involved in the processing to cancel processing operations. Every thread independently logs error conditions, too. After all threads terminate, the Job Coordinator gathers all the errors and warnings from all the threads and generates the response. The response of the `Process` command contains a collection of errors from all processing threads. You should look closer at the returned result of the `Process` command, and use the information it provides to investigate the cause of the processing failure.

NOTE

Sometimes a progress report might lose some trace events and important information about errors. Therefore, we recommend that you analyze the return result of the `Process` command in the bottom of the Processing dialog.

You should analyze the return result of the `Process` command from the bottom up. The last error usually is the one that caused the processing to fail. The rest of the errors usually report from higher levels of execution.

Error handling is a costly operation. It could take some time for every processing thread to notice the cancel flag raised by another thread. Some of the threads could be sleeping, waiting for some resource to become available, and therefore not checking for any flag at all. For example, a Read Data thread can go into the sleep state waiting for a SQL query result.

CHAPTER 22

Using SQL Server Integration Services to Load Data

IN THIS CHAPTER

- Using SSIS
- Using Direct-Load ETL

Data warehousing applications require complex procedures for data transformation and analysis. The typical life cycle of data in such applications comprises four stages:

1. An online transaction processing (OLTP) system collects the data.
2. The data is loaded from the OLTP system into the data warehouse through the process of extraction, transformation, and loading (ETL).
3. The data is loaded from the data warehouse into a multidimensional model that enables fast access for analysis of the data.
4. The data is available to the end user through reports built on top of the model or, for ad-hoc analysis, through various analytical applications (Excel, ProClarity, and so on).

Figure 22.1 shows the typical ETL process of moving data from the OLTP system through the data warehouse to the multidimensional model. It also shows another way of directly loading data into Analysis Services: the ETL direct-load process in which SQL Server Integration Services (SSIS) pipes data from nonrelational data sources directly into the multidimensional model. The ETL direct-load process is helpful in the following situations:

- You have to load data from nonrelational data sources, such as web logs, XML documents, flat files, and so on.
- The data warehouse schema is complex and not well suited to map to a multidimensional model.

- A relational database management system (RDBMS) not supported by Analysis Services was used to build your data warehouse. (However, Analysis Services supports all major RDBMS versions.) To use your existing data warehouse with Analysis Services, you can define an SSIS package to populate the multidimensional model with data from your data warehouse.

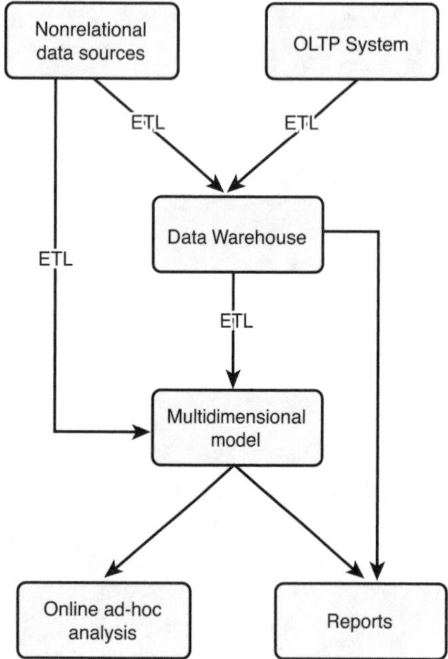

FIGURE 22.1 Data is moved from the OLTP system into the multidimensional model.

Using SSIS

SQL Server Integration Services allows you to create ETL packages. A single package contains a set of executables tasks that organized in the control flow: such as Bulk Insert Task, ActiveX Script Task.

One of the most important of these tasks is the data flow task. It defines logic for transforming the data. By itself, the data flow task consists of multiple components called transforms. Each of the transforms is responsible for a different type of data transformation, and they are tied into a pipeline defining the order of data flow. For example, you can create a package that iterates over tables in a relational database, checks which of the tables contain a new data, and loads that data into a multidimensional model. For building such a package, you would use the following:

- The for loop container.
- A table enumerator.

- A data flow task contains transforms of three different types:
    - **Source**—Reads data from a variety of sources such as relational databases, XML, binary, and flat files
    - **Data Flow Transformations**—Transforms data while moving it from source to destination (for example, aggregation, merge, and join)
    - **Destination**—Outputs data into different data stores

SSIS out of the box provides a large number of standard transforms. SSIS also provides an extensible infrastructure for building custom SSIS adapters, such as the third-party adapters available from Evolutionary Technologies International, Inc. (http://www.eti.com/) and Persistent Systems Private Limited (http://www.persistentsys.com/). You can even build your own adapters.

After building your package, you can run it directly from BI Development Studio to test it or you can use `dtexec.exe`. You can also use SQL Server Agent to schedule execution of your package.

Using Direct-Load ETL

To load and transform the data into Analysis Services, SSIS provides two data flow components: partition processing and dimension processing. Behind the scenes, SSIS loads the Analysis Services OLE DB provider into its process and uses it to upload data into the Analysis server. Figure 22.2 shows a diagram of this process.

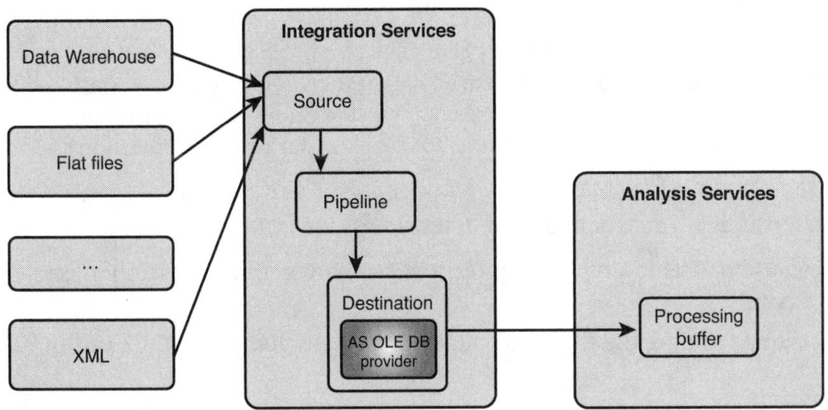

FIGURE 22.2 SSIS extracts data from the data warehouse, transforms it, and loads it into Analysis Services.

NOTE

You can run the package directly using `dtexec.exe/dtexecui.exe` or you can use SQL Server Agent's jobs infrastructure to schedule package execution.

The SSIS data flow component issues a processing command to Analysis Services. The command contains the data itself and instructs Analysis Services to process that data. If you run SQL Server Profiler to watch the commands executed during this pipeline processing, you will see the processing command as SSIS issues it. (However, you will not see the data in any of the events in SQL Server Profiler.) Analysis Services loads the incoming data into the processing buffer—the same buffer that receives the data from the relational data source (see Chapter 21, "Dimension and Partition Processing"). As the data is loaded into the buffer, Analysis Services continues the processing operation.

Within the pipeline, SSIS moves data from source to destination through buffers. By default, the buffer size is either 10MB or 10,000 records, whichever is smaller. Two properties of the data flow task determine the size of the buffers: `DefaultBufferMaxRows` and `DefaultBufferSize`.

NOTE

SSIS loads the Analysis Services OLE DB provider and acts like a client application with regard to the Analysis Services server. The Analysis Services OLE DB provider uses the XML/A protocol to send data. If you upload large amounts of data to the Analysis server, it is a good idea to enable binary XML and compression features for sending requests to Analysis Services. Change the value from `0` to `1` for the following Analysis Services server properties: `Network/Requests/EnableBinaryXML` and `Network/Requests/EnableCompression` (see Chapter 31, "Client/Server Architecture and Data Access").

Creating an SSIS Dimension-Loading Package

This section explains the process of building an SSIS package that loads data first into a dimension. You start by loading data into the `Warehouse` dimension of the FoodMart 2008 sample database. (Make sure that processing of the `Warehouse` dimension has not yet occurred. You can issue a `ProcessClear` command to clear the `Warehouse` dimension's processing if it has already taken place.)

For building such a package, you would use the following:

1. Open BI Dev Studio. Create a new SSIS project of type Integration Services Project, and give it a name.
2. In the package editor, drag the Data Flow task from the Toolbox onto the Control Flow tab.
3. On the Data Flow tab, drag OLE DB Source into the results pane of the Data Flow Task editor, as shown in Figure 22.3.
4. Right-click the OLE DB Source box and select Edit from the resulting menu.
5. In the OLE DB Source editor dialog, define the OLE DB connection manager for use by the OLE DB Source component. (The connection manager concept is similar to the concept of the Analysis Services `DataSource` object.)
6. Click the New button and create a new connection manager that points to the FoodMart 2005 sample SQL Server database.

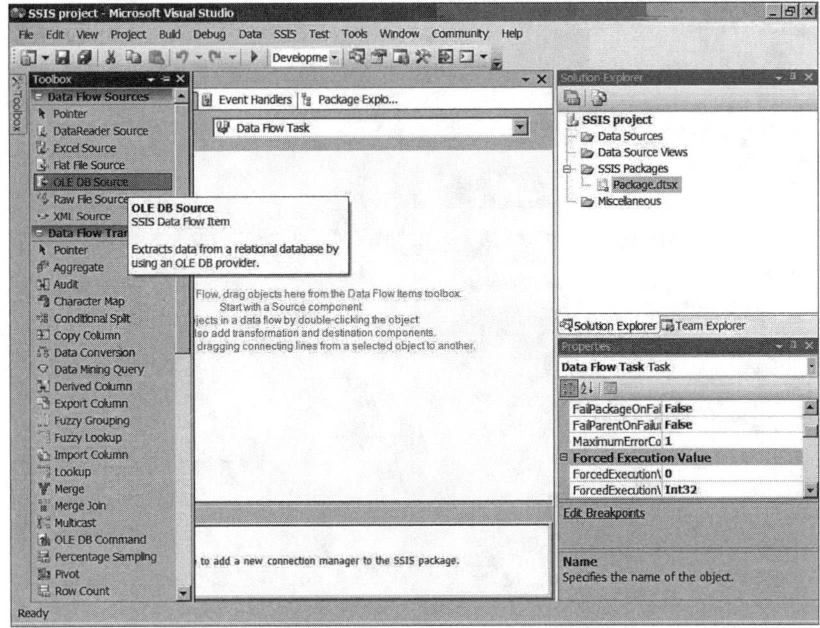

FIGURE 22.3 Drag and drop the OLE DB Source to define the source for your data flow.

7. In the Data Access Mode drop-down list, select Table or View. In the Name of the Table or the View drop-down list, select the `[dbo].[warehouse]` table (see Figure 22.4). This table loads data into the `Warehouse` dimension.
8. Click OK to go back to the Toolbox from which you dragged the OLE DB source. Drag the Dimension Processing data flow component (scroll down to find it) to the data flow editor.
9. Click the OLE DB Source box. (Two arrows appear below it.) Click the green arrow, move your mouse to the Dimension Processing box, and click again. The green arrow elongates to connect the OLE DB Source to the Dimension Processing box to show that the output of the OLE DB source flows into the Dimension Processing component.
10. Right-click the Dimension Processing box and select the Edit option from the resulting menu.
11. In the Dimension Processing Destination editor, define the Analysis Services dimension into which the SSIS package is going to load data.
12. Create a new connection manager that points to an instance of the Analysis server. Set the initial catalog to point to the FoodMart2005 sample database.
13. In the list below the Connection Manager box, select the `Warehouse` dimension (see Figure 22.5).
14. Click the Mappings node in the left pane and map the input columns (OLE DB Source table) to the destination columns (`Warehouse` dimension attributes), as shown in Figure 22.6.

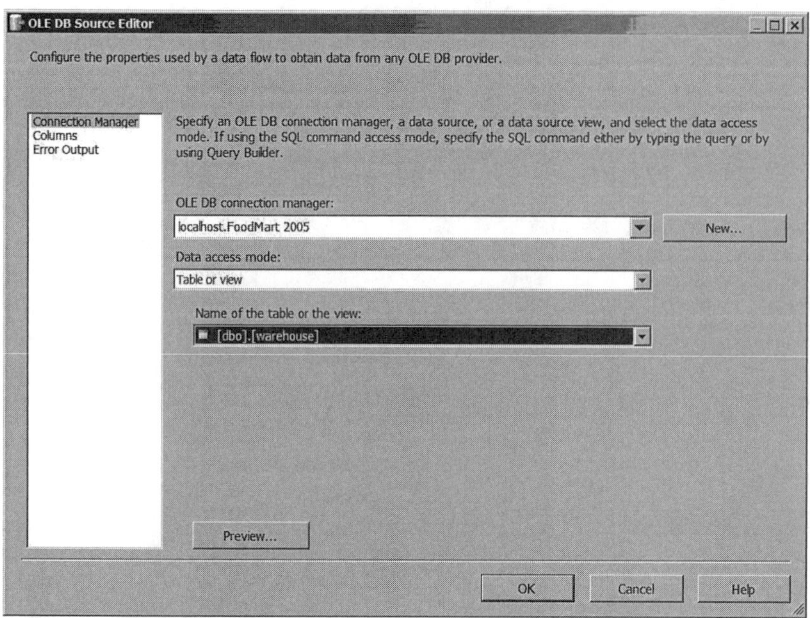

FIGURE 22.4 Create a new OLE DB connection manager and specify the data access mode.

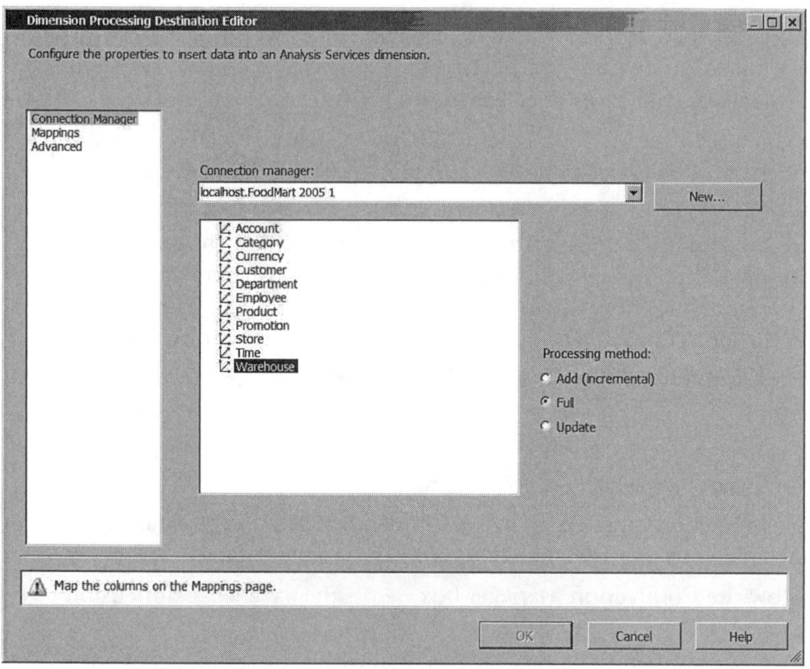

FIGURE 22.5 Select a dimension to load data into.

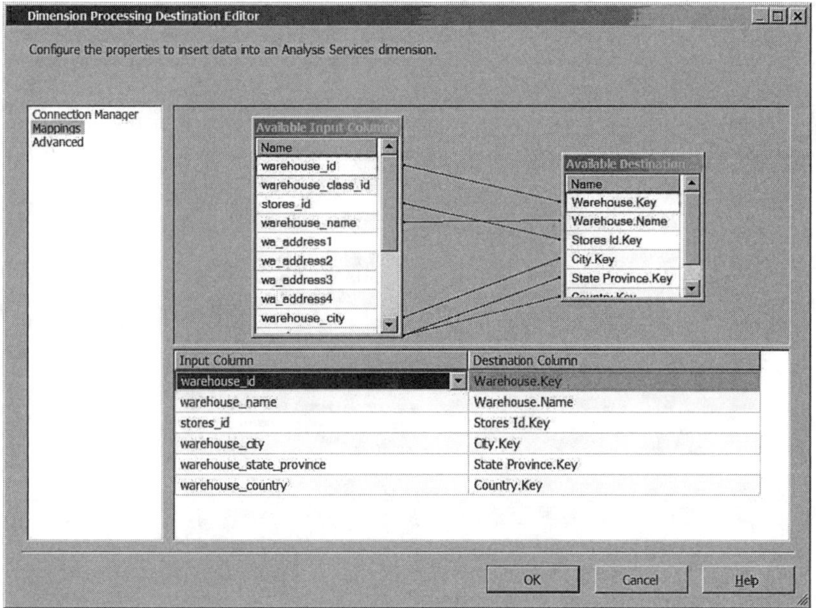

FIGURE 22.6 Define mappings between input and destination columns.

NOTE

For a dimension attribute based on a single column, Analysis Services specifies a single destination column for it in the form `AttributeName.Key`. If the dimension attribute also has a name column, Analysis Services specifies it in the form `AttributeName.Name`.

After you define all the mappings in the Dimension Processing Destination editor, you are ready to test your package. Close the Dimension Processing Destination editor and select Debug, Start Debugging from the resulting menu (or click F5).

At first, you will see two yellow boxes in the Data Flow tab of the package editor. As the package continues to execute, the boxes turn green one after another. Figure 22.7 shows the result.

At this point, you should be able to go to SQL Management Studio and browse the `Warehouse` dimension and its members.

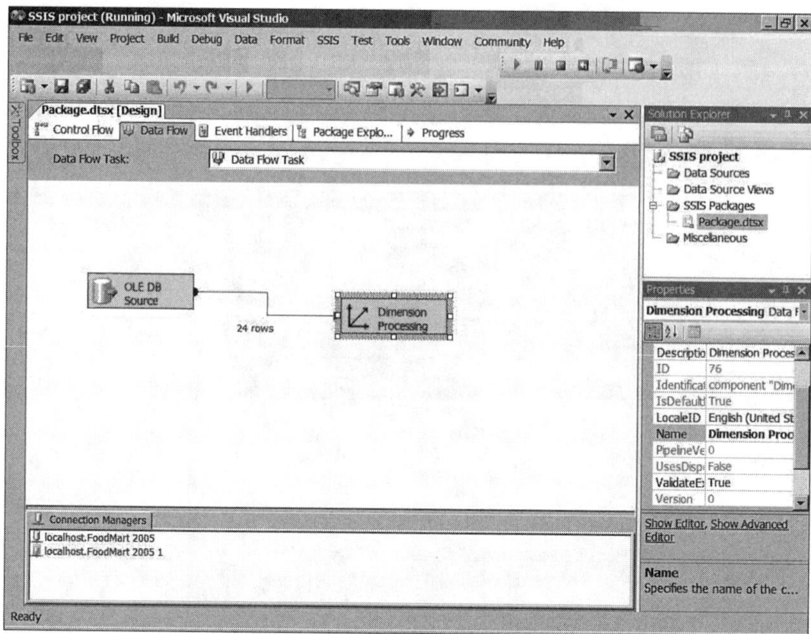

FIGURE 22.7 Use the debugging functionality of BI Dev Studio to test your dimension-loading package.

Creating an SSIS Partition-Loading Package

Now that you have built a dimension-loading package, go to SQL Management Studio and process your `Warehouse and Sales` cube using the Process Structure processing option. You will see all the dimensions of `Warehouse and Sales` cube as they are processed. Then, you can browse the cube, but you will not see any data because the data has not been loaded into partitions.

To build this package, follow these steps:

1. Delete the Dimension Processing data flow component in your SSIS project, and replace it with a Partition Processing data flow component from the Toolbox pane (refer to Figure 22.3 earlier in this chapter).
2. Add a flow arrow from the OLE DB Source data flow component to the Partition Processing component.
3. Modify your OLE DB Source data flow component to point to the `[dbo].[inventory_fact_1997]` table.
4. Right-click the Partition Processing box and select Edit from the resulting menu.
5. In the Partition Processing Destination editor, expand the `Warehouse and Sales` cube and select the `Inventory Fact 1997` partition in the `Warehouse` measure group (see Figure 22.8).

6. Click the Mappings node in the left pane and define the mappings from the source columns to the destination columns. (This is similar to step 14 in the earlier procedure.)

After you define all the mappings, you can test your package and load data into the `Inventory Fact 1997` partition. As soon as the package loads data into the partition, you can open SQL Management Studio and browse the `Warehouse and Sales` cube. This time you should see some values for the measures in the `Warehouse` measure group.

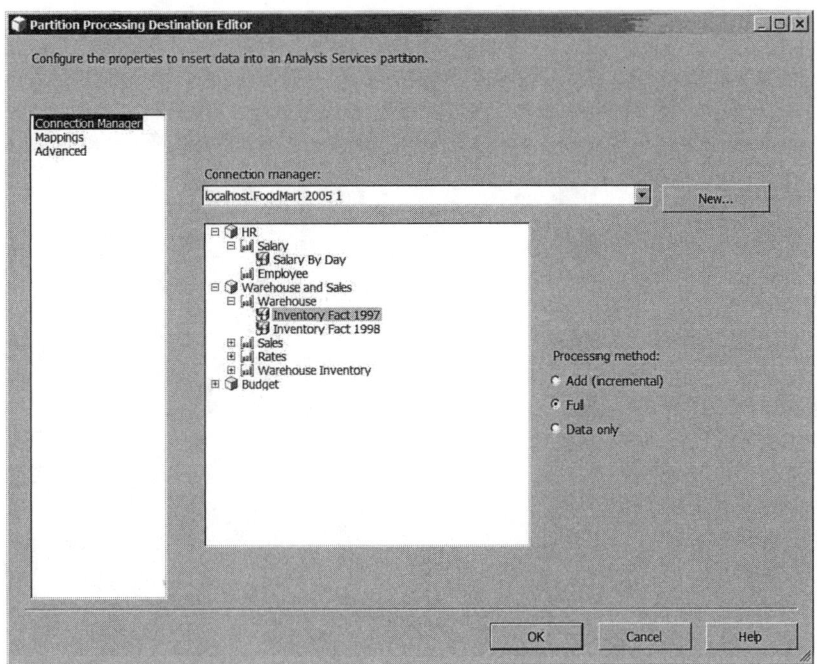

FIGURE 22.8 Select a destination partition for the SSIS package.

Mapping Composite Keys

If a dimension attribute key or name is bound to multiple columns in a relational table, it is a *composite key*. For example, in the `Customer` dimension, two columns form the basis of the `City` attribute's key: `customer.city` and `customer.state_province`. If you were to decide to use an SSIS package to load data into the `Customer` dimension, at the mapping stage you would see `City.Key(0)` and `City.Key(1)` in the destination columns. These destination columns correspond to the `customer.city` and `customer.state_province` input columns, respectively. (Open your Analysis Services database in BI Dev Studio to see how attributes map to the relational table columns.)

After you map the source column to the destination column, you no longer see the source column in the drop-down list. If you have a composite key in your dimension and you need to map a single relational column to several destination columns, you must tweak your OLE DB Source component to have a single column appear more than once in your OLE DB Source component. In the OLE DB Source editor, define the data access mode as SQL Command rather than Table or View (as shown in Figure 22.4). Then, compose a SQL command so that a `Select` statement contains the source column more than once. Alternatively, you can use the Derived Column transform to duplicate columns.

CHAPTER 23

Aggregation Design and Usage-Based Optimization

IN THIS CHAPTER

- Aggregations and Collection of Aggregations
- Designing Aggregations
- Query Usage Statistics
- Manual Design and Management of Aggregations
- Monitoring Aggregation Usage

Analysis Services has many objects, but physically it stores data only in dimensions and partitions. Partitions serve as storage for fact data. To provide fast access to the partition data, Analysis Services allows for creating two auxiliary data structures: partition indexes and aggregations. Aggregations and indexes are created at processing time. (For information about storing data, see Chapter 20, "Physical Data Model.")

Aggregations are data structures that store data that is precalculated (aggregated) based on the data stored in a specific partition. Because the size of an aggregation is usually smaller than the original data, you can query that aggregated data and get a much quicker response. Designing a subset of aggregations that best suits your query load is a nontrivial task. The discussion that follows will help you to understand the basic principles of aggregation.

Aggregations and Collection of Aggregations

Let's use the `Warehouse` measure group from the FoodMart 2008 sample database to explore the definition and usefulness of aggregations. Fact data stored in a partition is the same data as that in the fact table: a collection of measures and the dimension keys on the granularity level of the measure group. Figure 23.1 shows an example from the `Warehouse` measure group.

The diagram in Figure 23.2 takes the same data shown in Figure 23.1 and arranges it so that you can see the hierarchies of the `Product`, `Time`, `Store`, and `Warehouse` dimensions.

The lowest granularity (which is what's shown in Figure 23.1) is represented by the line connecting the lowest levels of the hierarchies.

Product_Id	Time_Id	Store_Id	Warehouse_Id	Units_Ordered	Units_shipped
350 (Swell Canned Peaches)	369 (1997-01-03)	2 (Store 2)	2 (Foster Products)	42	42
1397 (Sunset Paper Towels)	369 (1997-01-03)	2 (Store 2)	2 (Foster Products)	82	87

FIGURE 23.1 Data records stored in the `Warehouse` measure group.

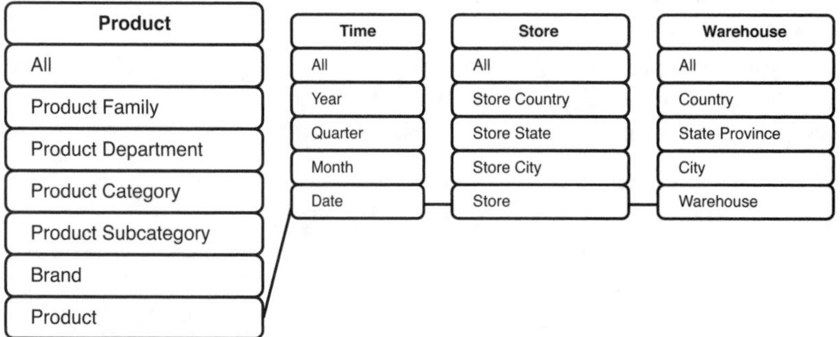

FIGURE 23.2 The line connects the levels that represent the lowest level granularity of the partition data.

If you aggregate data up to the `Brand` attribute in `Product` dimension, by the `Month` attribute in the `Time` dimension, by the `Store City` attribute in the `Store` dimension, and by the `City` attribute in the `Warehouse` dimension, you get the results shown in Figure 23.3.

Brand	Month	Store City	City	Units_Ordered	Units_shipped
Milk	February	Tacoma	Tacoma	47	47
Sugar	February	Seattle	Seattle	86	86

FIGURE 23.3 This data results from aggregating data up to the **`Brand`** attribute.

You can represent the granularity of the aggregation as the upper line in the dimension diagram in Figure 23.4.

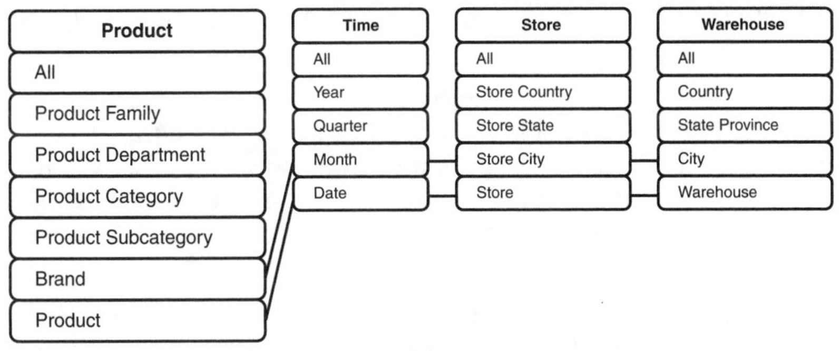

FIGURE 23.4 The upper line represents the granularity of our aggregation.

With partitions, you can store your data on the hard drive in a separate data structure (the aggregation). The next time there is a request for data of the same granularity as represented in the aggregation, the result is ready.

An aggregation is typically smaller than the fact data it is based on. The smallest aggregation is one that contains, in a single row, the grand totals or *all* levels for the data stored in the partition (see Figure 23.5).

Product	Time	Store	Warehouse	Units_Ordered	Units_shipped
All	All	All	All	227238	227238

FIGURE 23.5 This single row represents the grand totals and all levels of the partition data.

This aggregation gives us the grand total of units ordered and units shipped for all years, in all stores, for all products, and in all warehouses. When it's built, the aggregation will contain the single row shown in Figure 23.5. It will return responses to queries very quickly.

Designing Aggregations

If one aggregation increases query performance, why not build all the possible aggregations for the cube so that every query is answered by some aggregation? Because the number of potential aggregations is so large that if you were to build all of them, it would take a lot of time and a lot of space.

For example, we'll calculate how many potential aggregations you can have for just the `Warehouse` measure group in the `Warehouse and Sales` cube. (Figure 23.4 shows a diagram of the `Warehouse` measure group aggregations.) If you choose a single attribute from every dimension in the measure group, you would define the aggregation by `{ Product.attribute, Time.attribute, Store.attribute, Warehouse.Attribute }`. You can calculate the number of aggregations you could create; it would be the product of the number of dimension hierarchy levels across all dimensions: 7 × 5 × 5 × 5 = 874 – 1 (for the lowest level granularity) = 873. That's a lot!

Fortunately, you don't need to build that many aggregations to get a substantial performance gain for queries to your cube. As it happens, a query can be answered from an aggregation that is only a partial match. For example, if you were to send a query asking for data on the granularity of the `State Province` attribute of the `Warehouse` dimension, the result could come from the scanning and aggregating data from the aggregation on the `City` level.

This operation is a little longer than reading data from an exact match, but is much faster than reading and aggregating data from the lowest level of granularity. You can build a set of aggregations that covers a space of potential queries that speed the performance of your cube considerably. You can run the Aggregation Design Wizard to design a good set of aggregations that will provide good coverage for your cube.

Relational Reporting-Style Dimensions

If your dimension is a relational reporting-style dimension (that is, it doesn't have natural hierarchies), you'll need more aggregations to cover a space of queries. And these aggregations are a lot less efficient.

Dimensions in our sample database FoodMart 2008 have natural hierarchies defined and, therefore, relationships defined between attributes. When your dimensions have natural hierarchies, you don't need to include two attributes from the same dimension to build an aggregation. To make the calculations we presented in the earlier section, we didn't need more than a single attribute. It didn't make sense to include both the `Store State` and `Store City` attributes in a single aggregation.

If we were to create an aggregation that contains both attributes, the `Store State` attribute would be redundant. Data stored in this aggregation will be on the granularity of the `Store City` attribute. The `Store City` attribute is all you need to define the aggregation. You can see the redundancy for yourself in Figure 23.6.

On the other hand, if you don't have natural hierarchies in your dimension (relational reporting-style dimension), you can include more than a single attribute from a dimension when you define your aggregation definition. And because of that, you need to define many more aggregations for your measure group to achieve good performance for your cube.

In the earlier example, suppose that there is no relationship between the Store State and Store City attributes. Even though you can't have multiple cities with the same name in a state, you can have a city with same name located in several states (Portland, for example, in Oregon and Maine, to name two). In Figure 23.7, you can see that an aggregation that contains more than a single attribute from a dimension is valid rather than redundant.

You can calculate how many aggregations you need to maximize query performance in a cube that has relational reporting-style dimensions. For this calculation, an aggregation definition is represented as a series of digits, where every attribute in every dimension is represented by either 1 or 0. 1 represents the presence of the attribute; 0 represents its absence in the aggregation definition. These digits are grouped according to dimensions, with the groups separated by commas.

Brand	Month	Store State	Store City	City	Units_Ordered	Units_shipped
Booker	February	WA	Tacoma	Tacoma	47	47
Carlson	February	WA	Seattle	Seattle	86	86

FIGURE 23.6 The Store State and Store City attributes define an aggregation that is the same as one without the Store State attribute.

Brand	Month	Store State	Store City	City	Units_Ordered	Units_shipped
Booker	February	WA	Tacoma	Tacoma	47	47
Carlson	February	OR	Portland	Portland	144	144
Carlson	February	MN	Portland	Portland	23	23

FIGURE 23.7 The Store State and Store City attributes define a valid aggregation.

For example, this series of digits represents an aggregation in the Warehouse measure group: 001000,0000,0000,0000. The first group of digits represents attributes from the Product dimension. The digit 1 in the third position indicates that third attribute of the dimension, Product Category, participates in the aggregation. In the next group, there is no attribute from the `Time`, `Store`, or `Warehouse` dimensions. The absence of attributes indicates that these dimensions are aggregated to the highest level. You can think of this as if the granularity of the data is set to the All level for a dimension that has all its attributes set to `0`.

You can calculate the total number of different series of digits like this one for the `Warehouse` measure group. Use the following formula: 2 to the power of (num `Product` attributes + num `Time` attributes + num `Store` attributes + num `Warehouse` attributes) = 2 to the power of (6 + 4 + 4 + 4) = 262,144—a huge number.

The total number of aggregations is a little smaller than that because even in a relational reporting-style dimension, all the attributes are related to the key attribute. If the key attribute of the dimension participates in the aggregation, it doesn't make sense for any other attribute from the same dimension to participate.

Use the following formula to calculate the number of potential aggregations in the `Warehouse` measure group:

2 to the power of (5 + 3 + 3 + 3) [the aggregations that contain nonkey attributes] +

2 to the power of (3 + 3 + 3) [the aggregations that contain the key attribute of the `Product` dimension and nonkey attributes from other dimensions] +

2 to the power of (5 + 3 + 3) [the key attribute of the `Time` dimension] +

2 to the power of (5 + 3 + 3) [the key attribute of the `Store` dimension] +

2 to the power of (5 + 3 + 3) [the key attribute of the `Warehouse` dimension] =

22,528

This is a huge number. We considered only 4 dimensions with a total number of 18 attributes. You can see now that it's very expensive to optimize your cube when you have relational reporting-style dimensions. Even with a small number of attributes, it's really expensive to maintain good overall query performance with relational reporting-style dimensions.

It's even harder to optimize cube performance with relational reporting-style dimensions because queries can't reuse data from smaller aggregations. For example, in the earlier dimension with natural hierarchies, a query to the `Store State` attribute could use data from the aggregation with the `Store City` attribute. When you have a relational reporting-style dimension, a query can use data from only the aggregation with the `Store State` attribute if it exists. Otherwise, the data for the query has to come from the fact data.

Flexible Versus Rigid Aggregations

Depending on the way you defined relationships between attributes in a dimension, Analysis Services assigns a type (either rigid or flexible) to an aggregation. The type is assigned based on a set of rules about those relationships. Flexible aggregations are dropped from the partition as a result of an update of the dimension; rigid aggregations remain.

The logic Analysis Services applies to determine that an aggregation is rigid is this: For every attribute that participates in the aggregation, the relationship chain to the granularity attribute of the dimension is rigid; that is, all the relationships in the chain are rigid. On the other hand, if any relationship is flexible, the aggregation itself is flexible. For example, for the aggregation shown in Figure 23.2, the attribute relationship chains are as follows:

- **In the `Product` dimension**—`Product Subcategory` to `Brand`, `Brand` to `Product`
- **In the `Time` dimension**—`Month` to `Date`
- **In the `Store` dimension**—`Store City` to `Store`
- **In the `Warehouse` dimension**—`City` to `Warehouse`

If any of these relationships is flexible, the aggregation is considered flexible. If all the relationships are rigid, the aggregation is a rigid one. As it happens, this aggregation is a flexible one.

With a flexible aggregation, members can move from one parent to another during a dimension update. The aggregate totals based on one of the parent attributes would be invalid. And the flexible aggregation would be invalid. Analysis Services drops flexible aggregations during dimension updates to make sure that the aggregate numbers are correct.

NOTE

You can force the rebuilding of flexible aggregations during an incremental update of a dimension. Specify the `ProcessAffectedObjects` option in the dimension processing command. If you didn't specify this option, you can use the `ProcessIndex` command for your dimension; or you can rely on lazy processing to build flexible aggregations in the background. Any of these is an expensive solution.

However, you can use the `ProcessAdd` command to add only new members to a dimension. Using `ProcessAdd` eliminates the need to drop any aggregations. Along with that, you can use the `ProcessAdd` command to modify the properties of existing members.

Aggregation Objects and Aggregation Design Objects

In Analysis Services, physical aggregations belong to individual partitions. However, you logically define aggregation objects as part of an aggregation design object that belongs to a measure group. Figure 23.8 contains a diagram of these relationships.

23

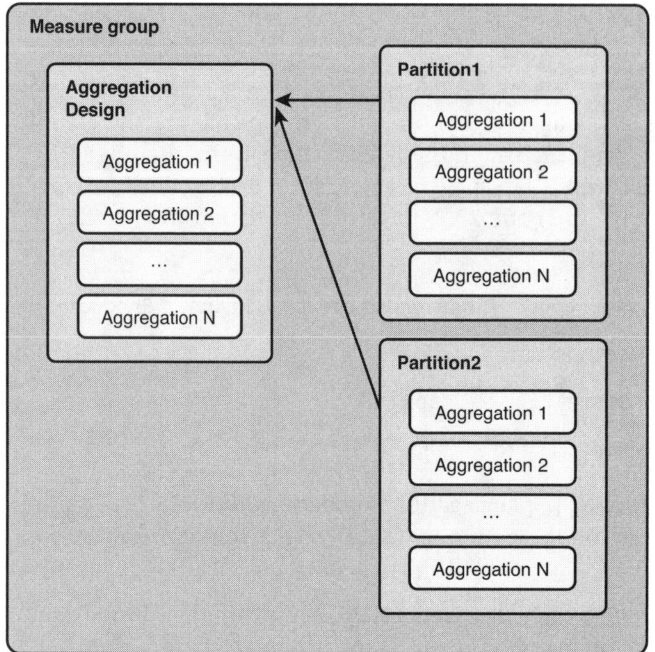

FIGURE 23.8 Partitions can reference the same aggregation design object.

This metadata design allows a single `AggregationDesign` object and its aggregation objects to be shared easily by multiple partitions. An aggregation object contains a collection of dimensions; every dimension element can contain zero or more attributes. A partition uses the `AggregationDesignID` property to reference an aggregation design object.

Using Data Definition Language to Define Aggregations

Listing 23.1 shows the Data Definition Language (DDL) that defines an aggregation in the `Warehouse` measure group. The aggregation has two attributes: the `Year` attribute (referenced by the `The Year`) from the `Time` dimension, and the `Product Category` attribute from the `Product` dimension.

LISTING 23.1 DDL for an Aggregation

```
<Aggregation>
     <ID>Aggregation 1</ID>
     <Name>Aggregation 1</Name>
     <Dimensions>
          <Dimension>
               <CubeDimensionID>Time</CubeDimensionID>
               <Attributes>
                    <Attribute>
                         <AttributeID>The_Year</AttributeID>
                    </Attribute>
               </Attributes>
          </Dimension>
          <Dimension>
```

```
            <CubeDimensionID>Warehouse</CubeDimensionID>
        </Dimension>
        <Dimension>
            <CubeDimensionID>Product</CubeDimensionID>
            <Attributes>
                <Attribute>
                    <AttributeID>Product Category</AttributeID>
                </Attribute>
            </Attributes>
        </Dimension>
        <Dimension>
            <CubeDimensionID>Store</CubeDimensionID>
        </Dimension>
    </Dimensions>
</Aggregation>
```


An AggregationDesign object contains a set of aggregations along with metadata that Analysis Services uses in the aggregation design algorithm to make qualified decisions. (For information about the aggregation design algorithm, see the "The Aggregation Design Algorithm" section later in this chapter.)

An Aggregations collection contains a set of aggregations. Analysis Services will not validate an Aggregations collection that contains duplicate aggregations. If you are planning to design aggregations yourself, make sure you don't have duplicate aggregations.

A Dimensions collection contains estimated counts for every attribute in every dimension in the measure group. The Analysis Services aggregation design algorithm uses the estimated counts to calculate potential size of aggregation. When you design an AggregationDesign object manually, you don't have to include a Dimensions collection.

Listing 23.2 shows the DDL definition for an AggregationDesign object in the Warehouse measure group with two collections: Aggregations and Dimensions. (We've included the Dimensions collection so that you can see what it's like.)

LISTING 23.2 DDL for an **AggregationDesign** Object

```
<AggregationDesign>
    <ID>AggDesign</ID>
    <Name>AggDesign</Name>
    <Dimensions>
        <Dimension>
            <CubeDimensionID>Time</CubeDimensionID>
            <Attributes>
                <Attribute>
                    <AttributeID>Time By Day</AttributeID>
                    <EstimatedCount>730</EstimatedCount>
                </Attribute>
                <Attribute>
                     <AttributeID>The Day</AttributeID>
                     <EstimatedCount>7</EstimatedCount>
                </Attribute>
.....
```

```
            </Attributes>
        </Dimension>
    </Dimensions>
    <Aggregations>
        <Aggregation>
            <ID>Aggregation 1</ID>
            <Name>Aggregation 1</Name>
            <Dimensions>
....
</AggregationDesign>
```

After you create an aggregation design object and set the `AggregationDesignID` property of the partition, you create physical aggregations for partition by initiating the processing of the partition. (Execution of the `ProcessFull` command, for example, would create aggregations.)

Partition aggregations are created during the last stage of partition processing (index processing). If you already have data loaded into the partition, you can change or add aggregations to your aggregation design object and use the `ProcessIndex` command to process the aggregations separately without reprocessing the data. You can also use `ProcessClearIndexes` to drop indexes and aggregations from your parturition.

NOTE

Changing the `AggregationDesign` object or the `AggregationDesignID` property of the partition will not cause the partition to drop the existing set of physical aggregations. You get into a situation where the metadata differs from the partition data. The set of aggregations defined for the partition differs from the set of aggregations processed for it. You can use the `LastProcessed` and `LastSchemaUpdate` partition properties along with the `LastSchemaUpdate` property of the `AggregationDesign` object to determine whether the logical aggregation design is out of sync with the physical aggregations.

The Aggregation Design Algorithm

You don't have to design aggregations for your cube manually. Analysis Services provides the Aggregation Design Wizard, which will design a set of aggregations for your cube. You can run the Aggregation Design Wizard either from Business Intelligence Development Studio (BI Dev Studio) or from SQL Server Management Studio.

To make decisions about the best set of aggregations, the aggregation design algorithm must have an estimated count of the members in all the attributes in all the dimensions in the measure group. If the `EstimatedCount` property of a dimension attribute isn't set, the Aggregation Design Wizard tries to count the members in the attribute by submitting a query to the relational database (such as `select distinct count...`). If your dimensions are large and have many attributes, the wizard's estimation phase can take a while.

After the estimates are obtained from the relational database, the Aggregation Design Wizard updates the `EstimatedCount` property of an attribute object. The next time you run the wizard, it won't ask you to supply an estimated count of members. If you designed your aggregations using a smaller (development) version of the database, it makes sense to reset the estimated counts. When you run the Aggregation Design Wizard on the production version of the database, the wizard will get better estimates.

Nonaggregatable Attributes

Some dimension attributes can't be aggregated; that is, they are *nonaggregatable*. For example, you wouldn't want to aggregate currencies across the `Currency Code` attribute. At any point in time, only a single currency is valid. In aggregation design, such an attribute needs to participate in all the aggregations in the measure group.

Set the `IsAggregatable` property of the attribute to `FALSE` to instruct the aggregation design algorithm to include this attribute in all the aggregations it designs.

NOTE

Change the `IsAggregatable` property with care, because setting it to `FALSE` will affect all the default members. In addition, we don't recommend that you have more than one nonaggregatable attribute in a dimension.

Dimension and Attribute Properties

The `Cube Dimension Attribute` object has an `AggregationUsage` property that is taken into account by the aggregation design algorithm when it designs aggregations. Table 23.1 lists the values this property takes.

TABLE 23.1 **`AggregationUsage`** Values

Name	Description
`Full`	The attribute will be inserted into any aggregation designed by the aggregation design algorithm.
`None`	The attribute won't be considered by the aggregation design algorithm at all.
`Unrestricted`	The aggregation design algorithm will always consider this attribute as a potential candidate.
`Default`	The default value for the `Cube` attribute. If a dimension attribute has no user-defined hierarchy, none of the attributes in the dimension is considered at all by the aggregation design algorithm. If the `Cube` attribute is part of a user-defined hierarchy, this value is treated as `Unrestricted`.

Query Usage Statistics

In addition to the ability to design aggregations based on only the structure of dimensions and attributes, Analysis Services enables you to take into account statistical information about queries when you design aggregations.

The Usage-Based Optimization Wizard runs exactly the same aggregation design algorithm, but it also enables you to influence your aggregation design by providing it with statistical information that is collected in the query log. To launch the Usage-Based Optimization Wizard, in SQL Server Management Studio, right-click the node for the partition you're working on and select Usage Based Optimization from the resulting menu.

The wizard connects to a *query log*, a relational table where Analysis Services logs statistical information about user queries. It enables you to select a subset of the query log that will automatically be entered into the aggregation design algorithm. This information enables the algorithm to design better suiting aggregations for your cube.

The Usage-Based Optimization Wizard runs a slight variation of the aggregation design algorithm. The algorithm moves gradually through the space of potential aggregations. It starts from the top—the aggregation that contains grand totals across all dimensions—and gradually makes its way down to the lower-granularity aggregations. As it progresses through the aggregation space, it considers each aggregation to determine whether adding it to the existing the set of aggregations. Greater weight is given to aggregations that will improve the performance of the subset of queries you selected in the wizard.

Interesting to mention a new option in the SQL Server 2008 version of the Usage-Based Optimization Wizard: If you run the wizard, on the "Completing the wizard" page you will find an option to merge new aggregations to the one existing already. For example: Run the Usage-Based Optimization Wizard for `Inventory Fact 1997` partition in the `Warehouse` measure group, and you will be able to merge new aggregations with aggregations of an existing aggregation design for that partition. This option enables you to incrementally update an existing aggregation design with new aggregations based on the usage of aggregations by the queries.

Setting Up a Query Log

To run the Usage-Based Optimization Wizard, you need to configure Analysis Services to write statistical information into a query log. A query log is a table in the SQL Server database. To set up a query log, you must change several server properties, described in Table 23.2.

TABLE 23.2 **QueryLog** Server Properties

Name	Description
`Log\QueryLog\QueryLogSampling`	Defines the frequency with which information is logged to the query log. The default value is `10`; that is, every tenth query is logged. To log every query, set this property to 1.

TABLE 23.2 **QueryLog** Server Properties

Name	Description
`Log\QueryLog\QueryLogConnectionString`	By default, this property is empty—Analysis Services doesn't log any queries to a query log. You can change this property to a valid connection string pointing to a valid copy of a SQL Server database. If `CreateQuery LogTable` value is set to `1`, Analysis Server creates a new table in the SQL Server database unless one with the same name already exists.
`Log\QueryLog\QueryLogTableName`	The name of the table in the SQL Server database that holds the Analysis Services query log. By default, this property is set to `OlapQueryLog`.
`Log\QueryLog\CreateQueryLogTable`	If this property is set to `1`, Analysis Services attempts to create a new table in the SQL Server database that the `QueryLog ConnectionString` property points to. If the table already exists, Analysis Services continues logging queries into it. By default, this property is set to `0`.

NOTE

The Analysis Services account must have sufficient privileges to create a query log table. We recommend that you create a dedicated SQL Server database to hold the Analysis Services query log. If your SQL Server database is not available for Analysis Services to log queries against, you won't see any notice of this in the user interface. Monitor the Windows event log for events that indicate query log errors.

When Analysis Services starts, it tries to connect to the SQL Server instance that holds the query log. If that server instance isn't available at that time, Analysis Services waits for 60 seconds (the default amount of time) before it proceeds. If you use Service Control Manager (SCM) to start Analysis Services, SCM might time out before Analysis Services starts. Nevertheless, it will eventually start. Use the server properties in Table 23.2 to set up a query log table, use the cube browser to browse the `Warehouse and Sales` cube, and then query the table to see it contents. The result you see should be similar to Figure 23.9.

MSOLAP_Database	MSOLAP_Object...	MSOLAP_User	Dataset	StartTime	Duration
FoodMart 2008	EDWARDM3.Fo...	REDMOND\edwardm	00,000000000,000000,0000000,000100,00	2008-10-09 23...	0
FoodMart 2008	EDWARDM3.Fo...	REDMOND\edwardm	00,000000000,000000,0000000,000000,00	2008-10-09 23...	0
FoodMart 2008	EDWARDM3.Fo...	REDMOND\edwardm	100000,00	2008-10-09 23...	0
FoodMart 2008	EDWARDM3.Fo...	REDMOND\edwardm	00,000000000,000100,0000000,000100,00	2008-10-09 23...	53
FoodMart 2008	EDWARDM3.Fo...	REDMOND\edwardm	000000,00000,0000000,0000000	2008-10-09 23...	0
FoodMart 2008	EDWARDM3.Fo...	REDMOND\edwardm	000100,00000,0000000,0000000	2008-10-09 23...	5
FoodMart 2008	EDWARDM3.Fo...	REDMOND\edwardm	000000,00000,0000000,0000000	2008-10-09 23...	0
FoodMart 2008	EDWARDM3.Fo...	REDMOND\edwardm	000000,00000,0000000,0000100	2008-10-09 23...	0
FoodMart 2008	EDWARDM3.Fo...	REDMOND\edwardm	100000,00	2008-10-09 23...	0
FoodMart 2008	EDWARDM3.Fo...	REDMOND\edwardm	000000,00000,0000000,0000100	2008-10-09 23...	0
FoodMart 2008	EDWARDM3.Fo...	REDMOND\edwardm	00,000000000,000000,0000000,000000,00	2008-10-09 23...	0
FoodMart 2008	EDWARDM3.Fo...	REDMOND\edwardm	000000,00001,0000000,0000100	2008-10-09 23...	0

FIGURE 23.9 The query log table for the `Warehouse and Sales` cube.

Table 23.3 describes the query log table columns.

TABLE 23.3 Columns in a Query Log Table

Column	Description
`MSOLAP_Database`	The name of the database
`MSOLAP_ObjectPath`	A period-separated list of database, cube, and measure group IDs that identify all the records that belong to specific measure group
`MSOLAP_Username`	The name of the user who queries Analysis Services
`StartTime`	The time the query starts
`Duration`	The duration of the request in milliseconds
`Dataset`	Contains the granularity of the MDX query

Take as an example one of the values in the `Dataset` column:

```
001101,00111,00001111,0011100
```

Every position in this series of digits represents a dimension attribute, in the order of its appearance in the DDL when the cube dimension was created. The dimensions are separated by commas. If an attribute doesn't participate in a query, a `0` occupies its position; if the attribute was requested as part of the query, a `1` occupies its position.

NOTE

A `1` always appears in the position of a nonaggregatable attribute.

Analysis Services not only logs data sets to a query log, it also deletes certain records from the query log table. Every time there is a structural change to a measure group or to any of the dimensions participating in it, Analysis Services deletes all the queries associated with the measure group.

Manual Design and Management of Aggregations

New in Analysis Services 2008 is ability to manually design and manage aggregations. Based on the customer feedback and the popularity of Aggregation Manager sample application, several improvements have been made to the BI Dev Studio to enable you to visually review and create new aggregations directly without running the Aggregation Design Algorithm Wizard or the Usage-Based Optimization Wizard. You can now also discover aggregation design objects and assign aggregation designs to a subset of partitions in the measure group.

For manual design of aggregations, BI Dev Studio introduces the Aggregations tab in the cube editor dialog. For example, open the sample FoodMart 2008 project in BI Dev Studio. Double-click the `Warehouse and Sales` cube to open the cube editor. Click the Aggregations tab and you will see list of the measure groups and aggregation design objects that belong to the measure groups, similar to what is shown in Figure 23.10.

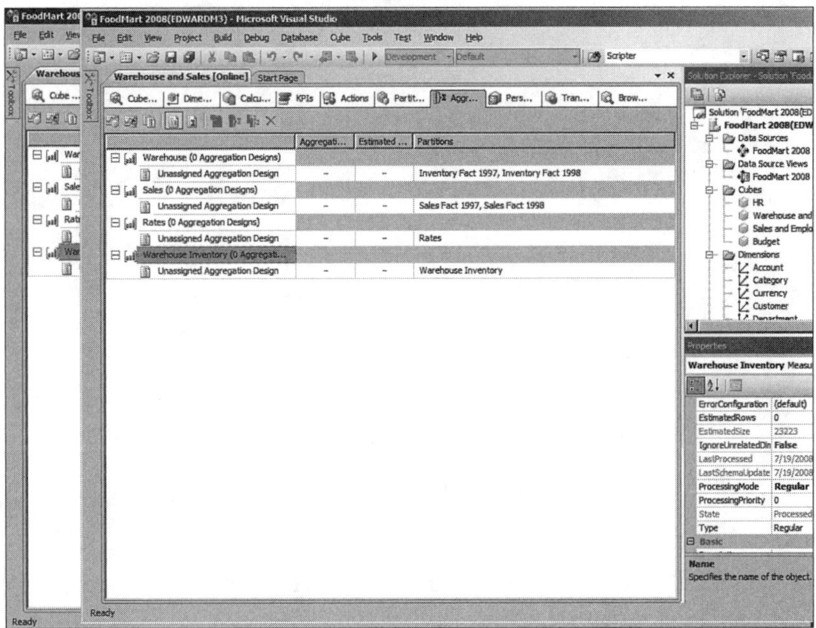

FIGURE 23.10 The Aggregations tab of the `Warehouse and Sales` cube.

If no aggregation designs exist in the measure group, you will see "Unassigned Aggregation Design" under the measure group node.

The right-click menu on the measure group presents you with several options:

- **Design Aggregations**—To run the aggregation design algorithm.
- **Usage-Based Optimization**—To run the usage-based optimization algorithm.

- **Assign Aggregation Design**—To assign an aggregation design to a partition (new in Analysis Services 2008).

To see the manual aggregation Advanced view, click the Advanced View toolbar button. The button icon is little hard to distinguish. Hover over the toolbar buttons to discover their designation through the tooltips.

When in Advanced view, select the Warehouse measure group and AggregationDesign in the drop-down boxes to see aggregations of the `AggregationDesign` object. If you expand the dimension nodes on the left of the Advanced pane, you will see a view similar to that shown in Figure 23.11.

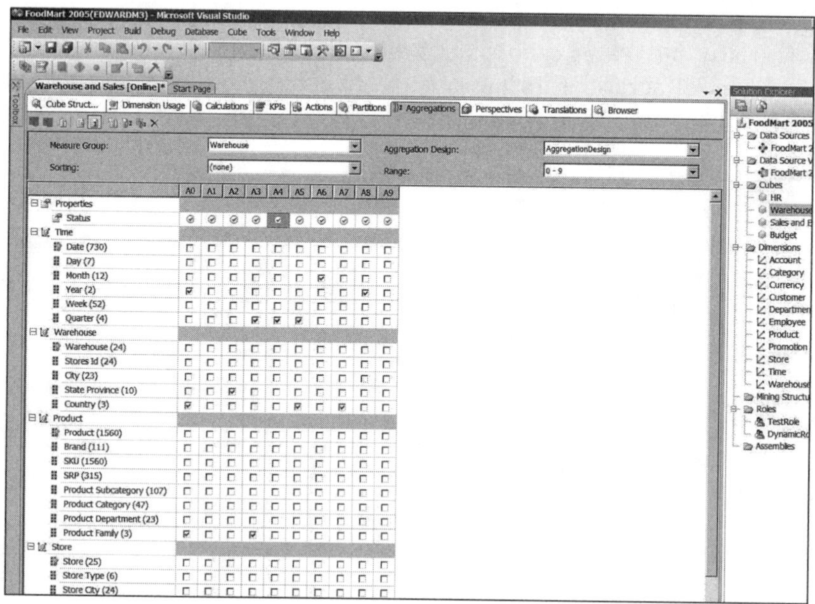

FIGURE 23.11 The Advanced view in the Aggregations tab.

On the left, you see list of dimensions and their attributes. In parentheses, you see the estimated count of members in each attribute based on the `EstimatedSize` attribute property. Each aggregation in the aggregation design represented by the column with check boxes checked whether the corresponding attribute participates in the aggregation. Aggregation names did not fit in the column captions, and Analysis Services designers chose to represent aggregation names with short abbreviations (the letter A and followed by the aggregation ordinal). For example, the third aggregation in the aggregation design is shown as a column with caption A3. To see the real name of the aggregation, just hover your cursor over the aggregation column caption.

Clicking the gray space under the aggregation enables you to select a particular aggregation. When you do that, additional toolbar buttons become enabled: Copy Aggregation, Delete. You can also access the same functionality through the right-click menu. In addition, in Advanced view you can create new aggregations and new aggregation designs.

SQL Management Studio 2008 enables you to see aggregation designs and assign designs to aggregations. To do so, open SQL Management Studio and expand the object's tree to measure group level. Under a measure group, the new Aggregation Designs node appears. If you have any aggregations designed for partitions in your measure group, aggregation design names appear under that node, too. In our sample FoodMart 2008 database, if you navigate to the `Warehouse` measure group in the `Warehouse and Sales` cube, you see `AggregationDesign` aggregation design. Right-clicking an aggregation design reveals several options, Assign Aggregation Design being one of them. If you select this option, you will open a screen similar to that shown in the Figure 23.12.

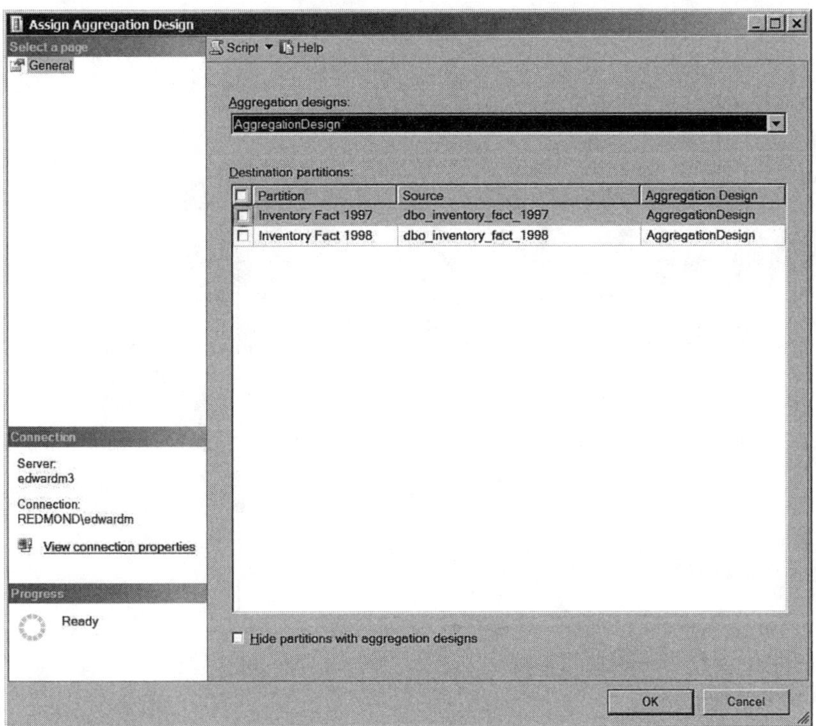

FIGURE 23.12 Assign aggregation designs to partitions.

Monitoring Aggregation Usage

You can use SQL Server Profiler to monitor query execution events to determine whether the aggregations you've designed and built are going to help your queries. You can see whether a specific query is being answered from the aggregation. (For information about SQL Server Profiler, see Chapter 38, "Using Trace to Monitor and Audit Analysis Services.")

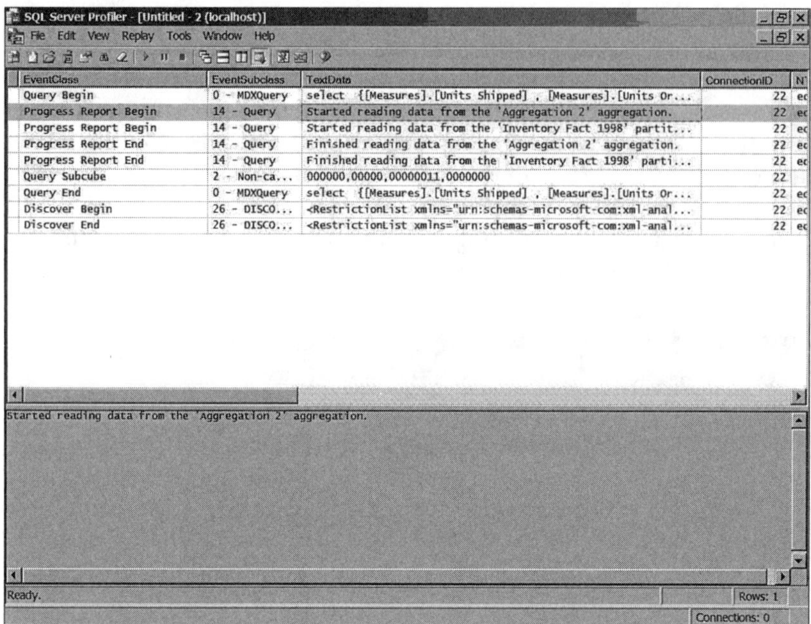

FIGURE 23.13 Use SQL Server Profiler to trace events that occur during the execution of an MDX query.

The following MDX query produces the events in the following SQL Server Profiler trace:

```
select
{[Measures].[Units Shipped] ,
[Measures].[Units Ordered]
}
on 0,
{ [Product].[Products].[Product Department].[Alcoholic Beverages] } on 1
from [Warehouse and Sales]
```

The first `Progress Report Begin Event` reported `"Started reading data from the 'Aggregation 2' aggregation."` in the `TextData` column. This event indicates that the query was resolved from an aggregation for the `Inventory Fact 1997` partition (not visible in the figure). Because we didn't create aggregations for the `Inventory Fact 1998` partition, the MDX query generates a second `Progress Report Begin Event` with a `TextData` column: `"Started reading data from the 'Inventory Fact 1998' partition."`

The third event, `Query Subcube`, is used to log information about the query in the query log table. The `TextData` column contains the same information about the query in the same format as the query log table.

CHAPTER 24

Proactive Caching and Real-Time Updates

IN THIS CHAPTER

- Data Latency and Proactive Caching
- Timings and Proactive Caching
- Proactive Caching Scenarios
- Change Notifications and Object Processing During Proactive Caching
- General Consideration for Proactive Caching
- Monitoring Proactive Caching Activity

When you build an Analysis Services application, an important consideration is how the application makes sure that the Analysis Services data is the most recent data from the relational database. It is also important for the application to manage how often Analysis Services receives updates from the relational database (in other words, the latency of the data).

In Figure 24.1, you can see a diagram of a typical reporting application that uses an online transaction processing (OLTP) system, ETL (Extract, Transform, and Load), a data warehouse, and Analysis Services. The overall latency of the system is the cumulative total from the time the update was entered into the OLTP system until the new data is available to the client application to query.

Applications typically implement updates to the data warehouse and updates to Analysis Services as part of a batch operation, usually daily or weekly. With daily or weekly updates, the latency of the data in Analysis Services could be too large.

Another separate type of applications that require very low or no latency for showing updates. Users in these applications need almost immediate access to the most recent data. These applications go under name of Real-Time OLAP applications and require additional logic for updates are consistent across dimensions and facts.

With Analysis Services, you can use proactive caching to make it easier to build lower-latency applications.

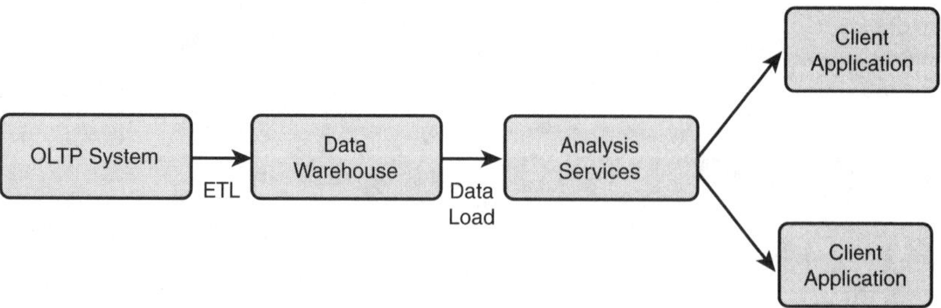

FIGURE 24.1 OLTP data goes through ETL and the data warehouse before it is loaded into Analysis Services.

Data Latency and Proactive Caching

Proactive caching is the part of the infrastructure of Analysis Services that enables you to define rules to detect changes in the relational database and rules for automatic updates of objects when Analysis Services is notified that a change has been received. To implement a low-latency system without built-in server functionality, you must implement custom logic that detects changes in the data warehouse and sends processing commands to update Analysis Services objects. Such an application triggers processing of Analysis Services objects every time new data comes into the relational database. That requires unnecessary processing and consumes a lot of Analysis Services resources.

Analysis Services features proactive caching technology to implement a low-latency system. Internally, the implementation of proactive caching can be seen as the retention of two versions of each object: the current one and a new one (a multidimensional online analytical processing [MOLAP] cache). After the new version has been processed, it becomes the current one. See the example in Figure 24.2.

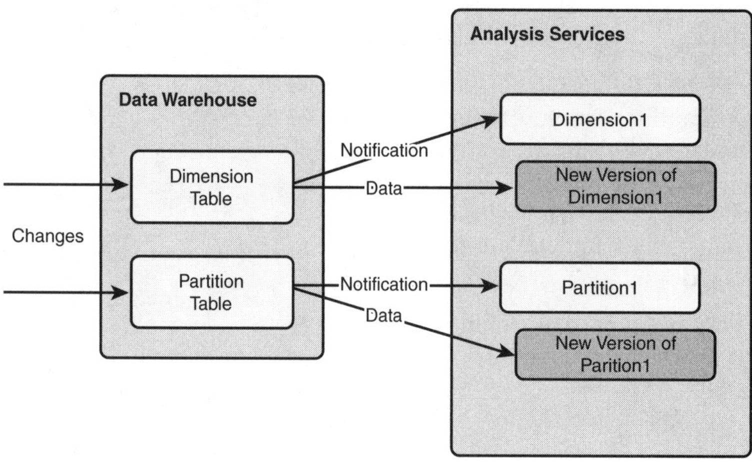

FIGURE 24.2 Proactive caching receives notifications and builds new version of dimensions and partitions.

The `Dimension1` and `Partition1` objects both have proactive caching turned on. Analysis Services listens for notifications from relational database. When Analysis Services is notified of a change, it starts processing new `Dimension1` and `Partition1` objects. When processing completes, the resulting new `Dimension1` and `Partition1` objects become the current objects and are available for the client application to query.

Depending on the latency of data you want to achieve in your multidimensional model, you can choose between two modes of transitions between the current and new versions of an object: MOLAP to MOLAP or MOLAP to ROLAP (relational online analytical processing) to MOLAP:

- In the MOLAP to MOLAP transition mode, the `Partition` or `Dimension` object stays in MOLAP mode for its lifetime. When Analysis Services is notified of a change, it processes a new MOLAP version of the object. After processing completes, the new version is available. In this mode, the latency of the data is dependent on the time it takes to process the new MOLAP version of the object.
- In the MOLAP-ROLAP-MOLAP mode, when Analysis Services is notified of a change, it changes the storage mode of the object from MOLAP to ROLAP and starts to build a MOLAP version of the same object (MOLAP cache). When the MOLAP cache is available, Analysis Services swaps the MOLAP and ROLAP versions of the object. Queries are then resolved from the MOLAP version. While the object is in ROLAP mode, you might see the drop in performance, but this mode of proactive caching guarantees that the client application receives the most recent data.

24

NOTE

We don't recommend using proactive caching settings that trigger a MOLAP to ROLAP to MOLAP transition. If a dimension changes from MOLAP storage mode to ROLAP, all the MOLAP `Partition` objects in the `Measure Groups` using the dimension automatically change to ROLAP mode, which slows down your system.

With proactive caching, you can define automated behavior for updating Analysis Services partitions or dimensions, based on notification of changes in underlying data warehouse tables. You can define proactive caching by using a `ProactiveCaching` object that belongs to a partition or dimension. The `ProactiveCaching` object defines how changes are detected in the data warehouse. It also defines the timings and policies for the frequency of updates after notification of a change. Listing 24.1 is an example of a `ProactiveCaching` object Data Definition Language (DDL) definition.

LISTING 24.1 DDL Definition of a **ProactiveCaching** Object

```
<ProactiveCaching>
    <SilenceInterval>PT10S</SilenceInterval>
    <Latency>-PT1S</Latency>
    <SilenceOverrideInterval>PT10M</SilenceOverrideInterval>
```

```
    <ForceRebuildInterval>-PT1S</ForceRebuildInterval>
    <Enabled>true</Enabled>
    <OnlineMode>OnCacheComplete</OnlineMode>
  <AggregationStorage>MolapOnly</AggregationStorage>
    <Source xsi:type="ProactiveCachingInheritedBinding" />
</ProactiveCaching>
```

Most of the properties of a `ProactiveCaching` object define the frequency of notification to Analysis Services about data changes and at the time that the MOLAP cache should be dropped and rebuilt. Later in this chapter, we cover each property.

Timings and Proactive Caching

Quite a few intricate timing issues are involved in defining a well-balanced system that performs well and enables you to see recent updates—that is, it doesn't spend most of the time processing the MOLAP cache.

Update Frequency

If you were to define a proactive caching scheme that would rebuild a MOLAP cache after every single update from the relational database, you might find that updates are coming too often. Suppose that Analysis Services starts to process a partition soon after a new notification arrives. Then a second notification arrives. The system examines the list of objects currently being processed and cancels the ongoing processing of the partition because Analysis Services doesn't allow multiple processing operations to run for the same object at the same time. If updates are frequent, your system will keep canceling the processing of the MOLAP cache. Figure 24.3 shows a diagram of this cycle of beginning and canceling processing.

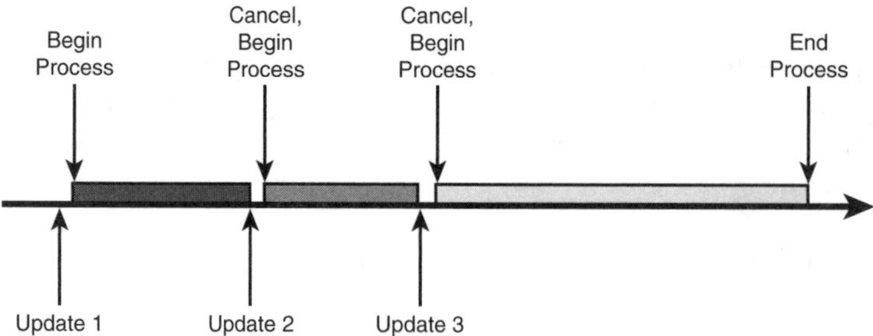

FIGURE 24.3 Multiple notifications in a short period of time delay object updates.

The processing of the object begins after the first update. That processing cannot complete because another update arrives, causing proactive caching to start processing the MOLAP cache. That processing cannot finish because of a third update. And so on. The `Proactive`

Caching object solves this problem with its SilenceInterval and SilenceOverride Interval properties:

- The SilenceInterval property specifies the amount of time, after it receives a notification, that Analysis Services waits before it starts building a new version of the object—*quiet time*. If Analysis Services receives another notification during quiet time, it just ignores it. The default value -1 (infinite) means *ignore notifications*.
- The SilenceOverrideInterval property specifies the time after which Analysis Services starts to process a new version of the object, even if updates come so frequently that there is no quiet time, as defined by the SilenceInterval property. The SilenceOverrideInterval property ensures that the object eventually will be updated, regardless of the stream of updates. The default value -1 (infinite) means *no override*.

Long-Running MOLAP Cache Processing

In cases where processing of the MOLAP cache takes a long time, you might prefer to sacrifice performance in favor of reducing latency (MOLAP to ROLAP to MOLAP mode of proactive caching). Proactive caching provides a Latency property to define how much time should pass after notification and before the storage mode of the object is switched from MOLAP to ROLAP. The default behavior -1 (infinite) means *never revert to ROLAP mode.*

Two additional properties, OnlineMode and AggregationStorage, control how an object behaves when it is converted to ROLAP:

- The OnlineMode property specifies whether to allow users to query dimensions or partitions while the object is in ROLAP mode. It takes two values: Immediate and OnCacheComplete.
  - With OnlineMode set to Immediate, a user can query the object immediately after it changed to ROLAP; queries are resolved from the ROLAP storage.
  - With OnlineMode set to OnCacheComplete, a user can't query the object until the MOLAP cache is built. If the time set by the Latency property has expired, the object is temporarily unavailable for query by users. The default value is Immediate. Be careful setting this property to Immediate on a Dimension object. You don't want it to change to ROLAP mode, because you would lose data in your MOLAP partitions.
- The AggregationStorage property defines whether Analysis Services creates (or starts using existing) ROLAP aggregations when a partition is switched to ROLAP mode. AggregationStorage takes one of two values: Regular or MolapOnly.
  - When you set AggregationStorage to Regular, Analysis Services converts the Partition object to ROLAP mode, but builds ROLAP aggregations (creates indexed views in SQL Server).
  - When you set AggregationStorage to MolapOnly, Analysis Services doesn't create ROLAP aggregations.

NOTE

ROLAP aggregations are usually implemented as indexed views in a SQL Server relational database. (See Chapter 23, "Aggregation Design and Usage-Based Optimization," for more information.)

In some situations, you will want to schedule reprocessing of the MOLAP cache regardless of whether a notification is received. In other words, you want to define how "stale" your MOLAP cache can be. For that, you can use the `ForceRebuildInterval` property. In this property, you can specify the length of time after the last cache was built that rebuilding of a new cache can start. The default value `-1` (infinite) means *no periodic rebuild*.

Proactive Caching Scenarios

Four proactive caching timing properties—`SilenceInterval`, `SilenceOverrideInterval`, `ForceRebuildInterval`, and `Latency`—can render your system useless when you use them together without caution. Analysis Services provides a user interface that enables you to choose from a number of scenarios that combine meaningful settings for proactive caching properties.

You can find this user interface in SQL Server Management Studio and in Business Intelligence Development Studio (BI Dev Studio). In SQL Server Management Studio, you can access it through the Cube Properties, Partition Properties, and Dimension Properties dialog boxes. BI Dev Studio provides access through the Partitions tab. Figure 24.4 shows the user interface you will see if you right-click the `Store` dimension in SQL Server Management Studio, select Properties from the resulting menu, and then select the Proactive Caching page.

Slide the bar on this page to select a scenario with preset timing values. You can click the Options button to see the values for the proactive caching in more detail.

MOLAP Scenario

The MOLAP scenario sets the storage mode for a partition or dimension to MOLAP. In this scenario, proactive caching is disabled.

Scheduled MOLAP Scenario

The values for properties in this scenario are as follows:

- `SilenceInterval = -1` (infinite)
- `SilenceOverrideInterval = -1` (infinite)
- `Latency = -1` (infinite)
- `ForceRebuildInterval = 1 day`

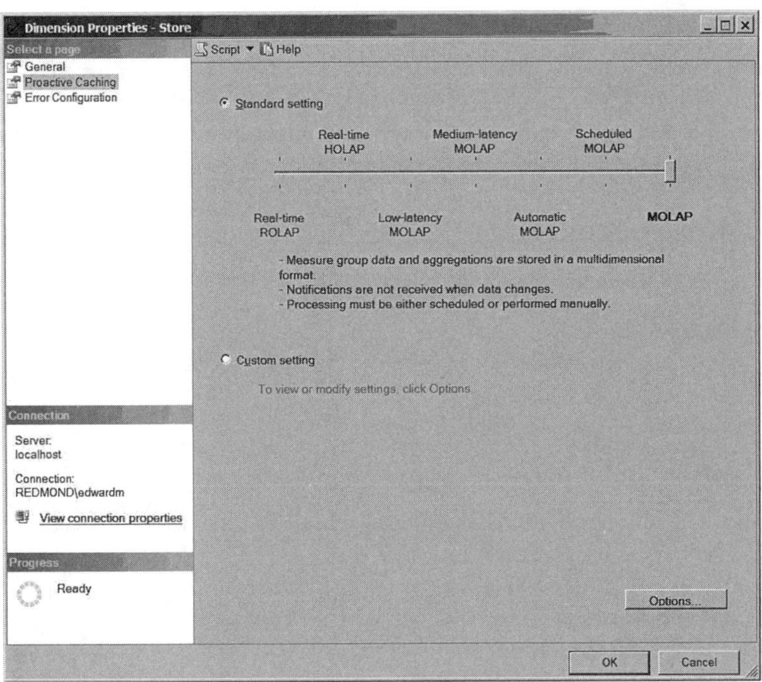

FIGURE 24.4 The Proactive Caching page enables you to define proactive caching properties.

If you select this scenario, Analysis Services will reprocess the MOLAP cache for the `Store` dimension daily.

NOTE

Use this property with caution. Don't expect Analysis Services to start processing a new version of the object at some specific hour in the day. The calculation Analysis Services makes to start processing depends on the `LastProcessed` timestamp on the object. Analysis Services simply checks whether the sum of the values of `LastProcessed` and `ForceRebuildInterval` is smaller than the value of the current time. For example, you can't rely on this property to start your processing at midnight. The start time for processing depends on how long the previous processing takes.

Use SQL Server Agent to schedule processing of an object at a specific time.

Automatic MOLAP Scenario

The values for properties in this scenario are as follows:

- `SilenceInterval` = `10 sec`
- `SilenceOverrideInterval` = `10 min`
- `Latency` = `-1` (infinite)

- `ForceRebuildInterval` = -1 (infinite)

In this scenario, Analysis Services doesn't react to a stream of updates separated by an interval of fewer than 10 seconds. Nonetheless, it will start reprocessing the cache 10 minutes after it receives the first notification. This scenario works well when batch updates are pushed by the ETL process into your data warehouse.

Medium-Latency MOLAP Scenario

The values for properties in this scenario are as follows:

- `SilenceInterval` = `10 sec`
- `SilenceOverrideInterval` = `10 min`
- `Latency` = `4 hours`
- `ForceRebuildInterval` = -1 (infinite)

This scenario is similar to the automatic MOLAP scenario, but after four hours the MOLAP cache expires and the object switches to the ROLAP mode.

Low-Latency MOLAP Scenario

The values for properties in this scenario are as follows:

- `SilenceInterval` = `10 sec`
- `SilenceOverrideInterval` = `10 min`
- `Latency` = `30 minutes`
- `ForceRebuildInterval` = -1 (infinite)

This scenario forces switching to ROLAP mode after 30 minutes. If the processing operation takes longer than 30 minutes, users will see a drop in performance.

Real-Time HOLAP Scenario

Real-time HOLAP (hybrid online analytical processing) scenarios are valid for setting proactive caching only to partitions, not to dimensions. The values for properties in this scenario are as follows:

- `SilenceInterval` = `0 sec`
- `SilenceOverrideInterval` = N/A
- `Latency` = `0 sec`
- `ForceRebuildInterval` = -1 (infinite)

In this scenario, Analysis Services sets the storage mode for the partition as HOLAP. The partition data is in ROLAP mode, and the aggregations are in MOLAP mode. MOLAP aggregations are rebuilt immediately after a notification arrives because the `SilenceInterval` property is set to `0`.

Real-Time ROLAP Scenario

In the real-time ROLAP scenario, the storage for the partitions and dimensions is set to ROLAP. The values for properties in this scenario are as follows:

- `SilenceInterval` = `-1`
- `SilenceOverrideInterval` = N/A
- `Latency` = `0 sec`
- `ForceRebuildInterval` = `-1` (infinite)

The real-time ROLAP scenario enables applications to show the user the latest version of the data available in the relational database. In the ROLAP mode, Analysis Services keeps internal caches so that it can improve the performance of similar queries. The data Analysis Services shows to the user can get out of sync with the data in the relational database. However, in the real-time ROLAP scenario, Analysis Services drops ROLAP caches when it receives a change notification because the `Latency` property is set to `0`.

24

NOTE

If you know that your system behaves different from the settings in one of the scenarios, we recommend that you pick the scenario closest to your requirements and use the Storage Options dialog box to modify the values of the proactive caching properties.

Change Notifications and Object Processing During Proactive Caching

Proactive caching, for the most part, is driven by the capability of Analysis Services to receive notifications about data changes in the relational database. Beyond that, for low-latency systems, you have to figure out *how* data has changed.

Scheduling Processing and Updates

Internally, Analysis Server keeps a list of DSV (Data Source View) `TableID` values for every object that has proactive caching enabled. (For information about DSVs, see Chapter 18, "DSVs and Object Bindings.") When a notification about a change in the relational table arrives, Analysis Services flags the DSV `TableID` as changed. Analysis Services uses this information to determine which objects need to be updated. In the example in Figure 24.5, notifications arrived at `TableID1` and `TableID3`, so the corresponding objects `Dim1` and `Part1` need to be updated.

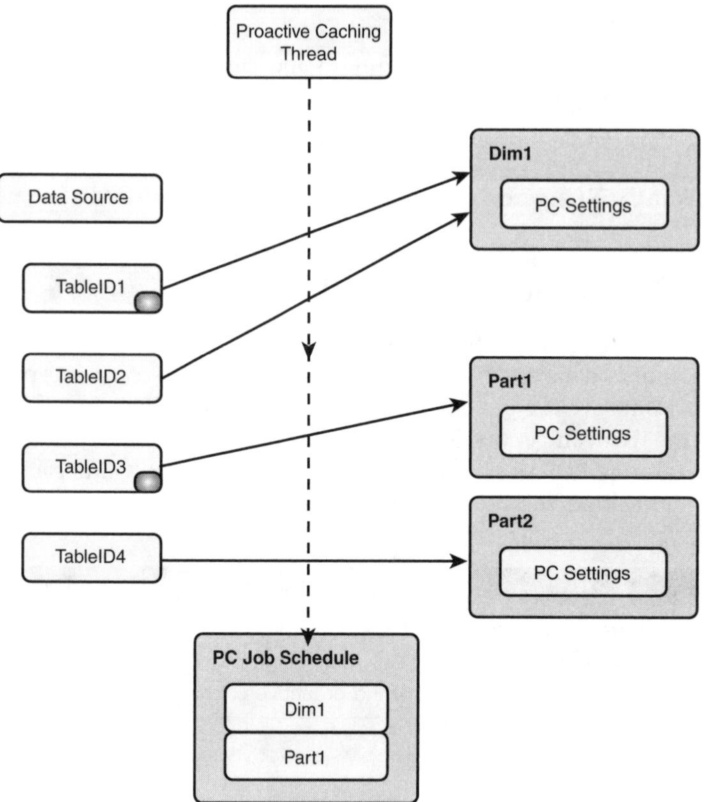

FIGURE 24.5 Objects that need to be updated are indicated by `TableID1` and `TableID3`.

The updates to the objects are scheduled according to this simple algorithm:

1. The proactive caching thread periodically scans all the `TableID` values associated with a data source and determines which objects are candidates for updating.
2. The proactive caching thread determines whether the object needs to be processed based on the proactive caching timing settings. If it does, Analysis Services enters the object into the processing queue.
3. All objects that have the same proactive cache settings are grouped into a single batch command. In a batch command, dimensions are always processed first; partitions are processed after the dimensions.

Proactive caching also applies a heuristic in cases where

- Several objects have similar settings.
- Some of them need to be reprocessed because the notification came and the silence interval expired.
- Some other objects don't need to be reprocessed.

In this sort of case, the proactive caching subsystem might process all of them together. In our example, suppose that `Dim1`, `Part1`, and `Part2` have the same proactive cache timing settings and Analysis Services receives notification for all of them. For `Part1` and `Part2`, the silence interval has expired, but it hasn't for `Dim1`. Proactive caching schedules processing of all three (`Part1`, `Part2`, and `Dim1`). It schedules them together because if new records were added to both the dimension and partition tables, processing of the partition would fail if the dimension hadn't been updated with new members.

Change Notification Types

You can use SQL Server Management Studio and BI Dev Studio to define notification options. You can choose from three mechanisms that trigger notifications to Analysis Services about changes in a relational database:

- Analysis Services subscribes to SQL Server trace events for a specific table.
- Your application sends a `NotifyTableChange` command to notify Analysis Services.
- Analysis Services uses user-defined SQL queries to poll the relational tables.

For example, open SQL Server Management Studio and go to the Proactive Caching page of the Properties dialog box for the `Store` dimension. Click the Options button and click the Notifications tab. In Figure 24.6, you can see the three options just described.

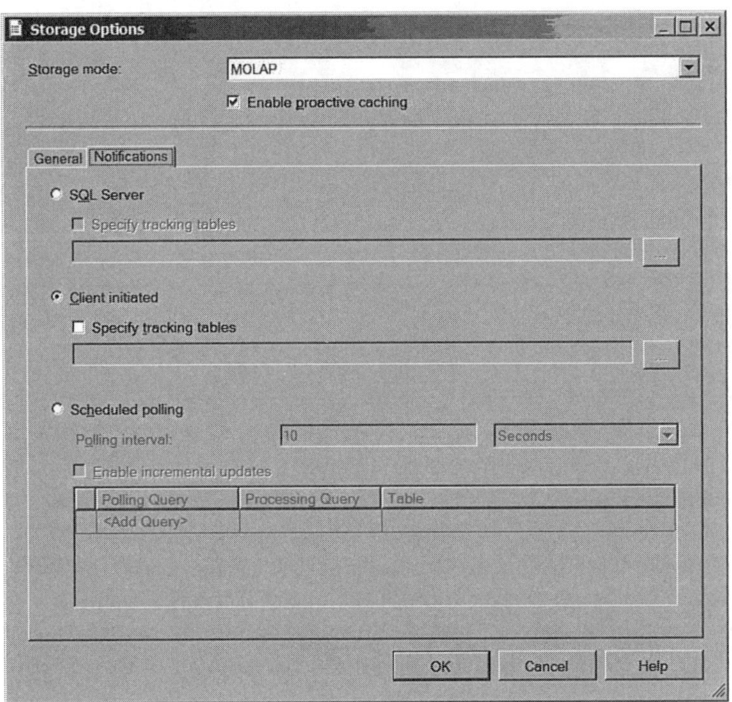

FIGURE 24.6 Define notifications for proactive caching in the Storage Options dialog box.

SQL Server

Analysis Services subscribes to SQL Server trace events that notify it of every change in the entire SQL Server database. Alternatively, you can select a table or set of tables to listen to.

There are several disadvantages to using SQL Server notifications. To subscribe to SQL Server trace events, the service account of Analysis Services must have system administrator privileges.

Delivery of the trace events is not guaranteed. Under such a heavy load, SQL Server might skip some events.

Client Initiated

This is the default option in the Proactive Caching dialog box. The client application can send a `NotifyTableChange` XML/A command to Analysis Services to force notification for a single or multiple `TableID` values. For example, when you design an update script for your data warehouse, after your commands for updating relational tables, you add a command that sends a XML/A `NotifyTableChange` request to Analysis Services. Listing 24.2 shows an example of the command that notifies Analysis Services of updates in the objects that depend on the `store` table.

LISTING 24.2 **NotifyTableChange** XML/A Request

```
<NotifyTableChange
xmlns="http://schemas.microsoft.com/analysisservices/2003/engine">
    <Object>
        <DatabaseID>FoodMart 2005</DatabaseID>
        <DataSourceID>FoodMart 2005</DataSourceID>
    </Object>
    <TableNotifications>
        <TableNotification>
            <DbSchemaName>dbo</DbSchemaName>
            <DbTableName>store</DbTableName>
        </TableNotification>
    </TableNotifications>
</NotifyTableChange>
```

Scheduled Polling Notification Mechanism

You can instruct Analysis Services to send an SQL query to the relational database to detect changes. The query needs to return a single value. Analysis Services compares this value to the value obtained in the previous execution of the query. If the new value is different, notification for proactive caching is triggered. In our example for the `Store` dimension, you can use the following polling query to retrieve the number of rows in the `store` table:

```
Select count (*) from dbo.store
```

The polling query is stored with the `TableID` data structure. Figure 24.7 shows a diagram that illustrates this process.

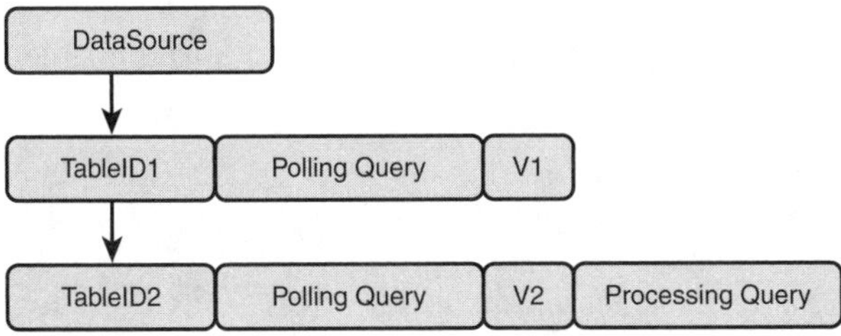

FIGURE 24.7 Polling queries and processing queries are stored along with the `TableID` data structure.

The proactive caching thread iterates over the `TableID` data structures and determines which tables need to be polled. For each table, it sends a polling query to the relational database. In our example, the result of this query is the number of rows in the `store` table, Analysis Services compares this number with the saved number (`V1`, in our case). A difference in the numbers triggers a notification. After the scheduled time period, Analysis Services sends the same query again. If you've inserted new rows into the `store` table, the query will return a larger number of rows. You can use the `RefreshInterval` property of the `ProactiveCaching` object to schedule how often Analysis Services sends the polling query.

NOTE

For a partition, it is enough to provide a single polling query. However, for a snowflake dimension, you might need to define several polling queries.

Incremental Updates Versus Full Updates

By default, Analysis Services performs full processing of partitions and incremental processing of dimensions using `ProcessUpdate`. (For information about different processing types, see Chapter 21, "Dimension and Partition Processing.") You can configure proactive caching to use incremental updates for partitions and the `ProcessAdd` for dimensions. To do this, you need to provide the `ProcessingQuery` property of the `ProactiveCaching` object for Analysis Services to use for the incremental update of a dimension or partition. For a defining processing query, Analysis Services enables you to write a parameterized SQL query in which the first parameter is an old value of the polling query and the second parameter is the new value.

In the following example, you need to set up proactive caching to reprocess the `Inventory Fact 1997` partition when new records are inserted into the fact table. The values of `time_id` fields for those new records will correspond to the time they were entered into the system. Therefore, you can define your polling query to retrieve the latest value of the `time_id` column:

```
Select Max(time_id) from inventory_fact_1997
```

The following processing query returns the records that have been inserted into the table since the previous poll:

```
Select * from inventory_fact_1997
Where ? <= time_id  and time_id > ?
```

While it is sending this query to the relational database, Analysis Services sends along two parameters, represented by question marks. These values are the old and new values of the `time_id`.

General Considerations for Proactive Caching

Proactive caching is not a magical caching system—it processes objects to create a cache. Because proactive caching processes MOLAP caches behind the scenes, processing consumes a lot of resources. It's a good idea to minimize the number of times and the number of objects for which you define proactive caching.

For example, if you have a lot of data, we recommend that you partition your measure group and define proactive caching only for the partition that holds data for the latest period of time. Another way (or additional way) to speed up processing is to use incremental updates rather than full updates.

It can take some time for you to understand the pattern of behavior—how often updates are being triggered—in your application. Make sure that you use the same proactive caching timings across the objects in a single cube so that Analysis Services can group the processing of those objects into a single batch. Doing so will improve the performance of you system.

You can also use cube objects to specify proactive caching settings. These settings are used as defaults when you create partitions. You should stay away from setting proactive caching on a cube object; otherwise, you might end up with proactive caching enabled for every new partition you create.

Monitoring Proactive Caching Activity

You can use the SQL Server Profiler application to monitor proactive caching activity. (For information about using SQL Server Profiler, see Chapter 38, "Using Trace to Monitor and Audit Analysis Services.") Figure 24.8 shows an example of trace events captured during proactive caching.

In this example, we set proactive caching for the `Store` dimension to the scheduled MOLAP scenario. The first event you see in the figure indicates executions of the `Alter` command, which changes proactive caching settings for the `Store` dimension.

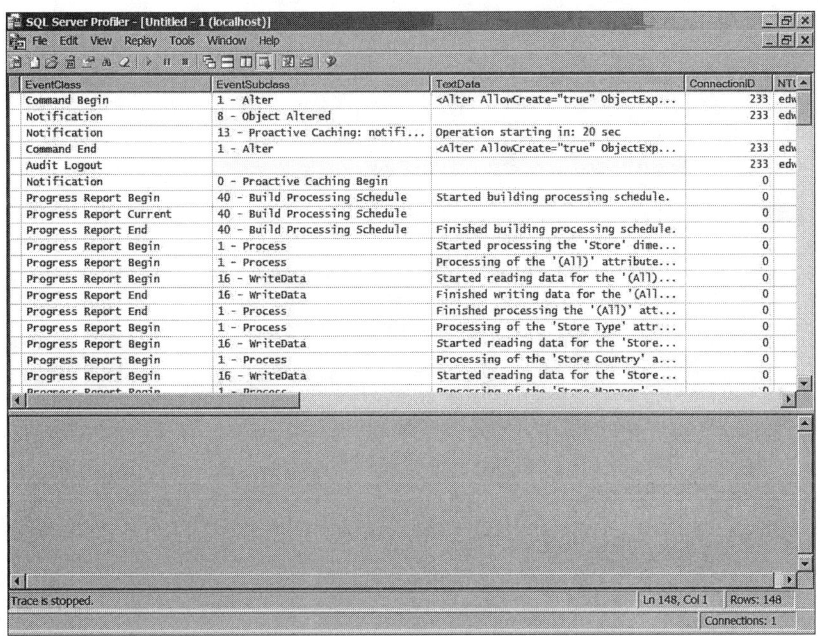

FIGURE 24.8 You can use SQL Server Profiler to monitor proactive caching events.

Just after that, you see a `Notification` event with the event subclass `"8 - Object Altered"`, and then you see another `Notification` event with the event subclass `"13 - Proactive Caching: notifiable"`. In the Text Data column for that event, you see a message indicating the time that the next processing will start. All events related to proactive caching are reported in the `Notification` class of events with different event subclasses.

After about 20 seconds (in the example, we set the `ForceRebuildInterval` property to `20 sec`), we see that processing of the `Store` dimension has begun. You see that all `Progress Report` events have the `ConnectionID` property set to `0`. That is because proactive caching operations are running as part of an internal subsystem within Analysis Server.

CHAPTER 25

Building Scalable Analysis Services Applications

IN THIS CHAPTER

Analysis Services supports multiple functionalities that increase the scalability and flexibility of your system by distributing data among servers. A distributed data system helps you to better:

- Increase the number of users that can simultaneously use the server
- Increase the volume of data stored in the system
- Extend the data model by including dimensions and measure groups from external models

Approaches to Scalability

You can approach scalability from two directions: scale up or scale out. With a scale-up approach, you increase the processing power of a single computer. With a scale-out approach, you increase the number of computers that contain your data. Both approaches have pros and cons. In the following sections, we look at these approaches to scalability from the perspective of Analysis Services.

The Scale-Up Approach

To scale your system, you add more processing power to a single physical computer or you transfer your application to another, more powerful computer. To scale data volumes, you add additional space to your hardware storage or increase the speed of storing data. The following lists describe in more detail the advantages of a scale-up solution.

The advantages to this solution are as follows:

- **Simplified multidimensional model**—With a single computer, you don't need to distribute and integrate data among different computers.
- **Simplified management model**—You manage only a single Analysis Server. All data-manipulating and data-loading scripts are targeted at a single computer. Moving data from a staging server to a production server is a simple process. With a scale-up approach, it's relatively easy to back up your database. It's easier to restore the application state from the backup. It's also easier to monitor your application. With a single computer, it's easier to find causes for slowdowns.
- **Simpler network configurations**—You don't need to configure the network to support a distributed infrastructure.

But this solution has its disadvantages:

- **Hardware cost**—At a certain point, scaling up to move your application to more and more powerful computers gets you into the price range of enterprise-level hardware. Enterprise-level hardware that enables you to scale to large data volumes is substantially more expensive than lightweight database hardware.
- **Single point of failure**—A single computer with attached storage is prone to failure more than the scale-out solution, which runs on multiple computers. To ensure high availability for your system, you need to pay an additional premium for fault-tolerant or highly reliable hardware.
- **Application growth**—It's hard to predict the growth of data volumes for your application or the number of users your application will have to support. With a scale-up approach, you have the burden of having to choose the right hardware for your application. Capacity planning is a delicate and risky task.
- **Scalability limits**—Relying on a single computer means that at some point you might run into the limitations of a single hardware component. For example, you might run into bandwidth limitation with your hardware storage solution.
- **Application configuration cost**—Running Analysis Services on enterprise-level hardware requires additional application configuration tuning.

The Scale-Out Approach

With a scale-out approach, your application and your data are distributed across several computers that work together to load data into the system and answer user queries. To scale your system, you add additional computers to your application. The disadvantages of a scale-out solution are the opposite of the advantages of those of the scale-up solution. In the following list, we discuss only the advantages:

- **Hardware costs**—To scale out your application, you use commodity hardware that is a fraction of the cost of enterprise-level hardware.

- **No single point of failure**—Failure of a single computer in a distributed architecture doesn't necessarily mean that the entire application fails. The other computers in the system can take on the work of the failed computer.
- **True scalability**—You scale the application by adding new computers. With an appropriate distributed network infrastructure, you should be able to scale your application far beyond any scale-up solution.

OLAP Farm

A scale-out approach to increasing the capacity of online analytical processing (OLAP) applications is known as an OLAP farm. Analysis Services provides a number of features that enable you to build an OLAP farm, a collection of computers that work together to support a multidimensional model. Figure 25.1 shows a diagram of the architecture of an OLAP farm.

You build your OLAP farm around the master server, which contains metadata and manages the whole system. The front-end servers communicate with the client computers and execute client requests. Front-end servers are typically configured to run under a network load-balancing cluster. A client application establishes a connection to a virtual IP address. That connection is redirected to one of the front-end servers. The front-end server parses and resolves the queries from the client application, and executes all the calculations defined in your cube.

Data Storage

There are two approaches to data storage in an OLAP farm:

- You can use a synchronization mechanism to have your data statically replicated across all the front-end servers. (For information about synchronization, see Chapter 40, "Deployment Strategies.") In this mode, each computer holds an exact replica of the database. Any change to the database requires an explicit operation to update the database on each server with the new data. The data on a server is not updated until some external operation distributes the updates.
- You can use link dimensions and link measure groups to load data from the master server to the front-end servers dynamically. In this scenario, each front-end server checks for updates and automatically refreshes its state if changes on the master server require an update. For a discussion of linked dimensions and linked measure groups, see the "Linked Dimensions and Measure Groups" section later in this chapter.

To execute a query, the front-end server first determines whether the answer is already available in its local cache. If not, with the static replication model, it retrieves data from the local storage.

NOTE

A front-end server needs a fast CPU for making calculations and a lot of memory for caching the results.

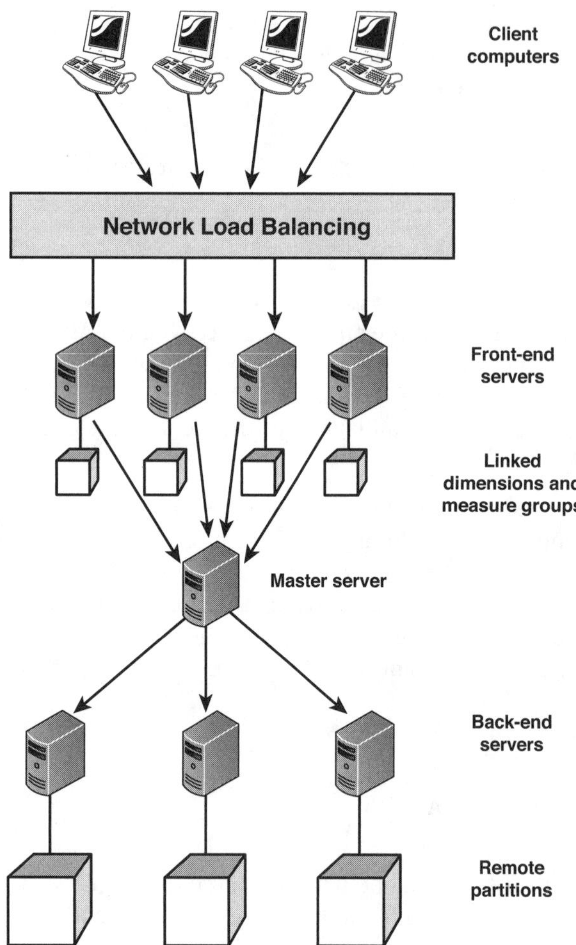

FIGURE 25.1 An OLAP farm uses front-end servers with linked dimensions and measure groups that point to the master server.

With the dynamic data-storage model with a master server, you have the option of adding more back-end servers to your OLAP farm to distribute data storage. The back-end servers enable you to load large data volumes into the system and enable the master server to efficiently retrieve the data requested by the front-end servers.

You use the remote-partitions feature of Analysis Services to distribute data between multiple back-end servers. Remote partitions enable you to load and store data on remote servers. The master server is the central computer in an OLAP farm. It defines the conceptual data model, and loads and retrieves the data for responses to user requests. Unfortunately, the architecture of the current version of Analysis Services doesn't enable you to remove the master server and point the front-end servers directly at the back-end servers. Therefore, the master server can become a bottleneck. Make sure to allocate enough resources for the master server so that it can handle the workload.

NOTE

An OLAP farm doesn't support the capability to write back data to all the servers in the farm. You can only write back data to the master server. With a dynamic data-loading solution, the front-end servers automatically get the new data. If your architecture is built on data replication, you have to resynchronize your data or flash caches on your front-end servers after a writeback operation.

The distributed architecture system is very flexible. You can scale your system according to the type of workload your system generally experiences. If you need to support more client connections, you add more front-end servers. If you need to store larger volumes of data, you add more back-end servers.

With the OLAP farm architecture that includes back-end servers, the total storage performance of the system is the sum of the performance of each back-end server storage system. The total amount of memory available for caching data is the sum of memory available for caching on the front-end servers, back-end servers, and the master server.

Network Load Balancing

The simplest way to build a scale-out distributed system is to set up a static OLAP farm with several front-end servers running side by side with the same replicated data or use Shared Scalable Database (SSD) feature of Analysis Services to point front-end servers to a single copy of a database. You can use Microsoft Clustering Services to distribute client connections among servers. Figure 25.2 shows a diagram of an example of such a distributed application.

Each client application connects to a single virtual IP address. The network load-balancing component ensures that the client connection is redirected to one of the Analysis Services servers. With this arrangement, you can increase the number of users supported by your application by simply adding a server to your cluster.

In Analysis Services, building load-balancing applications is possible with the `Synchronization` command, which enables you to easily synchronize the state of two servers. (For information about synchronization, see Chapter 40.)

In Analysis Services 2008, you can use SSD to point front-end servers to a single read-only copy of your database resides on a shared storage subsystem (SAN, NAS, and so on). You use the master server in this scenario to process a new version of the database, and then detach and copy it to a shared storage. Then, you issue a command for all front-end servers to detach from an old copy and attach to a new copy of a database.

Linked Dimensions and Measure Groups

To support an OLAP farm distributed scenario and enable users to share data between databases, Analysis Services implements linked dimensions and linked measure groups. Linked dimensions and measure groups enable you to load data into a dimension or

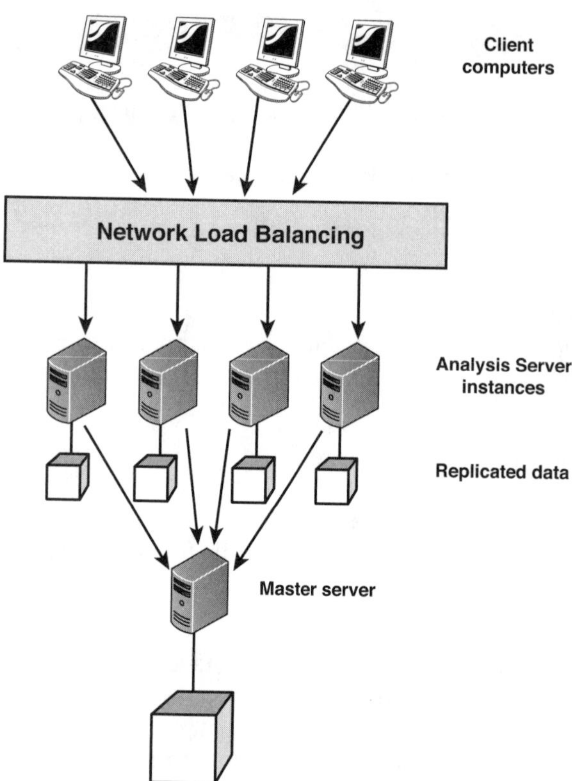

FIGURE 25.2 In a distributed application, each server points to a single copy of a database.

measure group from a remote Analysis Services database on demand. You can link dimensions and measure groups from a database on your server, from another instance of Analysis Services on the same computer, or from Analysis Services running on a remote server.

Two servers implement the link object. One of the servers, the publisher, stores the data. The other server, the subscriber, doesn't store data, but requests the data from the publisher and passes it to the user. To enable the subscriber server to connect to the publisher server, you have to configure both servers. You also need to make sure that the user account the subscriber uses to connect to the publisher has sufficient permissions on the publisher.

Analysis Services supports two modes of linking the metadata of the linked object: dynamic and static. The differences between these two modes play a role only during the creation of the object. After you create the linked object, regardless of the mode used, it behaves in the same way. In the dynamic mode, the subscriber retrieves the metadata of the linked object from the publisher during creation. To create a linked object in the static mode, you define the metadata of the linked object as part of the `Create` command you send to the subscriber. You could define the metadata as a subset of the metadata defined on the publisher. For example, you could issue a `Create` command to the subscriber that creates a linked measure group with a subset of the measures from that same measure group on the publisher.

You can use either of two Analysis Services policies to detect data changes in the publisher of a linked object: by query and by interval. With the by-query policy, during execution of every query, Analysis Services determines whether the object on the publisher has changed. With the by-interval policy, you can define a time interval after which Analysis Services checks whether the object on the publisher has changed.

Updates to the Source of a Linked Object

Analysis Services has different linked object behavior based on the type of change that occurs to the object on the publisher. The changes can be either structural or nonstructural. If there has been a structural change to the source of the linked object, you need to relink the objects from the publisher to the subscriber. For example, if you delete or add a new attribute to a dimension, the linked dimension becomes invalid and you need to relink it. When it creates a linked object, Analysis Services stores the linked object's metadata on the subscriber server.

Depending on the refresh policy, Analysis Services compares the metadata of the linked dimension on the subscriber to the metadata of the source dimension on the publisher. If it detects a structural change, Analysis Services returns an error; before you can use the linked dimension again, you have to delete and relink it. If the change is not structural, you don't need to relink the linked dimension.

For example, if you incrementally update a dimension on the publisher, Analysis Services treats the change as nonstructural. If you query your linked dimension, Analysis Services detects a version change and the query fails with the following error message: `Errors in the OLAP storage engine: The version of the linked dimension, with the name of 'Product', on the remote instance has changed. Repeat the operation to resolve the issue.`

However, under the hood, after the first query fails, Analysis Services updates the metadata of the linked dimension. The next time you issue a query to it, the query will succeed.

Linked Dimensions

In a more specific application of linked objects, Analysis Services enables you to use linked dimensions for reusing existing dimensions. With Analysis Services, you can create a linked dimension object that points to an existing dimension. Linked dimensions enable you to reuse a single version of a dimension across your organization. For example, you could use linked dimensions to have a standard version of the `Product` dimension across all the Analysis Servers installed in your network. When you link a dimension from the publisher, you don't have the flexibility to link only some attributes and not others.

As with other metadata objects, you create linked dimensions by issuing a Data Definition Language (DDL) request. The main difference between the DDL requests for regular and linked dimensions is the type of the `Source` object, which provides all the information required to link a dimension. The `Source` object of a linked dimension is of the

DimensionBinding type. Listing 25.1 is an example of using a Source object DDL to link to the Product dimension in our FoodMart 2008 sample database.

Table 25.1 describes the properties of the Source object.

TABLE 25.1 Properties of the Source Object

Name	Description
DataSourceID	The ID of the data source that points to the source database on the publisher.
DimensionID	References the ID of the source dimension in the publisher database.
Persistence	Defines the way the dimension is stored. This property takes two values: Metadata and NotPersisted.
RefreshPolicy	Defines the policy for Analysis Services to detect changes in the source of the linked dimension. The values are ByQuery and ByInterval. If this property is set to ByQuery, Analysis Services checks during every query to determine whether the source dimension has changed. (Not every client query will generate a query to the source dimension; the linked dimension will cache data retrieved from the source.) If this property is set to ByInterval, Analysis Services determines for every query whether the interval specified in the RefreshInterval property has expired, and it checks the version of the source. The default value is ByQuery.
RefreshInterval	Defines the amount of time before Analysis Services detects a change in the source of the linked object.

LISTING 25.1 DDL of a **Source** Object for the **Product** Dimension

```
<Source xsi:type="DimensionBinding">
     <DataSourceID>Food Mart 2008</DataSourceID>
     <DimensionID>Product</DimensionID>
     <Persistence>Metadata</Persistence>
     <RefreshInterval>PT1S</RefreshInterval>
</Source>
```

Analysis Services enables you to make limited changes to linked objects. The Persistence property of the Source object controls this functionality. If you specify the NotPersisted value to this property as part of the Create statement when you create a linked dimension, you need to send only a little information about the linked object. Analysis Services automatically fills in the rest of the properties based on the definition of the object on the publisher (dynamic linking). In Listing 25.2, you can see the DDL that creates a ProductStandard linked dimension.

LISTING 25.2 DDL to Create a Linked Dimension

```
<Create xmlns="http://schemas.microsoft.com/analysisservices/2003/engine">
    <ParentObject>
        <DatabaseID>FoodMart 2008 Linked</DatabaseID>
    </ParentObject>
    <ObjectDefinition>
        <Dimension xmlns:xsd="http://www.w3.org/2001/XMLSchema"
➥xmlns:xsi="http://www.w3.org/2001/XMLSchema-instance">
            <ID>ProductStandard</ID>
            <Name>ProductStandard</Name>
            <Source xsi:type="DimensionBinding">
                <DataSourceID>Food Mart 2008</DataSourceID>
                <DimensionID>Product</DimensionID>
                <RefreshInterval>PT1S</RefreshInterval>
                <Persistence>NotPersisted</Persistence>
            </Source>
        </Dimension>
    </ObjectDefinition>
</Create>
```


If the `Persistence` property is set to `NotPersisted` during the creation of the linked dimension, Analysis Services connects to the source database and retrieves metadata from it. It stores the metadata on the subscriber server. From this point on, you can't change the metadata of the linked dimension (with the exception of changing the dimension name).

Setting the `Persistence` property to `Metadata` (static linking) enables you to change some of the properties of the linked dimension. For example, you can remove some of the hierarchies from the linked dimension. If you set the `Persistence` property to `Metadata`, you also have to include the entire dimension definition in the `Create` statement for the linked dimension, including all the attributes and all the hierarchies.

NOTE

Business Intelligence Development Studio (BI Dev Studio) creates linked objects with the `Persistence` property to set to `Metadata`. To retrieve the dimension definition, BI Dev Studio connects to the source, obtains the metadata of the source object, and then constructs the `Create` statement for the linked object.

When you create a linked dimension, it initially contains only the metadata definition. While it is processing the linked dimension, Analysis Services verifies the metadata and creates all the necessary data structures (see Chapter 20, "The Physical Data Model"). The data structures remain empty until the first time a user queries the data. When Analysis Services receives a query for the dimension data, it first determines whether the data is available in the cache. If there is data in the cache, Analysis Services treats the linked dimension as a multidimensional online analytical processing (MOLAP) dimension. If Analysis Services can't locate data in the cache, it sends a request to the publisher server. The publisher server then iterates over all the relevant data structures, gathers data for only the requested dimension members, and sends the data to the subscriber server.

The subscriber server inserts the data it received into the data structures at exactly the same ordinal position as it was stored in the publisher server and registers the data with the dimension cache. At that moment, the dimension is considered populated; the subscriber server starts to treat it as a MOLAP dimension.

Linked dimensions that are often used and relatively small might be fully cached on the subscriber. You will see optimal query performance with these dimensions cached. As the result of this caching, the key store and other dimension stores contain only the records that appear in the dimension cache. Therefore, Analysis Services uses the dimension cache as a registry of the linked dimension data. This leads to an unfortunate side effect. In Analysis Services, the information about populated records is lost after the cache is cleaned. The subscriber might have the entire dimension structure fully populated, but the fact that it's populated is lost. As a result, the subscriber has to request data again from the publisher.

When you have linked a dimension to the corresponding dimension on the publisher, you can use it as if the dimension belonged to the subscriber database. You can include the linked dimension in your cube and associate it with a measure group, and you can load real data into your partitions. You can use a linked dimension in any measure group, not only in a linked measure group. For example, you can link the `Employee` dimension from your Human Resources server when your HR department needs information about employees in your organization. The `Geography` dimension is another dimension that you might use centrally in your organization to get a common view of the data on cities and ZIP Codes across the United States. The advantages of such reuse are as follows:

- A single standard version of the dimension eliminates the need to duplicate the dimension multiple times on each server.
- Updates to the dimension are centralized. A new version becomes available to all the servers at once. There are no delays and no discrepancies between versions.

Nevertheless, there is a disadvantage. You can suffer some performance degradation retrieving dimension data across the network from another server and recycling the subscriber requires to bring dimension again.

Linked Measure Groups

Linked measure groups enable you to reuse data from existing physical measure groups on another computer, in another database, or in another cube in the same database. The functionality of a linked measure group is close to that of the virtual cube in Analysis Services 2000, but it's far more powerful.

A linked measure group enables you to build virtual cubes that originate not only from one database, but also from different databases on the same server, or from different databases on different servers. There are two ways to create a linked measure group: link it from the same database or link it from a remote database.

When you link a measure group from another server, you have to link the dimensions you intend to use in your linked measure group before you link the measure group on the subscriber. You don't need to link all the dimensions from the publisher database.

For example, assume that you have two databases, `Publisher DB` and `Subscriber DB`, and that each has a cube: `Cube1` and `Cube2`, respectively. You can reuse data from the `MG1` measure group on the publisher and create a linked measure group `MG1` in `Cube2` on the subscriber. Before you can create this linked measure group, you have to link the dimensions used in the measure group on the publisher database: `Dim1` and `Dim2`. Figure 25.3 illustrates this example.

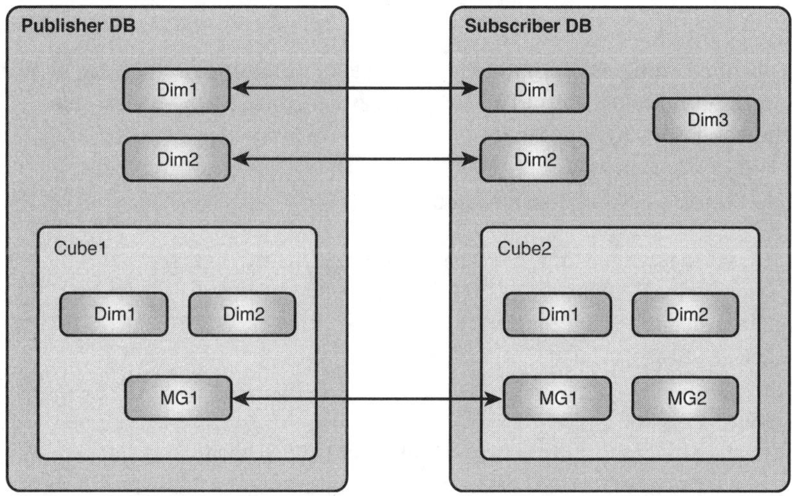

FIGURE 25.3 The linked measure group was created after dimensions used in the measure group were linked.

To link a measure group within one database, you don't need to create new linked dimensions. You can use dimensions from that database in your linked measure group. For example, assume that you have a database, DB, and two cubes: Cube1 and Cube2. If you want to reuse data from MG1 of Cube1 in Cube2, you can create a linked measure group and use the dimensions Dim1 and Dim2 that already exist in your database DB. You can see a diagram of this example in Figure 25.4.

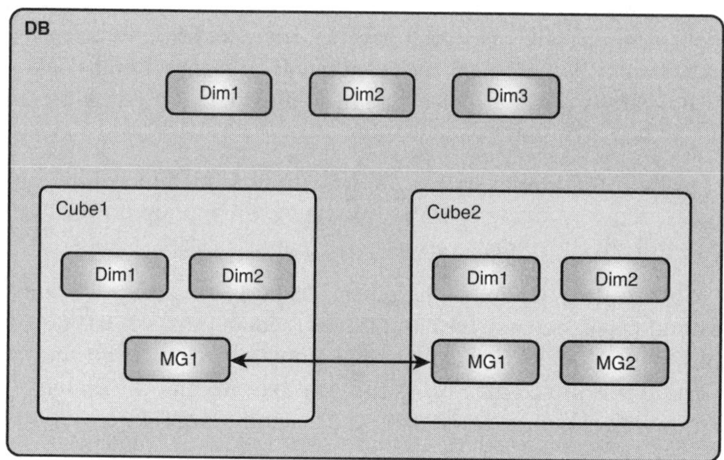

FIGURE 25.4 You can link a measure group within a single database.

Listing 25.3 shows part of a sample DDL that creates a Linked Sales measure group in a new database, FoodMart 2008 Linked, from the Sales measure group in the Warehouse and Sales cube of the FoodMart 2008 database.

LISTING 25.3 DDL to Create a Linked Measure Group

```
<Create xmlns="http://schemas.microsoft.com/analysisservices/2003/engine">
     <ParentObject>
          <DatabaseID>FoodMart 2008 Linked</DatabaseID>
          <CubeID>Linked Sales</CubeID>
     </ParentObject>
     <ObjectDefinition>
          <MeasureGroup xmlns:xsd="http://www.w3.org/2001/XMLSchema"
➥xmlns:xsi="http://www.w3.org/2001/XMLSchema-instance">
               <ID>Linked Sales</ID>
               <Name>Sales</Name>
 .......
              <Source>
                    <DataSourceID>Food Mart 2008</DataSourceID>
                    <CubeID>Warehouse and Sales</CubeID>
                    <MeasureGroupID>Sales </MeasureGroupID>
                    <Persistence>Metadata</Persistence>
```

```
                    <RefreshInterval>PT1S</RefreshInterval>
                    </Filter>
                </Source>
            </MeasureGroup>
        </ObjectDefinition>
</Create>
```

The DDL to create a linked measure group is similar to the DDL to create a linked dimension. There are three additional properties of the `Source` object, as described in Table 25.2.

TABLE 25.2 Properties of the **Source** Object

Name	Description
`CubeID`	References the ID of the cube in the publisher database
`MeasureGroupID`	References the ID of the source measure group in the publisher database
`Filter`	A Multidimensional Expressions (MDX) statement that restricts the data you can access in the linked measure group

25

During processing of the linked measure group, Analysis Services verifies the metadata of the linked measure group, but it doesn't load data into the measure group. Similar to the case of linked dimensions during query resolution, Analysis Services first determines whether the results are available in the measure group cache of the subscriber. If the data is present in the cache, Analysis Services uses it to form the result. If the data is not in the cache, the request for data is redirected to the publisher server and resolved according to the standard request resolution procedure. The publisher server determines whether results are available in its cache. If they are not, the publisher reads data from storage and registers the results in the publisher's cache. After that, the publisher sends the data to the subscriber. The subscriber deserializes the response, registers it with the measure group cache of the subscriber, and then returns the query result.

NOTE

When you link a measure group that is inside the same database as the source and the linked measure group has the same dimensionality as the source measure group, Analysis Services won't register results of a query twice. It registers the results only in the cache of the source measure group.

To expand your multidimensional model, you can associate more dimensions with the linked measure group than exist in the original measure group: You associate dimensions as indirect dimensions. You can also specify a subset of the measures you want to use in the subscriber measure group. For example, you can set up a `Market` measure group on one of your servers with information about the state of the market. You can create linked measure groups to enable your customers to link to your data. Your customers can use data in your measure group to analyze their sales against the market figures you provide.

NOTE

If you change source measure groups often, you might find it useful to create separate cubes, one per measure group, and create a single cube that joins all the measure groups you need as linked measure groups. This way you can avoid a situation where you change one measure group and Analysis Services drops the caches for the whole cube. If the data in one of the measure groups changes, the caches of cube with the linked measure groups won't be affected.

Remote Partitions

You can use the remote-partitions feature of Analysis Services to build a distributed back-end solution. Doing so enables you to scale a volume of stored data and increase the speed of processing and query performance.

In a remote-partitions scenario, you work with two kinds of servers: a single master server and one or more remote servers. The master server serves as a primary storage of meta-data, provides access to the data for client applications, and performs all the management operations. The remote servers contain partitions with data—remote partitions.

To create a remote partition, you create a database on a remote server and set up a data source object that points to the master server. The remote Analysis Services uses this connection to get information, such as dimension data, from the master server. On the master server, you create a data source object that points to the remote server. Then you create a partition using a DDL similar to the DDL you use to create a regular partition. The difference is that you specify a `RemoteDatasourceID` property that points to the data source you just created.

As an example, let's assume that you have two servers: the master server (localhost) and the remote server (localhost\slave). You create a remote partition, `Inventory Fact 1997`, in the FoodMart 2008 database. See Figure 25.5 for a diagram of this example.

To set up the remote partition `Inventory Fact 1997` on the remote server, follow these steps:

1. Create a new database, Remote DB, on the remote server.
2. Create a new data source object on the remote server that uses the Microsoft OLE DB Provider for Analysis Services 10.0 to point to the FoodMart 2008 database on the master server. Listing 25.4 is the DDL of the `Create` command.

LISTING 25.4 DDL to Create a Data Source Pointing to the Master Server

```
<Create xmlns="http://schemas.microsoft.com/analysisservices/2003/engine">
    <ParentObject>
```

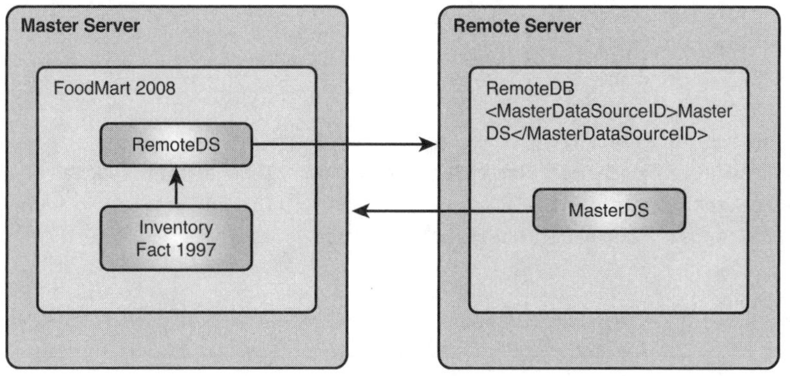

FIGURE 25.5 The partition `Inventory Fact 1997` is a remote partition.

```
        <DatabaseID>Remote DB</DatabaseID>
    </ParentObject>
    <ObjectDefinition>
        <DataSource xmlns:xsd="http://www.w3.org/2001/XMLSchema" xmlns:xsi=
➥"http://www.w3.org/2001/XMLSchema-instance" xsi:type="RelationalDataSource">
            <ID>MasterDS</ID>
            <Name>MasterDS</Name>
            <ConnectionString>Provider=MSOLAP.4;Data Source=localhost;Integrated
➥ Security=SSPI;Initial Catalog=FoodMart 2008</ConnectionString>
            <ImpersonationInfo>
                <ImpersonationMode>ImpersonateServiceAccount
➥</ImpersonationMode>
            </ImpersonationInfo>
        </DataSource>
    </ObjectDefinition>
</Create>
```

3. Change the `MasterDataSourceID` property of the Remote DB database to point to the newly created `MasterDS` data source object. You can do this by submitting the `Alter` command shown in Listing 25.5.

LISTING 25.5 DDL to Alter a Database to Add **`MasterDataSourceID`**

```
<Alter AllowCreate="true" ObjectExpansion="ObjectProperties"
➥ xmlns="http://schemas.microsoft.com/analysisservices/2003/engine">
    <Object>
        <DatabaseID>Remote DB</DatabaseID>
    </Object>
    <ObjectDefinition>
        <Database xmlns:xsd="http://www.w3.org/2001/XMLSchema"
➥ xmlns:xsi="http://www.w3.org/2001/XMLSchema-instance">
```

```
            <ID>Remote DB</ID>
            <Name>Remote DB</Name>
        <Language>1033</Language>
        <Collation>Latin1_General_CI_AS</Collation>
        <DataSourceImpersonationInfo>
            <ImpersonationMode>ImpersonateServiceAccount</ImpersonationMode>
        </DataSourceImpersonationInfo>
        <MasterDataSourceID>MasterDS</MasterDataSourceID>
    </Database>
    </ObjectDefinition>
</Alter>
```

4. In the FoodMart 2008 database on the master server, create a new data source, `RemoteDS`, with the following connection string to point to the Remote DB database on the remote server:

   ```
   Provider=MSOLAP.4;Data Source=localhost\Slave; Integrated Security=SSPI;
     ➥Initial Catalog=Remote DB
   ```

5. On the master server, modify the `Inventory Fact 1997` partition by setting the `RemoteDataSourceID` property to `RemoteDS`.
6. Issue the `Process` command to the master server to process your `Inventory Fact 1997` partition. After this partition is processed, you can see new the objects created by the master server in the RemoteDB database on the remote server.

NOTE

Make sure that user account under which the master server establishes the connection to the remote server has administrative rights on the remote server. You can either specify an appropriate user account in the `DataSourceImpersonationInfo` property of the DataSource object, or make sure that the existing service account for your master server has administrative rights on the remote server.

Processing Remote Partitions

To process a remote partition, you issue the `Process` command on the master server. When the master server receives the `Process` command, it generates an internal XML/A request to create the necessary objects on a remote server and sends this command to the remote server. The request defines the type of linked dimensions used in the measure group that contains this partition. These linked dimensions have a special refresh policy that supports storing the dimension data on the remote server. An internal request also defines the cube, measure group, and partition it needs to process.

In the first stage of partition processing, the remote server analyzes partition granularity and requests all the dimension data it needs from the master server. The remote server uses this data to decode the keys of the granularity attributes into `DataIDs` and build indexes. After the dimension data is loaded into the remote server, the remote server processes the partition data. (For more information, see Chapter 21, "Dimension and Partition Processing.")

At the end of the remote-partition processing, the remote server contains a multidimensional cube with linked dimensions, a regular measure group with partitions that contain data. Then, the remote server sends metadata information about the partition—such as the partition slice, partition size, indexes built for the partition, and so on—to the master server. This information enables the master server to avoid performing a round trip to the remote server for query execution and to make decisions about whether the requested data is stored on that remote partition.

The processing of multiple remote partitions is coordinated by the master server. It sends the `Process` commands to all the remote servers and coordinates the processing transactions between itself and each of them. A single processing transaction involves several remote servers. After the transaction is committed, a new version of the data from all remote servers becomes available to the users simultaneously, across all the servers. (For information about querying remote partitions, see Chapter 30, "Architecture of Query Execution—Retrieving Data from Storage.")

Using Business Intelligence Development Studio to Create Linked Dimensions

It's simple to define a new linked dimension. We'll use our sample FoodMart 2008 project. In BI Dev Studio, change the name of the project we've been working with from FoodMart 2008 to FoodMart 2008 Linked. Right-click the project node and select Properties from the resulting menu. On the deployment page of the Project's Properties dialog box, change Target Database to FoodMart 2008 Linked. Save the changes and deploy the solution.

Now your Analysis Server contains two databases: FoodMart 2008 and FoodMart 2008 Linked. We're going to link the `Product` dimension from FoodMart 2008 as a `ProductStandard` dimension into the FoodMart 2008 Linked database:

1. Right-click the `Dimensions` node in the Solution Explorer and select New Linked Dimension from the resulting menu. The Linked Object Wizard opens.
2. In the wizard, advance to the Select Data Source page, where you can create a new data source that points to the database you want to link your dimension to.
3. For our example, create a new data source that points to the FoodMart 2008 sample database you've deployed to the local server.
4. Advance to the Select Objects page and select the `Product` dimension.
5. Click Finish on the Completing the Wizard page. A new linked dimension appears in your database. It's named `Product 1`, so change the name to `ProductStandard`.
6. Open the `Warehouse and Sales` cube in the cube editor and add the `ProductStandard` dimension to `Warehouse and Sales` cube. Use the Dimension Usage tab to define the relationship between the `ProductStandard` dimension and the `Warehouse` measure group. Figure 25.6 shows the Define Relationship dialog box that appears on top of the cube editor.

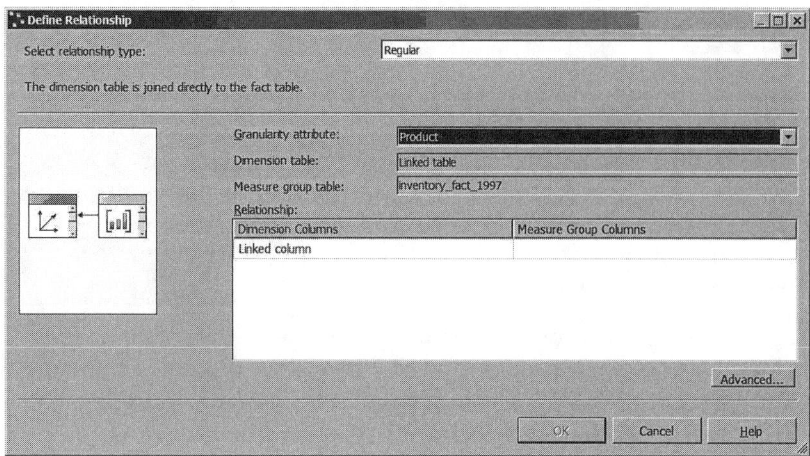

FIGURE 25.6 Create a link between a linked dimension and a local measure group in the Define Relationship dialog box.

7. Set the granularity attribute to `Product`.
8. The Relationship table's Dimension column is already populated with the name `Linked column`. Enter Product ID in the Measure Group Column and click OK.
9. Deploy your FoodMart 2008 Linked database and process the `Warehouse and Sales` cube.

When you browse the `Warehouse and Sales` cube, you'll see the `ProductStandard` dimension in your cube. It has exactly the same members as the `Product` dimension, the same hierarchies as the `Product` dimension, and shows the same totals as the `Product` dimension.

Using BI Dev Studio to a Create Virtual Cube

BI Dev Studio enables you to create linked measure groups and dimensions in a single wizard. In the FoodMart 2008 Linked database example, open the `Warehouse and Sales` cube in the cube editor and click the New Linked Object icon to launch the Linked Object Wizard. The Select Object page is different from what it was when you opened it to create linked dimensions. On this page, you see not only the dimensions you can link to, but measure groups, too. Figure 25.7 shows the Select Objects page of the wizard as you should see it.

In this illustration, you can see that you can't link to the `Product` dimension twice. This is not an Analysis Services limitation. BI Dev Studio prevents you from making a mistake and wasting server resources by creating multiple versions of linked dimensions with the same source. BI Dev Studio enables you to choose not only dimensions and measure groups, but also some other objects, such as actions and calculations.

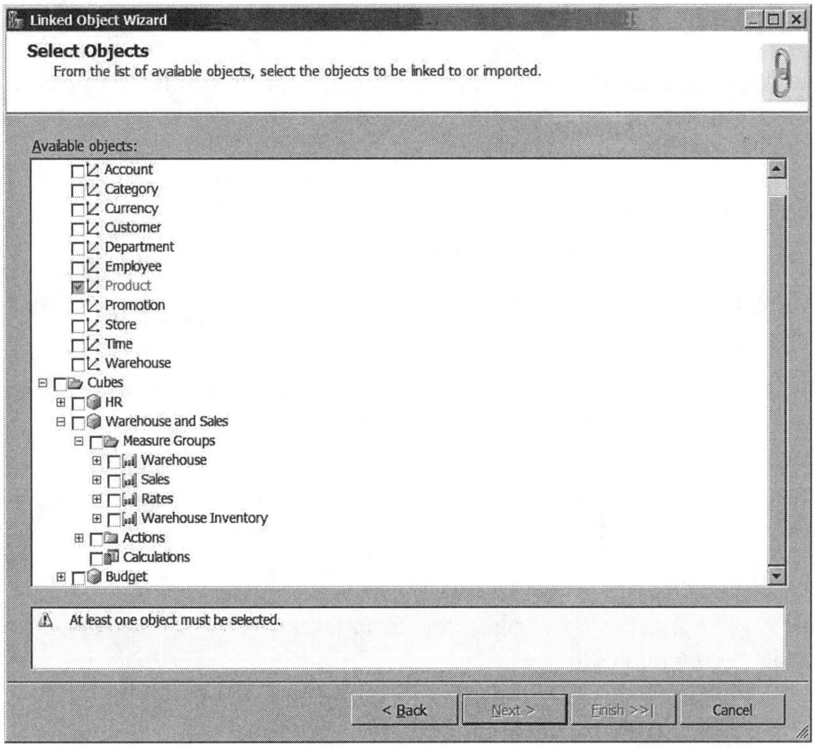

FIGURE 25.7 You can select objects to link on the Select Objects page.

NOTE

Analysis Services enables you to create only linked dimensions and linked measure groups. Any other object you select is simply re-created in the target database by BI Dev Studio. For example, if you click Calculations under the `Warehouse and Sales` cube, BI Dev Studio appends all the calculations from the source cube into the calculation script of the target database.

Select the `Sales` measure group and the `Store` and `Time` dimensions, and then advance to the Completing the Wizard page. On this page, you can see that all the dimensions and measures in your linked measure group have been renamed. BI Dev Studio renamed them to prevent name clashes in the target database.

When you complete the wizard, you will verify a new measure group created in your FoodMart 2008 Linked database: `Sales 1`. In the dimension usage pane, the `Sales 1` measure group is associated with the `ProductStandard`, `Store1`, and `Time 1` dimensions. BI Dev Studio is doing quite a bit of work for you.

Shared Scalable Databases

Analysis Services 2008 introduces new set of functionality that makes it easier to implement variation of the farm where multiple front-end servers are sharing a single copy of a database residing on the read-only shared storage (SAN, NAS, and so on). The front-end servers in this configuration are running as part of the network load-balancing cluster and presented to the user as a single server.

To make this scenario possible, Analysis Services introduces several new technologies:

- **Read-only**—Ability to mark database as read-only to disallow any updates to a database to make it possible for several servers to point to it.
- **Attach\detach for a database**—Ability to detach database from a server into and ability for several servers to attach to a single read-only copy of a database.
- **Database location**—To make it possible for a database to reside in a separate folder outside of the data folder, such that front-end servers can attach to a single database and not to share the entire data folder.

The scenario for creating shared database is as follows:

1. Process a new copy of the database, or just update an existing one by processing some of its objects on a processing server.
2. Detach new version of the database from the processing server and copy it to a shared location
3. Detach all front-end servers from the old copy of the database, and then attach then to a new copy in read-only mode.

Attach\Detach, Read-Only, and `DbStorageLocation`

Attach\Detach, Read-Only, and `DbStorageLocation` all three features tightly integrated. And we are going to talk about them together. For instance, you cannot mark database as read-only without detaching and attaching it first.

Detach

Attach and detach functionality is similar to backup and restore functionality; it is the ability to create an independent copy of a database and then bring it online to Analysis Services. The difference to a backup operation is that the database detach results in the database no longer being available to users to query. As a result of the detach operation, Analysis Services separates all the files that belong to a database being detached into a single (a database) folder. By default, your database folder is located under the Analysis Services Data folder. For instance, if you are detaching our sample database, the resulting folder containing all the FoodMart 2008 files would be: `C:\Program Files\Microsoft SQL Server\MSAS10.MSSQLSERVER\OLAP\Data\FoodMart 2008.0.db`. In addition to all your database data and metadata files, you will find one more file in your database folder after detaching it: the detach log file. In our example of detaching the FoodMart 2008 database, you will find a `FoodMart 2008.detach_log` in your database folder. Analysis Services uses this file to determine whether you can attach a database from a particular folder.

If you are using detach and attach functionality as a backup or deployment strategy for your application, make sure to copy an entire database folder with all its content.

SQL Server Management Studio provides a simple way to detach a database. Right-click the name of the database you want to detach in the Object Explorer and select Detach. Figure 25.8 shows the Detach dialog box as you should see it when trying to detach the sample FoodMart 2008 database.

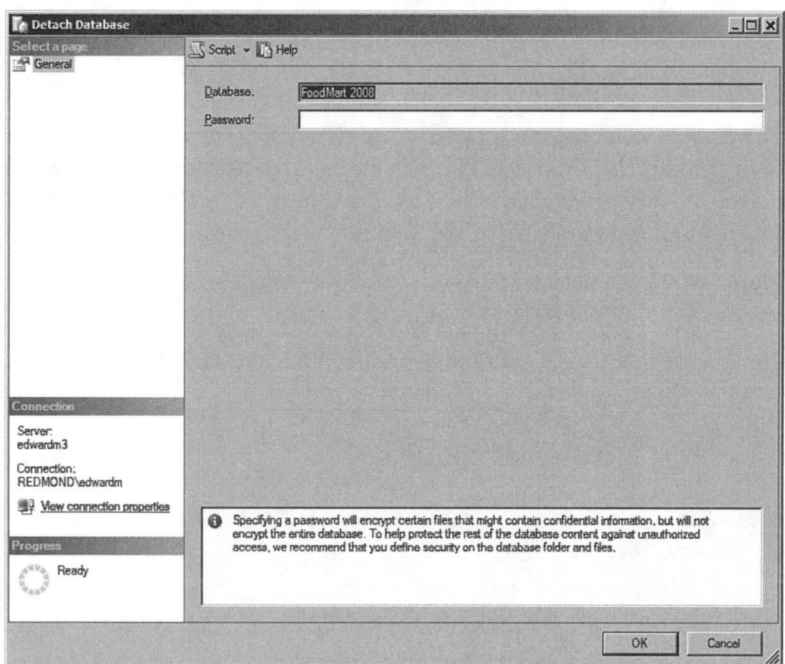

FIGURE 25.8 Detach dialog for the FoodMart 2008 database.

The DDL of the `Detach` command is extremely simple and allows you to specify only two parameters: an ID of the database to detach and optionally a password to be used to encrypt sensitive information stored with your database.

Listing 25.6 shows the DDL of the `Detach` command for detaching a FoodMart2008 database.

LISTING 25.6 DDL to Detach a FoodMart 2008 Database

```
<Detach xmlns="http://schemas.microsoft.com/analysisservices/2003/engine">
    <Object>
```

```
        <DatabaseID>FoodMart 2008</DatabaseID>
        <Password>2008</ Password>
    </Object>
</Detach>
```

Attach

Attaching a database is a pretty straightforward operation. To attach a database to Analysis Services, you need to specify a folder from which you will be attaching a database and optionally a password and a `ReadWriteMode` property.

The `ReadWriteMode` property of the `Attach` command can assume one of the two values:

- **`ReadOnly`**—The database is attached to Analysis Server in read-only mode.
- **`ReadWrite`**—The default value for the property. The database is attached to Analysis Server in read-write mode. The administrator is free to add\delete\process any of the objects. The database is "exclusively" attached to an instance of Analysis Services, and any attempt to attach it to another server instance will result in an error.

Let's consider an example where we detach the FoodMart 2008 database, copy it to the `C:\tmp` folder, and attach it to Analysis Services.

Listing 25.7 shows the DDL of the `Attach` command to attach a FoodMart 2008 database from `C:\tmp` folder.

LISTING 25.7 DDL to Attach a FoodMart 2008 Database

```
<Attach xmlns="http://schemas.microsoft.com/analysisservices/2003/engine">
    <Folder>C:\tmp\FoodMart 2008.0.db</Folder>
    <ReadWriteMode xmlns="http://schemas.microsoft.com
/analysisservices/2008/engine/100">ReadWrite</ReadWriteMode>
    <Password>2008</Password>
</Attach>
```

In our sample DDL, we could have omitted the `ReadWriteMode` property. In this case, the database is attached as read-write. In this example, we attached a database that was stored in the C:\tmp\FoodMart 2008.0.db folder, which is outside of the Analysis Services data directory. While executing this command, Analysis Services does not copy database files into the Analysis Services's data folder, and all database data and metadata files remain in the original directory.

If you try to attach a database without specifying a password, you will receive an error message. In our example of trying to attach a password-protected FoodMart2008 database, the error message would look like this: `Errors in the encryption library: The file \\?\ C:\tmp\FoodMart 2008.0.db\FoodMart 2008.detach_log is encrypted. You must provide a password.`

Read-Only

As mentioned previously, after attaching a database in read-only mode (by specifying ReadOnly value of the ReadWriteMode property of the Attach command), a database becomes a read-only database. Users can query this database, but cannot modify it in any way. For example, you cannot change database name or add a dimension; you cannot also process data in the read-only database. The only administrative operation allowed on the read-only database is a `Detach` command. To indicate the current state of the database, a database object has an additional `ReadWriteMode` property (similar to the property you specify in the `Attach` command). It could assume one of the two values—ReadOnly or ReadWrite.

NOTE

You cannot create a new database in the read-only mode; the only way to convert database into read-only state is to detach it from Analysis Services and attach it back latter.

DbStorageLocation

Analysis Services 2008 introduces ability to store all data and metadata related to different databases in different folders. This removes a limitation requiring all Analysis Services metadata and dimension data to reside in a single disk location. With previous versions of Analysis Services, you could only specify alternative locations for partition data using `StorageLocation` partition property. Analysis Services 2008 provides similar property of a `Database` object – `DbStorageLocation`, which indicates location of the database. By default, data is stored in the Analysis Services data directory if this property is not defined.

In our previous example, after detaching and attaching a database from C:\tmp, the DbStorageLocation property is set to \\?\C:\tmp.

NOTE

You should exercise extreme caution changing this property. Unintended change of it will resolve in data loss of your entire database. If you issue an `Alter` command that changes the DbStorageLocation, Analysis Server will delete all the files in the old location and will create a new database folder in the new location. The `Alter` command doesn't load data into Analysis Services; therefore, the new database folder will contain only metadata files and data will be lost. To protect you from the accidental data loss, SQL Server Management Studio doesn't allow to change the DbStorageLocation property. To change the database storage location, we recommend first detaching a database, copying it to desired location, and then attaching it back.

PART VI

Analysis Server Architecture

IN THIS PART

CHAPTER 26

Server Architecture and Command Execution

IN THIS CHAPTER

All Analysis Services commands are formatted using the XML for Analysis (XML/A) protocol, covered in detail in Chapter 32, "XML for Analysis." XML/A supports two types of requests: `Execute`, which executes commands on the server; and `Discover`, which retrieves metadata from the server.

Command Execution

During execution, a command from a client application passes through many server subsystems. Some of the subsystems work with all the commands that arrive at the server; others are responsible for only certain types of commands.

For example, a Data Definition Language (DDL) command such as `Create`, `Alter`, `Delete`, or `Process` is treated differently and involves different subsystems than does a data-retrieval command, such as the `Select` command. The server architecture diagram in Figure 26.1 shows how Analysis Services processes a command and illustrates the server subsystem responsible for each step of the process.

The diagram in Figure 26.1 illustrates the execution process for three types of requests. The first seven items in the diagram describe a sequence that the three types have in common:

1. The server listens for a client request on the TCP/IP port.

2. When the client establishes a connection with the server, Analysis Services creates the `Connection` object, allocates a data buffer, and authenticates the user.

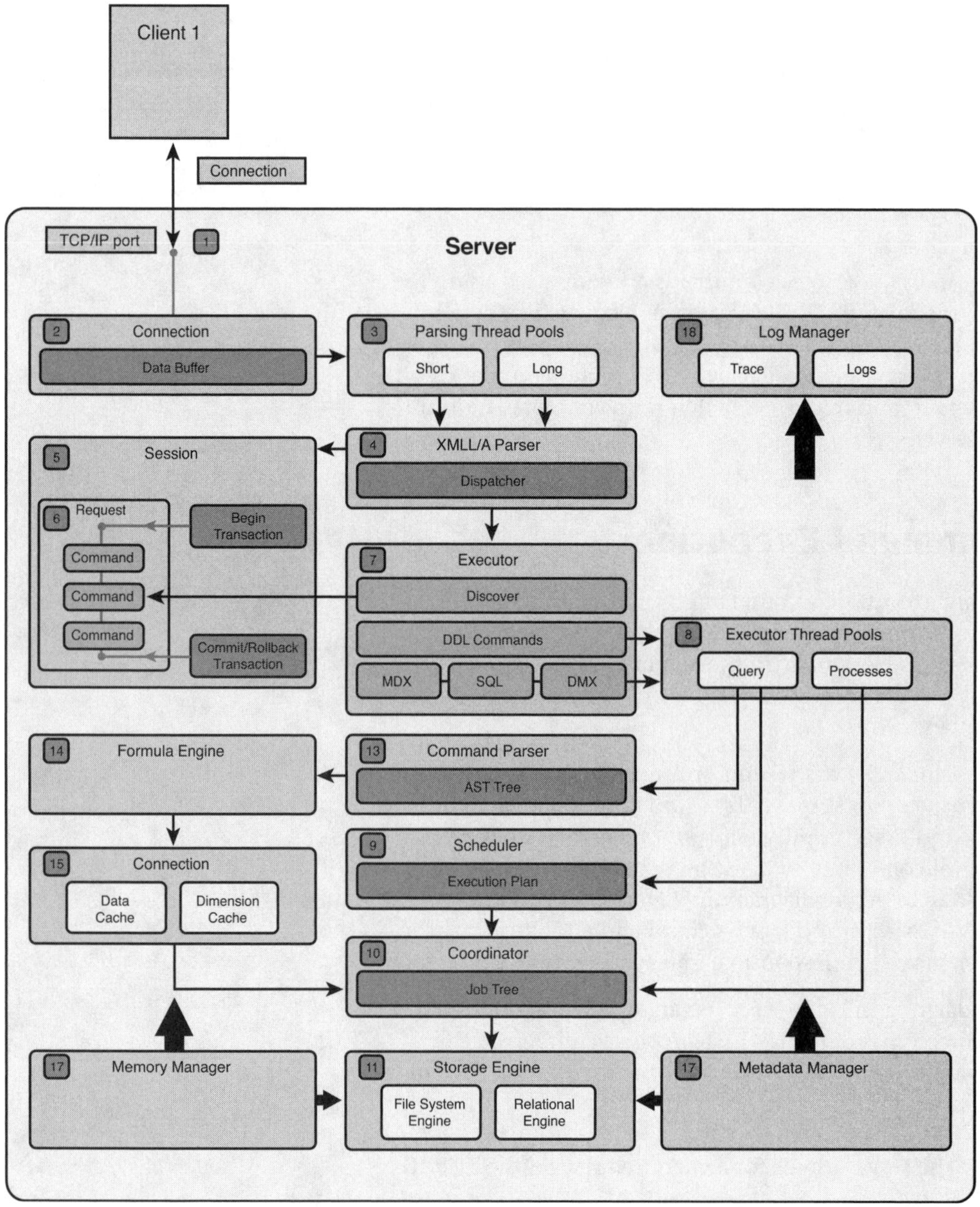

FIGURE 26.1 Server subsystems are responsible for the different steps in processing a command.

3. The server retrieves the thread from the parsing thread pool and passes it to the XML/A parser. There are two groups of threads in the parsing thread pool: a thread pool for short requests, and a thread pool for long requests. If the request fits into a single packet, the server retrieves the thread from the short pool. A thread for a larger request is retrieved from the long pool.
4. The XML/A parser starts parsing and analyzes the Simple Object Access Protocol (SOAP) headers to determine the session to which the request belongs. (For more information about SOAP headers, see Chapter 32, "XML for Analysis.")
5. The XML/A parser calls the session manager, which detects the existing session the request belongs to or it creates a new session. (For information about session management, see the next section in this chapter.)
6. After the session manager assigns a session to the request, responsibility for executing the request is passed to that session, the context for command execution is created, and a transaction is defined. (For information about transactions, see the "Commands That Control Transactions" section later in this chapter.)
7. The XML/A parser passes execution of the request to the dispatcher, which determines what type of command the request contains. It then sends the execution to the executor, which is where the paths of the three different types of requests diverge.
    - If the request is a `Discover` request, it executes immediately and returns results to the session, which then returns them to the client application (the end of the road). A `Discover` request typically doesn't require a lot of system resources for execution, so it can execute on the same thread used to parse the request. This allows the server to execute such requests quickly rather than spending time marshaling the request to another thread; the speed of execution generally doesn't depend on the load of the server.
    - If the request is a DDL command—a command for managing the server, such as for managing transactions, canceling requests, backup and restore, and many others—or a query command (commands that contain Multidimensional Expressions [MDX], Data Mining Extensions [DMX], or Structured Query Language [SQL] statements), the executor uses the thread pool to schedule execution.
8. For DDL commands and MDX, SQL, and DMX requests, the server takes a thread from the execution thread pool and schedules execution of the command.

Here the paths of the remaining two types of requests diverge. MDX, DMX, and SQL requests pass to the command parser. We'll pick up that sequence at number 12.

9. DDL commands pass to the execution scheduler. The execution scheduler creates an execution plan (a list of jobs that must be executed and their dependencies). Then execution passes to the job coordinator.
10. The job coordinator builds a job tree, requests the threads necessary for executing the jobs from the execution thread pool, initializes the threads, and then executes the jobs.

11. The storage engine executes the jobs. The storage engine retrieves the data from either the relational engine or the file system, processes it, and stores it in the file system of Analysis Services.

Execution of the DDL command is finished. Now we'll go back to the execution thread pool. From there, the queries (MDX, SQL, and DMX statements) pass to the command parser.

12. The command parser creates a semantic tree (Abstract Syntax Tree [AST]) for the request, and determines which query language the request contains. Execution of MDX and SQL requests passes to the formula engine; DMX requests go to the data-mining engine. We didn't include the data-mining engine in the diagram because we won't cover it in detail in this book. (For information about the formula engine, see Chapter 29, "Architecture of Query Execution—Calculating MDX Expressions.")
13. The formula engine uses the AST to build a tree of the MDX objects and to determine what data is needed to calculate the result of the query.
14. The formula engine sends the request to the cache system to search for data that might be stored in the cache. Dimension data is stored in the dimension cache; fact data is stored in the data cache. The data then returns to the formula engine, which computes the result of the request and sends it back to the client application. That's the end of the line for that request.

    If the requested data is not in the cache, the cache system generates an internal request for the data and sends the request through the Job Coordinator to the storage engine, following algorithm similar with execution of the DDL commands. (For information about the architecture of cache system, see Chapter 29.)

    After the data is retrieved from the storage engine, it passes to the cache. The formula engine finds it there, computes the response, and sends it back to the client application.

Three subsystems support all the modules in the system:

- The metadata manager stores all the metadata for the multidimensional model and passes it to any subsystem as needed.

- The memory manager allocates all the memory in the system and manages it for optimal use.

  For information about the memory manager, see Chapter 27, "Memory Management."

- The log manager enables any subsystem to give the user (or the client application) information about the condition of the server and progress of the execution of a command. The log manager passes the information to the trace system or writes it to various kinds of logs. An administrator can configure the sets of logs. At a minimum, critical information is written to the server log, such as information about starting and stopping of the server and critical errors. For information about the trace system, Chapter 38, "Using Trace to Monitor and Audit Analysis Services."

Session Management

Analysis Services uses sessions to manage state, the current set of updated data (writeback data) and calculations available while it executes a command. A command received by Analysis Services can be executed in a stateless session, in which the command executes independent of other commands, or in a stateful session, in which the command's execution can depend on the results or activities of another command in that session. For example, you can create a calculated member that is temporarily available to you, and then send a request that uses the calculated member. The request depends on the previous command that created the calculated member. Therefore, the session is stateful. (For information about calculated members, see Chapter 12, "Cube-Based MDX Calculations.")

The session manager subsystem of Analysis Services manages sessions on the server. A `Session` object makes it possible to share data between requests. There is a many-to-many relationship among client connections and session objects created on the server. You can create many sessions from a single client connection; a client can work with a single session through multiple connections. The only limitation is that the users who initiate connections should have the same credentials. Figure 26.2 illustrates client applications connecting to the server through session objects, one session object for each connection.

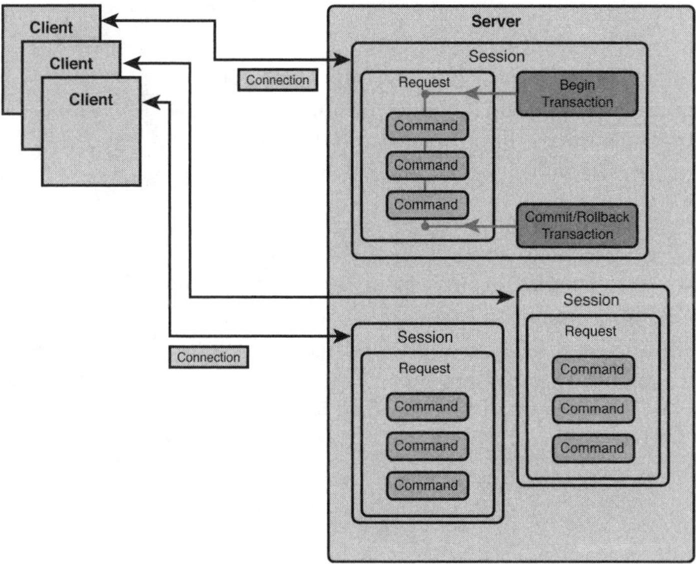

FIGURE 26.2 Sessions on the server are managed by the session manager subsystem.

When a client application connects to the server, the session manager creates a `Session` object; Analysis Services assigns a unique identifier to that `Session` object, and establishes the connection. The client application can create a new session, work with an existing one, or not create a session. (For information about the application programming interface [API] that enables a client application to create and end sessions, see Chapter 32.)

Information that can be shared between requests is stored on the session and remains on the server as long as the session is alive. The client application can end the session, and the session manager can delete the session when time expires. Because a single connection can work with multiple sessions, closing the connection doesn't automatically close the session. The client application can reconnect and work with the same session. However, the server can close a session if it is not in use for the timeout specified in the `IdleOrphanSessionTimeout` server configuration property. It's not a good idea to rely on the server to close a session. The system works more efficiently when the client application deletes the session when it disconnects from the server.

Analysis Services assigns a unique name to the `Session` object so that the client application can retrieve the name later (for example, using a `DISCOVER_SESSIONS` request) and use it for subsequent requests.

If a client application doesn't create a new session when it establishes a connection, Analysis Services creates a new `Session` object for it, but the object's lifetime is the same as the lifetime of the request.

A session works with only one request at a time, except for commands to start a trace (for information about traces, see Chapter 38) and requests to cancel execution of the previous request (which we discuss later in this chapter).

A session executes requests sequentially. However, an `Execute` request can contain just one command or group of commands wrapped in a `Batch` command. The server treats the commands in a batch as a single unit for execution. A request that contains a `Batch` command, as with other requests that contain a single command, executes sequentially. However, commands contained within the `Batch` command can execute either sequentially or in parallel, depending on the definition of the `Batch` command. (For more information, see the "`Batch` Command" section later in this chapter.)

In addition to the `Session` object that services a group of commands, Analysis Services creates an `Execution Context` object that contains the information and resources required to execute a single request. The lifetime of the `Execution Context` object is the same as the lifetime of the request. After the request is completed, the `Execution Context` is released and the resources are returned to the system.

Server State Management

Commands that arrive to Analysis Services can be divided into two categories:

- Commands that don't change the state of the server, such as MDX requests for data
- Commands that do change the state of objects on the server, such as `Create`, `Alter`, `Delete`, `Process`, and many other commands

Commands that change the objects of a database execute atomically: After the command successfully executes, the object of the database it worked with transforms into a new state, and all subsequent commands work with the new version of the object. If a command fails or is canceled, all the changes to the object roll back. The object remains in its previous state; subsequent commands work with the old version of the object. For a command that works with multiple properties of an object, at the command's completion either all the properties are changed or all of them remain the same.

Analysis Services uses the mechanism of transactions to support this atomic behavior. A transaction is an undividable list of commands that must fully execute or not execute at all. The transaction mechanism helps maintain the integrity of the system and prevents the concurrent execution of commands from driving the server into an inconsistent state. A user can initiate an explicit transaction on the session or the server starts an implicit transaction for each request. If the server starts an implicit transaction to execute a request, the server commits the transaction when execution is complete. If the execution completes successfully, the server makes the changes permanent; if the command fails, the server rolls back the transaction.

Executing Commands That Change Analysis Services Objects

Analysis Services uses an XML-based data definition language, within XML/A commands, to create, delete, and update its objects. The syntax of the Data Definition Language (DDL) depends heavily on the definition of the objects used in the conceptual data model. Data management commands usually contain three parts:

- A reference to the object with which the command operates
- A DDL definition of the object
- The parameters used to execute the command

The reference to the object usually contains the identifier for that object, and a list of the identifiers for its parent objects. (The list can contain identifiers in no particular order.)

You can use data definition commands only with major objects. (See Chapter 4, "The Conceptual Data Model," for more information about major and minor objects.) Therefore, object references refer only to major objects. Listing 26.1 shows a reference of the `Sales` measure group object.

LISTING 26.1 Reference Section of a Command That Operates on the **`Sales`** Measure Group

```
<DatabaseID>Foodmart 2008</DatabaseID>
<CubeID>Warehouse and Sales</CubeID>
<MeasureGroupID>Sales</MeasureGroupID>
```

All the data definition commands have a lot in common, but each command has its own set of parameters. We'll examine the most important data definition commands: `Create`, `Alter`, `Delete`, and `Process`.

Creating Objects

To support object creation, Analysis Services provides the `Create` command, which loads the definition of the object to the server. Listing 26.2 shows the syntax of the `Create` command.

LISTING 26.2 The Syntax of the **Create** Command

```
<Create Scope="Session" AllowOverwrite="false">
     <ParentObject>object_reference</ParentObject>
     <ObjectDefinition>
         object_definition
         .......
     </ObjectDefinition>
</Create>
```

The `Create` command contains a reference to the parent object, inside of which you create a new object. For example, when creating a cube or dimension, the parent object is a database. The `object_definition` section contains the DDL definition of a cube or dimension.

You can specify two parameters on a `Create` command: `Scope` and `AllowOverwrite`. The `Scope` parameter creates cubes and dimensions on a session, so those objects are available only to the user of the current session. To do this, specify the `Scope` parameter on the `Create` command and set it to `"Session"`. If you have not specified this parameter, Analysis Services creates a server object that is available to all the users that have access rights to it.

Use the `AllowOverwrite` parameter to specify how the `Create` command should behave when an object with the same ID already exists on the server. If you create an object with an identifier that matches an object that already exists on the server, Analysis Services can either remove the existing object and replace it with a new one or return an error.

If you define `AllowOverwrite="true"` (allowing Analysis Services to replace an existing object with a new one), but an error happens during execution of the command, the new object won't be created, and the old object won't be removed, because commands are executed atomically. (We discuss atomic execution of the commands later in this chapter.)

When the `Create` command overwrites an existing object, the old object is deleted, and a completely new object with the same identifier and a version number of `1` is created on the server. If the old object had data associated with it—for example, a dimension or cube—you have to process the new object before users can access the data.

Editing Objects

You can use the `Alter` command to change objects that already exist in the system. The `Alter` command replaces the old definition of the object with a new one. Listing 26.3 shows the syntax of the `Alter` command.

LISTING 26.3 The Syntax of the **Alter** Command

```
<Alter Scope="Session" AllowCreate="True"
   ObjectExpansion="ObjectProperties">
   <ParentObject>object_reference</ParentObject>
   <ObjectDefinition>object_definition</ObjectDefinition>
</Alter>
```

Similar to the `Create` command, you specify the parent object for the object to be edited by the `Alter` command, and then specify the definition of the object to be edited. When Analysis Services receives an `Alter` command, it first analyzes which changes are necessary for transformation of the object from the old state to the new one, and then performs those changes.

You can specify three parameters on the `Alter` command: `Scope`, `AllowCreate`, and `ObjectExpansion`. The `Scope` parameter alters cubes and dimensions on a session, so changes to those objects will be available only to the user of the current session. To do this, you specify the `Scope="Session"` parameter on the `Alter` command. If you have not specified this parameter, Analysis Services alters a server object so that the changes are available to all the users that have access rights to that object.

You can use the `AllowCreate` parameter to tell the system to create an object if it doesn't yet exist. In this case, Analysis Services treats the `Alter` command as a `Create` command. If an object with the specified identifier already exists on the system, however, the `Alter` command behaves differently from the `Create` command. In this case, instead of deleting the old object and creating a new one with the same identifier and a version number of `1`, the `Alter` command creates a new version of the specified object and increments the version number for that object. In addition, unlike the `Create` command, you might not need to reprocess an object changed with the `Alter` command. For example, if you need to change the name or description of the object, there is no need to reprocess the data associated with that object.

The `ObjectExpansion` parameter defines the depth of the new definition for the object. You can specify one of two values for this parameter in the `Alter` command:

- **`ObjectProperties`**—Indicates that the command is allowed to update only properties on the current object itself, without modifying any its child major objects. In this case, `ObjectProperties` refers to the object's simple properties, such as `Name` or `Description`, and its child minor objects.
- **`ExpandFull`**—Indicates that the command is allowed to update not just the current object itself, but also all its child major and minor objects.

In Chapter 4, we discussed minor and major objects, and indicated that you can alter minor objects only within the context of a change to the parent major object. The `Alter` command, correspondingly, can alter a minor object, but only within the context of the major object that contains it.

Deleting Objects

You can use the `Delete` command to delete objects that exist in Analysis Services. Listing 26.4 shows the syntax of the `Delete` command.

LISTING 26.4 The Syntax of the **Delete** Command

```
<Delete IgnoreFailures = "False">
      <Object>object_reference</Object>
</Delete>
```

The syntax of this command is a little different from the syntax of `Alter` and `Create` commands because you don't need to provide the `ObjectDefinition` element. To delete an object, you need to specify only the reference of the object that you are deleting.

You can also specify the `IgnoreFailures` parameter, which allows Analysis Services to ignore some of the errors that it might encounter during execution of the `Delete` command and continue deleting the object. For example, setting this parameter to `True` allows Analysis Services to ignore communication errors, so it can delete objects even if Analysis Services cannot establish a connection to other databases that might be required for this object; if your cube has a remote partition on a machine that is no longer available, you can still delete the cube. Of course, Analysis Services cannot absolutely ignore all errors.

Processing Objects

Commands for creating, altering, and deleting objects are needed for defining and supporting the multidimensional model. However, these commands alone are not enough to allow users to work with the model. Before the user can retrieve multidimensional data from Analysis Services, the data must first be loaded from the source and converted to the multidimensional format. The `Process` command loads the data into the objects you defined. Listing 26.5 shows the syntax used by the `Process` command.

TABLE 26.2 Types of the **Process** Command

Name	Applies To	Description
`ProcessFull`	`Database`, `Dimension`, `Cube`, `>easureGroup`, `Partition`, `MiningStructure`, `MiningModel`	Loads the new data into an `Cube`, `Partition`, has data loaded, it will dropped and new data will be loaded. In addition to loading data.
`ProcessAdd`	`Dimension`, `Partition`	Data that has not previously been loaded is added to the object.

TABLE 26.2 Types of the **Process** Command

Name	Applies To	Description
ProcessUpdate	Dimension	Analysis Services reloads data to the dimension and detects what data was changed. If Analysis Services detects that data changed during the Process command affects other objects, such as aggregations or partitions, it changes the state of those objects.
ProcessIndexes	Dimension, Cube, MeasureGroup, Partition	Analysis Services rebuilds the indexes of data stored in the object.
ProcessData	Dimension, Cube, MeasureGroup, Partition	Loads only data into the object and doesn't build Partition indexes.
ProcessDefault	Database, Dimension, Cube, MeasureGroup, Partition, MiningStructure, MiningModel	Loads data into the object and build indexes of the data, if the data was not loaded into the object or if the index wasn't built. If the object was already processed and had indexes, the Process command won't do anything.
ProcessScriptCache		Rebuilds the MDX global scope cache. (See Chapter 28 for more information.)
ProcessClear	Database, Dimension, Cube, MeasureGroup, Partition, MiningStructure, MiningModel	The Process command will drop the data from the object.
ProcessStructure	Cube, MiningStructure	The Process command processes dimensions of a cube and changes the state of all cube measure groups into the browsable state. After execution of this command, the user can issue queries to the cube, and retrieve dimension data, but not cube data.

TABLE 26.1 The Elements of the **Process** Command

Name	Description
`Object`	Reference to the object to be processed.
`Type`	Specifies the type of processing to perform. Table 26.2 lists the types of processing supported by Analysis Services.
`Bindings`	Defines mapping of the multidimensional object to the relational data source applied during processing command execution. (For more information about `Bindings`, see Chapter 17, "Loading Data from a Relational Database.") The `Bindings` element is optional in the `Process` command. When `Bindings` are not defined, Analysis Services uses the `Source` property of the object being processed. Bindings defined as part of the `Process` command are called out-of-line `Bindings` (OOL) and overwrite bindings defined in the `Source` property of the object.
`Datasource`	Data source that contains the data to be loaded into the object. (For more information about `Datasource`, see Chapter 17.) The `Datasource` element is optional in the `Process` command. When `Datasource` is not defined, Analysis Services uses the `Datasource` object of the current database. The `DataSource` defined as part of the `Process` command is called OOL `DataSource` and overwrites data source definition of the database.
`DatasourceView`	The data source view that contains the schema used during command execution. (For more information about data source views, see Chapter 17.) The `DatasourceView` element is optional in the `Process` command. When `DatasourceView` is not defined, Analysis Services uses the `DatasourceView` object of the current database. `DatasourceView` defined as part of the `Process` command is called OOL DSV and overwrites the DSV definition of the database.
`ErrorConfiguration`	Error configuration objects that specify rules by which Analysis Services handles errors related to referential integrity of the data during command execution. (See Chapter 21, "Dimension and Partition Processing," for more information about referential integrity errors.) The `ErrorConfiguration` element is optional in the `Process` command. When it is not defined, Analysis Services uses the `ErrorConfiguration` property of the object being processed.
`WriteBackTableCreation`	Indicates whether the writeback table should be used or created (if it doesn't exist).

LISTING 26.5 The Syntax of the **Process** Command

```
<Process>
    <Type>processing_type</Type>
```

```
    <Object>object_reference</Object>
    <Bindings>ool_bindings</Bindings>
    <DataSource>ool_ds</DataSource>
    <DataSourceView>ool_dsv</DataSourceView>
    <ErrorConfiguration>error_config</ErrorConfiguration>
    <WriteBackTableCreation>wb_tbl_creation</WriteBackTableCreation>
</Process>
```

You can use the elements shown in Table 26.1 when you define the `Process` command.

Analysis Services supports different types of processing with the `Process` command, which enables you to load different data structures of Analysis Services. Table 26.2 shows the types of properties supported in this version of Analysis Services.

In many cases, processing of data depends on how the physical data model is implemented and which kind of data is loaded. We discussed how Analysis Services performs processing in Chapter 21.

Analysis Services tracks version information for both the metadata and data of a major object. When it executes the `Process` command, Analysis Services increments the version information for the data stored in the partition. This change can affect not only the current object, but also other objects that depend on it. To analyze the dependencies of other objects on the object currently been processed, you can use impact analysis, a feature that we discuss later in this chapter.

Commands That Control Transactions

There are many scenarios in which requests coming from a client application should be grouped together, and changes made by individual commands be committed only if the changes of all the other commands in a group are committed. For example, suppose that you need to change the structure of a cube, process it after the change, and make the changes to the cube permanent only if the processing succeeds.

In the database field, a series of operations that should execute together must be either entirely completed or aborted is called a transaction. To enable transaction support, Analysis Services provides the `BeginTransaction`, `CommitTransaction`, and `RollbackTransaction` commands. You can deduce the purposes of these commands by their names:

- `BeginTransaction` begins a transaction on the server.
- `CommitTransaction` persists all the changes done to server objects by the commands running inside the transaction.
- `RollbackTransaction` discards all changes done to the objects so that they remain in the same state they were in before the transaction started.

The syntax for these commands is simple:

```
<BeginTransaction/>
<CommitTransaction/>
<RollbackTransaction/>
```

When Analysis Services receives a `BeginTransaction` command, it checks whether there is an existing `Transaction` object on the current session. If there isn't, Analysis Services creates a new `Transaction` object and assigns it a unique identifier. If there is an existing `Transaction` object on the current session, Analysis Services increments the internal counter for that `Transaction` object. The current version of Analysis Services doesn't support nested transactions. All subsequent operations execute inside the transaction. A user (or multiple users) working with different sessions don't see changes occurring inside the transaction; the changes aren't visible until they are committed. After the transaction is committed, users can see the updated objects.

You should call the `CommitTransaction` command as many times as you call the `BeginTransaction` command, before the `CommitTransaction` command commits the changes. However, if the changes are to be rolled back, the `RollbackTransaction` command rolls back the changes no matter how many times `BeginTransaction` was called before `RollbackTransaction` (as shown in Figure 26.3). If you try to roll back a transaction before it starts, Analysis Services returns an error.

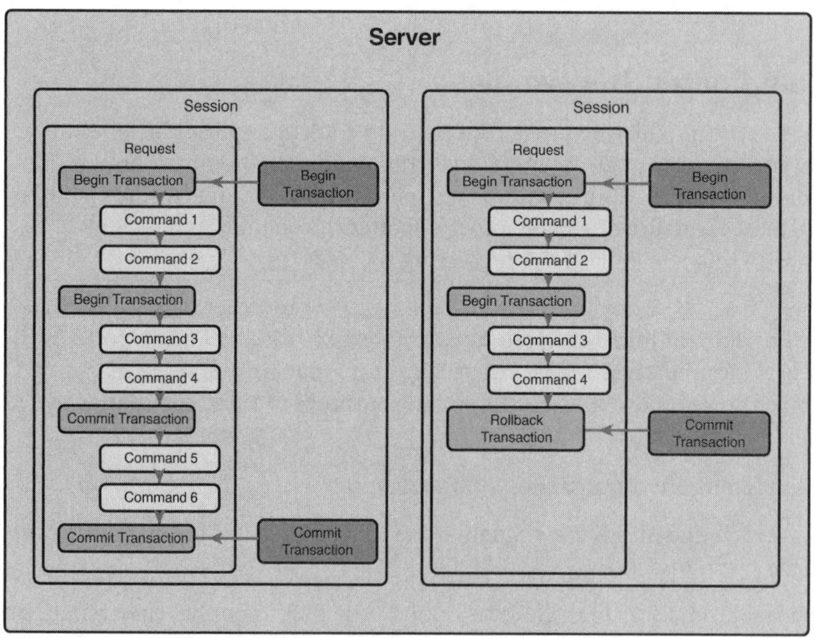

FIGURE 26.3 If all commands execute successfully, they are committed; if one command in the transaction fails, they all roll back.

Managing Concurrency

Analysis Services doesn't serialize commands coming to the server from different connections to different sessions; they execute in parallel. It's possible that different commands would try to change the same object at the same time. To prevent this, Analysis Services uses a lock mechanism.

Locking Objects

Before a command starts to change an object, it puts a lock on it. Other commands that might need to change this object must wait until the lock lifts. For example, a command that alters a dimension puts a lock on the dimension object. If a request from another user's session comes for a dimension update, it has to wait until the first one completes and the lock lifts. When a command is running inside a transaction, the lock doesn't lift until the whole transaction completes. The locking mechanism prevents concurrent commands from updating the same object at the same time. However, when two users try to change objects that depend on each other a deadlock can occur. Figure 26.4 shows sequence of operations that can lead to a deadlock:

1. Clients 1 and 2 each create a session on the server: Session A and Session B, respectively.
2. Client 1 begins a transaction on Session A and issues three commands. Client 2 begins a transaction on its session and issues a set of commands.
3. The first command from Client 1 puts a lock on Dimension A. The first command from Client 2 puts a lock on Dimension B.
4. Client 1 needs to work with Dimension B and Cube 1, so it tries to lock those objects, but the command from Client 2 already locked Dimension B.
5. The second command from Client 2 also needs to work with Cube 1, along with Cube 2. However, the first client has locked Cube 1.

Now we have a classic deadlock situation: Client 1 can't complete its work because it is waiting for the lock on Dimension B to lift. However, this lock won't lift because the commands from Client 2 won't complete; they are waiting for lock on Cube 1, set by Command 2 from Client 1.

Analysis Services provides two ways to exit from a deadlock situation:

- Each command executed on the server has a timeout associated with it. If the command doesn't complete its execution during the time allowed, the server automatically cancels it and rolls back the transaction in which the command is executing. The default command timeout is 60 minutes. (You can change the length of the timeout in the `ServerTimeout` server configuration property or you can use the `Timeout` property in a request to specify a shorter timeout.)
- An hour might seem like a long time for the life of a lock, and Analysis Services can detect whether more than one transaction is waiting for an object locked by a transaction. The server would cancel and roll back one of the transactions that was waiting for a lock to be lifted.

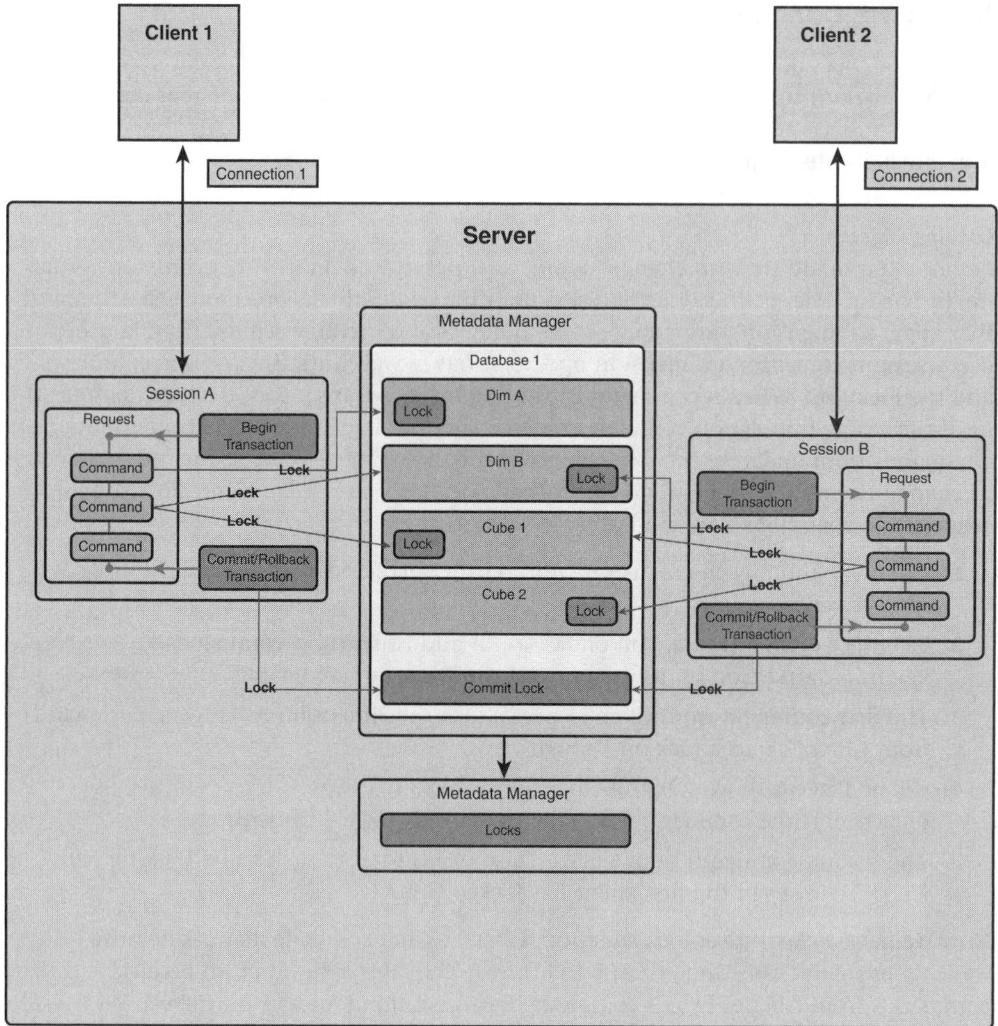

FIGURE 26.4 Multiple sessions can cause a deadlock on the server.

Using a Commit Lock for Transaction Synchronization

After the commands executed inside a transaction complete, they are committed to the server. It's very important that two different transactions from different users don't commit simultaneously. It's also important that, when committing the transaction, no query is running against the changing database because the query should return consistent data. To guarantee that a query works with the same version of the objects and that two transactions do not commit at the same time, Analysis Services uses a commit lock on the database object.

A commit lock can be either exclusive or shared. Before a session commits a transaction, it tries to acquire an exclusive commit lock on the database. If exclusive commit lock is granted to a session, no other session can obtain a commit lock for this database object. All query requests (but not DDL commands) are trying to acquire a shared commit lock.

Multiple requests can simultaneously obtain a shared commit lock if no exclusive commit lock has been granted to another request. If a transaction requests an exclusive commit lock, it has to wait until all previously granted shared locks lift and no other transaction has previously requested an exclusive commit lock. If these conditions are met and the transaction successfully acquires a commit lock, the session quickly commits all the objects and lifts the commit lock. However, if the conditions are not met, the transaction goes into the queue for a commit lock.

A transaction has to stay in the queue until all the requests currently running on the server complete, and potentially some requests can take a long time. During this time, the database is unavailable to new query requests because there is a command waiting in the queue for an exclusive lock. The server won't execute any command until our transaction is committed. To prevent this, you can specify a value for the `ForceCommitTimeout` property, which limits the time required to commit the transaction. If this timeout expires while an operation is running and preventing the transaction from committing, the server cancels all outstanding queries that are currently running.

NOTE

Because Analysis Services creates an implicit transaction for each command, all operations on the server execute according to this logic, even if the client application does not call the `BeginTransaction` command.

Locking Commands

When you have a complex system in which you need to coordinate operations in Analysis Services with operations in other servers, such as SQL Server or other instances of Analysis Services, you might need to manage transactions explicitly. For example, suppose that you want to update a table in SQL Server and process a partition based on this table in a single transaction. Analysis Services uses the `Lock` and `Unlock` commands, whose syntax is shown in Listing 26.6.

LISTING 26.6 The Syntax of the **Lock** and **Unlock** Commands

```
<Lock>
     <ID>lock_id</ID>
     <Object>object_reference<Object>
     <Mode>lock_mode</Mode>
</Lock>
<Unlock>
     <ID>lock_id</ID>
</Unlock>
```

To lock a database, you include in your code a unique identifier for the `Database` object and identifier of the lock object. Analysis Services checks whether the user has the appropriate permissions to lock the database. (Only server or database administrators can lock a database.) If the user does have permission, Analysis Services grants the lock or adds the request to the queue to wait for a lock. Analysis Services supports two types of locks: exclusive locks and shared locks:

- An exclusive lock prevents other sessions from obtaining a lock of either type until the current lock lifts. It prevents any command from another session from executing. You can obtain an exclusive lock by specifying `CommitExclusive` in the `lock_mode` element of the `Lock` command.
- A shared lock prevents any transaction from obtaining an exclusive lock on a database. However, requests coming to the database continue to execute and other sessions can obtain a shared lock. You can obtain a shared lock by specifying `CommitShared` in the `lock_mode` of the `Lock` command.

NOTE

A `Lock` command doesn't stop execution of other commands even if they change data or metadata objects. The `Lock` command affects the committing of transactions for only a very short time; and more precisely, it affects only getting a commit lock.

Canceling a Command Execution

If a command is issued by mistake or takes a long time to complete, the user might want to cancel it. To make this possible, Analysis Services provides the `Cancel` command. You call this command asynchronously, from a different connection, because the connection that executes the command is waiting for a response to be sent back to the client and cannot execute other commands. You can cancel your own command that is currently running on the server, or a server or database administrator can cancel sessions or connections when he notices that there are sessions or connections that are no longer in use.

To cancel your own command that is currently running on the server, you can create another connection, as a `SessionID` specify the identifier of the session the command to cancel runs on and issue a `Cancel` command. (For information about how to specify the session you need to work with as part of an XML/A request, see Chapter 32.) In this case, the `Cancel` command has the following syntax:

```
<Cancel/>.
```

To delete a session, a server administrator can use the `Cancel` command with the properties shown in Listing 26.7.

LISTING 26.7 A **Cancel** Command Issued to Delete a Session

```
<Cancel>
    <SessionID>SessionID</SessionID> ¦
    <SPID>SPID</SPID>
</Cancel>
```

To delete a connection, you can issue the `Cancel` command in Listing 26.8.

LISTING 26.8 The Syntax of a **Cancel** Command to Delete a Connection

```
<Cancel>
    <ConnectionID>ConnectionID</ConnectionID>
    <CancelAssociated>false</CancelAssociated>
</Cancel>
```

NOTE

Only a server administrator can end a connection or cancel a session. A database administrator can cancel a session that executes commands against his database. An end user can close his own connection or session or stop his own command.

When a server administrator deletes a connection, he can also cancel all the sessions associated with it by setting the `CancelAssociated` property to `True`. The session isn't immediately canceled. On the server, the `Cancel` command turns on a flag that signals to the session that it should stop all operations and returns to the client application. All server operations periodically check this flag; if it's turned on, the server starts the canceling process.

Because a command can use a number of threads during execution, each thread discovers that it should cancel the execution and raise a special error. If one of the threads is waiting for responses from other servers (that is, waiting for external data), interrupting this request can take a while. The cancel operation can take a long time from the moment the flag is turned on until the moment the server returns the response to the client.

If the `Cancel` flag is set too late, the server might not detect it before successfully completing the request. Think about the `Cancel` command as a hint to the server to complete the execution of the command, rather than a request that has to complete shortly. When Analysis Services is working with external databases and is waiting for them to send data, the responsiveness of the `Cancel` command depends on whether the external database supports asynchronous interruption of the request. If it does, as does SQL Server for example, Analysis Services sends an asynchronous interruption request and the operation quickly cancels. When this functionality is not supported, Analysis Services has to wait for the completion of the request, which can take some time.

Checking the Cancel flag within the inner loop of an operation can slow down the whole system. Therefore, Analysis Services checks the Cancel flag less frequently. You can change the frequency of how often the server should check for the Cancel flag by setting the CoordinatorCancelCount server configuration property. You can use this configuration property to make the server more or less responsive to the Cancel command. However, raising the responsiveness to the Cancel command can slow down the system.

To commit a transaction, Analysis Services might need to cancel all the requests running on the database, thereby blocking the completion of the transaction. Internally, this operation is done through the canceling mechanism we just discussed. A Cancel flag is turned on in all the sessions currently executing requests to the database, which causes the cancellation of those requests. As we discussed previously, canceling of all the requests happens when ForceCommitTimeout expires. Because the canceling itself can take some time, it is possible for an operation that needs to commit to cancel itself because its own command timeout expires. Therefore, we recommend that you set CommandTimeout larger than ForceCommitTimeout.

Batch Command

One of the important capabilities of Analysis Services is its facility to group commands into a single batch, treating them as a single unit of execution. You can group a number of commands together and send them to Analysis Services in a single request, framed within the Batch command. The Batch command provides a simple syntax for transactional execution of group of commands. Listing 26.9 shows the syntax of the Batch command.

LISTING 26.9 The Syntax of the **Batch** Command

```
<Batch Transaction="true" ProcessAffectedObjects="false">
      <Bindings>ool_bindings</Bindings>
      <DataSource>ool_ds</DataSource>
      <DataSourceView>ool_dsv</DataSourceView>
      <ErrorConfiguration>error_config</ErrorConfiguration>
      <Command1>cmd_1</Command1>
      <Command2>cmd_2</Command2>
      <Command3>cmd_3</Command3>
...
</Batch>
```

Within the Batch command, you can list all the commands that you want to execute, and other properties applicable to all the commands in a batch. For example, you can specify DataSource, DataSourceView, and Bindings objects, and ErrorConfiguration objects used during processing. (We discussed those properties in Chapter 21.)

Each `Batch` command contains `Transaction` and `ProcessAffectedObjects` parameters. The `Transaction` parameter defines how to execute commands contained by the `Batch` command if the user's session did not define a transaction. By default, this property is set to `TRUE`, which means that all the commands contained in the `Batch` command execute in a single transaction, and that the results from executing all the commands are committed only if all the commands execute successfully. In this case, a user gets a response from the server about successful completion of the batch. The response also contains messages produced by each individual command during execution.

If at least one command fails, execution of the entire batch stops, and the results of the commands that succeeded are not committed to the server. In this case, a user gets error notification that contains error messages from all the commands. The response might look like the one shown in Listing 26.10, which contains information about execution of the batch and execution of each individual command.

LISTING 26.10 A Sample Response from a Transactional **Batch** Command

```
<Envelope>
    <Body>
        <ExecuteResponse>
            <return>
                <results xmlns="http://schemas.microsoft.com/
➥analysisservices/2003/xmla-multipleresults">
                    <root xmlns="urn:schemas-microsoft-com:xml-
➥analysis:empty">
                        (output from cmd_1)
                    </root>
                    <root xmlns="urn:schemas-microsoft-com:xml-analysis:
➥empty">
                        (output from cmd_1)
                    </root>
                    <root xmlns="urn:schemas-microsoft-com:xml-analysis:
➥empty">
                        <Exception xmlns="urn:schemas-microsoft-com:
➥xml-analysis:exception" />
                        <Messages xmlns="urn:schemas-microsoft-com:
➥xml-analysis:exception">
                            <Error ErrorCode="3239313412" Description=
"Errors in the metadata manager. Either the cube with the ID of 'foo'
does not exist in the database with the ID of 'FoodMart 2008',
or the user does not have permissions to access the object."
Source="Microsoft SQL Server 2008 Analysis Services" HelpFile="" />
                        </Messages>
                    </root>
                </results>
```

26

```
            </return>
        </ExecuteResponse>
    </Body>
</Envelope>
```

When a batch is not marked as transactional, each command executes independently. If it completes successfully, its result is committed to the server. If an individual command fails, the server executes the next command in the batch. A nontransactional `Batch` command succeeds if the server was able to parse it and start execution of the first command. The response from batch execution contains a message (including error messages) from each individual command, as shown in Listing 26.11.

LISTING 26.11 A Sample Response from a Nontransactional **Batch** Command

```
<Envelope>
    <Body>
        <ExecuteResponse>
            <return xmlns="urn:schemas-microsoft-com:xml-analysis">
              <results
xmlns="http://schemas.microsoft.com/analysisservices/2003/
xmla-multipleresults">
                <root xmlns="urn:schemas-microsoft-com:xml-analysis:
➥empty">
                  <Exception xmlns="urn:schemas-microsoft-com:xml-analysis:
➥exception" />
                  <Messages xmlns="urn:schemas-microsoft-com:xml-analysis:
➥exception">
                    <Error ErrorCode="3239313412" Description="
Errors in the metadata manager. Either the cube with the ID of 'Bar'
does not exist in the database with the ID of 'FoodMart 2008',
or the user does not have permissions to access the object."
Source="Microsoft SQL Server 2008 Analysis Services" HelpFile="" />
                  </Messages>
                </root>
                <root xmlns="urn:schemas-microsoft-com:xml-analysis:
➥empty">
                   <Exception xmlns="urn:schemas-microsoft-com:
➥xml-analysis:exception" />
                     <Messages xmlns="urn:schemas-microsoft-com:
➥xml-analysis:exception">
                        <Error ErrorCode="3239313412" Description="Errors
in the metadata manager. Either the cube with the ID of 'foo'
 does not exist in the database with the ID of 'FoodMart 2008',
 or the user does not have permissions to access the object.
" Source="Microsoft SQL Server 2008 Analysis Services" HelpFile="" />
```

```
                        </Messages>
                    </root>
                </results>
            </return>
        </ExecuteResponse>
    </Body>
</Envelope>
```

You can use the `ProcessAffectedObjects` parameter to indicate when you want Analysis Services to automatically process objects affected by the execution of commands in the `Batch` command that change the state of server objects. For example, if you issue a `ProcessUpdate` command to a dimension, all the aggregations that refer to this dimension must also be rebuilt. By setting `ProcessAffectedObjects` to `TRUE`, you configure the `Batch` command to not only execute the `Process` command contained in the `Batch` command for this dimension, but also to rebuild the aggregations that refer to this dimension.

Although the `ProcessAffectedObjects` parameter is helpful and allows you to keep all the objects in working condition, use it with care. The `ProcessAffectedObjects` parameter could trigger many changes, and the system might start to perform a large number of operations and use great deal of your resources, which you might not expect because you've issued a command with just a single request. In addition, by explicitly specifying what objects are to be processed, you can maintain better control over what objects and resources are involved in a `Batch` command. If you already created a batch in which you have carefully planned the order of execution of commands, and then include the `ProcessAffectedObjects` parameter, your careful planning will be overwritten by the server as it takes over the execution of the batch.

To figure out which objects are affected by a change, you can use the `Impact Analysis` property on an XML/A `Execute` method. (We discuss how to set properties in XML/A requests in Chapter 32.) If you set the `ImpactAnalysis` property, the server will only simulate execution of the commands, but won't perform any changes; however, it will return a list of objects affected by the change when this command actually executes. It will also return the state of the affected objects if the command executes. For example, to figure out all the objects affected by processing of a `Time` dimension in the FoodMart 2008 database, you can issue the XML/A request shown in Listing 26.12.

LISTING 26.12 An Example of an **`ImpactAnalysis`** Request

```
<Execute xmlns="urn:schemas-microsoft-com:xml-analysis">
  <Command>
    <Batch Transaction="false"
➥xmlns="http://schemas.microsoft.com/analysisservices/2003/engine">
      <Process>
        <Type>ProcessFull</Type>
        <Object>
          <DatabaseID>FoodMart 2008</DatabaseID>
```

```
        <DimensionID>Time By Day</DimensionID>
      </Object >
    </Process>
  </Batch>
</Command>
<Properties>
  <PropertyList>
    <ImpactAnalysis>true</ImpactAnalysis>
  </PropertyList>
</Properties>
</Execute>
```

This request returns a long list of the affected objects. We have cut the list to make it fit; you can see the shortened list in Listing 26.13.

LISTING 26.13 An Example of the Response for **ImpactAnalysis**

```
<return xmlns="urn:schemas-microsoft-com:xml-analysis">
  <results xmlns="http://schemas.microsoft.com/analysisservices
/2003/xmla-multipleresults">
      <row>
        <Object>
          <Object>
            <CubeID>Budget</CubeID>
            <DatabaseID>FoodMart 2008</DatabaseID>
          </Object>
        </Object>
        <Impact>Unprocessed</Impact>
        <Severity>Warning</Severity>
        <Faultcode>-1056964608</Faultcode>
        <Description>Object will be unprocessed/cleared.</Description>
      </row>
      <row>
        <Object>
          <Object>
            <MeasureGroupID>Expense Fact</MeasureGroupID>
            <CubeID>Budget</CubeID>
            <DatabaseID>FoodMart 2008</DatabaseID>
          </Object>
        </Object>
        <Impact>Unprocessed</Impact>
        <Severity>Warning</Severity>
        <Faultcode>-1056964608</Faultcode>
        <Description>Object will be unprocessed/cleared.</Description>
      </row>
```

```
      <row>
        <Object>
          <Object>
            <MeasureGroupID>Warehouse Inventory</MeasureGroupID>
            <CubeID>FoodMart2008</CubeID>
            <DatabaseID>FoodMart 2008</DatabaseID>
          </Object>
        </Object>
        <Impact>Unprocessed</Impact>
        <Severity>Warning</Severity>
        <Faultcode>-1056964608</Faultcode>
        <Description>Object will be unprocessed/cleared.</Description>
      </row>
...
    </root>
  </results>
</return>
```

Inside the batch, you can group commands in blocks. Block commands are a useful mechanism that helps optimize the server's performance when doing complex processing operations because it allows you to define the order in which commands execute. To maximize capabilities of the server, you can bind commands inside the block that will execute in parallel, by using the `<Parallel>` element, as shown in Listing 26.14.

LISTING 26.14 The Syntax of the Parallel Execution Block

```
<Parallel maxParallel=n >
     <Command1>cmd_1</Command1>
     <Command2>cmd_2</Command2>
     <Command3>cmd_3</Command3>
</Parallel>
```

With this command, you tell the server to execute commands from the list in parallel. If you define the `maxParallel` parameter on the `Parallel` block, Analysis Services tries to execute as many commands in parallel as specified by the `maxParallel` parameter. If `maxParallel` is not specified, the server tries to execute all the commands in the block at the same time. After all commands in the parallel block are completed, the command next to the block starts to execute. When executing the commands, Analysis Services estimates the resources it has, the resources required for execution, and then decides how many commands it can execute in parallel. Therefore, the `maxParallel` property is only a hint for the server.

Analysis Services supports parallel execution of the same type of commands on the same type of objects; for example, the block can contain only dimension-processing commands, but it cannot contain both dimension-processing commands and cube-processing commands. You would need two blocks to perform both operations.

Parallel blocks can be used only in transactional batches. Failure of one of the commands causes the failure of all the commands in the `Batch`, regardless of whether the command was inside of the parallel block. You will get responses to your request in the same order as the commands that sent them were specified in the block, not in the order in which the commands executed.

If you need to perform an operation on an object that involves a large number of operations on other objects (for example, processing of the whole database, which causes processing of cubes, dimensions, and other objects), we recommend that you design blocks of commands manually. Try to avoid commands with automatic execution of a large number of objects because the server will try to execute, in parallel, as many operations as possible, and it might be not as efficient as if you configured the execution manually.

CHAPTER 27

Memory Management

IN THIS CHAPTER

Memory is the main system resource managed by Analysis Services to support the multidimensional data model. Efficient use of memory enables efficient access to data stored in the multidimensional model.

Analysis Services implements a model of memory management called the economical model. With the economical model, Analysis Services assigns a price per kilobyte that each data structure allocated in memory has to pay to hold that memory. When memory usage in the whole system grows, the price also grows. When a data structure is used by operations important for the system performance—for example, during a user's queries—it "earns" an income. Analysis Services unloads the data structure from memory (sometimes swapping it to disk, other times deleting the data stored in the data structure) when it is not used often enough and the price on memory is high. This approach to memory management enables Analysis Services to keep most of the useful data structures in memory and to clean data structures that aren't actively used by the system.

To prevent memory fragmentation and to enable efficient use of memory, Analysis Services keeps track of all the memory used by different subsystems. Each subsystem uses the Memory Manager to allocate the memory, instead of using the `malloc` and `free` operators provided by the operating system.

Analysis Services has two subsystems that manage memory: the Memory Manager (which is responsible for memory allocations) and the Memory Governor (which is responsible for distribution of the memory among the different operations performed by Analysis Services).

Economic Memory Management Model

As mentioned at the beginning of this chapter, Analysis Services uses an economical model to manage memory. It defines the price per kilobyte depending on the amount of available memory. Analysis Services uses two configuration properties to assign the price on memory: `LowMemoryLimit` and `TotalMemoryLimit`.

Analysis Services assigns the price to memory according to the scheme shown in Figure 27.1. Initially, the price of memory is zero, and all subsystems can allocate and release any amount of memory they need for functioning. The memory remains free until the amount of used memory reaches the `LowMemoryLimit`. After the amount of used memory reaches the `LowMemoryLimit`, the price on memory starts to grow. It grows linearly from zero to the value defined by the `MidMemoryPrice` configuration property—the memory price at the midpoint between the `LowMemoryLimit` and `TotalMemoryLimit`. After the amount of free memory reaches the midpoint, the price continues to grow, but it grows with much greater speed until the amount of used memory reaches the `TotalMemoryLimit` and the price reaches the `HighMemoryPrice` value. The price of memory can never exceed `HighMemoryPrice`.

The memory price defines two important facts: how much memory Analysis Services can allocate to execute a given operation, and how much memory a subsystem that uses the memory has to release back to the server. Analysis Services is tuned to work with default values of configuration properties, and we don't recommend you to change any values without experimenting. If you see that your system uses an amount of memory close to `TotalMemoryLimit`, you might want to experiment and increase the value of `MidMemoryPrice` and `HighMemoryPrice` so that Analysis Services will clean memory more intensively.

Server Performance and Memory Manager

Memory Manager is responsible for providing all servers' subsystems with memory. It allocates memory, assigns the price to memory, and cleans memory that can be released when the amount of used memory reaches a certain limit.

Memory Holders

Objects that allocate memory and provide it to different Analysis Services operations are called *memory holders*. Each memory holder implements an interface that provides Memory Manager with statistical information about the amount of memory used by a memory holder and the percentage of allocated memory actively used to support server operations. Periodically, the Memory Manager queries memory holders and collects its statistics. You can send a `DISCOVER_MEMORYUSAGE` to the server and get information about the current state of all memory holders, or you can use performance monitor counters to monitor the general state of memory. (You cannot see the state of individual memory holders with performance monitor counters.)

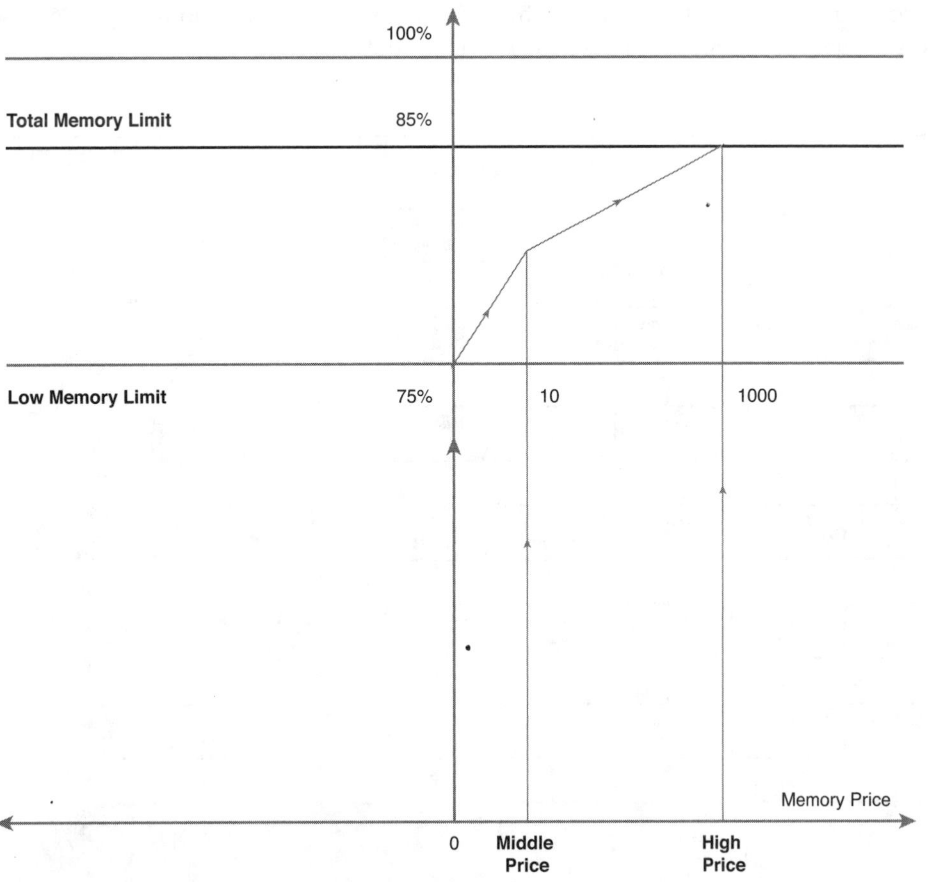

FIGURE 27.1 The price on memory is zero until the `LowMemoryLimit` is reached. The price grows linearly until it reaches *`MidMemoryPrice`*. It continues to grow linearly, but much faster, to `HighMemoryPrice` when `TotalMemoryLimit` is reached.

Analysis Services supports two types of memory holders: shrinkable and nonshrinkable (also known as allocators). Shrinkable memory holders can return part of the memory to the system when needed. For example, caches can be cleaned when memory is needed for other more important operations, file stores, and other objects that can be swapped to the disk when they are rarely used. (For more information about file stores, see Chapter 20, "The Physical Data Model.") Nonshrinkable memory holders provide memory to different subsystems and can't return that memory to the system until the component releases it.

The Memory Manager keeps lists of the memory holders. Shrinkable and nonshrinkable memory holders are stored separately. The system can have many memory holders. Therefore, during a single cleaning period, Analysis Services would not iterate all existing memory holders. It iterates memory holders from only a single list. You can monitor performance monitor counters to detect the size of the shrinkable and nonshrinkable memory. Figure 27.2 shows the lists of the memory holders.

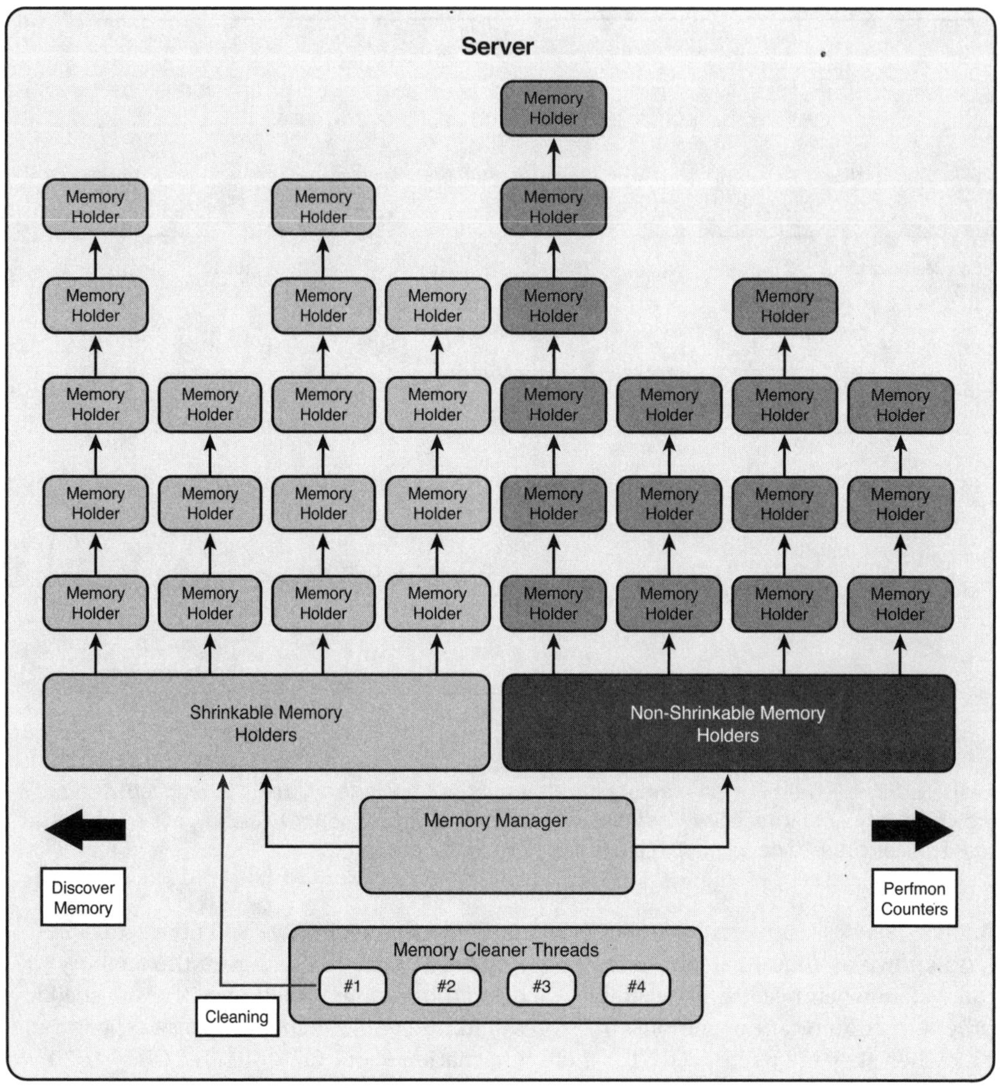

FIGURE 27.2 Memory Manager keeps lists of the memory holders, so shrinkable and nonshrinkable memory holders are stored separately.

You can retrieve statistics about memory usage using a `DISCOVER_MEMORY` request or monitoring key performance monitor counters.

Memory Cleanup

After the amount of memory used by the system rises above the `LowMemoryLimit`, Analysis Services periodically (the period is defined by the `Cleaning Period-LimitSystemFileCache Period` configuration property) wakes up a special cleaning thread, which iterates over the memory holders in one memory holder list, collects statistics about each memory holder, and sends an internal request to shrinkable memory holders to clean some memory. When a shrinkable memory holder gets this request, it calculates the tax, which it has to pay, and readjusts its balance. If the balance is negative, the memory holder returns memory to the system. When making a decision about the amount of memory a memory holder has to release to the system, it uses the strategy specific to each type of memory holder (we discuss the strategy later in this chapter) that would enable the memory holder to get to the positive balance in the next cleaning period.

When the used memory is getting close to the `TotalMemoryLimit` (by default, "close" is 12% percent below the `TotalMemoryLimit`), the Memory Manager starts additional cleaning threads. This lowers the performance of the system because a large part of CPU time is now used for cleaning.

When memory reaches the `TotalMemoryLimit`, the Memory Manager starts to work in crisis mode. In crisis mode, Analysis Services starts as many threads as there are processors on the machine and raises the priority of those threads. The cleaning operation practically blocks all other server operations until enough memory is released. When a shrinkable memory holder gets a command about a crisis release of memory, it has to release all the memory that it can release, regardless of its balance. It also reinitializes its data structures.

When release of the memory decreases the amount of memory used in the system to below the `LowMemoryLimit`, the Memory Manager drops the memory price to zero, and the Memory Manager starts to work in sleepy mode. It does not send requests to shrink the memory, and only periodically pings memory holders and adjusts the memory state statistics.

NOTE

The system can react slowly to the changes of the memory conditions, so it is theoretically possible that memory usage could go above the amount defined by the `TotalMemoryLimit` when memory is allocated faster than the cleaning threads can clean the memory. Similarly, the memory can be cleaned very aggressively and usage could go below the amount defined by the `LowMemoryLimit`.

Analysis Services monitors an event that the operating system sends when a computer runs out of memory and increases the memory price when it detects an out-of-memory condition. In this case, the memory price grows even faster, which speeds up the release of the memory to the system.

To calculate the amount of memory that a memory holder can keep and the amount of memory it needs to release, the economical memory management system uses five parameters. The initial values of those parameters are defined in the `MemoryModel` section of the server configuration properties. Table 27.1 describes the parameters of the memory model.

TABLE 27.1 Parameters of the Memory Model

Parameter	**Description**
`Tax`	The percent of the memory price that a memory holder has to pay for each kilobyte of memory it owns, starting from the previous time it paid taxes. For example, Analysis Services calculates cache tax based on the amount of memory used by the whole cache.
`Income`	The income from each kilobyte used by Analysis Services to support a user's operation. For example, the cache earns an income each time data was retrieved from it, and only the amount of data that was requested and found in the cache brings an income.
`MaximumBalance`	The maximum income that can be accumulated by a memory holder. After reaching this maximum, the memory holder accumulates no more income. The `MaximumBalance` parameter prevents memory holders from accumulating a huge positive balance and becoming unresponsive to the decrease of available memory.
`MinimumBalance`	The minimum balance that can be accumulated by a memory holder. After reaching this minimum, the memory holder's balance is no longer decreased. The `MinimumBalance` parameter prevents memory holders from accumulating a huge negative balance and becoming unresponsive to the increase of available memory.
`InitialBonus`	When a memory holder is created, it gets initial income so that it will not have to return the memory to the system during its first cleaning period. The `InitialBonus` parameter defines how many periods this memory holder can keep memory while it has not started to perform any useful work.

Managing Memory of Different Subsystems

Analysis Services uses the economic memory management model to manage memory for different subsystems. Important subsystems such as cache system, files stores, sessions, and many others are integrated with the Memory Manager. Let's look at how each of these subsystems reacts to changes in the memory conditions.

Cache System Memory Model

Data access performance in the multidimensional model heavily depends on the availability of data in the cache. Analysis Services supports a few levels of caching. Dimension and measure group caches store the data retrieved from the storage engine by the formula engine. Formula engine caches store data calculated by the formula engine. A flat data cache—a special kind of formula engine cache that stores values of individual cells—is also calculated by the formula engine.

All cache types have similar data structures; therefore, for simplicity, we call them all *cache*. For each request, a cache contains two data structures: a subcube that defines the structure of the data being retrieved and a datacache structure that contains the results of the request. We discuss all types of caches in Chapter 29, "Architecture of Query Execution—Calculating MDX Expressions." In this chapter, we discuss how Memory Manager works with caches.

Analysis Services looks up data in the cache, calculates or retrieves it from storage if it is not found in the cache, and stores new data in the cache. When the amount of used memory reaches the `LowMemoryLimit`, Memory Manager must decide what data should remain in the cache and what data should be cleaned. Obviously, the Memory Manager saves the data that is used often and deletes the data that is rarely used.

Each datacache structure and corresponding subcube form a memory holder. If the datacache is used during execution of a query, it gets an income according to the amount of memory used. When the cleaning period comes, the cache calculates the tax based on the current memory price and the amount of memory used for the datacache and its subcube. If the balance is positive, the cache remains in the system; otherwise, it is released.

All datacaches are registered in the datacache registry—an index that enables fast lookup of the datacache by subcube. The datacache registry is a memory holder, too. When Memory Manager operates in regular mode, it cleans datacaches and subcubes, but does not clean the index. However, when Memory Manager declares a crisis mode, Analysis Services cleans all datacaches, subcubes, and the datacache registry itself.

Managing Memory of File Stores

One of the most important data structures in Analysis Services is the file store, which Analysis Services uses to store most of the dimension data. (For more information about file stores, see Chapter 20.) The productivity of the file stores affects the productivity of the whole system. Access to the data stored in file stores is most efficient when all of it is loaded into memory.

Because it would be inefficient to have a memory holder for each page of the file store, the whole file store is a memory holder. When pages of a store are used, the memory holder gets income. The memory holder pays tax for all the memory allocated for all pages of the store. In addition, it gets an income when the system uses data from any page of the file store.

To detect the pages that have to be swapped out of memory, Analysis Services uses the page hit counter. When Memory Manager pings the file store, and the file store analyzes its current balance and the price of memory, the file store makes a decision to clean a part of the memory it holds. Therefore, the file store swaps the least-used pages to a disk, and the most-used pages remain in memory. This way, the memory used by file stores depends on the state of the memory usage in the whole system. If the server is busy with work that hits the caches and does not retrieve data from dimensions, after some period of time all the dimension file stores might be swapped to disk and the cache will accumulate a large amount of data. If usage of the caches decreases, the caches will be cleaned, and more pages of the file stores will be loaded in memory.

Managing Memory Used by User Sessions

Session objects are memory holders and are driven by the economical memory model. Similar to the caches, Session Manager is also a memory holder. When the memory price grows, Analysis Services ends sessions that do not bring an income. However, Analysis Services has minimum time during which a session cannot end, even when it has a negative balance. You can reset this value by changing the `MinIdleSessionTimeout` configuration property. After this time expires, sessions that have not been used for a while and have negative balance are deleted, memory is released, and all state stored on the session is lost. However, before the whole session terminates, Analysis Services tries to release the memory assigned to different objects stored inside the session object, which can be deleted without changing the session state. However, if a session has a negative balance after this procedure, Session Manager ends the session.

Other Memory Holders

Analysis Services has other subsystems that are governed by the economic model of memory management and are shrinkable memory holders. However, other components are implemented as nonshrinkable memory holders. Such components might allocate all the memory available on the system, causing the memory price to grow and shrinkable memory holders to release their memory, thus decreasing the productivity of the server. This situation can sometimes lead servers using Analysis Services to produce out-of-memory errors.

Memory Allocators

To prevent fragmentation, Analysis Services never allocates memory using functions provided by the operating system. It uses Memory Manager to allocate all its data structures. This enables Memory Manager to keep track of all the memory used in the system, to have more granular control over memory allocations, and to perform allocations more efficiently. For example, when allocating a data structure that contains a large amount of data, it makes sense to allocate it by pages. To provide memory to different subsystems and memory holders (shrinkable and noshrinkable), Analysis Services uses allocators—nonshrinkable memory holders.

NOTE

External components that run inside Analysis Services, such as OLE DB providers, are not integrated with Memory Manager and do not use Analysis Services allocators to allocate memory.

Analysis Services supports six types of allocations, which are supported by six types of allocators, described in Table 27.2.

TABLE 27.2 Types of Allocators

Type	Description
`PageAllocator`	Provides memory as fixed-size pages. Analysis Services supports three page sizes: Big Pages are 64KB, Middle Pages are 8KB, and Small Pages are 1KB.
`VectorAllocator`	Enables the allocation of contiguous memory for arrays, where each element of the array has the same size.
`StringAllocator`	Enables the allocation of text strings. Strings have a separate allocator because the designers of Analysis Services took patterns of string usage into consideration.
`ObjectAllocator`	Enables the creation of objects of a certain internal class. This type of allocator leads to lower memory fragmentation because if one object is deleted, another object of the same size can be allocated in its place.
`ArenaAllocator`	Enables the fast allocation of memory portions, but does not release this memory by chunks. `ArenaAllocator` holds a bookmark on the beginning of the allocated memory and can release all the memory up to the bookmark.
`GeneralAllocator`	Enables the allocation of memory of arbitrary size.

In addition, Analysis Services supports different levels of allocations that define the lifetime and locality of allocated memory. There are five levels, as described in Table 27.3.

TABLE 27.3 Levels of Memory Allocations

Level	Description
`Global`	Memory is allocated for the server-level subsystems, such as the thread pools, the error-handling subsystem, and so on. `ObjectAllocators` are available only on the `Global` level.
`MajorObjects`	Memory belongs to the metadata's major objects. This means that memory allocated on this level is released when a major object is destroyed. For example, a dimension has its own allocators and all attributes, hierarchies, and dimension caches are allocated from the dimension allocator. All this memory is released when a new version of the dimension is created. Therefore, memory is fragmented only during the lifetime of the dimension. For the new version of the dimension, previously accumulated fragmentation goes away.
`Session`	Memory belongs to the session object and all the memory is released when the session ends. For example, session scopes (discussed in Chapter 29) are allocated with session allocators.
`Request`	Memory belongs to the current user request. After execution of the request is completed, all information associated with this request is destroyed (except for the data stored in the caches). This way, execution of user requests does not fragment the memory.
`Thread`	Memory is associated with the thread. This memory is released when a thread is returned to the pool. This level does not require synchronization because the allocators occur on the same thread. Therefore, thread allocators are the best-performing allocators of the system, particularly the `Arena` allocator, which can be released just once before the thread is returned to the thread pool.

Each level of memory allocation has all the types of allocators (except for the `ObjectAllocator`, which is supported only on the `Global` level). Depending on the operations it is performing, Analysis Services uses different types and levels of allocators.

Effective Memory Distribution with Memory Governor

Memory Governor defines the order of memory allocations for different operations. Analysis Services can execute many operations in parallel; however, if an operation requires a larger amount of memory, it can be blocked even with free CPU cycles. To prevent such a situation from happening, Analysis Services has the Memory Governor, which is responsible for governing allocation of the memory to different components of the system.

Objects that Memory Governor can manage are memory holders that implement the memory holder interface. Typically, Analysis Services uses Memory Governor to coordinate memory used by the jobs (memory holders) of Job Coordinator. (For more information about Job Coordinator, see Chapter 26, "Server Architecture and Command Execution.")

When a job is created, Analysis Services assigns it an `InitialBonus`. Before Analysis Services starts execution of a job, it calculates the minimum amount of memory that the job needs for execution and the maximum amount of memory it can use during execution. After this, the job requests memory from Memory Governor and provides those minimum and maximum values and its current balance. Based on the balance of the job, memory price, and amount of memory available in the system, Memory Governor calculates the amount of memory that it can provide to the job. If this amount is between the requested minimum and the maximum, Memory Governor reserves memory for the job, and the job starts its execution. However, if there is not enough memory, Memory Governor blocks the request until another job completes, returns memory to the system, and notifies Memory Governor about the release of memory. Then Memory Governor recalculates the amount of memory needed for the first job in the queue of requests for memory, and unblocks it if there is now enough memory to execute the job. Figure 27.3 demonstrates the scheme by which Memory Governor operates.

The initial amount of memory that Memory Governor can distribute among the jobs is defined by the `MemoryLimit` configuration property in the `ProcessPlan` section. If the minimum amount of memory required for a job execution is larger than the `MemoryLimit`, Analysis Services cannot execute the job and returns an error to the user. You can turn off this error by setting the `MemoryLimitErrorEnabled` configuration property to `FALSE` and enable the job to complete by expropriating all the memory from Memory Governor. However, turning off the `MemoryLimitErrorEnabled` property does not guarantee that job will succeed, because it is quite possible that the system still will not have enough memory for its execution.

A job can be executed as a whole or in phases. Some jobs can be executed as a whole and, on completion, return allocated memory to Memory Governor. For jobs that execute in phases, when one phase is completed, the job reevaluates the income based on the work it performed during the completed phase, and the tax it must pay to hold the memory. After the job calculates the new balance, it also recalculates the maximum and the minimum amounts of memory needed for the next phase. After that, the job gets approval from Memory Governor to continue its work and the amount of memory that it can use to continue execution. This algorithm enables the system to rebalance the memory among the currently executing jobs, based on the changing conditions in the system.

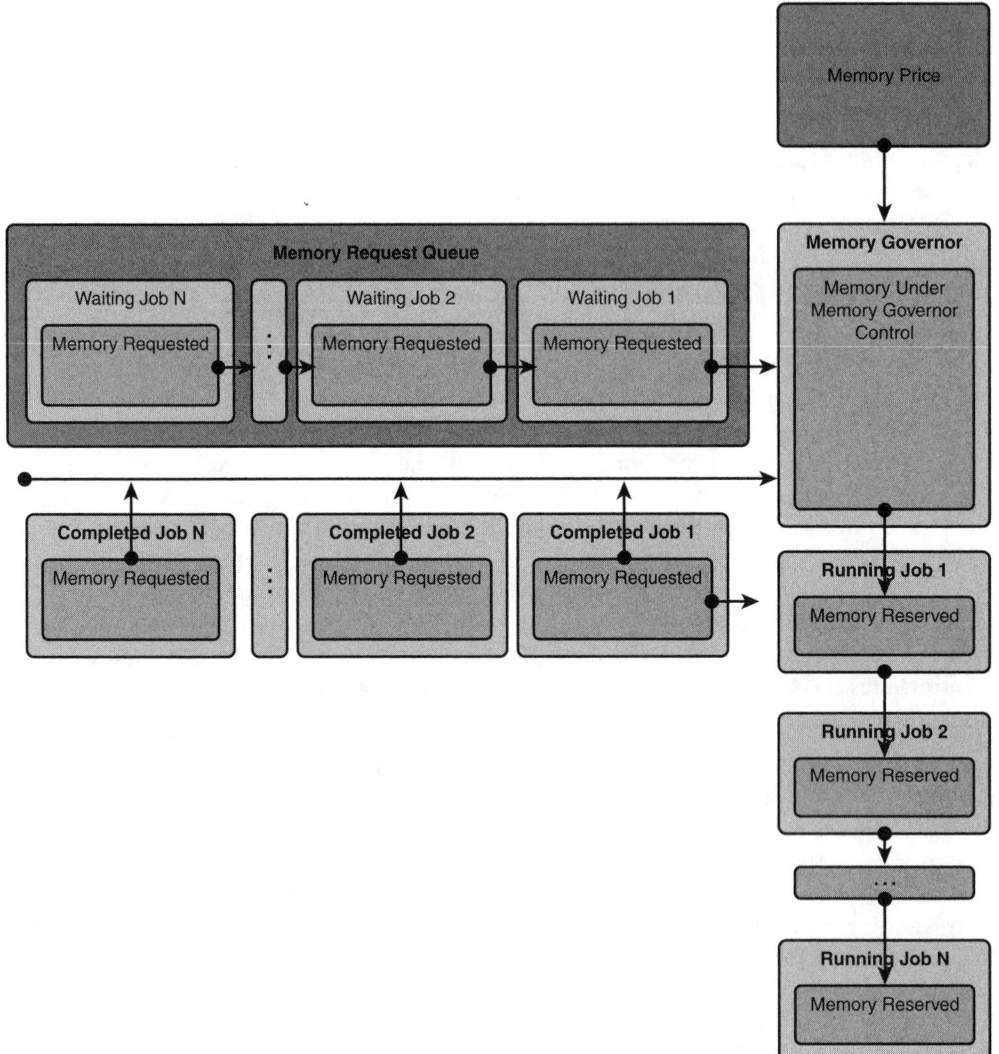

FIGURE 27.3 Memory Governor calculates the amount of memory that it can provide to a job. If memory is available, Memory Governor reserves it and the job starts its execution; otherwise, the job waits in the memory request queue until another job completes and returns memory to the Memory Governor.

Obviously, Memory Governor does not guarantee that Analysis Services has enough memory to execute any job, because not all subsystems are controlled by Memory Governor. For example, a query-resolution job is not governed by Memory Governor because it has higher priority than processing operations. The system works best when Analysis Services executes only the jobs controlled by Memory Governor, such as processing partitions and dimensions, building aggregations, and building indexes, simultaneously. However, even when jobs not controlled by Memory Governor are executed at the same time as commands it controls, some balance will be maintained because memory for all commands is allocated through Memory Manager, and Memory Manager controls the state of the system by raising the price on memory.

Memory Governor makes decisions about providing memory to a job based on the current state of the system, which enables Analysis Services to execute any set of jobs in parallel. However, Memory Governor does not base its decisions on operations not yet submitted to the system. On the other hand, the designer of the multidimensional model usually knows all the operations that have to be performed and can plan the execution much more efficiently. We recommend that you plan the execution of complex commands and design a well-balanced `Batch` command, which will provide Analysis Services with the sequence of operations that must be performed to achieve the best performance. (For more information about the `Batch` command, see Chapter 26.)

Memory Models of Attribute and Partition Processing

The memory models of attribute and partition processing look very much alike. Therefore, we will discuss how Memory Governor reserves memory during attribute and partition processing by considering only a partition example.

In the first phase of partition processing, Analysis Services analyzes the amount of memory that it will need to process a partition. (We discussed all phases of processing in Chapter 21, "Dimension and Partition Processing.") A partition-processing job is a memory holder and is controlled by the economical memory management model. However, it is not enough to use only the economical model. If Analysis Services would give all the available memory to the job of processing a partition, it would not have enough memory for other operations. You can use configuration properties to set up the conditions under which Analysis Services makes the initial calculation of memory needed for processing:

- **`BufferMemoryLimit`**—Defines maximum amount of memory that Analysis Services can use to execute the processing of one partition or one attribute
- **`BufferRecordLimit`**—Defines the maximum number of records that can be stored in the buffer of a single segment

Partitions are processed by a segment and Analysis Services uses two buffers: one to process records and another one to compress records. To calculate the required memory, the processing job evaluates the size of a single record in the processing buffer. The following formula enables you to calculate the number of records that a processing job puts into the buffer:

```
Nmax = (BufferMemoryLimit/RecordSize)/2.
```

This way you can find the maximum number of records that Analysis Services can put into the buffer, knowing the amount of memory that processing can use. If this number is larger than the allowed number of records in the buffer—`BufferRecordLimit`—Analysis

Services uses `BufferRecordLimit` as the maximum. Therefore, the formula to calculate the maximum and minimum number of records in the buffer is as follows:

```
Nmax = Min((BufferMemoryLimit/RecordSize)/2, BufferRecordLimit)
Nmin = 65536
```

Analysis Services never has a segment smaller than `65536`.

To look up `DataIDs` in a dimension, the process data job loads key hash tables into memory for all attributes used in the measure group. If your measure group has many large dimensions, Analysis Services might consume large portions of memory during partition processing. If memory is limited, Analysis Services will process partition in several passes (see Chapter 21). To calculate the minimum amount of memory required to process a partition, Analysis Services adds the amount of memory required to load the largest hash table to the minimum amount of memory required to allocate both buffers. To calculate the maximum amount of memory, Analysis Services adds the amount of memory required to load all the hash tables to the maximum amount of memory required to allocate buffers.

Now you can calculate the maximum and the minimum amounts of memory that processing has to request from Memory Governor:

```
Qmax = 2 * (Nmax/Nmin + 1)*Nmin*RecordSize + QHashTables
Qmin = 2 * Nmin*RecordSize + QLargestHashTable
```

Memory Governor reserves memory based on the memory price and balance of the processing operation. So, the number of records in the buffer is calculated by the following formula. (`Q` is the amount of memory actually reserved by Memory Governor for the processing operation.)

```
N = Max((Q/RecordSize)/Nmin ) * Nmin, Nmin)
```

Now Analysis Services can allocate the memory for the datacache buffer and start processing the partition. After the first segment is processed, the processing job reevaluates its balance. It calculates the tax as the memory price multiplied by the `Tax` property of the memory model and then multiplied by the amount of memory allocated for the datacache buffer.

Analysis Services uses a special approach to calculate the income of the processing job (as opposed to the other cases where it need to calculate the income). The income is calculated as the number of records that were processed, multiplied by the `Income` property of the memory model. After reevaluation of its balance, the processing job requests permission from Memory Governor to continue processing, and provides the minimum and the maximum amount of required memory and the new balance. Memory Governor returns the amount of memory it can reserve to process the next segment, which will be used to calculate the new size of the buffer. If the datacache buffer of the previous segment is too large, reevaluation for the next segment will happen after a long period of time, so the system will react slowly to the change of memory state. However, if the datacache buffer of the previous segment is too small, Analysis Services cannot perform optimization related to clustering, and the future performance of requests for querying segment is lowered. The designers of Analysis Services defined the default value of the `BufferRecordLimit` to meet both requirements.

Saving the data loaded from the data source also requires memory. You can use two server configuration properties—`CacheRowsetToDisk` and `CacheRowsetRows`—to customize an amount of memory needed:

- **`CacheRowsetToDisk`**—Specifies whether Analysis Services should use a disk to store records retrieved from the data source. If this property is set to `TRUE`, Analysis Services will not require additional memory to store those records, but the data will be swapped to disk and performance of processing can suffer. On the other hand, setting this property to `FALSE` will require additional memory, but it can improve the performance of the processing.
- **`CacheRowsetRows`**—Defines the number of records stored in the buffer during reading the records from the source. The amount of memory required to allocate the buffer is calculated as the number of records multiplied by the record size. You can calculate the approximate size of the record if you know the data type of the columns requested by the SQL query during processing.

When a lot of memory is available during the processing operation, the `CacheRowsetToDisk` property won't affect performance of the system because data is loaded into the file store, which won't be swapped to the disk because of low memory price. However, if there is memory pressure during the processing, data might be swapped to a disk, and efficiency will be lost. In that case, setting `CacheRowsetToDisk` to `FALSE` might provide better performance. We recommend changing this property only after you experiment on your system and establish that you have improved the processing performance of your set of data.

Memory Model of Building Aggregations

The speed of building aggregations depends largely on the availability of memory. If there is enough memory to keep data from all the aggregations, building aggregations can be a few times faster than if there is not enough memory and aggregations have to be swapped to disk.

While building aggregations, Analysis Services calculates the required memory, based on the `AggregationMemoryLimitMin` and `AggregationMemoryLimitMax` server configuration properties. These properties define the minimum and the maximum amounts of memory that the aggregation job requests from Memory Governor. Memory Governor evaluates the current memory price, the balance of the building aggregation job, and the amount of available memory, and reserves the memory that this job can use.

Analysis Services builds aggregations per segment of partition. It reads the data from the segment and builds the aggregations that can be built from the fact data (lowest granularity data). If this aggregation can be used to build other aggregations, Analysis Services will start to build those aggregations as a next step. Analysis Services recursively builds aggregations until it reaches an aggregation from which no other aggregations can be built, and saves this aggregation to the aggregations buffer.

When Analysis Services completes writing every aggregation to the buffer, the build-aggregation job reevaluates its balance. It calculates the income by multiplying the number of records in the built aggregation by the `Income` property of the memory model. Analysis Services calculates the tax as the current memory price multiplied by the size of the aggregations buffer used to store those records, and multiplies the `Tax` property of the memory model.

After reevaluation of the balance, the build-aggregation job requests permission from Memory Governor to build the next aggregation, and provides the minimum and the maximum amount of required memory and the new balance. Memory Governor returns the amount of memory it can reserve, which will be used to calculate the new size of the aggregations buffer to build the next aggregation. If the new size of the aggregations buffer cannot fit an aggregation, the content of the buffer is swapped into a temporary file, and memory is released and is populated with new data.

After the last aggregation of the last segment is built, Analysis Services starts to merge the data stored on the disk and in memory, and then stores merged aggregations to disk. This process of merging slows down building aggregations. If you can avoid this step, the build-aggregation job will take significantly less time. You can avoid this step by increasing the memory allocated for the build-aggregation job, by decreasing the number of designed aggregations, or by decreasing the size of the partition.

Memory Model of Building Indexes

The memory model of building indexes is a good example of when the amount of memory required for a job can be calculated precisely and does not require any additional information from the user (from the configuration file). When Analysis Services builds indexes, it has to decode data of a segment (see Chapter 21). Analysis Services already calculated the number of records during partition processing, and it knows the size of a record; therefore, it can easily calculate the amount of required memory.

To build indexes, Analysis Services has to load decoding tables into memory; otherwise, the decoding will be not efficient and the building of indexes will take a very long time. (For more information about decoding tables, see Chapter 20.) Therefore, the building indexes job should reserve memory for all the decoding tables and should lock those tables in memory, until decoding is completed. The build indexes job calculates the amount of memory needed to keep the current segment and decoding tables in memory, approximates the amount of memory required to build indexes, and then requests this memory from Memory Governor.

Because partitions from the same measure group require the same decoding tables, Analysis Services can build indexes for partitions from the same measure group in parallel, without large memory usage overhead.

If not enough memory is available to load all decoding tables, Analysis Services cannot build indexes at all. You should review the attributes of the dimensions in the measure group and disable indexes on some rarely used attributes by setting the `AttributeHierarchyOptimizedState` property value to `NonOptimized`. (You can get more information about this property in Chapter 5, "Dimensions in the Conceptual Model.")

The least effective are indexes for attributes with a large number of members, because they require large amounts of memory during building, and users rarely slice by such attributes in a query.

The build indexes job has only one phase and never reevaluates the required amount of memory. Therefore, the build-indexes job will not release memory to Memory Governor until it fully completes.

CHAPTER 28 Thread Management

IN THIS CHAPTER

Analysis Services uses threads provided by the Windows operating system to perform parallel execution of commands. The Thread Management subsystem of Analysis Services is responsible for keeping, controlling, and reusing threads. Efficiency of thread management affects efficiency of the entire system, and the creation of a large number of threads can lead to performance degradations due to factors such as unnecessary context switches and competition for system resources. On the other hand, a low number of threads can lead to CPU and disk underutilization.

The Thread Management subsystem uses thread pool objects to store and manage the threads. A thread pool requests threads from the operating system, stores them, and provides those threads to other server subsystems. Each subsystem places a request for a thread (multiple threads) in the thread pool's queue. The thread pool supplies threads based on the availability of threads and the priority of incoming requests.

Analysis Services has four thread pools:

- Short-command parsing pool
- Long-command parsing pool
- Query-execution pool
- Process-execution pool

To increase system throughput, the Analysis Services system designers chose to have multiple thread pools. Having different thread pools adds balance to the system and prevents long-running operations from blocking short-running commands. For example, Analysis Services does not stop accepting user connections while performing a processing operation. However, this approach increases the complexity of the system and requires caution when changing the configuration settings of a thread pool, which might require changing the settings of other thread pools to keep the system in balance. Understanding the inner workings of thread pools can help you fine-tune and troubleshoot your system's throughput.

Thread Pools

Analysis Services uses four thread pools to support three major operation types:

- Command execution (parser)
- Calculation execution (formula engine)
- Access to data stored on the server (storage engine)

Parsing is supported by two pools: short-running requests (parsed by threads from the short-command parsing pool) and long-running requests (parsed by the threads from the long-command parsing pool).

Analysis Services chooses commands that do not require the use of a lot of system resources being executed by threads from the short-command parsing pool. Threads from the short-command parsing pool parse the command, immediately execute it, and generate the response. Discover requests, and metadata operations that include the creation or deletion of objects, are good examples of such commands. Those commands spend a larger portion of their execution time on the result serialization because data for such requests typically is already loaded in memory (which allows for faster execution). Therefore, threads from the short-command parsing pool are used for a relatively short period of time and return to the pool in a short cycle. The short-command parsing pool enables independent and fast retrieval of a server's metadata and system statistics at any time, even when Analysis Services is under heavy load.

Commands that require a lot of system resources and use other server subsystems (such as the formula engine and storage engine) are parsed by the threads from the long-command parsing pool. Threads from the long-command parsing pool parse the command and immediately turn control over to another thread (from a different thread pool). However, the parsing thread is not returned to the thread pool until a command finishes execution and the results are passed back to the client. The turnaround speed of threads in the long-command parsing pool varies depending on the duration of the request. In many cases, throughput of Multidimensional Expressions (MDX) queries and processing commands depends on the number of idle threads available in the long-command parsing pool. If you decrease the number of threads in this pool, the parsing stage might become bottlenecked at command execution. However, you might notice that individual commands are running faster because they have more resources available during the later stages of execution.

The query-execution pool supplies threads to the formula engine subsystem that performs calculations of MDX. We chose to separate this pool from the process-execution pool to allow for calculation execution, even when the storage engine is busy executing other requests. Threads in this pool are often performing CPU-intensive operations.

Analysis Services uses the process-execution pool to perform storage engine operations, such as retrieving data from the disk, aggregating data, or loading data into the system. Threads in this pool are often performing I/O operations or operations involving access to external systems, such as loading data from relational databases. Therefore, the system needs more threads in this pool because they are often waiting for external operations to be completed.

Architecture of a Thread Pool

All types of thread pools have the same architecture and are configured using similar configuration properties. Analysis Services implements a thread pool using the I/O Completion Port mechanism, which is provided by the Windows operating system (see Figure 28.1). It initializes every pool with a minimum number of threads specified by the server's `MinThreads` property. Upon Analysis Services startup, these threads are initialized and attached to the I/O Completion Port, and once initialized the pool becomes ready to support requests for threads. Each thread pool has three queues to support requests with different priorities:

- High-priority queue
- Normal-priority queue
- Low-priority queue

When a request for a thread arrives at the pool, it is placed in the queue according to the priority of the request. Most requests have normal priority and are placed in the normal-priority queue. If the thread pool has available threads, I/O Completion Port provides threads to the first request in a queue with highest priority. The I/O Completion Port mechanism is designed in a way that it supplies a thread only if the number of concurrently executed threads being processed by a single CPU is less than a certain value. This value is defined by the Analysis Services `Concurrency` property. However, you cannot assume that the number of threads executed by a single CPU is always less than the value of the `Concurrency` property. The reason you cannot make this assumption is because the I/O Completion Port has information which threads are blocked by I/O operations (such as reading data from the disk or network) and does not count them as active and allows creation of new threads. Therefore, the total number of threads in the pool (active and blocked) exceeds the `Concurrency` value. When the I/O operation completes and threads become active again, the number of active threads might exceed the `Concurrency` value. Because the system cannot predict such situations, it is not easy to specify an optimal `Concurrency` value. If the `Concurrency` value is too low, the CPU can be underutilized, and as a result the performance of the execution can be degraded. If the `Concurrency` value is too high, the number of threads executing in parallel will be too high, which can lead to performance degradation resulting from competition for resources and context switches.

After the thread pool is finished serving requests from the highest-priority queue, it starts to serve the requests from the lower-priority queue. To prevent situations when only the

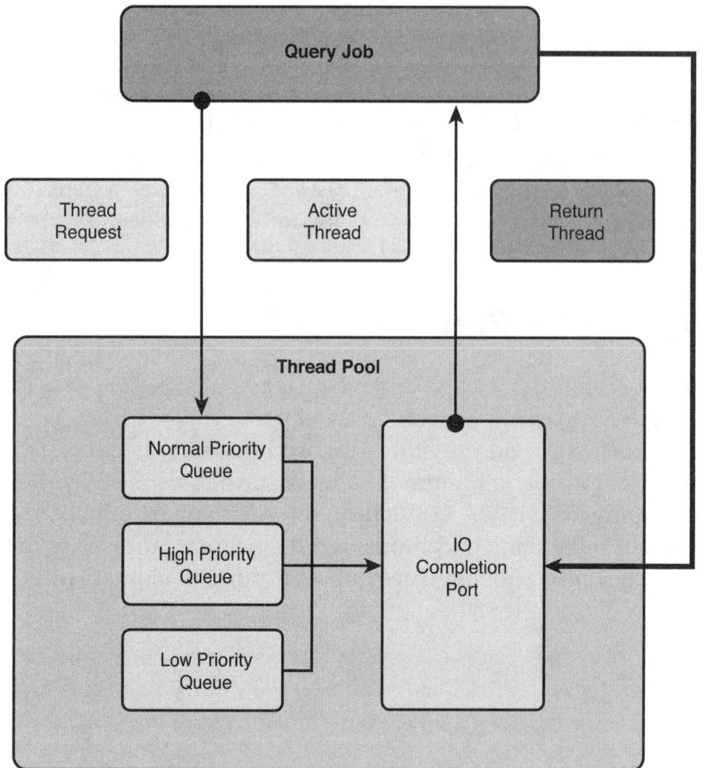

FIGURE 28.1 Thread pool architecture.

highest-priority requests get executed, the thread pool serves requests from the lower-priority pool even when the higher-priority pool is not empty. You can configure the ratio of requests served from the lower-priority pool to the higher-priority pool by using the Analysis Services `PriorityRatio` property.

Analysis Services gives its internal requests higher priority than user requests. For example, when relational online analytical processing (ROLAP) or the data-mining query requests data stored on the same instance of Analysis Services, it issues the request for data to itself, and this request is assigned highest priority.

If more than a single thread is needed to complete an operation, Analysis Services calculates the number of required threads and requests all of them simultaneously. This behavior is necessary to prevent a situation called thread starvation, where multiple operations are holding to some threads and cannot complete without getting more, and thus no operation can finish execution and release its threads.

In rare cases, a server cannot accurately predict the number of required threads and requests an additional thread from the pool after the operation has already started. In this case, if the pool has idle threads and can immediately provide them to the operation, the operation continues execution. Otherwise, execution of the operation fails with an error. This mechanism guarantees execution of the operation without thread starvation.

However, even with all of those layers of built-in defense, thread starvation may still occur. For example, during a ROLAP or data-mining query, the server calculates the number of required threads, accesses them from the pool, and begins execution. One of the threads might request data using an OLE DB provider that connects back to the instance of Analysis Services. If at that time the thread pool does not have idle threads, the command will be blocked. As mentioned earlier, Analysis Services tries to detect these situations and puts additional requests in the high-priority queue, but starvation can still can occur.

When Analysis Services needs more threads than currently exist in the thread pool, it creates new threads and attaches them to the I/O Completion Port. The number of threads in a thread pool is limited by the Analysis Services `MaxThreads` property. However, Analysis Services does not completely stop creating new threads even when it reaches the maximum thread limit. When it receives a request in the high-priority queue, it slowly starts to create new threads to prevent a deadlock. The server creates those threads with a long delay to give itself time to recover and prevent overuse of system resources based on the heavy load. When the system load subsides and the queues have no requests, Analysis Services starts releasing threads from the pool until the total number reaches the `MinThreads` value.

The main system resource used by the thread is memory (allocated for the thread call stack). By default, each thread allocates 1MB for the stack. Therefore, a large number of threads uses considerable memory. To lower a thread pool's memory use while maintaining a large number of threads, you can change the Analysis Services `StackSizeKB` property. However, change this value with great care, because lowering a stack size can lead to internal errors and system exceptions during query execution.

Managing Threads by Different Subsystems

Analysis Services subsystems calculate the number of threads required for an operation before its execution. Different types of operations may be configured differently based on the number of threads they require. For example, during query execution, Analysis Services needs to read data from partition segments in parallel and requires one thread per segment. However, if the partition contains a large number of segments, too many threads will run in parallel. Therefore, it is not practical to read all the segments simultaneously. The number of partition segments read in parallel is limited by the Analysis Services `CoordinatorQueryMaxThreads` property. The number of partitions scanned in parallel is limited by the Analysis Services `CoordinatorExecutionMode` property. Thus, the number of threads required to execute a query can be calculated as the number of partitions scanned in parallel multiplied by the number of segments of a partition scanned in parallel. If the `CoordinatorExecutionMode` property is set to a negative number, its absolute value is multiplied by the number of CPUs. The default value of the `CoordinatorExecutionMode` property is –4. On an eight-processor machine, Analysis Services scans 8 * 4 partitions in parallel and requests 8 * 4 * 16 threads (where 16 is the default value of the `CoordinatorQueryMaxThreads` property). Because by default each thread requires 1MB of memory for the stack, the system must allocate 0.5GB of memory to support 512 threads. Fortunately, this will not happen because Analysis Services limits the number of active threads by value of the `Concurrency` property.

While building indexes, Analysis Services faces challenges similar to query execution and uses a similar approach. The value of the Analysis Services `CoordinatorBuildMaxThreads` property defines the number of segments that are indexed in parallel.

During the processing operation, Analysis Services also uses the `CoordinatorExecutionMode` property to limit the number of partitions processed in parallel. As mentioned in Chapter 21, "Dimension and Partition Processing," Analysis Services uses three threads for the processing of a single partition. When processing a large number of partitions on the eight-processor machine, Analysis Services might create 8 * 4 * 3 threads, but the `Concurrency` value comes into play here again and limits number of active threads.

CHAPTER 29

Architecture of Query Execution—Calculating MDX Expressions

IN THIS CHAPTER

- Query Execution Stages
- Parsing an MDX Request
- Creation of Calculation Scopes
- Building a Virtual Set Operation Tree
- Optimizing Multidimensional Space by Removing Empty Tuples
- Calculating Cell Values
- Cache Subsystem

A multidimensional database consists of many parts, but at its heart are two major components: the storage engine and the formula engine. The storage engine writes data to and reads data from the disk. The formula engine accepts Multidimensional Expressions (MDX) requests, executes them, and sends requests to the storage engine to retrieve data. The user or client application interacts with the formula engine, and the formula engine in turn interacts with the storage engine.

In this chapter, we delve deeper in the discussion how the formula engine processes MDX query commands, and examine which data structures and algorithms it uses to retrieve and calculate necessary results in the shortest possible time. In Chapter 30, "Architecture of Query Execution—Retrieving Data from Storage," we discuss how the storage engine processes request for data from the formula engine.

Optimization of MDX calculations was one of the most important goals of Analysis Services 2008. Another goal of this release was not only to improve the performance of certain queries but also to make the system's behavior more consistent and predictable. With those goals in mind, Analysis Services developers redesigned the calculation engine, building on top of the successful design approaches introduced in the preceding version. In this redesign, some areas that we discuss shortly were changed, and new optimizations were introduced.

Query Execution Stages

When a client's request comes to Analysis Services, it passes through multiple stages. First, Analysis Services has to parse and analyze the Simple Object Analysis Protocol (SOAP) and XML for Analysis (XML/A) portions of the request, retrieve the MDX statement, and parse it. (We discussed the phases that precede the parsing of an MDX statement in Chapter 26, "Server Architecture and Command Execution.") After the system has determined what query language is used in the request, and if it detects that request contains an MDX query, it passes the execution of the request to the server subsystem responsible for execution of the MDX request—the formula engine.

The server architecture diagram in Figure 29.1 shows how Analysis Services processes an MDX query and illustrates the server subsystem responsible for each step of the process.

The process shown in Figure 29.1 traces the execution of MDX queries by the formula engine subsystem:

1. The command parser parses the MDX statement and produces an Abstract Syntax Tree (AST).
2. Analysis Services traverses the AST, resolves the names of the objects referenced in the query, and validates the signatures of the functions. This phase produces an expression tree.
3. After an expression tree is created, Analysis Services generates a collection of `Scope` objects. Each `Scope` object contains calculations that have a certain level of availability. For example, calculations created in MDX script reside in the global scope, calculations created in the sessions reside in the session scope, and so on. (For more information about MDX calculations, see Chapter 12, "Cube-Based MDX Calculations.")
4. Analysis Services performs static analysis of each node of the expression tree and produces a normalized tree. This is a new step in the query execution introduced in Analysis Services 2008; we discuss it later in this chapter.
5. Analysis Services executes the query. It starts the execution by evaluating the multidimensional space covered by the query. As a result of evaluating axes definitions, Analysis Services produces a virtual set operation tree. (We talk about the virtual set operation tree later in this chapter.)
6. Analysis Services iterates over the multidimensional space defined by the normalized tree and calculates cell values. While calculating cell values, Analysis Services first builds logical execution plan, which enables the system to walk through different allowed code paths and choose the most optimal one.
7. Analysis Services creates a physical execution plan.
8. If the query has a `NON EMPTY` operator, Analysis Services optimizes the multidimensional space and removes empty tuples. For more information about `NON EMPTY` operator, see Chapter 11, "Advanced MDX."

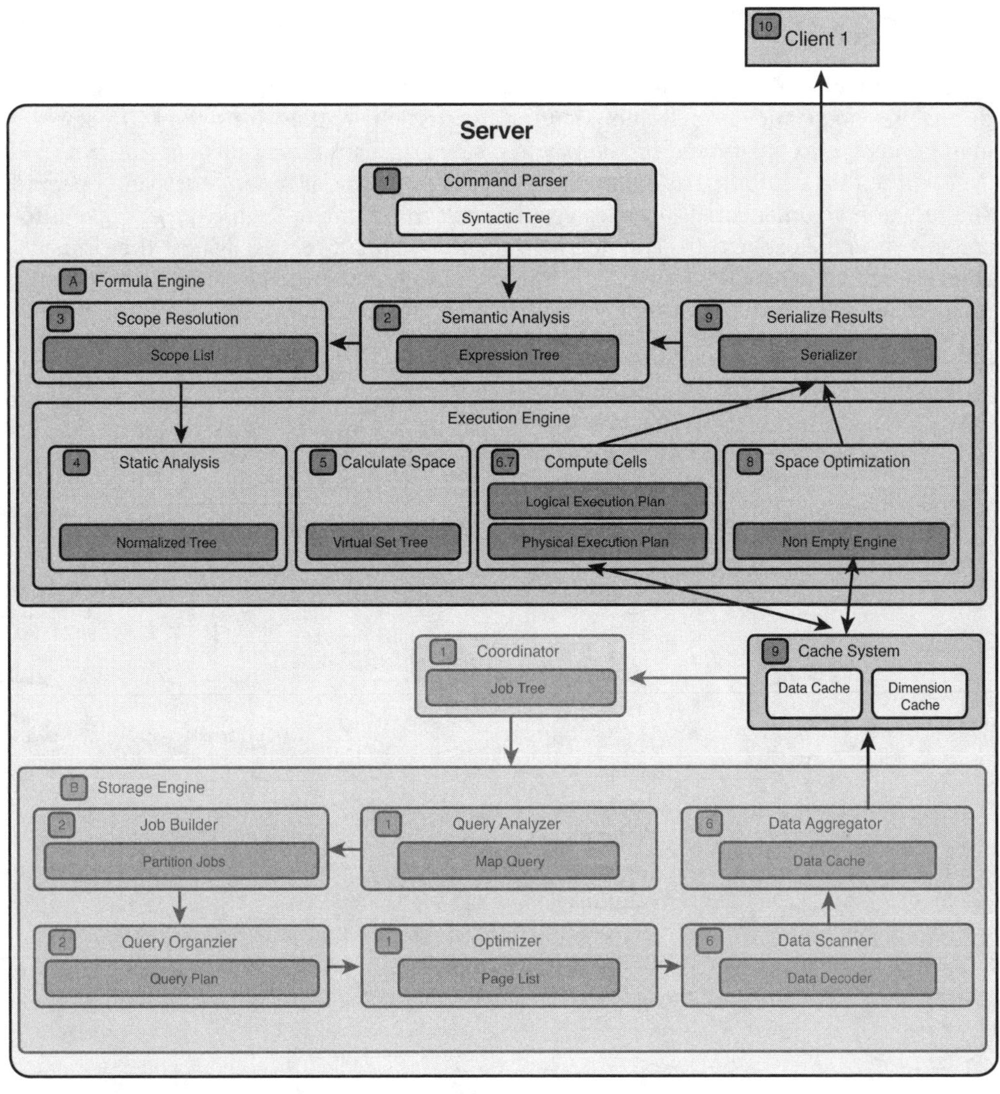

FIGURE 29.1 The query execution process.

9. The physical execution plan send requests to the cache subsystem that either retrieves values from the cache or sends a request to the storage engine subsystem.
10. Analysis Services serializes cell values and cell properties and sends the result of the query to the client.

29

Parsing an MDX Request

Analysis Services 2008 parses an MDX request in three phases: syntactical analysis, semantic analysis, and static normalization. During the first phase, it analyzes the MDX statement, finds syntax errors, and produces a tree-based data structure called an Abstract Syntax Tree (AST). An AST has operators and MDX functions as inner nodes, and operands and function arguments as leaf nodes. At this stage, the formula engine doesn't take into account structure of the cube, and doesn't validate the MDX request against the Unified Dimensional Model (UDM). For example, if you send the MDX query in Listing 29.1 to Analysis Services, it will produce the AST shown in Figure 29.2.

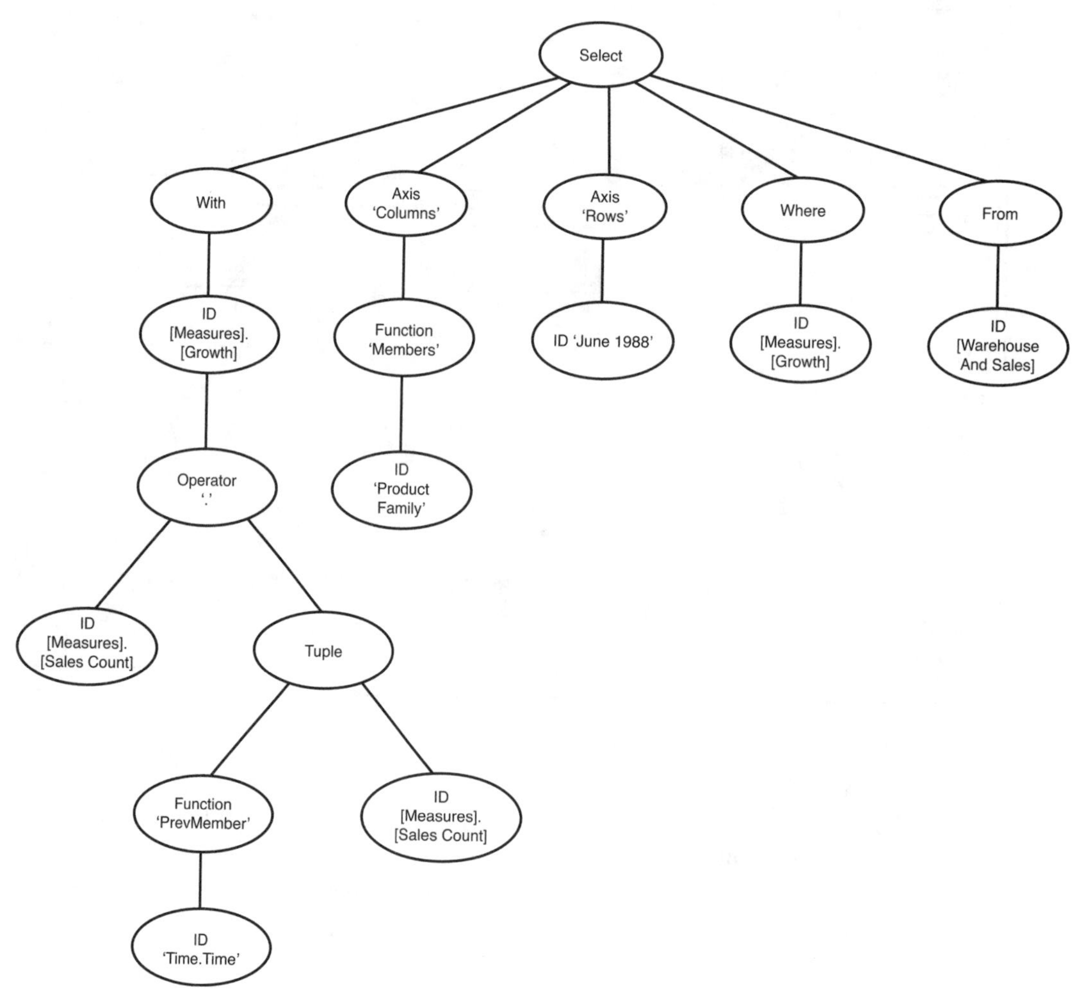

FIGURE 29.2 AST—result of the syntactical analysis.

LISTING 29.1 A Simple MDX Query

```
WITH member measures.growth as
[Measures].[Sales Count]-([Time].[Time].PrevMember,[Measures].[Sales Count])
SELECT [Product].[Products].[Product Family].members on COLUMNS,
[Time].[Time].[Month].&[6]&[1998] on ROWS FROM [Warehouse and Sales]
WHERE measures.growth
 CELL PROPERTIES VALUE
```

In the second parsing phase, Analysis Services traverses an AST, performs semantic analysis of the expression, resolves the names of the objects referenced in the query, and validates the signatures of the functions. During this phase, Analysis Services also collects information about all MDX calculations that can be used by the query and produces calculation scopes. (We discuss calculation scopes in the next section of this chapter.) The semantic analysis phase produces an expression tree. Each node on the expression tree is an object that represents an MDX function or object in the UDM. For the sample query in Listing 29.1, Analysis Services generates the expression tree shown in Figure 29.3.

In the third phase, the formula engine iterates the expression tree, performs static binding operations, and produces a normalized tree. Static tree normalization is a new feature of Analysis Services 2008. It includes implicit type conversions (type conversions were discussed in Chapter 10, "MDX Concepts") of all the nodes in the tree and does another static operation that we call constant folding—the conversion of a function to an MDX object. One of the examples of the constant folding is conversion from the `Time.Level(1)` expression to the equivalent `Time.Year` expression. In the preceding version, Analysis Services performed type conversions during the cell calculation phase, which in some queries could cause serious performance problems. Static normalization of MDX expressions during parsing allows relatively inexpensive (before any data is retrieved or calculated) mapping between types of the objects used as function parameters and MDX functions that accept those parameters. For the query in Listing 29.1, Analysis Services generates the normalized expression tree shown in Figure 29.4.

As the result of the static type conversion, new nodes (shown in Figure 29.4 in gray) are inserted into the tree: `MDXValue()`, `MDXValue()`, `MDSet`, and `MDXCurrentMember`. By adding an `MDXValue` node to the normalized tree, Analysis Services implicitly converts the expression `[Time].[Time].PrevMember` to the `[Time].[Time].CurrentMember.PrevMember`, because the function `.PrevMember` operates on a member and not on the hierarchy `[Time].[Time]`.

29

Creation of Calculation Scopes

After the second phase of parsing—semantical analysis—Analysis Services evaluates MDX calculations that can be applied to the query. All calculations are stored in `Scope` objects. A `Scope` object contains a collection of all kinds of calculations that Analysis Services supports, such as calculated members, named sets, calculated cells (this collection stores

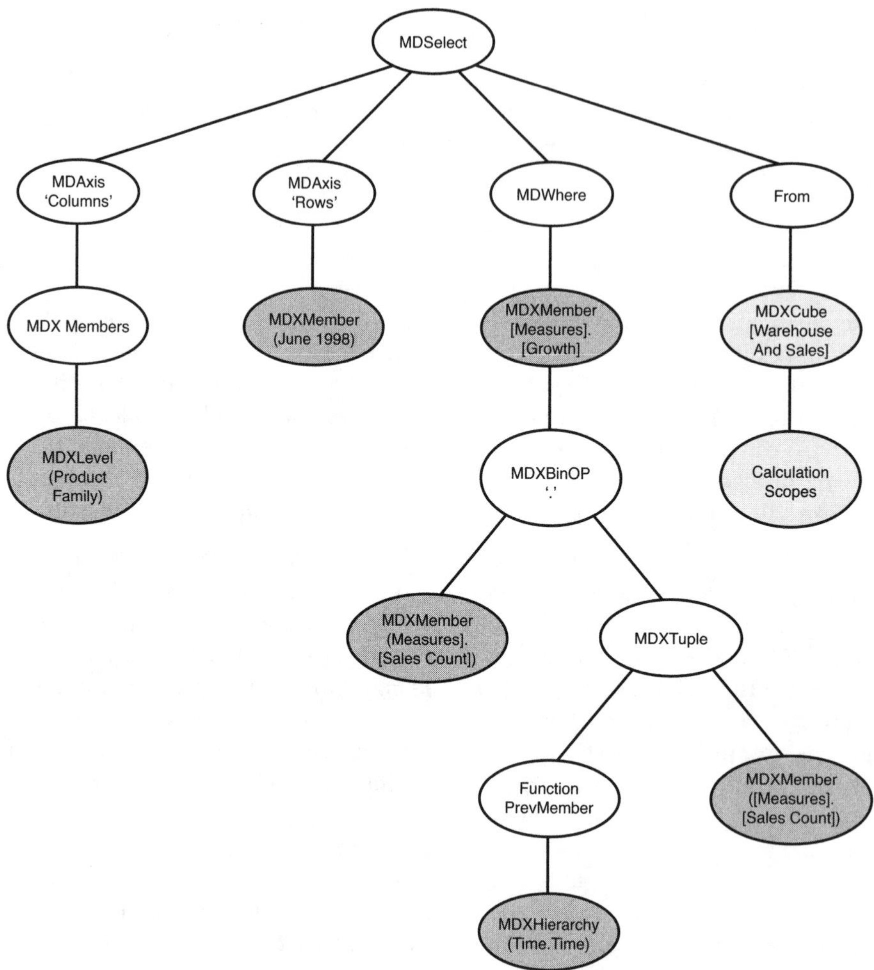

FIGURE 29.3 Expression tree—result of the semantic analysis.

not just calculated cells, but all assignment operators, unary operators, custom rollups, and semi-additive measures), visual totals, key performance indicators (KPIs), and actions. The `Scope` object also contains information about the default members for all dimensions in the cube.

Calculations can have different levels of availability; therefore, there are different types of scopes:

- Global scope contains calculations defined in MDX scripts, cube metadata objects such as actions and KPIs, and dimension calculations.
- Session scope contains calculations created by a user in a session (for example, calculated members created by the `CREATE MEMBER` statement).
- Query scope contains calculations created in a query using a `WITH` clause.

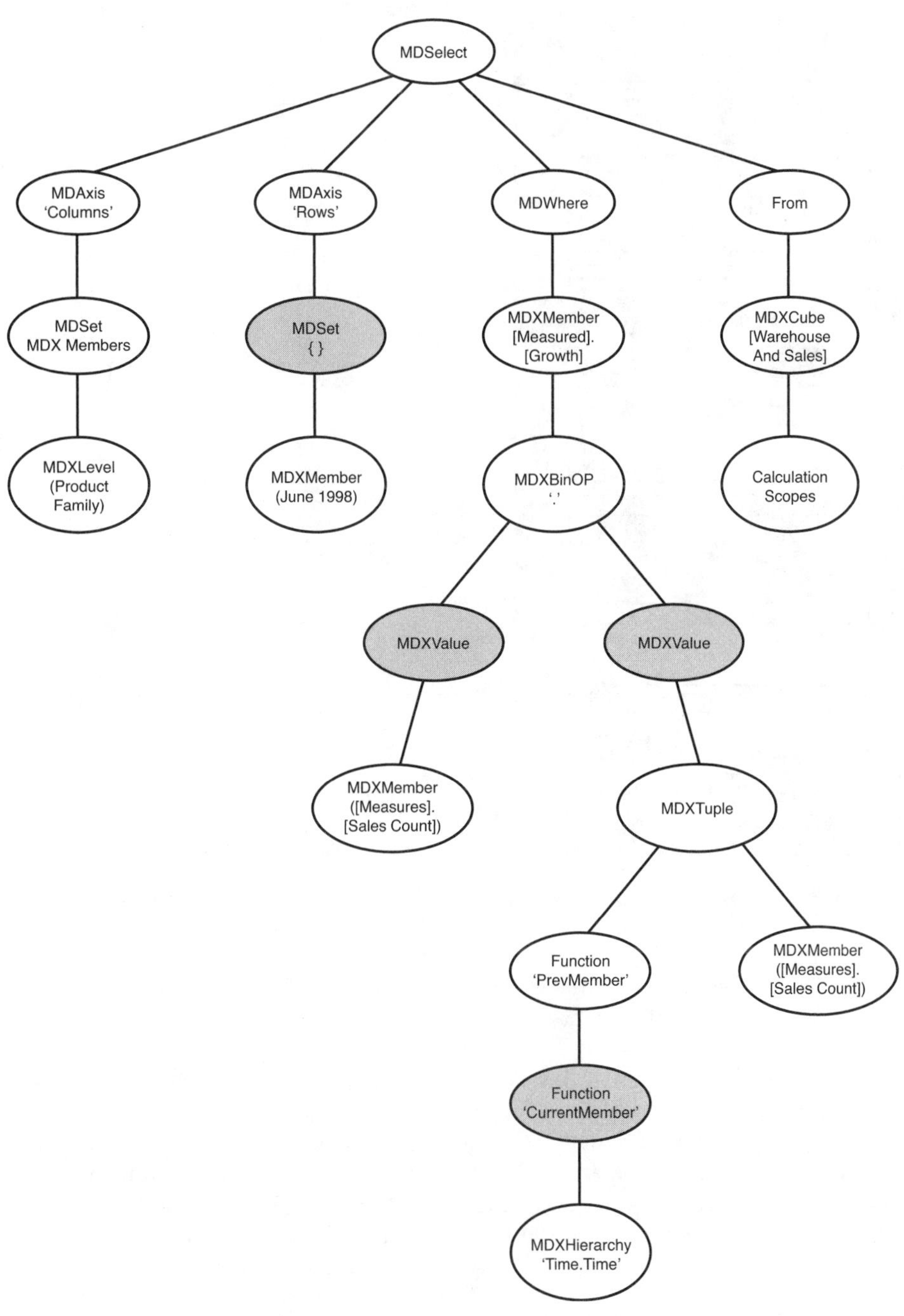

FIGURE 29.4 Normalized expression tree—result of the type conversion.

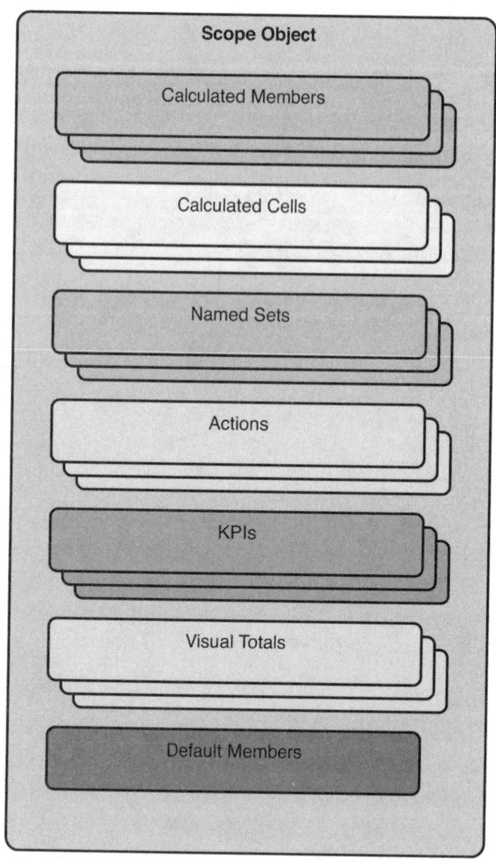

FIGURE 29.5 The `Scope` object contains all the calculations that Analysis Services supports.

- Subcube scope contains a restriction subcube defined by the SubSelect clause or the `CREATE SUBCUBE` statement.

All these types of scope derive from each other and make up a stack, with global scope on the bottom and, in the most general case, subcube scope on top. The type of the `Scope` object on the top of the scope stack depends on the MDX statement being executed. If the current statement is a `SELECT` statement with `subselect`, the subcube scope is on the top. If it's a regular `SELECT` statement, the query scope is on top of the stack. If the query is a `CREATE` statement, session scope is on top of the stack. Figure 29.6 shows the stack of scopes. Each scope has a reference to its *parent*—the scope immediately below the current one in the stack.

When Analysis Services performs lookups for calculations that might reside in any of the scopes, it starts to iterate from the top of the stack, following parent references. This makes calculations defined in any scope available during the query execution.

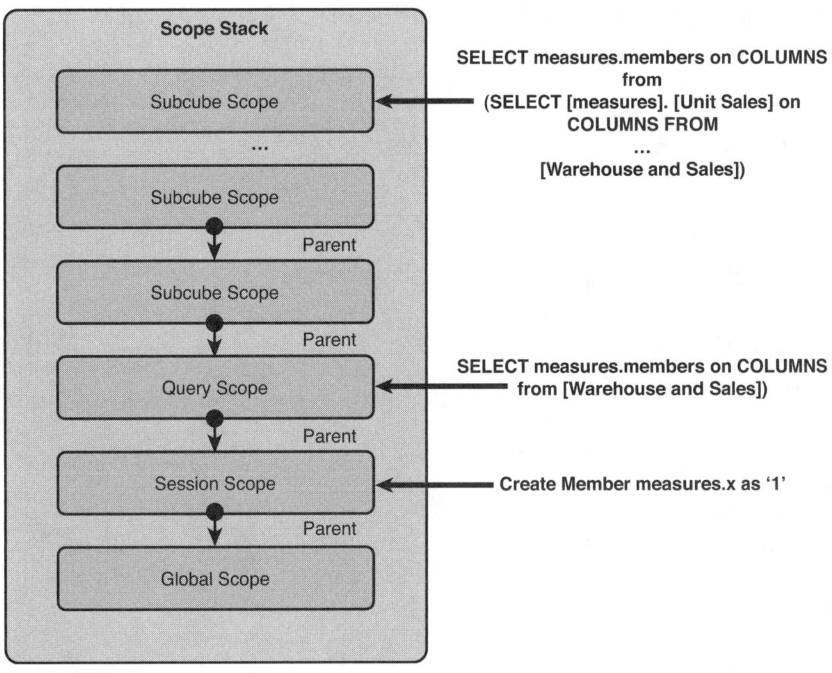

FIGURE 29.6 All these types of scope make up a stack, with global scope on the bottom and subcube, query, or session scope on the top.

Global Scope and Global Scope Cache

Cube and dimension calculations defined in the metadata of the cube or dimensions are accessible to all the users who have access to the cube or dimensions. Therefore, Analysis Services tries not to reevaluate expressions for calculations during every MDX query; instead, it creates a cache and stores `Scope` objects in it. However, evaluation of calculations depends on the security permissions of the user who executes the query. If this user doesn't have access to certain dimension members, he cannot access those members from an MDX script or dimension calculation. (For more information about dimension security, see Chapter 36, "Securing Dimension Data.") Therefore, Analysis Services caches the global scopes per combination of security roles to which the current user belongs, or even per user if any of the calculations stored in the scope use dynamic security. (Dynamic security is also discussed in Chapter 36.)

The *global scope cache* is a hash table integrated with Memory Manager. (It can be unloaded from memory if the Memory Manager detects that the system is low on resources.) The key to this hash table is a string that contains names of the roles to which the current user belongs. If at least one of the calculation objects uses the `UserName` function or the client-passed `EffectiveUserName` connection string property, Analysis Services uses the username as the key to the global scope cache. Figure 29.7 shows diagram of global scope cache.

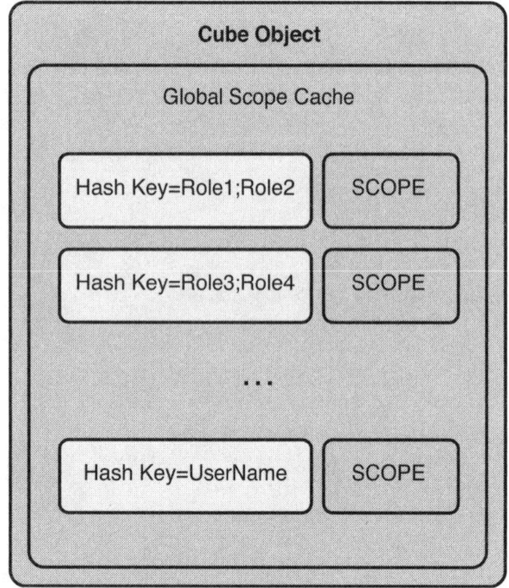

FIGURE 29.7 The global scope cache is a hash table with keys that contain name of the roles the current user belongs to or name of the user.

When a user that belongs to a certain role combination connects to the system for the first time, a global `Scope` object is built. This object is used for subsequent requests from the same user or users that belong to that group of roles.

Session Scope and Session Scope Cache

A user can use a single session to query multiple cubes; therefore, each session has a collection of `Scope` objects. The key into this collection is the cube name. When a user issues a statement that creates a calculation in the session, Analysis Services detects to which cube this calculation applies. If the session scope cache doesn't have the session scope associated with that cube, Analysis Services creates a new `Scope` object and inserts it into the session scope cache. In addition to the session scope, Analysis Services looks up the global `Scope` object in the global scope cache of the cube, and creates one if one is not found in the global scope cache. The session scope cache contains references to both the session scope and global scope of a cube, as shown in Figure 29.8.

Global and Session Scope Lifetime

As with other types of caches, Analysis Services has to make sure that the cache of session scopes and the global scope cache are not stale and detect conditions when users from different sessions changes state of a cube.

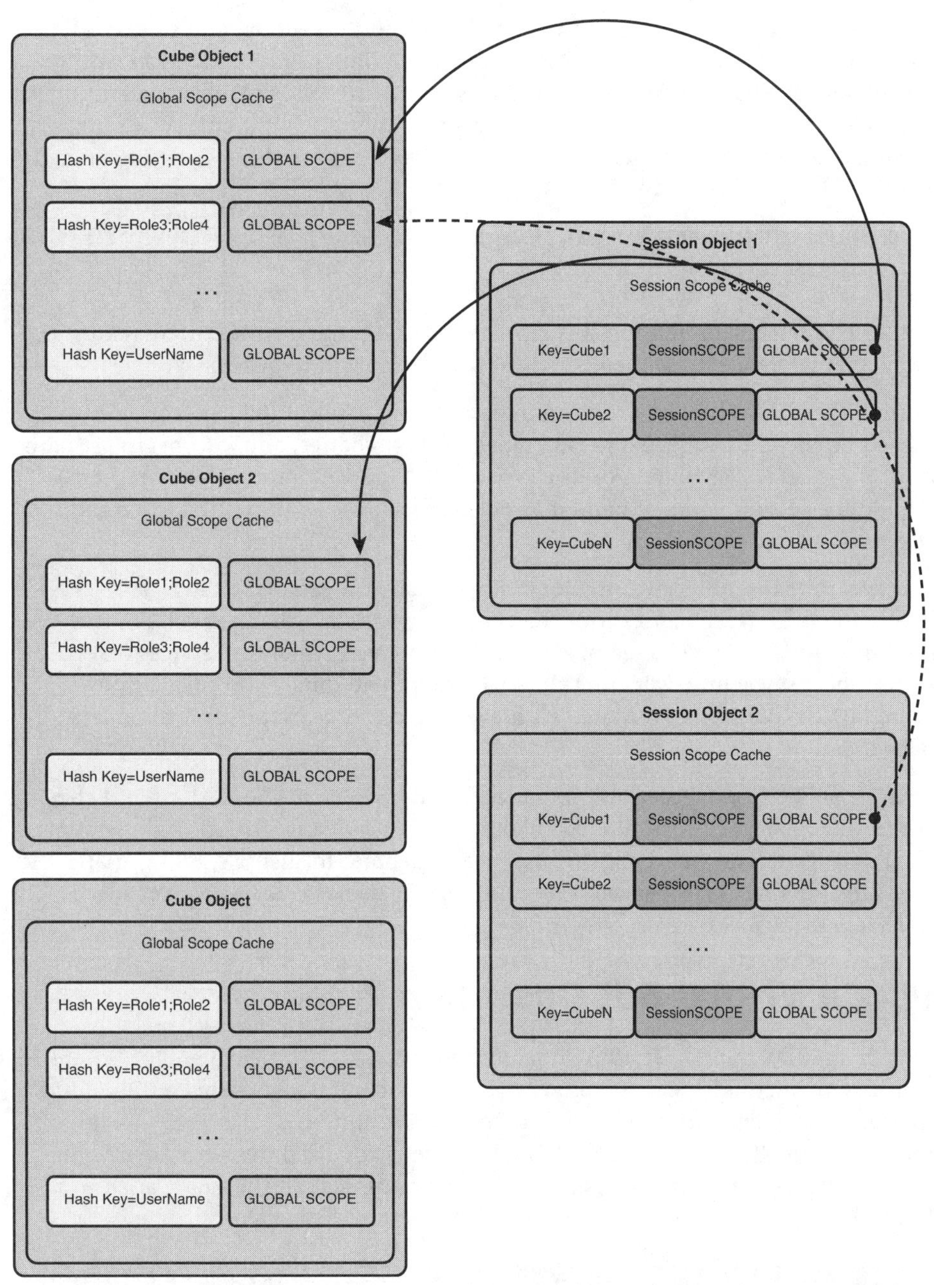

FIGURE 29.8 The session scope cache contains references to both the session scope and global scope of a cube.

Different types of changes may happen to the objects, and the global and session scope can withstand some changes. (For example, a change of dimension description won't affect calculations.) When you incrementally process a partition, existing calculations can continue to work, but results of MDX expressions might be different. For example, the following code can return different results if transactions for today's sales are added to the cube:

```
TopCount(CrossJoin([Customer].[Customer].Members, [Product].[Products].Members), 5,
[Measures].[Unit Sales])
```

On the other hand, if the dimension was reprocessed and some members were removed, calculations that reference those members won't work and will return an error.

To support all these different scenarios, Analysis Services has a complex mechanism that detects objects that were changed and the impact of that change, and informs the session manager of the change. Depending on the type of the change, the session manager can either rebuild the session scope or mark it as deleted. Figure 29.9 shows the mechanism of refreshing session scopes.

When the session manager receives the request to update the sessions, it iterates over all the sessions, and tries to refresh sessions that have scope for the changed cube in the session scope cache. When a change of the cube is not severe, Analysis Services first rebuilds the global scope by revaluating the MDX script and dimension calculations, extracts the MDX expressions associated with every calculation in the session scope, and reevaluates them.

If a cube is severely changed, the session manager iterates over all the sessions and checks whether the session scope for the altered cube has at least one calculation. Such sessions are marked as deleted, and when another user request comes to such a session, Analysis Services returns error message: `Current session is no longer valid due to structural changes in the database.`

Building a Virtual Set Operation Tree

The results of an MDX query contain two major sections: axes definition and cells definition. After it completes parsing of a query, Analysis Services starts to evaluate the multidimensional space covered by this query and produces first section of the results—axes definition. Therefore, it iterates over the branch of the normalized tree associated with each axes. Because axes in MDX are always defined by sets, we call the axis branch of a normalized tree a virtual set operation tree.

NOTE

Analysis Services works with sets not only to define the multidimensional space of a query, but also executes MDX expressions that contain sets in many other situations. For example, in dimension security, named sets and MDX expressions are defined in MDX scripts. A virtual set operation tree is also used in all these cases.

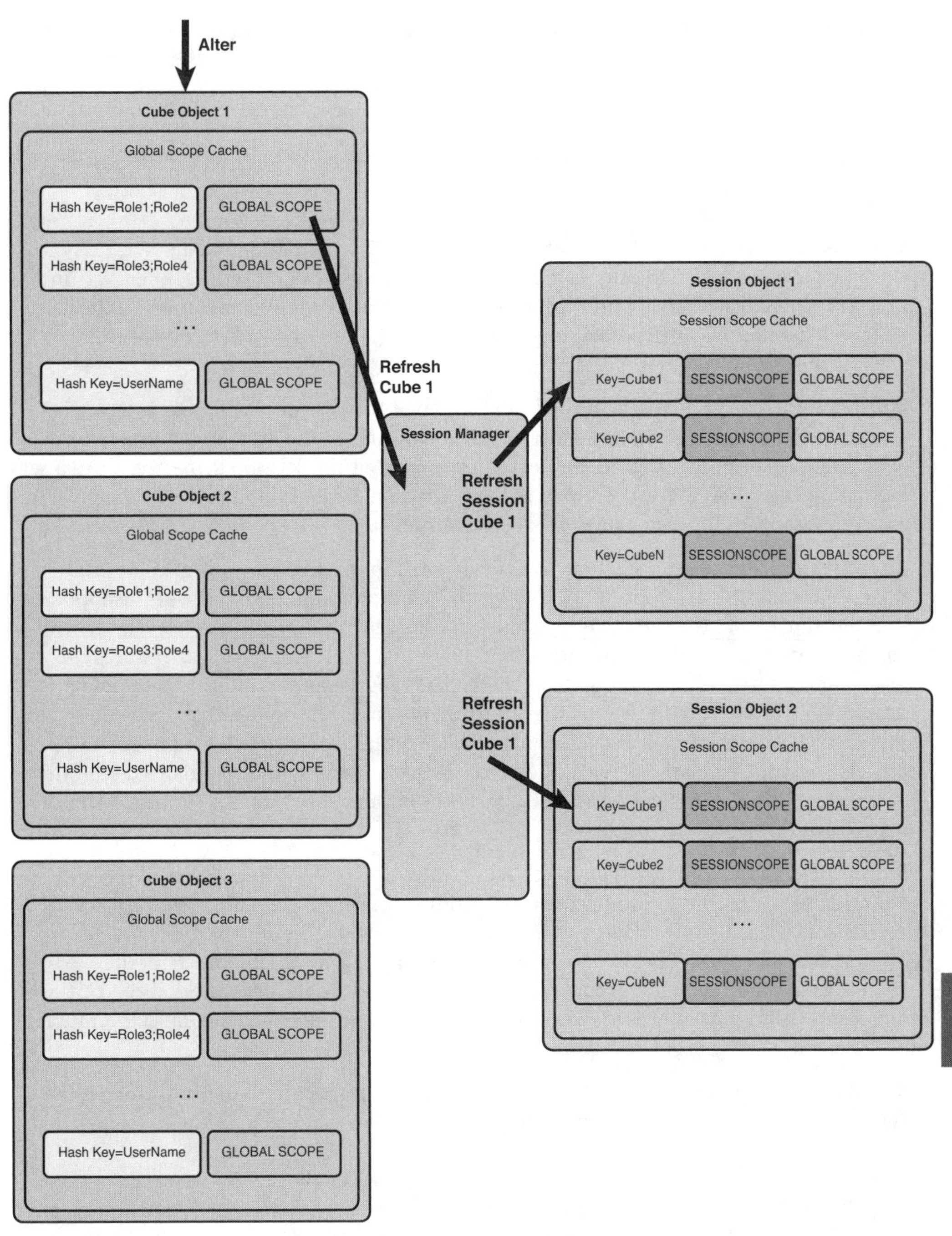

FIGURE 29.9 When a cube is altered or reprocessed, Analysis Services sends the request to the session manager to refresh or delete affected sessions.

When an MDX expression consists of several sets nested within one another, the result of each set sometimes pipelines to another set, producing a virtual set without creating a temporary data structure to hold the intermediate result. For example, consider the following MDX expression:

```
TopCount(CrossJoin([Customer].[Customer].Members, [Product].[Products].Members), 5,
[Measures].[Unit Sales]).
```

If Analysis Services were to first create a data structure to hold all members returned by the `CrossJoin` function, in our example it would have to hold 23,360,704 members in memory. Then, it would discard most of them and return only five members to the user. With sets pipelining, Analysis Services doesn't store the intermediate results of the `CrossJoin` function.

Pipelining the output of a set into the next set saves the cost of writing out intermediate results, and that savings can be significant. If the output of the set is saved in a temporary data structure for processing by the next set, we say that the set is *materialized*. Virtual set evaluation has a lower cost than materialization and is chosen by Analysis Services whenever the algorithm for the evaluation of sets permits it.

Internally, the virtual set operation tree is evaluated in top-to-bottom order. To simplify the code responsible for coordination of virtual set evaluation, each `Set` object supports a uniform `TupleIterator` interface that hides the implementation details of each set. The `TupleIterator` interface has two functions: `Start` and `Next`. Analysis Services uses the `Start` function to initialize the state of the `TupleIterator` and to allocate internal data structures. The `Next` function calls the `Next` function of each input set, and executes code specific to the given `Set`. If the algorithm implemented for a set allows input tuples to be processed completely when they are received, input tuples are not materialized, and the evaluation is pipelined. Sometimes the algorithm implemented for the set might need to materialize the set.

In our TopCount example, Analysis Services creates a virtual set tree that contains the following sets, `TopCountSet` and `Crossjoin`, and two `SliceSets` (for `[Customer].[Customer].Members` and `[Product].[Products].Members` expressions). To evaluate the expression, Analysis Services doesn't create a data structure that holds all the members of the hierarchy `Customer` and hierarchy `Products`. Instead, it creates a data structure to hold all the members resulting from `CrossJoin`. However, it creates an intermediate data structure for the results of the `TopCount` function.

In addition to the `TupleIterator` interface, Analysis Services internally implements the `TupleContainer`, `TupleCounter`, and `TupleRanker` interfaces:

- `TupleContainer` provides information about whether a set contains a certain tuple. Performance of some sets can be greatly optimized if Analysis Services won't materialize the set to answer this question. For example, it's much faster to find out whether sets that make up a `CrossJoin` set contain a tuple than to perform the `CrossJoin` function and lookup for a tuple in a much larger set.

- TupleCounter provides access to the number of tuples in the set. For some types of sets, the number of tuples is known in advance or easy to calculate; for others, Analysis Services has to materialize the set to find the number of its tuples.
- TupleRanker provides access to the ordinal position of the tuple in the set or tuple's rank. Similar to TupleCounter, for some sets it's easy and fast to find out the tuple's ordinal position; for others, the set has to be materialized.

Optimizing Multidimensional Space by Removing Empty Tuples

The logical space of a cube that can be addressed from an MDX query is large. It includes combinations of all the members of all the hierarchies, regardless of whether any data for those combinations exists. There are many scenarios in which you might like to remove a coordinate (tuple) that would result in empty cells at the intersection of coordinates on the other axes. To do this, you can use a NON_EMPTY operator or a NonEmpty function, as discussed in Chapter 11.

Analysis Services uses the same algorithm to implement both the NON_EMPTY operator and the NonEmpty function, so we'll explain both of them with an example of the NON_EMPTY operator. Analysis Services has two approaches to implementation of the NON_EMPTY operator. Using the first one—the naïve approach—Analysis Services simply iterates over all the tuples on the axis with NON EMPTY operator, calculates the values of the cells on intersection of the current tuple with all combinations of tuples on other axes, and only then removes empty cells. In a large and sparse data set, this algorithm will take a long time and consume a lot of memory.

The second approach—the data-bound approach—is based on the idea that the physical space of the cube is much smaller than its logical space and only not-empty values are physically stored in the cube. Therefore, this algorithm first issues a request to the storage engine subsystem to retrieve not-null values covering the coordinate space defined by the query, and then projects those not-null values on the axes.

This approach is much faster than the first one, especially when the data set is large and sparse. In most scenarios, Analysis Services 2008 uses the data-bound approach. Even when there are calculations covering the space over which Analysis Services performs a NON EMPTY operation, it will use a physical plan (as we discuss shortly) to retrieve necessary data first and then use the data-bound approach. There is a small set of scenarios when Analysis Services can not use data-bound approach and fall back to the naiïve one. For example, when a NON EMPTY algorithm is applied to multidimensional space with recursive MDX calculation or many overlapping calculations, Analysis Services might choose to use a naiïve algorithm.

Analysis Services always starts execution of NON_EMPTY with the data-bound approach, and then it analyzes the multidimensional space defined by the query and falls back to the naiïve algorithm if it's impossible to stay with the data-bound approach. If you are monitoring traces using the SQL Server Profiler, you can see whether Analysis Services executes your query using a naiïve algorithm by checking whether the `IntegerData` column for the `Calculate Non Empty Begin` event is equal to `11`. Another way to see whether Analysis Services uses a naiïve algorithm is by checking the perfmon counter `MSAS 2008:MDX\Total NON EMPTY Unoptimized`.

Calculating Cell Values

Similarly to the preceding version, Analysis Services 2008 calculates MDX expressions on the subcubes that cover the requested space. It does not calculate the value for each individual cell (which is what the calculation engine of Analysis Services 2000 does). Thus, Analysis Services 2008 provides a "block-computation" approach. The block-computation approach provides a number of obvious benefits, such as reducing the cost of determining which calculations apply to each individual cell, and reducing the cost of initializing data structures for each cell. It also enables Analysis Services to take advantage of data sparsity, so typical for online analytical processing (OLAP) data, and enables optimizations on the cells that have empty values.

When Analysis Services needs to calculate the result of a query or calculate an MDX expression, it builds calculation plans, which then execute. To build the calculation plan, the system breaks the space of the cube into subcubes. These subcubes must satisfy a rule: All cells of a subcube have the same calculation.

An execution plan in Analysis Services 2008 has two parts: a logical plan and a physical plan. A logical plan is a tree of nodes with operators that will be performed over a subcube. A logical plan's operator takes a subcube as an input parameter, performs a transformation over it, and produces a modified subcube on the output. Eventually, a logical plan produces subcubes that the formula engine sends to the storage engine to retrieve the data. Based on the logical plan, Analysis Services creates multiple physical plans to define the sequence of data processing. After physical plans have been created, Analysis Services finds the most efficient one and executes it.

Logical Plan Construction

To execute an MDX expression, the calculation engine analyzes the multidimensional space that the query or expression requested, and generates one or more data structures called *subcubes*—data structures that define part of the multidimensional space. For each subcube, Analysis Services iterates over all the scopes available in the current context and retrieves calculations that apply to the subcube. During this operation, it divides the subcube into smaller portions, each covered by a single calculation. The pair—subcube and calculation formula—is an original building block of the logical plan. Even if Analysis Services doesn't find any calculations associated with a subcube, it creates a logical plan with a virtual formula that specifies how to retrieve data from the storage engine subsystem.

For example, suppose that you have a simple cube with dimension D1, and three measures: M1, M2, and M3. The cube contains the following MDX script:

```
Calculate;
M1=M1*M2;
```

Suppose also that a user issues the following query, which retrieves the values of all measures:

```
SELECT measures.members ON COLUMNS,
       D1.Members ON ROWS FROM cube
```

Analysis Services builds the logical execution plans, as shown in Figure 29.10.

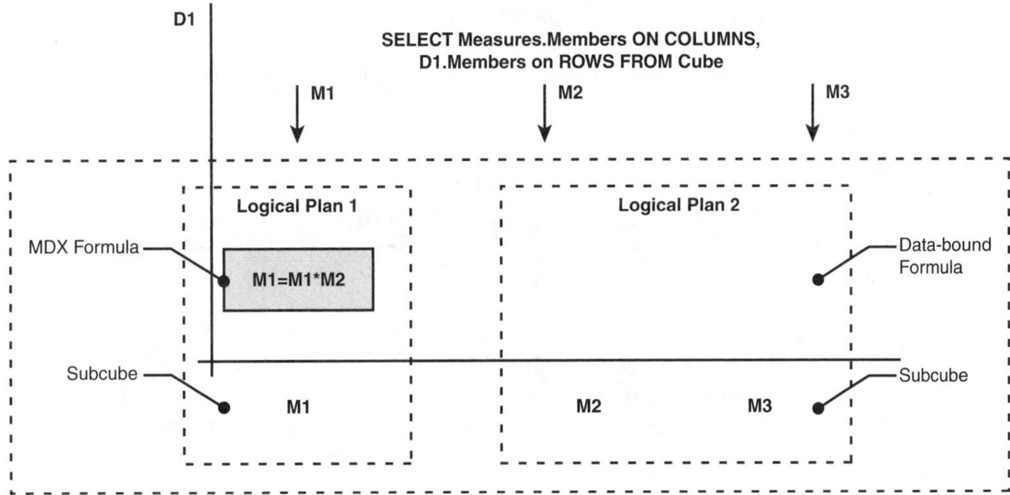

FIGURE 29.10 Analysis Services analyzes the request and builds two logical execution plans.

As mentioned earlier, each node of logical execution plan contains an operation that needs to be performed on the given subcube. For example, Analysis Services builds Logical Plan 1 for the M1=M1*M2 expression, as shown in Figure 29.11.

While building a logical plan, Analysis Services calculates several properties of the logical operator that it will use in later stages of execution. `DefaultValue`, `Static` or `Dynamic`, and varying attributes are properties of the logical plan operators. The `DefaultValue` property carries information about the value that will most often be encountered in the requested subspace. For example, if the system can predict that a required dataset is relatively sparse, the `DefaultValue` property will contain the value `EMPTY`—by definition, sparse data contains a lot of empty values. For example, data stored in the OLAP storage engine is usually sparse; in the FoodMart database, there are no values for each product sold to each customer at any possible period of time. In many other cases, the system can automatically derive the default value. For example, for a IIF operator, `"True"` or `"False"` can be default values. Obviously, there are plenty of scenarios when a required dataset is dense

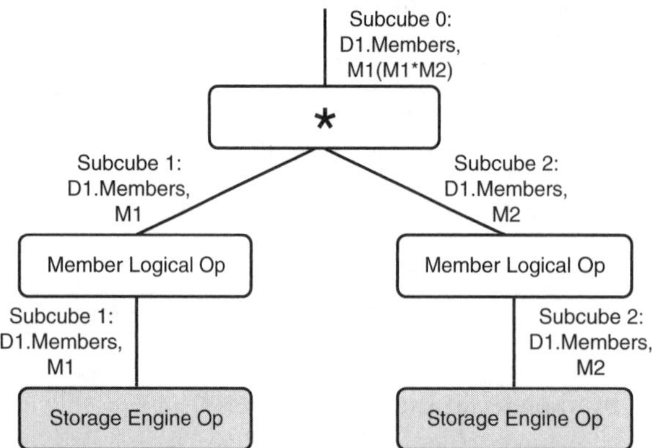

FIGURE 29.11 Logical plan for the multiplication operator.

and the system just cannot derive the `DefaultValue`; in such cases, the default value will be a `N/A` value.

An expression is static when it would yield the same value in any coordinate of the subcube. For example, the expression `[Time].[Time].[Month].Members.Count` is static because the number of months doesn't depend on any other dimension of the cube. On the other hand, the `M1.Value` expression is dynamic because its value depends on the coordinate of the cube in which it evaluated.

Even when an expression is dynamic it can be invariant (static) in the context of some attributes, but variant for others. For example, the expression `[Time].[Time].PrevMember` doesn't depend on either the `Product` or `Store` dimension, but it depends on the `Time` dimension. Execution of the query in Listing 29.2 (with results shown in Figure 29.12) demonstrates that the results of the `PrevMember` function depend only on the `Time` dimension.

LISTING 29.2 A Simple MDX Query

```
WITH
  MEMBER measures.x AS
    [Time].[Time].PrevMember.Name
SELECT
  [Product].[Products].[Product Family].MEMBERS ON COLUMNS
 ,{
    [Time].[Time].[Month].[June]
   ,[Time].[Time].[Month].[July]
   ,[Time].[Time].[Month].[August]
  } ON ROWS
FROM [Warehouse and Sales]
WHERE
  measures.x
```

In this example, the `Month` attribute is a varying attribute for the `Time.Time.PrevMember` expression. Knowledge of varying and invarying attributes allows Analysis Services to dramatically shrink the number of cells for which it needs to evaluate an expression. Now the system does not need to evaluate an expression in the context of all the cells of the subspace (in our example, nine times). Instead, it can do so only for members of the varying attributes (three times in our example). To achieve this goal, Analysis Services creates a join table transform—a logical operator that maps original members of the varying attribute used in the query to the results of the expression. For our example, Analysis Services builds the join table shown in Figure 29.13.

	Drink	Food	Non-Consumable
June	May	May	May
July	June	June	June
August	July	July	July

FIGURE 29.12 Results of the `PrevMember` expression depend only on the `Time` dimension.

Input	Output
June	May
July	June
August	July

FIGURE 29.13 Join table for the `PrevMember` expression.

In some scenarios, Analysis Services does not need to use a join table to perform operations over the subspace. Sometimes it can use a simple static transform that maps a single member to another member (for example, to map from the calculated member to the physical member). At other times, the system cannot use a join table transform (for example, when operating over unnatural hierarchies). In such cases, Analysis Services tries to break an original subcube into smaller portions and tries to apply either a join table transform or static member transform on each subcube. This approach will produce many small subcubes and as a result, formula engine will send many queries to storage engine subsystem. Analysis Services implements optimized logical operators for most MDX functions however, some functions don't have specialized logical operators and use a generic one. For example, stored procedure calls do not have their own logical operators, because the system does not have any information about their behavior. To view a list of functions that have advanced logical operators, refer to the Books Online article, "Performance Improvements for MDX in SQL Server 2008 Analysis Services," at http://msdn.microsoft.com/en-us/library/bb934106.aspx.

Physical Plan Construction

After it builds the logical execution plans, Analysis Services starts to build physical plans. It iterates each logical plan in the top-down approach, and for each logical operator creates a physical one. The formula engine can choose one of three physical operands supported by Analysis Services 2008:

- **iterator**—Iterates over the cell values
- **lookup**—Extracts a single cell from collection of cells
- **datacache**—Materializes in memory a set of cells required by operation

The system analyzes different properties of the logical operand, such as `DefaultValue`, `Static/Dynamic`, and varying attributes and MDX functions corresponding to the operand and chooses the right physical operand for this position of the physical plan. For example, to perform multiplication operations over the multidimensional space, Analysis Services needs to perform the following steps. First it has to retrieve results of a left-hand operand and results of the right hand one (see Figure 29.11). Then, it needs to iterate over the first set of values and for each cell retrieve the corresponding cell from the second one and then perform mathematical operation on two values, or it does the opposite (iterates over the second set of values and retrieves the corresponding one from the first set of values). With both algorithms, the results will be exactly the same, but performance might differ. Imagine a currency-conversion operation, where for each product you need to multiple the value of its sale over the current conversion rate. In many cases, the number of products is much larger than the conversion rates, and it will be much faster to iterate over products and look up into much smaller result set—the currency rates (see Figure 29.14). Therefore, when choosing the type of the physical operand, Analysis Services iterates over sparse results and looks up into dense ones.

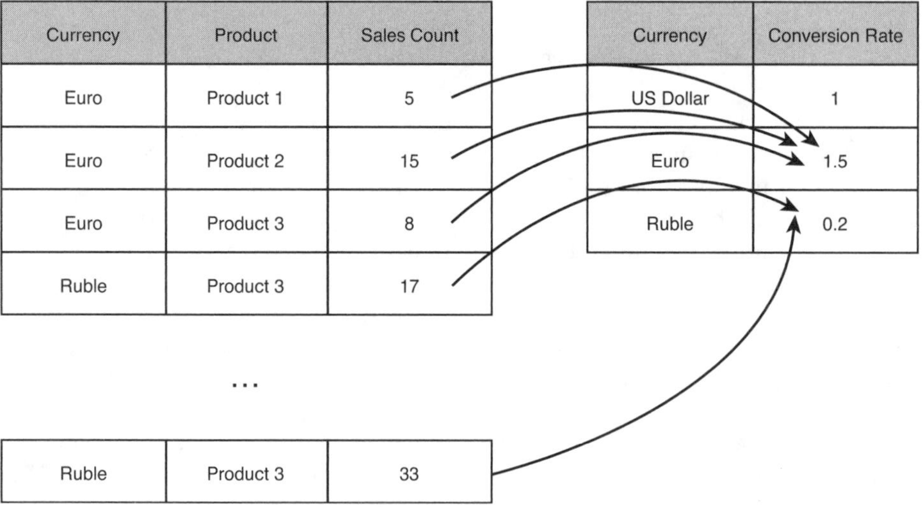

FIGURE 29.14 A currency-conversion operation.

For the multiplication operation, Analysis Services creates the physical plan shown in Figure 29.15.

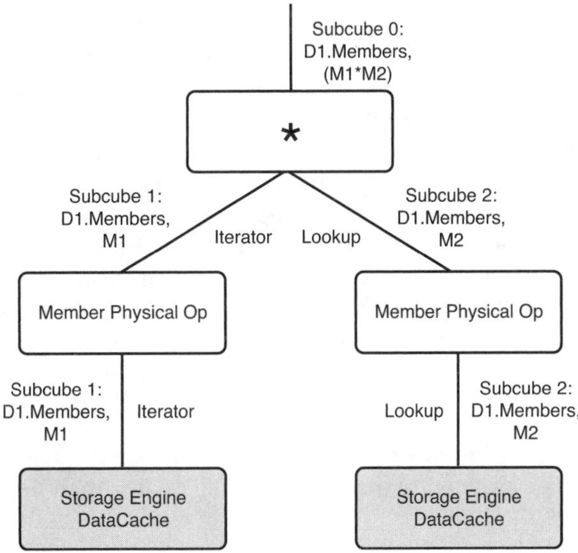

FIGURE 29.15 The physical plan for the multiplication operation.

Execution of the Physical Plan

After physical plan is built, Analysis Services starts to execute it from the bottom up. First, it tries to retrieve results from the formula cache. (We discuss the formula cache later in this chapter.) If results are found in the cache, Analysis Services passes them to the subsystem that serializes the results.

If results are not found, Analysis Services executes the code corresponding to the physical operand. If the operand is responsible for data retrieval from the storage engine subcube, the system sends the request to the storage engine subsystem. For operations involving calculation, the physical operand will perform the necessary calculations, such as multiplication.

In most scenarios, a block-computation approach to query execution is much more efficient than a cell-by-cell approach. When testing your system, however, you might want to experiment and compare the performance of these two approaches. For those rare cases, you can use the keyword `HINT LAZY` to disable block computation of a calculation expression. Because in most cases you do not need to disable block computation, this hint is turned off by default. Turn it on using server configuration property `Configuration Settings\OLAP\Query\LazyEnabled`.

The separation of logical and physical plans enables Analysis Services to postpone the execution of expensive operations, such as data retrieval or operations over large datasets, until an optimal execution plan is created. However, sometimes the system needs to perform relatively expensive operations during the logical plan construction. For example, while building a logical plan for an `IIF` operator, Analysis Services might need to execute a condition operator to decide which branch will be used. This permits the system to split up the space in two parts and build a logical and then physical plan only for the part of multidimensional space that satisfies the condition. This approach works very well for some formulas, but can have a negative impact on others. You can change system behavior by providing hints to the `IIF` expression. Analysis Services 2008 supports two hints: `EAGER` and `STRICT`. The `EAGER` hint means that the system will keep an original subcube and won't split it based on the condition of the `IIF` operator. The `STRICT` hint means the opposite and recommends the system to split the space. With hints, you are just providing the recommendations to the system, but Analysis Services will make the final decision.

Cache Subsystem

Performance of data access depends on the availability of this data in the cache. Analysis Services supports a few levels of caching:

- Dimension and measure group caches to cache the data retrieved from the storage engine
- Formula caches to store data calculated by the formula engine

Dimension and Measure Group Caches

When the formula engine needs to get data from the storage engine, it first sends the request to the cache system, which returns data if it exists in the cache; otherwise, the cache system requests data from the storage engine and saves it in the cache. Analysis Services supports this scheme for two types of caches: the dimension cache, which contains results of queries for dimension data; and the measure group cache, which contains the results of queries to get cell values. Each dimension and each measure group has its own cache.

The measure group cache and dimension cache have the same data structure; therefore, we will call both of them the *data cache registry*. When the formula engine needs to request data from the data cache registry, it generates a subcube that defines the subspace required for the calculations. In the best case, this subcube contains a single slice of data and its granularity. For example, if the formula engine needs to retrieve data about sales in the United States by the months of 1997, it generates a subcube that defines the granularity on the `Stores` and `Months` attributes, and a slice on `USA` and `1997` members. The granularity defines the list of attributes from which data is requested, and the slice defines a list of members from those attributes.

The result of the request is a data structure called a *data cache*. A data cache is a compressed data store. Its rows correspond to the nonempty coordinates of the multidimensional space returned by the request, and its columns correspond to the attributes requested by the subcube and, in the case of a request for measure group data, all the members in that measure group. See Chapter 20, "The Physical Data Model," for more information about compressed stores.

The cache system pairs each request subcube and its corresponding data cache into a `CacheItem` object. The data cache registry is a collection of the `CacheItems` and an index that enables fast access to the data stored in the cache. Figure 29.16 shows the scheme by which the data cache registry functions.

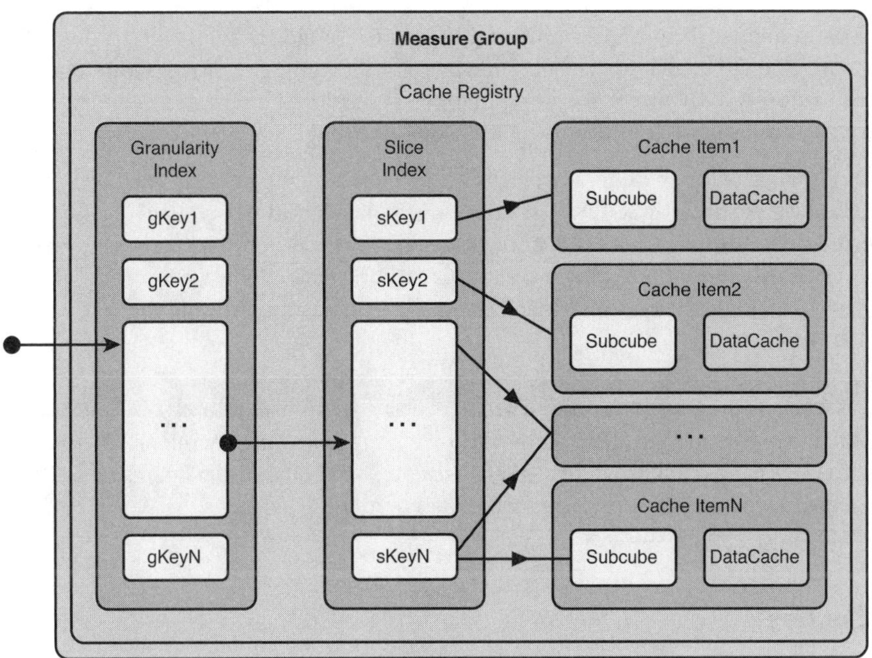

FIGURE 29.16 Structure of the data cache registry.

Requests come to the cache registry as subcubes, and the registry uses indexes to find the subcube and the data cache that corresponds to the subcube. If Analysis Services finds a subcube that completely matches the requested one, the data cache is returned to the caller. If Analysis Services finds the subcube in the registry that represents a superset of the data requested in the request subcube, it generates a new data cache and filters records corresponding to the requested subcube into it. Then, Analysis Services registers a new subcube and data cache in the registry. For example, assume that the data cache registry already contains a subcube representing all members of the `Month` attribute, and the next request to the cache registry uses a subcube for the months of the year 1998. Analysis Services will find the `CacheItem` with data for all the months, and then filter out the data cache records corresponding to the months of 1998 into another data cache object.

The data cache registry can also aggregate data and create data cache objects with higher-granularity data from the data of lower granularity. For example, assume that the data cache registry already contains a subcube representing all members of the `Month` attribute, and the next request to the cache registry uses a subcube for the year 1998. Analysis Services will find the `CacheItem` with data for all the months, filter out the data cache records corresponding to months of 1998, and then aggregate them into another data cache object that will contain a single record corresponding to the year 1998.

You can use the performance counters in `MSAS 2008:Cache` to monitor usage of the cache system. If the cache doesn't contain data, the data cache registry requests this data from the storage engine. After the data is retrieved, it registers the new subcube and data cache in the registry.

This way, all the requests from the formula engine to the storage engine come through the cache subsystem. The data cache registry is integrated with Memory Manager and adjusts itself when the amount of available memory changes. (For more information about data cache registry cleanup, see Chapter 27, "Memory Management.")

You can find out whether your query retrieves data from the cache by monitoring the `Query Subcube` trace event with SQL Server Profiler. If you see that `EventSubclass` is `Non-cache data`, the query missed the cache, and the request was executed by retrieving data from the storage. However, when you see the `GetDataFromCache` event with `EventSubclass` equal to `Get data from measure group cache`, the internal request was answered from the cache.

NOTE

A single MDX query can send multiple requests to the storage engine. Therefore, it's possible that you will see multiple `QuerySubcube` events, and some of the internal requests will be answered from the cache and others from the storage.

Formula Caches

Data structures for formula caches that the formula engine uses to store calculated values are very similar to the data cache registry used to cache data retrieved from the multidimensional store. Each `Scope` object has its own formula cache registry. When Analysis Services retrieves data from the formula cache registry, it iterates the stack of `Scope` objects available in the current context.

Similar to the data cache registry, the formula cache registry holds subcubes produced by the calculation execution plans and data caches that contain the results of calculations. The formula cache registry also contains an index that enables fast access to the data stored in the cache.

The Calculation execution plans that fall back to individual calculation of cell values do not use the formula cache registry. For the results provided by this type of calculation execution plan, Analysis Services has a special cache called the *flat cache*. Instead of storing a subcube for each individual cell, Analysis Services stores the following information about the cell: coordinate of the cell (its tuple), calculation pass, and calculated value associated with that cell. Figure 29.17 demonstrates the structure of the formula cache registry and the flat cache.

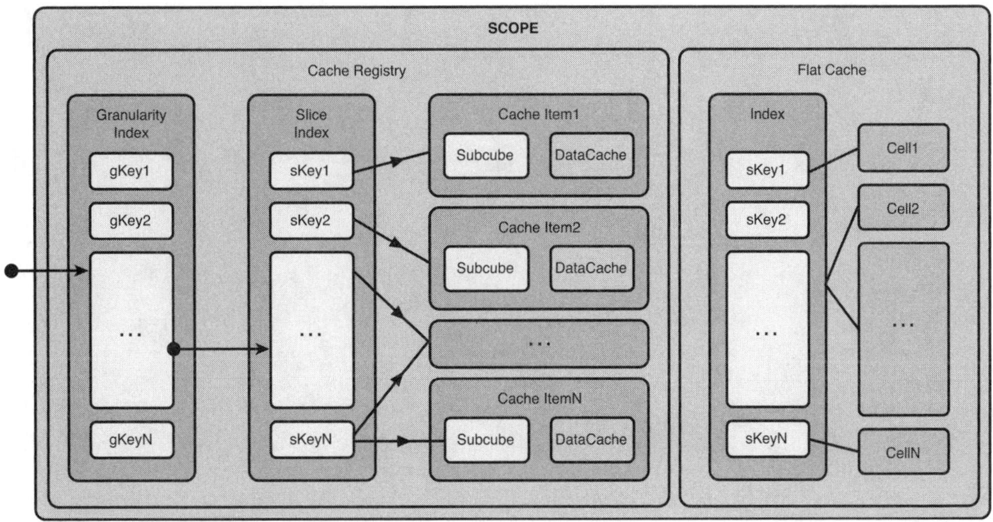

FIGURE 29.17 The formula cache registry.

You can monitor trace events to the formula caches in the same way you monitor trace events to the data cache registry. If your query was resolved from the cache, you will see the `GetDataFromCache` trace event in the SQL Server Profiler with the type of the cache shown in the `EventSubclass` column.

CHAPTER 30

Architecture of Query Execution—Retrieving Data from Storage

IN THIS CHAPTER

Efficient execution of Multidimensional Expressions (MDX) requests is the main responsibility of the formula engine and the storage engine subsystems. In the preceding chapter, we discussed the stages a query passes through the formula engine and the data structures Analysis Services uses to calculate the results of MDX queries. In this chapter, we discuss how Analysis Services retrieves data from multidimensional storage and how it handles requests for data stored in different types of partitions and dimensions.

When the formula engine needs to retrieve data stored in the multidimensional store, it forms an internal request to the cache system, which returns data immediately if it exists in the cache; otherwise, the cache system requests data from the storage engine. In this chapter, we delve deeper in our discussion about what happens when the storage engine receives an internal request for data.

The storage engine subsystem supports two types of internal requests for data: requests for dimension data and requests for measure group data. The formula engine subsystem detects what data is requested by a user, forms a dimension or measure group subcube, and passes it to the cache subsystem, which passes the request to the measure group or dimension object that contains the requested data. The difference between measure group and dimension subcubes is only in the attributes that each references: A measure group subcube references attributes of all the dimensions included into a measure group, whereas a dimension subcube references attributes of the dimension.

Analysis Services executes a request for measure group data similarly to the way it executes a request for dimension data. Therefore, we discuss the execution of a request for measure group data and provide you with information that you can use to deduce how Analysis Services retrieves dimension data.

Query Execution Stages

When an internal request comes to the storage engine subsystem, it passes through multiple stages. The server architecture diagram in Figure 30.1 shows how Analysis Services processes this request and illustrates the server subsystems responsible for each step of the process.

The process shown in Figure 30.1 traces the data retrieval from the multidimensional storage by the storage engine subsystem:

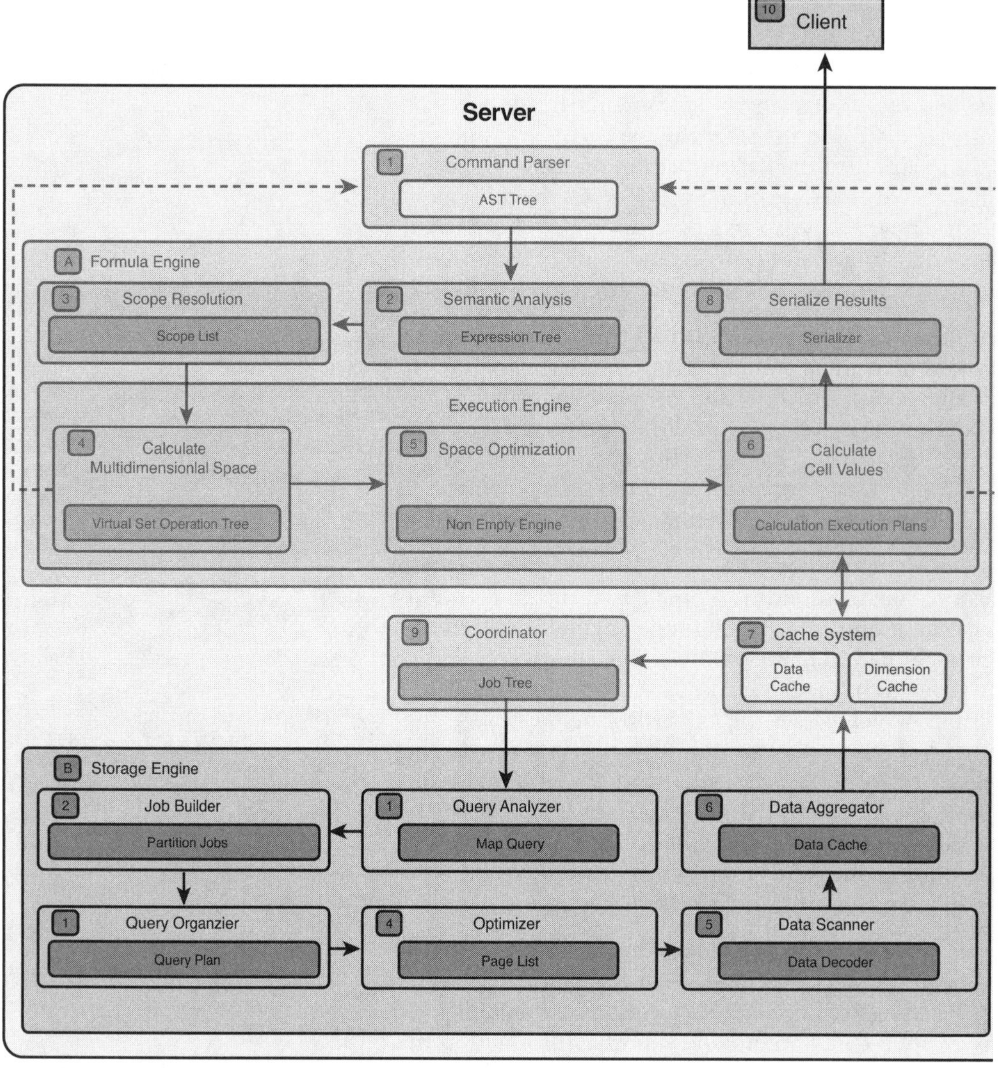

FIGURE 30.1 Query execution process by the storage engine subsystem.

1. Analysis Services analyzes the request and detects the type of the request: It checks the types of dimensions included in a measure group and detects whether at least one of the dimensions included in the request is an indirect dimension. (For more information about indirect dimensions, see Chapter 8, "Advanced Modeling.") In this stage, Analysis Services forms a data structure called a `MapQuery`. The `MapQuery` contains the requested subcube, additional information about the request (such as the type of the request), and a placeholder where the result will be accumulated.
2. Analysis Services analyzes partition slices of all the measure group's partitions and constructs a list of partitions that might contain requested data. (For more information about partition slices, see Chapter 20, "Physical Data Model," and Chapter 21, "Dimension and Partition Processing.") At this stage, Analysis Services creates the Query Partition jobs that it will use in the later stages to read data from partitions.
3. Analysis Services starts the execution of Query Partition jobs. Each job creates a query plan that defines the strategy to optimize retrieval of data from the partition.
4. Analysis Services iterates over partition segments and uses the bitmap indexes to build a list of pages in a segment that it will scan later to retrieve query results. (For more information about indexes, see Chapters 20 and 21.)
5. Analysis Services reads the pages from disk and passes data to the data decoder, which uses decoding tables (see Chapter 20 for more information about data decoding) to decode attributes necessary to generate the response. The data decoder optimizes the data decoding and filters out not requested data.
6. Analysis Services merges results from all the partitions into a single `Datacache` object. It aggregates data to the level defined by the request subcube. For example, if the partition has `Date` as a granularity attribute but a user has requested data about sales in January, Analysis Services aggregates the value of all the records that contain days in January into a record that contains aggregated values for the whole month of January. Aggregation can be very simple for regular measure groups and can be complex for measure groups that include a many-to-many dimension or measure with `AggregateFunction DISTINCT_COUNT`. We discuss all these types of aggregations later in this chapter.

Querying Different Types of Measure Groups

Starting from the third phase—Query Organizer—retrieval of data from the partition depends on the partition type and follows different code paths for different types of partitions. In the following sections, we discuss data retrieval from relational online analytical processing (ROLAP) and multidimensional online analytical processing (MOLAP) partitions. In addition, Analysis Services follows different algorithms when it retrieves data from measure groups that have `DISTINCT_COUNT` measures, measure groups that have many-to-many dimensions, and regular measure groups.

Querying Regular Measure Groups

After Analysis Services detects that the request doesn't reference many-to-many dimensions and the measure group doesn't contain a `DISTINCT_COUNT` measure, it creates a Query Measure Group job. During its initialization, Analysis Services iterates over all the partitions, verifies partition slices, and checks whether the subcube of the partition slice intersects with the request subcube, which indicates whether partition contains the requested data. For all partitions that contain requested data, Analysis Services creates Query Partition jobs. If no partition slice was defined and indexes weren't built for this partition, Analysis Services creates Query Partition jobs for all the partitions in a measure group. Figure 30.2 demonstrates the scheme Analysis Services uses to query the partitions of a regular measure group.

When Analysis Services creates a Query Partition job, it detects whether requested data is fact data and stored inside this partition, or it's aggregated data and stored inside of one of the aggregations. Therefore, if server configuration enables aggregations, Analysis Services iterates over available aggregations and checks whether an aggregation contains requested data. The mechanism of data lookup in an aggregation is similar to the mechanism used to retrieve data from the cache registry. (For more information about the cache subsystem, see Chapter 29, "Architecture of Query Execution—Calculating MDX Expressions.")

After Analysis Services detects the part of partition that contains requested data, it uses partition metadata to build a query plan. While building a query plan, Analysis Services makes the following optimizations:

- Analysis Services analyzes attribute relationships and deducts attributes that weren't specified in a subcube slice by related attributes that where specified. For example, if a subcube in a request contains a slice by Seattle, Analysis Services sets a slice on `Washington` and on `US`.

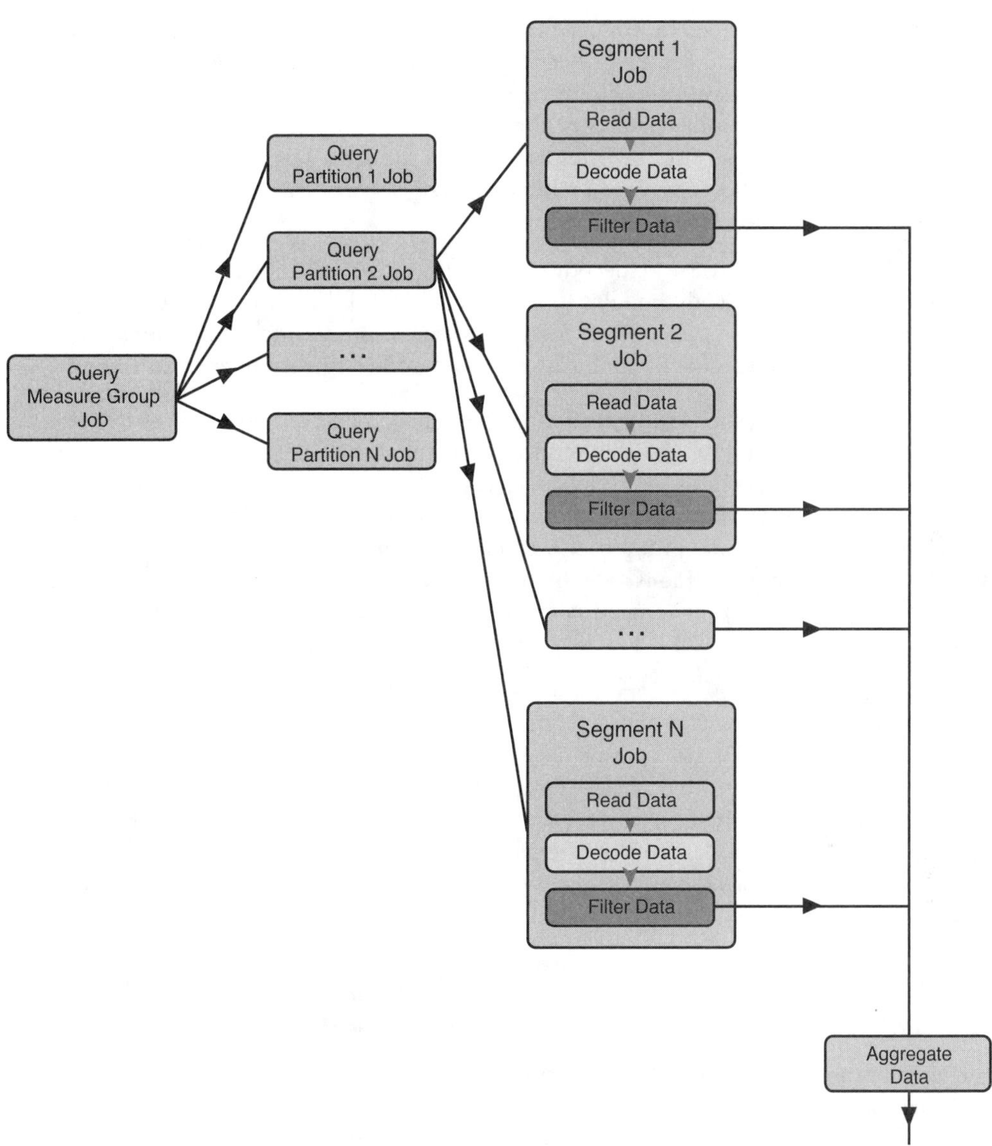

FIGURE 30.2 The scheme Analysis Services uses to query partitions of a regular measure group.

- Analysis Services validates whether partition contains requested data. It uses minimum and maximum values of `DataIDs` that were created during index building. If the `DataIDs` requested in a subcube don't fit into this range, Analysis Services completes the Query Partition job and doesn't scan the current partition for data.
- Analysis Services optimizes the subcube to include only slices for data in the partition. This optimization is typically done for requests that contain a set of slices (this

type of request is called an *OR query*). For example, if a user requests data about customers that live in Seattle or Redmond, the subcube will contain a set with two members: `Seattle` and `Redmond`. If the partition metadata contains information that the current partition has data only about customers that live in Redmond and Bellevue, Analysis Services rewrites the original subcube. The updated subcube will contain a single slice—`Redmond`—which Analysis Services can handle much more efficiently than a slice with a set of members.

- Analysis Services detects the decoding tables that it will use during query execution. It tries to use fewer decoding tables to decode more attributes. Because decoding tables are built using native hierarchies, Analysis Services tries to find native hierarchies with larger number of levels that can help to decode larger number of attributes.

If Analysis Services has successfully initialized the Query Partition job, it references it into a Query Measure Group job. Analysis Services then starts the Query Measure Group job, and Job Coordinator executes multiple Query Partition jobs in parallel. Analysis Services uses the `CoordinatorExecutionMode` server configuration property to define the number of partitions from one measure group that it can query in parallel. By default, the value of the `CoordinatorExecutionMode` is –4, which means 4 multiplied by number of the processors on the machine. If you change this value to 0, Analysis Services will try to run all the jobs in parallel. And if you set it to the positive number, Analysis Services will use it as number of jobs to run in parallel.

Partitions are `MapStore` objects and divided into segments by 64K records. To read data from each segment of a partition, Analysis Services creates a Segment job. However, a partition can contain hundreds of segments, and Analysis Services can't start all this jobs in parallel. You can use the `CoordinatorQueryMaxThreads` server configuration property to configure the number of segments of one partition that Analysis Services queries in parallel. By default, each Analysis Services doesn't start more than 16 Segment jobs per partition simultaneously, and starts more jobs only when one of the running jobs completes.

A Segment job requires a single thread, which Analysis Services retrieves from the thread pool (see Chapter 28, "Thread Pool"). The number of threads in a pool is limited, so the number of started jobs can't exceed the number of available threads in the thread pool.

The large number of jobs executed in parallel can overload the system and lower the server performance, because jobs will compete for resources. This typically happens with a machine that has a large number of CPUs, where by default the number of jobs running in parallel can became really high. If you notice that your system slows down because of a large number of jobs executing at the same time, we recommend lowering the number of partitions or segments queried in parallel.

Another negative effect of this architecture can show up in the system with many users. When a query from one user utilizes all system resources, a query from other users can wait a long time before it gets resources required for execution. To make the system more responsive to queries from multiple users, you can use the server configuration property `CoordinatorQueryBalancingFactor`. When the `CoordinatorQueryBalancingFactor` property is set to a value larger than 0, Analysis Services limits the number of threads used by a single request, and so resources are left for other users' requests. Because this property can negatively affect performance of individual queries, use it with caution.

If bitmap indexes were created for a given segment and attribute, Analysis Services uses indexes to detect which pages of the segment to read. For example, if a query requests data about sales of customers that lived in Redmond in 1998, Analysis Services needs to use indexes of the `City` and `Year` attributes to find pages that contain data. If indexes are not found for the given attributes, Analysis Services must scan all the pages of the segment.

After Analysis Services detects pages that contain data, it reads data from the granularity attribute of the partition or aggregation and decodes data to the granularity defined in the request using the data decoder. Analysis Services creates the data decoder using information about the segment's compression stored in the segment's header. Reading the segment's header, Analysis Services might find out that the current segment doesn't contain the requested data and will then skip this segment.

Analysis Services starts decoding from attributes specified in a slice of requested subcube to filter records by this slice. Among attributes used in a slice, Analysis Services first chooses the attribute with a larger number of members because this attribute has better selectivity. (That is, it has a better chance to filter out a large number of records.) In our example, Analysis Services first decodes the `City` attribute, and skips records that don't contain data for Redmond. Then Analysis Services decodes the `Year` attribute and skips records that don't have information for the year 1998.

In the last phase, Analysis Services aggregates all records that weren't filtered out and passes them to the `MapQuery` object. The `MapQuery` object collects data from all the segments of all the partitions and forms the resulting `Datacache` object.

Querying ROLAP Partitions

ROLAP partitions don't store data; they contain only metadata that Analysis Services uses to generate a query to a relational data source. In the first phase of data retrieval, Analysis Services analyzes the partition slice and detects whether the partition contains the requested data. If the slice matches the request subcube, Analysis Services creates the Query ROLAP Partition job.

Data retrieval from a ROLAP partition during query execution is similar to loading of relational data into a MOLAP partition during partition processing. (For more information about partition processing, see Chapter 21.) But whereas Analysis Services processes the MOLAP partition in three phases—read data, process data, and write data—during a ROLAP query, it skips the third phase: write data. Analysis Services generates a SQL request to the relational source by translating the request subcube into SQL. It translates slices defined in a subcube into a `WHERE` clause of a SQL query and granularity into a `SELECT` clause.

NOTE

Speed of data retrieval from a ROLAP partition depends on the speed of reading data from the relational database. To improve the efficiency of the ROLAP request, we recommend that you review the indexing scheme of your relational database.

Analysis Services sends the generated SQL query to the relational database and reads data into a read data buffer. Then it processes the buffer by converting granularity attribute keys to `DataID` of dimension members and fills a process buffer. Analysis Services doesn't write the content of the process buffer to disk, but passes it to the `MapQuery` object as a result of the Query ROLAP Partition job.

Querying Measure Groups with DISTINCT_COUNT Measures

Analysis Services uses a different algorithm to retrieve data from a measure group that has a `DISTINCT_COUNT` measure than the algorithm it uses to retrieve data from a regular measure group. During processing of the partitions of such a measure group, Analysis Services detects the minimum and maximum unique values of the `DISTINCT_COUNT` measure, which we call the *range of distinct count values for a partition*. For example, if you have a `Unique Customer DISTINCT_COUNT` measure in your measure group, Analysis Services collects the range of distinct count values of customer IDs while processing partitions.

At query time, Analysis Services compiles a list of the partitions in a measure group that contain requested data (similar to the process for a regular measure group). Then it analyzes minimal and maximal distinct values for every partition and looks for partitions that contain an intersection of those ranges. Therefore, in the previous example, if you designed partitions so that the first partition contains all customers with IDs from 1 to 10000 and the second partition contains customers with IDs from 10001 to 20000, the ranges of those two partitions won't intersect, and partitions can be queried independently of each other. If you request the number of unique customers that lived in Redmond in 1998, Analysis Services can get the number of customers from the first partition and the number of customers from the second partition and aggregate them. However, if data stored in the first partition and in the second partition is mixed and both partitions contain customers with IDs from 1 to 20000, the ranges of distinct values of both partitions intersect. Therefore, Analysis Services can't simply aggregate two values. It must scan both partitions, because if records for the customer with ID 9500 exist in both partitions, they should be counted just one time.

While analyzing partitions, Analysis Services groups partitions that have intersecting ranges and creates a list of groups. Partitions from different groups don't have intersected ranges and can be queried independently of each other.

For each group of partitions, Analysis Services creates a `MapQuery` object that will be used to accumulate the result. It creates a Query Range Group job and a Query Partition job for each partition of the group, as shown in Figure 30.3.

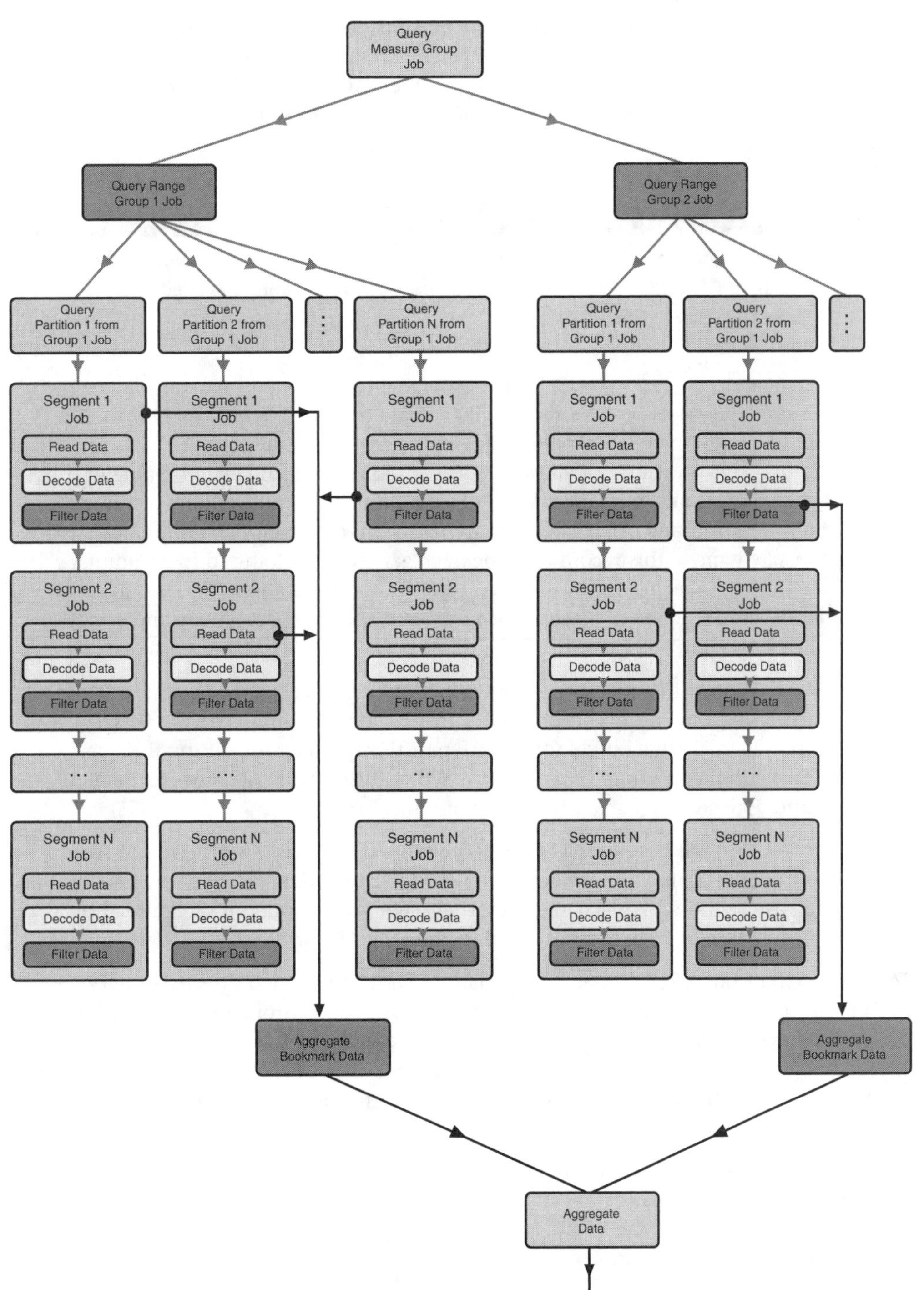

FIGURE 30.3 The scheme Analysis Services uses to query partitions of a measure group that has a `DISTINCT_COUNT` measure.

Analysis Services retrieves data from the partitions inside the range group in parallel. It loads data from each partition into a buffer. Because data in partitions with the DISTINCT_COUNT measure are sorted by distinct values, Analysis Services can easily find the maximal value that was loaded into buffers of all the partitions and put a bookmark on that value in each buffer.

NOTE

You cannot configure the number of partitions to be read in parallel when a measure group contains a DISTINCT_COUNT measure; all partitions that were assigned to a group will be processed in parallel.

In the next stage, Analysis Services moves all the data prior to the bookmark into the aggregate bookmark data buffer. Analysis Services aggregates values for non–DISTINCT_COUNT measures of all the records in this buffer, and assigns value of the DISTINCT_COUNT measures to 1. The new record contains data for a certain customer, which won't appear in any other range group, partition, or buffer. Therefore, Analysis Services can safely move this record into the aggregate data buffer used to accumulate the result from all the range groups. In the aggregate data buffer, Analysis Services aggregates all the records and produces the results for non–DISTINCT_COUNT measures and count of distinct values.

If one of the partitions in a measure group with a DISTINCT_COUNT measures is a ROLAP partition, things become more complicated. During the processing, Analysis Services cannot detect distinct value ranges for ROLAP partitions. Therefore, during the query, Analysis Services builds a group of partition based on distinct value ranges for MOLAP partitions and adds ROLAP partitions to each group.

The Query Partition job generates a SQL query with a WHERE clause restricting distinct values to minimal and maximal values of the group's range. Analysis Services also adds an ORDER BY clause to the SQL query to ensure that records are produced by the relational database in the same order as records saved in the MOLAP partitions.

To retrieve data from a ROLAP partition, Analysis Services uses two threads: one to read from the relational source and the second one to convert data from a relational to multidimensional format. While retrieving data from a measure group that contains a DISTINCT_COUNT measure, Analysis Services simultaneously scans all partitions in a same group, so it won't release ROLAP partition job threads to the thread pool until it completes scanning all data.

To avoid deadlocks, Analysis Services doesn't start a Query Range Group job until it can get all the threads for all partitions in a group. If there are many ROLAP partitions, it can require a considerable number of threads to start execution of the request, and so the number of concurrent requests executed on the system at the same time will decrease.

Querying Remote Partitions and Linked Measure Groups

Two features in Analysis Services enable you to store data on another machine and retrieve it during query execution: remote partitions and linked dimensions and measure groups.

Querying the Remote Partitions

When the storage engine subsystem gets an internal request for data, it analyzes the partitions that contain data. The partition slice of remote partitions is stored on the master server; therefore, Analysis Services can detect whether a remote partition contains requested data without communicating with the remote server.

Then Analysis Services creates a `MapQuery` object and generates an internal XML/A request inside of which it serializes the content of the `MapQuery` object. When the remote server receives such a request, it deserializes the `MapQuery` object and looks up data in the cache. If the cache doesn't contain the requested data, the remote server executes the request following the algorithm used by a master server for local partitions. The remote server creates a `Datacache` object that contains the requested data from all the remote partitions located on that server. It serializes content of the `Datacache` object into an XML/A response and sends it back to the master server.

When the master server receives the response from the remote server, it retrieves the `Datacache` object and passes it to the `MapQuery` object to aggregate with the `Datacache` objects from local partitions and partitions from other remote servers.

NOTE

If your measure group has a `DISTINCT_COUNT` measure, all the partitions in the same distinct value range are scanned simultaneously. If possible, avoid situations in which partitions from the same distinct value range group are located on different server, because this will cause multiple round trips between the master and remote machines. The query execution will be very efficient if you place partitions from a single distinct value range group on the same machine.

Querying Linked Measure Groups

When the storage engine subsystem receives a request for data stored in a linked measure group, it generates an internal XML/A request inside of which it serializes the content of the request subcube. When the publisher server receives the request, it deserializes the request subcube and looks up data in the cache registry. If the cache doesn't contain the requested data, the publisher server executes the request following the algorithm we discussed earlier. The publisher server creates a `Datacache` object that contains requested data from all the partitions in this measure group and serializes it into an XML/A response to the subscriber server.

NOTE

The resulting `Datacache` object is cached in the cache registry of both the publisher and subscriber servers.

Querying Measure Groups with Indirect Dimensions

Analysis Services has to perform a complex algorithm to retrieve data from a measure group that contains an indirect dimension. (For more information about indirect dimensions, see Chapter 8.) A typical example of an indirect dimension is a many-to-many dimension, so we will discuss the algorithm of data retrieval from a measure group that has a many-to-many dimension. Figure 30.4 shows this algorithm.

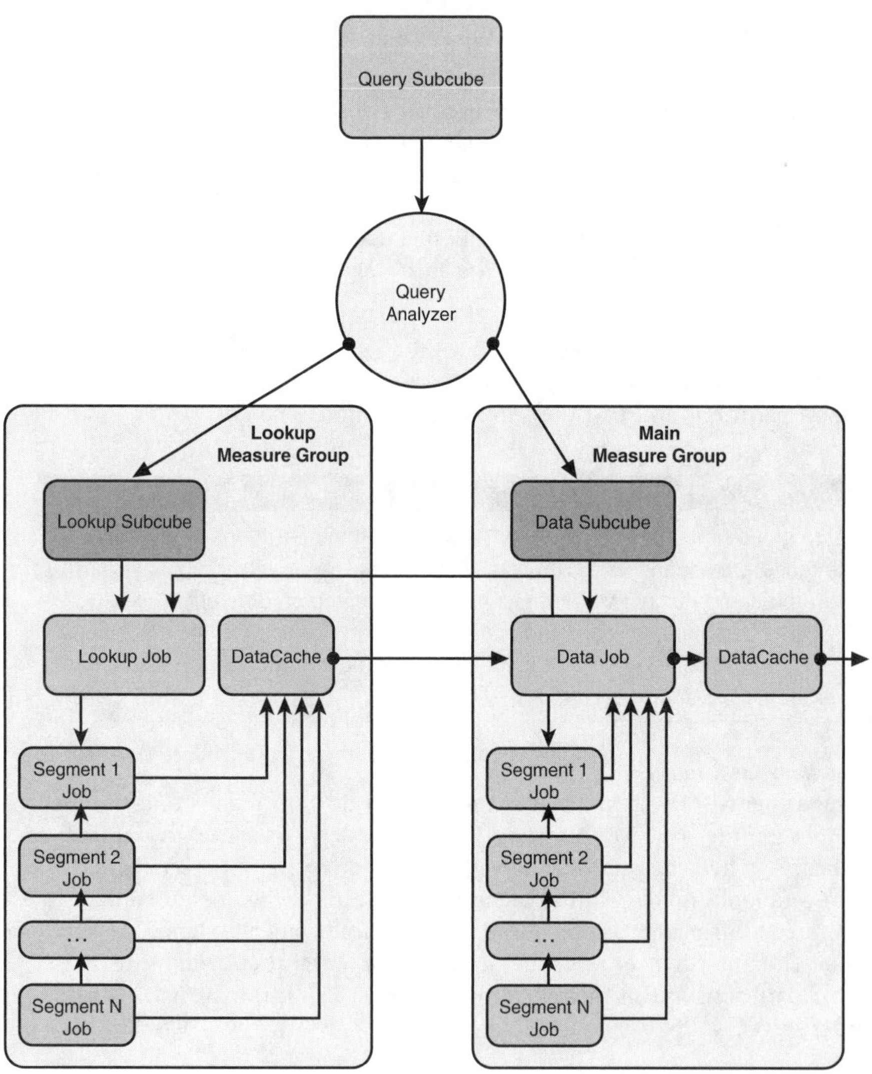

FIGURE 30.4 Algorithm of data retrieval from a measure group with a many-to-many dimension.

First, Analysis Services use the Query Analyzer to analyze the request and divide it in two parts: the request to the main measure group (the measure group that contains a many-to-many dimension) and the request to the lookup measure group (the intermediate measure group), which builds a lookup table used to resolve indirect dimensions.

For example, assume that you have a cube with two measure groups. The main measure group contains information about sales to customers, so it has a `Customer` dimension and a `Sales` measure that contains the amount customers have paid. To analyze sales by demographic groups, your cube has the `Demographic` measure group that contains the `Customers` and `Demographic Group` dimensions. Note that the same customer can belong to a few different demographic groups. When a user sends a query to produce sales by demographic groups, the storage engine subsystem gets a request to the main measure group, `Sales`, with a subcube that has granularity on the `Demographic Group` dimension. This request comes to the Query Analyzer subsystem, which detects that it includes a many-to-many dimension—`Demographic Groups`. Analysis Services breaks this request into two parts: the request to the `Sales` measure group to bring data for sales of all the customers, and the lookup request to the lookup measure group to bring data about the demographic groups of customers.

Analysis Services creates subcubes for both the requests and two jobs: Data and Lookup jobs. It also creates a dependency between the Data job and the Lookup job to make sure that the Data job doesn't start until the Lookup job completes.

Analysis Services then starts the jobs. The Job Coordinator subsystem starts the Lookup job first, and it scans segments of partitions in the intermediate measure group (as discussed earlier in this chapter). Analysis Services collects the result in the `Datacache` object and passes it to the Data job. The `Datacache` object contains two columns: `Customers` and `Demographic Group`.

The Data job uses a lookup `Datacache` to build a table that it will use to look up a list of all the demographic groups for each customer. Then, Analysis Services scans data of the main measure group, and creates the `Datacache` objects for each partition's segment, which has two columns: `Customers` and `Sales`. The Data job creates a new `Datacache` object with two columns: `Demographic Groups` and `Sales`. For each customer in the `Datacaches`, it looks up a record in the lookup `Datacache`, and then generates a record with the `DataID` of the demographic group that corresponds to the current customer and sales of that customer. If a customer belongs to multiple demographic groups, Analysis Services creates a new record for each demographic group for this customer. In the next phase, Analysis Services aggregates data from every segment into the resulting `Datacache`. After all the segments produce data, the `Datacache` contains the result.

If your cube contains a large number of sales transactions, your measure group could potentially contain hundreds of millions of records. However, if the number of customers is not very large and there are just a few demographic groups, this scheme works efficiently and scales well for a large number of sales. However, if the number of customers and the number of demographic groups grows, you may encounter performance problems because the lookup `Datacache` can become very large and will take a lot of memory (or might even not fit into memory). Therefore, we recommend that you avoid using large measure groups as an intermediate measure group for many-to-many dimensions.

The result of our example contains the sales for every demographic group. However, if you aggregate all the sales for all the demographic groups, you will get a total of sales greater than the total sales to all the customers. This happens because a customer can belong to multiple demographic groups, and sales by such a customer will be aggregated into all demographic groups he belongs to. Therefore, the result of a query to the measure group with the many-to-many dimension is not really aggregatable.

PART VII

Accessing Data in Analysis Services

IN THIS PART

CHAPTER 31

Client/Server Architecture and Data Access

IN THIS CHAPTER

Analysis Services supports several types of data access architectures. The most straightforward architecture is made up of a client and a server, generally located on distinct computers, communicating directly with each other. If you want to communicate via the Internet, we need to introduce a middleware component, Internet Information Services (IIS), which serves as a bridge between the client and the server. Analysis Services also supports an offline scenario, in which you browse your data within a *local cube*; this architecture combines the client and server on the same computer and inside the same process.

Using TCP/IP for Data Access

When both the client and the server are located within the same domain, connections to Analysis Services are usually made through TCP/IP. In this case, messages traverse a four-layer protocol stack (see Figure 31.1):

- Internet Protocol (IP) is responsible for addressing and defining the route from one computer to another.
- Transmission Control Protocol (TCP) is used for transferring blocks of data that don't bear semantic loading.
- Simple Object Access Protocol (SOAP) is a lightweight protocol that uses an Extensible Markup Language (XML) messaging framework to transfer information between applications.

- XML for Analysis (XML/A) defines methods of access to multidimensional data and online analytical processing (OLAP) metadata.

NOTE

Analysis Services supports both IPv4 and IPv6. The default is IPv4, but you can change the configuration of your server to use IPv6 or to use both IPv4 and IPv6.

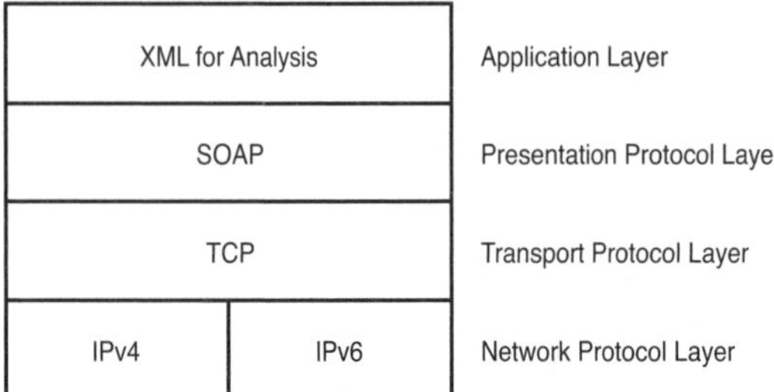

FIGURE 31.1 The protocol stack.

SOAP defines an XML-based format for the exchange of messages between applications. The SOAP specification defines a standard way of invoking objects, rules for defining and transferring data types, and methods of handling errors. This messaging framework is highly extensible and is independent of implementation-specific semantics such as the programming model. SOAP version 1.1 can use any transport protocol, including TCP, to transfer its messages and attachments.

Proposed by Microsoft and Hyperion Solutions, XML/A is an open standard for communication between an OLAP server and client applications. It is built on top of SOAP to transfer data, including multidimensional data, between a client and a server.

Using Binary XML and Compression for Data Access

XML/A and SOAP are standard text-based protocols that significantly simplify implementation of both client and server message exchange. However, you might have to pay for this simplification with a performance hit because of the workload needed to transfer and decode the text messages. Analysis Services deals with this problem by transferring some of the data in binary format and compressing the data before it goes through the wire. Clients can transfer information to the server and vice versa in three modes:

- **Text format**—Plain text requests and responses using XML/A and SOAP protocols.
- **Binary format**—Tags of XML elements and attributes are encoded in binary format; numeric values are not converted to strings but are transferred as is over the wire. This solves a number of problems: Content going over the wire is less verbose; parsing of XML is easier and faster; and most important, the precision of numeric

values, especially those in `double` and `float` data types, is not lost through conversion to strings.

- **Compressed format**—Contents of request and response are compressed using a proprietary compression algorithm.

The binary and compressed formats are proprietary formats. Therefore, only the libraries shipped with Analysis Services can use those formats to communicate with a server.

The OLE DB provider shipped with Analysis Services supports data exchange in both binary and compressed formats. ADOMD.NET *(ActiveX Data Objects Multidimensional)* and AMO *(Analysis Management Objects)* can generate requests only in text format or compressed formats, but they can receive data in binary and compressed format, and in text format. Because requests sent by ADOMD.NET are usually small, you won't notice any degradation in performance (comparing to OLEDB) with ADOMD.NET. It's possible in future versions of Analysis Services that AMO will be optimized to take advantage of the binary format when it sends requests to the server.

When it establishes a connection to the server, a client component negotiates with the server to determine which format of the protocol can be used during communication. Before that negotiation, the client application doesn't have information about which formats the server supports. In the first request, the client specifies the format of the request and the format of the response it supports, and the server responds with the best available formats.

By default, the OLEDB provider requests that both request and response are in binary and compressed format; AMO and ADOMD.NET specify that the request format is text and compressed and the response format is binary and compressed. By default, the server supports all of these formats. You can configure (on both the client and the server) the format in which the client communicates with the server. On the client, you use the `Protocol Format` and `Transport Compression` properties to manipulate those settings; on the server, you use the `EnableBinaryXML` and `EnableCompression` configuration properties to allow or disallow certain formats.

Using HTTP for Data Access

Analysis Services uses Windows NT integrated security to authenticate all incoming TCP/IP requests and listens on a port that can be hidden behind a firewall. Therefore, it is generally not possible to use a TCP/IP connection to establish a connection to a server in another domain or outside of your network. You can do this, however, with HTTP/HTTPS supported by Microsoft Analysis Services.

Using HTTP/HTTPS for accessing data in Analysis Services has one more advantage: It allows full decoupling of client and server. Because HTTP, SOAP, and XML/A are standard, well-documented protocols, the client components can be implemented independent of the server.

Analysis Services uses Microsoft IIS as a middleware component to enable access to data via HTTP. The process of data exchange between client and the server (and illustrated in Figure 31.2) is as follows:

1. The client sends an HTTP POST request to IIS using the IIS server name and the path to a service component known as the pump (binary name `msmdpump.dll`) as the URL.
2. IIS receives the request, authenticates the sender, and creates a security context in which the code in the pump will be executed.
3. IIS starts the pump and uses the Internet Server API (ISAPI) to communicate with it.
4. The pump connects to Analysis Services via TCP/IP and sends the data received from the client without any changes.

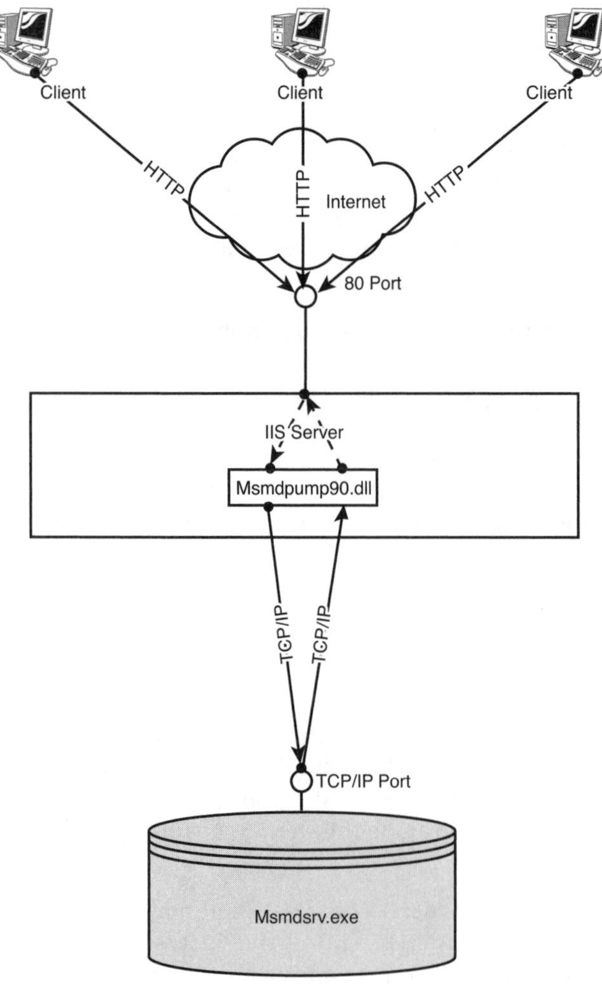

FIGURE 31.2 The diagram shows the process of the client working with the server over the Internet.

5. Analysis Services executes the request and sends a response to the pump, which passes the response to the client.

Analysis Services allows configurations where IIS and Analysis Services run on different computers. But when the system is configured this way and you're using integrated Windows authentication with IIS, you should take into consideration that, by default, the Windows operating system doesn't allow delegation. (That is, when a server impersonates a client, it can access resources only on the local computer.)

If you want to run the client, IIS, and Analysis Services on separate computers, and you want to use integrated Windows authentication, you have to configure the system to use Kerberos authentication and configure the domain to allow delegation.

When you use the HTTP and HTTPS protocols from client libraries that are shipped with Analysis Services, the content of the requests and responses can be sent in binary and compressed format similar to those used by the TCP/IP protocol.

Offline Access to Data

The data access scenarios outlined in earlier sections assume that a direct—or indirect—connection can be established between the server and client. This is not always possible. Your users might need to access data when they are disconnected from the local network or from the Internet (for example, when they're on an airplane or otherwise unable to connect).

In such situations, you can use a local cube. A local cube is usually a snapshot of server data, which can be saved as a file on a laptop or desktop computer. The cube file is created while the connection to Analysis Services or another source of data, such as SQL Server, is live. The cube can contain a portion of the data in the original data source or, space allowing, all the data.

NOTE

You can't use SQL Server Management Studio or Business Intelligence Development Studio to create a local cube, but you can use Microsoft Office or some other third-party tool.

The local cube then becomes the data source for the client component. This arrangement makes it possible for the user to browse the data offline—while on the plane—or to send it to customers or management via email. The user can't, however, change the data in the local cube. In addition, local cubes have certain performance and functional limitations compared to server cubes. Figure 31.3 shows the components that make it possible to work with local cube files.

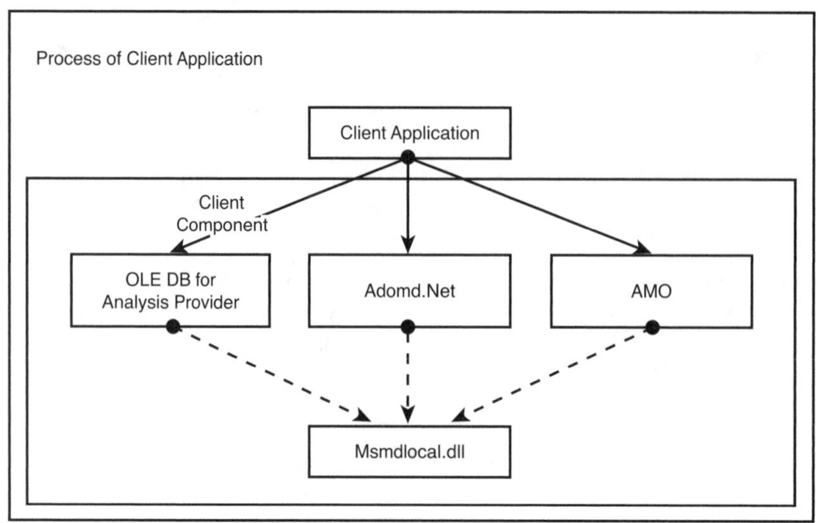

FIGURE 31.3 Components that can be used to work with local cubes.

When you browse the data stored in a local file, you use the same client application requests that you would use if you were connected to an instance of Analysis Server.

Client Components Shipped with Analysis Services

Microsoft SQL Server Analysis Services supports various methods of building client application to access data stored on a server. You can build your client application with client components shipped with SQL Server, or you can use XML for Analysis (XML/A) to create your own components and use HTTP to connect to the server.

When you're considering the right component to use in the application you're writing, ask yourself the following questions:

- Is it possible to install the additional components on all the client computers?
- Do all the client computers run on the Windows operating system?
- Will my application be used to analyze data or to administer Analysis Services?
- Will I write my application in native or managed code?

Depending on the answers to these questions, you can choose the component or technology that best suits your business needs.

Using XML for Analysis to Build Your Application

Because XML/A is an open standard and the HTTP protocol is well documented, the client application doesn't need any additional components. To build your client application, you can choose from a large number of existing tools that create and parse XML documents (for example, the .NET Framework and MSXML). Figure 31.4 shows an illustration of the creation and processing of XML/A requests and responses.

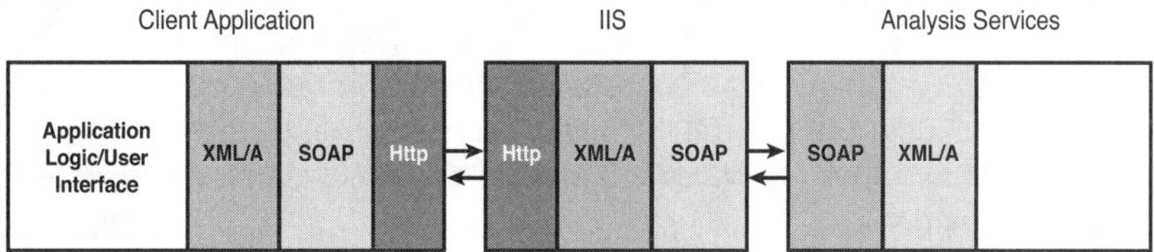

FIGURE 31.4 Processing of XML/A requests.

The client application generates an XML stream, which represents an XML/A request wrapped in a SOAP envelope. It then sends the message to the IIS server via HTTP. IIS parses the HTTP headers and passes the rest to Analysis Services, which parses the XML/A request wrapped in the SOAP envelope. Analysis Services makes the calculations and generates an XML/A response, also wrapped in a SOAP envelope. IIS adds the HTTP headers and sends the response back to the client. In your application, you can use any generic tool to work with HTTP and parse SOAP and XML responses, or you can write your own.

With this approach to data access, you don't need to install a special component on the client computer, and you don't need to worry about which operating system or hardware the client uses. However, you might lose a bit in performance because you have the extra step of passing data through HTTP.

Using Analysis Services Libraries to Build Your Application

Analysis Services ships with four libraries that you can use to build your client applications. Using these libraries, you can recover the performance loss you get with HTTP and XML/A. You also gain some benefits from optimizations built in to the libraries. As long as you can install the library on the client computer, and you know that your applications will be operating in a Windows environment, one of these four libraries is likely to be the best choice for you.

If you're creating an analytical application, you can use the Analysis Services OLE DB provider or ADOMD.NET. For an application written in native code, use the Analysis Services OLE DB provider; for writing a new application in managed code, use ADOMD.NET.

In most cases, if your application is intended for the administration of Analysis Services, you use AMO. Use the DSO (Decision Support Objects) library only when you have to maintain a legacy Analysis Services 2000 system and have to manage legacy cubes migrated from Analysis Services 2000. Table 31.1 shows which library works best for each purpose.

TABLE 31.1 Libraries Delivered with Analysis Services

	Native Code	Managed Code
Query Management	OLE DB for OLAP/ADOMD/ADO	ADOMD.NET
Administration	DSO	AMO

Query Management for Applications Written in Native Code

As with earlier versions of Analysis Services, you can access data by using the interfaces of OLE DB. OLE DB is a collection of standard interfaces, based on COM, that make it possible for client applications to access data from various data sources. OLE DB for OLAP was released in 1997, and is based on OLE DB, but is designed specifically for access to multidimensional data. OLE DB for Data Mining (OLE DB DM), an extension to the existing standard, was released in 2000. Analysis Services supports all three, collectively known as Analysis Services OLE DB provider.

The OLE DB provider is the optimal way of connecting to Analysis Services from client applications written in native code. A disadvantage of OLE DB, other than that it is pretty complex, is that you can't use OLE DB interfaces in certain applications, such as those written in Visual Basic and scripting languages, such as VBScript, JScript, and other languages that use automation.

Visual Basic works only with classes that implement the `IDispatch` interface; OLE DB classes implement the `IUnknown` interface. If you want to write your application in Visual Basic or another language that supports automation, you need another layer above the OLE DB provider: ADO or ADOMD. These layers accept calls from client applications and delegate them to OLE DB or Analysis Services OLE DB, which in turn communicates directly with the data source.

This way of accessing data stored in Analysis Services is not new, but it makes it possible for the majority of applications existing today to work. Figure 31.5 shows how ADO and ADOMD work with the providers.

Query Management for Applications Written in Managed Code

In developing the .NET Framework technology, Microsoft updated its approach to data access technology with ADO.NET, not only adding the capability to work with managed code, but also reviewing the architecture and principles of data access. ADO is a layer above OLE DB providers, delegating all calls to OLE DB. With ADO.NET, Microsoft introduced the concept of the ADO.NET provider—a managed assembly that implements the standard interfaces defined by ADO.NET, allowing you to work with data stored in a specific database.

Microsoft has released three ADO.NET providers with the .NET Framework: `SqlClient`, `OracleClient`, and `OledbClient`. The first two providers enable your application to work with data stored in SQL Server and Oracle databases, respectively. The third provider is a logical continuation of ADO and enables your application to work with existing OLE DB providers.

ADO.NET providers are written for working with a specific data source, and are the most efficient means for working with that database. If there is a specific provider for the data source you're working with, we recommend that you use it instead of the more universal `OledbClient`.

If you are writing your application in managed code, we advise you to use ADOMD.NET to access data stored on Analysis Server. ADOMD.NET is not a layer above the OLE DB

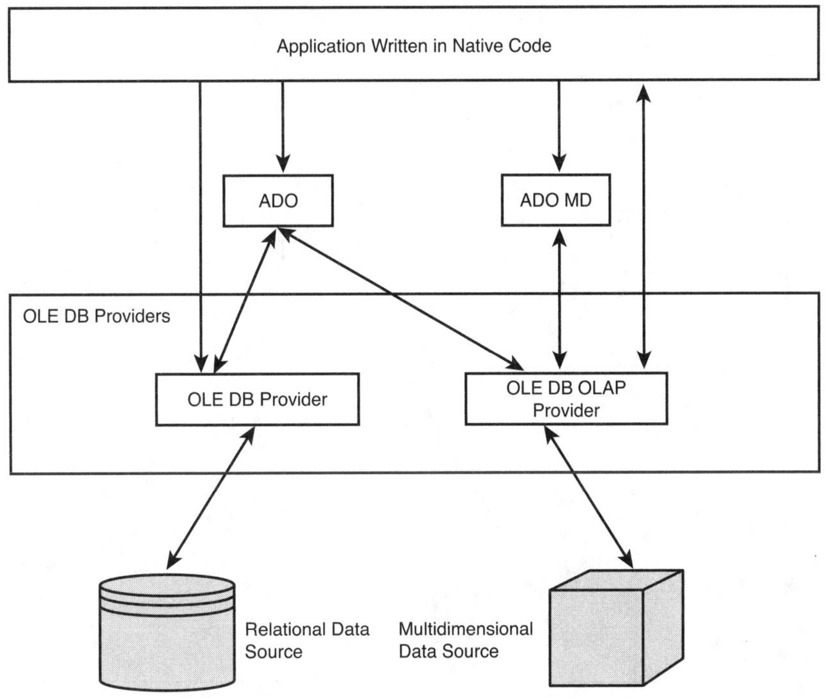

FIGURE 31.5 Access to data using OLE DB and ADO technologies.

provider, but communicates directly with Analysis Server. Figure 31.6 shows ADOMD.NET in the general picture of data access technologies from managed applications.

Using DSO and AMO for Administrative Applications

You can use the DSO library to maintain already existing applications. This library delegates all requests to a library specifically intended for administering Microsoft SQL Server Analysis Services: AMO. AMO is written in managed code and is intended for use with applications written in managed code, but it can be used from native code, too. Figure 31.7 shows how applications written in managed code and those written in native code use these libraries.

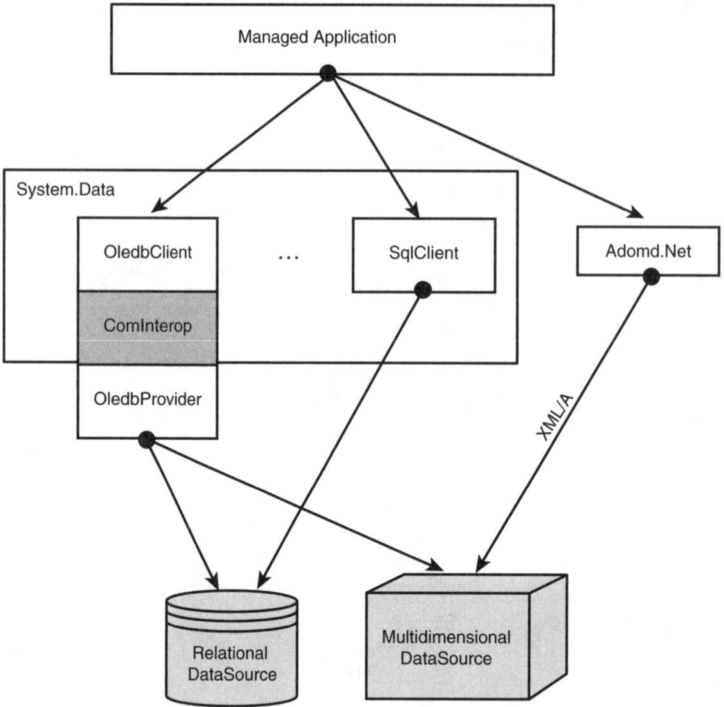

FIGURE 31.6 The diagram of the data access components that can be used from an application written in managed code.

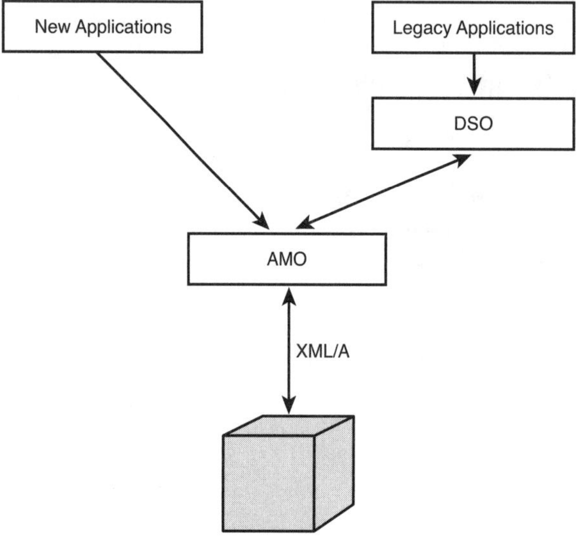

FIGURE 31.7 Components for administering Analysis Services.

CHAPTER 32

XML for Analysis

IN THIS CHAPTER

- State Management
- XML/A Methods
- Handling Errors and Warnings

XML for Analysis (XML/A) is a standard protocol for access to multidimensional data. It enables any client applications access to any multidimensional database that supports XML/A.

XML/A was designed as a web-based data access standard. It was intended to serve as "glue" between applications and distributed multidimensional data sources over the web and enterprise networks. In Analysis Services 2005, the role of XML/A was extended from web access to that of a standard protocol enabling data access to Analysis Services. (You can find the XML/A specification at http://www.xmla.org.)

XML/A derives much of its underlying foundation from the OLE DB standard. For example, all the schema rowsets defined by OLE DB and the OLE DB for OLAP specification are supported by XML/A. The properties are similar, but in the transition from OLE DB to XML/A, significant changes had to be made to fit into a web-based, stateless world.

XML/A defines a standard XML format for messages and the representation of multidimensional data types. It uses XML and Simple Object Access Protocol (SOAP) to generate messages and process the results. SOAP, originally based on Hypertext Transfer Protocol (HTTP), defines a format based on XML for the exchange of messages between applications. It replaces such protocols as Remote Procedure Call (RPC), Common Object Request Broker Architecture (CORBA), and Distributed Component Object Model (DCOM), which are not suitable for the exchange of information via the Internet. Version 1.1 of SOAP can use other transport protocols, such as Transport Control Protocol (TCP). SOAP defines the format of requests, whereas XML/A defines the messages needed for access to data.

State Management

XML/A was initially intended for use with the HTTP protocol. By definition, HTTP is stateless; it does not save the state between requests. Therefore, one of the main goals for the designers of XML/A was to provide a way for a client application to work within the boundaries of a single request without being dependent on information created by another request.

The XML/A designers reviewed the OLE DB interfaces and found that the information that is usually shared between requests is the `DataSource` and `Session` properties that were specified by the client application when the `DataSource` and `Session` objects were created and used by the OLE DB provider during execution of queries.

So, they decided to allow a client application to specify the properties needed to execute a specific request as part of the request itself instead of specifying them once when `DataSource` or `Session` objects are created and saving them on the server. Each XML/A method has a `Properties` parameter that contains a list of the properties that affect the execution of that request. The following example shows what the `Property` parameter of an XML/A method looks like in XML format:

```
<Properties>
    <PropertyList>
        <Catalog>Foodmart 2008</Catalog>
        <Timeout>10000</Timeout>
    </PropertyList>
</Properties>
```

Because a client application usually doesn't specify very many properties, it doesn't have a big impact on the size of the request and, therefore, on performance. However, some of the Analysis Services functionality requires that a larger amount of data be saved on the server.

For example, the What-If Analysis feature can temporarily change the data on Analysis Services and enables you to query this changed data with another request (see Chapter 16, "Writing Data into Analysis Services"). Another example of saving large objects on the server is the creation of temporary calculated members that are available to other requests from the same user (see Chapter 12, "Cube-Based MDX Calculations"). To enable saving information between the requests, XML/A provides sessions.

XML/A enables you to associate group of requests with a session. Analysis Services assigns each session a unique identifier, and all subsequent requests use this identifier to get access to data stored on the session. Although support for sessions is not mandatory for an XML/A provider, Analysis Services does support sessions. It implements sessions by providing a `Session` object (see Chapter 26, "Server Architecture and Command Execution," and Chapter 29, "Architecture of Query Execution—Calculating MDX Expressions"). The data shared by requests is stored in the `Session` object. In our first example—the What-If Analysis—the changed data is stored in the `Session` object, and the original data is not overwritten. In our second example, the temporary calculated members created by the client application are stored in the `Session` object and available to Multidimensional Expressions (MDX) requests sent by the same client.

To work with sessions requests in XML/A, use the SOAP headers `Begin Session`, `Session`, and `End Session`. A client application that initiates a session sends its request with the header `Begin Session`:

```
<Header>
    <BeginSession mustUnderstand="1" xmlns="urn:schemas-microsoft-com: xml-analysis" />
</Header>
```

Analysis Services creates a `Session` object, and assigns it a unique identifier, which is returned to the client in the header of the response:

```
<Header>
    <Session SessionId="CB3D45DF-E576-4943-9047-B63AA7EA3EB4" />
</Header>
```

Subsequent requests can pass this identifier to the server in a header `Session` so that they can use the information stored in the `Session` object:

```
<Header>
    <XA:Session mustUnderstand="1" SessionId="CB3D45DF-E576-4943-9047-
➥B63AA7EA3EB4" xmlns:XA="urn:schemas-microsoft-com:xml-analysis" />
</Header>
```

After the client application completes its work with the session, it sends a request for termination of the session using the header `End Session`. At that point, the saved information in the `Sessions` object is deleted, and no longer available to requests:

```
<Header>
    <XA:EndSession mustUnderstand="1" SessionId="CB3D45DF-E576-4943-9047-
➥B63AA7EA3EB4" xmlns:XA="urn:schemas-microsoft-com: xml-analysis" />
</Header>
```

If a session contains a large amount of data, the server can easily run out of memory unless the server can control the session's lifetime. The XML/A specification recommends that the client application be prepared for a session to end on the server at any moment and to have a mechanism in place to reconnect and reestablish its work. Analysis Services has a mechanism for control over sessions: Session Manager, which deletes sessions in the background when certain conditions are met.

To understand how Session Manager works, you need to understand the relationship between connections and sessions (see Figure 32.1). Theoretically, there is a many-to-many relationship between connections opened to Analysis Services and sessions created on the server by client applications. Therefore, a user can work with multiple sessions through one established connection, and client applications can use multiple connections to work with a single session. In practice, however, only connections opened by single user (a user with the same credentials) can be used to work with a single session.

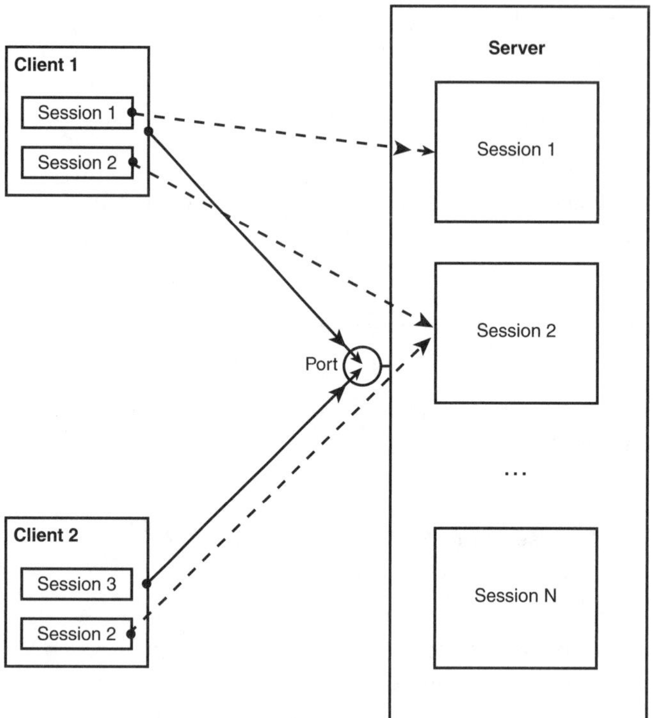

FIGURE 32.1 The relationships between connections and sessions.

When a session is not closed by a client application for a long time, Analysis Services can end it. Session Manager can end a session in the following cases:

- When the last connection that was using a session is closed and the time specified by the `IdleOrphanSessionTimeout` server configuration property elapses.
- When no client application has used the session for the time specified in the `MaxIdleSessionTimeout` session configuration property.
- When the connection is not used during time specified by the `IdleConnectionTimeout` configuration property, the server ends the connection. Because the session won't have any connections associated with it, it will be deleted after the time specified in `IdleOrphanSessionTimeout` expires.
- If the server is overloaded, and Memory Manager determines that it is necessary to free some resources, and the session was not used in the time specified by the `MinIdleSessionTimeout` configuration property.

- If the session contains information that is no longer valid. This could be the case when calculated members or calculated cells are created in the cube by the user, and the cube has undergone serious structural changes. For example, a structural change such as the deletion of a dimension used in the calculation stored in the session would trigger termination of the session.

XML/A Methods

XML/A defines two methods: `Discover`, which retrieves metadata from the server; and `Execute`, which causes the server to perform some command.

The Discover Method

The `Discover` method enables the client application to read metadata that contains necessary information about the XML/A provider. For example, that metadata might contain a list of accessible sources of data, a list of properties supported by the XML/A provider, the keywords that the provider recognizes, or a list of all the databases accessible to the client.

The following is the signature for the `Discover` method:

```
Discover (in RequestType as EnumString,
in Restrictions as Array,
in Propertiesas Array,
out Resultset as Rowset)
```

The result of a `Discover` request is an XML document in `Rowset` format. The `Discover` method supports the following parameters.

RequestType

Use the `RequestType` parameter to specify the information returned by the `Discover` method.

The XML/A specification defines six `Discover` request types. (See the XML/A specification for a complete list of request types.) In addition, the XML/A provider supports all schema rowsets defined by the OLE DB for OLAP and the OLE DB for data-mining specifications. Analysis Services defines additional provider-specific `Discover` request types.

This parameter is very similar to its counterpart in OLE DB, but there are some differences. For the OLE DB method `GetSchemaRowset`, the `RequestType` is of data type GUID; for XML/A, it is a string that contains the name of the request type rather than its GUID.

Restrictions

Use the `Restrictions` parameter to limit the information returned by `Discover`. You can construct a collection of restrictions and pass it to the server in an XML/A request.

With the `Restrictions` parameter in OLE DB, the list of restrictions is indexed; in XML/A, you can use keywords to list the restrictions in any order. This greater flexibility can simplify the creation of requests.

Properties

The Properties parameter is an array of properties defined by the XML/A specification, by OLE DB, or by the XML/A provider. These properties are transferred in a request to reduce the need to store state on the Internet. The Properties parameter acts the same in XML/A as it does in OLE DB. OLE DB stores parameters on the server for use in requests, whereas XML/A sends the parameters with each request.

The following example is a request the client sends to the server to request a list of all the cubes in a certain database.

First generate a SOAP *envelope*—the XML element that any SOAP message starts with:

```
<Envelope xmlns = "http://schemas.xmlsoap.org/soap/envelope/">
```

Next create the body of the SOAP message:

```
<Body>
```

Then the Discover method of XML/A:

```
<Discover xmlns = "urn:schemas-microsoft-com:xml-analysis">
```

Define the parameter, RequestType, which requests a list of cubes from the XML/A provider:

```
<RequestType>MDSCHEMA_CUBES</RequestType>
```

Limit the request to cubes with the name Warehouse and Sales in the FoodMart 2008 database:

```
<Restrictions>
        <RestrictionList>
            <CATALOG_NAME>Foodmart 2008</CATALOG_NAME>
            <CUBE_NAME>Warehouse and Sales</CUBE_NAME>
        </RestrictionList>
</Restrictions>
```

Create a collection of properties, specifying the database that the request will be sent to and a time interval after which the request will be stopped if it is not completed:

```
            <Properties>
                <PropertyList>
                    <Catalog>Foodmart 2008</Catalog>
                        <Timeout>10000</Timeout>
                </PropertyList>
            </Properties>
        </Discover>
    </Body>
</Envelope>
```

The result of this request is a rowset in XML format. It consists of two parts: the schema and the data. The schema contains information about the columns in the rowset—their names and data types. The schema plays the same role as the `GetColumnInfo` call in OLE DB. The client application uses the schema to prepare the necessary structures for storing/displaying the data returned in the XML document. The data in the returned XML document contains values for each field in the rowset.

The returned XML document, like the request, contains a SOAP envelope and a body:

```
<soap:Envelope xmlns:soap ="http://schemas.xmlsoap.org/soap/envelope/">
        <soap:Body>
```

Next is an XML element with the name of the method that produced the result—`DiscoverResponse`—with a namespace attribute:

```
<DiscoverResponse xmlns = "urn:schemas-microsoft-com:xml-analysis">
<return>
```

The namespace attribute of the next element specifies that the response is a rowset, defined by the XML/A specification:

```
                    <root xmlns = "urn:schemas-microsoft-com:xml-
➥analysis:rowset"xmlns:xsi = "http://www.w3.org/2001/XMLSchema-instance" xmlns:xsd =
➥"http://www.w3.org/2001/XMLSchema">
```

Then the XML schema:

```
                    <root xmlns = "urn:schemas-microsoft-com:xml-analysis:rowset"
➥xmlns:xsi = "http://www.w3.org/2001/XMLSchema-instance"xmlns:xsd =
➥"http://www.w3.org/2001/XMLSchema">
                         <xsd:schema targetNamespace = "urn:schemas-microsoft-
➥com:xml-analysis:rowset" xmlns:sql = "urn:schemas-microsoft-com:xml-sql"
➥elementFormDefault = "qualified">
                              <xsd:element name = "root">
                                   <xsd:complexType>
                                        <xsd:sequence minOccurs = "0" maxOccurs=
➥"unbounded">
                                             <xsd:element name = "row" type = "row"/>
                                        </xsd:sequence>
                                   </xsd:complexType>
                              </xsd:element>
                              <xsd:simpleType name = "uuid">
                                   <xsd:restriction base = "xsd:string">
                                        <xsd:pattern value = " [0-9a-zA-Z] {8} -
➥[0-9a-zA-Z] {4} - [0-9a-zA-Z] {4} - [0-9a-zA-Z] {4} - [0-9a-zA-Z] {12} "/>
```

```
                                    </xsd:restriction>
                                </xsd:simpleType>
    <xsd:sequence>
```

The name and type attributes return the name of the column and the type of data it contains. The returned rowset could contain two or more columns with the same name. However, XML cannot have two elements with the same name. To enable the client application to distinguish between columns with the same name, sql:field contains attributes with unique names, and name contains a name that can be shown the client. The following shows the use of these attributes to distinguish columns in our example:

```
        <xsd:element sql:field = "CATALOG_NAME" name = "CATALOG_NAME" type =
➥"xsd:string"/>
        <xsd:element sql:field = "SCHEMA_NAME" name = "SCHEMA_NAME" type =
➥"xsd:string" minOccurs = "0"/>
        <xsd:element sql:field = "CUBE_NAME" name = "CUBE_NAME" type =
➥"xsd:string" minOccurs = "0"/>
        <xsd:element sql:field = "CUBE_TYPE" name = "CUBE_TYPE" type =
➥"xsd:string" minOccurs = "0"/>
        <xsd:element sql:field = "CUBE_GUID" name = "CUBE_GUID" type = "uuid"
➥minOccurs = "0"/>
        <xsd:element sql:field = "CREATED_ON" name = "CREATED_ON" type =
➥"xsd:dateTime" minOccurs = "0"/>
        <xsd:element sql:field = "LAST_SCHEMA_UPDATE" name = "LAST_SCHEMA_UPDATE"
➥type = "xsd:dateTime" minOccurs = "0"/>
        <xsd:element sql:field = "SCHEMA_UPDATED_BY" name = "SCHEMA_UPDATED_BY"
➥type = "xsd:string" minOccurs = "0"/>
        <xsd:element sql:field = "LAST_DATA_UPDATE" name = "LAST_DATA_UPDATE"
➥type = "xsd:dateTime" minOccurs = "0"/>
        <xsd:element sql:field = "DATA_UPDATED_BY" name = "DATA_UPDATED_BY" type
➥= "xsd:string" minOccurs = "0"/>
        <xsd:element sql:field = "DESCRIPTION" name = "DESCRIPTION" type =
➥"xsd:string" minOccurs = "0"/>
        <xsd:element sql:field = "IS_DRILLTHROUGH_ENABLED" name =
➥"IS_DRILLTHROUGH_ENABLED" type = "xsd:boolean" minOccurs = "0"/>
        <xsd:element sql:field = "IS_LINKABLE" name = "IS_LINKABLE" type =
➥"xsd:boolean" minOccurs = "0"/>
        <xsd:element sql:field = "IS_WRITE_ENABLED" name = "IS_WRITE_ENABLED"
➥type = "xsd:boolean" minOccurs = "0"/>
        <xsd:element sql:field = "IS_SQL_ENABLED" name = "IS_SQL_ENABLED" type =
➥"xsd:boolean" minOccurs = "0"/>
        <xsd:element sql:field = "CUBE_CAPTION" name = "CUBE_CAPTION" type =
➥"xsd:string" minOccurs = "0"/>
<xsd:element sql:field="BASE_CUBE_NAME" name="BASE_CUBE_NAME" type="xsd:string"
➥minOccurs="0" />
```

```
        <xsd:element sql:field = "SOURCE_CUBE" name = "xsd:unsignedShort" type =
➥"xsd:string" minOccurs = "0"/>
    </xsd:sequence>
</xsd:complexType>
```

The returned data follows the schema. In our example, the client application receives the following:

```
<row>
    <CATALOG_NAME>Foodmart 2008</CATALOG_NAME>
    <CUBE_NAME>Warehouse and Sales</CUBE_NAME>
    <CUBE_TYPE>CUBE</CUBE_TYPE>
    <LAST_SCHEMA_UPDATE>2004-10-07T16:14:21</LAST_SCHEMA_UPDATE>
    <LAST_DATA_UPDATE>2004-10-07T16:14:35</LAST_DATA_UPDATE>
    <DESCRIPTION/>
    <IS_DRILLTHROUGH_ENABLED>true</IS_DRILLTHROUGH_ENABLED>
    <IS_LINKABLE>false</IS_LINKABLE>
    <IS_WRITE_ENABLED>false</IS_WRITE_ENABLED>
    <IS_SQL_ENABLED>true</IS_SQL_ENABLED>
    <CUBE_CAPTION>Warehouse and Sales</CUBE_CAPTION>
    <SOURCE_CUBE>1</SOURCE_CUBE>
</row>
```

Each line begins with a row element and is followed by a list of rowset columns with their corresponding values. If the value of an element equals `NULL`, the XML/A provider can serialize the empty element or simply skip it. Currently, Analysis Server always skips the empty elements in columns that are empty for all rows, but serializes an empty element if the value of that element is empty only in the current row. In the preceding example, `SCHEMA_NAME` is skipped, but the `<DESCRIPTION/>` element is present but empty.

The Execute Method

The `Execute` method enables the client application to send to the server a command that will result in some action; for example, to execute an MDX query or create a database on the server.

The following is the signature for the `Execute` method:

```
Execute (IN  Command as String,
             Properties as Array,
             OUT     Resultset as Resultset)
```

The result of the `Execute` method is an XML document, which can contain one of three data types: `Rowset`, `MDDataset`, and an empty result. The `MDDataset` format was specifically designed for defining multidimensional data. It resembles the `IMDDataset` interface defined by the OLE DB for OLAP specification.

The type of the result depends on the `Command` parameter and the content of the `Format` property passed by the client to the `Execute` method. If no `Format` property is specified, the result is the same as if `Format` were defined as native.

Table 32.1 shows the type of result based on the `Command` parameter and the value of the property `Format`.

TABLE 32.1 Resultset by Format and Command

	Format Property		
	Native	*Multidimensional*	*Tabular*
MDX `Select`	`MDDataset`	`MDDataset`	`Rowset`
DMX `Select`	`Rowset`		`Rowset`
SQL `Select`	`Rowset`		`Rowset`
DDL command	Empty result	Empty result	Empty result

The `Execute` method supports the following parameters.

`Command`

The `Command` parameter contains an XML document that contains information about the command to be executed on the server. Commonly used commands fall into two categories:

- Data Manipulation Language (DML) commands request information that is stored or calculated on the server. MDX, Data Mining Extensions (DMX), and SQL requests are examples of such commands.
- Data Definition Language (DDL) commands create and manipulate objects on the server. `<Create>`, `<Alter>`, and `<Delete>` are examples of this type of command. DDL commands were designed especially for Microsoft Analysis Services. They are not supported by other XML/A providers; nor are they defined by the XML/A 1.1 specification.

A command sent to the server must be a valid XML element. All requests to the server written in MDX, DMX, or SQL must be wrapped in a `<Statement>` element.

`Properties`

The `Properties` parameter of the `Execute` method is similar to the `Properties` parameter of the `Discover` method. It contains a collection of properties that enable you to control various aspects of execution. (See the "The `Discover` Method" section earlier in this chapter for a discussion of the `Properties` parameter.)

The following example is a request that the client sends to the server to execute a simple MDX statement that returns the values of all the measures in the cube:

```
SELECT measures.members ON COLUMNS FROM [Warehouse and Sales]
```

To generate the `Execute` method, we need to form a SOAP envelope:

```
<Envelope xmlns="http://schemas.xmlsoap.org/soap/envelope/">
```

Next, the body of the request:

```
<Body>
```

The next element specifies the method that will be called; in this case, it is Execute:

```
<Execute xmlns="urn:schemas-microsoft-com:xml-analysis">
```


This element is followed by elements for each parameter passed into the method.

The first parameter, Command, contains a Statement element that wraps an MDX request:

```
<Command>
        <Statement> SELECT measures.members ON COLUMNS FROM [Warehouse and
Sales]</Statement>
</Command>
```

Next comes a list of properties with information that identifies the database to which the request is sent and the format for the result:

```
<Properties>
     <PropertyList>
               <Catalog>Foodmart 2008</Catalog>
               <Format>Multidimensional</Format>
               <Content>Data</Content>
     </PropertyList>
</Properties>
    </Execute >
  </Body >
</Envelope >
```

Result in the MDDataset Format The result of the request containing the MDX query will be, by default, an XML document in MDDatataset format. The result in MDDataset format contains an XML schema, as does a resultset in Rowset format. However, whereas the schema in Rowset contains information about the columns in the rowset, the schema in MDDataset contains only information about the XML elements and remains the same for result of all the multidimensional queries. Even though the schema is returned to the client application by default, you can write your client application to exclude the schema by specifying the Content property with a value of Data.

The information contained in the MDDataset result is arranged in three sections:

- **OlapInfo**—Information about the structure of result to be returned. OlapInfo serves the same purpose as ColumnInfo in a rowset. OlapInfo contains the following blocks:
    - **CubeInfo**—A list of the cube elements. In the current version of Analysis Services, only requests to a single cube are supported. Therefore, the CubeInfo list usually contains just one element, which specifies the cube's name and the

time of the last update of its data and structural change. In future versions, this limitation might be lifted.

- **AxisInfo**—Information about axes, hierarchies, tuples, members, and member properties.
- **CellInfo**—Information about cell properties.

- **Axes**—Information about the axes, tuples, and members that define the multidimensional space in the result.
- **Cells**—Information about the resulting cells (the value in each cell and other cell properties, such as FormattedValue and FormatString).

The AxisInfo Section The AxisInfo section contains information about the hierarchies located along an axis and about the properties of the members of those hierarchies that will be returned as result of the request. Each hierarchy has a HierarchyInfo element with a name attribute containing a unique name of the hierarchy. Each of the member properties in the hierarchy is a child element of HierarchyInfo. In Analysis Services, member properties can be of different data types, so the property has a type attribute that contains its data type.

The member properties returned by the request fall into two categories:

- Standard and are always returned by Analysis Services: MEMBER_CAPTION, MEMBER_UNIQUE_NAME, LEVEL_UNIQUE_NAME, LEVEL_NUMBER, and DISPLAY_INFO.
- Custom properties depend on the DIMENSION PROPERTY clause in the MDX statement. (For more information, see Chapter 11, "Advanced MDX.")

All the standard properties have the XML element names that are defined by the XML/A specification. This designation simplifies the XML format and improves its readability. For example, UName would replace MEMBER_UNIQUE_NAME, and Caption would replace MEMBER_CAPTION.

In addition to the axes defined by MDX Select statement, the server can return one more axis: SlicerAxis, which contains the elements specified in the Where clause and default members of hierarchies that were not used in the request but are present in the cube. However, under certain circumstances, Analysis Services might not return a SlicerAxis (for example, if the Where clause contained a set with more than one tuple).

The CellInfo Section The CellInfo section contains information about cell properties. Each property has Name and Type attributes. If the data type of a property is constant throughout the resultset, the server specifies that data type in the attribute of that property in the CellInfo section. If the data type is variable, the server specifies it in the CellData section for each cell. For example, CellOrdinal is always unsignedInt, regardless of the cell, but Value can be type string in one cell and int in another.

The cell properties returned by the MDX request fall into two categories:

- Standard properties that Analysis Services returns by default with for each request: VALUE, FORMATTED_VALUE, and CELL_ORDINAL

- Additional properties that you specify in the CELL PROPERTIES clause of an MDX query

As is the case with the member properties, there are standard cell properties for which XML element names are defined in the XML/A specification. (For example, FmtValue corresponds to the FORMATTED_VALUE cell property.)

The following example analyzes the format of an XML/A response containing an MDDataset resultset:

The result of our request starts with the elements Envelope and Body:

```
<Envelope xmlns="http://schemas.xmlsoap.org/soap/envelope/">
     <Body>
```

Next comes an element that specifies the method used in the request:

```
          <ExecuteResponse xmlns="urn:schemas-microsoft-com:xml-analysis">
               <return>
                    <root xmlns="urn:schemas-microsoft-com:xml-analysis:mddataset"
➥xmlns:xsi="http://www.w3.org/2001/XMLSchema-instance"
➥xmlns:xsd="http://www.w3.org/2001/XMLSchema">
```

If we hadn't specified that we want only data and not the XML schema, the schema would appear here, right before OlapInfo:

```
<OlapInfo>
     <CubeInfo>
          <Cube>
               <CubeName>Warehouse and Sales</CubeName>
               <LastDataUpdate xmlns="http://schemas.microsoft.com/analysis
➥services/2003/engine">2004-09-28T17:18:40
               </LastDataUpdate>
               <LastSchemaUpdate xmlns="http://schemas.microsoft.com/analysis
➥services/2003/engine">2004-09-28T17:17:32
               </LastSchemaUpdate>
          </Cube>
     </CubeInfo>
```

The hierarchy is identified by its unique name (in this example, Measures):

```
<AxesInfo>
<AxisInfo name="Axis0">
     <HierarchyInfo name="[Measures]">
          <UName name="[Measures].[MEMBER_UNIQUE_NAME]" type="xsd:string"/>
          <Caption name="[Measures].[MEMBER_CAPTION]" type="xsd:string"/>
          <LName name="[Measures].[LEVEL_UNIQUE_NAME]" type="xsd:string"/>
          <LNum name="[Measures].[LEVEL_NUMBER]" type="xsd:int"/>
          <DisplayInfo name="[Measures].[DISPLAY_INFO]" type="xsd:unsignedInt"/>
     </HierarchyInfo>
```

```
</AxisInfo>
```

In addition to the axes defined by the MDX `Select` statement, the server returns one more axis, `SlicerAxis`:

```
<AxisInfo name="SlicerAxis">
        ...
</AxisInfo>
</AxesInfo>
```

The `CellInfo` section contains information about cell properties:

```
<CellInfo>
     <Value name="VALUE"/>
     <FmtValue name="FORMATTED_VALUE" type="xsd:string"/>
     <CellOrdinal name="CELL_ORDINAL" type="xsd:unsignedInt"/>
</CellInfo>
</OlapInfo>
```

The Axes Section After the application receives the data about the structure of the result, it can start reading the result itself. The `Axes` section contains a list of all the axes, in the same order as they were specified in the MDX statement, followed by `SlicerAxis`. The XML/A specification defines three possible formats for the serialization of an axis:

- `ClusterFormat`
- `TupleFormat`
- `CustomFormat`

Because Analysis Services supports only `TupleFormat`, we limit the discussion to this format.

The response to our request, therefore, would look like this:

```
<Axes>
     <Axis name="Axis0">
```

Each axis contains a list of tuples; each tuple contains one or more members:

```
<Tuples>
     <Tuple>
```

The `Hierarchy` attribute of the `Member` element specifies the hierarchy the member belongs to. It can have child elements for each `member` property.

```
               <Member Hierarchy="[Measures]">
                    <UName>[Measures].[Unit Sales]</UName>
                    <Caption>Unit Sales</Caption>
                    <LName>[Measures].[MeasuresLevel]</LName>
                    <LNum>0</LNum>
```

```
                    <DisplayInfo>0</DisplayInfo>
                </Member>
            </Tuple>
            <Tuple>
                <Member Hierarchy="[Measures]">
                    <UName>[Measures].[Store Cost]</UName>
                    <Caption>Store Cost</Caption>
                    <LName>[Measures].[MeasuresLevel]</LName>
                    <LNum>0</LNum>
<DisplayInfo>131072</DisplayInfo>
</Member>
            </Tuple>
                ...
        </Tuples>
</Axis>
...
</Axes>
```

The `CellData` Section The `CellData` section contains the values of the cell properties. The properties that have a constant data type do not have the `type` attribute in this section; it was defined in the `CellInfo` section. Cell properties with a variable data type, such as `Value`, have an attribute type for each cell:

```
<CellData>
```

Each `Cell` element has a `CellOrdinal` attribute, which specifies an index that describes the placement of the cell among all the cells in the result. A cell that has a `NULL` value can be skipped in the resultset, but it would nonetheless have a `CellOrdinal` property associated with it:

```
    <Cell CellOrdinal="0">
        <Value xsi:type="xsd:double">2.66773E5</Value>
        <FmtValue>266,773.00</FmtValue>
    </Cell>
    ...
</CellData>
```

Handling Errors and Warnings

A well-designed system should always have an effective mechanism for handling errors and warnings. The following four categories describe the errors and warnings generated by the XML/A provider. Your approach to error handling depends on the type of error.

- **Errors that occur during the execution of the request, but before server starts to serialize the response**

In such a case, it could be that the provider was not able to parse the SOAP envelope of the request. For example, the method name was misspelled. Or maybe a method was called successfully, but the error occurred during execution of the method. As another example, if an MDX command that contains a syntax error is passed into the `Execute` method, the XML/A provider will generate an error.

- **Errors that occur during the execution of the request, after part of the request have already been generated by the server**

  For example, the `<Batch>` command might have multiple subcommands. If one of them succeeds and a result is generated, but the second one fails, the XML/A provider will generate an exception.

- **Errors in the response**

  In such a case, execution of the request succeeds, but the error occurs when the server is creating the response. For example, if one of the cells contained in the resultset has a secured value, the XML/A provider will generate a cell error.

- **Warnings that are issued when some problem occurs that does not prevent the execution from completing**

  For example, if during creation of the cube the locale specified by the user is not supported, the server creates a cube using a default locale. Because the cube is usable, Analysis Services does not fail the execution of the command and does not roll back the cube-creation transaction. Everything might look normal, but the data will not be in the locale the user expects—and she probably won't know it. The warning lets her know about the different locale settings used by the server.

Errors That Result in the Failure of the Whole Method

For errors that result in the failure of the whole method (category 1), the XML/A error-handling mechanism is built on top of SOAP. It uses the `SOAP FAULT` message that carries error information within a SOAP message response. Table 32.2 shows three child elements of the `Fault` element that can offer information about the error contained in the SOAP message.

TABLE 32.2 Child Elements of the **Fault** Element

<Fault> Child Element	**Description**
`<faultcode>`	Identifies the fault that occurred by an error code number
`<faultstring>`	An explanation of the fault
`<detail>`	Application-specific information about the error

According to the XML/A specification, the `<detail>` element should contain one or more `Error` elements that provide detailed information about the error that occurred. Table 32.3 describes the four attributes of the `Error` element.

TABLE 32.3 Attributes of the **Error** Element

<Error> Attribute	Description
ErrorCode	An unsigned integer number that identifies the error
Description	An explanation of the error
Source	The name of the component that generated an error
HelpFile	The path or URL to the help file that describes the error

The following example shows a response that the client application will receive if it sends a request with a typo in the method name:

```
<soap:Envelope xmlns:soap="http://schemas.xmlsoap.org/soap/envelope/">
  <soap:Body>
    <soap:Fault xmlns="http://schemas.xmlsoap.org/soap/envelope/">
      <faultcode>XMLAnalysisError.0xc10f0007</faultcode>
      <faultstring>The BadXMLAMethod element at line 3, column 66 (namespace
➥urn:schemas-microsoft-com:xml-analysis) cannot appear under Envelope/Body.
➥</faultstring>
      <detail>
        <Error ErrorCode="3238985735" Description="The BadXMLAMethod element at line
➥3, column 66 (namespace urn:schemas-microsoft-com:xml-analysis) cannot appear under
➥Envelope/Body." Source="Microsoft SQL Server 2008 Analysis Services" HelpFile="" />
      </detail>
    </soap:Fault>
  </soap:Body>
</soap:Envelope>
```

MDX Errors

When an error occurs in the execution of an MDX statement, you can take advantage of a more powerful mechanism for error handling than you get with SOAP. Analysis Services provides information about syntax errors that occur during the parsing of an MDX statement. For example, such information could be the location of the error in the command; it would be contained in the child element `Location` within the `Error` element.

In this example, we send an MDX request to the server in which we reference a hierarchy that does not exist in the cube. Analysis Services generates an `Error` element that contains information about the error and its location:

```
<Statement>SELECT x.members ON COLUMNS FROM [Warehouse And Sales]</Statement>
<soap:Envelope xmlns:soap="http://schemas.xmlsoap.org/soap/envelope/">
  <soap:Body>
    <soap:Fault xmlns="http://schemas.xmlsoap.org/soap/envelope/">
      <faultcode>XMLAnalysisError.0xc10a0006</faultcode>
      <faultstring>Query (1, 9) The dimension '[x]' was not found in the cube when
➥the string, [x], was parsed.</faultstring>
```

```
      <detail>
        <Error ErrorCode="3238658054" Description="Query (1, 9) The dimension '[x]'
➥was not found in the cube when the string, [x], was parsed." Source="Microsoft SQL
➥Server 2008 Analysis Services" HelpFile="">
          <Location xmlns="http://schemas.microsoft.com/analysisservices/2003/engine">
            <Start>
              <Line>1</Line>
              <Column>9</Column>
            </Start>
            <End>
              <Line>1</Line>
              <Column>9</Column>
            </End>
            <LineOffset>0</LineOffset>
            <TextLength>1</TextLength>
          </Location>
        </Error>
      </detail>
    </soap:Fault>
  </soap:Body>
</soap:Envelope>
```

Errors That Occur After Serialization of the Response Has Started

Because the SOAP specification allows the SOAP body to have only one child element, if an error occurs after the server has started to produce the result, a SOAP fault cannot be created. In such cases, Analysis Services generates an `<Exception>` element.

An exception can occur at any point of execution of a method. If the server has already started to serialize the response and has produced multiple nested XML elements at the time of the error, the server has to close all open tags (to produce valid XML) and serialize the error information.

To mark the exact place where the problem occurred, an `<Exception>` element is placed at the spot. After the server has closed all the open XML elements, it serializes the error information in a `<Message>` element. (There could be more than one message element in the response.) If you are familiar with exception handling in the .NET Framework or other languages that support exceptions, the following analogy will help: The `Exception` element is similar to a `throw` statement; the `Message` element corresponds to the `catch` statement.

The following example demonstrates how exception/message elements work:

```
<Axes>
     <Axis name="Axis0">
...
```

```
        </Tuple>
        <Tuple>
             <Member Hierarchy="[Data Stores].[ByLocation]">
                  <UName>
                      [Data Stores].[ByLocation].[State].&amp;[CA].&amp;[City 09]
                      </UName>
                  <Caption>City 09</Caption>
                  <LName>[Data Stores].[ByLocation].[City]</LName>
                  <LNum>2</LNum>
                  <DisplayInfo>131073</DisplayInfo>
            </Member>
        </Tuple>
        <Tuple>
             <Member Hierarchy="[Data Stores].[ByLocation]">
                  <UName>[Data Stores].[ByLocation].[State].&amp;[CA]</UName>
                  <Exception xmlns="urn:schemas-microsoft-com:xml-analysis
:exception" />
             </Member>
        </Tuple>
    </Tuples>
</Axis>
</Axes>
<Messages xmlns="urn:schemas-microsoft-com:xml-analysis:exception">
     <Error ErrorCode="3238658205" Description="The string, ******, is not a valid
➥expression for the Pattern argument of the VisualTotals function. Use the asterisk
➥(*) character." Source="Microsoft SQL Server 2008 Analysis Services" HelpFile="" />
</Messages>
</root>
```


Errors That Occur During Cell Calculation

When an error occurs during the calculation of a cell value, there is a good chance that the other cells are, nonetheless, valid and contain useful data. In this case, Analysis Services does not generate a `Fault` element; instead, it places an `Error` element as a data value of the failed cell.

The following MDX statement creates a calculated member using the MDX function `Order`, which accepts only the `Set` expression as the first parameter, not a string expression. Execution of this statement results in an `MDDataset` resultset with cell data that contains some `Error` elements:

```
WITH member measures.x AS 'Order("string",4)' select {x} ON COLUMNSFROM [Warehouse
➥and Sales]
          <CellData>
            <Cell CellOrdinal="0">
```

```
            <Value>
              <Error>
                <ErrorCode>3238658121</ErrorCode>
                <Description> The ORDER function expects a tuple set expression
➥for the 1 argument. A string or numeric expression was used. </Description>
              </Error>
            </Value>
            <FmtValue>
              <Error>
                <ErrorCode>3238658121</ErrorCode>
                <Description> The ORDER function expects a tuple set expression
➥for the 1 argument. A string or numeric expression was used. </Description>
              </Error>
            </FmtValue>
          </Cell>
        </CellData>
```

Warnings

In many cases, the server doesn't need to fail the request, but it does need to provide some information to the client application. The `Messages` list can contain the child element `Warning` that provides information about the warning—its severity, description, source, and help file or a URL that points to help information.

The following example shows an XML/A response containing information about a warning that occurred during the execution of a request. A `Messages` section that contains warning information might look like this:

```
            </CellData>
            <Messages xmlns="urn:schemas-microsoft-com:xml-analysis:exception">
              <Warning WarningCode="1090584599" Description="The 'Arabic' locale
➥for UI is not supported." Source="Microsoft SQL Server 2008 Analysis Services"
➥HelpFile="" />
              <Warning WarningCode="1090584599" Description="The 'Arabic' locale
➥for UI is not supported." Source="Microsoft SQL Server 2008 Analysis Services"
➥HelpFile="" />
            </Messages>
          </root>
        </return>
      </ExecuteResponse>
    </soap:Body>
  </soap:Envelope>
```

CHAPTER 33

ADOMD.NET

IN THIS CHAPTER

- Creating an ADOMD.NET Project
- Writing Analytical Applications
- ADOMD.NET Connections
- Working with Metadata Objects
- `AdomdCommand`
- Using the `CellSet` Object to Work with Multidimensional Data
- Working with Data in Tabular Format
- Which Should You Use: `AdomdDataReader` or `CellSet`?
- Using Parameters in MDX Requests
- Asynchronous Execution and Cancellation of Commands
- Error Handling

ADOMD.NET is both an ADO.NET provider for Analysis Services and an object model designed to simplify access to multidimensional data stored in Microsoft SQL Server Analysis Services. You use this object model to develop analytical applications, and not for administering Analysis Services. ADOMD.NET provides users a view of the data in the data source. Only the data that the security restrictions allow this user to see is available to him.

In this chapter, we provide an overview of the classes in the object model and various examples of their use. We not only show you what the code looks like, we also explain what is happening under the covers of the function calls. We also give you advice about which objects to use for different scenarios.

Creating an ADOMD.NET Project

First, we're going to create a project in Microsoft Visual Studio. You don't have to use Visual Studio to use ADOMD.NET, but your life as a developer will be easier if you do. We explain how to use ADOMD.NET with Visual Studio in great detail for any reader who is not familiar with Visual Studio.

Open Visual Studio and create a new project in the New Project dialog box, shown in Figure 33.1.

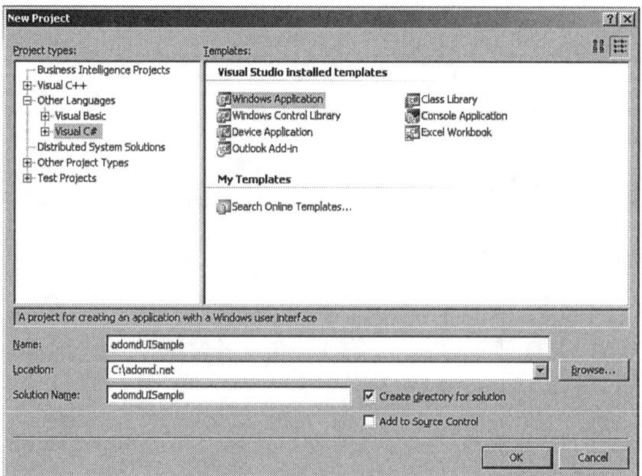

FIGURE 33.1 The New Project dialog box is your starting point.

NOTE

There are various ways to create a project. The most straightforward way is from the File menu: Click File, point to New, and then click Project.

Under Project Types, select the language you want to use. Our examples are written in C#, so choose C# as the language for your project. In some of the samples in this chapter, we use Windows user interface controls; in others, we show plain console applications with text output. For the first type of application, under Visual Studio Installed Templates, select Windows Forms Application (for the second type, you would select Console Application). In the Name box, name the project **AdomdUISample**. Click OK to create the project.

Before you can start using ADOMD.NET in your code, you have to reference the assembly that contains ADOMD.NET. Right-click References in the tree view on the left, and then click Add Reference, as shown in Figure 33.2.

The Add Reference dialog box appears, as shown in Figure 33.3.

Use this dialog box to select Microsoft.AnalysisServices.AdomdClient as a referenced assembly. Now right-click the Form box on the right, and then click View Code.

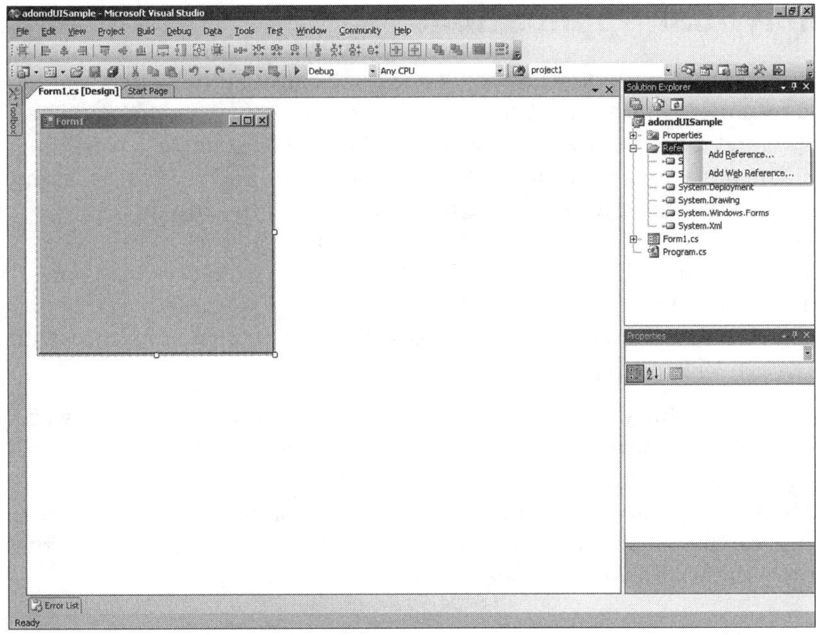

FIGURE 33.2 Click Add Reference.

Add Reference

.NET | COM | Projects | Browse | Recent

Component Name	Version	Runtime	Path
ExceptionMessageBox	10.0.0.0	v2.0.50727	C:\Program F
extensibility	7.0.3300.0	v1.0.3705	C:\Program F
IEExecRemote	2.0.0.0	v2.0.50727	C:\Windows\
IEHost	2.0.0.0	v2.0.50727	C:\Windows\
IIEHost	2.0.0.0	v2.0.50727	C:\Windows\
ISymWrapper	2.0.0.0	v2.0.50727	C:\Windows\
Microsoft Analysis Services Time Dimension Ge...	10.0.0.0	v2.0.50727	C:\Program F
Microsoft.AnalysisServices.AdomdClient	10.0.0.0	v2.0.50727	C:\Program F
Microsoft.AnalysisServices.AdomdServer	9.0.0.0	v2.0.50727	C:\Program F
Microsoft.AnalysisServices.System.DataMining	10.0.0.0	v2.0.50727	C:\Program F
Microsoft.Build.Conversion.v3.5	3.5.0.0	v2.0.50727	C:\Program F
Microsoft.Build.Engine	2.0.0.0	v2.0.50727	C:\Windows\
Microsoft.Build.Engine	3.5.0.0	v2.0.50727	C:\Program F

OK | Cancel

FIGURE 33.3 The Add Reference dialog box shows a list of assemblies that can be referenced.

Now we're almost ready to create our application with ADOMD.NET, but first we need to import the namespace for the ADOMD.NET classes. So, at the beginning of the file, add the `using` clause for `Microsoft.AnalysisServices.AdomdClient`:

```
using Microsoft.AnalysisServices.AdomdClient;
```

Writing Analytical Applications

A typical user who works with multidimensional data goes through a process that is different from that used by a user of relational data. From the first view of aggregated data, he is likely to drill down and request more and more detailed data. For example, a marketing manager of a retail enterprise might start by looking at global sales, and then focus on just Europe. Then, he might drill down further to see the data from France, and then maybe from just Calais, and even from one specific store. Then, he might go back to the global view and look at just one product the company sells. And he might drill down the same path to find out how much of that product the store in Calais sold last month or the month before. He rarely asks for a static report; he works in constant communication with the server.

Thus, an application for working with multidimensional data requires more flexibility and a higher level of interactivity. The application has to connect to a multidimensional data source, discover the structure of the stored data, and allow the user to query and drill down into the data. Most applications intended for the analysis of multidimensional data, even nontrivial ones, can be visualized by the diagram in Figure 33.4. You can easily write such an application with the ADOMD.NET object model.

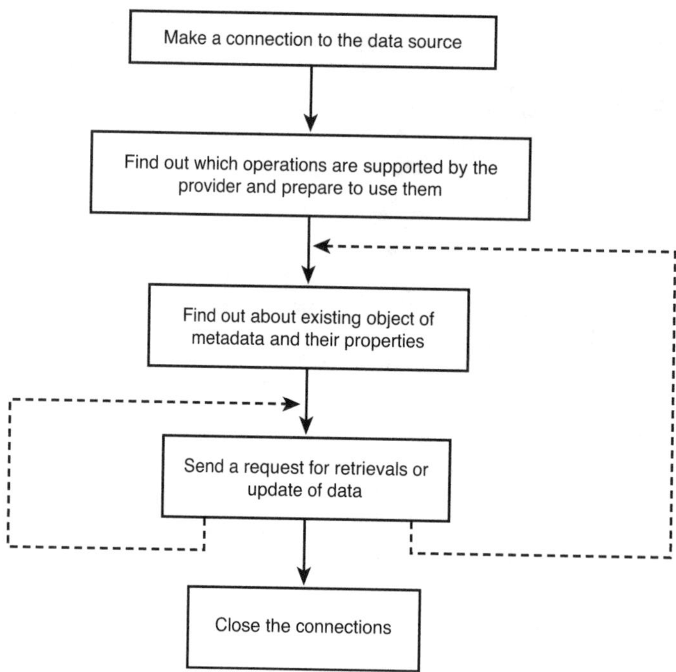

FIGURE 33.4 A client application uses this process to browse multidimensional data.

ADOMD.NET Connections

In a typical data access system, the first step is to establish a connection to a source of data. A client application that works with Microsoft SQL Server Analysis Services follows the same rule, and establishes a connection to the data source. To establish this connection, ADOMD.NET provides the class `AdomdConnection`, which is similar to the connection classes of `SqlClient`, `OledbClient`, and other ADO.NET providers.

`AdomdConnection` implements the `IDBConnection` interface and supports the majority of methods defined by the interface, as shown in Figure 33.5.

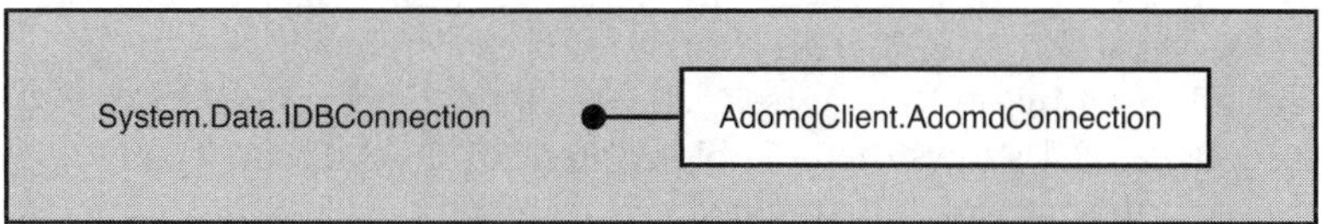

FIGURE 33.5 The `ADOMDConnection` object implements the `IDBConnection` interface.

As shown in Listing 33.1, the client application uses the `ConnectionString` properly of `AdomdConnection` class to specify information needed to make a connection—for example, the name of the server or of the database.

LISTING 33.1 Opening and Closing Connections

```
//Create a connection string with connection properties.
String conString = "Datasource=localhost; Initial Catalog=Foodmart 2008";

// Create a connection object.
AdomdConnection con = new AdomdConnection();

//Set the connection string on the connection object.
con.ConnectionString = conString;

//Open a connection.
con.Open();

//Do the necessary operations.

//Close the connection.
con.Close();
```

As you can see, this code is similar to the code of an application that uses ADO DB and ADO.NET. In designing ADOMD.NET, we did our utmost to make sure that all the object models we provide with Analysis Services—ADOMD.NET, AMO, and the OLE DB provider—support the same set of properties.

All the properties supported by ADOMD.NET fall into two categories:

- Properties necessary for establishing a connection with a server and that have to be, consequently, processed by ADOMD.NET on the client. An example from this category is the property `Datasource`, which contains the name of a source of data.
- Properties responsible for various operations on the server and that, therefore, must be sent to the server. An example from this category is the property `Initial Catalog`, which contains the name of the database on the server.

During the execution of the method `Open`, ADOMD.NET parses the content of the `ConnectionString` property and separates the properties into two groups: those that will be used on the client, and those that will be packed in an XML for Analysis (XML/A) message and sent to the server. Then, ADOMD.NET analyzes the content of the `Datasource` property and, depending on the content, chooses a type of connection to a data source and opens it. Table 33.1 shows the possible content of the `Datasource` property and the type of connection that would be opened.

TABLE 33.1 **`Datasource`** Property Content and Corresponding Connections

Content of the `Datasource` Property	Connection
Filename with the extension `.cub`	Connection with a local cube
URL beginning with http:// or https://	HTTP connection
Name (or IP address) of a computer or instance	TCP/IP connection
`local` or `localhost`	TCP/IP connection to the same computer

Analysis Services supports multiple servers working on one computer (multi-instancing). Each instance listens on a different port. If you're connecting to a multi-instancing computer via TCP/IP, you cannot use just the name of the computer for the name of the server.

If a user is connecting to a computer running multiple instances, she has to use the name of the instance in addition to the name or IP address of the computer. If she is connecting to the default instance, she can use just the name (or IP address) of the computer—`localhost` or `local` if the client and server are on the same computer. ADOMD.NET would use the following BNF (Backus-Naur Form notation) to parse the content of the `Datasource` property:

```
Datasource::= <host name>[\instance name ¦: port number]
<host name>::= <computer name>¦<IP address> ¦ localhost ¦ local
```

If the user knows on which port the instance listens, she can specify the port number—for example, `Datasource = localhost:1092`. But more often, the user doesn't know the port number, but she does know the name of the instance. So, she would specify the name of the instance—for example, `Datasource = localhost\myinstance`. In such a case, ADOMD.NET carries out a more complex operation. It sends a `Discover_Instances` request for the port number of the Redirector, with restrictions on the name of the instance. The reply would be a rowset with one row containing the number of the port that ADOMD.NET will use to establish the connection. Figure 33.6 shows an illustration of this operation.

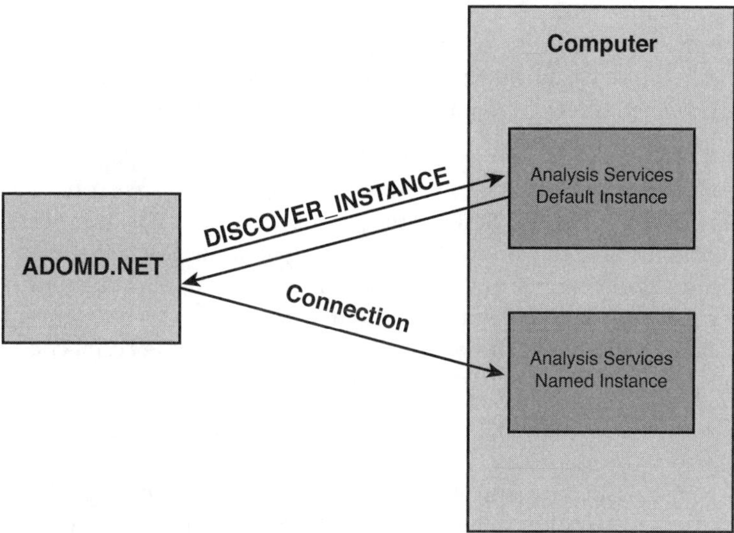

FIGURE 33.6 Find the port number by the name of the instance.

If you are going to work with a local cube, you can just specify the path of the file that contains the local cube (for example, `Datasource=c:\mycube.cub`).

NOTE

ADOMD.NET allows only local cubes in files with a `.cub` extension.

If you have your data stored on a domain different from the client or outside your network, the client connects to the server via HTTP. To do this, you can specify a `Datasource` property that contains the URL to the XML/A provider. For Analysis Services, this URL is the full path to the `msmdpump100.dll` installed on Internet Information Services (IIS). For example, if you create the virtual directory `msolap` on IIS and copy `msmdpump100.dll` there, you use the following URL in the `Datasource` property: http://<computer_name>/msolap/msmdpump100.dll. If you are connecting to an XML/A provider different from Analysis Services, you can similarly specify its URL in the `Datasource` property. For example, if you are connecting to XML/A SDK version 1.1, you can use the following URL: http://<computername>/xmla/msxisapi.dll.

NOTE

ADOMD.NET 2008 officially supports only Analysis Services 2005, 2008, and XML/A SDK 1.1 as XML/A providers.

Analysis Services supports integrated security, which means that the user is not required to specify a username and password to establish a connection. If the connection is made through HTTP or HTTPS, however, the client application can take advantage of the authentication mechanisms provided by IIS.

Some of the authentication modes supported by IIS require a username and password. For example, if IIS directory security is set up for Basic Authentication, the user has to provide her username and password to be able to work with Analysis Services. ADOMD.NET provides `UserID` and `Password` connection string properties to the client application. When the username and password are specified by the client application, ADOMD.NET always includes them in the HTTP request. Those properties are ignored if the connection ADOMD.NET is establishing to the data source is not via HTTP.

There is a reason behind this behavior. When ADOMD.NET forms an HTTP request, it doesn't have information about the security settings specified on IIS: It doesn't know whether IIS is configured to use Basic Authentication or Windows Authentication. To minimize round trips, ADOMD.NET packs all the available information into the request and sends it to the server. If IIS has been configured to authenticate with a method that does not require user credentials, the credentials are ignored. If the user has not specified a username and password (or has provided wrong ones) and IIS is configured to require user credentials, IIS reports an error in the HTTP response, and ADOMD.NET throws an `AdomdConnectionException`. The client application should be able to handle this exception and provide a user interface that allows the user to enter a username and password.

NOTE

This requirement in ADOMD.NET is different from the requirement in the Analysis Services OLE DB provider. If the OLE DB provider fails to establish a connection to the data source, the OLE DB provider displays a connection dialog box (unless the connection string property `Prompt` is set not to allow that), in which the user can enter a data source, username, and password.

While ADOMD.NET is opening a connection to the server, it creates a new session. By default, ADOMD.NET creates one session for each connection, but allows multiple connections to use the same session. To enable the use of one session by multiple connections, use the `AdomdConnection.SessionID` property. The `SessionID` property should be set before the subsequent connection is opened.

Listing 33.2 shows how one session can be used by two connections. In this example, we're getting a little ahead of ourselves by using metadata objects of the ADOMD.NET object model (described in the next section of this chapter). If you like, you can skip this example and return to it later.

LISTING 33.2 Multiple Connections Using the Same Session

```
//Create the first connection object.
AdomdConnection con = new AdomdConnection();
con.ConnectionString = "Datasource=localhost; Initial Catalog=Foodmart 2008;";
con.Open();

//Create a command and send a request that will create a new calculated member
//on the session.
AdomdCommand command = con.CreateCommand();
command.CommandText = "CREATE MEMBER [Warehouse and Sales].Measures.MyCalcMember as
1";
command.ExecuteNonQuery();

//Check to make sure that the calculated member was created.
if (null != con.Cubes["Warehouse and Sales"].Measures.Find("MyCalcMember"))
     Console.WriteLine(" Measure 'MyCalcMember' is created on the session from the
➥ first connection. ");
else
      Console.WriteLine(" Measure 'MyCalcMember' is not created on the session from
➥ the firstconnection. ");

//Create the second connection object.
AdomdConnection con2 = new AdomdConnection();
con2.ConnectionString = "Datasource=localhost; Initial Catalog=Foodmart 2008;";

//Set the session identifier of the first connection in the second
//connection object.
con2.SessionID = con.SessionID;
// Open the second connection
con2.Open();

//Check to make sure that the calculated member created by first connection
//is available on the second connection.
if (null != con2.Cubes["Warehouse and Sales"].Measures.Find("MyCalcMember"))
      Console.WriteLine(" Measure 'MyCalcMember' is available on the session from
➥ the second connection. ");
else
      Console.WriteLine(" Measure 'MyCalcMember' is not available on the session
from the second connection. ");

//Close the second connection.
con2.Close();
```

```
//Close the first connection.
con.Close();
```

If the user or the client application has not specified the database to connect to, the server connects to the first database it finds. After communication has been established, you can use the `AdomdConnection.Database` property to find out what database the current connection is to. Then, you can use the `AdomdConnection.ChangeDatabase()` command to change the current database. If you want to allow the user to choose the database, you use the `AdomdConnection.GetSchemaDataset` method. `GetSchemaDataset` is a sufficiently universal method that enables the client application to request any schema `rowset` or `Discover` request type from the server.

In Listing 33.3, we connect to a server without specifying a database. We ask the server to give the user a list of all existing databases, and then we change the connection to the database the user chooses (see Figure 33.7).

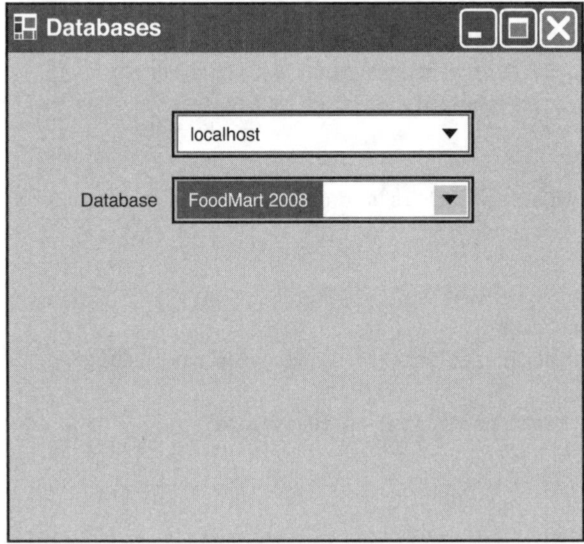

FIGURE 33.7 The user interface allows the user to choose a database.

LISTING 33.3 Listing All Existing Databases and Changing the Current Database of the Connection to the One Selected by the User

```
namespace AdomdIterateDatabases
{
    partial class AdomdIterateDatabasesForm: Form
```

```
{
      private AdomdConnection con = new AdomdConnection();
      private Boolean areDatabasesPopulated = false;

      //This function produces a list of names of the existing databases on
      //the server whose name was entered by the user in serverBox TextBox.
      private void PopulateDatabases()
      {
            if (areDatabasesPopulated)
                  return;
            //if connection is already open, close it.
            if (con.State == ConnectionState.Open)
                  con.Close();
            con.ConnectionString = "Datasource = " + serverBox. Text;
            try
            {
                   //Open the connection.
                    databaseBox.Enabled = true;
                    databaseBox.Items.Clear();
                   //Retrieve DataSet that contains all the databases.
                   DataSet catalogs = con.GetSchemaDataSet("DBSCHEMA_CATALOGS",
➥ null);
                   //All the results will be located in the first table
                   //of the dataset.
                   //Populate the combo box with the names of the databases.
                   foreach(DataRow row in catalogs.Tables[0].Rows)
                   {
                         databaseBox.Items.Add(row["CATALOG_NAME"]);
                    }
                    areDatabasesPopulated = true;
                    return;
            }
            catch(AdomdConnectionException conException)
            {
                  //If there was a connection error, pass it to the user.
                  MessageBox.Show(conException.Message,"Connection Error");
            }
            catch(AdomdErrorResponseException errException)
            {
                   //If there was an error in the request, pass it to the user.
                   MessageBox.Show(errException.Message, "Error Response");
            }
            catch(Exception ex)
            {
```

33

```
                MessageBox.Show(ex.Message, "Error");
            }
        }
        public Form1()
        {
            InitializeComponent();
        }

        //This method will be called when the user selects a database from
        //the combo box.
        private void databaseBox_SelectedIndexChanged(object sender, EventArgs e)
        {
            //The user has chosen one database.
            //Change the current database to the database chosen by the user.
            ComboBox comboBox = (ComboBox)sender;
            string selectedDatabase = (string)comboBox.SelectedItem;
            if ( null != selectedDatabase )
                con.ChangeDatabase(selectedDatabase);
        }

        //This method will be called when the user expands a combo box.
        private void databaseBox_DropDown(object sender, System. EventArgs e)
        {
            //Call the function to make a list of all the databases.
            PopulateDatabases();
        }

        private void serverBox_TextChanged(object sender, EventArgs e)
        {
            //If the user chose a different server name,
            //the list of databases should be repopulated.
            areDatabasesPopulated = false;
        }
    }
}
```

Working with Metadata Objects

ADOMD.NET provides a rich model for navigating the client view of metadata objects that exist on the server. Such objects allow the client application to use simple programming interfaces to work with cubes, dimensions, hierarchies, members, and many other objects.

Figure 33.8 shows the hierarchy of all the metadata objects exposed through ADOMD.NET interfaces.

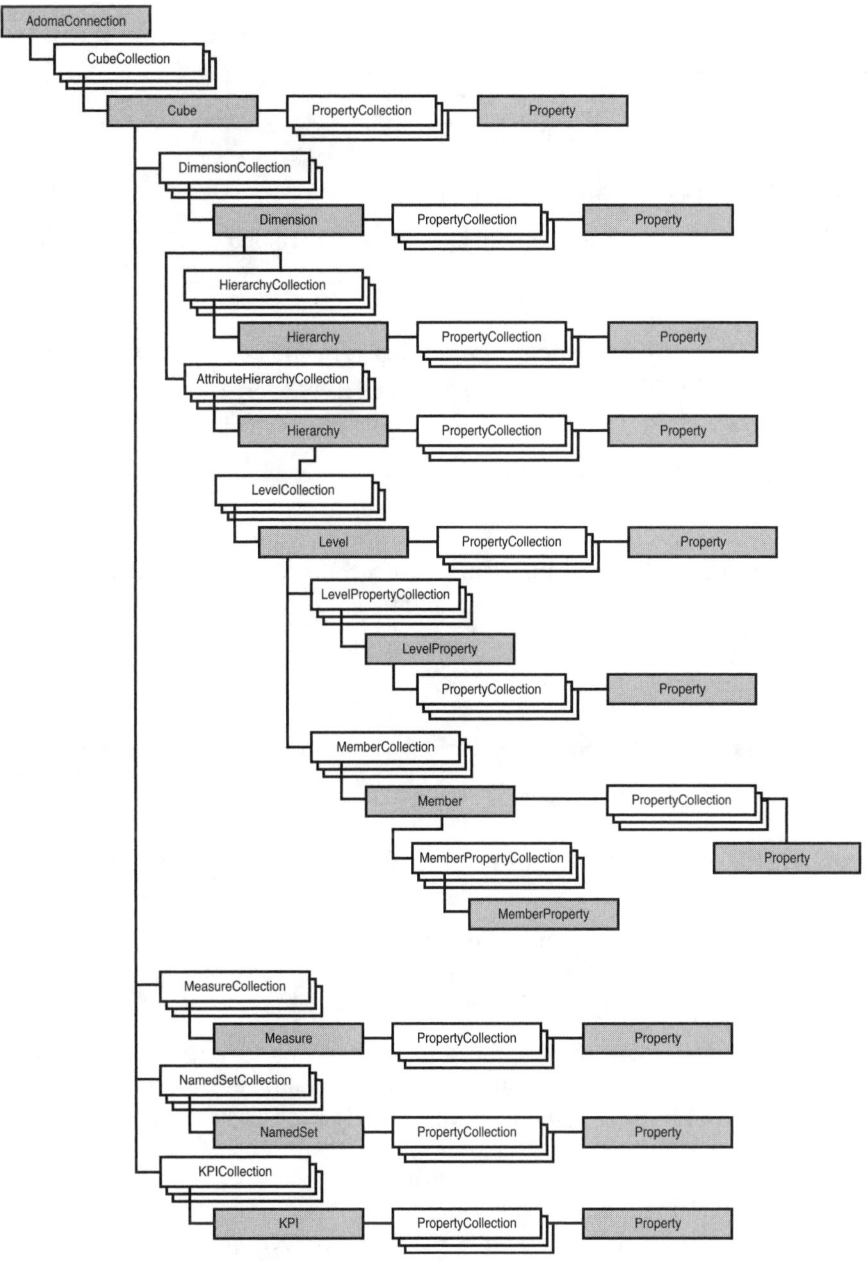

FIGURE 33.8 This hierarchy of metadata objects is supported by ADOMD.NET.

Operations on Collections

The properties and methods that client application code can use to operate with collections are the same for all ADOMD.NET collections, as shown in Figure 33.9.

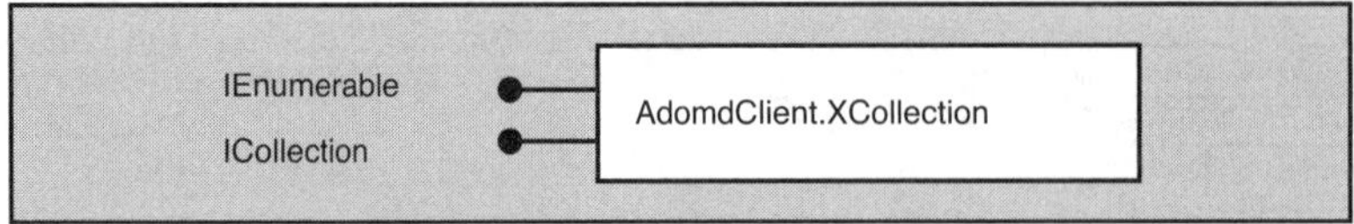

FIGURE 33.9 All ADOMD.NET collections implement `IEnumerable` and `ICollection` interfaces.

Each collection in ADOMD.NET implements the `IEnumerable` and `ICollection` interfaces and all the methods and properties supported by those interfaces described here.

Count

`Count` returns the number of elements in the collection.

Item

`Item` (`indexer` in C#) provides access to the elements of a collection. ADOMD.NET provides two overloads for this method: by index and by name. For example, in C#, access to the elements of a collection can be expressed with this code:

```
Dimension dim = cube.Dimensions[0];
```

This call returns the first element of the collection. Or you could use the following:

```
Dimension dim = cube.Dimensions["Customer"];
```

This call returns an element of a collection with the name `Customer`. Note that it uses a name rather than a unique name.

Access to an element of a collection by index is more efficient than by name. If you have the opportunity, use the first method. (In some of our following examples, we use access by name, but we have done that only for the sake of simplicity.)

If no element with that name exists in the collection, or if an index oversteps the bounds of a collection, an exception is thrown. Because exception handling always slows down the system, use these methods only if you know that the element exists in the collection.

Find

`Find` returns the specified element of the collection. Unlike `Item`, it does not throw an exception, but returns `null` if the object doesn't exist in the collection. For example

```
Dimension dim = cube.Dimensions.Find("Customer");
```

returns an object with the name `Customer`, but

```
Dimension dim = cube.Dimensions.Find("foo");
```

returns `null`.

GetEnumerator

`GetEnumerator` returns the `Enumerator` object, which is used for the iteration of a collection. Let's look at a small piece of a code that iterates the collection:

```
// Get an Enumerator object
IEnumerator enumerator = con.Cubes.GetEnumerator();
CubeDef cube;
//Iterate the elements of the collection through the end of the collection
while(enumerator.MoveNext())
{
     cube = enumerator.Current;
     Console.WriteLine(cube.Name);
}
```

C# and VB .NET provide special keywords for the iteration of collections: `foreach` (C#) and `for each` (VB .NET):

```
foreach(CubeDef cube in con.Cubes)
{
     Console.WriteLine("Cube Name: " + cube.Name);
}
```

The starting point of an application iterating over Analysis Services metadata objects is a collection of cubes. This collection contains all the cubes created and processed on the server to which the user has read access. Listing 33.4 iterates objects of the database from the cube down to the level, and prints the names, unique names (if there are such), and captions of the objects.

LISTING 33.4 Iteration of Metadata Objects

```
//Connect to the server.
AdomdConnection con = new AdomdConnection();
con.ConnectionString = "Datasource=localhost; Initial Catalog=FoodMart 2008;";
con.Open();

//Iterate the objects in the collection of cubes.
foreach(CubeDef cube in con.Cubes)
{
     Console.WriteLine("Cube Name: " + cube.Name);

     //Iterate the objects in the measures collection.
     foreach(Dimension dim in cube.Dimensions)
     {
```

33

```
            Console.WriteLine("Dimension Unique Name: " + dim.UniqueName);

            // Iterate the objects in hierarchy collection.
            foreach(Hierarchy hier in dim.Hierarchies)
            {
                Console.WriteLine("Hierarchy Unique Name: " + hier. UniqueName);
                //Iterate objects in the levels collection.
                foreach(Level level in hier.Levels)
                {
                    Console.WriteLine("Level Unique Name: " + level.UniqueName);
                }
            }
        }
}
//Close the connection.
con.Close();
```

Internally, all collections are implemented in the same way. To populate a collection, ADOMD.NET sends the appropriate XML/A `Discover` request to the server. For example, to populate a collection of cubes, ADOMD.NET sends an `MDSchema_Cubes` request. Then, it creates as many `CubeDef` objects as rows were returned in the resulting rowset. ADOMD.NET objects are not created at the same time the collection is created, but are created on demand—when the client application's code calls the property of the collection that gets the object for the first time. Table 33.2 shows the relationships between ADOMD.NET objects and the schema rowset requests they send. (Any collection marked with an asterisk [*] sends a different kind of request. We discuss them in a later section, "Working with a Collection of Members (`MemberCollection`).")

TABLE 33.2 ADOMD.NET Collections and the Schema Rowset Requests Sent to Populate Them

ADOMD.NET Collection	Schema Rowset Request
CubeCollection	MDSCHEMA_CUBES
DimensionCollection	MDSCHEMA_DIMENSIONS
KPICollection	MDSCHEMA_KPIS
MeasureCollection	MDSCHEMA_MEASURES
NamedSetCollection	MDSCHEMA_SETS
HierarchyCollection	MDSCHEMA_HIERARCHIES
AttributeHierarchyCollection	MDSCHEMA_HIERARCHIES
LevelCollection	MDSCHEMA_LEVELS
LevelPropertyCollection	MDSCHEMA_PROPERTIES
MemberProperties *	MDSCHEMA_MEMBERS
MemberCollection *	MDSCHEMA_MEMBERS

TABLE 33.2 ADOMD.NET Collections and the Schema Rowset Requests Sent to Populate Them

ADOMD.NET Collection	Schema Rowset Request
MiningModelCollection	DMSCHEMA_MINING_MODELS
MiningStructureCollection	DMSCHEMA_MINING_STRUCTURES
MiningContentNodeCollection	DMSCHEMA_MINING_MODEL_CONTENT
MiningServiceCollection	DMSCHEMA_MINING_SERVICES
MiningModelColumnCollection	DMSCHEMA_MINING_COLUMNS
MiningServiceParameterCollection	DMSCHEMA_MINING_SERVICE_PARAMETERS
MiningStructureColumnCollection	DMSCHEMA_MINING_STRUCTURE_COLUMNS

ADOMD.NET objects expose only the subset of columns returned by the schema rowsets as named properties. However, it is practically impossible to create a property for each column in each rowset. To help us deal with this, each object model class has a collection named `Properties`.

The `Properties` collection has as many elements as the corresponding schema rowset has columns. The name of each element corresponds to the name of a column in the schema rowset. If the client application needs to find information about the object that is not available from a named property of the object, the data can always be retrieved from the `Properties` collection as long as you know the name of the column. Listing 33.5 shows how to retrieve a dimension's ordinal using the `Properties` collection of the `Dimension` object.

LISTING 33.5 Retrieving a Dimension's Ordinal

```
AdomdConnection con = new AdomdConnection();
con.ConnectionString = "Datasource=localhost; Initial Catalog=Foodmart 2008;";
con.Open();
CubeDef cube = con.Cubes["Warehouse and Sales"];
foreach(Dimension dim in cube.Dimensions)
{
      Console.WriteLine("Dimension: '" + dim.Name + "' Ordinal= " +
dim.Properties["DIMENSION_ORDINAL"].Value.ToString());
}
con.Close();
```

Caching Metadata on the Client

Usually it takes much less processor and network time to send a small number of larger requests to the server than to send a large number of small requests. Sending a separate request to populate each collection makes sense only when your client application needs to work with a very limited number of objects (for example, if it iterates only members of a single level from a single hierarchy). In reality, however, most client applications eventually iterate an object hierarchy touching almost all the metadata objects.

ADOMD.NET has a special caching mechanism to decrease the number of round trips between client and server. Caching occurs only on objects that are frequently used and do not demand huge memory consumption, such as dimensions, hierarchies, and levels.

We do not apply caching to members because doing so can entail loading a huge quantity of information that probably would not be used. Neither do we cache small collections of measures, named sets, and key performance indicators (KPIs) because they are not often used and may vary for each request to the server. For example, if a client application sends a request to the server to create a calculated measure, the result of that request will change the contents of `MeasureCollection` on the server. So, using `MeasureCollection` from the cache would produce an incorrect response.

Here's how the caching of metadata works. The `Cube Def` object stores three data structures: one for all the dimensions in the cube, another for all the hierarchies of the cube, and a third for all the levels of the cube. As soon as a client application requests the first dimension of a cube, all the dimensions are requested. When it requests the first hierarchy, all the hierarchies are requested, and so on. ADOMD.NET stores data and relationships between objects; the relationships help to define what hierarchy belongs to what dimension, connecting them by the column `DIMENSION_UNIQUE_NAME`. Figure 33.10 shows the structures that ADOMD.NET uses to cache metadata.

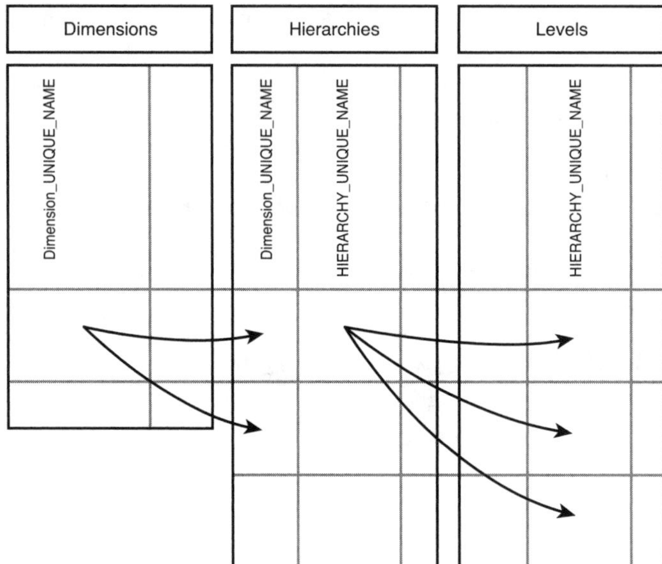

FIGURE 33.10 ADOMD.NET caches metadata.

Unfortunately, while your query is running, another connection can update the cube on the server. When this happens, the results returned from a cache will differ from the results that come back from the server. To make sure that doesn't happen, ADOMD.NET uses the algorithm shown in Figure 33.11.

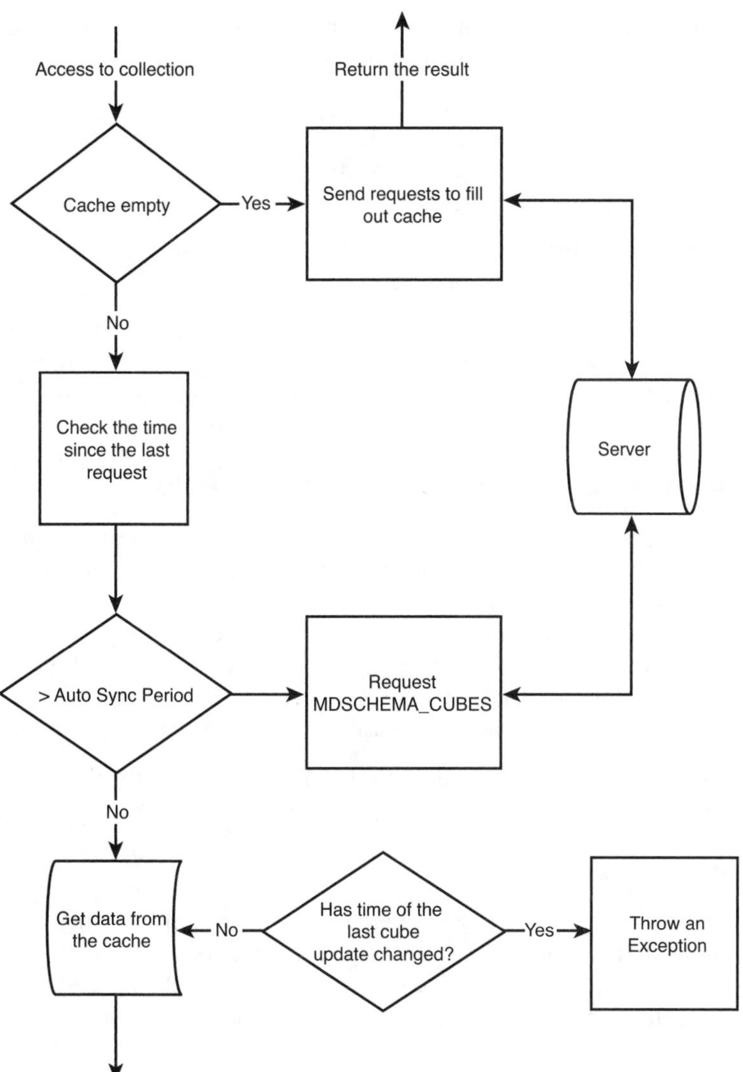

FIGURE 33.11 ADOMD.NET uses this algorithm for retrieving objects from the metadata cache.

When client code calls a property or method on the collection, ADOMD.NET checks whether the cache is empty. If the cache is empty, ADOMD.NET sends a `Discover` request to the server, and then populates the cache. If the cache is not empty, ADOMD.NET checks the time that has elapsed between the previous request to the server and this one.

If the number of milliseconds elapsed is greater than that specified by the `Auto Sync Period` connection string property, the cache could be stale. (If this property is not specified in the connection string, ADOMD.NET uses 10 milliseconds as default value.) So, ADOMD.NET sends an `MDSCHEMA_CUBES` request to the server to determine whether the cube has been changed. If the cube has not been updated on the server during this period, the object stored in the cache is passed to the client. If the cube has changed, however, ADOMD.NET throws an `AdomdCacheExpiredException`.

When you are developing an application that works with metadata objects, you should be ready to catch an `AdomdCacheExpiredException` and correctly process it. The `AdomdCacheExpiredException` serves two purposes:

- To notify the client application that no metadata collection can be used until the method `RefreshMetadata` is called on the `AdomdConnection` object.
- To enable the client application to update the user interface so that it reflects the changes that occurred on the server. For example, if your client application shows a tree of the metadata objects and one of the dimensions has been renamed on the server, you would want to refresh the tree view to reflect the name change.

Working with a Collection of Members (`MemberCollection`)

The collection of members differs radically from other collections that contain metadata. The main distinction is the potential size of the collection. Even the number of dimensions, hierarchies, and levels that you would find in very large systems can be measured in hundreds or thousands, but this information can easily fit in the memory of the client computer. On the other hand, the number of members at the bottom level of one dimension could easily reach millions. If we load all the members of that level on a client's computer to cache a collection of members, we could easily overload the client computer.

A correctly designed client application, however, doesn't demand all the members of a level simultaneously. Usually the client needs only enough members to fit the screen of the user (or two screens, if you want the application to read a little bit ahead and prepare the data in advance for the next display).

If you want to show a limited number of members, there is no need to bring all the members of the level to the client computer. The client application does not usually really need all the information contained in all 20 columns of the `MDSCHEMA_MEMBERS` schema rowset. (Most of the time, the properties you'll want are `Name`, `Unique Name`, `Caption`, and `Type`.)

To meet the needs of the typical developer who doesn't want all those properties, ADOMD.NET provides an interface for access to a subset of members. There are four overloads for the functions `Level.GetMembers` and `Member.GetChildren`, which return `MemberCollection`. Because the operation of loading members can take a significant amount of time, the ADOMD.NET designers created this interface such that, unlike the other interfaces for access to collections, `MemberCollection` is retrieved by the method instead of by the property.

- `Level.GetMembers()` returns all members of a level, with a limited set of properties.

- `Level.GetMembers(long start, long count)` returns number of members specified by `<count>` parameter, starting at `start` member.
- `Level.GetMembers(long start, long count, params MemberFilter [] filters)` returns number of members specified by `<count>` parameter, starting at `start` member and limited by the `filters`.
- `Level.GetMembers(long start, long count, string [] properties, params MemberFilter [] filters)`. In addition to filtering, the client application can specify which `MemberProperties` should be returned by the server.
- `Member. GetChildren()` returns all children of a member, with a limited set of properties.
- `Member. GetChildren(long start, long count)` returns number of child members specified by `<count>` parameter, starting with `start` member. `count` is the maximum number of returned members.
- `Member. GetChildren(long start, long count, params MemberFilter [] filters)` returns number of child members specified by `<count>` parameter, starting with `start` member and limited by the `filters`.
- `Member. GetChildren(long start, long count, string [] properties, params MemberFilter [] filters)`, in addition to applying the filter, specifies which properties of the member should be requested from the server.

We are now going to give you some examples that show how each of these functions works. Listing 33.6 returns all the members of the `Store` level, but the collection `MemberProperty` remains empty until further operations by the client application. We talk about that later in the "Handling Object Symmetry" section.

LISTING 33.6 **`Level.GetMembers()`**

```
//Open a connection to the server.
AdomdConnection con = new AdomdConnection();
con.ConnectionString = "Datasource=localhost; Initial Catalog=Foodmart 2008;";
con.Open();

//Go to the level.
Level lvl = con.Cubes["Warehouse and Sales"].Dimensions["Store"].
➥Hierarchies["Stores"].Levels ["Store"];

//Receive a collection of the members of the level.
MemberCollection allMembers = lvl.GetMembers();

//Print all the elements of the collection.
foreach(Member member in allMembers)
{
    Console.WriteLine(member.UniqueName + ";");
```

```
}
// Verify that the MemberProperty collection is empty, despite
//existing custom member properties at each element at the level "Store".
 Member firstMember = allMembers[0];
 foreach(MemberProperty memberProperty in firstMember.MemberProperties)
 {
     Console.WriteLine(memberProperty.UniqueName);
}

//Close the connection
con.Close();
```

The code in this example prints the members of the `Store` level. This is quite a long list—all the stores in our data warehouse:

```
[Store].[Stores].[Store].&[19];
[Store].[Stores].[Store].&[20];
[Store].[Stores].[Store].&[9];
[Store].[Stores].[Store].&[21];
[Store].[Stores].[Store].&[1];
[Store].[Stores].[Store].&[5];
[Store].[Stores].[Store].&[10];
[Store].[Stores].[Store].&[8];
[Store].[Stores].[Store].&[4];
[Store].[Stores].[Store].&[12];
[Store].[Stores].[Store].&[18];
[Store].[Stores].[Store].&[0];
[Store].[Stores].[Store].&[6];
[Store].[Stores].[Store].&[7];
[Store].[Stores].[Store].&[24];
[Store].[Stores].[Store].&[14];
[Store].[Stores].[Store].&[11];
[Store].[Stores].[Store].&[13];
[Store].[Stores].[Store].&[2];
[Store].[Stores].[Store].&[3];
[Store].[Stores].[Store].&[15];
[Store].[Stores].[Store].&[16];
[Store].[Stores].[Store].&[17];
[Store].[Stores].[Store].&[22];
[Store].[Stores].[Store].&[23];
```

Similar to the previous example, Listing 33.7 returns the members of the `Store Name` level, but the number of returned members is limited to the `start` and `count` parameters. The `count` parameter is the maximum number of returned members. If the caller passed a `count` that is greater than the maximum number of members in the level, ADOMD.NET returns the members that are there.

LISTING 33.7 **Level.GetMembers(long start, long count)**

```
//Set an initial element of the member and number of returned elements.
long start = 3;
long count = 10;

//Open a connection to the server.
AdomdConnection con = new AdomdConnection();
con.ConnectionString = "Datasource=localhost; Initial Catalog=Foodmart 2008; ";
con.Open();

//Go to the level.
Level lvl = con.Cubes["Warehouse and
Sales"].Dimensions["Store"].Hierarchies["Stores"].
➥Levels["Store"];

//Receive a collection of the members of the level, which starts with member
//number 3 and contains 10 members.
MemberCollection allMembers = lvl.GetMembers(start, count);

//Print all the elements of the collection.
foreach(Member member in allMembers)
{
      Console.WriteLine(member.UniqueName + ";");
}
//Verify that the collection MemberProperty is empty, despite the existence of
//custom member properties at each member at the level "Store".
 Member firstMember = allMembers[0];
 foreach(MemberProperty memberProperty in firstMember.MemberProperties)
 {
     Console.WriteLine(memberProperty.UniqueName);
}

//Close the connection
con.Close();
```

This code results in the following list of the unique names of the members. This list of names is a subset of the names returned by the first example:

```
[Store].[Stores].[Store].&[21];
[Store].[Stores].[Store].&[1];
[Store].[Stores].[Store].&[5];
[Store].[Stores].[Store].&[10];
[Store].[Stores].[Store].&[8];
[Store].[Stores].[Store].&[4];
```

```
[Store].[Stores].[Store].&[12];
[Store].[Stores].[Store].&[18];
[Store].[Stores].[Store].&[0];
[Store].[Stores].[Store].&[6];
```

ADOMD.NET enables the client application to set more interesting restrictions and filters for returned elements. For example, you can request all the elements with a member property that begins with the letter *R*. You use the object `MemberFilter`. Listing 33.8 shows an example.

LISTING 33.8 **`Level.GetMembers(long start, long count, string [] properties, MemberFilter filter)`**

```
//Open a connection to the server.
AdomdConnection con = new AdomdConnection();
con.ConnectionString = "Datasource=localhost; Initial Catalog=Foodmart 2008;";
con.Open();

//Get the level.
Level lvl = con.Cubes["Warehouse and
Sales"].Dimensions["Store"].Hierarchies["Store"].
➥ Levels["Store"];

//Set restrictions for the size of the collection.
//In this case, we want to get all the elements that satisfy the filter.
long start = 0;
long count = lvl.MemberCount;

//Create the filter object.
//Choose the elements of the dimension member property "Store Manager" that begin
// with the letter "R".
MemberFilter memberFilter = new MemberFilter("Store Manager",
➥ MemberFilterType.BeginsWith, "R");

//Request members.
MemberCollection allMembers = lvl.GetMembers(start, count, memberFilter);

//Print all the elements of the collection.
foreach(Member member in allMembers)
{
    Console.WriteLine(member.UniqueName + ";");
}

//Close the connection.
con.Close();
```

This request returns only one member. The name of the manager of store number 19 begins with the letter *R* (Ruth):

```
[Store].[Stores].[Store].&[19];
```

In the example, we used the `BeginsWith` attribute to filter the response. One call of the `GetMembers` method can contain multiple filters; each filter can contain only one attribute. You can choose from the following filter attributes:

- `Equals` to limit the returned members to those of a specified value
- `BeginsWith` to limit the returned members to those that start with a specified substring
- `EndsWith` to limit the returned members to those that end with a specified substring
- `Contains` to limit the returned members to those that contain a specified substring

In Listing 33.8, you had to trust our word that the name of the manager of store number 19 in the city of Vancouver is Ruth. Using the overload method `GetMembers(long start, long count, string [] properties, params MemberFilter [] filters)`, you can prove to yourself (trusting only to the accuracy of the data) that Ruth is the manager. The overload method `GetMembers` allows the application to request the names that `MemberProperties` collection will be populated with. When you specify `properties`, you can specify both custom member properties and built-in (intrinsic) member properties. In Listing 33.9, we take a look at how to request all available custom member properties.

LISTING 33.9 **`GetMembers(long start, long count, string [] properties, params MemberFilter [] filters)`**

```
//Open a connection to a source of data.
AdomdConnection con = new AdomdConnection();
con.ConnectionString = "Datasource=localhost; Initial Catalog=Foodmart 2008;";
con.Open();

//Get the level
Level lvl = con.Cubes["Warehouse and Sales"].Dimensions["Store"].
➥Hierarchies["Stores"].Levels["Store"];
long start = 0;
long count = lvl.MemberCount;
MemberFilter mf = new MemberFilter("Store Manager", MemberFilterType.BeginsWith,
➥ "R");

//Create an array of member properties
string[] properties = new string [lvl.LevelProperties.Count];
int i = 0;
```

```
//Iterate MemberProperties and store the unique names of member properties
foreach(LevelProperty levelProperty in lvl.LevelProperties)
{
     properties[i++] = levelProperty.UniqueName;
}

//Get the members and the member properties that are interesting to us
MemberCollection allMembers = lvl.GetMembers(start, count, properties, mf);

//Print the list of members
foreach(Member member in allMembers)
{
     Console.WriteLine(member.UniqueName + ";");
}
//If there is at least one member in the collection, print its member property
if (allMembers.Count> 0)
{
     Member firstMember = allMembers[0];
     foreach(MemberProperty memberProperty in firstMember.MemberProperties)
     {
          Console.WriteLine(memberProperty.UniqueName + "=" +
memberProperty.Value);
    }
}
//Close the connection
con.Close();
```

As we predicted, the result is one member, and it is the same as in the previous example: Store 19.

```
[Store].[Stores].[Store].&[19];
```

We also printed these member properties: `Store City`, `Store Manager`, `Store Sqft`, and `Store Type`:

```
[Store].[Stores].[Store].&[19];
[Store].[Stores].[Store].[Store City]=Vancouver
[Store].[Stores].[Store].[Store Manager]=Ruth
[Store].[Stores].[Store].[Store Sqft]=23112
[Store].[Stores].[Store].[Store Type]=Deluxe Supermarket
```

We have reviewed here ways to iterate the members of a level. ADOMD.NET has similar methods for the iteration of the collection of children of a specific member. You have to modify the earlier examples only slightly to see how the `GetChildren` function works.

Working with Metadata That Is Not Presented in the Form of Objects

Analysis Services keeps a lot of metadata about the model, but not all of this metadata is represented by objects of the ADOMD.NET object model. To get access to this kind of metadata information, you can use the `AdomdConnection.GetSchemaDataSet`.

This method is similar to the `GetSchema` method in OLE DB or `OledbClient.GetOLEDB SchemaDataTable`: It allows client application to retrieve any schema rowset or `Discover` supported by the server. ADOMD.NET provides three overloads for the `GetSchemaDataSet` method:

33

```
public DataSet GetSchemaDataSet(Guid schema, object[] restrictions)
public DataSet GetSchemaDataSet(String schemaName, AdomdRestrictionCollection
➥ restrictions)
public DataSet GetSchemaDataSet(String schemaName, String schemaNamespace,
➥ AdomdRestrictionCollection restrictions)
```

The first overload is modeled after the `GetSchema` method of OLE DB and allows the caller to pass the GUID of the schema with an array of restrictions. The second one is modeled after the `Discover` method of XML/A, and takes the name of the schema rowset to be retrieved; it also accepts a collection of restrictions. Each restriction is identified by the name, so there is no need to preserve the order of the restrictions in the collection.

Future versions of Analysis Services might extend the list of supported schema rowsets or XML/A `Discover` requests. To support the compatibility between the new server and old client, those schema rowsets probably will be implemented in the new namespace. The last overload of the `GetSchemaDataSet` method is designed to enable the client application to use current version of ADOMD.NET to work with future versions of the server. It allows a client application to pass not only the name of the request, but also the namespace in which this request was implemented. Let's look at an example (see Listing 33.10) that demonstrates how to retrieve a list of `Action` objects (actions are not represented by the ADOMD.NET object) using `GetSchemaDataSet`.

LISTING 33.10 Iterating Actions Using the **`GetSchemaDataSet`** Method

```
//Open a connection to the server.
AdomdConnection con = new AdomdConnection();
con.ConnectionString = "Datasource=localhost; Initial Catalog=Foodmart 2008;
➥ Safety Options=1";
con.Open();


//Create a collection of restrictions for GetSchemaDataSet.

AdomdRestrictionCollection restrictions = new AdomdRestrictionCollection();
```

```
restrictions.Add("CATALOG_NAME", "Foodmart 2008");
restrictions.Add("CUBE_NAME", "Warehouse and Sales");
restrictions.Add("COORDINATE", "[Store].[Store City].[Los Angeles] ");
int coordinateType = 4; // MDACTION_COORDINATE_MEMBER
restrictions.Add("COORDINATE_TYPE", coordinateType.ToString());
restrictions.Add("INVOCATION", 0);

//Call the method GetSchemaDataSet.
DataSet ds = con.GetSchemaDataSet("MDSCHEMA_ACTIONS", restrictions);

//Iterate all the rows in the first table of the dataset.
//Print the contents of each column.
foreach(DataRow row in ds.Tables[0].Rows)
{
     foreach(DataColumn column in ds.Tables[0].Columns)
     {
          Console.WriteLine(column.Caption + "=" + row[column]);
     }
}

//Close the connection.
con.Close();
```

The result of this code is the following information about the `Action` object we created in Chapter 15, "Key Performance Indicators, Actions, and the `DRILLTHROUGH` Statement":

```
CATALOG_NAME=FoodMart 2008
SCHEMA_NAME=
CUBE_NAME=Warehouse and Sales
ACTION_NAME=Store Locations
ACTION_TYPE=1
COORDINATE=[Store].[Store City].[Los Angeles]
COORDINATE_TYPE=4
ACTION_CAPTION=View Map for Los Angeles
DESCRIPTION=This action displays a map with the location of a store pinned on it
CONTENT=http://maps.msn.com/home.aspx?plce1=Los Angeles,CA,USA
APPLICATION="Internet Explorer"
INVOCATION=1
```

If you are familiar with `OledbClient` ADO.NET provider, you might ask why `OledbClient` returns `DataTable` and ADOMD.NET returns `DataSet` when retrieving schema rowset. The designers of ADOMD.NET took this approach because `OledbClient` does not support nested rowsets (that is, when one of the columns of the rowset is a rowset itself). Nested rowsets don't exist among schema rowsets in the OLE DB specification or in OLE DB for online analytical processing (OLAP), but are very often used in data mining and in some of the Discover requests defined by the XML/A specification. For example, Discover_Schemas_Rowsets returns a nested rowset.

DataSet is the most obvious choice for an object to store such information in because it can hold tables and their relations. Listing 33.11 shows how to iterate nested rowsets in a case where the client application does not have advance information about the columns and the relationships between them. In this example, we call DISCOVER_ROWSETS to retrieve information about MDSCHEMA_ACTIONS: its columns, column types, and names of the restrictions.

LISTING 33.11 Retrieving Information About **MDSCHEMA_ACTIONS**

```
public void WriteDiscoverSchemaRowsets()
{
     //Open a connection to the server.
     AdomdConnection con = new AdomdConnection();
     con.ConnectionString = "Datasource=localhost; Initial Catalog=Foodmart 2008;";
     con.Open();

     //Create a restriction collection that will limit the result to information
     //about the Actions schema rowset.
     AdomdRestrictionCollection restrictions = new AdomdRestrictionCollection();
     restrictions.Add("SchemaName", "MDSCHEMA_ACTIONS");

     //Call the method GetSchemaDataSet.
     DataSet ds = con.GetSchemaDataSet("DISCOVER_SCHEMA_ROWSETS", restrictions);

     //Get the first table. ADOMD.NET will always return it even if the result
     //is empty.
     DataTable dt = ds.Tables[0];

     //To improve performance, we will create an array in which we will store
     //DataRelation for each column that contains DataRelation and null if
     //the column contains data values.
     DataRelation[] drMap = new DataRelation[dt.Columns.Count];
     int iColumn = 0;
     //Iterate all the columns and relationships in the DataTable.
     //This is certainly not very convenient. It would be better if the column
     //stored additional information whether it contains reference or data. But
     //unfortunately that's not the way it works.
     foreach(DataColumn column in dt.Columns)
     {
          foreach(DataRelation dataRelation in ds.Relations)
          {
               if (IsParentRelationColumn(dataRelation, column))
```

```
            {
                drMap[iColumn] = dataRelation;
                break;
            }
        }
        iColumn ++;
    }

    //Iterate the rows of the first datatable and print their values.
    foreach(DataRow row in dt.Rows)
    {
        iColumn = 0;
        foreach(DataColumn column in dt.Columns)
        {
            if (drMap[iColumn] != null)
            {
                Console.WriteLine(column.ColumnName);
                //Navigate to the nested table through relationship.
                foreach(DataRow childRow in row.GetChildRows(drMap[iColumn]))
                {
                    foreach(DataColumn childColumn in childRow.Table.Columns)
                    {
                        //If the column is a data column rather than a
                        //relationship column, print the data value.
                        if (! IsChildRelationColumn(drMap[iColumn],
➥ childColumn))
                        {
                            object field = childRow[childColumn];
                            Console.WriteLine(" " +
➥ childColumn.Caption + "=" + field.ToString());
                        }
                    }
                }
            }
            else
            {
                object field = row [column];
                Console.WriteLine(column.Caption + "=" + field.ToString());
            }
            iColumn++;
        }
    }
    //Close the connection
    con.Close();
}
//The helper function that detects whether the column is a child of the relation.
```

```
static private bool IsChildRelationColumn(DataRelation dataRelation, DataColumn
➥ dataColumn)
{
     foreach(DataColumn relationColumn in dataRelation.ChildColumns)
     {
          if (dataColumn == relationColumn)
          {
                return true;
          }
     }
     return false;
}

//The helper function that detects whether a column is a child of a relation.
static private bool IsParentRelationColumn(DataRelation dataRelation, DataColumn
➥ dataColumn)
{
      foreach(DataColumn relationColumn in dataRelation.ParentColumns)
      {
          if (dataColumn == relationColumn)
          {
               return true;
           }
     }
     return false;
}
```

So, the result we get is the following data about the `Actions` schema rowset:

```
SchemaName=MDSCHEMA_ACTIONS
SchemaGuid=a07ccd08—8148-11d0-87bb-00c04fc33942
Restriction
      Name=CATALOG_NAME
      Type=xsd:string
      Name=SCHEMA_NAME
      Type=xsd:string
      Name=CUBE_NAME
      Type=xsd:string
      Name=ACTION_NAME
      Type=xsd:string
      Name=ACTION_TYPE
      Type=xsd:int
      Name=COORDINATE
      Type=xsd:string
      Name=COORDINATE_TYPE
```

```
        Type=xsd:int
        Name=INVOCATION
        Type=xsd:int
        Name=CUBE_SOURCE
        Type=xsd:unsignedShort
Description =
RestrictionsMask=511
```

AdomdCommand

To send a command to the server that will result in some action, ADOMD.NET provides the `AdomdCommand` class. In the simple case, the command accepts a string containing a Multidimensional Expressions (MDX), Data Mining Expressions (DMX), or SQL query forms an XML/A `Execute` request and sends it to Analysis Services. Similar to `AdomdConnection`, `AdomdCommand` implements the standard `IDbCommand` interface, as shown in Figure 33.12.

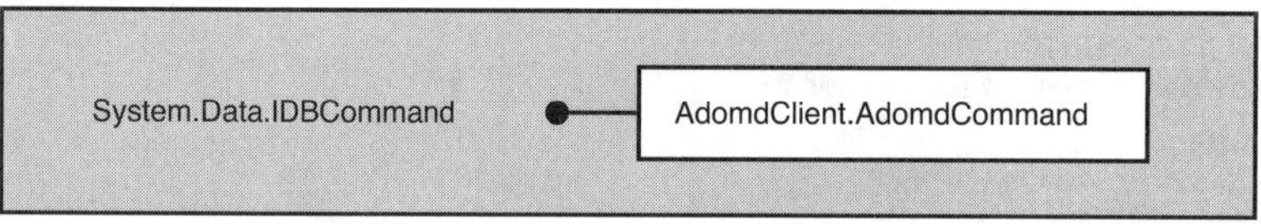

FIGURE 33.12 The `ADOMDCommand` object implements the `IDbCommand` interface.

Properties

`AdomdCommand` always works with `AdomdConnection`. However, there are various ways of creating these objects. One of them is to create `AdomdConnection` and `AdomdCommand` objects and then use the `Connection` property of the `AdomdCommand` object to pass the connection to the command, as shown in Listing 33.12.

LISTING 33.12 Sending the Query to Analysis Services

```
//Open a connection to the server.
String conString = "Datasource=localhost; Initial Catalog=Foodmart 2008";
AdomdConnection con = new AdomdConnection();
con.ConnectionString = conString;
con.Open();

// Create the object AdomdCommand.
AdomdCommand command = new AdomdCommand();
command.Connection = con;

//Define the text the request.
```

```
command.CommandText = "SELECT Measures.Members ON COLUMNS FROM [Warehouse and
Sales]";

//Execute command...
//...
// Close the connection.
con.Close();
```


In most cases, the request sent to the server is small enough. For example, even the longest MDX request will hardly exceed two or three pages of text. However, some Data Definition Language (DDL) requests that can be sent to the server using ADOMD.NET are quite large and can take much more memory on the client computer. It is not optimal to construct such a request as a string and send it through the `CommandText` property.

For large DDL requests, ADOMD.NET provides the `CommandStream` property, which accepts the object that implements the `IStream` interface. Because only well-formed XML can be sent to the server, ADOMD.NET has to perform some operations to determine whether the stream contains XML or just plain text. To do this, ADOMD.NET uses a simple algorithm that reads the first symbol of the request. If the first character is <, ADOMD.NET assumes that stream contains an XML element. But if the first character is some other symbol, ADOMD.NET wraps the request with the `<Statement>` element before it sends the request to the server.

ADOMD.NET allows only one of two properties to be set: either `CommandText` or `CommandStream`. Listing 33.13 uses `CommandStream`.

LISTING 33.13 Using **`CommandStream`**

```
//Open a connection to the server.
AdomdConnection con = new AdomdConnection();
con.ConnectionString = "Datasource=localhost;";
con.Open();

//Open a stream for reading a file that contains the XML for creating a cube
System.IO.StreamReader sr = new System.IO.StreamReader
➥("..\\..\\Foodmart2008Metadata.xml"", true);
AdomdCommand command = con.CreateCommand();
command.CommandStream = sr.BaseStream;

// Execute the command
command.ExecuteNonQuery();

// Close the stream
sr.Close();
```

```
//Close the connection.
con.Close();
```

Methods

After the command is defined, it has to be executed. There are various ways to execute of a command, depending on what result you expect:

- `ExecuteCellSet` executes the command and receives a result in the form of a multidimensional cellset. (We discuss multidimensional cellsets in the "Using the `CellSet` Object to Work with Multidimensional Data" section later in this chapter.)
- `ExecuteReader` executes the command and receives a result in the form of the `AdomdDatareader` class.
- `ExecuteXmlReader` returns a result in the form of an XML/A result (either `Rowset` or `MDDataSet`).
- `ExecuteNonQuery` executes the command, but does not return a result.
- `Execute` returns an object whose type depends on the request that has been executed: `CellSet`, `AdomdDataReader`, or `NULL`.

ExecuteCellSet

`ExecuteCellSet` executes the command and returns the `CellSet` object, which is intended for work with multidimensional data. The `CellSet` object, in the simplest case, is created by the `ExecuteCellSet` command and comes back to the user already initialized and populated with data. This command can be used only for executing MDX queries. If you use it to execute a SQL or data-mining query, ADOMD.NET will not return a result and will instead throw an exception (see Listing 33.14).

LISTING 33.14 Executing an MDX Query and Retrieving a **Cellset**

```
// Connect to the server.
AdomdConnection con = new AdomdConnection();
con.ConnectionString = "Datasource=localhost; Initial Catalog=Foodmart 2008";
con.Open();

//Create a simple MDX request.
String cmdText = "SELECT Measures.Members ON COLUMNS FROM [Warehouse and Sales]";
AdomdCommand command = new AdomdCommand(cmdText,con);

//Execute a method that returns CellSet.
CellSet cellset = command.ExecuteCellSet();

//Close the connection.
con.Close();
```

ExecuteDataReader

The ExecuteDataReader method executes a command and returns an AdomdDataReader object, which is used for navigating the information received from the server in the form of a forward-only recordset. (We discuss the AdomdDataReader object later, in the "Working with Data in Tabular Format" section.) Listing 33.15 is a simple code example that shows the use of this method.

LISTING 33.15 Executing a Command and Retrieving a Result in the **DataReader** Format

```
// Connect to the server.
AdomdConnection con = new AdomdConnection();
con.ConnectionString = "Datasource = localhost; Initial Catalog=Foodmart 2008";
con.Open();

// Create a simple MDX statement.
AdomdCommand command = (AdomdCommand)con.CreateCommand();
string query = "SELECT Measures.Members ON COLUMNS FROM [Warehouse and Sales]";
command.CommandText = query;

//Execute the method that returns IDataReader.
IDataReader reader = command.ExecuteReader();

// Read the metadata about the columns in the returned result.
DataTable schemaTable = reader.GetSchemaTable();
Console.WriteLine("Schema");
for(int iSchRow = 0; iSchRow<schemaTable.Rows.Count; iSchRow ++)
{
for(int iSchCol = 0; iSchCol<schemaTable.Columns.Count; iSchCol ++)
     {
     Console.WriteLine(schemaTable.Rows[iSchRow][iSchCol].ToString() + " ");
     }
}
// Read the result.
while(reader.Read())
{
     for(int iCol = 0; iCol <reader.FieldCount; iCol ++)
     {
            Console.WriteLine(reader.GetValue(iCol).ToString());
            Console.WriteLine(reader.GetDataTypeName(iCol));
     }
}
// Close DataReader.
reader.Close();
// Close the connection.
con.Close();
```

ExecuteXmlReader

The ExecuteXmlReader method executes a command and returns XmlReader, containing an XML/A resultset. The main purpose of this method, although not the only one, is to save the result for subsequent work after the connection is closed (see Listing 33.16).

LISTING 33.16 Executing a Command and Retrieving the Result in XML Format

```
//Open a connection to a source of data.
AdomdConnection con = new AdomdConnection();
con.ConnectionString = "Datasource=localhost; Initial Catalog=Foodmart 2008;";
con.Open();

//Create a command.
AdomdCommand command = con.CreateCommand();
command.CommandText = "SELECT Measures.Members ON COLUMNS FROM [Warehouse and
Sales]";

//Execute the command and get XmlReader.
XmlReader reader = command.ExecuteXmlReader();

//Write the XML into a file.
string xml = reader.ReadOuterXml();
System.IO.StreamWriter writer = new System.IO.StreamWriter("cellSetXml.xml", false);
writer.Write(xml);
//Close the file.
writer.Close();
//Close XmlReader.
reader.Close();
//Close the connection.
con.Close();
```

At some later time, the saved result can be opened and loaded into the CellSet object:

```
//Open XmlReader from the XML file.
XmlTextReader reader = new XmlTextReader("cellSetXml.xml");
//Load the XML into the CellSet object.
CellSet cellSet = CellSet.LoadXml(reader);

//Close XmlReader.
reader.Close();
```

NOTE

Because ExecuteXmlReader reads data directly from a stream based on the connection to the server, XmlReader must be closed before any other operations on this connection can be executed. Otherwise, it blocks the work of other commands, and an exception is thrown.

ExecuteNonQuery

The ExecuteNonQuery method is used to execute Create, Drop, Update, Call, and other requests that do not return results, but change the state on the server. Unlike the SqlClient provider, this method never returns a result and cannot be used for a direct call to stored procedures (see Listing 33.17).

LISTING 33.17 Executing Commands That Do Not Return Results

```
//Connect to the server.
AdomdConnection con = new AdomdConnection();
con.ConnectionString= "Datasource=localhost; Initial Catalog=Foodmart 2008";
con.Open();

//Create a command that will send a request for a creation of a calculated member.
String cmdText = "CREATE Member [Warehouse and Sales].Measures.MyCalcMember as 1 ";
AdomdCommand command = new AdomdCommand(cmdText,con);

//Execute the command, without expecting a returned result.
command.ExecuteNonQuery();

//Close the connection.
con.Close();
```

The result of this code is a calculated member, created on the server and accessible to all the commands of the current session.

Execute

Use of the methods described in the preceding sections requires that the client application be aware of the type of request sent. There are a number of client applications for which this does not present a problem—such an application generates the query and, therefore, is aware of its type before it sends the query to the server.

However, there are other applications that accept the text of requests from the user, or from other components of the system, and cannot determine what type of request should be executed. For such applications, we have the method Execute, which returns a result as a loosely typed object. Let's look at an example of the use of Execute in Listing 33.18.

LISTING 33.18 Executing Commands and Retrieving the Result in the Default Format

```
//Connect to the server.
AdomdConnection con = new AdomdConnection();
con.ConnectionString = "Datasource=localhost; Initial Catalog=Foodmart 2008";
con.Open();

//Create a command that sends a simple MDX request.
String cmdText = "SELECT measures.members ON COLUMNS FROM [Warehouse and Sales]";
AdomdCommand command = new AdomdCommand(cmdText, con);

//Execute a command and return an object of any type.
Object result = command.Execute();

//Analyze the type of object returned.
if (null == result )
{
     //No result
}
else if (result is CellSet)
{
     //Work with CellSet.
     CellSet cellset = (CellSet)result;
}
else if (result is AdomdDataReader)
{
     //Work with DataReader.
     AdomdDataReader dataReader = (AdomdDataReader) result;
}

//Close the connection.
con.Close();
```

Using the `CellSet` Object to Work with Multidimensional Data

The `CellSet` object is one of the key objects in ADOMD.NET. You use it to manipulate multidimensional data on the client. As discussed in the "`AdomdCommand`" section earlier in the chapter, `CellSet` is created as the result of execution of the `AdomdCommand.ExecuteCellSet` method, but it can also be created by loading XML from a file or from another XML/A data source. `CellSet` represents a set of the collections necessary for the iteration of data on the client. To draw a parallel with ADO.NET, `CellSet` is a multidimensional `DataSet`. If you take a look at the diagram of the hierarchy of objects represented in

Figure 33.13, you might on the one hand conclude that the `CellSet` object hierarchy is similar to the multidimensional result defined by the XML/A specification (See the "XML/A Methods" section in Chapter 32, "XML for Analysis," for further discussion.) On the other hand, you might be reminded of the hierarchy of ADOMD objects.

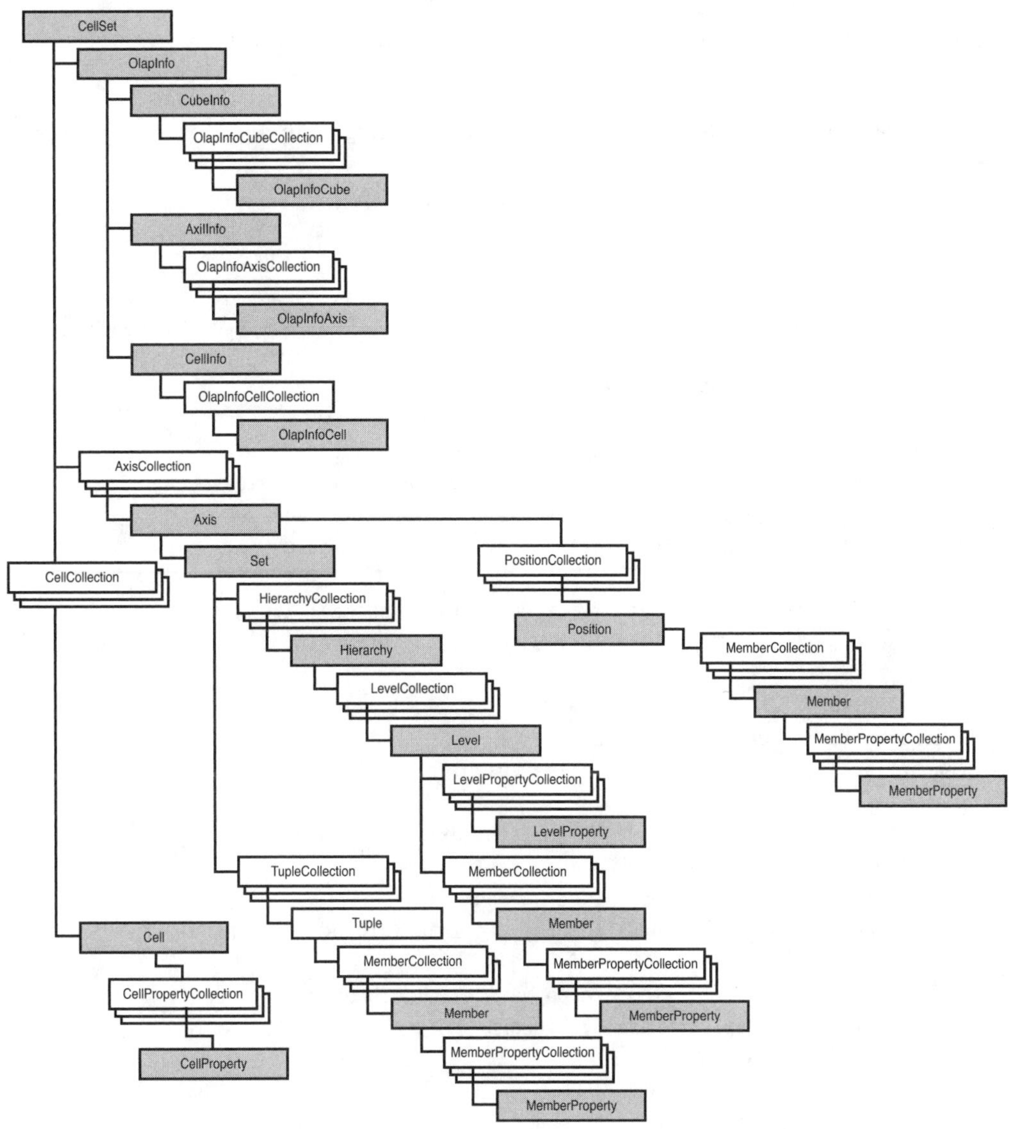

FIGURE 33.13 The hierarchy of `CellSet` objects supported by ADOMD.NET.

One of the new objects in ADOMD.NET is `OlapInfo`, which enables the application to receive metadata about a `CellSet` object. This can be useful for applications that are not aware of the content of the MDX query that is sent to the server. `OlapInfo` contains metadata for the cube, hierarchies, members, and properties of the members used in the request, and for the cell properties requested in the MDX query. The `OlapInfo` object in `CellSet` has the same structure as the `OlapInfo` element in XML/A. Listing 33.19 shows an example of the `OlapInfo` object in use.

LISTING 33.19 Iterating the **`OlapInfo`** Section of the **`CellSet`** Object

```
// Open a connection to the server.
AdomdConnection con = new AdomdConnection("Datasource=localhost; Initial Catalog=
➥Foodmart 2008;");
con.Open();

//Send a simple MDX statement.
AdomdCommand command = con.CreateCommand();
command.CommandText = "SELECT Measures.Members ON COLUMNS FROM [Warehouse and
Sales]";
CellSet cellset = command.ExecuteCellSet();

//Iterate the metadata of the cubes used in the request.
//In the current version of Microsoft SQL Server Analysis Services,
// only one cube can be used in the request.
foreach(OlapInfoCube cubeInfo in cellset.OlapInfo.CubeInfo.Cubes)
{
     Console.WriteLine("CubeName = " + cubeInfo.CubeName);
     Console.WriteLine("Cube was last updated on " + cubeInfo.LastDataUpdate);
}

// Iterate the metadata for the axes.
foreach(OlapInfoAxis axisInfo in cellset.OlapInfo.AxesInfo.Axes)
{
     // For each axis, print the name of the axis.
     Console.WriteLine("AxisName = " + axisInfo.Name);
     //Iterate the hierarchies on the current axis.
     foreach(OlapInfoHierarchy hierarchyInfo in axisInfo.Hierarchies)
      {
           Console.WriteLine("HierarchyName = " + hierarchyInfo.Name);
           foreach(OlapInfoProperty hierarchyPropertyInfo in
➥hierarchyInfo.HierarchyProperties)
          {
               Console.WriteLine("HierarchyProperty = " +
➥hierarchyPropertyInfo.Name);
          }
     }
}
```

```
//Iterate the cell properties that are used in the request.
foreach(OlapInfoProperty cellPropertyInfo in
➥cellset.OlapInfo.CellInfo.CellProperties)
{
    Console.WriteLine("CellPropertyName = " + cellPropertyInfo.Name);
}

//Close the connection.
con.Close();
```


Executing this sample code yields a result that contains the name of the cube, the time it was last changed, the names of the axes used in the query, the unique names of the hierarchies for each axis, and properties of the members and cells returned by the query:

```
CubeName = Warehouse and Sales
Cube was last updated on 8/10/2006 7:06:21 PM
AxisName = Axis0
HierarchyName = [Measures]
HierarchyProperty = MEMBER_UNIQUE_NAME
HierarchyProperty = MEMBER_CAPTION
HierarchyProperty = LEVEL_UNIQUE_NAME
HierarchyProperty = LEVEL_NUMBER
HierarchyProperty = DISPLAY_INFO
CellPropertyName = CellOrdinal
CellPropertyName = VALUE
CellPropertyName = FORMATTED_VALUE
```

In addition to containing the `OlapInfo` object, `CellSet` contains a collection of axis objects—a subset of the multidimensional space that the server returned as a result of the execution of the MDX query. Along each axis is a set of tuples, each of which is a collection of members.

If you look closely at the structure of the hierarchy of the result, it will remind you of the structure of most MDX queries sent to the server. In designing ADOMD.NET, we set a goal of unifying ADOMD.NET and MDX. On the other hand, we wanted to keep to a minimum the changes that a developer would need to make to port an application from ADOMD to ADOMD.NET. To accomplish all this, we created another branch in our object model, `PositionCollection`, which accurately mimics the structure of objects used in ADOMD. `CellSet` also contains `CellCollection`—a collection of the values of cells and their properties.

There are lots of ways you can display multidimensional data. Regardless of your choice of user interface, the job of displaying data remains the same. We're going to use the simple approach of displaying data in a grid control. Unfortunately you will not find the grid control you need in the current versions of Visual Studio .NET. The `DataGrid` control—a managed control provided by Visual Studio for displaying data—is not designed for displaying a multidimensional data. And, the Microsoft `FlexGrid`—a native control for displaying data in grid format—is no longer distributed with Visual Studio. Therefore, we have published a sample `Grid` control to demonstrate the display of multidimensional data. This `Grid` control is a legacy control, written in native code, that we use for demonstration purposes only. If you want to play around with it, you can download the sample database, code samples, and other information from the web at http://www.samspublishing.com or from http://www.e-tservice.com.

To place the results of an MDX query in a grid, follow these steps:

1. Create a new project in Visual Studio .NET. (See the "Creating an ADOMD.NET Project" section earlier in this chapter.)
2. Right-click References in the tree view on the left, and then click Add Reference.
3. On the COM tab of the References dialog box, select the INView ActiveX Control module.
4. Open Form1 in form design mode.
5. In the Toolbox, right-click Data and select Choose Items.
6. On the COM Components tab of the Choose Toolbox Items dialog box, select INView Control.
7. Drag the grid to the form.

You have now created a toolbar with an Execute button and a text box for entering query text.

When the user clicks the Execute button, a connection to the server is created, and the query is executed. To simplify the sample, we support only queries that request two axes from the server (see Listing 33.20).

LISTING 33.20 Displaying Multidimensional Data in a Grid

```
private void toolStripButtonExecute_Click(object sender, EventArgs e)
{
     if (queryBox.Text.Length <= 0)
         return;
      try
      {
            //Open a connection to a server.
            AdomdConnection con = new AdomdConnection("Datasource=localhost;
➥ Initial Catalog=Foodmart 2008;");
            con.Open();
            AdomdCommand command = con.CreateCommand();
            command.CommandText = queryBox.Text;
            //Execute a command and get a cellset back.
            CellSet cellset = command.ExecuteCellSet();
            //Display the result in the grid.
            DisplayResult(cellset);
```

```
            //Close the connection.
            con.Close();
        }
        catch (AdomdException ex)
        {
            //Display an error message if an exception occurred.
            MessageBox.Show(ex.Message);
        }
}
```


After the query has been successfully executed, we display the result in the grid. The grid contains of three major areas: headings for the columns area, headings for the rows area, and the data area. We populate the column headings with the captions of the members located along the COLUMNS axis and the row heading area with the captions of the members located along the ROWS axis. Because the CellSet object contains hierarchical data and can have members of more than one hierarchy located along the axis, we create as many columns or rows in the headings as the number of the hierarchies along the axis.

We can now place the FormattedValue properties in the cells of the data area of the grid. The user can type a query such that it will not return a FormattedValue property; in that case, the code in our example causes an exception. If you want to have more robust code, you might want to check whether FormattedValue property is available before calling the Cell.FormattedValue property (see Listing 33.21).

LISTING 33.21 Fetching the Properties of a **Hierarchy** Object

```
//Display the result for the user.
private void DisplayResult(CellSet cellset)
{
     //Validate the result.
     if (cellset.Axes.Count != 2)
         throw new InvalidOperationException("This sample doesn't support queries
➥ that don't return two axes");

     //Calculate the number of the columns.
     int colCount = (0 == cellset.Axes[0].Set.Tuples.Count) ? 1 :
➥cellset.Axes[0]. Set.Tuples.Count;
     //Calculate the number of the rows.
     int rowCount = (0 == cellset.Axes[1].Set.Tuples.Count) ? 1 :
➥cellset.Axes[1].Set.Tuples.Count;
     //Calculate the number of the rows in the column captions.
     int colCaption = (0 == cellset.Axes[1].Set.Hierarchies.Count) ? 1 :
➥cellset.Axes[1].Set.Hierarchies.Count;
     //Calculate the number of the columns in the row captions.
```

```
    int rowCaption = (0 == cellset.Axes[0].Set.Hierarchies.Count) ? 1 :
➥cellset.Axes[0].Set.Hierarchies.Count;
    InitializeGrid(colCount, rowCount, colCaption, rowCaption);
    //Show the columns captions.
    DisplayCaptions(cellset.Axes[0], true);
    //Show the rows captions.
    DisplayCaptions(cellset.Axes[1], false);
    //Show the data.
    DisplayData(cellset);
}
//Display the columns captions.
private void DisplayCaptions(Axis axis, bool displayColumns)
{
    //Iterate over all hiearchies on the column axis.
    for (int iHierarchy = 0; iHierarchy < axis.Set.Hierarchies.Count; iHierarchy++)
    {
        //Iterate over all tuples on the column axis.
        //We want to merge the cells of the header if the member is
➥ duplicated along the hierarchy.
        int cSkippedTuples = 1;
        for (int iTuple = 0; iTuple < axis.Set.Tuples.Count;
➥iTuple += cSkippedTuples)
        {
            //Calculate how many cells should be merged.
            cSkippedTuples = CalculateSkippedCells(axis, iHierarchy, iTuple);
            INVIEWLib.Cell cell = null;
            if (displayColumns)
            {
                //Get the cell on the grid in the columns heading area.
                //if member was used more then once along the hierarchy, merge
                //the cells in the header.
                cell = this.colGrid.get_Cell(iHierarchy + 1, iTuple + 1 ) as
➥ INVIEWLib.Cell;
                cell.SetSize(1, cSkippedTuples);
            }
            else
            {
                //Get the cell on the grid in the rows heading area.
               //if member was used more then once along the hierarchy,
➥ merge the cells in the header.
                cell = this.rowGrid.get_Cell( iTuple + 1, iHierarchy + 1)
➥ as INVIEWLib.Cell;
                cell.SetSize(cSkippedTuples, 1);
            }
            //Put the Member.Caption property on the grid
```

```
                Member member = axis.Set.Tuples[iTuple].Members[iHierarchy];
                cell.Text = member.Caption;
            }
        }
    }

    //Helper function that calculated the number of cells in the grid headers that
    //should be merged.
    private int CalculateSkippedCells(Axis axis, int iHierarchy, int iTuple)
    {
        int cCells = 1;
        Member member = axis.Set.Tuples[iTuple].Members[iHierarchy];
        //Iterate over the members following a current one.
        for(int iCurrentTuple = iTuple + 1; iCurrentTuple < axis.Set.Tuples.Count;
➥ iCurrentTuple++)
        {
            //Compare Unique names of the current member and members that follows it.
            //Break when we found a member that differs from the current one.
            if (member.UniqueName != axis.Set.Tuples[iCurrentTuple].Members
➥[iHierarchy].UniqueName)
                break;
            cCells++;
        }
        //return number of cells that can be merged.
        return cCells;
    }

    //Display the data values.
    private void DisplayData(CellSet cellset)
    {
        //Iterate over the tuples in the columns and rows axes.
        for (int iCol = 0; iCol < cellset.Axes[0].Set.Tuples.Count; iCol++)
        {
            for (int iRow = 0; iRow < cellset.Axes[1].Set.Tuples.Count; iRow++)
            {
                //Get the cell on the grid in the data area.
                INVIEWLib.Cell cell = this.dataGrid.get_Cell(iRow + 1, iCol + 1)
➥ as INVIEWLib.Cell;
                //Put the Formatted value property of the cell on the grid.
                cell.Text = cellset.Cells[iCol, iRow].FormattedValue;
            }
        }
    }
```

33

This code draws a grid with data returned from Analysis Services, as shown in Figure 33.14.

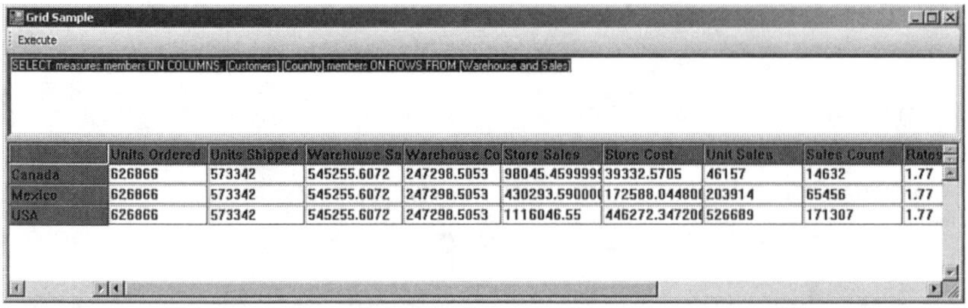

FIGURE 33.14 The `Grid` control displaying the result of the execution of the multidimensional query.

Handling Object Symmetry

Objects contained in a `CellSet` object have similar interfaces and follow the same rules as metadata objects; we call this *object symmetry*. A client application can retrieve some classes of objects in two ways: by iterating the `CellSet` object and by iterating metadata objects. For example, `Hierarchy`, `Member`, and `MemberProperty` objects can be retrieved as a result of an MDX query or by navigating metadata objects. ADOMD.NET usually sends a schema rowset request to request a metadata object. A schema rowset request generally retrieves more information from the server then an MDX query.

Let's take the `Hierarchy` object as an example. It has properties such as `Name`, `UniqueName`, `Description`, `HierarchyOrigin`, and others. When the `Hierarchy` object is obtained by iterating the metadata objects, its properties are populated from result of the execution of an `MDSCHEMA_HIERARCHIES` schema rowset request. If the `Hierarchy` object is obtained as a result of an MDX query, however, the object contains only its unique name. (See the discussion of `MDDataSet` in Chapter 32.)

This raises a question: When the client application requests the `Caption` property of the `Hierarchy` object, how does ADOMD.NET provide this information? ADOMD would throw a `NotImplemented` exception, but ADOMD.NET is designed to solve the problem and provide the client application with the information it requested. In our example, ADOMD.NET will send an `MDSCHEMA_HIERARCHIES` request to the server if the schema is not in the cache.

At first glance, this is very convenient for the programmer who creates the client application, because she doesn't need to write complex code. On the other hand, an apparently simple operation could lead to a round trip to the server. If performance is critical, try to avoid calls to the following properties of the `Hierarchy` object:

- `Name`
- `Description`

- ParentDimension
- DefaultMember
- DisplayFolder
- Caption
- HierarchyOrigin
- Levels
- Properties

The code in Listing 33.22 demonstrates a simple way of accessing properties that are not part of the multidimensional result returned by the server.

LISTING 33.22 Fetching Object Properties That Are Not Part of a Multidimensional Result

```
//Open a connection to the server.
AdomdConnection con = new AdomdConnection("Datasource=localhost; Initial
➥Catalog=Foodmart 2008;");
con.Open();

//Execute a simple MDX statement.
AdomdCommand command = con.CreateCommand();
command.CommandText = "SELECT Measures.Members ON COLUMNS FROM [Warehouse and
Sales]";

//Execute the command and get the CellSet object.
CellSet cellSet = command.ExecuteCellSet();

//Iterate the axes and their hierarchies and get properties of each hierarchy.
foreach(Axis axis in cellSet.Axes)
{
     foreach(Hierarchy hier in axis.Set.Hierarchies)
     {
          Console.WriteLine(hier.Caption);
          Console.WriteLine(hier.Description);
     }
}
//Close the connection.
con.Close();
```

You probably have already noticed that the `Member` object differs from other objects in the object model. The main difference is the possible number of members in the collection. There are usually many more members in the system than there are hierarchies or levels, so sending a round-trip request to the server to bring additional properties of each member can cause severe performance problems.

To warn application designers of the potential problem, ADOMD.NET throws an `InvalidOperationException` when the client application tries to get properties for which there is no information on the client. If you really want to access member properties, you can call the `FetchAllProperties` method and then use the property you need. Listing 33.23 illustrates this approach.

LISTING 33.23 Fetching the Properties of the Member Object That Are Not Part of a Multidimensional Result

```
//Open a connection to the server.
AdomdConnection con = new AdomdConnection("Datasource=localhost; Initial
➥ Catalog=Foodmart 2008;");
con.Open();

//Execute an MDX statement.
AdomdCommand command = con.CreateCommand();
command.CommandText = " SELECT {[Measures].[Store Cost],
➥[Measures].[Store Sales]} ON COLUMNS FROM [Warehouse and Sales]";
CellSet cellSet = command.ExecuteCellSet();

//Iterate the axes and tuples on each axis.
foreach(Axis axis in cellSet.Axes)
{
     foreach(Tuple tuple in axis.Set.Tuples)
     {
          Member member = tuple.Members[0];
          try
          {
               //Try to get the member.Type property; this will cause an exception.
               Console.WriteLine(member.Type);
          }
          catch(InvalidOperationException ex)
          {
               Console.WriteLine(ex.Message);
               // Send a request to the server to bring all the properties of
               // the current member.
               member.FetchAllProperties();
               //Successfully print the property member.Type.
               Console.WriteLine(member.Type);
          }
     }
}
//Close the connection
con.Close();
```

This code could cause a performance loss, but you can avoid that. If your client application generates MDX queries, you can specify the properties you want to retrieve from the server in the `DIMENSION PROPERTIES` clause of your MDX statement. So, in the preceding example, you could change the request to the following and ADOMD.NET would neither throw an exception nor send additional requests to the server:

```
SELECT measures.members DIMENSION PROPERTIES MEMBER_TYPE ON COLUMNS FROM [Ware-
house and Sales]
```


Working with Data in Tabular Format

Because ADOMD.NET is an ADO.NET provider, it supports most of the same interfaces as other ADO.NET providers. A client application can use the same approach for data access through ADOMD.NET as it would use with other ADO.NET providers.

ADO.NET provides two models for working with data: connected and disconnected. To work with data in the connected mode, ADO.NET provides the `IDataReader` interface that enables the application to read data from the stream. To support the disconnected scenario, ADO.NET provides the `DataSet` class that stores data in memory and does not depend on the data source.

The data in a `DataSet` object can be loaded from an XML document or by using a special object—specifically, an adapter: `DataAdapter`. Figure 33.15 shows the operations that can occur when a client application loads data into a `DataSet` object.

First, the client application instantiates the `DataAdapter` class and passes it a connection string that can be used to establish a connection to the data source and the text of the command to be executed. Under the hood, `DataAdapter` creates an `AdomdCommand` object and an `AdomdConnection` object. Then, it establishes the connection, executes the command, and retrieves the result in the form of an `AdomdDataReader` object. `AdomdDataAdapter` then reads the data from the `AdomdDataReader` object and writes that data into the `DataSet` object.

NOTE

The `DataSet` object is a component delivered with the .NET Framework and is not part of the ADO.NET provider. Therefore, it does not fall within the scope of this book. We cover it only in the context of other ADOMD.NET objects.

`AdomdDataAdapter` is a special object that connects the data source and the `DataSet` object. It implements the `IDbDataAdapter` interface and inherits from the `System.Data.DbDataAdapter` class, as shown in Figure 33.16.

Listing 33.24 provides an example that populates the `DataSet` object with the data retrieved from the Analysis Server.

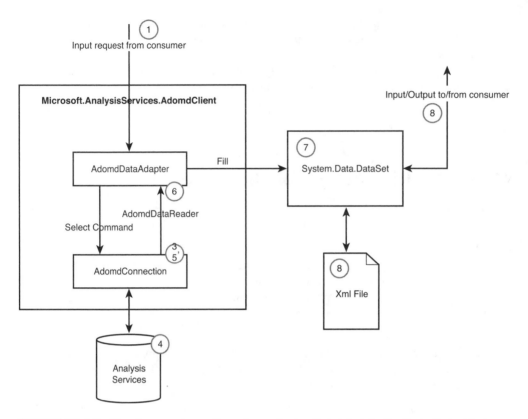

FIGURE 33.15 The diagram shows the schema for loading data into the `DataSet` object.

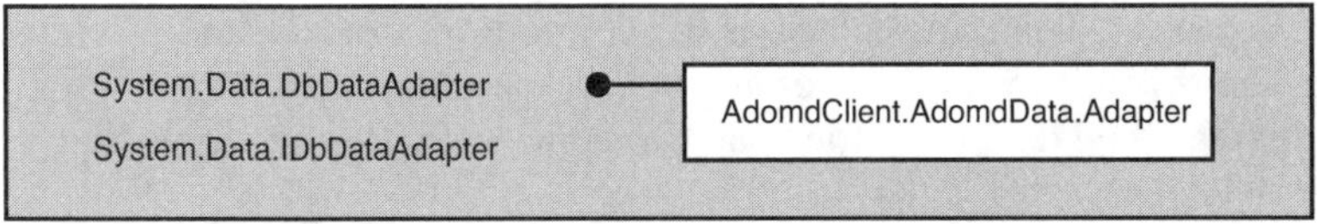

FIGURE 33.16 The `ADOMDDataAdapter` object inherits from the `DbDataAdapter` object and implements the `IDbDataAdapter` interface.

LISTING 33.24 Populating a Dataset with the Results of a Query Sent to Analysis Services

```
string commandText = "SELECT Measures.Members ON COLUMNS FROM [Warehouse and Sales]";
string connectionString = "Datasource=localhost; Initial Catalog=Foodmart 2008;";
AdomdDataAdapter dataAdapter = new AdomdDataAdapter(commandText, connectionString);
DataSet ds = new DataSet();
dataAdapter.Fill(ds);
```

As you can see, this piece of code is very simple. Practically all the work of loading the data occurs during the execution of the `Fill` method, which opens a connection, sends a request to the server, and closes the connection. If you need to create more than one

DataSet object from a single source of data, you probably want to use the same connection multiple times and maintain the life of the connection yourself instead of having DataAdapter do it for you (see Listing 33.25).

LISTING 33.25 You Can Pass an Existing **AdomdCommand** Object to a Data Adapter

```
string commandText = "SELECT Measures.Members ON COLUMNS FROM [Warehouse and Sales]";
string connectionString = "Datasource=localhost; Initial Catalog=Foodmart 2008;";
AdomdConnection con = new AdomdConnection(connectionString);
con.Open();
AdomdCommand command = new AdomdCommand(commandText, con);
AdomdDataAdapter dataAdapter = new AdomdDataAdapter(command);
DataSet ds = new DataSet();
dataAdapter.Fill(ds);
con.Close();
```


NOTE

The current version of ADOMD.NET supports the DataAdapter and DataSet objects only for reading data from the server, not for writing. If you need your application to change data on the server (to write back and perform what-if analysis), use the MDX command UPDATE.

AdomdDataReader

In the preceding section, we described the process of loading data into the DataSet object. However, a client application often needs to read data, display it in the user interface, or manipulate it in some other way, rather than store it in memory. In this case, you would not use the DataSet object. You can use AdomdDataReader, which iterates data in a forward-only fashion. This object iterates the stream of data while receiving it from the server, and allows the client application to work with parts of the data before it loads the full resultset. AdomdDataReader implements the standard IDataReader and IDataRecord interfaces, as shown in Figure 33.17.

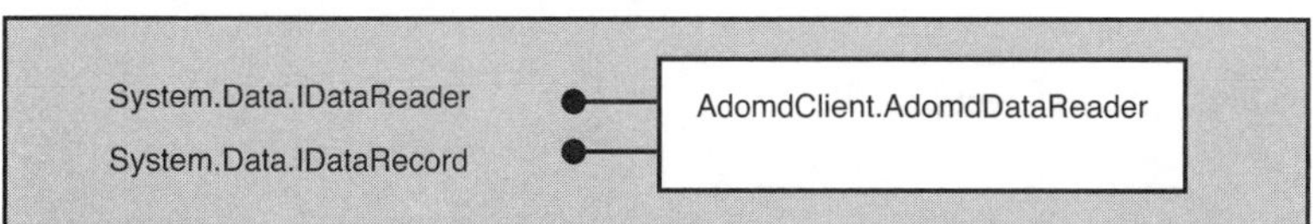

FIGURE 33.17 The ADOMDDataReader object implements the IDataReader and IDataRecord interfaces.

To iterate the result in IDataReader format is simple enough, and the result looks very similar to what you would get from iterating data using SqlClient or OledbClient. Listing

33.26 shows a straightforward way of using `IDataReader`. Because the interface is well documented, you will not have any problem finding more information in case you want to use the interface for something more sophisticated.

LISTING 33.26 Using **DataReader** to Iterate the Results of a Query

```
//Open the connection to the server.
AdomdConnection con = new AdomdConnection();
con.ConnectionString = "Datasource = localhost;Initial Catalog=Foodmart 2008;";
con.Open();

//Create and execute an MDX query.
AdomdCommand command = con.CreateCommand();
command.CommandText = "SELECT Measures.Members ON COLUMNS FROM [Warehouse and
Sales]";
AdomdDataReader reader = command.ExecuteReader();

//Read the metadata about the columns.
DataTable schemaTable = reader.GetSchemaTable();
Console.WriteLine("Schema Information about resultset");
foreach(DataRow schRow in schemaTable.Rows)
{
     foreach(DataColumn schColumn in schemaTable.Columns)
     {
          Console.Write(schColumn.ColumnName + ":");
          Console.WriteLine(schRow[schColumn].ToString());
     }
}
//Another way to access that metadata is to call the
//AdomdDataReader.GetName() method, but if the result contains no rows,
//this approach won't work.
Console.WriteLine("Name of the columns");
for(int iCol = 0; iCol)
{
     Console.WriteLine(reader.GetName(iCol));
}
//Iterate the values.
Console.WriteLine("Values in the resultset");
while(reader.Read())
{
     for(int iCol = 0; iCol <reader.FieldCount; iCol ++)
     {
          Console.Write("Value: " + reader.GetValue(iCol));
          Console.WriteLine("Type: " + reader.GetDataTypeName(iCol));
     }
```

```
}
//Close the DataReader.
reader.Close();
//Close the connection.

con.Close();
```

As a result, we receive the following data. First, we obtain metadata about the columns in the resultset:

```
Schema Information about resultset
ColumnName:[Measures].[Store Cost]
ColumnOrdinal:0
ColumnSize:0
NumericPrecision:0
NumericScale:0
DataType:System.Object
ProviderType:System.Object
IsLong:False
AllowDBNull:True
IsReadOnly:True
IsRowVersion:False
IsUnique:False
IsKeyColumn:False
IsAutoIncrement:False
BaseSchemaName:
BaseCatalogName:
BaseTableName:
BaseColumnName:
ColumnName:[Measures].[Store Sales]
ColumnOrdinal:1
ColumnSize:0
NumericPrecision:0
NumericScale:0
DataType:System.Object
ProviderType:System.Object
IsLong:False
AllowDBNull:True
IsReadOnly:True
IsRowVersion:False
IsUnique:False
IsKeyColumn:False
IsAutoIncrement:False
```

```
BaseSchemaName:
BaseCatalogName:
BaseTableName:
BaseColumnName:
```

From the second approach, we get the names of the columns:

```
Name of the columns
[Measures].[Store Cost]
[Measures].[Store Sales]
```

And finally, we receive the values of the fields in the resultset:

```
Values in the resultset
Value: 658192.962500003Type: Object
Value: 1644385.6Type: Object
```

CAUTION

There is one very important restriction to remember while using `AdomdDataReader`: It keeps the connection with the server open the whole time it is reading the data. This means that other commands cannot use the same connection to execute their requests while `AdomdDataReader` is open. If another command tries to use the same connection to execute a request while `AdomdDataReader` is open, ADOMD.NET throws an exception.

Using Visual Studio User Interface Elements to Work with OLAP Data

Visual Studio is tightly integrated with the .NET Framework and provides developers with powerful tools to use in creating user interface elements for data access. One of those tools is the `DataGridView` class, which is used for binding data with the user interface. This control is not well suited to work with data in the multidimensional format, but it is very useful for displaying data in tabular format. To create an example that displays data on the screen, follow these steps:

1. Create a new project in Visual Studio .NET. (See the "Creating an ADOMD.NET Project" section earlier in this chapter.)
2. Open Form1 in form design mode.
3. In the Toolbox, choose `DataGridView` and drag it onto your form.
4. In the Toolbox, choose Button and drag it onto the form. Name your button **Populate Grid**. (We'll use this button to create requests to Analysis Services and populate the grid.)
5. Add `Microsoft.AnalysisServices.AdomdClient.dll` in the References list.
6. Add the `using` clause for `Microsoft.Analysis Services.AdomdClient`.
7. Go back to the Form Designer, double-click the Populate button, and copy and paste the code from Listing 33.27.

LISTING 33.27 Populate Grid with Data

```
private void Populate_Click(object sender, EventArgs e)
{
     //Connect to the server.
     AdomdConnection con = new AdomdConnection();
     con.ConnectionString = "Datasource=localhost;Initial Catalog=Foodmart 2008";
     con.Open();
     string query = "SELECT {[Measures].[Unit Sales], [Measures].[Sales Count],
[Measures].[Store Sales]} ON COLUMNS FROM [Warehouse and Sales]";
     //Create a DataAdapter object and specify the text of your MDX statement
➥ and the connection object.
     AdomdDataAdapter da = new AdomdDataAdapter(query, con);
     //Create a data table and fill it with the results of your query
     DataTable dataTable = new DataTable();
     da.Fill(dataTable);
     //Close the connection.
     con.Close();
     //Fill the grid with data from the table.
     dataGridView1.DataSource = dataTable;
}
```

This code draws a simple grid that contains the data received from Analysis Services, as shown in Figure 33.18.

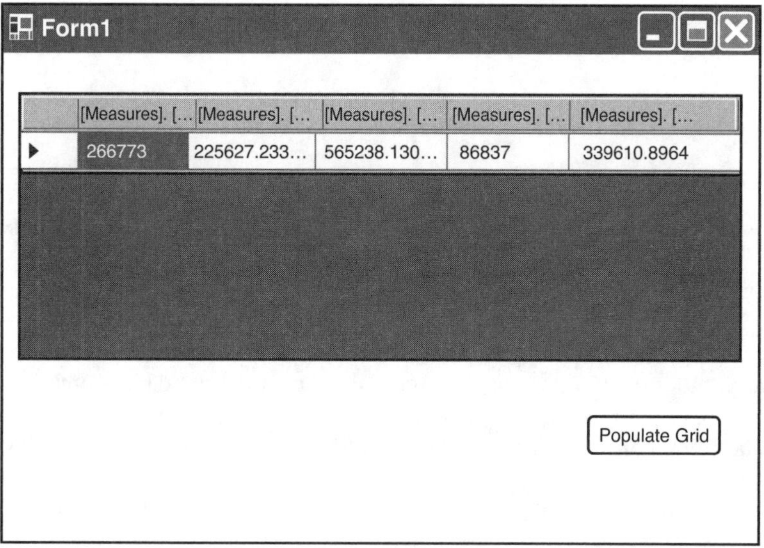

FIGURE 33.18 The user interface displays a simple `DataGrid`.

Which Should You Use: AdomdDataReader or CellSet?

Let's suppose you're planning to write a client application that must manipulate multidimensional data. You're thinking of using AdomdDataReader. But then you start thinking that maybe CellSet would be better. In this section, we give you the information you need to weigh the pros and cons of each approach, according to what you need your application to do. When reviewing different methods for manipulation of multidimensional data and different objects of the object model for operations with data, you might ask, "Which is the recommended method?." The answer to that question depends on the requirements of your application and the scenarios in which it will be used.

AdomdDataReader is the best choice when

- Your application can have a constant connection with the data source.
- The requests that your application generates can result in very large responses.
- You do not need to get absolutely all the member and cell properties specified in the MDX request that your application sends to the server.
- You are sending SQL or DMX queries. You do not have any other option but AdomdDataReader because these requests cannot result in a CellSet object.
- You want to use a Visual Studio user interface component, such as a DataGrid or WebGrid, because the result doesn't need to look like a multidimensional result.

CellSet is the best choice when

- You have to get all the member and cell properties that are included in the MDX request that your application generates.
- You need to keep the relationship between objects and their hierarchies specific to multidimensional data in the display of the data.
- You need to use data elements more than once.
- Your client application needs to work with the results of various commands simultaneously.
- The result of the executed command is not very big and can fit in the memory of the client computer.
- To minimize the number of simultaneously open connections to the data source, you want make it possible to use one connection for several components of the application or make one connection available for use by several users.

The long and short of the matter is that CellSet is generally best for work with multidimensional data, whereas AdomdDataReader is best when you need fast access to large amounts of data.

Using Parameters in MDX Requests

The client application you write will often generate the text of MDX requests based on user input. One part of the request usually remains constant for all requests, and the other part varies from request to request, depending on the data the user enters.

In Analysis Services 2000, you had to create your MDX requests by concatenating strings prepared in advance with strings entered by the user. This way of creating MDX requests was not convenient, and sometimes it could be dangerous because a user could try to outwit the system by entering incorrect text; for example, he could try to break security by MDX injection.

Starting from Analysis Services 2005, there is a faster, more reliable way of operating with data entered by the user: parametric queries. ADOMD.NET allows the client application to use the `AdomdParametersCollection` specified in the `AdomdCommand` object to pass parameters to the server. `AdomdParametersCollection` consists of `AdomdParameter` objects. `AdomdParameter` implements the `IDataParameter` interface (as shown in Figure 33.19) and allows you to pass parameters of any scalar type to the query.

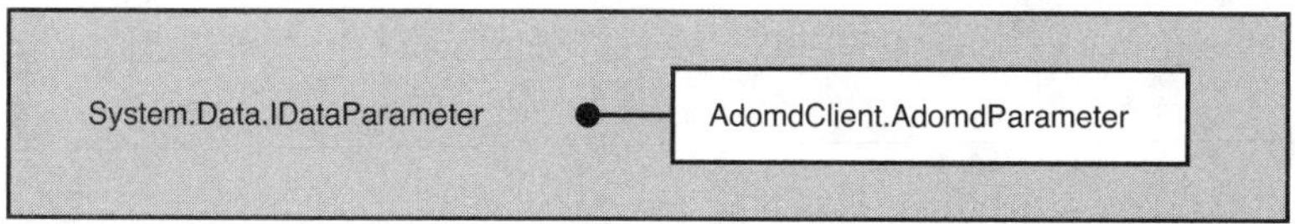

FIGURE 33.19 The `ADOMDDataParameter` object implements the `IDataParameter` interface.

Let's look at an example to see how parameters can be used in an application. In this example, the application displays a certain number of the products that were the most popular in each possible product family. This application allows the user to choose the product family she's interested in and the number of top products that she wants to see. To implement this, our application creates an MDX query and, instead of specifying the product family and the number of products, embeds the following:

```
SELECT TopCount(Descendants(StrToMember(@productFamilyMember,
➥CONSTRAINED), [Product].[Product Name] ), @topCount,
➥[Measures].[Unit Sales] ) ON COLUMNS FROM [Warehouse and Sales]
```

The parameters must be scalar types, but they can represent different MDX objects, such as `Member` or `Set`, so the template should contain a function that translates a scalar type—a string—to MDX. In Listing 33.28, we use `StrToMember`; but in similar cases, you could use `StrToSet` or `StrToTuple`. You don't need to translate the numeric parameter that specifies the number of the products because the MDX function `TopCount` expects a numeric value.

LISTING 33.28 Sending Parametric Queries to Analysis Services Using ADOMD.NET

```
using System;
```

```
using System.Collections.Generic;
using System.ComponentModel;
using System.Data;
using System.Drawing;
using System.Windows.Forms;
using Microsoft.AnalysisServices.AdomdClient;

namespace AdomdParametricQuery
{
    partial class Form1: Form
    {
        private AdomdConnection con = new AdomdConnection();
        private TupleCollection productFamiliesTuples = null;

        public Form1()
        {
            InitializeComponent();
            //During initialization of the form, we create a connection
            //to the server.
            this.con.ConnectionString = "Datasource=localhost; Initial Catalog=
➥Foodmart 2008";
            this.con.Open();
            //Fill out the combo box with all the product families.
        PopulateProductFamilies();
        }


        //Fill in the combo box with all the possible product families. In order
        //to do this, generate the following MDX request to send to the server:
        //SELECT [Product].[Products].[Product Family].members ON COLUMNS
➥FROM [Warehouse and Sales]
        private  void PopulateProductFamilies()
        {
            AdomdCommand command = this.con.CreateComman();
            command.CommandText =
"SELECT [Product].[Products].[Product Family].members
➥ ON COLUMNS FROM [Warehouse and Sales]";
            CellSet cellSet = command.ExecuteCellSet();
            productFamiliesTuples = cellSet.Axes[0].Set.Tuples;
             foreach(Tuple tuple in productFamiliesTuples)
             {
            productFamiliesBox1.Items.Add(tuple.Members[0].Caption);
            }
            productFamiliesBox1.SelectedIndex = 0;
            return;
        }
```

```
        // When the user clicks the Execute button, the MDX query to request
        //the best-selling product is sent, using the product family that the
        //user chose, and the expected number of products, also chosen by
        //the user.
        private void Execute_Click(object sender, EventArgs e)
        {
            //Create the command object.
            AdomdCommand command = this.con.CreateCommand();
            // Make sure that the MDX request contains special labels for
            //the parameters.
            command.CommandText = "SELECT topcount
➥(Descendants(StrToMember(@productFamilyMember), [Product].[Products].[Product] )
➥, @topCount, [Measures].[Unit Sales] ) ON COLUMNS FROM [Warehouse and Sales]";
            // The product family chosen by the user.
            //Find the unique name of the tuple that represent the product family
            //the user chose in the first request.
            string chosenProductFamily = this.productFamiliesTuples
➥[productFamiliesBox1.SelectedIndex].Members[0].UniqueName;
            //Create parameters.
            command.Parameters.Add("productFamilyMember", chosenProductFamily);
            command.Parameters.Add("topCount", topCountBox.Value);
            //Send the request.
            CellSet topProductsCellSet = command.ExecuteCellSet();
            topProductsBox1.Items.Clear();
            //Fill out the list box with the products returned by this MDX request.
            foreach(Tuple tuple in topProductsCellSet.Axes[0].Set.Tuples)
            {
                topProductsBox1.Items.Add(tuple.Members[0].Caption);
            }
        }
    }
}
```

This code produces the user interface shown in Figure 33.20.

Asynchronous Execution and Cancellation of Commands

When you create software that provides a user interface, it is important to make sure that the user can continue to work with the application while a long-running operation is being executed. You also need to provide the user with an opportunity to cancel the long-running operation.

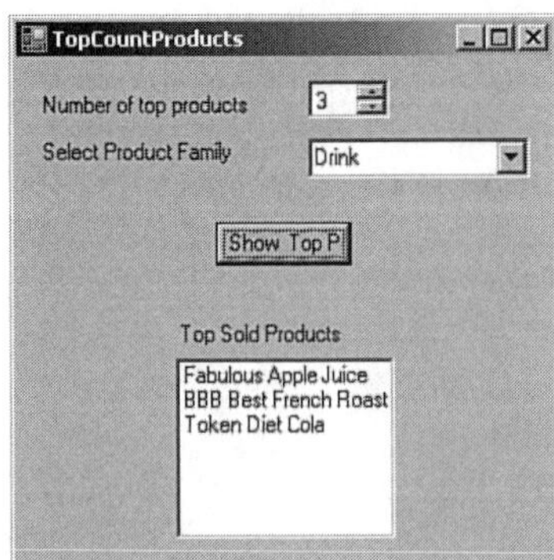

FIGURE 33.20 The user interface displays the top-selling products in the product family the user selected.

Client applications that support canceling do not usually execute commands in the main thread, but instead create a special worker thread specifically for the purpose of executing long-running operations while the user is working on something else.

ADOMD.NET provides the `AdomdCommand.Cancel` method that allows a client application to cancel a command that it sent to the server. ADOMD.NET cancels the commands by creating a new connection to the server and sending a `<Cancel>` XML/A request. (This method works only in the context of one user's session on the server. Another user cannot cancel the first user's command. For more information about the `Cancel` command, see Chapter 26, "Server Architecture and Command Execution.") A client application should call `Cancel` on a thread different from the one on which execution was started because ADOMD.NET methods that execute queries—`ExecuteCellSet`, `ExecuteDataReader`, `Execute`, and so on—don't return to the caller until execution of the command is complete. We will create a simple client application that makes it possible for the user to cancel a command. Before we begin, however, we want to point out that the operation of connecting to a data source can take a long time and things will work better if it is executed in separate thread. For the sake of simplicity, we do not show that in the example.

Listing 33.29 shows the execution and cancellation of a command in asynchronous mode. This client application has three buttons: Open Connection (to open a connection), Execute (to execute the command), and Cancel (to cancel the command). It also has a simple list box for displaying the member names on the screen. (We could have used a grid control, but we didn't, to avoid complicating the example.)

When you work with multiple threads, it is important to provide synchronization between objects and to prevent multiple threads from using the same resource simultaneously. We do this by turning the buttons on and off. For example, the Execute button is disabled while the connection is being made. The Cancel button is disabled when the user clicks the Execute button and remains disabled until the command starts to execute. At this point, the Execute button is disabled and the Cancel button is enabled. This prevents the possibility that the command would be executed twice.

This approach to synchronization is a bit oversimplified; you can choose other methods of synchronization available in the .NET Framework, such as using the `Lock` method of the `System.object` class. We use the `BackgroundWorker` class, provided by the .NET Framework 2.0, to create the worker thread and execute the command in the background.

If you click the Cancel button and issue the `Cancel` command more than one time, Analysis Services might generate an error that the command has already been canceled. ADOMD.NET propagates this error to the caller as an exception. In our sample application, we capture all the exceptions thrown by the `command.Cancel` method.

LISTING 33.29 Executing a Query Asynchronously and Canceling the Query

```
using System;
using System.Collections.Generic;
using System.ComponentModel;
using System.Data;
using System.Drawing;
using System.Windows.Forms;
using Microsoft.AnalysisServices.AdomdClient;

namespace QueryCancel
{
      partial class Form1: Form
      {
            AdomdConnection connection = null;
            AdomdCommand command = null;
            BackgroundWorker backgroundWorker = null;

            public Form1()
            {
                  InitializeComponent();
                  //Before the connection is established, only the Connection
                  //button is enabled.
                  connectionButton.Enabled = true;
                  cancelButton.Enabled = false;
                  executeButton.Enabled = false;
                  //Create BackgroundWorker
                  this.backgroundWorker = new BackgroundWorker();
                  this.backgroundWorker.WorkerReportsProgress = false;
                  this.backgroundWorker.WorkerSupportsCancellation = true;
                  this.backgroundWorker.RunWorkerCompleted + = OnCompleted;
                  this.backgroundWorker.DoWork + = OnDoWork;
}

          // This function is called when the user clicks the Connection button.
private void connectionButton_Click(object sender, EventArgs e)
```

```
        {
        //Open a connection to the server
            this.connection = new AdomdConnection();
      this.connection.ConnectionString = "Datasource=localhost;
➥Initial Catalog
=Foodmart 2005;";
                this.connection.Open();
        //When the connection is opened, it is possible to execute the command,
        //but not possible to cancel it
                connectionButton.Enabled = false;
                executeButton.Enabled = true;
}
        // The function is called when the user clicks the Execute button
          private void executeButton_Click(object sender, EventArgs e)
          {
             // Create a command
                this.command = this.connection.CreateCommand();
                this.command.CommandText =
 @"SELECT NON EMPTY
[Customer].[Customers].[Customer].Members
➥ON COLUMNS FROM [Warehouse and Sales]";
             //Before starting the worker thread, disable the Execute button,
             //so the user won't be able to click it twice.
              //Enable the cancel button
                cancelButton.Enabled = true;
                executeButton.Enabled = false;
        //Start the worker thread, pass the AdomdCommand object as a parameter
        //to the function, which will be called on the worker thread
                this.backgroundWorker.RunWorkerAsync(this.command);
}
          //This function is called on the background thread.
          void OnDoWork(object sender, DoWorkEventArgs doWorkArgs)
          {
             //Retrieve the AdomdCommand object from the parameter.
                BackgroundWorker backgroundWorker;
                backgroundWorker = sender as BackgroundWorker;
                AdomdCommand commandOnThread = (AdomdCommand)doWorkArgs.Argument;
        //Start the MDX query.
             CellSet cellSet = commandOnThread. ExecuteCellSet();
                //If during execution, the user clicks the Cancel button,
                //a flag backgroundWorker.CancellationPending is set to TRUE.
        if(backgroundWorker.CancellationPending)
                    doWorkArgs.Cancel = true;
                else
                    doWorkArgs.Result = cellSet;
}
```

```
        //The function is called by the class BackgroundWorker on the main thread
        // when the function running in the background completes
        void OnCompleted(object sender,
                  RunWorkerCompletedEventArgs completedArgs)
          {
        //If there was an error, notify the user.
                if(completedArgs.Error! = null)
                {
                     statusLabel.Text = "Error Occured";
                      MessageBox.Show(completedArgs.Error.Message,
➥completedArgs.Error.Source);
}
    else if (completedArgs.Cancelled)
                {
                      statusLabel.Text = "Cancelled";
                      MessageBox.Show(" Command has been canceled by user ");
}
          else
                {
            //The command completed successfully.
                      CellSet cellSetResult = (CellSet)completedArgs.Result;
                   //Populate the list box with the names of the members.
foreach(Tuple tuple in cellSetResult.Axes[0].Set.Tuples)
                      {
                            TupleBox1.Items.Add(tuple.Members[0].Caption);
}
                      statusLabel.Text = "Completed";
}
              //Execution of the command is completed, close the connection and
              // reset all the buttons.
                if (null! = this.connection && this.connection.State ==
➥ ConnectionState.Open)
                      this.connection.Close();
                this.connection = null;
                connectionButton.Enabled = true;
                cancelButton.Enabled = false;
                executeButton.Enabled = false;
}
        // The function is called when the user clicks the Cancel button.
        private void cancelButton_Click(object sender, EventArgs e)
        {
                // Call the Cancel method, which sends a cancel request to the
server.
                try
                {
                      this.command.Cancel();
```

```
                }
                catch (AdomdException  ex)
                {
                    //If you send two Cancel commands one after another
                    //Analysis Services might return an error on the second one,
                    // notifying that command is already cancelled.
                    //We catch corresponding exception to prevent users from seeing
                    //it. In this example we assume that Cancel command can't
                    //throw other exceptions that would be caught by this
                    //statement as well.
                }
               //Inform BackgroundWorker that command has been canceled.
              this.backgroundWorker.CancelAsync();
            }
        }
    }
}
```

Execution of this sample code generates the user interface shown in Figure 33.21.

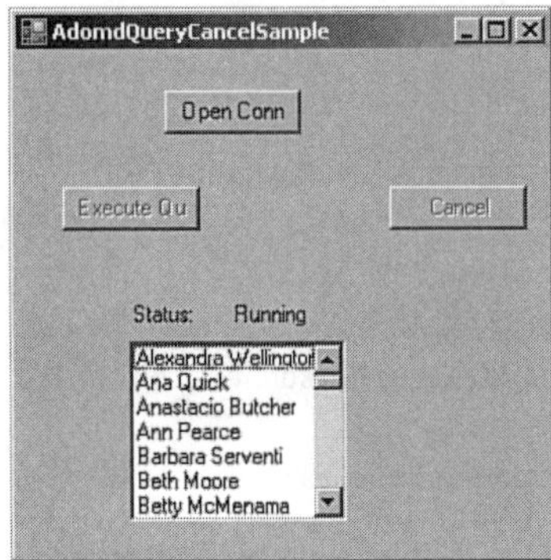

FIGURE 33.21 The user interface that enables you to execute and cancel commands.

Error Handling

One of the most important aspects of software development is the ability to process errors. This ability is especially important in a client/server scenario, where failures can occur not only because of bugs in the code, but also because of various circumstances beyond your control, such as network failures, server turnoff, wrong data entered by the user, and so on. Therefore, we cannot discuss about ADOMD.NET without covering error handling.

In this section, we discuss the classes responsible for error handling and show you how to use them. The more often you use them and the more familiar you become with them, the less time you will spend debugging your application.

Following the methodology of error handling offered by the .NET Framework, ADOMD.NET uses an exception-handling mechanism to work with errors. When an error is encountered, an exception is thrown by the object model, and the client application has to catch and process it. The client application either continues the execution or passes the error message to the user.

Because you are already familiar with programming languages in the .NET family, you know that you should put the code that might cause an exception inside `try` instructions, and wrap the error-handling code in a `catch` instruction. The .NET Framework also provides the `finally` instruction, in which you should place code that has to be executed regardless of whether an exception is thrown. For example, a program written in C# would look like this:


```
try
{
    // Execute some code.
}
catch(Exception exception)
{
    // Handle the error
}
finally
{
    // Operations for clearing resources, for example, to close the connections
}
```

ADOMD.NET has a special class for error handling: `AdomdException`. A client application that calls ADOMD.NET objects should be ready to catch this kind of exception from any call to ADOMD.NET. The application should also be prepared for other standard types of exceptions to be thrown by ADOMD.NET, such as `NotSupportedException`, `InvalidOperation Exception`, and `ArgumentNullException`. These types of exceptions usually imply misuse of the object model; that is, the problem is in the client application code.

To enable the client application to handle different types of errors in dissimilar ways, ADOMD.NET provides special classes derived from `AdomdException`. The remainder of the chapter discusses those special classes.

AdomdErrorResponseException

`AdomdErrorResponseException` is thrown when a request sent to the server has failed and the server has returned an error message to the client. An erroneous MDX request can be one of the many reasons for this exception. An `AdomdErrorResponseException` object contains a collection of the `AdomdError` objects. Each `AdomdError` object gives information about the error—its code, message, and path or URL to the file containing the help information about the error. An `AdomdError` object also contains information about the location in the request where the syntax error occurred. Figure 33.22 displays the hierarchy of objects contained in `AdomdErrorResponseException`.

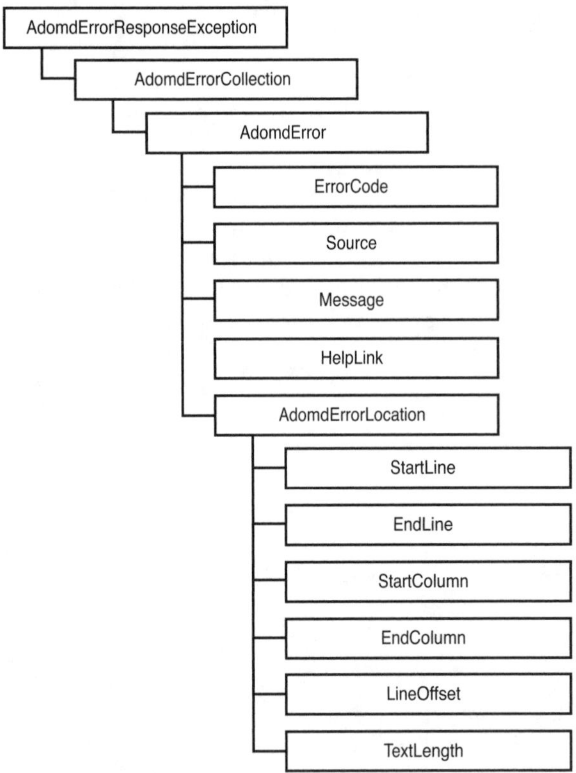

FIGURE 33.22 The hierarchy of objects in `AdomdErrorResponseException`.

It is possible that the request has been executed successfully, but some of the cells in the response contain errors. This could happen for various reasons; for example, the current user doesn't have permissions to see the content of a cell or the calculation of the cell value contains an error.

In a case like this, the client application should not interrupt execution, but should process the error and move to the other cells, because they can often contain useful information. To support such a scenario, the client application should be ready to catch an exception when it calls any property of a cell object. `Value` or any other property of `Cell` could lead to an `AdomdErrorResponseException`. Listing 33.30 is an example of handling an error that occurs when a cell value is calculated.

LISTING 33.30 Handling an Error That Occurs When a Cell Value Is Calculated

```
//Open a connection to the server.
AdomdConnection con = new AdomdConnection("Datasource=localhost; Initial Catalog=
➥foodmart 2008;");
```

```
con.Open();

//Create a command that contains a calculated member with an error.
//The method Order accepts only set or tuple of the set as parameters, and we try to
//pass numeric expression.
AdomdCommand command = con.CreateCommand();
command.CommandText = " WITH member measures.x AS 'Order("string",4)'
SELECT {x} ON COLUMNS FROM [Warehouse and Sales]";
CellSet cellset =
command.ExecuteCellSet();

//Iterate all the cells and print their values.
foreach(Cell cell in cellset.Cells)
{
     try
     {
          Console.WriteLine(cell.Value);
     }
     catch(AdomdErrorResponseException errorCell)
     {
          //If there was an error, iterate the error collection and print the
          // error message.
          Console.WriteLine(" Error in the cell ");
          foreach(AdomdError cellError in errorCell.Errors)
          {
               Console.WriteLine(cellError.Message);
          }
     }
     catch(AdomdException ex)
     {
          Console.Write(ex.Message);
     }
}

//Close the connection.
con.Close();
```

This code produces the following message:

```
Error in the cell
The ORDER function expects a tuple set expression for the 1 argument. A string or
numeric expression was used.
```

AdomdUnknownResponseException

AdomdUnknownResponseException is thrown when ADOMD.NET parses the response sent by the server. This can happen if the request has been sent to an XML/A provider with a version of XML/A that is not supported by the client. Often, such errors are fatal; the client application should not continue to execute, but should instead notify the user.

AdomdConnectionException

AdomdConnectionException is thrown when the connection with the server cannot be opened or has been interrupted. A good example of the use of this type of exception is if the connection to the server fails, the client application can display a user interface in which the user can specify missing connection information, such as the server name, user ID, and password. AdomdConnectionException has the ExceptionCause property, which provides information to the client application about the cause of the failure. In this version of ADMOMD.NET, the ExceptionCause property can return two values: AuthenticationFailed and Unspecified. Those properties provide a client application with the information that the connection cannot be established because of security issues or for some other reason.

AdomdCacheExpiredException

AdomdCacheExpiredException notifies the client application that the metadata cache has expired. We talked about this type of exception earlier, in the section "Caching Metadata on the Client" (see Listing 33.31).

LISTING 33.31 Catching Exceptions Thrown by ADOMD.NET

```
    AdomdConnection con = new AdomdConnection("Datasource=localhost;
➥ Initial Catalog=foodmart 2008;");
    try
    {
            //Open a connection to the server.
            con.Open();

            //Do some operations.
            //...
     }
     catch(AdomdConnectionException conException)
     {
            Console.WriteLine(conException.Message);
     }
     catch(AdomdErrorResponseException errorException)
     {
            //If there was an error, iterate the error collection and print the
            //error message
            foreach (AdomdError cellError in errorException.Errors)
```

```
        {
            Console.WriteLine(errorException.Message);
        }
    }
    catch(AdomdUnknownResponseException ex)
    {
        Console.WriteLine(ex.Message);
    }
    catch(AdomdCacheExpiredException cacheExeption)
    {
        Console.WriteLine(cacheExeption.Message);
        //refresh the controls
        //...
    }
    finally
    {
        //Close the connection
        if ( con.State == ConnectionState.Open )
            con.Close();
    }
}
```

33

CHAPTER 34

Analysis Management Objects

IN THIS CHAPTER

Analysis Management Objects (AMO) exposes a hierarchical object model for administering Analysis Services. A client application can use AMO to control the server and to create and maintain online analytical processing (OLAP) and data-mining objects. You can use it to automate all the functionality available through the Analysis Services user interface, such as processing partitions, backing up and restoring data, and many others. Business Intelligence Development Studio (BI Dev Studio) and SQL Server Management Studio use AMO to implement the user interface.

In this chapter, we give you an overview of the classes of the object model and some samples of their use. We also describe different modes provided by AMO for the administration of Analysis Services.

AMO is a managed assembly designed to be used from a managed application written in any .NET language, but it can also be used from one written in native code. For the sake of simplicity, we wrote the samples in this chapter in C#.

AMO Object Model

When they were planning the AMO object model, the designers had three goals in mind:

- The first, and most obvious, was to provide an object model that could replace Decision Support Objects (DSO) as an object model for administering Analysis Services.

- Second, and almost as obvious, was to create an object model that would be faster and more intuitive than DSO.
- Finally, they wanted to expose all the Analysis Services functionality in the new object model.

The hierarchy of objects exposed through the AMO model is the same as the hierarchy of the objects on the server, defined by DDL (Data Definition Language). (For details about DDL, see Chapters 4, "The Conceptual Data Model," and 26, "Server Architecture and Command Execution.") Under the hood, AMO uses XML for Analysis (XML/A) DDL requests to operate Analysis Services.

Figure 34.1 shows the hierarchy of objects exposed through AMO.

Types of AMO Objects

All the objects provided by AMO can be divided in two categories: major objects and minor objects. Interfaces implemented by AMO objects and the collections that contain them depend heavily on the category the object belongs to. Objects that belong to the same category are derived from the same interfaces and implement the same subset of methods and properties.

Major Objects

A major object can be created, updated, and deleted independently of its parent collections. For example, you can create a database object and later add it to the collection of databases that belong to the server object. These objects contain `Name` and `ID` properties, and can be referenced by those properties. There is, however, a semantic difference between the two properties:

- `ID` is a management property. It is given to an object when it is created and cannot be changed during the life of that object.
- The `Name` property of an object can be changed after the object is created. The object's `Name` property is exposed to the analytical client applications.

These distinctions between the `Name` and `ID` properties enable you to implement features such as object renaming, copying, and pasting. Both the `Name` and `ID` properties generally have to be unique among the child elements of the same collection. In some exceptional cases, `Name` and `ID` have to be unique among the objects that are grandchildren of the same parent. For example, `Name` and `ID` have to be unique for all dimensions in the database, but can be duplicated in different databases. But, all the measures in a `Cube` object (not just in the same `Measure Group`) must have unique `Name` and `ID` properties. Therefore, if you are generating your own values for `ID`, you have to take care to create values that you can maintain as unique over the lifetime of the object.

Major objects can be divided further:

- Processable major objects have to be deployed to the server and processed (loaded from or connected to data from a relational source) before they can be used by the analytical client applications. `Cube`, `Dimension`, and `Database` objects are good examples of processable major objects.

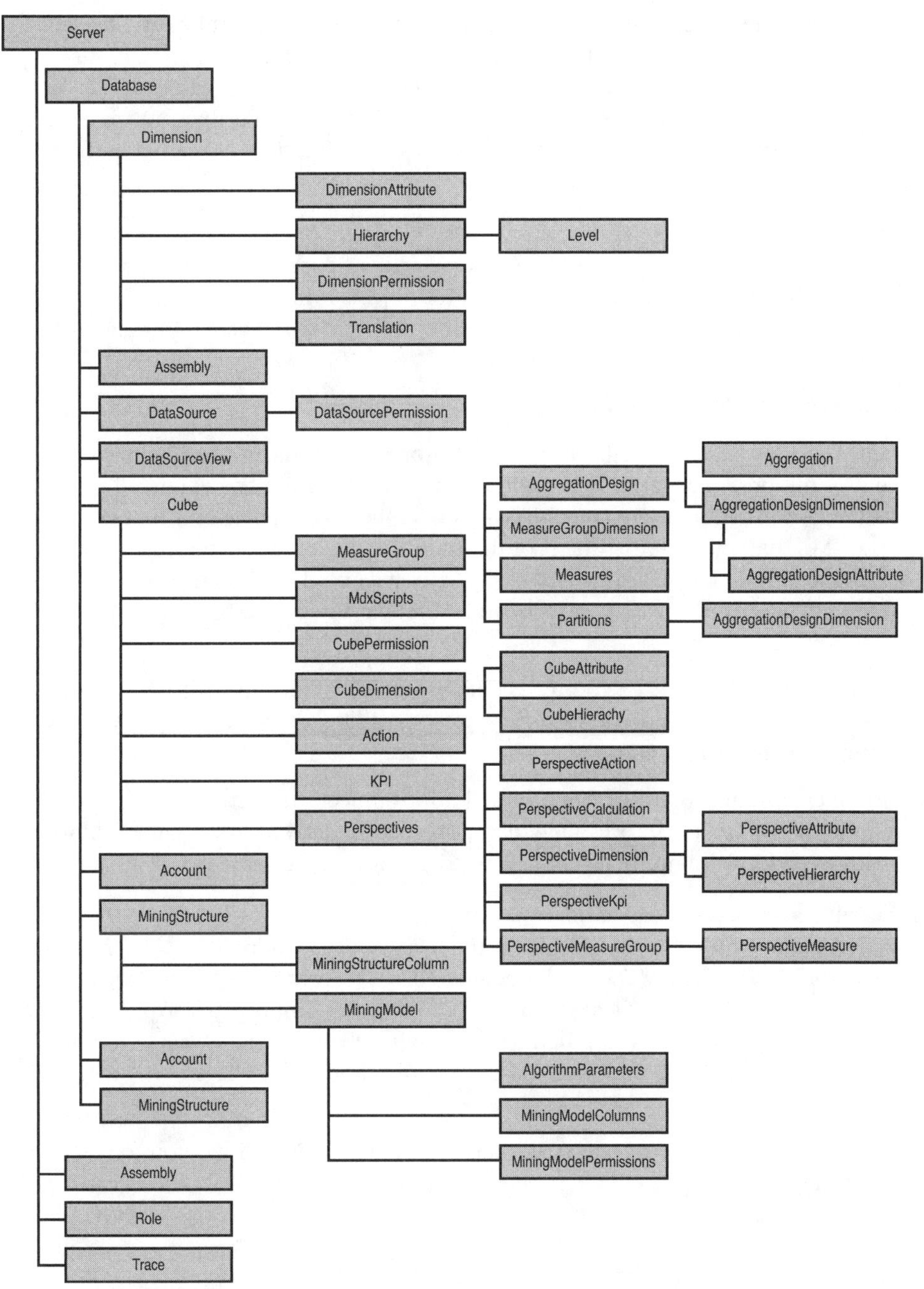

FIGURE 34.1 The hierarchy of objects exposed through AMO.

- Nonprocessable major objects have only to be deployed before they can be used. They are pure metadata objects; they do not work with data. For example, the `Assembly` object is a nonprocessable major object: It can be created on the server independent of its parents (`Server` or `Database`), but because it does not have data associated with it, it does not have to be processed before it can be used by the client applications.

Minor Objects

A minor object can be created, updated, or deleted only as part of an operation on its parent object. The `Name` and `ID` properties of minor objects follow the same rules as major objects. That is, the value of the `ID` property cannot be changed over the lifetime of the object, but the value of the `Name` property can.

Minor objects can be divided further:

- Named minor objects contain `Name` and `ID` properties, and can be referenced by them. A minor object can also contain a `Description` property—extended human-readable information about the object—and an `Annotation` property that contains valid XML that allows enrichment of the model and provides extensible information about the object. The `Hierarchy` object is a good example of a named minor object because it cannot be created on its own; it can be created only as part of its parent `Dimension`.
- Unnamed minor objects exist only as part of the collection they belong to. They do not have `Name` or `ID` properties; for example, `Translation` or `Account` objects have neither `Name` nor `ID` properties.

From an implementation point of view, named minor objects are derived from the unnamed minor objects, nonprocessable major objects are derived from named minor objects, and processable major objects are derived from unprocessable major objects.

Unnamed Objects and Collections of Unnamed Objects

All unnamed minor objects are derived from the `System.ComponentModel.Component` class; therefore, all objects in the AMO object model are derived from the `System.ComponentModel.Component` class. The AMO classes are designed to be components, so a class can be used in a Rapid Application Development (RAD) environment such as Visual Studio .NET, in which they can be dragged and dropped onto a form and manipulated on a design surface.

All AMO objects also implement the `ICloneable` interface, which allows you to create new instances of the object with the same properties (see Figure 34.2). AMO objects can be created in two ways:

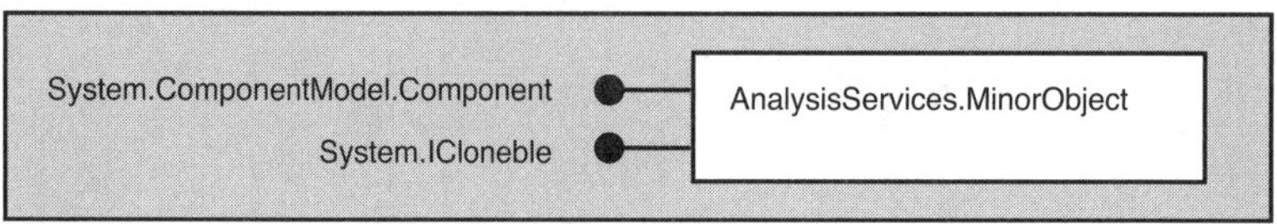

FIGURE 34.2 All AMO objects implement the `ICloneable` standard interface.

- AMO can load objects that exist on the server.
- A programmer can create objects and add them to the collections.

All AMO objects support the following methods:

- `Clone` creates a new object that is a copy of the current object.
- `Validate` validates the object by checking certain properties of the object. The validation process depends on the object. In the simplest case, AMO checks that the `Name` and `ID` properties contain only valid characters. AMO provides two overloads for this method. The first one validates the object and returns a Boolean value of `TRUE` if the object is valid and `FALSE` if the object not valid. The second overload comes into play if the object is not valid. It returns a string containing information about cause of the failure.
- `Parent` returns the parent object of the current object. For example, the parent object for a `Cube` object would be the database the cube belongs to. In addition to the `Parent` property, all objects have named parent properties for each major object that is a parent to it. For example, the `Cube` object has a `ParentDatabase` property and a `ParentServer` property that would return the cube's parent database and the cube's parent server, respectively.

All AMO collections have similar properties, and they all use identical methods of navigation and access to the objects stored in them. All AMO collections derive from the collection of unnamed objects and implement the standard interfaces `IEnumerable`, `ICollection`, and `IList`, as shown in Figure 34.3.

FIGURE 34.3 All AMO collections implement the `IEnumerable`, `ICollection`, and `IList` standard interfaces.

All AMO collections support the following methods:

- `Count` gets the number of elements contained in the collection.
- `Add` adds an object to the end of the collection.
- `CanAdd` validates that the object can be added to the collection. This method checks to make sure that the object passed by the client application is not null and that the object does not already exist in the collection.
- `Clear` removes all elements from the collection.
- `Contains` determines whether the collection contains a specified object.
- `IndexOf` gets the index in the collection of the object. If the object does not exist in the collection, it returns `-1`.

- `Insert` inserts the specified object into the collection at the specified index.
- `Item` (in C#, this method is called `indexer`) provides access to elements of a collection.
- `Move` moves an object from a specified index to another index.
- `Remove` removes the first occurrence of a specified object from the collection.
- `RemoveAt` removes an object from the collection at a specified index.

All AMO collections provide an overload for the `Item` property to access elements by specifying an index. For example, in C#, access to the elements of a collection can be achieved with the following code:

```
Database db = server.Databases[0];
```

This call returns the first `Database` object in the `Databases` collection.

Named Objects and Collections of Named Objects

Named objects are derived from the `INamedComponent` interface. This interface extends the functionality of `IModelComponent` and provides a way to support the `Name`, `ID`, `Description`, and `Annotation` properties. Named objects also implement the `IFormattable` interface to provide the functionality to format the value of the object into a string representation, as shown in Figure 34.4.

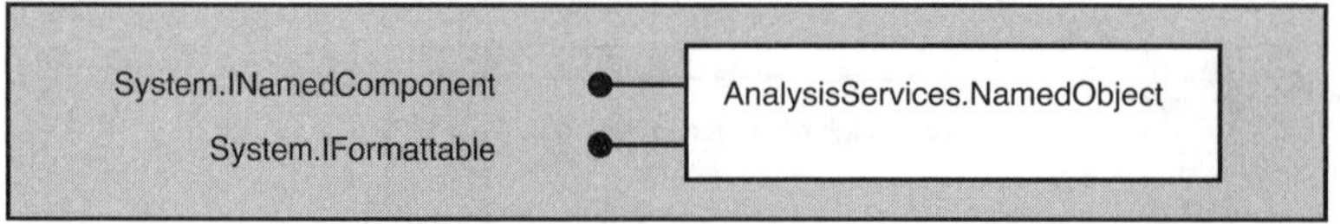

FIGURE 34.4 Named objects are derived from the `INamedComponent` interface and implement the `IFormattable` interface.

Named objects support the following properties:

- `Annotation` sets and gets an XML document that provides extensible information about the object.
- `Description` sets and gets the human-readable description about the object.
- `ID` sets and gets the ID of the object.
- `Name` sets and gets the name of the object.

Collections of named objects extend the functionality of the regular collections by providing an interface for inserting and retrieving objects by their `Name` or `ID` properties:

- `Add()` creates a new object with generated `Name` and `ID` properties and adds this object to the end of the collection.

- `Add(string name)` creates an object with the specified name and adds this object to the end of the collection. AMO automatically generates a value for the `ID` property.
- `Add(string name, string id)` creates an object with the specified name and ID and adds the object to the end of the collection.

NOTE

For optimal performance, we recommend that you pass an object's ID to the `Add` method. Creating objects by `Name` or letting AMO generate the `Name` and `ID` properties will not yield performance as good as you get when you create an object by `ID`.

- `Contains(string id)` determines whether the collection contains an object with the specified ID.
- `ContainsName(string name)` determines whether the collection contains an object with the specified name.
- `Find(string id)` provides access to an element of a collection by the `ID` property. This method is similar to the `Item` method, but AMO will not throw an exception if the collection does not contain an object with the specified `ID`. If no object with the specified ID exists in the collection, the method `Find` returns null. If you are not sure that the object exists in the collection, we recommend that you use this method instead of the `Item(indexer)` method.
- `FindByName` provides access to an element of the collection by the `Name` property. This method is similar to `GetByName`, but AMO will not throw an exception if the collection does not contain an object with the specified name. If no object with the specified name exists in the collection, the method `FindByName` returns null. If you are not sure that the object exists in the collection, we recommend that you use this method rather than the `GetByName` method.
- `GetByName(string name)` provides access to the elements of the collection by the `Name` property. This method is equivalent to the `Item` method, but uses the `Name` property of the object as an index rather than the `ID` property. If an element with that name does not exist in the collection, AMO throws an exception. Retrieving elements by `Name` is more expensive than retrieving them by `ID` or by an index.
- `GetNewID` generates a string that can be used as an ID to create a new object in the collection. AMO provides two overloads for this method. The user can specify a prefix, and AMO will generate a valid ID that starts with that prefix. If the user does not specify the prefix, AMO chooses a prefix based on the type of the collection. For example, `server.Databases.GetNewID()` generates an `ID` that starts with the `Database` substring.
- `GetNewName` generates a string that can be used as a name for a new object. AMO provides two overloads for this method. The user can specify a prefix, and AMO will generate a valid name that starts with that prefix. In this version, if the caller does not specify the prefix, AMO chooses a prefix based on the type of the collection. For

example, `server.Databases.GetNewName()` generates a name that starts with the `Database` substring.

- `IndexOf(string id)` gets the index in the collection of the object with the specified ID. If the object does not exist in the collection, it returns `-1`.
- `IndexOfName(string name)` gets the index in the collection of the object with the specified name. If the object does not exist in the collection, it returns `-1`.
- `IsValidID` validates the specified `ID` by checking that the string does not contain unsupported characters—such as a period (.), comma (,) and many others—is not a reserved word, and that an object with the same `ID` property value does not already exist in the collection. AMO provides two overloads for this method. One validates the `ID` and returns a Boolean value `TRUE` if the ID is valid and `FALSE` if the `ID` not valid. The second overload comes into play if the `ID` is not valid. It returns a string containing information about the cause of the failure.
- `IsValidName` validates the specified `Name` value by checking that the string does not contain unsupported characters—such as a period (.), comma (,), and many others—is not a reserved word, and that an object with the same `Name` property value does not already exist in the collection. AMO provides two overloads for this method. The first validates the `Name` property and returns a Boolean value of `TRUE` if the `Name` is valid and `FALSE` if the `Name` not valid. The second overload comes into play if the `Name` property is not valid. It returns a string containing information about cause of the failure.
- `Item` (in C#, this method is called `indexer`) provides access to the elements of the collection. In addition to being accessible by its index, a named object can be accessed by its `ID` property. If no element with that `ID` exists in the collection, AMO throws an exception. Exception handling always slows down the system, so for better performance, use this method only if you know that the object exists in the collection.
- `Remove` removes from the collection the object with the specified `ID` property. In addition to the overload of the `Remove` method that enables a client application to remove an object by specifying its object reference, collections of named objects have two other overloads for this method. The first overload removes only the specified object from the collection, but the second one allows the user to indicate whether she wants to also remove the objects that reference the specified object. If the collection does not contain an object with the specified `ID`, AMO throws an exception.

Major Objects and Collections of Major Objects

Major objects derive from the `IMajorObject` interface. This interface extends the functionality of `INamedComponent` interface and provides support for creation, deletion, and synchronization with the corresponding objects on the server, as shown in Figure 34.5.

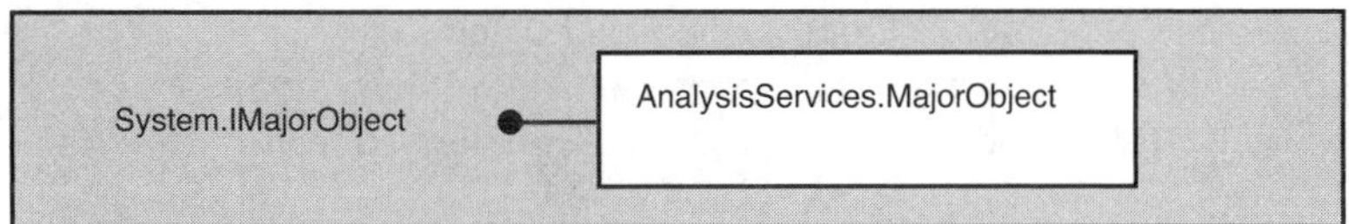

FIGURE 34.5 Major objects are derived from the IMajorObject interface.

Major objects support the following methods and properties:

- Drop sends a Delete statement to the server and removes an object from the parent collection. When you set the affectDependents parameter to TRUE, you are instructing AMO to send an Update request to the server for each of the objects affected by the deletion of the object. The Drop method might fail to delete an object because of a communication problem. You might want to make sure that such an object gets deleted regardless. To accomplish this, have the application pass the DropOptions.IgnoreFailures parameter to the Drop method.
- LastSchemaUpdate returns the date and time when the structure of the object was last changed on the server.
- Refresh synchronizes AMO and Analysis Services. If more than one user or client application is administering Analysis Services, it is easy to get into a situation in which a client application ends up with a reference to an AMO object that no longer has a corresponding object on the server or a situation in which the object on the server has changed.
- Update sends object definitions to the server. The client application can use the default overload of the Update method, which causes only the object itself and its properties to be updated on the server. A client application can also pass the UpdateOptions parameter, which specifies whether the dependent objects also need to be updated. (We discuss dependent objects in greater detail in the "Dependent and Referenced Objects" section later in this chapter.)

  In addition, a client application can pass an UpdateMode parameter, which specifies the operation that should be performed on the object: Create, Replace, Update, or any combination of those. This argument affects which DDL request AMO sends to the server: Create or Alter.

  An application can also pass the XmlaWarningCollection collection, which will be populated by the Update method if a warning occurs, and the ImpactDetailCollection collection, which will be populated with information about the changes of object state that will occur on the server if the Update operation succeeds. (You'll read more about this functionality in the "Impact Analysis" section later in this chapter.)

Collections of the major objects support the same interfaces and functionality as collections of all other named objects.

Processable Major Objects and Collections of Processable Major Objects

Processable major objects are those that have to be processed before they can be used by an analytical client application. All processable major objects are derived from the `IProcessable` interface (see Figure 34.6).

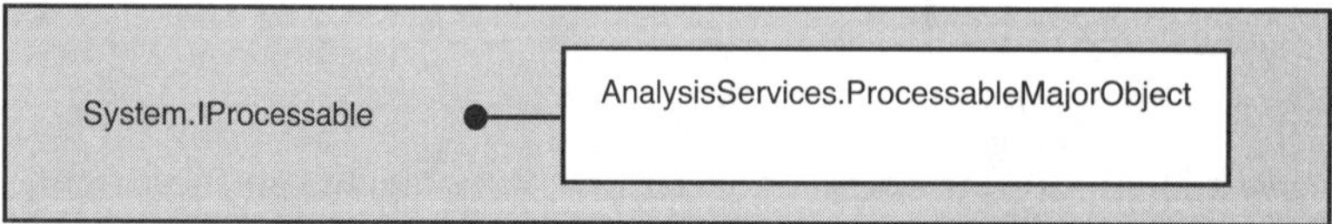

FIGURE 34.6 All processable major objects are derived from the `IProcessable` interface.

Processable major objects support the following methods and properties:

- `CanProcess` verifies that the object supports the type of processing that the client application is passing to this method. For example, because the `MeasureGroup` object does not support the `ProcessScriptCache` type of processing, the method `CanProcess` returns `FALSE`. Nevertheless, the `Cube` object does support this type, so calling the `CanProcess` method on the `Cube` object returns `TRUE`.
- `LastProcessed` returns the date and time when the object was last processed on the server.
- `Process` requests that the server process the object. AMO provides a few different overloads of this method. One of them allows sending a request to the server to calculate the potential impact of the processing operation, but does not actually perform processing. We cover impact analysis later in this chapter.

Collections of processable major objects support the same interfaces and functionality as collections of all other named objects.

Dependent and Referenced Objects

The complexity of AMO as an object model stems from the fact that many AMO objects are highly dependent on each other. A change to one object might affect not only that object, but a number of other objects, too.

To better understand the issue of dependencies, let's look at an example in which we have a database that has one dimension and two cubes. Both cubes include the same dimension. Each of the `Cube` objects contains a reference to the `Dimension` object, and each `Cube Dimension` object contains a reference to the hierarchies in the database dimension. Figure 34.7 illustrates these relationships.

Deletion of one of the hierarchies of the dimension can affect the structure of both cubes in either of two ways: Both cubes lose referential integrity because they have references to objects that no longer exist, or AMO navigates through the tree of objects that depend on the hierarchy and updates them in both cubes.

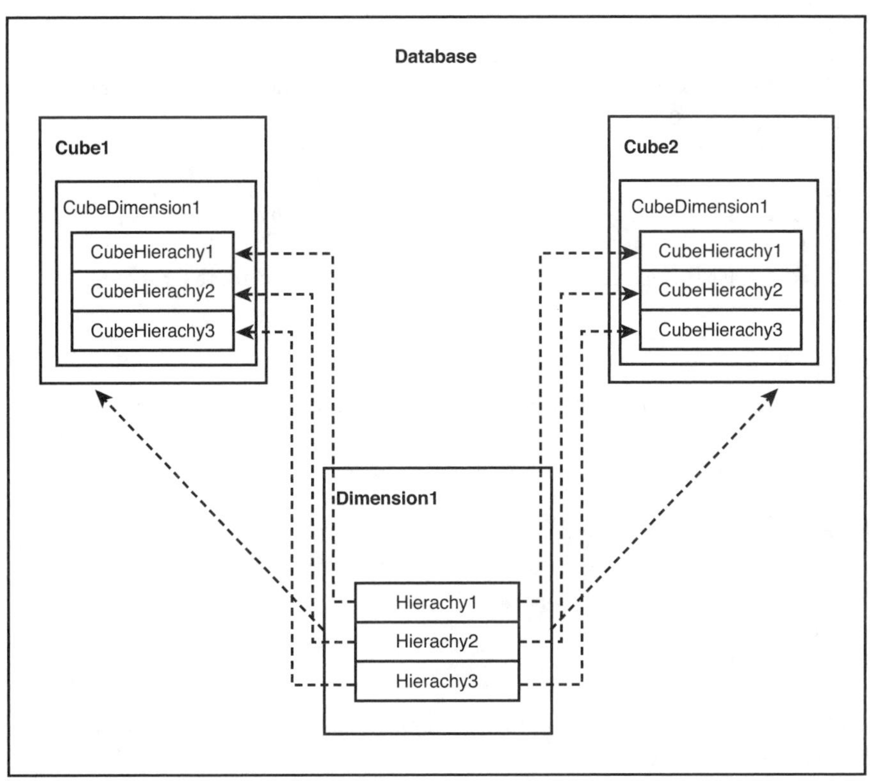

FIGURE 34.7 Hierarchies in the cube dimensions reference hierarchies in the database dimension.

Adding, deleting, or even rearranging the objects in a collection could cause structural changes in their dependent objects. When an object is added to, removed from, or moved inside a collection, AMO not only performs the requested operation, but also modifies any affected collections. For example, if a client application deletes a hierarchy from the collection of hierarchies on the database dimension, AMO also removes the referenced hierarchy from the collection of the cube hierarchies on each of the cubes that references the deleted hierarchy (see Listing 34.1).

LISTING 34.1 Dependency Among AMO Objects

```
using (Server srv = new Server())
{
    //Connect to the server.
    srv.Connect("localhost");
    //Use the database FoodMart 2008.
    Database db = srv.Databases.GetByName("FoodMart 2008");
    //Iterate all the cubes.
    Console.WriteLine("Before deletion");
```

```
    foreach(Cube cb in db.Cubes)
    {
        //Print the names of the hierarchies in the "Customer" cube dimension.
        CubeDimension dimCustomer = cb.Dimensions.FindByName("Customer");
        if (null!=dimCustomer)
        {
            foreach(CubeHierarchy hier in dimCustomer.Hierarchies)
            {
                Console.WriteLine(cb.ToString() + ": " + hier.ToString());
            }
        }
    }
    //Remove the hierarchy named "Customers" from the database dimension
    //named "Customer."
    Dimension dbDim = db.Dimensions.GetByName("Customer");
    Hierarchy dbHier = dbDim.Hierarchies.GetByName("Customers");
    dbDim.Hierarchies.Remove(dbHier);
    //Iterate all the cubes and make sure that no cube has the hierarchy
    //"Customers" in the dimension "Customer."
    Console.WriteLine("After deletion");
    foreach(Cube cb in db.Cubes)
    {
        CubeDimension dimCustomer = cb.Dimensions.FindByName("Customer");
        if (null!=dimCustomer)
        {
            foreach(CubeHierarchy hier in dimCustomer.Hierarchies)
            {
                Console.WriteLine(cb.ToString() + ": " + hier.ToString());
            }
        }
    }
}
```

After you run this sample code, you will see that the `Customers` hierarchy has also been removed from the collection of hierarchies in the `Customer` cube dimension.

Not all AMO objects depend on each other in the same way. Some objects have very strong dependencies on others; they cannot continue to exist if the objects they depend on get deleted. As you saw in the example, if the hierarchy of the database dimension is removed, the referenced hierarchy on the cube dimension is necessarily removed, too. However, other types of object have weaker interdependencies. If the objects they depend on get deleted, they are not deleted; they are changed. For example, if the dimension `Attribute` is deleted, the `Dimension` object is altered but not deleted.

When a client application calls the `Drop` method on a major object, AMO performs a cascading operation that deletes all the referenced AMO objects, too. But, there is a way to specify whether the <Delete> DDL statement that AMO sends to the server when the `Drop` method is executed includes only the original object on which the `Drop` method was performed or includes all the dependent and referenced objects. The client application passes the parameter `DropOptions` to the `Drop` method. By default, only the current object is deleted on the server.

Because AMO has already updated the tree of dependent objects on the client side, it is very likely the `Drop` method will result in failure because of the inconsistency between the objects on the client and the objects on the server. If the client application specifies `DropOptions.AlterOrDeleteDependents`, the DDL request that AMO sends to the server includes all the dependent objects. We recommend that you use the default setting of `DropOptions` only if you know for sure that no other dependent objects are involved in the deletion.

Other operations on the major AMO objects, such as `Update`, `Refresh`, `Drop`, or `Process`, provide a similar way for a client application to specify how deep the operation should go. For example, if a client application adds a new hierarchy to the database dimension and then calls method `Update` on the database object without specifying the `UpdateOptions` argument, only the database object will be updated on the server; the `Dimension` and `Cube` objects on the server will not be. On the other hand, if the caller specifies `UpdateOptions.AlterDependencies` or `UpdateOptions.ExpandFull` the changes to the `Cube` objects will be propagated to the server.

Sometimes it is useful for the user to understand the impact of the change he is about to make. Because the outcome of the AMO operation can affect other AMO objects in one way and objects on the server in a slightly different way, AMO provides two features that help the user to analyze the impact of the potential change:

- Impact analysis enables the user to analyze the effect of potential changes on the server. It usually provides the answer to these questions: Which processed objects will become unprocessed? Which of the server objects will have to be changed as a result of the current operation? Impact analysis is performed on the server.
- The Dependencies Calculator analyzes the effect that the deletion of an AMO object has on other AMO objects. The Dependencies Calculator works on the client and determines which of the client objects have to be deleted or altered by the operation, or which dependencies will be broken as a result of the operation.

Impact Analysis

To enable the user to understand the impact of the change she is about to make on the server before she actually performs the operation, AMO provides impact analysis functionality, which gives the client application an answer to this question: What is the impact of the following change on the server? Before a client application sends a request to delete an attribute, it can call an AMO method that will determine which other objects would be affected by the proposed change. The application, using the information returned by AMO, can then determine whether to first modify other objects before it tries to make the change under consideration.

AMO methods that can affect the state of objects on the server—such as `Update`, `Drop`, and `Process`—allow the client application to analyze the impact of those changes without performing the actual change. The `Update`, `Drop`, and `Process` methods have overloads that allow passing the `ImpactDetailCollection` parameter, which AMO populates with the information about the impact of the current operation. AMO also enables the client application to specify whether the command should commit the change to the server or just run impact analysis. Listing 34.2 shows the `Update` method called on the `Database` object after an attribute is removed from the dimension.

LISTING 34.2 Using Impact Analysis

```
//Create a server object.
using(Server srv = new Server())
{
     //Connect to the server.
     srv.Connect("localhost");
     //Choose the database.
     Database db = srv.Databases.GetByName("FoodMart 2008");
     //Remove attribute named Marital Status from the Customer dimension.
     Dimension dbDim = db.Dimensions.GetByName("Customer");
     DimensionAttribute attr = dbDim.Attributes.GetByName("Marital Status");
     dbDim.Attributes.Remove(attr);

     //Allocate the collection for the warning that might be returned to the
      //application.
     XmlaWarningCollection warnings = new XmlaWarningCollection();
     //Allocate the collection for the details of impact analysis.
     ImpactDetailCollection impactDetailCollection = new ImpactDetailCollection();
     //Analyze the objects that will be affected if the database were updated, but
     // don't update the database.
     db.Update(UpdateOptions.ExpandFull, UpdateMode.Default, warnings,
            impactDetailCollection ,true);

     //Iterate the collection of impact details and print: impacted objects,
     //their types,impact, and description of the impact.
     foreach(ImpactDetail impactDetail in impactDetailCollection)
     {
           Console.WriteLine(impactDetail.Object.Name + "\t" +
➥impactDetail.Impact.ToString() + "\t" +  impactDetail.Description);
     }
}
```

This code returns the printout shown in Figure 34.8.

The impact analysis is not performed on the client. AMO sends a request to the server—the same XML/A request that would be sent to perform the actual operation (for example,

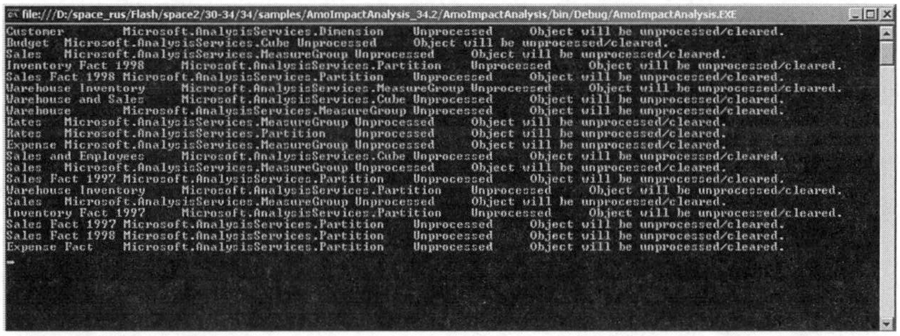

```
file:///D:/space_rus/Flash/space2/30-34/34/samples/AmoImpactAnalysis_34.2/AmoImpactAnalysis/bin/Debug/AmoImpactAnalysis.EXE
Customer        Microsoft.AnalysisServices.Dimension    Unprocessed     Object will be unprocessed/cleared.
Budget  Microsoft.AnalysisServices.Cube Unprocessed     Object will be unprocessed/cleared.
Sales   Microsoft.AnalysisServices.MeasureGroup Unprocessed     Object will be unprocessed/cleared.
Inventory Fact 1998     Microsoft.AnalysisServices.Partition    Unprocessed     Object will be unprocessed/cleared.
Sales Fact 1998 Microsoft.AnalysisServices.Partition    Unprocessed     Object will be unprocessed/cleared.
Warehouse Inventory     Microsoft.AnalysisServices.MeasureGroup Unprocessed     Object will be unprocessed/cleared.
Warehouse and Sales     Microsoft.AnalysisServices.Cube Unprocessed     Object will be unprocessed/cleared.
Warehouse       Microsoft.AnalysisServices.MeasureGroup Unprocessed     Object will be unprocessed/cleared.
Rates   Microsoft.AnalysisServices.MeasureGroup Unprocessed     Object will be unprocessed/cleared.
Rates   Microsoft.AnalysisServices.Partition    Unprocessed     Object will be unprocessed/cleared.
Expense Microsoft.AnalysisServices.MeasureGroup Unprocessed     Object will be unprocessed/cleared.
Sales and Employees     Microsoft.AnalysisServices.Cube Unprocessed     Object will be unprocessed/cleared.
Sales   Microsoft.AnalysisServices.MeasureGroup Unprocessed     Object will be unprocessed/cleared.
Sales Fact 1997 Microsoft.AnalysisServices.Partition    Unprocessed     Object will be unprocessed/cleared.
Warehouse Inventory     Microsoft.AnalysisServices.Partition    Unprocessed     Object will be unprocessed/cleared.
Sales   Microsoft.AnalysisServices.MeasureGroup Unprocessed     Object will be unprocessed/cleared.
Inventory Fact 1997     Microsoft.AnalysisServices.Partition    Unprocessed     Object will be unprocessed/cleared.
Sales Fact 1997 Microsoft.AnalysisServices.Partition    Unprocessed     Object will be unprocessed/cleared.
Sales Fact 1998 Microsoft.AnalysisServices.Partition    Unprocessed     Object will be unprocessed/cleared.
Expense Fact    Microsoft.AnalysisServices.Partition    Unprocessed     Object will be unprocessed/cleared.
```

FIGURE 34.8 The `Update` method populates a collection with the information about the impact of removing an attribute from a dimension.

<Alter>), except that it also contains an XML/A property, `ImpactAnalysis`, set to `1`. For a review of impact analysis functionality as it is performed on the server, see Chapter 26.

Dependencies Calculator

To help the user understand the impact of deleting an object on other AMO objects, AMO provides the `DependenciesCalculator` class. This class provides a client application with the method `GetDeleteDependents`, which analyzes the database object passed by the client code and the array of the objects to be deleted. It returns a `HashTable` containing `DependencyResult` objects that contain information about the dependencies. Each `DependencyResult` contains a dependent object, the type of dependency, and the description of the dependency. If you pass `TRUE` as a value of the `recursive` parameter, the Dependencies Calculator recursively calculates dependencies over the dependent objects.

Let's take a look at an example of the use of the Dependencies Calculator. Code in Listing 34.3 retrieves AMO objects that will be affected by the deletion of the `Customers` hierarchy from the database dimension `Customer`.

LISTING 34.3 Using the Dependencies Calculator

```
using (Server srv = new Server())
{
    //Connect to a server.
    srv.Connect("localhost");
    //Choose the FoodMart 2008 database and Customer dimension.
    Database db = srv.Databases.GetByName("FoodMart 2008");
    Dimension dim = db.Dimensions.GetByName("Customer");
    //Create DependenciesCalculator.
    DependenciesCalculator dependsCalculator = new DependenciesCalculator();
    //Analyze the objects affected by the deletion of the "Customers" hierarchy.
    object[] objects = new object[] { dim.Hierarchies.GetByName("Customers") };
    Hashtable dependencies = dependsCalculator.GetDeleteDependents(db, objects,
        false);
```

```
        Console.WriteLine("Dependencies");
        //Iterate over all the dependencies and print their descriptions.
        foreach (IEnumerable dependencyList in dependencies.Values)
        {
            foreach (DependencyResult dependency in dependencyList)
            {
                Console.WriteLine(dependency.Description);
            }
        }
}
```

This code returns information shown in Figure 34.9.

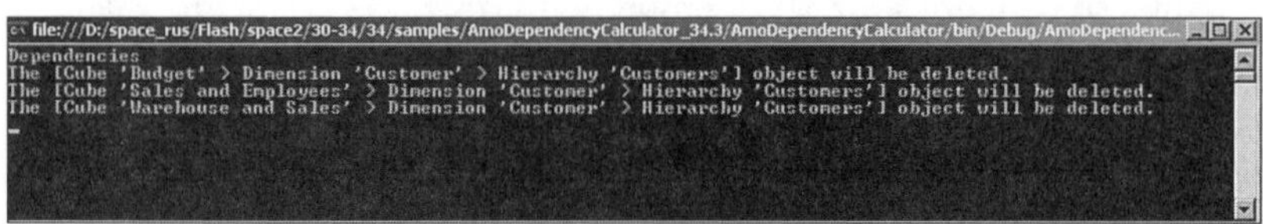

FIGURE 34.9 The **GetDeleteDependents** method populates a collection with information about objects dependent on the objects being deleted.

In this example, a strong dependency exists between the hierarchy of the database dimension and the hierarchies of the cube dimensions. That dependency will cause the hierarchies of the cube dimension to also be removed.

We can slightly modify the sample code as shown in Listing 34.4 to determine what effect deletion of the table in the `DataSourceView` on the other objects would have. We get a result that contains weaker dependencies; not all involved objects must be deleted, but will be invalidated instead.

LISTING 34.4 Using the Dependencies Calculator When Deleting a **DataSourceView** Object

```
using (Server srv = new Server())
{
    //Connect to the server.
    srv.Connect("localhost");
    //Choose the FoodMart 2008 database and Customers dimension.
    Database db = srv.Databases.GetByName("FoodMart 2008");
    //Create DependenciesCalculator.
    DependenciesCalculator dependsCalculator = new DependenciesCalculator();
    //Analyze the objects affected by the deletion of the DSV table.
    object[] objects = new object[] { db.DataSourceViews[0].Schema.Tables[0] };
    Hashtable dependencies = dependsCalculator.GetDeleteDependents(db, objects,
                             false);
    Console.WriteLine("Dependencies");
    //Iterate over all the dependencies and print their descriptions.
```

```
    foreach (IEnumerable dependencyList in dependencies.Values)
    {
        foreach (DependencyResult dependency in dependencyList)
        {
            Console.WriteLine(dependency.Description);
        }
    }
}
```

Removing a `DataSourceView` AMO object will not automatically delete dependent objects, but will invalidate them instead, as shown in Figure 34.10.

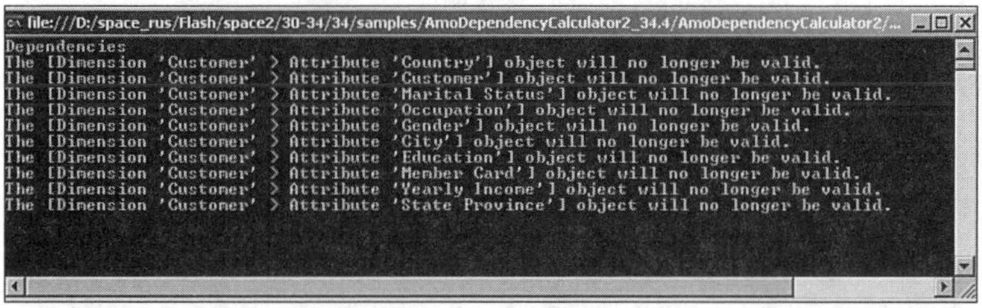
file:///D:/space_rus/Flash/space2/30-34/34/samples/AmoDependencyCalculator2_34.4/AmoDependencyCalculator2/...
Dependencies
The [Dimension 'Customer' > Attribute 'Country'] object will no longer be valid.
The [Dimension 'Customer' > Attribute 'Customer'] object will no longer be valid.
The [Dimension 'Customer' > Attribute 'Marital Status'] object will no longer be valid.
The [Dimension 'Customer' > Attribute 'Occupation'] object will no longer be valid.
The [Dimension 'Customer' > Attribute 'Gender'] object will no longer be valid.
The [Dimension 'Customer' > Attribute 'City'] object will no longer be valid.
The [Dimension 'Customer' > Attribute 'Education'] object will no longer be valid.
The [Dimension 'Customer' > Attribute 'Member Card'] object will no longer be valid.
The [Dimension 'Customer' > Attribute 'Yearly Income'] object will no longer be valid.
The [Dimension 'Customer' > Attribute 'State Province'] object will no longer be valid.

FIGURE 34.10 Removing a `DataSourceView` AMO object will not automatically delete dependent objects, but will invalidate them instead.

Creating a Visual Studio Project That Uses AMO

We are going to start by creating a project in Microsoft Visual Studio. You do not have to use Visual Studio to use AMO to create your application, but your life as a developer will be easier if you do. Creating an AMO project is similar to creating an ADOMD.NET project, so we do not go into a lot of detail here. Look back at the "Creating an ADOMD.NET Project" section in Chapter 33, "ADOMD.NET," if you need to refresh your memory.

Before you can start using AMO in your code, you have to register the assembly that contains AMO—Analysis Management Objects (`Microsoft.AnalysisServices.dll`)—and import the namespace for the AMO classes by adding the `using` clause for `Microsoft.AnalysisServices`:

```
using Microsoft.AnalysisServices;
```

Connecting to the Server

When it is working with AMO, the client application can connect to the server and work with it in connected mode. In connected mode, the client application sends updates to the server and regularly synchronizes with changes performed by other users. A good example of an application that works in connected mode is SQL Server Management Studio, which sends each operation carried out by the user to the server. The first step that any connected mode application should do is to establish a connection to the server.

As you might predict, AMO provides the `Server.Connect` method for making a connection to Analysis Services. You have a couple of choices about how you use this method. The client application can pass the method a connection string that contains various properties needed to make a connection—for example, the name of the server (see Listing 34.5).

LISTING 34.5 Connecting to the Server Using a Connection String

```
using (Server srv = new Server())
{
      string connectionString = "Datasource=localhost;";
      srv.Connect(connectionString);
      //Perform some operations.
      //...
}
```

If the client application does not need to pass any connection properties to the `Connect` method except the name of the server, it can just pass the server name as a parameter to the `Server.Connect` method. This approach was included in AMO for compatibility with Decision Support Objects (DSO) because DSO did not have a notion of the connection string and used just the server name for a connection. Nevertheless, it can come in handy. Listing 34.6 contains the code you use if you want to establish the connection this way.

LISTING 34.6 Connection to the Server Using Just the Name of the Server

```
using (Server srv = new Server())
{
      srv.Connect("localhost");
      //Perform some operations.
      //...
}
```

In designing AMO, we did our utmost to make sure that all the object models we provide with Analysis Services—ADOMD.NET, AMO, and the OLE DB provider—support the same set of properties. Actually AMO and ADOMD.NET carry out almost the same set of operations to establish a connection to the server internally, so we recommend that you read the "ADOMD.NET Connections" section in Chapter 33 for a detailed explanation of connection operations.

AMO and ADOMD.NET can share a session on the server, just as different instances of the `Server` object can share a session. If you want to connect to a session that already exists on the server, you can pass its `SessionID` property as a parameter to the `Server.Connect` method, as shown in Listing 34.7.

LISTING 34.7 Share the Session Between AMO and ADOMD.NET

```
using System;
using System.Collections.Generic;
using System.Text;
using System.Data;
using Microsoft.AnalysisServices;
using Microsoft.AnalysisServices.AdomdClient;

namespace AmoSessionShareSample
{
     class Program
     {
          static void Main(string[] args)
          {
               try
               {
                    //Create an ADOMD.NET Connection object.
                    Microsoft.AnalysisServices.AdomdClient.AdomdConnection
adomdConnection = new Microsoft.AnalysisServices.AdomdClient.AdomdConnection();
                    adomdConnection.ConnectionString = "Datasource=localhost;
                   Initial Catalog=FoodMart 2008;";
                    adomdConnection.Open();
                    //Create an AMO Server object.
                    Microsoft.AnalysisServices.Server server =
                         new Microsoft.AnalysisServices.Server();
                    //Connect to the server using the same session that the
                    //ADOMD.NET connection uses.
                    server.Connect("Datasource=localhost",
➥adomdConnection.SessionID);

                    Microsoft.AnalysisServices.Database database =
                        server.Databases.FindByName("FoodMart 2008");
                    //Create a new cube.
                    Microsoft.AnalysisServices.Cube cube = CreateCube(database);

                    //Start the transaction.
                    server.BeginTransaction();
                    //Update the cube.
                    cube.Update(UpdateOptions.ExpandFull);
                    //Process the cube.
                    cube.Process(ProcessType.ProcessDefault);
                   //Check that the new cube is available through the
                   // ADOMD.NET connection.
                   //It would not be available if the session weren't shared.
                   if (null != adomdConnection.Cubes.Find(cube.Name))
```

34

```
                        Console.WriteLine("The new cube created by AMO is
➥ available through ADOMD.");
                    //Roll back the transaction.
                    server.RollbackTransaction();
                    //Close the AMO connection;this call does not end the session.
                    server.Disconnect(false);
                    //Close the ADOMD.NET connection; this call does close
                    //the session.
                    adomdConnection.Close();
            }
            catch (AmoException amoException)
            {
                Console.WriteLine(amoException.Message);
            }
            catch (AdomdException adomdException)
            {
                 Console.WriteLine(adomdException.Message);
            }
    }
```

Canceling Long-Running Operations

When you write a client application that provides a user interface, you do not want to make your user wait, unable to continue working with the user interface, while a long-running operation finishes. Some of the operations that AMO performs, such as the processing of some databases, can take a long time. In addition, AMO executes all operations synchronously, which means that a call to a process method will not return a response until AMO has received the server response. To make sure that your user does not have to wait, we recommend that you use a different thread for executing long-running operations so that the user can continue to use the application during the operation.

It is also a good idea to enable users to cancel an operation. AMO provides the `Server.CancelCommand` method, which sends a request to the server to cancel the request. `CancelCommand` works similarly to the `Cancel` method in ADOMD.NET. When the client application calls `Server.CancelCommand`, AMO opens a new XML/A connection using the same connection properties that were used to establish the original connection. Then, AMO sends the `<Cancel>` request to the server. (It can take some time for the server to actually cancel the request.)

In the "Asynchronous Execution and Cancellation of Commands" section in Chapter 33, we presented a simple application that executes a query in one thread and cancels it in another. You can use AMO to write a similar application that processes a cube in one thread and cancels processing in another. This client application has three buttons:

Connect (to open a connection), Process (to process the cube), and Cancel (to cancel processing).

To prevent multiple threads from using the same resource simultaneously, we will use a simple synchronization approach—switching the buttons on and off. The `Process` button is disabled until the connection is created; the `Cancel` button is disabled until processing begins. This synchronization technique might not work for everyone. You can use any other synchronization technique, such as the `Lock` method of the `System.Object` class. Listing 34.8 uses the `BackgroundWorker` object provided by the .NET Framework.

LISTING 34.8 Asynchronous Processing of a Cube

```
using System;
using System.ComponentModel;
using System.Windows.Forms;
using Microsoft.AnalysisServices;

namespace AmoProcessCancel
{
     public partial class Form1: Form
     {
          Server server = null;
          BackgroundWorker backgroundWorker = null;

          public Form1()
          {
            InitializeComponent();
            //Before the connection is established, only the Connection
            //button is enabled.
            connectionButton.Enabled = true;
            cancelButton.Enabled = false;
            processButton.Enabled = false;
            //Create BackgroundWorker object.
            this.backgroundWorker = new BackgroundWorker();
            this.backgroundWorker.WorkerReportsProgress = false;
            this.backgroundWorker.WorkerSupportsCancellation = true;
            this.backgroundWorker.RunWorkerCompleted += OnCompleted;
            this.backgroundWorker.DoWork += OnDoWork;
          }

          //This function is called when the user clicks the Connection button.
          private void connectionButton_Click(object sender, EventArgs e)
          {
               //Open a connection to the server.
               this.server = new Server();
               this.server.Connect("Datasource=localhost;");
```

```
        //When the connection is opened it is possible to start
        //processing, but still impossible to cancel the process.
        connectionButton.Enabled = false;
        processButton.Enabled = true;

    }

    //This function is called when the user clicks the Process button.
    private void processButton_Click(object sender, EventArgs e)
    {
        //Get a database object and cube object.
        database = this.server.Databases.GetByName("FoodMart 2008");
        Cube cube = database.Cubes.GetByName("Warehouse and Sales");
        //Before starting the worker thread, disable the Process button so
        //the user won't be able to click it again.
        //Enable the Cancel button.
        cancelButton.Enabled = true;
        processButton.Enabled = false;
        //Start the worker thread, then pass the Cube object as a parameter
        // to the function that will be called on the worker thread.
        this.backgroundWorker.RunWorkerAsync(cube);
    }

    //This function is called when the user clicks the Cancel button.
    private void CancelButton_Click(object sender, EventArgs e)
    {
        //Call the Cancel method to send a cancel request to the server.
        try
        {
            this.server.CancelCommand(this.server.SessionID);
        }
      catch (OperationException ex)
      {
         //If you send the Cancel command twice Analysis Services
         //might return an error, that command is already cancelled.
         //We assume that Cancel command can't through other exceptions.
      }
        //Inform BackgroundWorker that the request has been canceled.
        this.backgroundWorker.CancelAsync();
    }

    //This function is called on the background thread.
    void OnDoWork(object sender, DoWorkEventArgs doWorkArgs)
  {
        //Retrieve the Cube object from the doWorkArgs parameter.
        BackgroundWorker backgroundWorker;
```

```
            backgroundWorker = sender as BackgroundWorker;
            Cube cube = (Cube)doWorkArgs.Argument;
            //Start processing.
            cube.Process(ProcessType.ProcessFull);
            //If the user clicks the Cancel button during processing,
            // set the flag backgroundWorker.CancellationPending to true.
            if(backgroundWorker.CancellationPending)
                doWorkArgs.Cancel = true;
            else
                doWorkArgs.Result = true;
        }

        //This function is called by the class BackgroundWorker on the main
        //thread when the function running in the background completes.
        void OnCompleted(object sender, RunWorkerCompletedEventArgs completedArgs)
        {
            //If there was an error, notify the user.
            if(completedArgs.Error != null)
            {
                MessageBox.Show(completedArgs.Error.Message,
                    completedArgs.Error.Source);
            }
            else if (completedArgs.Canceled)
            {
                 MessageBox.Show(" Processing has been canceled by the user.");
            }
            else
            {
                 //The processing completed successfully.
                 MessageBox.Show(" Processing has been completed.");
            }
            //Execution of the command has completed, close the connection
            //and reset all buttons.
            if (null != this.server && this.server.Connected)
            {
                this.server.Disconnect();
            }
            this.server = null;
            connectionButton.Enabled = true;
            cancelButton.Enabled = false;
            processButton.Enabled = false;
        }
    }
}
```

When the user clicks the Cancel button, the sample application calls the `server.CancelCommand` method, which issues the `Cancel` DDL command. You can read about the `Cancel` command in Chapter 26. The `Cancel` command does not immediately cancel the running command; on the server, the `Cancel` command turns on a flag that signals to the session that it should stop all operations and returns to the client application. All server operations periodically check this flag; if it is turned on, the server starts the canceling process. The response generated by the server differs depending on the processing stage being executed at the moment you clicked the Cancel button. Therefore, the sample application might show different message boxes every time you click the Cancel button. If you issue the `Cancel` command more than one time, Analysis Services might generate an error telling you that the command already been canceled; AMO propagates this error to the caller as an exception. This sample application captures all the exceptions thrown by `server.CancelCommand`.

AMO Object Loading

After a connection to the server is established, the client application can use AMO interfaces to enumerate all the metadata objects that exist on the server. AMO retrieves metadata information from the server by sending `DISCOVER_XML_METADATA` requests. However, it would not be very efficient to download the metadata information about all the objects on the server in one request.

AMO has an intelligent mechanism for downloading metadata from the server. The idea is that only the objects that are needed or requested by the application are downloaded to the client. For example, after establishing the connection to the server, AMO populates the `Databases` collection and other collections of major objects that are children of the server object (such as `Traces`, `Assemblies`, `Roles`, and `ServerProperties`), by sending a `DISCOVER_XML_METADATA` request with an `ObjectExpansion` restriction set to `ExpandObject`.

The server sends back the properties of the current object (`Server`) and the `Name`, `ID`, and several other properties (such as `CreatedTimestamp`, `LastSchemaUpdate`, `LastProcessed`, `State`, and `LastUpdated`) of the major objects it contains.

When the client code tries to access a property of one of those contained objects, AMO sends a request to the server for more information. If the requested property has already been retrieved, AMO returns the property value that is cached on the client. Listing 34.9 shows at what time which object will be downloaded from the server.

LISTING 34.9 Loading AMO Objects from the Server

```
using (Server srv = new Server())
{
    string connectionString = "Datasource=localhost;";
    //The following code will connect to the server and send a
    //DISCOVER_XML_METADATA request, then AMO will populate all the properties
    //of the server object and create collections of major contained objects.
    srv.Connect(connectionString);
```

```
    //The following line will not send a request to the server, the
    // Database collection already exists on the client.
    foreach(Database database in srv.Databases)
    {
        //The following line will not send a request to the server,
        //Name is already populated.
        Console.WriteLine(database.Name);
        //The following line will send a request to the server, to retrieve all
        //the properties of the Database object, including its children that are
        //major objects.
        Console.WriteLine(database.Translations[0].Language);
    }
}
```


Working with AMO in Disconnected Mode

A client application does not necessarily have to establish a connection to work with AMO objects. AMO can be operated in disconnected mode. The designers of the AMO object model created this mode mostly for applications such as BI Dev Studio that enable a team of database developers to design and develop data warehouse projects. The main idea behind working disconnected from the server is to allow an individual developer to work independently on her computer, being able to save her work to disk, even when the work is not completed or maybe even incorrect. However, when she is ready to move to the deployment stage, she can connect to the server and deploy the project to the server.

In disconnected mode, you can create a whole tree of AMO objects, starting with the `Database` object, without establishing a connection to the server. You can perform basic AMO operations, such as instantiation of objects, adding them to the collection, validation, and so on. Then, you can serialize (store) the whole hierarchy of objects and retrieve them later. But, while you're working in disconnected mode, any operation that requires sending a request to the server, such as `Update` and `Process`, will fail.

When a database developer is ready to deploy her work to the server, the client application can create a `Server` object, connect to Analysis Server, and add the database that was created in disconnected mode, with all the child objects of the `Database` object. Then, the application can send updates to the server, synchronize with the updates on the server done by another developer, and can then perform process operations and process objects.

Listing 34.10 demonstrates a scenario of working with AMO objects in disconnected mode. In this example, we also show the AMO methods `Serialize` and `Deserialize`, which allow the client application to store the definitions of AMO objects, in XML format, to the file. It is possible to read the XML and restore those objects later.

LISTING 34.10 Working with AMO Objects in Disconnected Mode

```
string fileName = "..\\..\\amoserializedb.xml";
```

```
//Call helper function that will create the database, including the whole tree
//of its child objects, such as data source, cube, dimensions, and so on.
Database db = CreateDatabase();
//Create an XML writer that will be used to serialize the AMO objects into a file.
System.Xml.XmlTextWriter writer =
          new System.Xml.XmlTextWriter(fileName, Encoding.UTF8);
//Save the definitions of the database and the tree of AMO objects into the file.
Utils.Serialize(writer, db, false);
writer.Close();

    // ...Do some operations.

//Create an XML text reader that will be used to deserialize the AMO objects.
System.Xml.XmlTextReader reader = new System.Xml.XmlTextReader(fileName);
//Read the objects from the file and create a Database object.
Database newDatabase = (Database)Utils.Deserialize(reader, new Database());
reader.Close();

//Create a Server object and connect to the Analysis Server.
using (Server srv = new Server())
{
     srv.Connect("localhost");
     //Add the newly created database to the DatabaseCollection, if no database
     //with the same ID already exists in the collection.
     if ( !srv.Databases.Contains(db.ID) )
     {
          srv.Databases.Add(db);
          db.Update();
     }
     else
         throw (new ApplicationException("Database " + db.ID +
                "already exists on the server"));
}
```

Using the Scripter Object

One of the interesting features of AMO is its capability to generate XML scripts that contain DDL commands—commands such as `Alter` and `Process`—that can be sent to the server later to perform specified operations. This functionality is useful in many scenarios, such as to allow a database administrator a simple way to create automation scripts.

AMO provides scripting functionality by introducing the `Scripter` object. The `Scripter` object has a method, `Script`, which streams XML into the `XmlWriter` created by the caller. As input, the `Script` method takes an array of `ScriptInfo` objects that contain information about the objects and DDL commands to be scripted. The sample code in Listing 34.11 creates a script with the `Alter` command to modify or create the FoodMart 2008 database. For more information about the `Alter` command, see Chapter 26.

LISTING 34.11 Script Database

```
//Create a Server object.
using (Server srv = new Server())
{
    string fileName = "..\\..\\scriptDBAlter.xml";
    //Connect to the server.
    srv.Connect("localhost");
    Database db = srv.Databases.FindByName("Foodmart 2008");
    //Create the scripter object.
    Scripter scripter = new Scripter();
    //Create an XML text writer, which will be used to script the command
    //into the file.
    System.Xml.XmlTextWriter writer =
        new System.Xml.XmlTextWriter(fileName,Encoding.UTF8);
    //Create a scriptInfo object.
    ScriptInfo scriptInfo = new ScriptInfo(db,
         ScriptAction.AlterWithAllowCreate, ScriptOptions.Default, false);
    //Create an array of the scriptInfo objects. In this example, the array
    //contains just one element.
    ScriptInfo []scriptInfos = new ScriptInfo[] { scriptInfo };
    //Create a scripter object.
    scripter.Script(scriptInfos, writer);
    //Close the XML writer.
    writer.Close();
}
```

In addition to the `Script` method, AMO provides a number of methods that simplify scripting: `ScriptCreate`, `ScriptAlter`, and `ScriptDelete`. These methods generate `ScriptInfo` objects with `ScriptAction.Create`, `ScriptAction.Alter`, or `ScriptAction.Delete`, and call the `Script` method. Listing 34.12 shows the `ScriptAlter` method.

LISTING 34.12 Using the **ScriptAlter** Command

```
//Create a server object.
using (Server srv = new Server())
{
    //Connect to the server.
    srv.Connect("localhost");
    Database db = srv.Databases.FindByName("Foodmart 2008");
```

```
    Scripter scripter = new Scripter();
    string fileName = "..\\..\\scriptDB.xml";
    //Create an XML text writer, which will be used to script the command.
    System.Xml.XmlTextWriter writer =
            new System.Xml.XmlTextWriter(fileName,Encoding.UTF8);
    //Create an array of major objects. In this example, the array contains
    //just one element.
     MajorObject[] objects = new MajorObject [] { db };
    //Script the Alter command.
    scripter.ScriptAlter(objects, writer, false);
    //Close the XML writer.
    writer.Close();
}
```

To simplify the scripting of objects even further, especially in cases where you have a single object to script or need to script processing operations and batches of the commands, the `Scripter` object has a number of static methods you can use:

- **`WriteStartBatch`**—Generates a `<Batch>` element for the DDL `Batch` command. For more information about the `Batch` command, see Chapter 26.
- **`WriteEndBatch`**—Generates a closing `</Batch>` element for the `Batch` command.
- **`WriteStartParallel`**—Generates a `<Parallel>` element, which you can use inside the `Batch` command to execute inner commands in parallel.
- **`WriteEndParallel`**—Generates a closing `</Parallel>` element.
- **`WriteCreate`**—Generates a DDL `Create` command.
- **`WriteAlter`**—Generates a DDL `Alter` command.
- **`WriteDelete`**—Generates a DDL `Delete` command.
- **`WriteProcess`**—Generates a DDL `Process` command.

For example, you can use the `WriteStartBatch` command to generate an opening XML element `Batch`, and then use `WriteProcess` in a loop to generate `Process` commands to process all databases or all the partitions in a measure group. Then, you close the `Batch` command with `WriteEndBatch` method, as shown in Listing 34.13.

LISTING 34.13 Scripting a **Batch** Operation Containing Multiple Processing Operations

```
//Create a Server object.
using (Server srv = new Server())
{
    //Connect to the server.
    srv.Connect("localhost");
    Scripter scripter = new Scripter();
    string fileName = "..\\..\\scriptDBBatch.xml";
```

```
    //Create an XML text writer, which will be used to script the command.
    System.Xml.XmlTextWriter writer =
          new System.Xml.XmlTextWriter(fileName,Encoding.UTF8);
    //Start a transactional batch.
    Scripter.WriteStartBatch(writer, true);
    foreach(Database db in srv.Databases)
    {
         //Script the processing of the database.
         Scripter.WriteProcess(writer, db, ProcessType.ProcessFull);
     }
    //End the batch.
    Scripter.WriteEndBatch ( writer );
    //Close XML writer
    writer.Close();
}
```


Using Traces

Analysis Services enables database administrators to monitor or trace a set of operations executed on the server. AMO allows application designers to take advantage of this functionality. Using the `Trace` object of AMO, you can write utilities that enable monitoring, auditing, and profiling of Analysis Services. Another application of traces is to enable the client application to process or display the events sent by the server during some of the operations. For example, during processing, the server can send important information about the status and progress of the processing operations.

The `Trace` object has `OnEvent` and `Stopped` methods that enable a client application to subscribe to a trace event and get notification when the event is fired or tracing is stopped. A client application can subscribe to the `Trace` event by executing the following code:

```
// Start the default trace
svr.SessionTrace.OnEvent
       += new TraceEventHandler(DefaultTrace_OnEvent);
svr.SessionTrace.Stopped
       += new TraceStoppedEventHandler(DefaultTrace_Stopped);
```

But, the trace will not be started until the `Start` method is called. During the execution of the `Start` method, AMO starts a new thread from which it establishes the connection to the server that will be used to subscribe to the server traces:

```
svr.SessionTrace.Start();
```

To stop tracing, the client application calls the Stop method, which will disconnect from the server and terminate the thread used for tracing:

```
    this.server.SessionTrace.OnEvent -= new
➥TraceEventHandler(sessionTrace_OnEvent);


this.server.SessionTrace.Stopped -= new
➥TraceStoppedEventHandler(sessionTrace_Stopped);

    this.server.SessionTrace.Stop();
```

Two categories of Trace objects are provided by AMO:

- Customizable traces enable a client application to subscribe to specific trace events. This category of traces is useful when you are creating applications for monitoring and profiling the server. To create or modify a custom Trace, a client application can use the Traces collection of the Server object.
- Default traces are produced by the server during certain server operations, such as processing. The client application does not have to create a new Trace object to get additional information from the server during processing. AMO provides the SessionTrace property on the Server object to enable client applications to subscribe to the processing events.

In the previous section ("Canceling Long-Running Operations"), we demonstrated how operations that have the potential to run for a long time can be run asynchronously and how to cancel such operations. Now we want to extend that example and demonstrate how to use the Trace object to display the progress of the processing operation.

Let's take the previous example and add tracing capabilities to it. In addition to the Connect and Process buttons, let's add a progress bar that shows the progress of the processing operation and a tree view that displays the events as they occur on the server during the processing of the cube. The user interface display will look like the one in Figure 34.11.

As in the previous example shown in Listing 34.14, we are using the button state for synchronization. Immediately after establishing the connection with the server, we will subscribe to the default trace events. We will display the trace events in the tree view control, and we will show a progress bar that reports the progress of the cube processing.

LISTING 34.14 Using the **Trace** Object to Display User Interface Controls

```
using System;
using System.ComponentModel;
using System.Drawing;
using System.Windows.Forms;
using System.Collections;
using System.Threading;
```

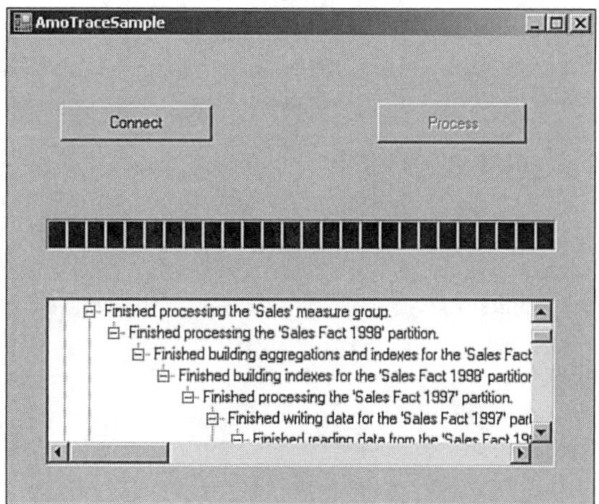

FIGURE 34.11 The UI displays a progress bar and a tree view showing events as they are received during the processing of the cube.

```
using Microsoft.AnalysisServices;

namespace AmoTraceSample
{
     public partial class AmoTraceForm : Form
     {
          Server server = null;
          BackgroundWorker backgroundWorker = null;
          TreeNode prevNode = null;
          ArrayList nodeStack = new ArrayList();
          enum AddNodeType
          {
               NodeBegin,
               NodeEnd,
               NodeInsert
          };
          enum ButtonState
          {
               None,
               Connect,
               Process
          }
```

As in Listing 34.8, we use the BackgroundWorker class provided by .NET Framework. We also use the button state for synchronization:

```
public AmoTraceForm()
{
     InitializeComponent();
     //Until the connection is established, only the
     //Connection button is enabled.
     SetButtonsState(ButtonState.Connect);
     //Create and initialize BackgroundWorker.
     InitializeBackgroundWorker();
}

//Reset the state of the buttons.
private void SetButtonsState(ButtonState state)
{
     switch (state)
     {
          case ButtonState.Connect:
               processButton.Enabled = false;
               connectionButton.Enabled = true;
               break;
          case ButtonState.Process:
               connectionButton.Enabled = false;
               processButton.Enabled = true;
               break;
          case ButtonState.None:
               connectionButton.Enabled = false;
               processButton.Enabled = false;
               break;
     }
}

private void InitializeBackgroundWorker()
{
     this.backgroundWorker = new BackgroundWorker();
     this.backgroundWorker.WorkerReportsProgress = false;
     this.backgroundWorker.WorkerSupportsCancellation = true;
     this.backgroundWorker.RunWorkerCompleted += OnCompleted;
     this.backgroundWorker.DoWork += OnDoWork;
}
```

When a user clicks the Connect button, we connect to the server:

```
private void connectionButton_Click(object sender, EventArgs e)
{
```

```
        //Open a connection to the server.
        this.server = new Server();
        this.server.Connect("Datasource=localhost;");
        SubscribeToSessionTrace();
        //Subscribe to the trace event.
        this.processProgress.Value = 0;
        this.reportTree.Nodes.Clear();
        //When the connection is opened, it is possible to
        //start processing, but still impossible to cancel the process.
        SetButtonsState(ButtonState.Process);
    }
```

After the connection to the server is established, we subscribe to the default trace events:

```
    //Set the event handler that will be called when the trace event is
    //fired.
    //Start tracing.
    private void SubscribeToSessionTrace()
    {
        this.server.SessionTrace.OnEvent +=
               new TraceEventHandler(sessionTrace_OnEvent);
        this.server.SessionTrace.Stopped +=
               new TraceStoppedEventHandler(sessionTrace_Stopped);
        this.server.SessionTrace.Start(); // this method is not blocking
    }
```

After the user clicks the Process button, our application takes the `Warehouse and Sales` cube of the FoodMart 2008 database and passes it to the function running on the background thread so that it can be processed:

```
    //This function is called when the user clicks the Process button.
    private void processButton_Click(object sender, EventArgs e)
    {
        //Get a database and a cube.
        Database database = this.server.Databases.GetByName("Foodmart 2008");
        Cube cube = database.Cubes.GetByName("Warehouse and Sales");
        //Before starting the worker thread, disable the Process button
        //so the user won't be able to click it again.
        SetButtonsState(ButtonState.None);
        //Start the worker thread, then pass the Cube object as a parameter
        //to the function that will be called on the worker thread.
        this.backgroundWorker.RunWorkerAsync(cube);
    }
```

On the background thread, we process the `Warehouse and Sales` cube:

```
    void OnDoWork(object sender, DoWorkEventArgs doWorkArgs)
```

```
{
    //Retrieve the Cube object from the doWorkArgs parameter.
    BackgroundWorker backgroundWorker;
    backgroundWorker = sender as BackgroundWorker;
    Cube cube = (Cube)doWorkArgs.Argument;
    //Start processing.
    cube.Process(ProcessType.ProcessFull);
    doWorkArgs.Result = true;
}
```

When processing is complete, unsubscribe from the trace events and close the connection. Trace events are sent back lazily, meaning that the processing operation may complete before you receive all the trace events. This is inconvenient but, unfortunately, there is no good solution to this problem. In the example, we solve it by waiting a bit before unsubscribing from trace events to give the server time to finish sending all the trace events:

```
void OnCompleted(object sender, RunWorkerCompletedEventArgs completedArgs)
{
    //If there was an error, notify the user.
    if(completedArgs.Error != null)
    {
        MessageBox.Show(completedArgs.Error.Message,
            completedArgs.Error.Source);
    }
    else
    {
        // The processing completed successfully.
        MessageBox.Show(" Processing has been completed. ");
    }
    //Execution of the command has completed, close the connection
    //and reset all buttons.
    if (null != this.server && this.server.Connected)
    {
        //Unsubscribe from the trace events, stop tracing.
        if (this.server.SessionTrace != null)
        {
            //Here we need to wait until all the trace events have
            //been retrieved.
            Thread.Sleep(500);
            UnsubscribeToSessionTrace();
        }
        //Disconnect from the server.
        this.server.Disconnect();
    }
    this.server = null;
    SetButtonsState(ButtonState.Connect);
```

```
}

//Unsubscribe from the trace events and stop tracing.
private void UnsubscribeFromSessionTrace()
{
     this.server.SessionTrace.OnEvent -=
           new TraceEventHandler(sessionTrace_OnEvent);
     this.server.SessionTrace.Stopped -=
           new TraceStoppedEventHandler(sessionTrace_Stopped);
     this.server.SessionTrace.Stop();
}
```

After processing starts, we start to receive various tracing events. We create a new node that appears on the reporting tree when the `ProgressReportBegin` event is received. When the sample application receives a `ProgressReportEnd` event, the node that was created during the `ProgressReportBegin` event is updated. We also increment the progress bar when the `ProgressReportCurrent` event is received:


```
///The function will be called when the Trace event is fired.
private void sessionTrace_OnEvent(object sender, TraceEventArgs e)
{
     try
     {
          //Increment the progress bar.
          if ( TraceEventClass.ProgressReportCurrent == e.EventClass )
               IncrementReport();

          //Create a new node on the report tree or update
          //the existing node.
          switch (e.EventClass)
          {
               case TraceEventClass.ProgressReportBegin:
                    AddNode(e.TextData.Trim(),AddNodeType.NodeBegin,
                        Color.Black);
                    return;
               case TraceEventClass.ProgressReportEnd:
                   AddNode(e.TextData.Trim(), AddNodeType.NodeEnd,
                        Color.Black);
                    return;
               case TraceEventClass.ProgressReportError:
                    AddNode(e.TextData.Trim(), AddNodeType.NodeInsert,
                        Color.Red);
                    break;
          }
     }
```

```
            catch (Exception ex)
            {
                MessageBox.Show(ex.Message);
            }
    }
```

Trace handling occurs on the thread created by AMO, not on the main thread. Therefore, if you want to use the trace event handler to manipulate the user interface controls that were created on the main thread, you have to marshal calls to the UI controls on the main thread. In this example, we use the `Invoke` method of each UI control—tree view and progress bar—but you can achieve the same results by different means:

```
        // Increment the progress report bar.
        //Since Trace events are called from the thread created by AMO,
        //thread marshaling is required to access the UI controls.
        delegate void IncrementReportDelegate();
        void IncrementReport()
        {
            if (processProgress.InvokeRequired)
            {
                IncrementReportDelegate d =
                    new IncrementReportDelegate(IncrementReport);
                this.Invoke(d);
            }
            else
            {
                processProgress.Increment(10);
            }
        }

        //Add or update the node of the report tree.
        //Because Trace events are called from the thread created by AMO,
        //thread marshaling is required to access the UI controls.
        delegate void AddNodeDelegate(string text, AddNodeType addNodeType,
               Color color);
        void AddNode(string text, AddNodeType addNodeType, Color color)
        {
            if (reportTree.InvokeRequired)
            {
                AddNodeDelegate d = new AddNodeDelegate(AddNode);
                this.Invoke(d, new object[] { text, addNodeType ,color});
            }
            else
            {
                TreeNode node;
                switch (addNodeType)
```

```
                {
                    case AddNodeType.NodeBegin:
                        node = new TreeNode(text);
                        if (null != this.prevNode)
                        {
                            this.prevNode.Nodes.Add(node);
                            this.prevNode.Expand();
                        }
                        else
                            this.reportTree.Nodes.Add(node);
                        this.prevNode = node;
                        this.nodeStack.Add(node);
                        break;
                    case AddNodeType.NodeEnd:
                node = (TreeNode)this.nodeStack[this.nodeStack.Count - 1];
                        node.Text = text;
                        this.prevNode = node.Parent;
                        this.nodeStack.Remove(node);
                        break;
                    case AddNodeType.NodeInsert:
                        node = new TreeNode(text);
                        if (null != this.prevNode)
                            this.prevNode.Nodes.Add(node);
                        else
                            this.reportTree.Nodes.Add(node);
                        this.prevNode = node;
                        this.nodeStack.Add(node);
                        break;
                    default:
                        node = null;
                        break;
                }
                node.ForeColor = color;
            }
        }

        //This method is called when the trace is stopped.
        private void sessionTrace_Stopped(ITrace sender, TraceStoppedEventArgs e)
        {
            if (e.StopCause == TraceStopCause.StoppedByException)
                throw e.Exception;
        }

    }
}
```

34

Error Handling

Errors are a fact of life and a fact of programming. One of the most important aspects of software development is the ability to process errors and protect users and application from unwanted behaviors. The ability to understand and handle errors gracefully is especially important when you are using a complex object model such as AMO, where things can take an unexpected turn because of network failure. Therefore, we cannot talk about AMO without talking about error handling.

In this section, we discuss the classes responsible for error handling and show you how to use those classes. The more often you use them, the less time you will spend debugging your application.

AMO is built on top of the .NET Framework, so it uses exceptions as error-handling mechanisms. When it calls any AMO method or property, an application should be prepared to get any one of the standard exceptions, such as `NotSupportedException`, `InvalidOperation Exception`, and `ArgumentNullException`. These exceptions usually indicate a misuse of the object model—a bug in the code of the client application.

AMO provides a base class for error handling: `AmoException` (shown in Figure 34.12). It also provides four classes derived from `AmoException`, which are designed to allow the client application to use different error-handling code for different kinds of errors. A client application that calls AMO objects should be ready to catch an `AmoException` or, if appropriate, the instance of the derived exception class.

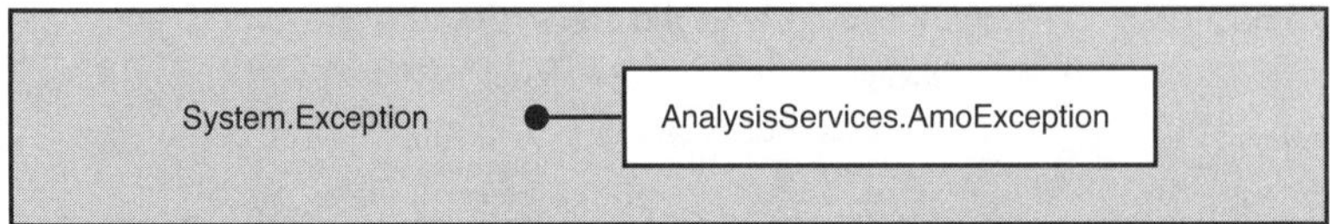

FIGURE 34.12 AMO provides a base class for error handling—`AmoException`—which is derived from the `System.Exception` class.

The following sections discuss the exception classes derived from `AmoException`.

OperationException

`OperationException` is thrown when the request sent to the server returns an error or a warning to the client. Because `OperationException` is designed to propagate errors and warnings returned by the server, and because Analysis Services can return multiple messages for the single request, `OperationException` contains a collection of `XmlaResult` objects. Each `XmlaResult` object can contain more than one message, so it can have an `XmlaMessageCollection`. Each `XmlaMessage` object is either an error or a warning. AMO provides two classes derived from `XmlaMessage`, one for each type of message: `XmlaWarning` and `XmlaError`. Figure 34.13 shows these relationships.

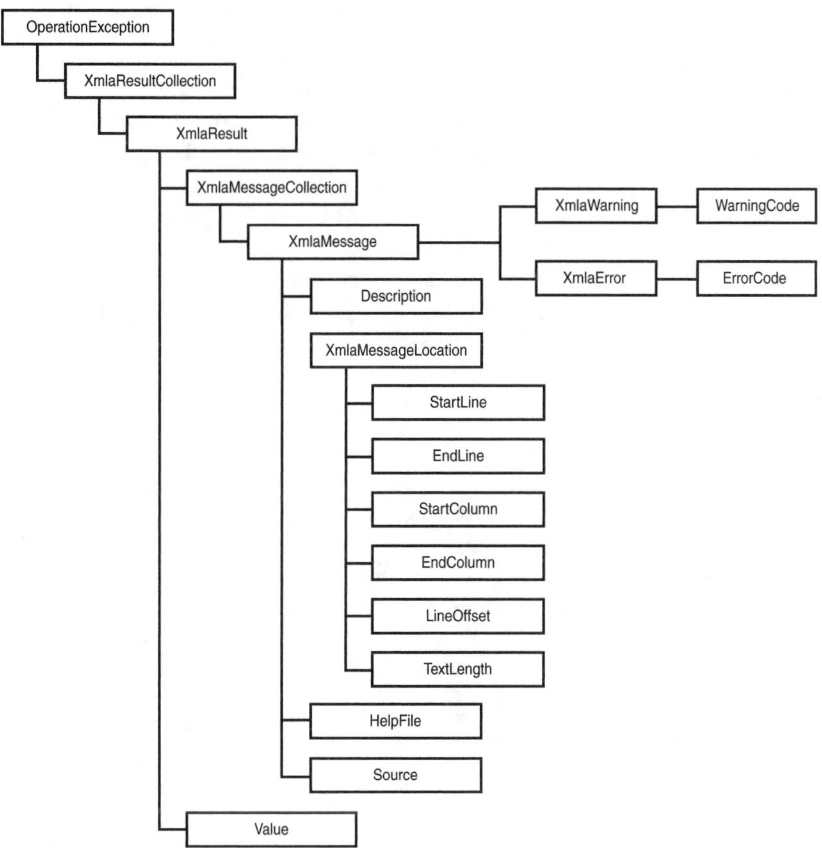

FIGURE 34.13 This diagram shows the hierarchy of objects exposed through `OperationException`.

ResponseFormatException

`ResponseFormatException` is thrown when AMO cannot understand the response sent by the server. This can happen if the request has been sent to an XML/A provider with a version of XML/A that is not supported by AMO. Such errors are always fatal, so the client application should cease its execution.

ConnectionException

`ConnectionException` is thrown when the connection with the server cannot be opened or has been interrupted. This kind of exception has the `ExceptionCause` property, which provides information to the client application if the connection cannot be established because of security issues or for some other reason.

In this version of AMO, the `ExceptionCause` property can return three values: `AuthenticationFailed`, `IncompatibleVersion`, and `Unspecified`. A good example of a use for `AuthenticationFailed` exception is if the connection to the server fails, the client application displays a user interface in which the user can enter missing connection information, such as server name. If AMO detects that version of the server it connects to is incompatible, it returns an `IncompatibleVersion` exception. Obviously, this exception will not happen when you use the current version of AMO to connect to current version of Analysis Services. In all other cases, the value of the `ExceptionCause` property is `Unspecified`.

OutOfSyncException

`OutOfSyncException` is thrown by AMO in rare situations when the objects on the client are out of sync with the objects on the server. This exception might occur if, while it is syncing with the server, AMO receives from the server a reference to objects that do not exist on the client. This situation usually happens if another user has changed the metadata on the server, and the metadata on the client (AMO) is now outdated (see Listing 34.15).

LISTING 34.15 Catching and Handling Exceptions

```
Server server = null;
try
{
     //Open a connection to the server.
     server = new Server();
     server.Connect("localhost");
     //...Do some AMO operations.
}
catch (ConnectionException conException)
{
     Console.WriteLine(conException.Message);
     //Show a dialog box requesting the server name from the user.
     //...
}
catch(OperationException operationException)
{
     foreach(XmlaResult result in operationException.Results)
     {
```

```
            foreach(XmlaMessage message in result.Messages)
            {
                 if(message is XmlaWarning)
                     Console.WriteLine(message.Description, "warning");
                 else
                     Console.WriteLine(message.Description, "error");
            }
      }
}
catch(ResponseFormatException ex)
{
     throw;
}
catch(OutOfSyncException outOfSyncException)
{
     throw;
}
finally
{
     if(server.Connected)
        server.Disconnect();
}
```

PART VIII

Security

IN THIS PART

CHAPTER 35

Security Model for Analysis Services

IN THIS CHAPTER

Business intelligence systems store information that is critical for making day-to-day decisions (and so, for making strategic decisions). This data usually contains information about customers, employees, or monetary transactions. Therefore, it's critically important to provide secure and reliable access to the data while still protecting the system from malicious access.

Analysis Services offers a state-of-the-art role-based security model based on Microsoft infrastructure. This model takes us into a discussion of the following areas: connection security, administrative security, data security, code access security, and external data access security:

- **Connection security** is a set of security settings and mechanisms that validates users who establish connections to the server that hosts Analysis Services. Connection security includes *authentication*, the mechanism that allows Analysis Server to recognize users that connect to it securely. Connection security also includes *authorization*, which is the process Analysis Services uses to associate a set of permissions with the user's identity.
- **Administrative security** defines permissions granted to an Analysis Services administrator and the process that the administrator uses to grant permissions to the users.
- **Data security** is a set of permissions that enables a user to access Analysis Services data. Analysis Services allows data access in different levels of granularity, it allows to manage access to cell data of the cube and to the dimension members.

- **External data access security** defines the permissions under which Analysis Services can access external data, such as relational databases. This type of security also defines the way Analysis Services accesses a file system to store and load its own data and back up files and to other instances of Analysis Services.
- **Code access security** enables an administrator to prevent external code from performing certain operations in your system. For example, Analysis Services applies code access security when it loads Common Language Runtime stored procedures. (For information about code access security, see Chapter 14, "Extending MDX with Stored Procedures.")

Figure 35.1 illustrates the Analysis Services security model with these five types of security.

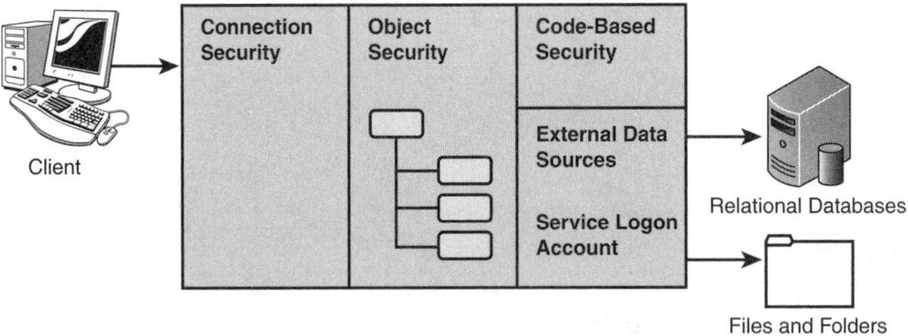

FIGURE 35.1 The Analysis Services security model.

Connection Security

When a user tries to connect to Analysis Services, Analysis Services first needs to verify the user's identity; that is, to authenticate the user. Analysis Services uses Microsoft Windows security mechanisms to authenticate users.

Analysis Services client applications can connect to Analysis Services using two protocols: TCP/IP and HTTP. (For information about TCP/IP and HTTP, see Chapter 31, "Client/Server Architecture and Data Access.") For a TCP/IP connection, Analysis Services supports only Windows authentication.

TCP/IP Connection Security

Analysis Services authenticates authorized users using Security Support Provider Interface (SSPI). SSPI serves as a bridge between Analysis Services and the operating system. It uses security packages that implement security interfaces. By default, Analysis Services uses the `Negotiate` protocol, which analyzes requests and chooses the most appropriate security protocol. You can configure Analysis Services to use a specific security protocol (for instance, `NTLM` or `Kerberos`). For that, you can use the Analysis Services `SecurityPackageList` server configuration property. On the client side, you can specify the desired protocol as part of the connection string. Currently, Analysis Services supports the following protocols: `Negotiate`, `NTLM`, `Kerberos`, and `Anonymous User`.

NOTE

To monitor the users logging in to your server, you can do a SQL Server Profiler trace to see the `AuditLogon` events generated by Analysis Services after it successfully authenticates each user. You can also use a `DISCOVER_CONNECTIONS` request to obtain a list of all the current connections.

You can enable anonymous access to your server by using `RequireClientAuthentication` server configuration property and `ImpersonationLevel` connection string property. By default, the `RequireClientAuthentication` property is set to `True`; set it to `False` to enable anonymous access. To grant anonymous users access to your server objects, add a built-in `ANONYMOUS LOGON` account to your database roles objects and configure data access security. (More information about object security is available later in this chapter.)

HTTP Security

After you set up HTTP access to Analysis Services, you can use authentication methods other than Windows authentication. (For information about setting up HTTP access, refer to http://www.microsoft.com/technet/prodtechnol/sql/2005/httpasws.mspx.)

Analysis Services uses a separate component—HTTP pump (`msmdmump.dll`)—to pass the data between client, IIS (Internet Information Server), and Analysis Services. Therefore, it supports all IIS authentication mechanisms:

- Integrated Windows authentication
- Anonymous access
- Basic authentication

NOTE

IIS determines the authentication mechanism for authenticating a user by reading the security settings on the virtual directory where the pump component is located.

Integrated Windows Authentication

When Integrated Windows authentication (formerly called *NTLM* or *Windows NT Challenge/Response authentication*) is set up for the pump. IIS authenticates the Windows user and impersonates the pump component with the user's credentials. The pump establishes a connection to the server hosting Analysis Services under the user's credentials to initiate an HTTP connection.

Constrained Delegation In certain scenarios, more than two computers are involved in executing a single request using integrated Windows authentication. These computers pass user credentials from one to another to keep executing the user request under the same credentials, delegating execution under the user's account.

Sometimes a corporate network is set up so that the user doesn't access Analysis Services through a single IIS server, but through two or more IIS servers that are chained. In the example illustrated in Figure 35.2, Computer1 runs IIS and connects to Computer2, which also runs IIS. Only then is the connection established to Analysis Services.

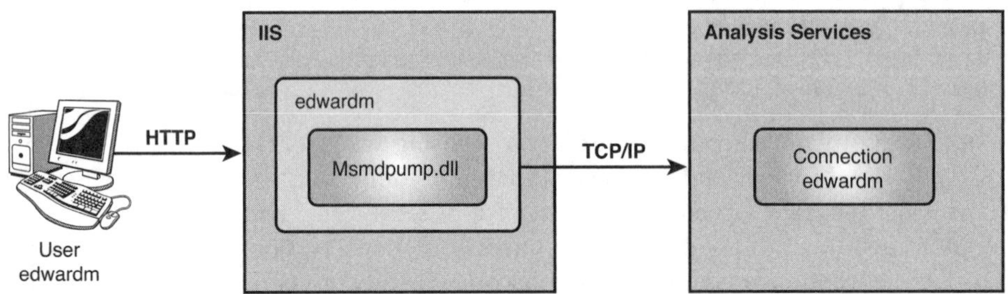

FIGURE 35.2 Setting up access to the corporate network can require a number of authentication hops.

IIS on Computer1 passes or delegates the impersonation of `edwardm` to Computer2 so that it can establish a connection to Analysis Services under `edwardm`'s credentials. This scenario is called *constrained delegation*.

By default, delegation is not enabled. You need the Kerberos authentication package to enable constrained delegation. You configure both computers to use the Kerberos authentication protocol to enable delegation. You can find step-by-step instructions for enabling constrained delegation using the Kerberos authentication package at http://www.mosha.com/msolap/articles/kerberos_delegation.htm.

Anonymous Access

By default, IIS uses the `IUSR_`*`ComputerName`* account to impersonate an anonymous user. However, you can provide your own account name and password for this account. In our example, `edwardm` tries to establish an HTTP connection to Analysis Services. IIS doesn't authenticate `edwardm`, but instead it impersonates the pump using `IUSR_ComputerName` account. Thus, the TCP/IP connection to Analysis Services is established under that account. If you're monitoring connections from SQL Server Profiler, you'll see the `IUSR_Machine` username in the `NTUserName` column for the `AuditLogin` event (see Figure 35.3).

Enabling anonymous access to Analysis Services through HTTP (as opposed to TCP/IP) does not require setting the `RequiredClientAuthentication` server configuration property to `TRUE`.

NOTE

If you enable anonymous authentication, IIS always attempts to authenticate the user with anonymous authentication first, even if you enable additional authentication methods.

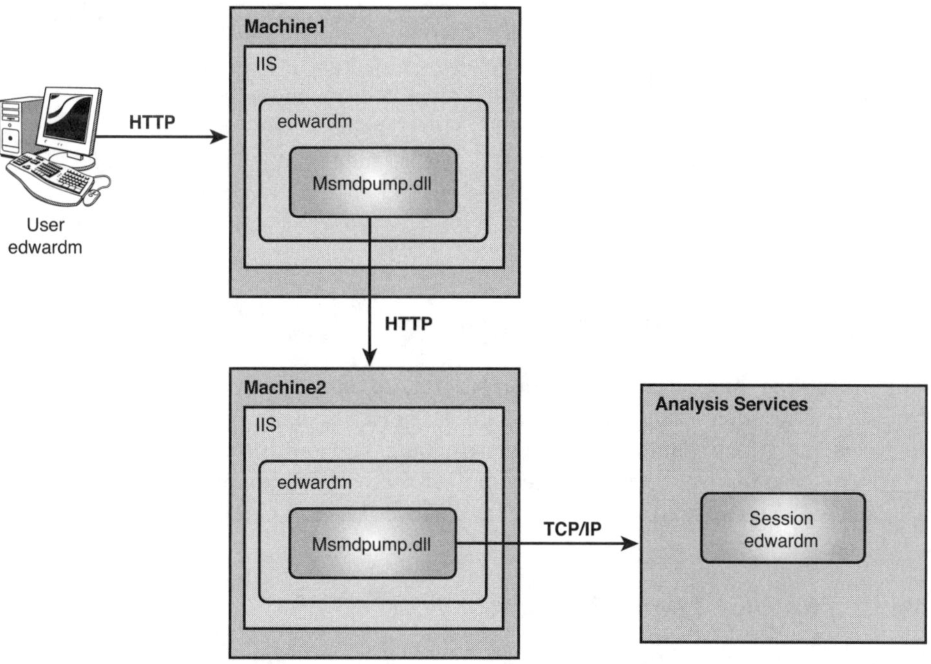

FIGURE 35.3 Anonymous authentication.

Basic Authentication

With basic authentication, the user can enter her username and password information as part of the connection string when she establishes a connection. `UserName` and `Password` passes from the client to IIS via HTTP headers in clear text; therefore, they can be easily intercepted. IIS uses the username and password to impersonate the user before the pump establishes the connection to Analysis Services.

In our example, illustrated in Figure 35.4, `edwardm` passes his credentials as part of the connection string. The pump establishes a connection to Analysis Services under `edwardm`'s credentials.

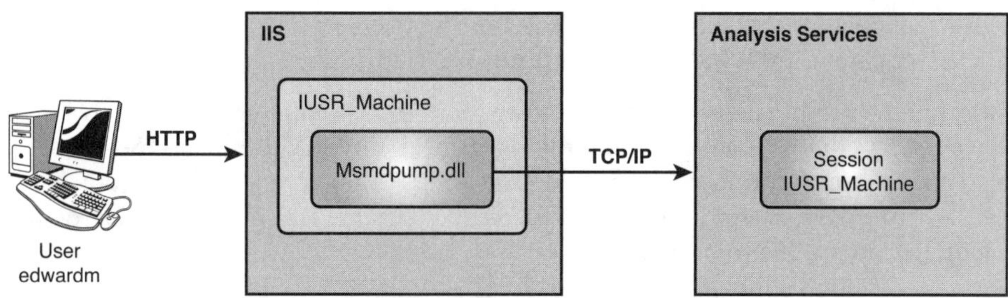

FIGURE 35.4 Basic authentication using HTTPS.

NOTE

HTTP is not secure and can be easily intercepted by a third party. Data transmitted over HTTP is not encrypted when basic authentication is used, so the username and password you include as part of the connection string can be easily seen. Basic authentication over HTTP is considered a highly volatile authentication mechanism. It's better to use the secure version of HTTP: *HTTPS*. HTTPS encrypts all data sent between a client application and IIS.

External Data Access Security

For many operations, Analysis Services requires access to various external sources and operating system resources. To load data in a cube, for example, Analysis Services might need to access a relational database and to store cube data it needs to access the file system. For Analysis Services to access external data successfully, you must set up the external data access security in such a way that Analysis Services can get access to all the resources it needs.

Choosing a Service Logon Account

Analysis Services runs as a Windows service. When you are running setup for SQL Server, you are asked to select the account your Analysis Services service will run under. You can choose one of the following three types of account: the built-in system account, a domain user account, or a local user account. For the built-in system account, you can use the `LocalSystem`, `LocalService`, or `NetworkService` account.

Each of these account types has benefits and drawbacks:

- A `LocalSystem` account is a high-privileged account that has access to all the resources of the computer. We do not recommend running Analysis Services under this type of account because in case of malicious attack compromised Analysis Services can grant complete control over your computer.
- A user domain account is the best choice. On one hand, it allows you to define access rights to system resources. On the other hand, it allows you to establish access to external data sources. For example, you can use this account to grant access to SQL Server data using Windows authentication.
- A local user account is an account you create on a local computer to run Analysis Services. You grant this account only the rights necessary to run Analysis Services. With a local user account, you can set up the access to operating system resources, but harder to grant access to external data sources because account local to particular machine is not visible to other machines.

Your choice of account type will be influenced by a number of considerations:

- If you provide a service logon account that allows too many privileges and a security attack compromises your service, an attacker could gain easy access to computer resources.

- A service account needs enough privileges for the Analysis Services service to function.
- A services account needs to have enough privileges to access external data sources (for instance, SQL Server).
- Integrated Windows authentication to gain access to SQL Server is considered a more secure method than SQL Server authentication.

NOTE

If you are using Analysis Services configuration properties to change data directories, make sure that the Analysis Services service account has read/write permissions to the folder. The same advice applies to the `LogDir`, `TempDir`, and `BackupDir` server properties. Take the same precaution when using the `StorageLocation` partition property to create partitions in custom folders.

Configuring Access to External Data Sources

Analysis Services allows administrator to configure access to external data sources. You can use the `ImpersonationInfo` property of a `DataSource` object to specify the security account under which Analysis Services establishes a connection to external data sources. Just before establishing the connection, Analysis Services impersonates the thread with the credentials of the account specified in the `ImpersonationInfo` property. Listing 35.1 shows the Data Definition Language (DDL) for an `ImpersonationInfo` property in a data source.

LISTING 35.1 DDL That Defines an **`ImpersonationInfo`** Object

```
<ImpersonationInfo>
     <ImpersonationMode>ImpersonateAccount</ImpersonationMode>
     <Account>MyUser</Account>
     <Password>AAAAAA</Password>
</ImpersonationInfo>
```

The following list describes the properties of the `ImpersonationInfo` object:

- `ImpersonationMode` defines the way the data source is impersonated. Values for the `ImpersonationMode` property include the following:
  - **`Default`**—The `ImpersonationMode` property inherits its value from the `DataSourceImpersonationInfo` object of the database parent object. If the `ImpersonationMode` property for the database is also set to `Default`, the established connection will be under the service account credentials.
  - **`ImpersonateAccount`**—Specifies that the connection will be established with the credentials specified in the `Account` and `Password` properties of the `ImpersonationInfo` object.

- **ImpersonateCurrentUser**—Specifies the use of the credentials of the current user; utilized only to run data mining queries.
- **ImpersonateServiceAccount**—Establishes the connection with the credentials of the account under which the Analysis Services server started.

- Account defines the name of the user account to use for impersonation.
- Password defines the password for the account specified in the Account property.

The DataSourceImpersonationInfo property of the Database object serves as a default for access to external sources if the ImpersonationInfo property is not specified for the DataSource object, or when the ImpersonationMode property is set to Default.DataSourceImpersonationInfo has exactly the same structure as the ImpersonationInfo object. Its only purpose is to serve as a default for data sources with ImpersonationMode set to Default.

Changing a Service Logon Account

Use the SQL Server Configuration Manager to change a service logon account. Although you can view and change a logon account for Analysis Services through the Windows Service Control Manager, we recommend that you *never* use it to change a service logon account.

NOTE

You can access the SQL Server Configuration Manager through the Start menu: Start, Microsoft SQL Server 2008, Configuration Tools, SQL Server Configuration Manager.

The main reason for using Configuration Manager is that, during installation, SQL Server setup grants Analysis Services access to all the file system folders and Registry entries necessary for it to be able to operate. If you change the service logon account using Windows Service Control Manager, the new service account might not have enough privileges to access the file system and system Registry, and that could lead to a situation in which you can't start Analysis Services.

SQL Server setup creates a local security group (SQLServer2005MSOLAPUser$MACHINE NAME$MSSQLSERVER in Analysis Services 2005 and SQLServerMSASUser$ MACHINENAME $MSSQLSERVER, in version 2008) and grants it all required file system and Registry permissions. The service logon account becomes a member of this group. When you change the service logon account using SQL Server Configuration Manager, it removes the old service account and inserts the new one into this group.

All file system folders are secured using that local security group. The alternative is to secure every folder using an Analysis Server logon account.

Security for Running Named Instances (SQL Server Browser)

To establish a connection to a named instance of Analysis Services, a client application first connects to Analysis Services Redirector, which runs inside the SQL Browser process. The SQL Browser service logon account is initially chosen during SQL Server installation. By default, SQL Server setup sets the SQL Browser account to `NetworkService`.

Security for Running on a Failover Cluster

SQL Server setup creates a local security group so that it can grant multiple permissions to multiple folders and Registry keys. However, if SQL Server is running on a failover cluster, you can't use a local security group to secure the folders that reside on a shared drive. After Analysis Services fails over to another node, Analysis Services won't be able to access folders on the shared drive. For that reason, during SQL Server setup on a failover cluster, setup prompts you for a name for the domain group. You also need to make sure that SQL Server setup can add the service logon account to this domain group.

Before installing Analysis Services on a failover cluster, you need a couple of things: Ask the domain administrator to create a new security group for you to use during cluster installation and to add your account as co-owner of the domain group. We recommend that you create a separate domain group to secure every installation on the failover cluster.

Object Security Model for Analysis Services

Analysis Services uses role-based security to grant multiple users the same level of access to different resources within a system. A role object contains a set of users who share the same security privileges. A user who belongs to a certain role can access the resources that role has permissions for.

Granting permissions to roles rather than to a certain user makes it easier to manage security. For example, suppose that you grant a set of permissions to all the managers in your organization. If a new manager is hired, you don't need to redefine her security settings. All you have to do is add her user account to the appropriate role.

The role-based security approach enables you to handle two tasks separately: define security permissions to different objects within Analysis Services, and add or delete users.

To define security permissions in Analysis Services, you use a `Role` object, which has a `Members` collection with user accounts of users having the same level of access.

Level of access to the different objects in Analysis Services is defined by the `Permission` object. You can specify the `Permission` object for the majority of the major objects in Analysis Services. The `Permission` object includes a reference to the `Role` object.

Server Administrator Security

After Analysis Server establishes a user's identity (authenticates the user), it determines the permissions to grant the user. All users of Analysis Services can be divided into three logical categories: server administrators, database administrators, and regular users.

Server administrators are responsible for managing the server; creating and deleting databases; and designing, developing, and maintaining security policies. Server administrators need access to all Analysis Services objects, and they can perform any operation in Analysis Services.

Only server administrators can do the following:

- Create databases
- Change server properties
- Query Dynamic Memory Views (DMVs)
- Cancel users' sessions and connections
- Register stored procedures

For granting a user administrative rights, Analysis Services architecture defines a single dedicated serverwide role: `Administrators`. Any user who is a member of the `Administrators` role is considered an Analysis Services administrator. Listing 35.2 contains the DDL to use to define membership in the `Administrators` role.

LISTING 35.2 DDL to Add Users to the **`Administrators`** Role

```
<Alter AllowCreate="true" ObjectExpansion="ObjectProperties"
➥xmlns="http://schemas.microsoft.com/analysisservices/2003/engine">
     <Object>
          <RoleID>Administrators</RoleID>
     </Object>
     <ObjectDefinition>
          <Role xmlns:xsd=http://www.w3.org/2001/XMLSchema
➥xmlns:xsi="http://www.w3.org/2001/XMLSchema-instance">
               <ID>Administrators</ID>
               <Name>Administrators</Name>
               <Members>
                    <Member>
                         <Name>MyAccount</Name>
                    </Member>
               </Members>
          </Role>
     </ObjectDefinition>
</Alter>
```

There can be only one Administrators role. If you try to create a new Administrators role, you get this error message: Server and server role objects cannot be created, deleted, or fully expanded.

When you add accounts to a role, you can add only valid Windows accounts. You can add domain accounts or groups. For example, you can add the domain user we've already established, REDMOND\edwardm. Analysis Services also allows you to add local computer user or group accounts, such as LocalMachine\Administrators, to the server Administrators role.

You can also add built-in accounts, such as Everyone (which grants access to any user—not a good idea from a security perspective) and NT AUTHORITY\SYSTEM, a local computer's service account.

During setup, you can add members to the server Administrators role (Provisioning page in setup). However, if you are an administrator for the local computer, you can still connect to Analysis Services because all members of the Windows LocalMachine\Administrators group are granted administrative rights to Analysis Services. (This is the equivalent of adding the LocalMachine\Administrators group to the Administrators role.) On Windows Vista and Windows Server 2008, even though you are a local machine administrator, you will have to run an administrative application connecting to Analysis Services under elevated Windows Administrative privileges ("Run as administrator"). We recommend you provision your server administrative role to avoid that.

In many organizations, the server computer administrator is not the same person who manages Analysis Services. If this is the case, you should add the Analysis Services administrator to the Administrators role, and then use the BuiltinAdminsAreServerAdmins configuration property to revoke the administrator rights of the LocalMachine\Administrators group.

NOTE

Revoking the rights of the LocalMachine\Administrators group by turning off the BuiltinAdminsAreServerAdmins server configuration doesn't provide full security protection. The operating system provides members of the LocalMachine\Administrators group with privileges that allow them access to the configuration file. Any computer administrator could potentially turn on the BuiltinAdminsAreServerAdmins property.

SQL Server Management Studio (SSMS) provides you with a user interface to manage the Administrators role through the Server Properties dialog box.

Database Roles and Permission Objects

All nonadministrative security within Analysis Services is managed through the Database role and Permission objects. Similar to the server Administrators role, you can add only valid Windows accounts to the Database role. Unlike the Administrators role, however, you can use the Database role to define a granular set of permissions to different objects in the database.

NOTE

The number of combinations of security permissions for a `Database` role can be very large. Therefore, we strongly recommend giving your `Role` objects meaningful names.

Most of the major objects and some of the minor objects enable you to define security rules using `Permission` objects. Each permission object has a set of distinct properties that regulate various types of access to the parent object (for example, read permissions, write permissions, read definition permissions).

Let's take a look at an example of setting permissions for users of the `Budget` cube. For all the users who need a read access to the cube, create a `BudgetCubeUsers` database role. Then, you create a `CubePermission` child object of the `Budget` cube, referencing the `BudgetCubeUsers` role object. Set the `Read` property of the `CubePermission` to `Allowed`.

Therefore, to grant access to an object, you need to do the following

1. Create the database `Role` object and specify its members.
2. Create the `Permission` object as a child of the object you want to secure.
3. Set the required type of access using the `Permission` object's properties.
4. Set a reference from the `Permission` object to the `Role` object.

Figure 35.5 shows a diagram of all the security permission objects in the Analysis Services object hierarchy.

We're going to show you the process you follow to create a `BudgetCubeUsers Database` role and grant it read access to the `Budget` cube. First, you create a `Database` role using the DDL statement shown in Listing 35.3.

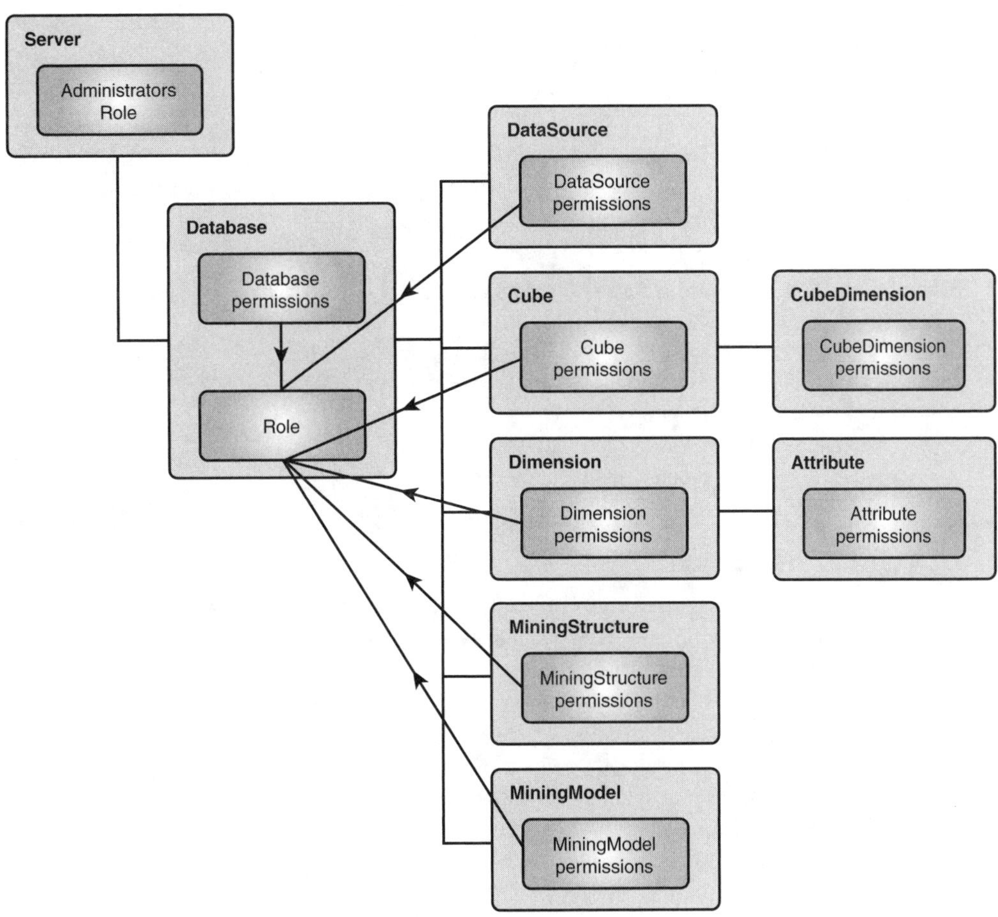

FIGURE 35.5 Hierarchy of permission objects.

LISTING 35.3 DDL to Create a **BudgetCubeUsers** Role

```
<Alter AllowCreate="true" ObjectExpansion="ObjectProperties"
➥xmlns="http://schemas.microsoft.com/analysisservices/2003/engine">
     <Object>
          <DatabaseID>FoodMart 2008</DatabaseID>
          <RoleID>Role</RoleID>
     </Object>
     <ObjectDefinition>
          <Role xmlns:xsd="http://www.w3.org/2001/XMLSchema"
➥xmlns:xsi="http://www.w3.org/2001/XMLSchema-instance">
               <ID>Role</ID>
               <Name>BudgetCubeUsers</Name>
               <Members>
               <Member>
                    <Name>MyUser</Name>
               </Member>
```

```
            </Members>
        </Role>
    </ObjectDefinition>
</Alter>
```

Then, you send the DDL statement in Listing 35.4 to create a CubePermission object and to grant Read access to the BudgetCubeUsers Database role.

LISTING 35.4 DDL to Create a **CubePermission** Object

```
<Alter AllowCreate="true" ObjectExpansion="ObjectProperties"
➥xmlns="http://schemas.microsoft.com/analysisservices/2003/engine">
    <Object>
        <DatabaseID>FoodMart 2008</DatabaseID>
        <CubeID>Budget</CubeID>
       <CubePermissionID>CubePermission</CubePermissionID>
    </Object>
    <ObjectDefinition>
        <CubePermission xmlns:xsd="http://www.w3.org/2001/XMLSchema"
➥xmlns:xsi="http://www.w3.org/2001/XMLSchema-instance">
            <ID>CubePermission</ID>
            <Name>CubePermission</Name>
            <RoleID>Role</RoleID>
            <Read>Allowed</Read>
            <ReadSourceData>None</ReadSourceData>
        </CubePermission>
    </ObjectDefinition>
</Alter>
```

Defining Object Permissions

The Permission object has a set of properties that allow for defining the type of access to various objects in the system. Like many other Analysis Server metadata objects, the Permission object has Name, ID, Description, and Annotations properties. The Permission object properties depend on the type of the parent object, but some of its properties are common for all Permission objects, as listed in Table 35.1.

TABLE 35.1 **Permission** Object Properties

Name	Description
ID	The ID of the permission object.
RoleID	Points to a database role object.
Read	Usually means that the user can browse the object from a client application. This property can take two values: None and Allowed.
Process	If set to True, members of the Database role can process the object and its child objects. This property can take two values: True and False.
ReadDefinition	Defines whether users can see the DDL definition of the object. The idea is that the DDL definition of the object might be the intellectual property of the object designer. (For example, a cube designer might not be willing to share his cube's calculation script.) In addition, the way a cube maps to the relational database might represent a security risk. (A cube designer might not be willing to allow users to see the names of the relational tables and columns.) This property can be set to None, Basic, or Allowed. If this property is set to Allowed, role members can retrieve the object's entire DDL definition using a DISCOVER_XML_METADATA call. When you create linked objects or local cubes, you might need just a portion of the object's DDL definition. In that case, you can specify the Basic value for the ReadDefinition property to allow partial discovery of the object's DDL. If ReadDefinition is set to Basic, Analysis Services does not reveal mappings to the relational database. If this property is set to None, the client cannot retrieve the object's DDL.
Write	When this property is set to Allowed, it grants permission to modify the content of the object. This property applies only to Dimension, Cube, and Mining Model objects. The possible values are None and Allowed.

35

A few rules define the way security applies to permission objects:

- **Inheritance**—If one of the permission properties is set on an object at a higher level, the properties also apply to the lower-level objects. For example, if you have allowed a Process permission on your database, you can also process all the cubes and dimensions in your database. An exception applies to this rule: A Read permission on the database means that users can see the database name, but don't have Read access to all the database cubes. To grant Read access to all the cubes in your database, you need to go through every cube and create a CubePermission object to explicitly grant access to each cube.

- **Union**—If a user belongs to multiple groups, the set of permissions for that user is the union of all the permissions for all the groups. For example, if a user belongs to RoleA, which has Read access to CubeA, and to RoleB, which has Read access to CubeB, the user can see both CubeA and CubeB.

DatabasePermission Object

The DatabasePermission object specifies access permissions to the entire database. If the Read property is set to Allowed, the user can see only the name of the database, not the names of the objects within the database. If you set the Process property to True, members of the Database role can process any object within the database.

You can also specify an Administer property for a DatabasePermission object. If you set this property to True, members of the role are considered database administrators. Database role members can perform any operation in the database. For example, the command shown in Listing 35.5 makes BudgetCubeUsers role members database administrators of the FoodMart 2008 database.

LISTING 35.5 DDL to Grant the **BudgetCubeUsers** Role Administrative Permissions to the FoodMart 2008 Database

```
<Alter AllowCreate="true" ObjectExpansion="ObjectProperties"
➥xmlns="http://schemas.microsoft.com/analysisservices/2003/engine">
    <Object>
        <DatabaseID>FoodMart 2008</DatabaseID>
        <DatabasePermissionID>DatabasePermission</DatabasePermissionID>
    </Object>
    <ObjectDefinition>
        <DatabasePermission xmlns:xsd="http://www.w3.org/2001/XMLSchema"
➥xmlns:xsi="http://www.w3.org/2001/XMLSchema-instance">
            <ID>DatabasePermission</ID>
            <Name>DatabasePermission</Name>
            <RoleID>Role</RoleID>
            <Administer>true</Administer>
        </DatabasePermission>
    </ObjectDefinition>
</Alter>
```

Database administrators can perform a variety of tasks with the database:

- Back up the database, and restore the database by overwriting the existing one with an earlier one. (To restore a new database, you must be a server administrator.)
- Query some of the DMVs. For example, send select * from $system.DISCOVER_SESSIONS to find all the existing sessions that are open against the current database.
- Cancel user sessions. After viewing the database sessions, a database administrator can send a Cancel command that ends a given session.

- Use the SQL Server Profiler application to monitor activities within your database. To see all the activities on the server, you must be a server administrator. You won't see `Discover` requests because they are performed as lightweight operations. Evaluating the permissions involved in every `Discover` request can slow down server operations. The Analysis Services designers opted in favor of performance in this case, sacrificing the database administrator's ability to see `Discover` requests.

DataSourcePermission Object

This object is used to set permissions for data source objects. Set the `ReadDefinition` property of the `DataSourcePermission` object to enable users to see the connection string used in the data source object and get information about the relational database to which this data source points.

A data source object enables you to connect to the relational database. If you specify the `ImpersonationMode` property of the data source object as the `ImpersonateService` account, Analysis Services establishes the connection under the Analysis Services service account. To allow any data source to be impersonated with the service account, you must have server administrator privileges.

DimensionPermission Object

The `DimensionPermission` object defines access to a dimension object. The `ReadDefinition` property controls access to the DDL of the dimension. The `Process` property controls whether members of the role can process the dimension.

Browsing the dimension object is not controlled by the `Read` property. Only database administrators can browse database dimensions separately from the cube.

Dimension members are typically browsed by accessing a cube from a client application. The `DimensionPermission` object provides default security settings for cube dimensions. If a `CubeDimensionPermission` object is not specified, Analysis Services uses the `DimensionPermissions` object to display cube dimensions.

The `AttributePermissions` collection enables you to define security for dimension attributes. (For information about the `AttributePermission` object, see Chapter 36, "Securing Dimension Data.")

CubePermission Object

The `CubePermission` object defines a set of access permissions for a cube object. To allow the members of a `Database` role access to a cube, all you need to do is create a `CubePermission` object and set the `Read` property to `Allowed`.

The `CubePermission` object has one property in addition to the set of properties common to `Permission` objects. The `ReadSourceData` property defines whether a user has access to raw data (not including cube or dimension calculations). This property is intended to solve the following problem.

The DrillThrough statement enables a user to drill down to the lowest level of detail. It ignores any cube or dimension calculations that might exist in a cube. You might or might not want to allow users to see data before those calculations are applied. The Read property controls access to the cube data that is a result of cube calculations. To enable users to see raw data, it's not enough to grant Read permissions. Therefore, the Analysis Services designers introduced a new type of permission: ReadSourceData. Turn on the ReadSourceData property to enable users to perform DrillThrough operations, create local cubes, and create linked objects.

The CubePermission object contains a CellPermission object that defines permission to view cell values. (For information about the CellPermission object, see Chapter 37, "Securing Cell Values.") It also contains a collection of CubeDimensionPermission objects that you can use to override the default settings of the DimensionPermission objects.

Managing Database Roles

Your primary tool for managing roles is the Edit Role dialog box in SQL Server Management Studio. Use it to define role membership and permissions for roles. To access the Edit Role dialog box, open SQL Management Studio and right-click the Role object you want to manage, and then select Properties from the resulting menu. Your screen should look like that shown in Figure 35.6.

Navigate through the navigation pane of the dialog box and click the different nodes to perform all the major management tasks associated with security. The Script button enables you to script the changes you've made to the role properties and to the permission objects. After you've scripted the actions in the dialog box, you will see the multiple commands in the script wrapped into a single batch.

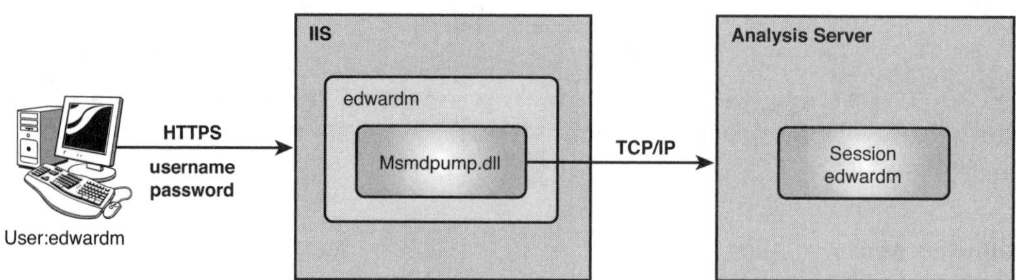

FIGURE 35.6 Use the Edit Role dialog box to manage membership and security permissions for Database roles.

CHAPTER 36

Securing Dimension Data

IN THIS CHAPTER

You can grant and deny access to data stored in Analysis Services using different levels of granularity. In previous chapters, we discussed how the administrator could grant or deny access to databases, cubes, and dimensions. In this chapter, we discuss how you can provide more granular levels of security that protect portions of the data stored in Analysis Services from some users while still making that data available to others. Analysis Services supports two models of security that enable you to restrict access to the data: dimension security and cell security.

- **Dimension security** enables the administrator to restrict access to the multidimensional space by preventing a user from accessing certain members of a dimension and the cell values associated with those members. For example, company policy might allow sales representatives to see the names and addresses of their customers, but not customers with whom other sales representatives work. In addition, dimension security enables the administrator to configure the system so that it aggregates total values from all the children of the current member or only from those children to which dimension security grants the user access.
- **Cell security** enables the administrator to hide values of certain cells in a cube from the user without actually restricting the multidimensional space. For example, a division manager should be able to see all employees of a company, but see salaries only for employees in his organization. The main difference between cell security and dimension security is that with cell security, the user can see the dimension

members associated with employees in a company and perhaps see sales figures for all employees but not salaries of all employees in the company.

Figure 36.1 shows the difference between dimension security and cell security. Dimension security removes coordinates from multidimensional space, whereas cell security hides values of cells.

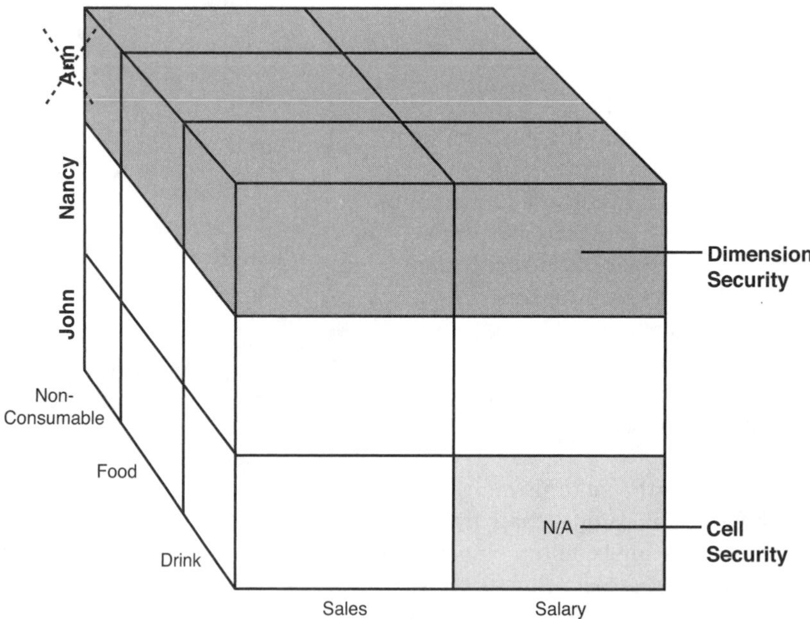

FIGURE 36.1 Dimension security removes coordinates from multidimensional space, whereas cell security hides values of cells.

For example, assume that you have a cube that has two measures, `Sales` and `Salary`, and a single dimension, `Employees`, which contains two managers:

- Ann (with two direct reports: Nancy and Tom)
- John (with two direct reports: Bob and Susann)

If you do not define dimension security or cell security settings on the cube, Ann would see the report shown in Figure 36.2.

With dimension security, you can allow managers to see information (including information about salaries) for their direct reports, but not information about other employees.

	Salary	Sales
ALL	13,500	1,250
Ann	4,000	400
Nancy	1,000	100
Tom	2,000	200
John	3,000	200
Bob	1,500	150
Susann	2,000	200

FIGURE 36.2 When there is no security defined, Ann can see all the employees in the organization and everybody's sales and salaries. The value of the ALL member is the sum of the `Sales` and `Salary` measures for all employees.

Dimension security can also allow managers to see total values as a value aggregated only from unrestricted children. With dimension security defined to support such a model, Ann would see the report shown in Figure 36.3.

	Salary	Sales
ALL	7,000	700
Ann	4,000	400
Nancy	1,000	100
Tom	2,000	200

FIGURE 36.3 Dimension security doesn't allow Ann to see employees reporting to John, and values for the member ALL don't take into account the `Sales` and `Salary` values for John and his team.

With cell security, however, you can allow all users to have access to all the names of employees in the organization, but allow managers to see only the values of sales for their direct reports. With cell security defined to support such a model, Ann would see the report shown in Figure 36.4.

	Salary	Sales
ALL	13,500	1,250
Ann	4,000	400
Nancy	1,000	100
Tom	2,000	200
John	N/A	200
Bob	N/A	150
Susann	N/A	200

FIGURE 36.4 Cell security allows Ann to see employees reporting to John, but not the values of their salaries. However, the `Salary` value for the member ALL contains the total for all employees and doesn't reflect cell security.

Defining Dimension Security

Dimension security fits in the role-based security model that we discussed in Chapter 35, "Security Model for Analysis Services." For each role, you define the dimension members that you either allow or deny access to. You can also specify whether you want the total values to include values corresponding to members denied by dimension security.

You can define dimension security for a database dimension or for a cube dimension (if you want dimensions of different cubes to have different security settings). On the server, you define dimension security by a collection of `AttributePermission` objects associated with either a `DimensionPermission` object or `CubeDimensionPermission` object, as shown in Figure 36.5.

`AttributePermission` is a minor object. In addition to the standard properties of most Analysis Services objects, such as `Name`, `ID`, `Description`, and `Annotation`, the `AttributePermission` object has the properties shown in Table 36.1.

TABLE 36.1 Properties of the **AttributePermission** Object

Property	Description
AllowedSet	Contains the Multidimensional Expressions (MDX) set expression that defines the members of an attribute allowed by dimension security.
AttributeID	Represents the unique identifier of the dimension attribute to which the AttributePermission object applies.
DefaultMember	Contains an MDX expression that defines a default member of an attribute. You should use this property if dimension security restricts the default member for a dimension attribute.
DeniedSet	Contains the MDX set expression that defines the members of an attribute restricted by dimension security.
VisualTotals	Indicates whether to consider dimension security when calculating aggregated values.

The AllowedSet and DeniedSet Properties

You define the members that you want to enable or restrict by specifying an MDX set expression in the AllowedSet and DeniedSet properties of an AttributePermission object. If you have not explicitly specified a set expression for the AllowedSet property, Analysis Services uses the <attribute hierarchy>.AllMembers set. If you have not explicitly specified a set expression for the DeniedSet property, Analysis Services uses the empty set ({}).

When you define AllowedSet or DeniedSet properties on an attribute, they affect not only members of the attribute on which you define them, but also members of other attributes in a dimension. Analysis Services performs auto-exist between the allowed/denied set of properties of the attribute on which you defined dimension security with other attributes of the dimension. For more information about auto-exist, see Chapter 11, "Advanced MDX."

However, rules for applying auto-exist differ slightly between the AllowedSet and DeniedSet properties. Dimension security allows members of the set included in the AllowedSet property if they are not explicitly denied and if they exist with members of

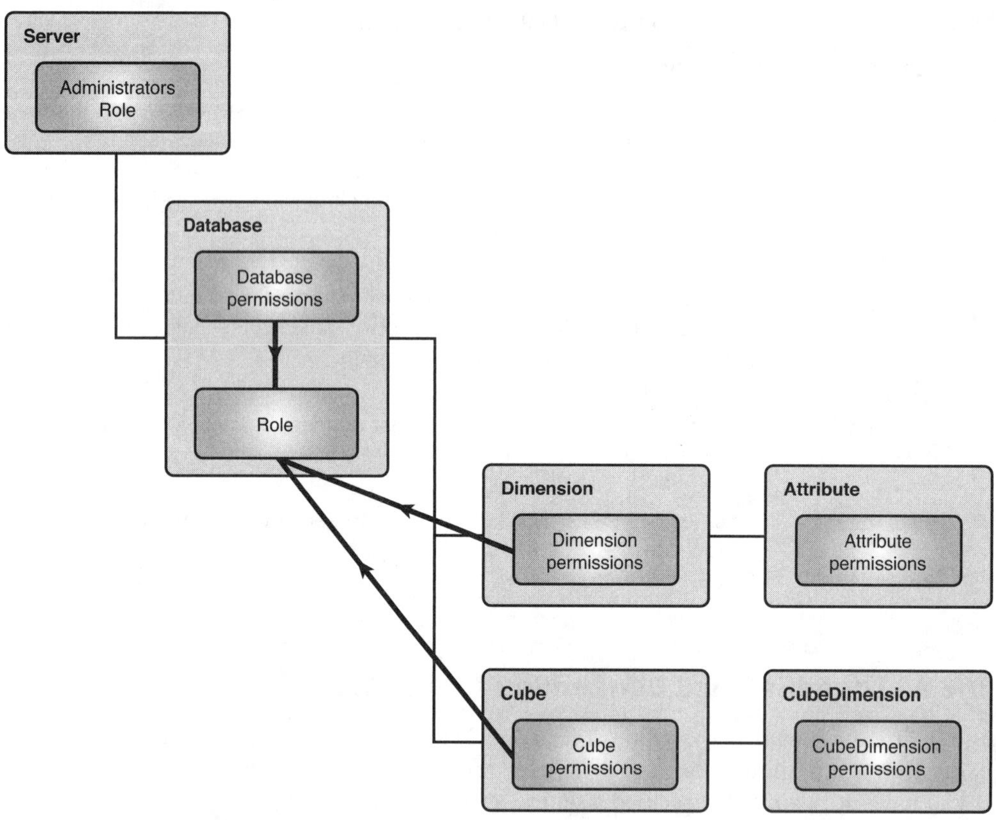

FIGURE 36.5 This hierarchy of objects used to define dimension security.

the set included in the `AllowedSet` properties of other attributes. For example, if you define dimension security on the `State` attribute of the `Customer` dimension of the FoodMart 2008 database by setting an `AllowedSet` property to `{[WA]}`, members of the `Country` attribute that exist with member `WA`—`[USA]`—is allowed, and other members are denied. For the `City` attribute, members that exist with member `WA`—cities in Washington state—are allowed, and cities in other states are denied. This rule enables you to allow a member, its descendants, and its ancestors. Figure 36.6 shows members of the `Customer` dimension and attributes to which they belong. Members allowed by dimension security are shaded.

When you define a `DeniedSet` property on an `AttributePermission` object, it affects members of other attributes in a slightly different way from that of the `AllowedSet` property. Members of the attributes to which the current attribute is not directly or indirectly related are not affected by the `DeniedSet` property. (Related attributes are those on top of the current attribute; for example, `Country` is related to `State`, but `State` is not related to `Country`.) However, members of the attributes to which the current attribute is related are restricted if they exist with members of the set defined by the `DeniedSet` property. This rule enables you to deny the member and its descendants but still allow its ancestors.

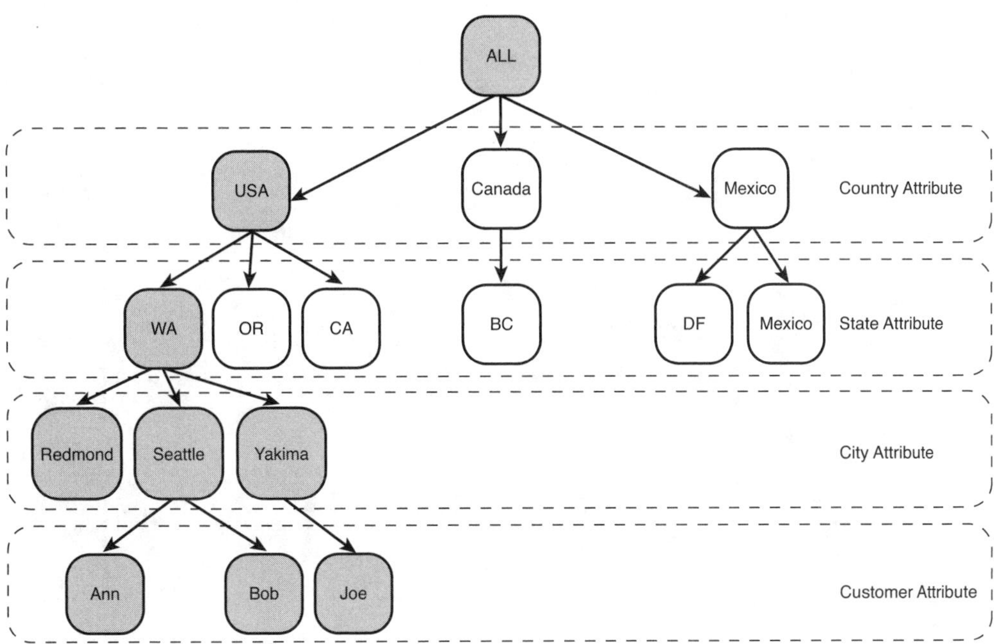

FIGURE 36.6 By allowing member WA on the `State` attribute, you allow all members on other attributes that exist with it.

If you define the `DeniedSet` property on the `State` attribute as `{[WA]}`, none of the members of the `Country` attribute are restricted, because `State` is not related to `Country`. (`Country` is instead related to `State`.) However, because `State` is related to `City`, members of the `City` attribute are restricted. Members that exist with member `[WA]`—cities in Washington state—are therefore restricted. The same rule applies to the members of the `Customer` attribute in that customers living in Washington state—associated with members that exist with member `[WA]`—are also restricted. Figure 36.7 shows members of the `Customer` dimension and attributes to which they belong; shaded members are those restricted by dimension security.

When the dimension is a parent-child dimension, you allow or deny not only the members of the sets defined in the `AllowedSet` and `DeniedSet` properties, respectively but also the descendants of each member, and allow ancestors of each member of the `AllowedSet`. For example, if you specify the set expression `{[Total Expenses]}` in the `DeniedSet` property of the `Accounts` attribute (a parent attribute of the dimension), you deny not only the `Total Expenses` member but also its descendants, as shown in Figure 36.8.

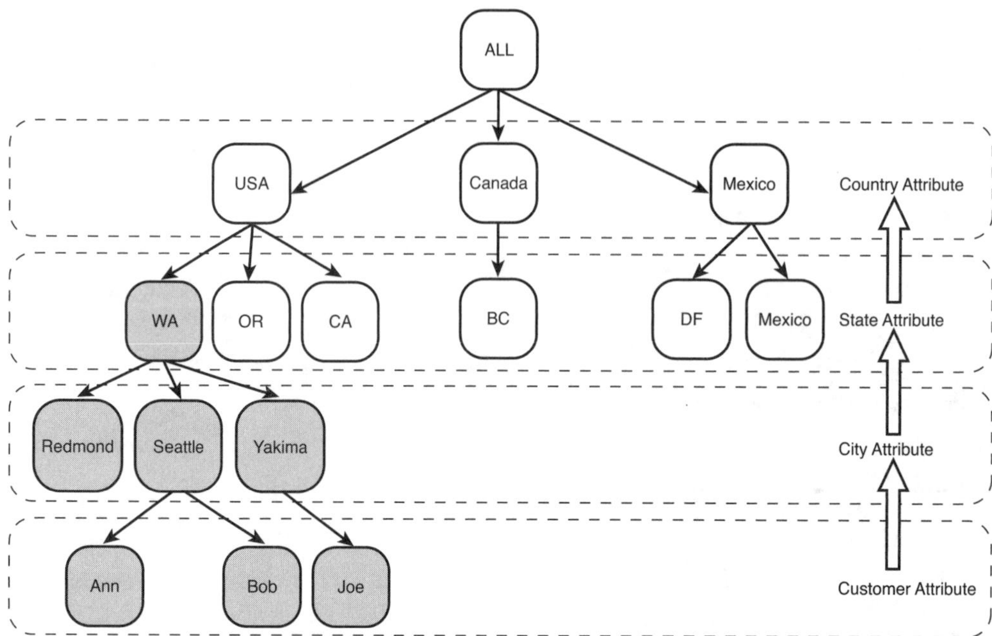

FIGURE 36.7 By denying member WA on the `State` attribute, you deny members of the attributes to which `State` is a related attribute and members that exist with WA.

When you apply dimension security on multiple attributes, sometimes it might be easier to think about the rules that we just discussed (how setting the dimension security on one attribute affects other attributes) in terms that are more mathematical. You can calculate the permitted set (the set of members permitted on an attribute) by the following formula:

```
PermittedSet(i) =
    Ancestors(
        Exists(
            Descendants(Allowed(i))-Descendants(Denied(i)),
            CrossJoin(
                Allowed(r¹)-Denied(r¹) - All(r¹),
                ...,
                Allowed(rⁿ)-Denied(rⁿ) - All(rⁿ),
                Allowed(u¹),
                ...,
                Allowed(uⁿ),
                Ascendants(
                Descendants(Allowed(pᵏ))-Descendants(Denied(pᵏ))
                                ) - ALL(pᵏ)
            )
        )
    )
```

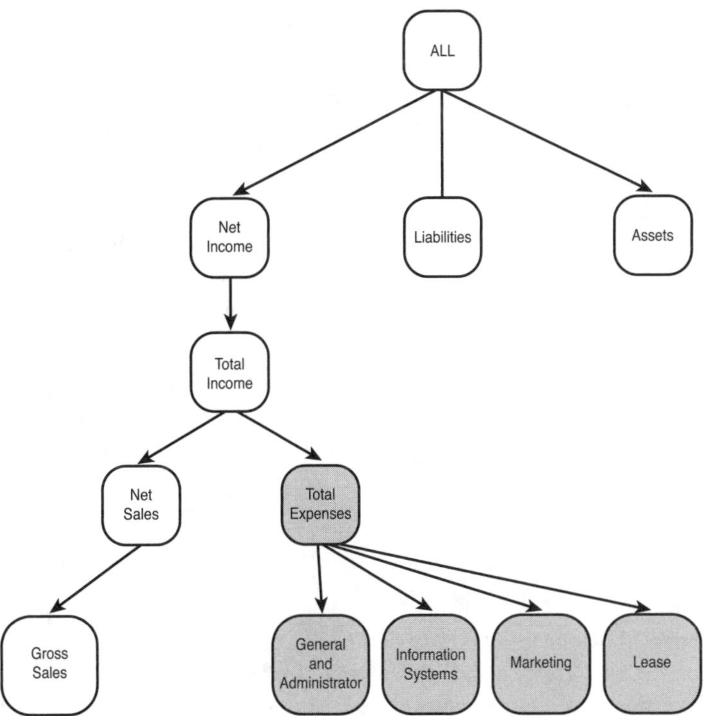

FIGURE 36.8 By denying the member `Total Expenses` on the `Accounts` attribute, you deny its descendants, too.

The preceding formula uses the following elements:

- `Allowed(i)` represents the allowed set; that is, the set for the `AllowedSet` property defined on the current attribute.
- `Denied(i)` represents the denied set; that is, the set for the `DeniedSet` property defined on the current attribute.
- `Allowed(r¹)-Denied(r¹),...,Allowed(rⁿ)-Denied(rⁿ)` represent the result of excepting the denied set from the allowed set for each attribute directly or indirectly related to the current attribute.
- `Allowed(u¹),...,Allowed(uⁿ)` represent the allowed sets on all other attributes—attributes not related to the current attribute.
- `Allowed(pᵏ)` represents the allowed set on the parent attribute, if the dimension is a parent-child dimension.

- `Denied(p^k)` represents the denied set on the parent attribute, if the dimension is a parent-child dimension.
- `Ancestors` represents the members of the given set and all the ancestors of each member of the given set. In case of attribute hierarchy, this function returns members of a given set and the `ALL` member.
- `Descendants` represents all the members of a given set and all their descendants. Because the attribute hierarchy has just two levels, the `Descendants` function for the attribute hierarchy retrieves only members of a given set. It is used in the formula when you are calculating dimension security on the parent attribute of the parent-child dimension.

You can use the formula to test the result you want to get from applying dimension security. For example, if you need to see which members of the `City` attribute are permitted after you restrict access to Washington state (shown in Figure 36.7), you can apply the formula as shown here:

```
PermittedSet(City) =
    Ancestors(
        Exists(
            //all descendants of members in attribute hierarchy City
            //is equivalent to the all the members of the level City
            Descendants(City.members)-Descendants({}),
            CrossJoin(
                //all the members of the related attribute Country
                //because there is no dimension security
                //defined on this attribute
                Country.members - {} - Country.All,
                //all the members of the related attribute State,
                // except members from the DeniedSet {WA}
                State.members - State.WA - State.All,
                //all the members of the not related attribute
                //Customer
                Customer.members
            )
        )
    )
```

The formula returns all the cities that "exist" with all the countries, all the customers, and all the states except the state of Washington.

The `VisualTotals` Property

When dimension security is not defined, the values for the lower granularities (or higher levels of the cube) are calculated by aggregating the values of the higher granularities (or lower levels of the cube). However, when you define dimension security, you have a choice of which value you want users to see as the total value. You can choose whether to aggregate the total value from all members of the cube or only from those not restricted by dimension security.

In an earlier example, when you defined the `DeniedSet` property on the `State` attribute as `{[WA]}`, as shown in Figure 36.9, should the value of the member `USA` be calculated as a sum of values from `WA`, `OR`, and `CA`, or should only the values from `OR` and `CA` be added together? Analysis Services enables you to specify the desired behavior by setting the `VisualTotals` property of the `AttributePermission` object. You set `VisualTotals` property to `TRUE` when you want only allowed members to participate in aggregation; otherwise, you set it to `FALSE`. For example, if you specify the set expression `{[WA]}` for the `DeniedSet` property on the `State` attribute, and set the `VisualTotals` property for that attribute to `TRUE`, the sales value for `USA` is equal to the sum of the sales in `CA` and `OR`. However, if you set the `VisualTotals` property of the `State` attribute to `FALSE`, the value for `USA` is the sum of sales in `WA`, `CA`, and `OR`. Figure 36.9 shows how the values are aggregated when the member `WA` is secured and the `VisualTotals` property is enabled.

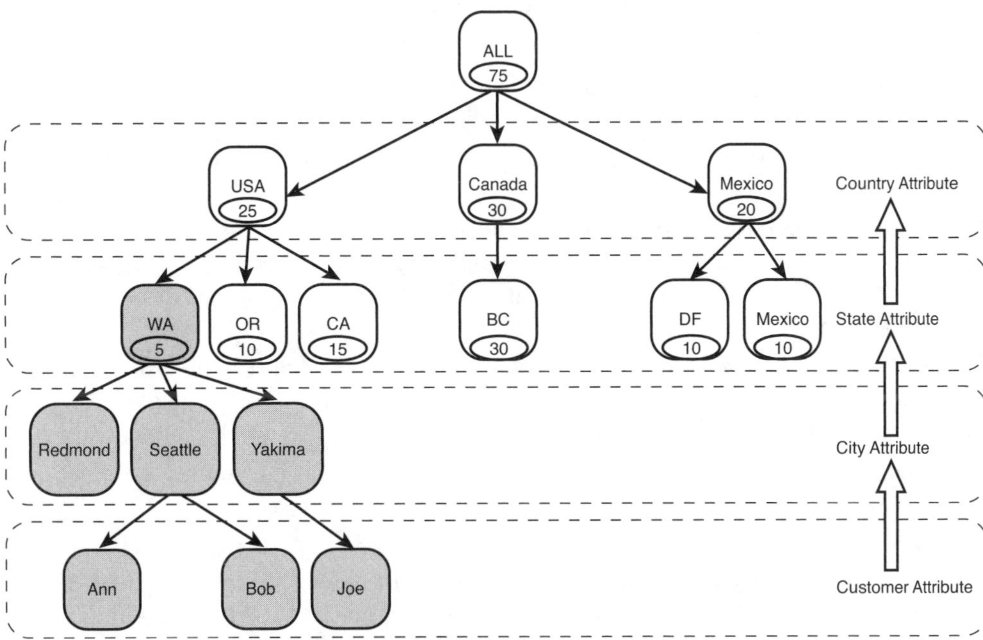

FIGURE 36.9 The **`VisualTotals`** property is enabled, so the sales value for USA is the sum of sales in CA and OR.

NOTE

You can set `VisualTotals` to `TRUE` or `FALSE` for different attributes of the dimension. Therefore, one attribute can have `VisualTotals` enabled while another attribute has it disabled.

Defining Dimension Security Using the User Interface

Now that you know what properties the `AttributePermission` object has, you can define a sample permission that doesn't allow a user to see customers located in the state of Washington. To do this, specify the following set expression in the `DeniedSet` property:

```
{[Customer].[State Province].&[WA]}
```

Each of the following methods enables you to define dimension security:

- Manually constructing and sending Data Definition Language (DDL) by using an `ALTER` command within an `Execute` request
- Using Analysis Management Objects (AMO) in a custom application to define attribute permissions
- Using the Role Designer user interface, provided by SQL Server Management Studio or BI Dev Studio, to define attribute permissions

The following are the steps that you need to perform in BI Dev Studio to set dimension security on the `Customer` dimension:

1. In BI Dev Studio, open the `FoodMart 2008` project.
2. In the Solution Explorer, double-click the `TestRole.role` role to open the Role Designer, or right-click the `Roles` node and select Create a New Role from the contextual menu.
3. Select the Dimension Data page in the Role Designer, and ensure that the Basic tab displays. You can use the Basic tab to either deselect members that you want to hide from the users of the role or to select members that you want to allow the users of your role to see.
4. In the Dimension drop-down list, choose the `Customer` database dimension. (If you want to define dimension security differently for dimensions of different cubes, you can select a cube dimension.)
5. In the Attribute Hierarchy drop-down list, choose the `State Province` attribute hierarchy.
6. In the Basic tab, deselect the `WA` member.
7. You can use the Advanced tab to specify the sets of members allowed or denied to users of that role. When you check or uncheck members in the Basic tab, the Advanced tab automatically updates. Figure 36.10 shows the Advanced tab of the Role Designer.

When you save your work and deploy the project, BI Dev Studio sends the DDL to the server, which then alters the cube and saves the `DimensionPermission` object. Listing 36.1 shows the portion of DDL related to the defining the dimension security.

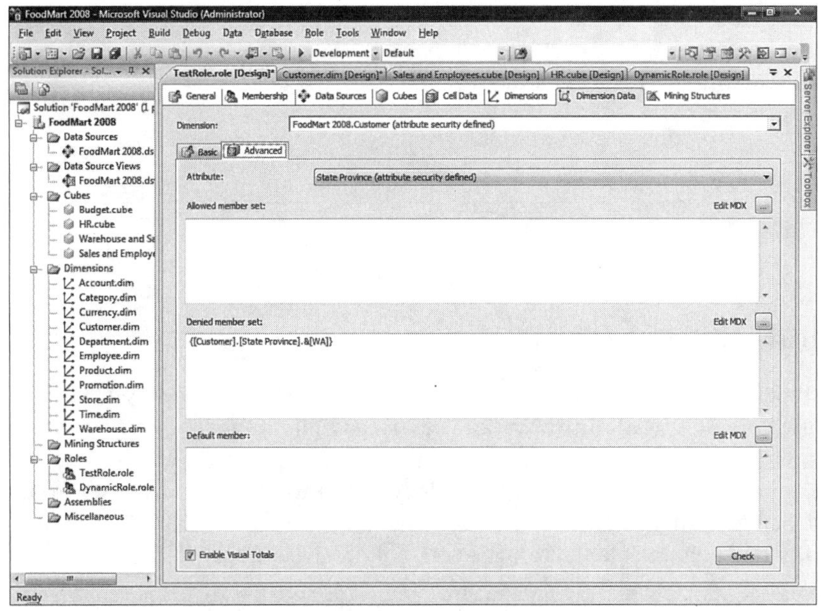

FIGURE 36.10 When you unchecked the WA member in the Basic tab, Analysis Services updated the Advanced tab of the role editor.

LISTING 36.1 DDL Request for Defining the **DimensionPermission** Object

```
<DimensionPermission>
     <Name>DimensionPermission</Name>
     <ID>DimensionPermission</ID>
     <CreatedTimestamp>2006-04-27T05:38:09</CreatedTimestamp>
     <LastSchemaUpdate>2006-05-08T21:45:36</LastSchemaUpdate>
     <ObjectVersion>14</ObjectVersion>
     <ObjectID>71D34D80-6C06-4B33-B606-29BC12CCD720</ObjectID>
     <Ordinal>14</Ordinal>
     <PersistLocation>0</PersistLocation>
     <System>false</System>
     <DataFileList/>
     <Description/>
     <RoleID>Role</RoleID>
     <ReadDefinition>None</ReadDefinition>
     <Process>false</Process>
     <Read>Allowed</Read>
     <Write>None</Write>
     <AttributePermissions>
          <AttributePermission>
               <AttributeID>State Province</AttributeID>
               <DefaultMember/>
```

```
            <AllowedSet/>
            <DeniedSet>{[Customer].[State Province].&amp;[WA]}</DeniedSet>
            <VisualTotals>0</VisualTotals>
        </AttributePermission>
    </AttributePermissions>
</DimensionPermission>
```

Testing Dimension Security

After you define dimension security on a role, you must make sure that it works as you expect it to. Because you are the administrator of the database, if you issue queries to the cube under your own credentials, you always have enough privileges to see the data without applying dimension security. To test this role, you can use the cube browser in BI Dev Studio or SQL Server Management, which enables you to browse the data as a particular user or a member of a certain role. To test the role, follow these steps:

1. Access the cube browser by double-clicking the `Warehouse and Sales` cube in the Solution Explorer and moving to the Browser tab in BI Dev Studio, or by right-clicking the cube name—`Warehouse and Sales`—in the Object Explorer of the SQL Server Management Studio and choosing Browse from the resulting menu.
2. Select the Choose User icon, which will show you the Security Context Properties dialog for the `Warehouse and Sales` cube.
3. In the resulting box, select the role from which you want to use to browse the data, as shown in Figure 36.11.

After you have chosen the role, you can browse the cube as if you were a member of that role. Drag the `Store Sales` measure and drop it in the data area of the browser, and then drag the `Customer` dimension and drop it in the rows area. When you drill down into the `Customer` dimension, as shown in Figure 36.12, you can see that the `USA` member has only two children—`CA` and `OR`—because `WA` is restricted. Notice also that the total value for `Store Sales` in the `USA` member equals `Store Sales` in `CA` plus `Store Sales` in `OR` (because we set the `VisualTotals` property of the `State Province` attribute to `TRUE`).

NOTE

You don't have to use the tools shipped with Analysis Services to test roles. If you have client application that enables you to specify a connection string property, you can define the `Roles` connection property as:

```
Roles=YourRoleName;
```

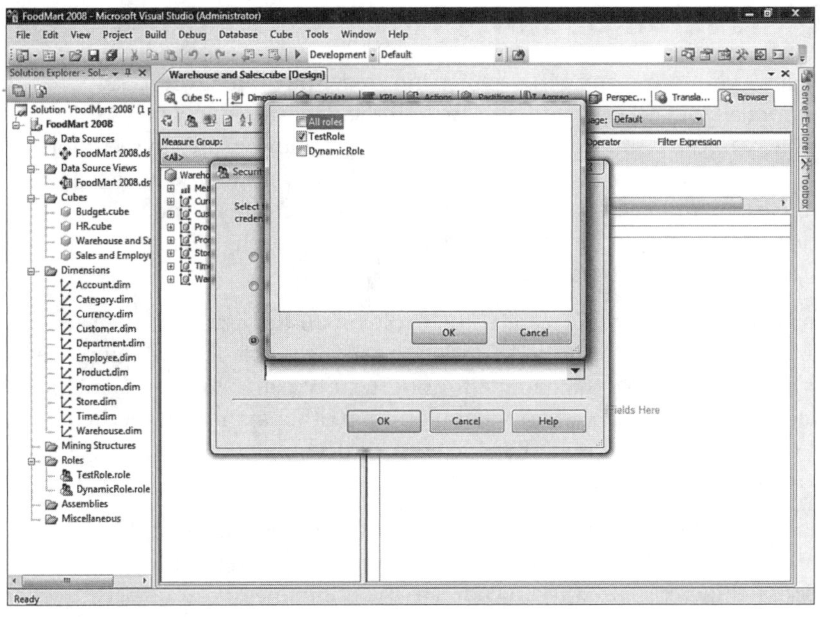

FIGURE 36.11 Select the role you want to test.

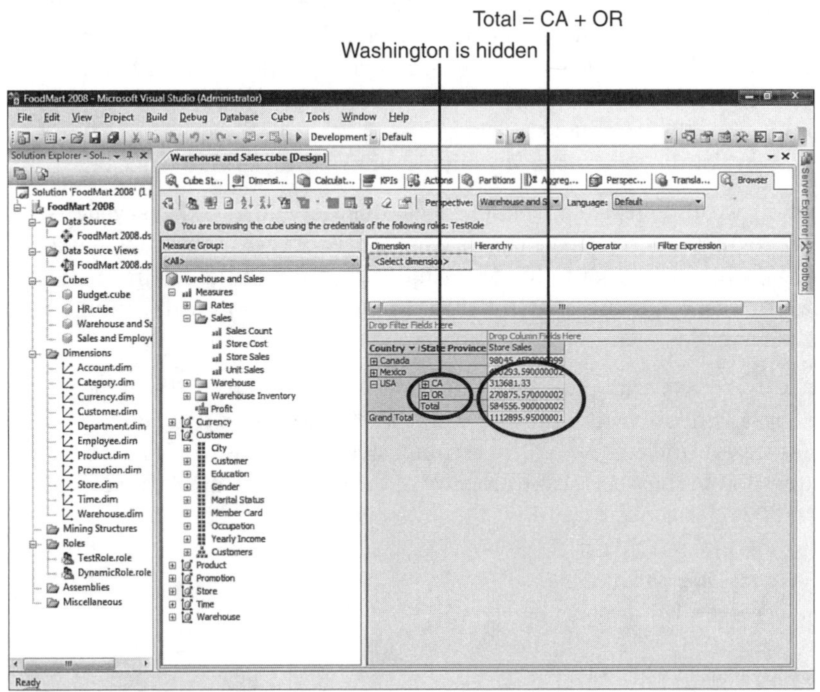

FIGURE 36.12 The WA member is not shown because it is restricted by dimension security, and the total value of USA equals the value of CA plus value of OR.

Dynamic Dimension Security

Analysis Services allows you to use any MDX expression to define dimension security. Therefore, you can model your security system based on the data stored in Analysis Services. For example, you can define an MDX expression that allows a user to see information about the store where she works, but not other stores. However, such scenarios don't fit well with the role-based approach because you would have to create an individual role for each user of the system. You can instead use a data-based approach, called *dynamic dimension security*, to address such scenarios.

With dynamic dimension security, you create a single role for all the users and use the `UserName` MDX function inside the security definition to tailor the role for each employee. When you deal with a large number of combinations of security permissions, this method has a definite advantage because it is easier to maintain than other approaches. When a new user is added to the system, you don't have to create a new role; the existing role is automatically adjusted.

The `UserName` function returns a string that contains the domain\username of the Windows user that connects to Analysis Services. You can use this string in the MDX expressions that define dimension security to compare the username of the current Windows user against the username of employees in your organization.

You can map the result from the `UserName` function to members of the cube in different ways. One of the simplest methods (that fits our purpose) is to add a column that contains the username of the employee and build a dimension attribute based on it. For example, we added the `user_name` column to the `dbo.employees` table in the `FoodMart 2008` relational database. We then created a new attribute, `User Name`, in the `Employee` dimension. The `KeyColumns` property of the `User Name` attribute is set to `employee.employee_id`, and the `NameColumns` property of the `User Name` attribute is set to `employee.user_name`.

As part of the example, we also created a new role, `DynamicRole`, and added `Everyone` as member of the role. We have also created a cube `Sales and Employees`. This cube has a measure group, `Sales`, which is similar to the `Sales` measure group contained in the `Warehouse and Sales` cube, but it also contains the `Employee` dimension with granularity set on the `Store` attribute.

Now you can use the `User Name` attribute to map the user who browses the cube to the member of the `Employee` dimension. You can also define a set of members that allows you to see only the store (or stores) where you work. To accomplish both actions, you can specify the following MDX expression in the `AllowedSet` property of the `Store` cube dimension:

```
Filter(
 [Store].[Store].[Store].members,
 [Store].[Store].currentmember.properties("key") =
Exists(
 [Employee].[Store].[Store].members,
StrToMemeber ("Employee.["+UserName()+"]", CONSTRAINED)
).Item(0).Properties("key") )
```

This expression uses the `StrToMemeber` MDX function to get a member of the `Employee` attribute hierarchy from the member of the `User Name` attribute hierarchy that you construct from the string returned by the `UserName` MDX function. The expression then maps the members of the `Employee` attribute hierarchy to the corresponding members of the `Store` attribute hierarchy. As the last step, the expression uses the `Filter` function to get member of the `Store` dimension that has a key corresponding to the key of `Employee` dimension member.

NOTE

The MDX expression used in the `AllowedSet` or `DeniedSet` property of an `AttributePermission` object must be valid. If your expression contains an error, dimension security disables access to all members of the dimension.

Now that we have dynamically defined dimension security, when you browse the data as a user of the `DynamicRole` role, you see only the data associated with your username. For example, Figure 36.13 displays data only for store 12, located in Mexico, because user Irina Gorbach (under whose credentials we are browsing) happens to work in that store.

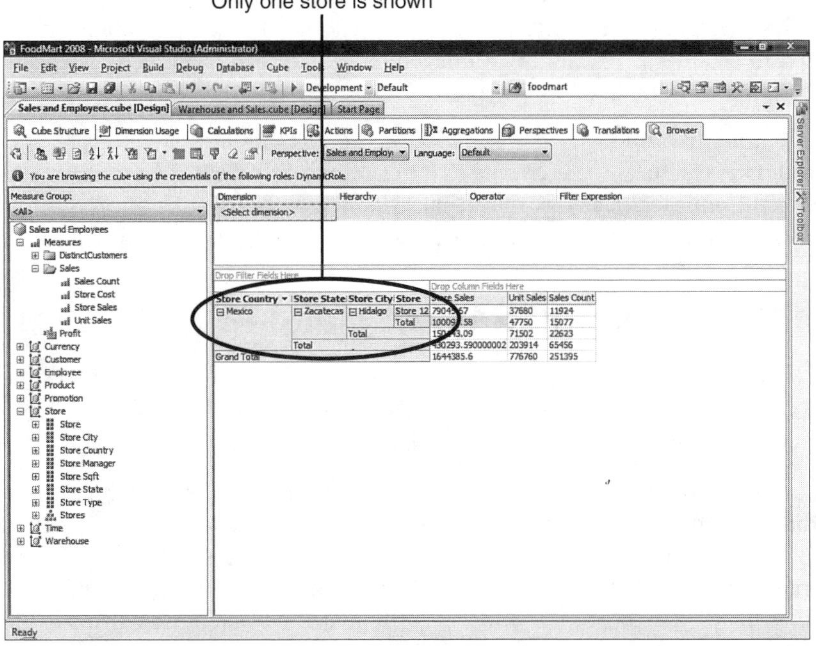

FIGURE 36.13 Members that do not correspond to the store where Irina Gorbach works are secured.

Dimension Security Architecture

A user who retrieves data from Analysis Services can belong to multiple roles. Therefore, when a user retrieves data, Analysis Services evaluates dimension security for each role to which that user belongs. If the system has many security roles defined, the possible combination of roles that different users belong to can be very large. Analysis Services has a scalable mechanism that enables fast evaluation of dimension security, which works even for very large dimensions.

Analysis Services does not create and load in memory a duplication of the dimension with allowed members, but instead keeps in memory a small data structure called `CubeAttributeSecurity`. The `CubeAttributeSecurity` data structure implements the interface that provides Analysis Services with information as to whether dimension security allows or denies a particular member.

Physical representation of the `CubeAttributeSecurity` data structure depends on many factors. In some cases, Analysis Services keeps a compressed bitmap and can deduce the information about the allowed or denied members from it; in other cases, it has to create a materialized bitmap that contains a bit for each attribute member. Even in the worst-case scenario, when Analysis Services has to materialize the bitmap, the number of bytes used by dimension security cannot be more then number of members in the dimension divided by eight. The bitmap used in `CubeAttributeSecurity` is a file store class (discussed in Chapter 20, "Physical Data Model") and can be swapped out on disk when Memory Manager (discussed in Chapter 27, "Memory Management") decides that some of the memory on the system has to be freed.

If a user belongs to more than one security role, Analysis Services iterates `CubeAttributeSecurity` structures for each role and performs a bitwise `OR` operation between bits returned from each `CubeAttributeSecurity` structure. This operation is very fast and doesn't require many resources, even when the user belongs to many roles.

Dimension Security, Cell Security, and MDX Scripts

Analysis Services applies dimension security before evaluating an MDX script because it must evaluate all expressions inside the MDX script within the context of dimension security. However, Analysis Services applies cell security *after* evaluating the MDX script.

When a user connects to Analysis Services, the system determines the roles to which the user belongs (in other words, the active roles) and checks whether the MDX script that corresponds to this combination of active roles is already in the global scope cache. (For more information about the global scope cache, see Chapter 29, "Architecture of Query Execution—Calculating MDX Expressions.") If this is the first time that a user with such a combination of roles has entered the system, Analysis Services must first evaluate the dimension security.

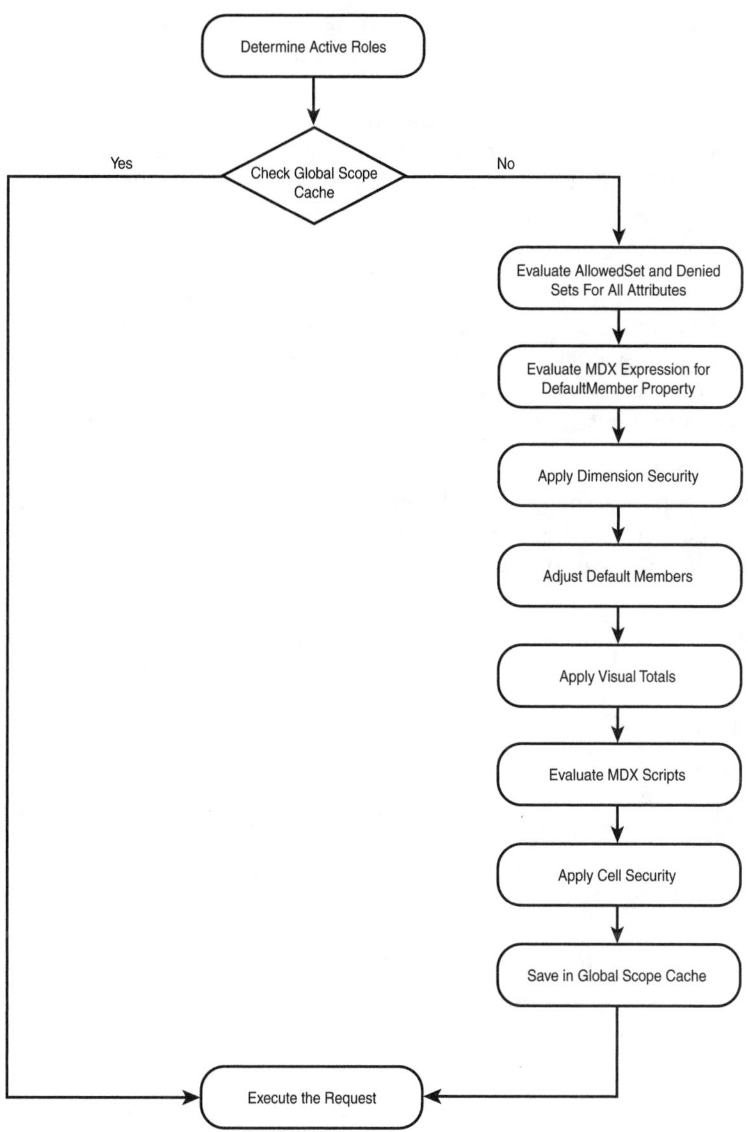

FIGURE 36.14 Analysis Services applies dimension security before the MDX script is evaluated, and applies cell security after the MDX script is evaluated.

To do so, Analysis Services iterates through all the AttributePermissions objects, evaluates the MDX expressions for the AllowedSet and DeniedSet properties of the AttributePermission object for each active role, and builds CubeAttributeSecurity structures. Analysis Services then evaluates MDX expressions of the DefaultMember property of the AttributePermissions object. If more than one role has the DefaultMember property defined, the default member of the first role wins. However, Analysis Services iterates the roles in a nondeterministic order, so you cannot predict which role will be first. Analysis Services then applies dimension security. From then on, all operations execute in the secured context.

If dimension security restricts any default member, the system cannot use it in subsequent operations. Therefore, Analysis Services changes default members for attributes that have a restricted default member. Typically, if an attribute is aggregatable, the member ALL is the default member; otherwise, any unrestricted member from the top level can become a default member.

Analysis Services applies any applicable visual totals, and finally evaluates the MDX script. After Analysis Services evaluates the script, it adds the script to the global scope cache. Figure 36.14 shows the process just described.

CHAPTER 37
Securing Cell Values

IN THIS CHAPTER

- Defining Cell Security
- Testing Cell Security
- Contingent Cell Security
- Dynamic Cell Security

Cell security enables an administrator to hide the values of certain cells in a cube from the user—as opposed to dimension security, which defines access permissions to the axes coordinates in multidimensional space. For example, a sales manager should be able to see values of the sales for his direct reports, but perhaps not allowed to see the sales for sales representatives from a different division. The difference with dimension security is that, with cell security, everybody can see the members associated with sales representatives, but only a certain group of people can see cell values associated with those members.

Defining Cell Security

Similar to dimension security, cell security fits in the role-based security model discussed in Chapter 35, "Security Model for Analysis Services." For each role, you can use Multidimensional Expressions (MDX) to define a cell or group of cells that is accessible by or denied to a user. On the server, cell security is defined by a collection of `CellPermission` objects; `CellPermission` is a property of the `CubePermission` object, as shown in Figure 37.1.

Each `CellPermission` object has the properties shown in Table 37.1.

Now that you know what properties the `CellPermission` object has, you can define a sample permission that allows a user to see sales of the stores located in Mexico and the United States, but doesn't allow him to see sales of stores in

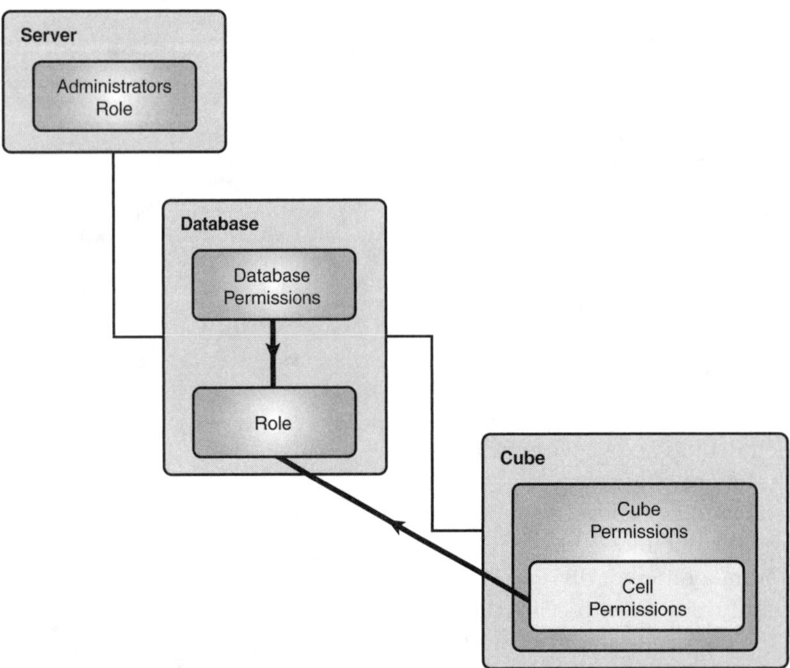

FIGURE 37.1 This hierarchy of objects is used to define cell security.

TABLE 37.1 Properties of the **CellPermission** Object

Name	Description
`Expression`	MDX expression that resolves to a Boolean `TRUE` or `FALSE` value. When the expression resolves to `TRUE`, a cell or group of cells covered by the expression is allowed by cell security. When the expression resolves to `FALSE`, the cells are denied.
`Access`	Can be one of the following values: `Read`: A user has read access to a cell; `ReadContingent`: A user has read access to a cell only if that user has access to the cells from which the current cell derives (we talk more about contingent cell access later in this chapter); `ReadWrite`: A user has access to the cell for read and write.

Canada but does allow him access to values of the units sold measure. To do this, you can use the following MDX code:

```
(NOT Measures.CurrentMember IS [Measures].[Store Sales])
OR (NOT [Store].[Store Country].CurrentMember
IS [Store].[Store Country].[Canada])
```

This expression allows the user to see values from all measures except `Store Sales`, and to show values for `Store Sales` for all countries except Canada.

You can define cell security using either Data Definition Language (DDL) statements or a user interface provided by SQL Server Management Studio or BI Dev Studio. The following steps describe how to apply cell security using BI Dev Studio.

1. In BI Dev Studio, open the `FoodMart 2008` project.
2. In the Solution Explorer, double-click the `Role.role` role to open the role editor.
3. Choose the `Cell Data` page.
4. In the Cube drop-down list, choose the `Warehouse and Sales` cube.
5. Check the Enable Read Permissions check box.
6. You can copy and paste the expression into the Allow Reading of Cube Content box, or click Edit MDX and use MDX Builder to construct an MDX statement.
7. After you have defined an MDX expression, you can make sure that it has the correct syntax by clicking the Check button.

Figure 37.2 shows the MDX Builder dialog with an MDX expression that allows access to all cells except those corresponding to sales in Canada.

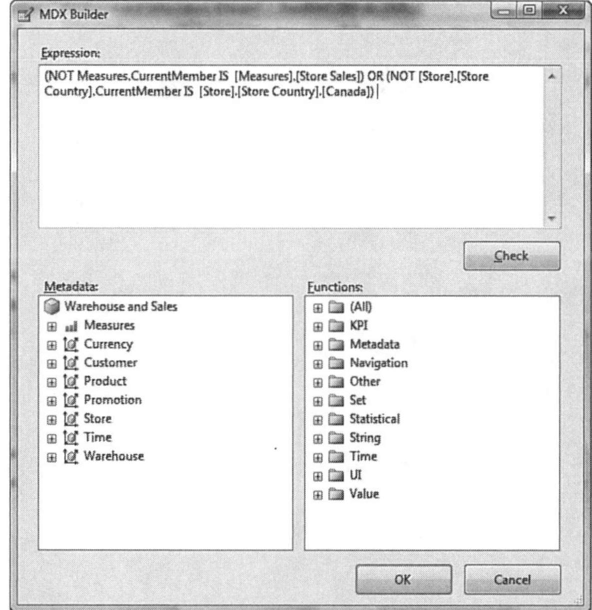

FIGURE 37.2 You use the MDX Builder dialog to define cell security of a cube.

37

When you save your work and deploy the project, BI Dev Studio sends the necessary `Alter` DDL command to the server, which then alters the cube and saves the `CubePermission` object. Listing 37.1 shows the portion of DDL related to defining the cell security.

LISTING 37.1 DDL Request for Defining a **`CubePermission`** Object

```
<CubePermission>
    <Name>CubePermission</Name>
    <ID>CubePermission</ID>
    <CreatedTimestamp>2006-05-03T04:31:52</CreatedTimestamp>
    <LastSchemaUpdate>2006-05-05T04:58:32</LastSchemaUpdate>
    <ObjectVersion>7</ObjectVersion>
    <ObjectID>4DB37960-3AEE-4B52-83AD-78C95C2E111E</ObjectID>
    <Ordinal>7</Ordinal>
    <PersistLocation>0</PersistLocation>
    <System>false</System>
    <DataFileList />
    <Description />
    <RoleID>Role</RoleID>
    <ReadDefinition>None</ReadDefinition>
    <Process>false</Process>
    <Read>Allowed</Read>
    <ReadSourceData>None</ReadSourceData>
    <Write>Allowed</Write>
    <DimensionPermissions />
    <CellPermissions>
        <CellPermission>
            <Description />
            <Access>Read</Access>
            <Expression>(NOT Measures.CurrentMember
 IS [Measures].[Store Sales]) OR
 (NOT [Store].[Store Country].CurrentMember
 IS [Store].[Store Country].[Canada])</Expression>
        </CellPermission>
    </CellPermissions>
</CubePermission>
```

Testing Cell Security

After you define cell security on a role, you need to make sure that it works as you expect it to. Because you are the administrator of the database, if you issue queries to the cube under your own credentials, you will have enough privileges to see all the data without cell security being applied. However, to test this role, you can follow the Test Cube

Security link located in the upper-right corner of the Cell Data pane of the role editor. The link opens the cube browser for you, which allows you to browse the data as a particular user or as a member of a certain role:

1. Select the Change User icon, which will show you a Security Context dialog box for the `Warehouse and Sales` cube.
2. On the resulting dialog, select the role you want to use to browse the data from the Roles box, as shown in Figure 37.3.

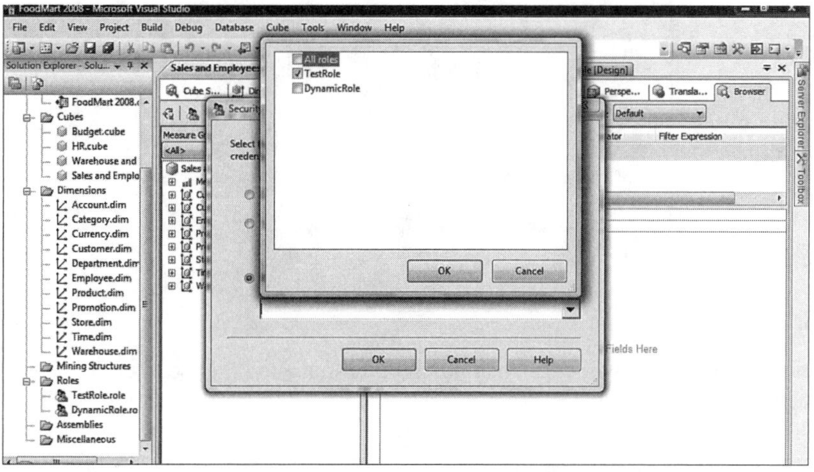

FIGURE 37.3 In the Security Context dialog, select the role you want to test.

After you have chosen the role, you can browse the cube as if you were a member of that role. Now drag the `Store Sales` measure and drop it in the data area of the browser, and then drag the `Store` dimension and drop it in the rows area. When you drill down into `Store` dimension, as shown in Figure 37.4, you can see that cells associated with the `USA` and `Mexico` members have valid values, but the value of the cell associated with `Canada` is `#N/A`.

By default, Analysis Services returns the `#N/A` (Not Available) string as a value for cells denied to the user by cell security. A client application can configure Analysis Services and specify the format in which it gets secured values by using the Secured Cell Value connection property. Instead of `#N/A`, secured values can be shown as `NULL`, `0`, `#SEC`, or a cell error.

NOTE

You don't have to use the tools shipped with Analysis Services to test the roles. If you have a client application that enables you to specify a connection string property, you can define the `Roles` or `EffectiveUserName` connection properties as follows: `Roles=TestRole;` or `EffectiveUserName=redmond\irinag;` (for example).

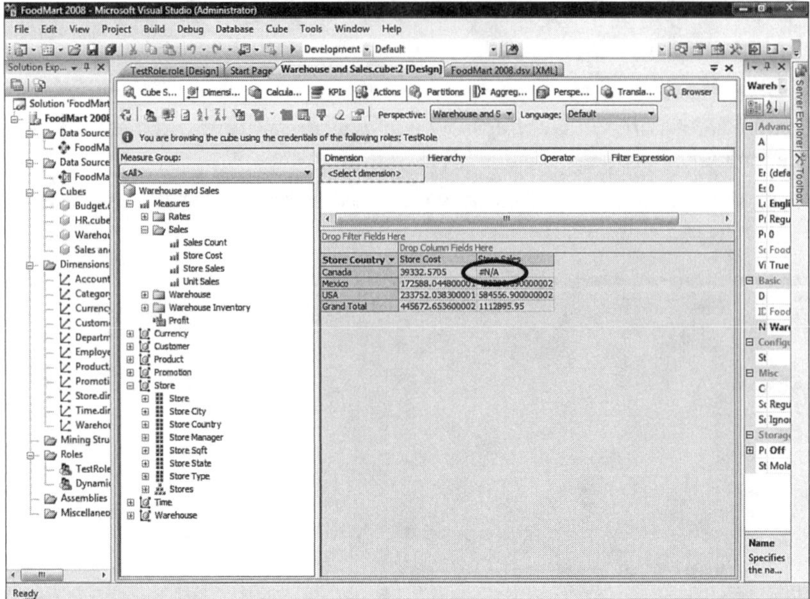

FIGURE 37.4 The cell for store sales in Canada has an error because it is secured from users of TestRole by the cell security.

Contingent Cell Security

When you specify Read as the access permission type of the CellPermission object, Analysis Services allows or denies the user rights to see the values covered by the MDX expression in the Expression property. However, this might expose more information than you intended. Consider, for example, the following calculated member:

```
[Measures].[Profit] = [Measures].[Store Sales] - [Measures].[Store Cost]
```

If you define cell security as in the previous example (which denied user access to values of store sales in Canada), you don't prevent the user from seeing the profit of sales in Canada or from seeing the cost of the stores in Canada. Therefore, a smart user can deduce the following information:

```
[Measures].[Store Sales] = [Measures].[Profit] + [Measures].[Store Cost]
```

If you want to prevent such a situation, you can modify the access type of the CellPermission object to deny access to the value of the Profit member in addition to the value of Store Sales. However, if you have many calculated members or other calculations, the process may become cumbersome. You can instead define the access type as ReadContingent and prevent the user from accessing Profit, because the cell that Profit depends on—Store Sales—is secured. You can do this in BI Dev Studio by moving the cell security expression from Enable Read Permission to the Allow Reading of Cell Content Contingent on Cell Security, as shown in Figure 37.5.

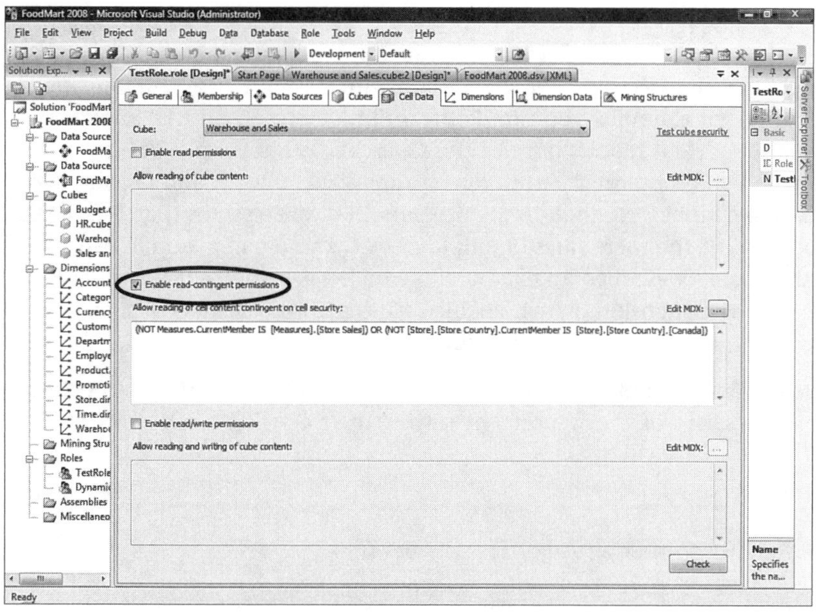

FIGURE 37.5 How to define contingent cell security.

When you browse the data as a user of `TestRole` after you have defined contingent cell security, you are denied from seeing not only `Store Sales` in Canada but also `Profit` of Canadian stores, as shown in Figure 37.6.

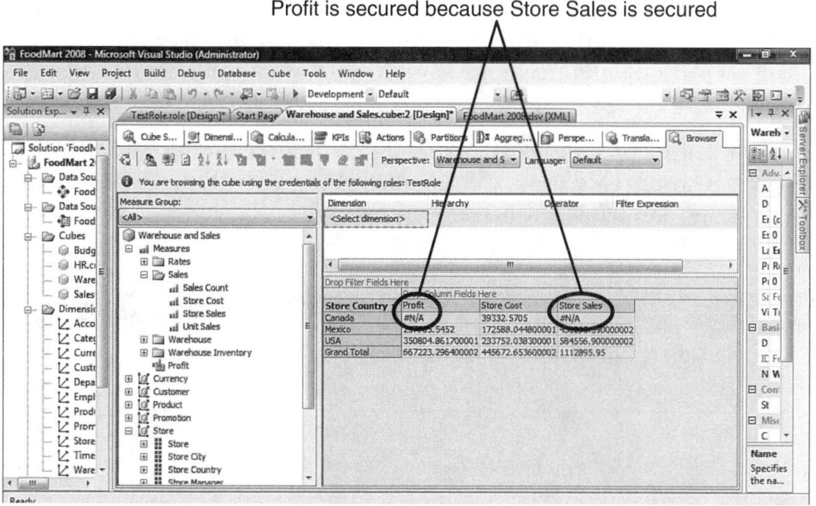
Profit is secured because Store Sales is secured

FIGURE 37.6 Cells for store sales and profit in Canada show an error.

Dynamic Cell Security

Similar to dynamic dimension security, you can design your system to use dynamic security within cell security. For example, you can define an MDX expression that allows managers to see salaries of their reports but not the salaries of other people. You can use the UserName function (which returns a string that contains the domain and username of the Windows user who connects to Analysis Services) in MDX expressions that define cell security to compare against the usernames of employees of your organization. Chapter 36, "Securing Dimension Data," described an example in which we created a User Name attribute on the Employee dimension, which enabled us to map the username of an employee to a member on the Employee dimension.

You can use the User Name attribute to define a permission expression that allows you to see your salary, and the salary of your reports, by setting the following MDX expression for cell security:

```
IsAncestor(
LinkMember([Employee].[User Name].[User Name].members(
"["+UserName()+"]"),[Employee].[Employees])
, [Employee].[Employees].CurrentMember)
OR LinkMember([Employee].[User Name].[User Name].members(
"["+UserName()+"]"),[Employee].[Employees])
 IS [employee].[Employees].CurrentMember
```

This expression uses the LinkMember MDX function to get a member on the Employees hierarchy from the member of the User Name attribute hierarchy. The cell is allowed if it is based on the member that corresponds to the employee who browses the cube or the member's ancestors.

Now after you have defined cell security, when you browse the data as a user of DynamicRole, you will see #N/A for all the employees that are not you and are not your reports, as shown in Figure 37.7.

While browsing a cube with the preceding expression set up as cell security, you might notice that performance becomes very slow. This happens because Analysis Services has to apply the cell security expression when calculating the value of each cell.

NOTE

If a complex MDX expression is specified as a cell security expression, it will slow down the server.

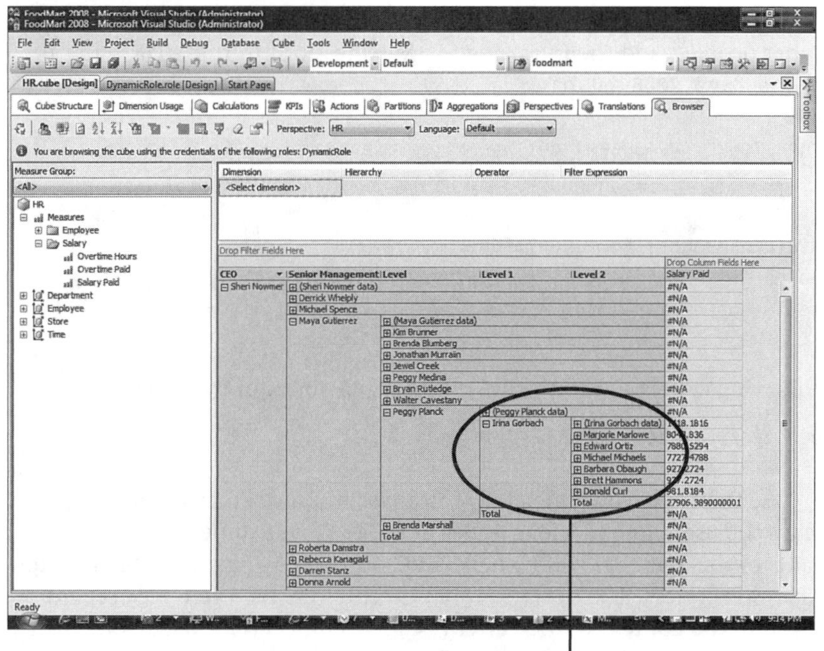

FIGURE 37.7 Cells corresponding to employees that are not Irina and not her reports are secured.

To improve the performance of this scenario (and many other scenarios), it is helpful to understand how Analysis Services works under the hood and the order of operation in which Analysis Services performs when it executes a client request and applies cell security. Chapter 36 covered this in detail. Here, we'll just say that expressions defined by cell security are evaluated after MDX scripts are evaluated. Therefore, expressions defined in MDX scripts can be used in cell security. (For more information about MDX scripts, see Chapter 12, "Cube-Based MDX Calculations.")

Armed with this knowledge, you can create the following combination of calculations: hidden calculated member on the `Measures` dimension (which value can be either `FALSE` or `TRUE`) to be used in cell security expression, and a `SCOPE` statement that defines a subcube for nonsecured values. Inside the `SCOPE` statement, assign the value of the hidden calculated member to `TRUE`. The `SCOPE` statement evaluates the subcube expression statically when MDX script is loaded, which means that the complex expression that maps the username to the member in the `Employee` dimension and calculates the descendants of this member will be performed only once—when the MDX script is calculated by Analysis Services. On the other hand, Analysis Services evaluates the fast exception `measures.cellsecurityexpression` for each requested cell.

To improve the performance of this scenario—to allow managers to see salaries of their reports, but not other people—add the following MDX expressions to the MDX script of the HR cube in the FoodMart 2008 database:

```
CREATE MEMBER CURRENTCUBE.[MEASURES].cellsecurityexpression
 AS false,
VISIBLE = 0;
SCOPE (Descendants(LinkMember([Employee].[User Name].
 [User Name].members("["+UserName()+"]"),[Employee].[Employees])));
    [MEASURES].cellsecurityexpression = true;
END SCOPE;
```

Then assign the following expression to the CellPermission object of DynamicRole:

```
measures.cellsecurityexpression
```

Now when you browse the cube, you will get very fast performance because the complex expression that maps the username to the member in the Employee dimension and calculates the descendants of this member will be performed only once—when the MDX script is calculated by Analysis Services. The operation that executes for each cell—cell security expression evaluation in the context of the current cell—is simple and calculated quickly.

PART IX
Management

IN THIS PART

CHAPTER 38

Using Trace to Monitor and Audit Analysis Services

IN THIS CHAPTER

- Trace Architecture
- Types of Trace Objects
- Creating Trace Command Options
- SQL Server Profiler
- Flight Recorder
- Tracing Processing Activity
- Query Execution Time Events

Whenever you're working with a server application, you naturally want to know, one could even say need to know, what's going on inside the application. To keep track of its inner workings, Analysis Services has a powerful mechanism: trace.

In end-user applications, you usually get information about what's going on in a message that appears on the screen. For example, if Microsoft Word cannot save your file, you immediately see a message telling you that. In the server applications space, however, the question is more complicated because server applications such as Analysis Services don't have a direct way to let you know what's going on. One way to solve the problem is to write the information into a dedicated file: the log file. Another solution is to use a more sophisticated mechanism: trace.

With logging, the system creates a log file. As events occur in the application, the system writes those events in the log file. Logs come in all shapes and sizes. Every server application developer decides what needs to be logged, how the log is organized, and the format of the event descriptions. The Microsoft Windows event log can serve as a good example of an advanced version of a log. In addition to writing its events into a log, Windows provides a common infrastructure that makes it possible for other applications to add their events to the Windows event log.

The Windows event log is built to be efficient. It doesn't contain a description of every error ever produced by an application. It contains only a pointer to a description of the event. Windows enables a user to do advanced searching through the log, and it allows other applications to access the log programmatically. But like any log, it has inherent problems:

- You have no control over what is being logged.
- A log typically has a rigid structure that resembles a relational table, which means that every event has the same number of columns.
- Logs usually don't have good mechanisms for controlling the problem of excessive increase in its size.
- There is no real-time message notification. The typical logging infrastructure doesn't give you immediate notification of events. The event is first written to the log file, and only then can you access it when you want to search for an event.

Trace Architecture

The end of our discussion of logging brings us naturally to the concept of trace. In contrast to logging, trace gives you a lot of control over the events that are gathered by the system and what the system does with them. In simple terms, you create a series of filters (trace objects) so that the system pays attention to only the events you specify. And you can specify that those events are stored in a trace file, sent to a client computer for display, or both. Let's start with a look at Analysis Services' trace architecture, shown in Figure 38.1.

Trace infrastructure is governed by the Trace Manager component of Analysis Services. To subscribe to a trace, any component of Analysis Services creates a `Trace` object and registers it with the Trace Manager. Properties of the `Trace` object define what events are produced.

Analysis Services uses a single-file `TraceDefinition` that contains the definition and parameters of all trace events. When subscribing to a trace, the subscriber creates a `Trace` object containing set of events she wants to see. Sets of these events from all the trace objects are merged by the Trace Manager and form a global filter that is used to determine which events are produced and should be entered into a single global linked list of events (`TraceQueue`). The subscriber reads events from the `TraceQueue` according to their `Trace` object definitions and streams them either over the network, where you can see them as they occur, or into a file, where you can view them at your convenience.

After an event has been received by all subscribers, it is discarded from the queue. In case of overload, Analysis Server might decide to discard trace events from the queue even before they are consumed by all subscribers.

There are three types of `Trace` objects (administrative trace, session trace, and flight recorder trace):

- The most common trace is the administrative trace, which is created when the user sends a `Create` command for a `Trace` object. It can send events to the user or write them into a trace file.
- A session trace is created automatically by the server for every session.

- A flight recorder trace collects historical data.

After an event is consumed by all the relevant traces, it is discarded.

NOTE

The system is optimized so that any event that is not consumed by a trace won't even be produced.

SQL Server gives you several options for consuming and analyzing trace events produced by Analysis Services. You can use a SQL Server Profiler to manually create traces and analyze trace events. You can also use the SQL Server Profiler object model to programmatically access live traces or open existing trace files.

Types of Trace Objects

All three `Trace` object types—administrative trace, session trace, and flight recorder trace—are represented in Figure 38.1. The following sections cover each one of them in more detail.

Administrative Trace

The administrative trace, created by the server or the database administrator, is the most common type of `Trace` object. It directs its output either to the network or into a file.

To create an administrative `Trace` object, the database administrator (DBA) sends a `Create` command. The database administrator then typically sends a `Subscribe` command to receive events over the network. If all the DBA needs is the events written to a trace file, the `Subscribe` command doesn't have to be sent, but the DBA does have to make sure that the trace file is specified in the `Create` command.

Session Trace

A session trace reports on events that are associated with one specific user session. There is no need to send a `Create` command because the trace is created by the server automatically as soon as you send a `Subscribe` command during a session.

Some limitations apply to a session trace. Because you don't use a `Create` command, you can't control trace properties, such as specifying the events that are included in the session `Trace` object definition. Nor can you stream a session trace into a file.

Flight Recorder Trace

The concept of the flight recorder trace is similar to that of the flight recorder you find in the airline industry. Each airplane carries a "black box" that automatically records the equipment's actions as they occur. The flight recorder trace works in a similar fashion. It records the actions of the server and server state automatically.

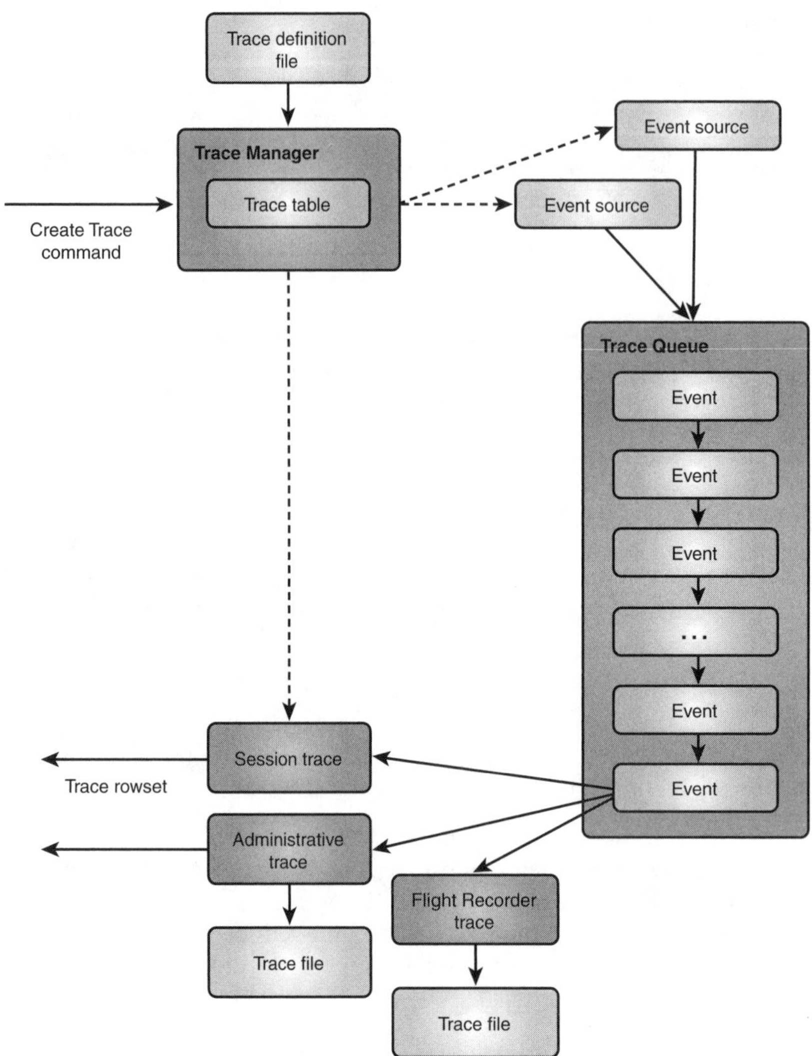

FIGURE 38.1 In this workflow diagram, you can see how trace events are produced and filtered.

Creating Trace Command Options

You use the options of the `Create` command to control the behavior of the trace. Listing 38.1 shows a representation of a trace Data Definition Language (DDL). You can refer back to it to see how to use the options described in Table 38.1.

TABLE 38.1 **Create** Command Options

Name	Description
Name	The name of the Trace object.
ID	A unique identifier for the Trace object.
LogFileName	The name of the trace file the server writes trace events into. If you don't specify the full name of the file, including its path, the server creates a trace file in the dedicated folder, LogDir.
LogFileSize	Use LogFileSize to control the maximum size for the trace file. When the file reaches that maximum size, the server can stop the trace or, if the LogFileRollover property has been set, start streaming to a different file with a similar name.
LogFileRollover	Directs the server to create a new file when the current trace file reaches its maximum size. The name of the new trace file is the original file's name with 001 appended to it. So, if your trace file named mylog.trc reaches its maximum size, the server creates a file named mylog001.trc, and continues to increment the appended number as long as the files fill up.
LogFileAppend	Controls what happens when you issue a Create command with a filename and the server finds an already-existing trace file with the same name. You can set this property to direct the server to overwrite the original file or to add the trace events to the original file.
AutoRestart	Determines whether the trace automatically restarts whenever the server restarts. Set this option to 1 if you want the Trace object to be re-created whenever the server restarts. Set this option to 0 if you want the Trace object to be discarded whenever the server shuts down.
Audit	Controls whether the trace infrastructure is permitted to discard events before it sends them. This option enables you to prevent the server from discarding events just because the server is overloaded. (The server isn't very discriminating about what events it discards in times like this.) Setting the Audit option to 1 ensures that the server sends trace events no matter how busy it is. However, if the server doesn't have the capacity to send the trace events to audit trace, it will shut itself down. So, if you set the Audit option, make sure that the trace isn't set to track very many events.

LISTING 38.1 A Trace DDL

```
<Trace>
    <ID>trace ID<ID>
    <Name>Trace Name<Name>
    <LogFileName>filename</LogFileName>
    <LogFileAppend>1¦0</>
    <LogFileSize>filesize</LogFileSize>
```

38

```
    <Audit>1¦0</Audit>
    <LogFileRollover>1¦0</LogFileRollover>
    <AutoRestart>1¦0</AutoRestart>
    <StopTime>stop_time</StopTime>
    <Events>  ... </Events>
    <Filters>filter_expression[, filter_expression]</Filters>
</Trace>
```

SQL Server Profiler

SQL Server Profiler was initially developed to trace SQL Server events, but the Analysis Services trace protocol, definitions, and file format are compatible with those of SQL Server. SQL Server Profiler can connect to Analysis Server as easily as it can to SQL Server. Follow these steps to open SQL Profiler and connect to your server:

1. Open SQL Server Profiler from the Start menu: Start, Microsoft SQL Server 2008, Performance Tools, SQL Server Profiler.
2. To connect to Analysis Services, select New Trace from the File menu.
3. From the Server Type drop-down list in the Connect to Server dialog box, select Analysis Services. In the Server Name text box, enter the name of your server and then click the Connect button.

Defining a Trace

When you have a connection, you can use the Trace Properties dialog box to define the properties of your trace and select the events you want to trace (see Figure 38.2).

On the General tab of the Trace Properties dialog box, you can name your trace and then use the check boxes to choose the trace's properties:

- In the Use the Template drop-down list, choose the template for your trace. The default is Standard. Choose Blank if you want no trace events selected by default. Choose Replay to select only the events that are relevant to replay functionality.
- Select Save to File to enable the trace to stream events into a file. After you select the check box, you can choose a name for the file in the Save As dialog box.

Use the Events Selection tab to select the events that you want your trace to capture. When you first see the Events tab, it contains the events that have been selected—according to the template you chose on the General tab. Figure 38.3 shows the results of selecting the Standard template.

You can select the check boxes in the columns to include specific information about each event in your trace. Table 38.2 contains descriptions of the most important columns. (Descriptions of all the columns are included in Books Online.)

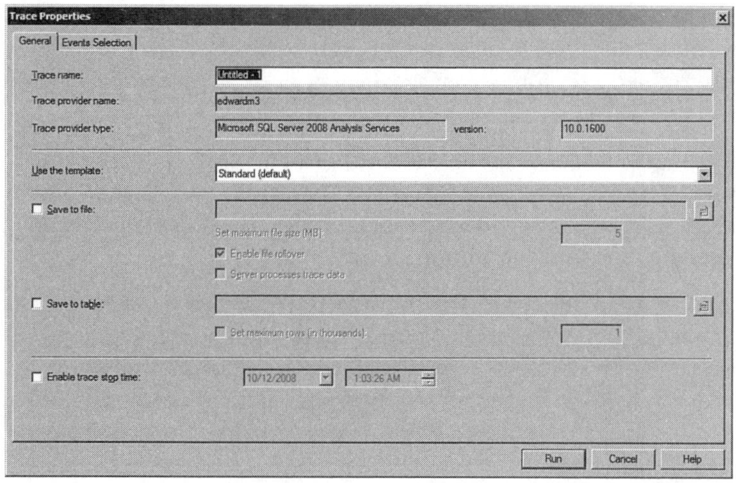

FIGURE 38.2 Use the Trace Properties dialog box to select options for your trace.

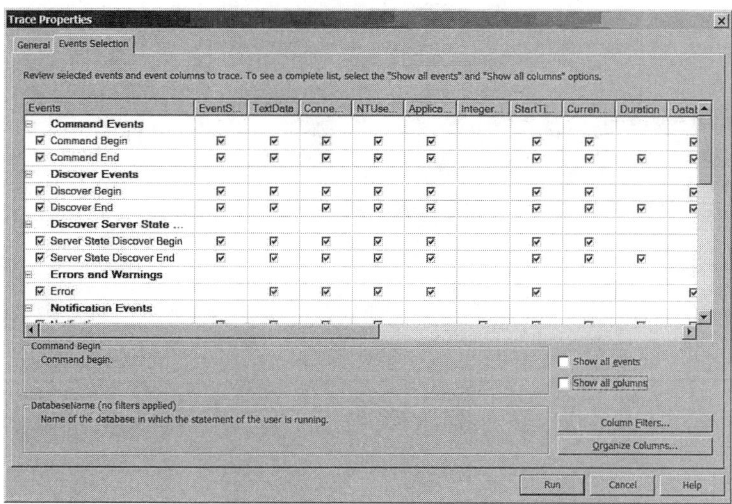

FIGURE 38.3 The Events Selection tab shows the events that will be traced.

TABLE 38.2 Important Columns on the Events Selection Tab

Name	Description
`EventSubclass`	An additional classification for the event. For example; the Progress Report event has the subclass `ExecuteSQL`.
`TextData`	Textual information about the event. For example, each `Command` or `Query` event contains the text of the command or query.
`IntegerData`	Numeric information of the event. For example, in a `Progress Report Current` event, the number represents the number of rows read.

The identification columns about objects, such as `ObjectName` and `ObjectID`, provide information that enables you to identify the objects affected by the event. For example, the object ID and the path to the object for a `Progress Report` event enable you to identify the object that is being processed.

Other columns, such as `ConnectionID`, `SessionID`, `SessionType`, and `SPID` (server process ID) contain information about user connections or sessions. The `ApplicationName` column contains the name of the application that opened the connection. The `ClientProcessID` column contains the numeric ID for that application.

You can select the Show All Events and Show All Columns check boxes in the lower-right corner of the dialog box to see hidden events and columns. These hidden events and columns are the ones that were not included in the template you selected on the General tab of the Trace Properties dialog box. Now you can select additional events and columns to add to your trace.

Running a Trace

Click the Run button in the Trace Properties dialog box to run your trace. So long as you don't have any other open user connections to Analysis Services, the SQL Server Profiler dialog box (shown in Figure 38.4) appears with the name you chose for your trace.

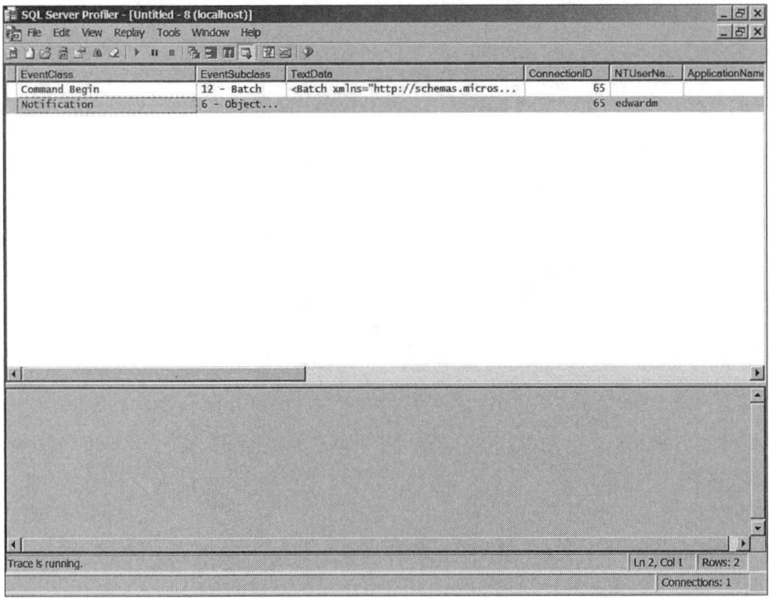

FIGURE 38.4 The SQL Server Profiler dialog box now shows the events captured by the trace.

Our trace has captured two events: `Command Begin` and `Notification`. The `Command Begin` event's `TextData` column contains the text of the `Create` command that created the trace. A `Notification` event is generated every time an object is created. The `Notification` event in Figure 38.4 was generated when we created the trace. The `SubClass` column,

`Object Created`, indicates the creation of the `Trace` object. Here you see a `Trace` object reporting its own creation. By default, the trace contains a filter condition that removes all events associated with SQL Server Profiler activity. In our example, we removed that filter condition.

If you open SQL Server Management Studio and then open a connection to your Analysis server, you'll see even more events in your trace. You can see the additional events from our sample trace in Figure 38.5.

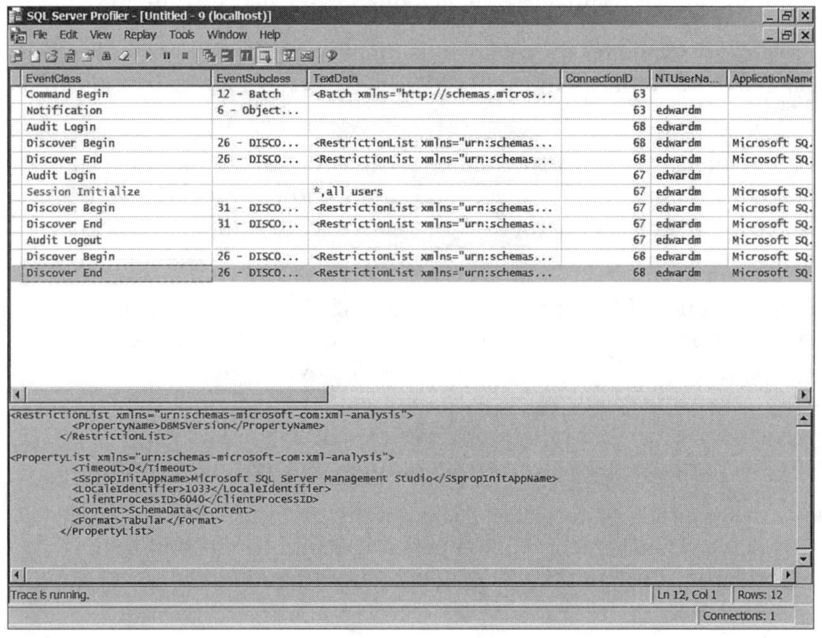

FIGURE 38.5 Additional events are listed in the trace after a connection with SQL Server Management Studio.

The events you see in Figure 38.5 fall into four categories, as described in Table 38.3.

TABLE 38.3 Event Categories

Security Audit	**Command Events**	**Query Events**	**Discover Events**	**Session Events**
`Audit Login/Logout`	Command Begin/End	Query Begin/End	Discover Begin/End	Existing Session
`Audit Object Permission`			Existing Connection	
`Audit Backup/Restore`			Session Initialize	

TABLE 38.3 Event Categories

Security Audit	Command Events	Query Events	Discover Events	Session Events
Audit Server Start/Stop				

You use events in the Security Audit, Command Events, Query Events, and Discover Events categories to investigate your server activity, such as who connected, which query was sent to the Analysis server, and which command or which discover request was submitted.

The Session Events category facilitates the replay functionality of SQL Server Profiler. The existing sessions and existing connections events enable SQL Server Profiler to replay the captured trace.

The `Audit Login` event indicates that the user application was able to establish a connection to Analysis Services and the Analysis server successfully authenticated the user. The user's name appears in the `NTUserName` column. The `ConnectionID` column contains a number that serves as the ID for the connection. In Figure 38.5, that ID is `68`.

In the `Event Subclass` column of the `Discover Begin` event, you'll find a `DISCOVER_PROPERTIES` request, which indicates that the client application was discovering the Analysis Services properties. If you click anywhere in the Discover Begin event row, you can see more details in the pane below. In our example, you'll see details of the `TextData` column: `<PropertyName>ProviderVersion</PropertyName>`. Now you know that SQL Server Management Studio has asked which version of Analysis Services is running.

In Figure 38.5, you can see another `Audit Login` event right after the `Discover End` event. This means that SQL Server Management Studio opened a second connection to the Analysis server. And, then it issued a `DISCOVER_XML_METADATA` to find out which objects the server has.

NOTE

Right after the `Audit Login` event indicating that a second connection has been opened, you can see a `Session Initialize` event. This event did not occur after the first connection was made because that connection wasn't used to request anything that required the server to calculate the permissions that were set for the user who opened the connection. (The connection just asked for information about Analysis Services.) However, the second connection asked for the list of objects, which did require the server to do those calculations.

Try sending various queries and commands to Analysis Services on your own to see what sort of activity is reported by events in the Command Events and Query Events categories. Don't forget to look at the `Event Subclass` and `Text Data` columns, which are where you'll find the most relevant information.

Flight Recorder

Suppose that you left your computer for a while, maybe to read this book some more, and SQL Server Profiler continued to run while it was connected to the Analysis server. While you're gone, the server from time to time issues `Discover` events on its own. When you return, you'll see those events identified by a `0` in the `ConnectionID` column. (A connection ID equal to `0` means that the event was generated by an internal connection on the server, without input from you.) These `Discover` requests are part of the flight recorder activity on the server. In the example illustrated in Figure 38.6, you can see that we stopped working for a while and when we came back, we had more rows in our SQL Server Profiler.

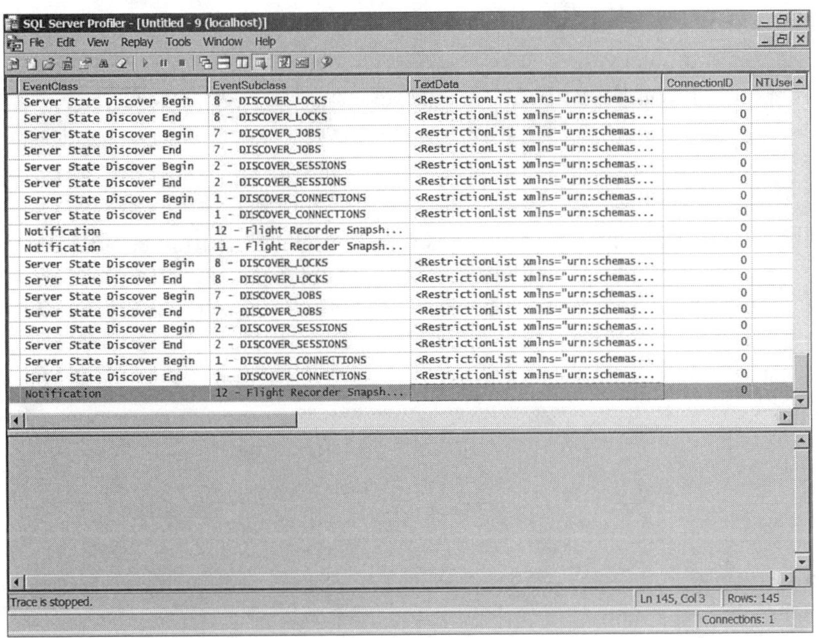

FIGURE 38.6 SQL Server Profiler records events initiated by the server on its own.

The flight recorder is just a `Trace` object, with a trace definition, that records a certain kind of server activity (depending on the type of request) for some specified period of time. It's configured to run automatically on your server. The flight recorder serves as sort of an archive of your server events so that you don't need to worry about not having a record of your recent server activity. You can use it to investigate or troubleshoot problems that occurred during the covered time. There are some problems associated with the flight recorder, however:

- The flight recorder cannot expand indefinitely, so it has to be restricted somehow. See the "Configuring Flight Recorder Behavior" section later in this chapter for information about restricting flight recorder size.
- The flight recorder records only activity that happened during the past hour (the default period of time the flight recorder records). So, much of the time you can't tell what happened by just looking at the record. Imagine that you suspect that some stale or inactive connections are consuming server resources. You can look at the flight recorder data for the current hour of server activity, but you won't be able to find information about connections that users made to the server a few days ago. The flight recorder trace file is of no help in such a situation.

How the Flight Recorder Works

To overcome the problem of not being able to tell exactly what happened when you look at the flight recorder record, you have to either make sure that the flight recorder trace spans several days (which is impractical because you would consume a lot of server space) or configure the server to take snapshots of server state as the flight recorder records. These snapshots would contain requests for information about the current server state.

The primary role of a server-state discover request is to give you information about the server state. The snapshots that you see in Figure 38.7 contain server-state discover requests. The events that result from these requests are recorded into the flight recorder trace file.

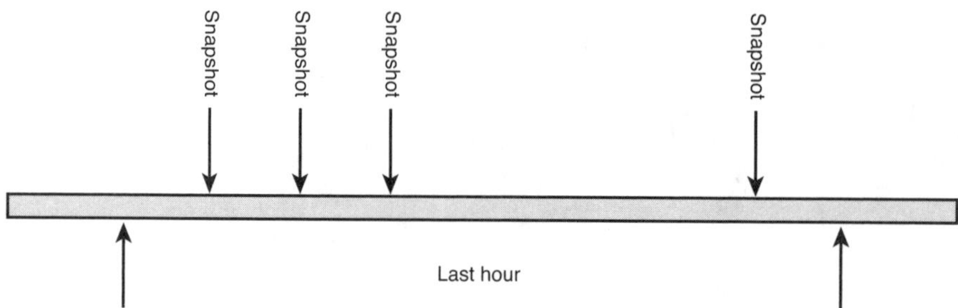

FIGURE 38.7 Taking periodic snapshots of server activity enables you to conserve server space.

In Figure 38.7, you see four snapshots taken during the past hour. In our example, the server sends four requests for each snapshot: `DISCOVER_SESSIONS`, `DISCOVER_CONNECTIONS`, `DISCOVER_JOBS`, and `DISCOVER_LOCKS`. (You can also see these requests listed in the SQL Server Profiler screen shown in Figure 38.8.)

NOTE

You can configure the server to include different requests and a higher or lower number of requests. Our example uses the default settings.

Configuring Flight Recorder Behavior

To configure flight recorder behavior, you edit the Analysis Services configuration file (`msmdsrv.ini`), usually located in `C:\Program Files\Microsoft SQL Server\MSSQL.1\OLAP\Config`. In a text editor, such as Microsoft Notepad, search for flightrecorder. The section is shown in Listing 38.2.

LISTING 38.2 The **`FlightRecorder`** Section of the Server Config File

```
<FlightRecorder>
    <Enabled>1</Enabled>
    <FileSizeMB>10</FileSizeMB>
    <LogDurationSec>3600</LogDurationSec>
    <SnapshotFrequencySec>120</SnapshotFrequencySec>
    <TraceDefinitionFile/>
    <SnapshotDefinitionFile/>
</FlightRecorder>
```

Table 38.4 gives the definitions of the properties that define the behavior of the flight recorder.

TABLE 38.4 Flight Recorder Properties

Property	Definition
`FileSize`	Controls the size of the flight recorder trace file
`LogDuration`	Controls the length of time the flight recorder records
`SnapshotFrequency`	Controls how frequently snapshots are taken
`SnapshotDefinitionFile`	Determines which `DISCOVER` requests are generated
`TraceDefinitionFile`	Determines which events are logged in the flight recorder trace file

38

NOTE

The `flightrecordertracedef.xml` and `flightrecordersnapshotdef.xml` files by default are located in the Analysis Services `bin` folder.

The current flight recorder trace file is called `FlightRecorderCurrent.trc`; it's located along with the `FlightRecorderBack.trc` file in the default Log folder. When the flight recorder reaches its limit, either by time or by file size, the server deletes `FlightRecorderBack.trc`. The server then renames the `FlightRecorderCurrent.trc` file to `FlightRecorderBack.trc` and starts recording a new time period. Because you have two files, the flight recorder needs twice the amount of space that you configured it for (if you set the `FileSize` property).

Discovering Server State

Server-state discover requests enable you to figure out the current state of the analysis server. Unfortunately, SQL Server Management Studio doesn't report the current users of Analysis Services or the queries or commands they are executing. No problem, however; you can use Analysis Services Dynamic Memory Views (DMV) functionality to discover list of users and current connections opened against Analysis Server. For example, open SQL Server Management Studio, and then open the DMX query editor and establish connection to Analysis Server. At this point, you can send a query like `select * from $system.DISCOVER_CONNECTIONS` to discover the list of connections. For more information about using DMVs, see Chapter 41, "Resource Management."

Tracing Processing Activity

Tracing processing activity, and tracing the resolution of queries (discussed in Chapter 16, "Writing Data Into Analysis Services"), can help you troubleshoot problems on the server. Although the Processing dialog box does an excellent job of capturing processing trace events, sometimes you need the full power and flexibility of SQL Server Profiler to troubleshoot processing problems.

The processing of three types of objects bring data to the Analysis server:

- Dimensions
- Partitions
- Mining models, which are partly resolved in the processing of dimensions and partitions

Reporting the Progress of Dimension Processing

When the server begins to process a dimension, it automatically creates a dimension-processing job. The beginning of a dimension-processing job appears in SQL Server Profiler as an event: `Progress Report Begin`. Other events keep you up-to-date on how the dimension process is going. With the `Progress Report Current` event, SQL Server Profiler includes such information about how many rows have been read.

If an error occurs, you'll see a `Progress Report Error` event in SQL Server Profiler. You'll see a description of the error and the error's numeric ID. And when the processing ends (that is, when all the attributes have been processed), SQL Server Profiler will show a `Progress Report End`.

Internally a dimension-processing operation spawns a processing job for every attribute in the dimension. These processing jobs generate the same events—`Progress Report Begin` and so on. Most of the time the processing of one attribute can run in parallel to the processing of other attributes. When one attribute is related to another, the second one is processed after the first one. For example, because all the attributes are related to the key attribute of the dimension, directly or indirectly, the key attribute is processed last.

Take a look Figure 38.8, which shows the steps that are typically reported during the processing of a single dimension attribute. Not all of these steps will necessarily be executed during the processing of a dimension attribute, so you might not see events associated with some of these steps in SQL Server Profiler. For example, only a grouping attribute needs to go through the discretization step. Another example: Only for attributes with a large number of members does the Analysis server need to create groups during processing. For such big attributes, you would see only `Progress Report` events with `GroupData` and `GroupDataRecord` subclasses.

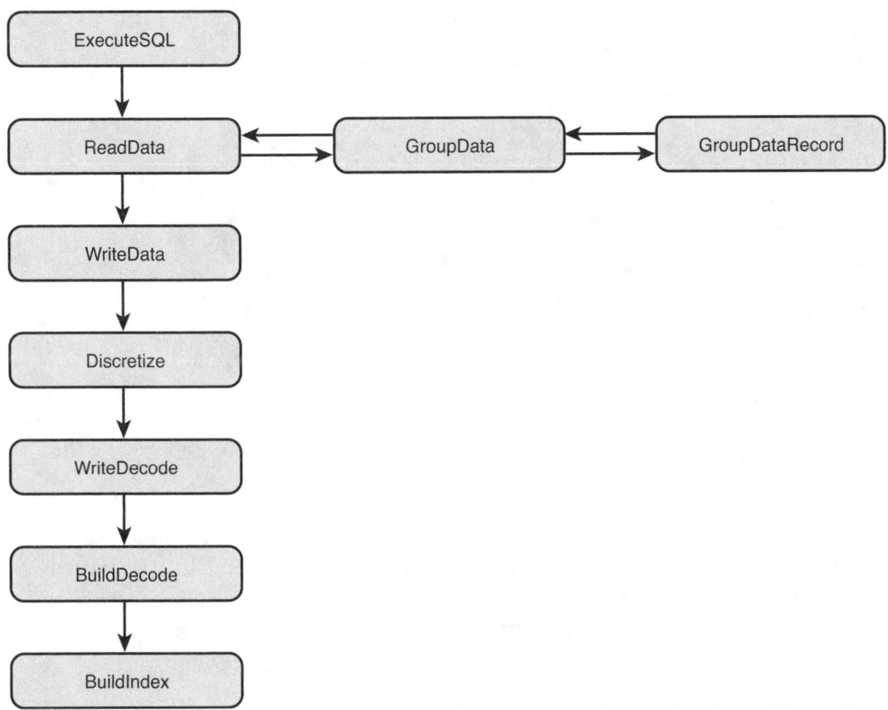

FIGURE 38.8 The trace of processing of a dimension attribute.

Because the processing of dimension attributes can take place asynchronously, you can feel like you're seeing a real tangle in SQL Server Profiler. You have to be careful about reading the events. The trick is to keep track of what appears in the `ObjectName` column. That's where you can see the object that is being processed and differentiate the reporting events of one attribute from those of another, even though the events generated are likely to be intermixed.

Let's go back to the example we introduced at the beginning of the chapter. Figure 38.9 shows what you might see in SQL Server Profiler during the processing of our `Product` dimension. Actually, you might not see it exactly this way. We moved the `ObjectName` column a little to the left so that it would fit in the illustration.

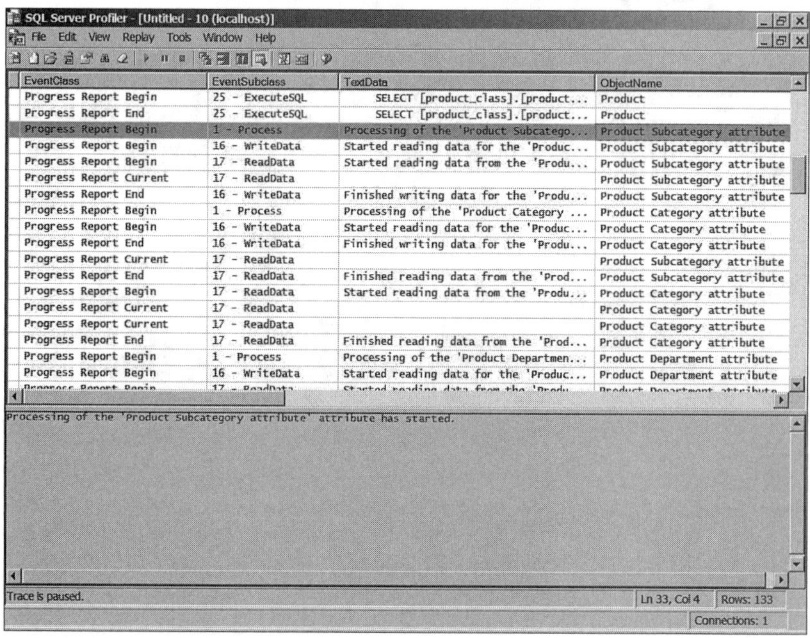

FIGURE 38.9 SQL Server Profiler shows events that report the progress of processing the attributes of the `Product` dimension.

Take a look at the columns `EventClass`, `EventSubclass`, and `ObjectName`. Where you see the name of the object being processed in the `ObjectName` column, you can tell that the events of the `ProductCategory` attribute and those of the `ProductSubcategory` attribute are intermixed. For the `Product` attribute, the `Progress Report Begin` event with a subclass of `ExecuteSQL` indicates the beginning of processing the attribute.

When the `ExecuteSQL` operation completes, the server issues another `Progress Report Begin` event with the subclass `ReadData`; and when that one is complete, the server issues another `Progress Report Begin` event with the subclass `WriteData`. If you look closely at Figure 38.9, you'll see that the description of the `WriteData` subclass is `Started reading` data. That's obviously not the right description; it's a result of a bug in Analysis Services. It wasn't fixed by the time we wrote this book, but it might be by the time you look at your own SQL Server Profiler.

You'll find something else interesting as you look closely at Figure 38.9. It looks like the server started writing data before it read the data. That is, you might see the Progress Report End event with the ReadData subclass come after the one with the WriteData subclass. This can occur because of the asynchronous nature of the execution. If a writing operation is fast, it can get its event into the queue before the reading operation.

Reporting the Progress of Partition Processing

Processing partitions is bit different from processing of dimensions, but not by much. Figure 38.10 shows the steps that are typically reported during processing of a partition. Like the processing of dimension attributes, it starts with executing SQL statements. In addition, partition processing also has ReadData and WriteData subclasses. However, unlike the processing of dimensions, the processing of partitions has an additional step. The server has to process aggregations, too, so you would see events for the BuildAggsAndIndexes step in SQL Server Profiler during processing of the partition.

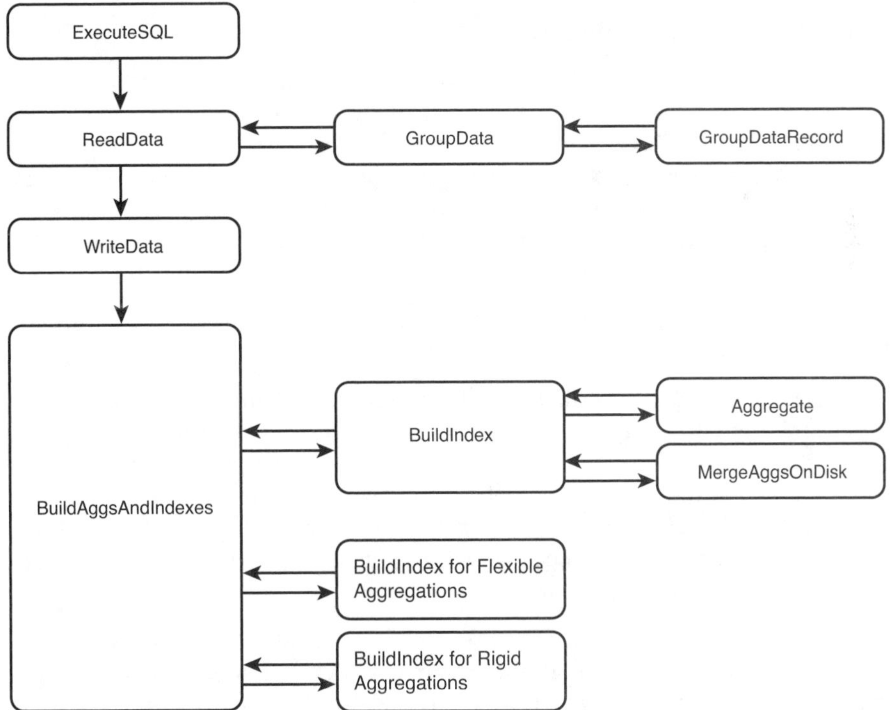

FIGURE 38.10 SQL Server Profiler shows events that report the progress of processing the partition.

38

Query Execution Time Events

When you're troubleshooting query performance, it's very helpful if you can see exactly what's happening while a query is being executed. For example, one query might be executed faster than the exact same query on a different cube. In addition, you're going to want to know which partitions are participating in the resolution of the query. You also are likely to want to know whether the query hit an aggregation. The information that can answer these questions is available to you through the query execution time events available in Analysis Services.

Analysis Services gives you a set of query-processing events such as `Query Subcube`, `Query Dimension`, and `Get Data from Aggregation`. These events were created specifically to report on events that happen during query resolution. In addition, you'll see some of the same progress report events that we used to monitor the processing of object. Internally it's the storage engine subsystem of Analysis Services that implements processing and access to the data files. During query execution, you'll see progress reports whenever the storage engine needs to scan a partition to retrieve data needed for a query.

Running a Simple Query

Let's see what happens with this simple query:

```
SELECT measures.members ON COLUMNS FROM [Warehouse and Sales]
```

Start SQL Server Profiler and click the See All Events check box so that you can see all the events and their columns. Now select all the query processing events. To make things easy, click the Organize Columns button and move the `ObjectPath` column so that it's right after the `TextData` column. Run a trace and then send a Multidimensional Expressions (MDX) query. You should then see SQL Server Profiler as it appears in Figure 38.11.

At the top of SQL Server Profiler, you can see a `Query Begin` event. This event informs you that the server has received your query.

The next event is the `Query Cube Begin Event`. On the surface, it might seem like the `Query Begin` event is simply telling you that query has been executed against the cube. `Query Cube Event` events, along with other query-processing events, has been added to Analysis Services to reveal more information about the inner workings of the system. These events provide information about the operations of the formula engine and tell you what code is currently executing. Specifically, the `Query Cube Begin Event` tells you that the formula engine started executing your query.

The next events indicate that server has begun serializing results back to the client. First it serializes the axes. When the server has all the information it needs about which members lie on the axes, it starts asynchronously streaming the results of the query to the client.

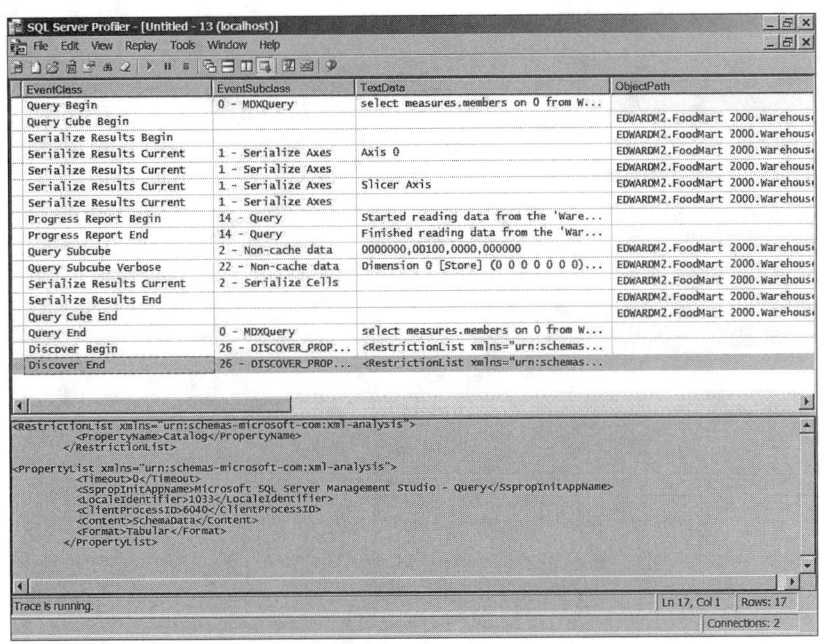

FIGURE 38.11 SQL Server Profiler shows the events for your MDX query.

After the serialization events comes a set of progress report events telling you that the storage engine is reading data from the `Warehouse and Sales` partition. After it generates `Query Subcube` and `Query Subcube Verbose` events, the server starts steaming cell data to the client.

Changing the Simple Query

With our sample MDX query, the `Warehouse and Sales` cube doesn't have any aggregations. If you were to design aggregations for the sample `Warehouse and Sales` cube and send the same query, SQL Server Profiler would show you additional events associated with the query resolved from the aggregations (shown in Figure 38.12). For more information about aggregations, see Chapter 23, "Aggregation Design and Usage-Based Optimization."

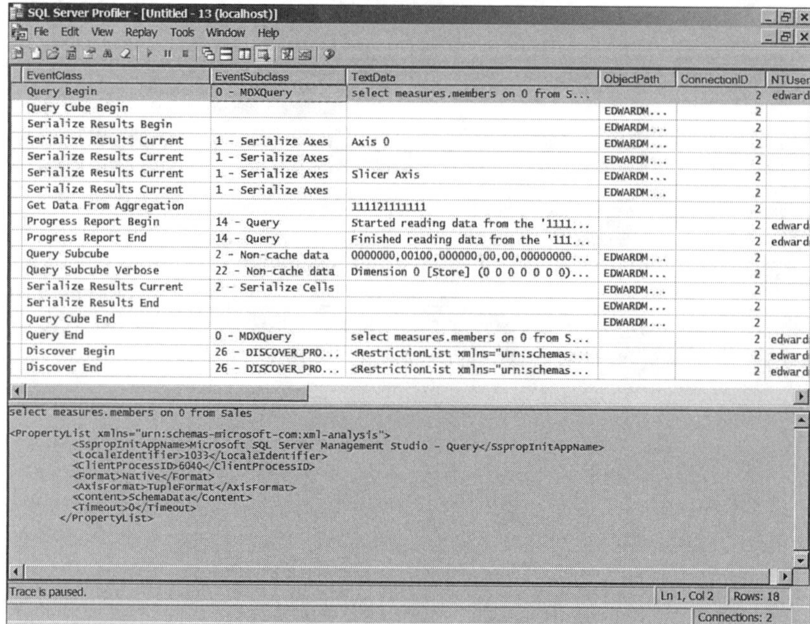

FIGURE 38.12 SQL Server Profiler shows the events for a query against the `Sales` cube.

In SQL Server Profiler, you see the `Query Begin` and `Query Cube Begin` events, just as you did with your earlier query. But now you have a new event that occurs just before the progress report events: the `Get Data from Aggregation` event. This event (and the `Progress Report` events) indicates that the query hit an aggregation and that the server used the aggregation in the resolution of the query.

If you look at the `Text Data` column of the `Progress Report Begin` and `Progress Report End` events, you'll see `Started (or Finished) reading data from the 11112111111 aggregation`. That string of numbers is the name of the aggregation that the query hit.

Running a More Complex Query

Now let's try a query that is a little bit more complex:

```
SELECT {[Measures].[Store Sales]} ON COLUMNS,
[Product].[Product Name].members ON ROWS
FROM [Warehouse and Sales]
```

With this query, SQL Server Profiler shows a different face (of course). You should see what is shown in Figure 38.13.

Just as with our other queries, SQL Server Profiler starts with the `Query Cube` and `Query Cube Begin` events. The serialize events follow, and they feature a new event indicating that the server had to serialize one more axis; we now have axis 0 and axis 1. If you

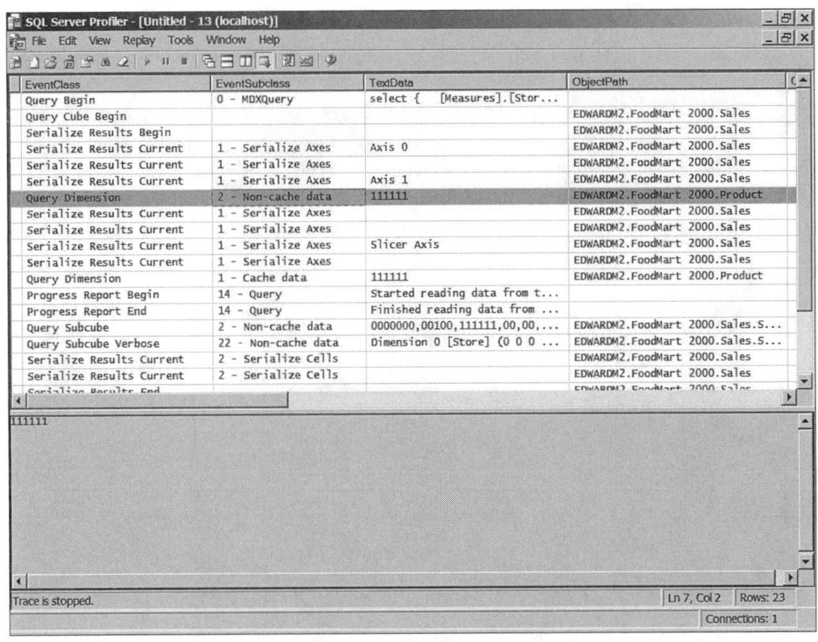

FIGURE 38.13 SQL Server Profiler shows the events of your complex query.

compare this figure to Figure 38.12, you'll see that Figure 38.13 is missing the `Get Data from Aggregation` event. We didn't hit an aggregation with this query.

Right in the middle of the serialize events, you see a new event: `Query Dimension`. To populate the axis rows, the formula engine has to query the storage engine for members of the `Product` dimension. The `ObjectPath` column for the `Query Dimension` event is where you can see the name of the dimension being queried.

Changing the Complex Query

Now let's complicate the query some more. To tell the truth, we haven't even scratched the surface of MDX queries. Queries such as these would appear only in the first few pages of any respectable MDX book. However, these queries are about right for illustrating the inner workings of Analysis Services.

We're not going to change our query very much. We're just going to ask the server to give us only products that were actually sold in the stores; in other words, the products that have no NULL sales. (You can find more details about MDX queries in Chapter 11, "Advanced MDX.")

```
SELECT {[Measures].[Store Sales]} ON COLUMNS ,
NON EMPTY [Product].[Product Name].members ON ROWS
FROM Sales
```

The events of this query appear in Figure 38.14.

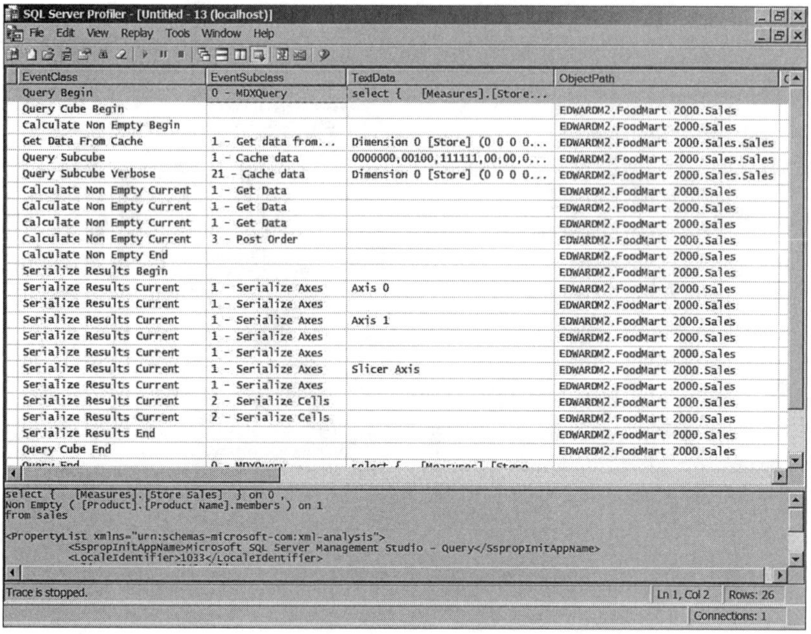

FIGURE 38.14 SQL Server Profiler shows the events for our new query.

Think back to the last query we sent. Now we have some events that occur after `Query Begin` and `Query Cube Begin`. These are new for us: `Calculate Non Empty Begin` and `Get Data from Cache`. The `Calculate Non Empty Begin` event indicates that the server has entered the `Calculate Non Empty` code path. The purpose of this code path is to have the server, as it resolves the query, eliminate any coordinates whose intersections contain no results. `Get Data from Cache` indicates just what it seems to indicate: The data that is retrieved is coming from a cache. The cache was created when our previous query read its data. Therefore, you don't see any `Progress Report` events here.

Two events, `Calculate Non Empty Begin` and `Get Data from Cache`, occur before the serialization events. The server can't populate the axes before it gets the result set, so the server first has to issue a request for the result set.

Changing Your Query Just a Little More

The query execution in the preceding example is pretty compact. Now we'll change our query just a little. Replace the `Non Empty` (an operator in MDX) with `NonEmpty` (a function in MDX). The operator/function difference is important in MDX. You can find details about these concepts in Chapter 11.

We didn't change much in the query, but this time there's quite a difference in the results presented in SQL Server Profiler (see Figure 38.15).

SQL Server Profiler - [Untitled - 13 (localhost)]

File Edit View Replay Tools Window Help

EventClass	EventSubclass	TextData	ObjectPath	Conne
Calculate Non Empty Begin			EDWARDM2.FoodMart 2000.Sales	
Get Data From Cache	1 - Get data from...	Dimension 0 [Store] (...	EDWARDM2.FoodMart 2000.Sales.Sales	
Query Subcube	1 - Cache data	0000000,00100,111111,...	EDWARDM2.FoodMart 2000.Sales.Sales	
Query Subcube Verbose	21 - Cache data	Dimension 0 [Store] (...	EDWARDM2.FoodMart 2000.Sales.Sales	
Calculate Non Empty Current	1 - Get Data		EDWARDM2.FoodMart 2000.Sales	
Calculate Non Empty Current	1 - Get Data		EDWARDM2.FoodMart 2000.Sales	
Calculate Non Empty Current	1 - Get Data		EDWARDM2.FoodMart 2000.Sales	
Calculate Non Empty Current	3 - Post Order		EDWARDM2.FoodMart 2000.Sales	
Calculate Non Empty End			EDWARDM2.FoodMart 2000.Sales	
Serialize Results Begin			EDWARDM2.FoodMart 2000.Sales	
Serialize Results Current	1 - Serialize Axes	Axis 0	EDWARDM2.FoodMart 2000.Sales	
Serialize Results Current	1 - Serialize Axes		EDWARDM2.FoodMart 2000.Sales	
Serialize Results Current	1 - Serialize Axes	Axis 1	EDWARDM2.FoodMart 2000.Sales	
Serialize Results Current	1 - Serialize Axes		EDWARDM2.FoodMart 2000.Sales	
Serialize Results Current	1 - Serialize Axes		EDWARDM2.FoodMart 2000.Sales	
Serialize Results Current	1 - Serialize Axes	Slicer Axis	EDWARDM2.FoodMart 2000.Sales	
Serialize Results Current	1 - Serialize Axes		EDWARDM2.FoodMart 2000.Sales	
Query Dimension	1 - Cache data	111111	EDWARDM2.FoodMart 2000.Product	
Get Data From Cache	1 - Get data from...	Dimension 0 [Store] (...	EDWARDM2.FoodMart 2000.Sales.Sales	
Query Subcube	1 - Cache data	0000000,00100,111111,...	EDWARDM2.FoodMart 2000.Sales.Sales	
Query Subcube Verbose	21 - Cache data	Dimension 0 [Store] (...	EDWARDM2.FoodMart 2000.Sales.Sales	
Serialize Results Current	2 - Serialize Cells		EDWARDM2.FoodMart 2000.Sales	
Serialize Results Current	2 - Serialize Cells		EDWARDM2.FoodMart 2000.Sales	

```
Dimension 0 [Store] (0 0 0 0 0 0 0) [Store Name attribute]:0 [Store Name - Store Manager]:0 [Store Name - Store Sqft]:0
Dimension 1 [Time] (0 0 3 0 0) [Month attribute]:0 [Quarter attribute]:0 [Year attribute]:[1997] [time_id]:0 [the_date]:
Dimension 2 [Product] (* * * * * *) [Product Name attribute]:* [Brand Name attribute]:* [Product Subcategory attribute]:*
Dimension 3 [Promotion Media] (0 0) [Media Type attribute]:0 [promotion_id]:0
Dimension 4 [Promotions] (0 0) [Promotion Name attribute]:0 [promotion_id 1]:0
Dimension 5 [Customers] (0 0 0 0 0 0 0 0 0) [Name attribute]:0 [Name - Education]:0 [Name - Gender]:0 [Name - Marital Sta
Dimension 6 [Education Level] (0 0) [Education Level attribute]:0 [customer_id]:0
```

Trace is running. Ln 21, Col 2 Rows: 30 Connections: 2

FIGURE 38.15 SQL Server Profiler shows the results of your query.

Even though the events are pretty much the same, this query produced an extra request for cell results—that is, data. The server makes an extra trip to retrieve data before it can populate the axes.

CHAPTER 39

Backup and Restore Operations

IN THIS CHAPTER

- Backing Up Data
- Backing Up Related Files
- Backup Strategies
- Automating Backup Operations
- Restoring Lost or Damaged Data
- MDX Extensions for Browsing Your File System

Backup and restore are two of the most important and most commonly executed administrative actions. These two operations are often spoken of together in the context of routine management operations. However, they aren't at all similar operations when you get right down to it.

Backing up data is a routine management operation, typically scheduled to run automatically on a regular basis. However, there is nothing routine about the restore operation. Restoring data is something done in times of crisis, when something unexpected happens to the system, such as hardware or software failures.

Despite these differences, we cover the two operations in one chapter because they are related in terms of their functions. You back up your data so that you can restore it if you ever need to.

Backing Up Data

Historically speaking, the backup functionality in Analysis Services 2005 became an integral part of Analysis Server. This is quite a valuable improvement over Analysis Services 2000, where it was a standalone application. Analysis Services 2008 brings a new level of scalability and performance due to a new, high-performance storage subsystem, comparable in performance with raw OS file operations.

The backup function in Analysis Services operates at the database level only. The functionality for backing up a single partition, a dimension, and for differential backups is reserved for future versions.

Planning Your Backup Operation

When you're planning to back up your database files, a number of factors determine which approach is best for your operation:

- The size of the database to be backed up
- The type of storage you use for dimensions and partitions (ROLAP/MOLAP/HOLAP)
- The amount of time allocated for the backup operation
- High-availability requirements

NOTE

You can't use the Analysis Services backup function to back up a relational database.

Figure 39.1 shows an example of different storage modes for Analysis Server objects. Analysis Server can back up multidimensional online analytical processing (MOLAP) objects, but it cannot back up relational online analytical processing (ROLAP) objects.

Three MOLAP partitions are shown in Figure 39.1. Two partitions (`Part1` and `Part2`) store their files in the `Data` directory. `Part3`'s files are located in `c:\dir3`. Analysis Server can back up these files.

The figure also shows two partitions: `Part1R` and `Part2R`. These partitions depend, respectively, on the SQL Server tables `Tab1R` and `Tab2R`. We use the `R` to indicate that these partitions are ROLAP partitions. Analysis Server cannot back up these files because they are relational. You have to back up relational databases on your own.

We have one more partition, `WrtB`, the writeback partition. It depends on a SQL Server table `WrtB`. Writeback partitions are ROLAP partitions; therefore, Analysis Server can't back them up, you must back up relational databases on your own.

So, when you are backing up an Analysis Services database, you should also consider backing up following;

- Server configuration file (`msmdsrv.ini`)
- ROLAP partition and dimension data
- Writeback data for supporting dimension and cell writeback
- Query log table
- Backup databases containing data for the remote partitions in case you have designed a scaled-out solution

Analysis Services backup will back up the following:

- Database metadata
- Partition and dimension data files located in the data folder
- Partition files located outside of the data folder in separate folders

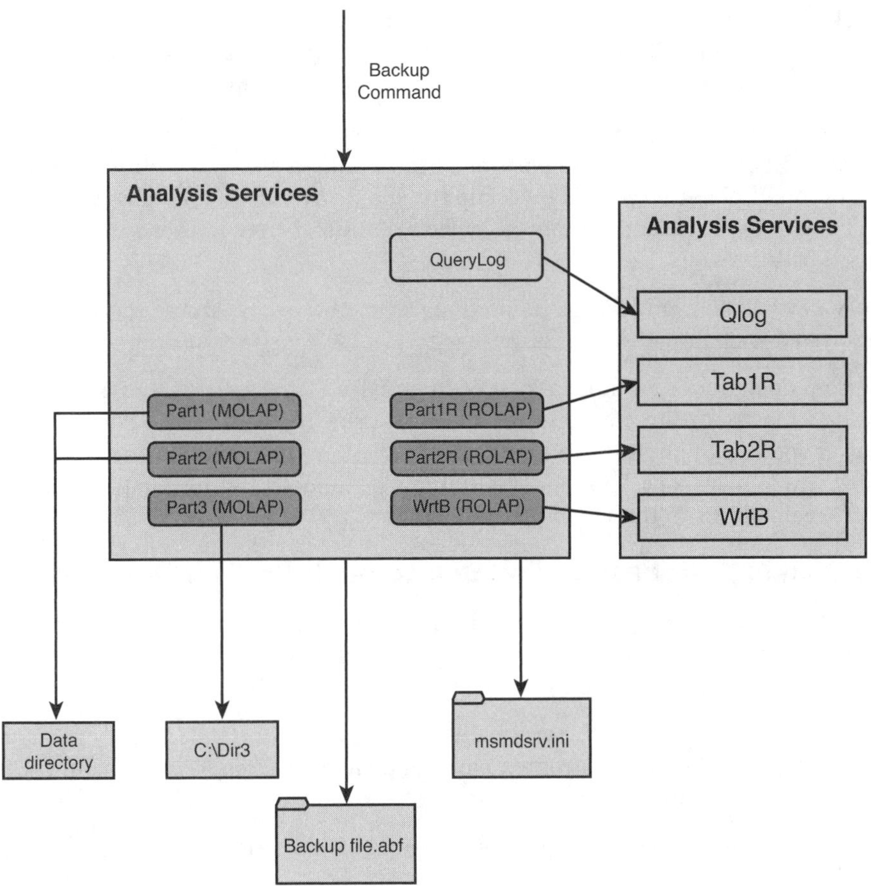

FIGURE 39.1 Analysis Server has different storage modes for objects.

We'll cover a couple different ways to run the backup operation. You can use our convenient Backup Database dialog box, or you can write a Data Definition Language (DDL) command and send it directly to the Analysis Server or write an Analysis Management Objects (AMO) application to perform a backup operation from your application.

In either case, the outcome of the backup operation on a database is a single file with the extension `.abf` (Analysis backup file). Analysis Server enforces this extension.

When they were designing the backup subsystem, the Analysis Services architects focused on a number of goals. The following list shows what they accomplished:

- Backup operation tasks work efficiently and quickly, consuming as few I/O resources and as little memory as possible. Ideally, backup performance should be bound only by the performance of the I/O subsystem.

- The backup operation is nonintrusive. While a backup operation is running, users can query data in Analysis Server. Users also should be able to process objects inside the database being backed up while a backup operation is running.
- Just like any other Analysis Services operation, the backup operation conforms to strict transactional rules. For example, one of those rules is that the versions of the objects of the database saved in the backup file should be consistent across the database. The backup file should contain no objects of different versions or partially processed partitions.
- The backup subsystem provides rich functionality so that users can use the backup operation in a wide range of business scenarios.
- The backup operation is an integral part of the Analysis Services security system, providing a means for the user to secure the data inside the backup file. For example, a user operating remotely can browse the file system on a remote computer to decide where to place a backup file. This eliminates the need for the database administrator to gain access to the server file system.

Using the Backup Database Dialog Box to Back Up Your Database

The Backup Database dialog box is a perfect training tool if you prefer the ease and convenience of the dialog box or if you're performing an Analysis Services backup operation for the first time. Here's how you can use the Backup Database dialog box.

Start in SQL Server Management Studio and right-click the name of the database you want to back up. Choose Back Up from the contextual menu. Figure 39.2 shows what you will see if you right-click the sample database, FoodMart 2008.

Use the right pane of this dialog box to provide information and select options for backing up a database:

- The Database text box contains the name of the database you're going to back up. Typically, this text box is already populated with the name of the database you right-clicked to get to this dialog box.
- The Backup File text box contains the name of the file your database will be backed up to. The default location for this file is the folder `C:\Program Files\Microsoft SQL Server\MSAS10.MSSQLSERVER\OLAP \Backup`. You can type the full path or click Browse to change the location of your backup file.

Beneath the Options label, you'll find some choices to make about your backup operation:

- Select the Allow File Overwrite check box to overwrite the existing backup file with the new one. If you don't want to overwrite the existing file, don't select this option and do choose a different name for the backup file you're creating. For example, if you back up FoodMart 2008 every day, you might name one file `FoodMart2008_Jan1`, and the next one `FoodMart2008_Jan2`. If you don't select this option, and give your backup file a name that matches a file that already exists, you'll get an error.
- Select the Apply Compression check box to compress your backup file. If you select this option, Analysis Server will spend additional time compressing the data. In

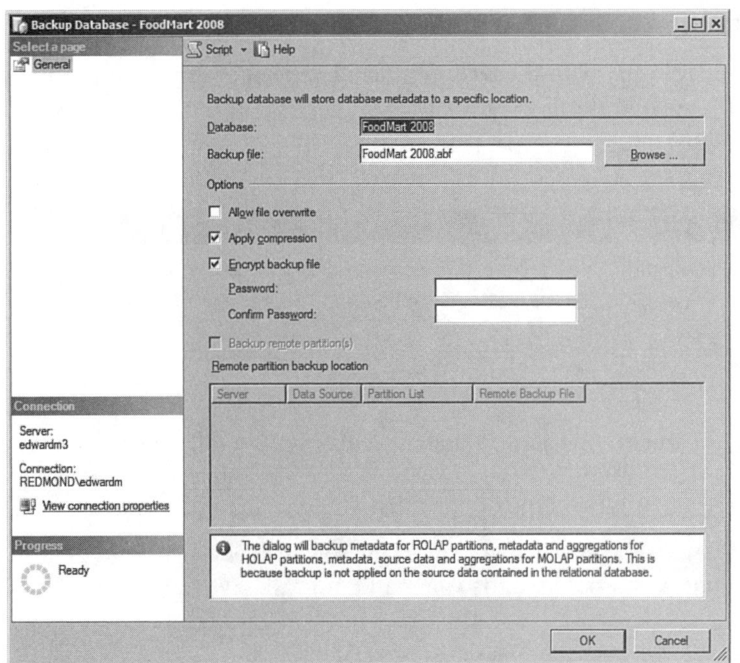

FIGURE 39.2 The Backup Database dialog box presents options for your backup file.

addition, some Analysis Services data is already stored in a compressed format, which means that you might not gain a lot of storage room by selecting this option.

- Select the Encrypt Backup File check box to encrypt your file. If you select this option, you'll have to type a password in the Password text box and type it again in the Confirm Password text box. Record this password in some safe place; you'll need it if you ever want to restore your database from this backup file.

  The last note here is about providing a password in the backup command. The password you provide will be used by Analysis Services to encrypt the backup file.

  Although Analysis Server doesn't enforce any password policies that relate to password length, numbers, and special characters used in the password, we recommend that you use general security precautions when selecting you password.

- Select the Backup Remote Partition(s) check box if your database has remote partitions and you want to back them up in this operation. If you select this operation, the locations of your remote partition backup files appear in the box below Remote Partition Backup Location.

When you're ready to submit your choices to the server, click OK. If you then look in the location where you saved your backup file, you will find your file with an `.abf` extension.

As an alternative to using the Backup Database dialog box, you can use a SQL Server Integration Services task to submit the command.

Using a DDL Command to Back Up Your Database

If you prefer, you can work directly with the DDL command instead of using the Backup Database interface to back up your database. The easiest way to explain this is to use the Script function of the dialog box.

NOTE

You could also use any text editor to write your own command. If you save it with the extension `.xmla`, you can use SQL Server Management Studio to send your command directly to Analysis Server.

Along the top of the right pane in the Backup Database dialog box, you'll find a series of buttons. Click the button labeled Script. If you move to SQL Server Management Studio, you'll see a command script that reflects the options that you selected in the dialog box.

If you right-clicked the FoodMart 2008 database and made no changes in the Backup Database dialog box options, you would see the command in Listing 39.1.

LISTING 39.1 A Simple DDL Command for Backing Up FoodMart 2008

```
<Backup xmlns="http://schemas.microsoft.com/analysisservices/2003/engine">
     <Object>
         <DatabaseID>FoodMart 2008</DatabaseID>
     </Object>
     <File>FoodMart 2008.abf</File>
</Backup>
```

Default options are not present in the scripted command. Because you selected the default for each option in the dialog box, the command contains just these few lines identifying the database to be backed up and the name of the backup file. If you had made other choices in the dialog box, the scripted command would be somewhat longer.

To issue this command, just click the Execute button. If you look in the folder `C:\Program Files\Microsoft SQL Server\MSAS10.MSSQLSERVER\OLAP \Backup`, you'll see that the `FoodMart 2008.abf` file has been created.

The designers of Analysis Server built in both simplicity (as shown in the preceding example) and power to execute backups for the most complex configurations. The power is provided by the options that you can add to the DDL command. The complete set of options for the Backup command appears in Listing 39.2, with the default values in bold.

LISTING 39.2 Complete Set of Options for the DDL **Backup** Command

```
<Backup>
<object>object_ref</object>
```

```
<File>BackupFile</File>
[<AllowOverwrite>true/false</AllowOverwrite>]
[<BackupRemotePartitions>true/false</BackupRemotePartitions>]
[<Locations>
          [<Location>
<File>BackupFile</File>
<DataSourceID>Datasource ID</DataSourceID>
          </Location>]
     </Locations>]
[<ApplyCompression>true/false</ApplyCompression>]
[<Password></Password>]
</Backup>
```

For an explanation of these options, see the preceding section, "Using the Backup Database Dialog Box to Back Up Your Database."

Backing Up Related Files

In addition to your database files, we recommend that you regularly back up several related files: configuration files, writeback files, and query logs. If you back up these files, too, you should be well covered for restore operations and any others that you might perform in the future.

Backing Up the Configuration File

For a full Analysis Server backup, we also recommend that you make a manual backup of the Analysis Server config file (`msmdsrv.ini`). By default, the config file is located in your `%Program files%\ Microsoft SQL Server\MSAS10.MSSQLSERVER\OLAP\Config` folder.

Backing Up the Query Log Database

The Query log is a mechanism that enables Analysis Server to collect statistics on the number of queries and types of queries that your users send. These statistics are presented in a SQL Server table, which you can examine when you want to know what your users are doing. You can use this information to build your aggregations and optimize the performance of your cubes.

39

NOTE

Earlier versions of Analysis Server supported Access databases and other relational databases for the Query log. However, Analysis Services supports only SQL Server databases (SQL Server versions 2000, 2005, and of course, 2008).

You can set the Query log feature in SQL Server Management Studio. Right-click your Analysis Server, and choose Properties from the contextual menu. In the Analysis Server Properties dialog box, look for three properties:

- `Log\QueryLog\CreateQueryLogTable` is set to `true` if Analysis Services is set to collect Query log data, and `false` if it is not.
- Click `Log\QueryLog\QueryLogConnectionString` to examine the connection string, which contains the SQL Server name and the name of the database.
- `Log\QueryLog\QueryLogTableName` shows the name of the SQL Server table that contains the Query log data.

Because the table that contains the Query log data is in a relational database, you must set up its backup operation separately from the backup operation for your multidimensional database.

Backing Up Writeback Tables

If you have enabled the writeback capability for one or more of your measure groups and dimensions, you'll want to make sure that you back up the writeback tables during your backup operation. For information about that setting, see Chapter 7, "Measures and Multidimensional Analysis."

Your first step is to determine whether writeback is defined in a measure group. To do that, expand the tree in the left pane of SQL Server Management Studio. A measure group that has writeback enabled will have a child folder under the Writeback folder that is the child of the folder for the measure group.

If you have measure groups with the writeback capability enabled, you'll want to make sure that your writeback tables are backed up along with your multidimensional database. The first thing you need to do is figure out is where the writeback table is located. You can use the Scripting functionality of SQL Server Management Studio to find the writeback table:

1. Right-click the writeback partition in the folder tree.
2. Select Script Writeback As, select Create To, and then select New Query Editor Window.
3. Look for `DataSourceID` and the `DbTableName` in the script that appears in the window (see Listing 39.3).

LISTING 39.3 Writeback Partition DDL Definition

```
<Partition>
<ID>WriteTable_Sales</ID>
<Name>WriteTable_Sales</Name>
<Source xsi:type="TableBinding">
<DataSourceID>FoodMart</DataSourceID>
<DbTableName>WriteTable_Sales</DbTableName>
</Source>
<StorageMode>Rolap</StorageMode>
<ProcessingMode>Regular</ProcessingMode>
<Type>Writeback</Type>
</Partition>
```

Now that you know the relational database and table names, you can back them up. You can create a full backup of the `FoodMart` relational database or make sure that content of `WriteTable_Sales` is stored along with the Analysis Server backup.

Backup Strategies

Let's look at some common backup scenarios—most, but not all, of which will use either the Backup Database dialog box or a DDL file.

Typical Backup Scenario

In a typical backup scenario, you build a system of scheduled backups. You can use SQL Server Integration Services to schedule them to run automatically without human interaction.

NOTE

SQL Server Integration Services enables you to execute and schedule any Analysis Services command.

It's a good idea to schedule backup operations immediately after your database is incrementally updated so that you always have the most recent version available for a restore operation, if one is needed.

High-Availability System Backup Scenario

When Analysis Server is part of a highly available application, there is, unavoidably, a stretch of time that users will find the system unavailable or will experience slowdowns while the files are being backed up. In this situation, even though the backup functionality operation is designed to be minimally intrusive, you can't avoid a little intrusiveness. Therefore, you need to do what you can to your backup operation to make the performance hit as small as possible.

Standalone Backup Server

One backup strategy for highly available systems is to maintain a standalone backup server on a separate computer. You set up a procedure to synchronize the state of the backup server with the state of the main production server. You can use the `Synchronize` command to set up this procedure. You can find detailed information about the synchronize functionality in Chapter 40, "Deployment Strategies."

One advantage of this strategy is that it results in a lighter load on the production server computer. After it synchronizes the state of the production computer with the state of the backup server, the `Synchronize` command is very efficient at determining which portions of the database have changed. It then sends to the backup server only the files that differ from the database on the main server.

In this operation, the production computer performs only read operations, and those only for portions of the database. Therefore, less interference occurs with ongoing user operations, and you have a lighter load on the production computer.

Physical Backups of Data Files

Various hardware and software vendors offer a number of packaged backup solutions that are based on making physical backups of the Analysis Services files. One advantage of these packaged solutions is that some of the vendors can achieve high efficiency and performance with file transfers. In addition, some of them are pretty successful in dealing with large amounts of data.

For a physical backup, you can use the new ability of Analysis Services 2008 to attach and detach the database. Simply detach the database you would like to preserve and move it to a different folder. Make a physical backup of that folder, and then attach the database back to the server.

If you decide to back up your entire data folder without detaching databases, you need to be aware of a couple of issues:

- If some of the partitions are not located in the data folder, it's hard for the backup application to find all the files required for backup.
- It's not possible to back up one database at a time. All Analysis Server data has to be backed up simultaneously.

Automating Backup Operations

Because the backup operation is a routine operation, automating it is a good practice. You can do this in several ways. You would choose one based on the design of your application. We cover just a few of them here.

SQL Server Agent

You can use the SQL Server Agent infrastructure to create a new job that includes a step that sends a `Backup` command to Analysis Services. To refresh your knowledge of the `Backup` command and how to generate a backup script, look back at the "Using a DDL Command to Back Up Your Database" section earlier in this chapter.

After you have your backup script, create a new job and then create a new step in that job. Set the step type to SQL Server Analysis Services Command. You can paste your `Backup` command into the command body, and then select the server that will receive the command.

SQL Server Integration Services

You can use SQL Server Integration Services (SSIS) to create a package that includes an `Analysis Services Execute DDL` task to send a command to back up your databases. First, create a new Integrations Services project in Business Intelligence Development Studio and drag an `Analysis Services Execute DDL` task onto the Control Flow pane. Then double-click your task and click General in the Analysis Services Execute DDL task editor, as shown in Figure 39.3.

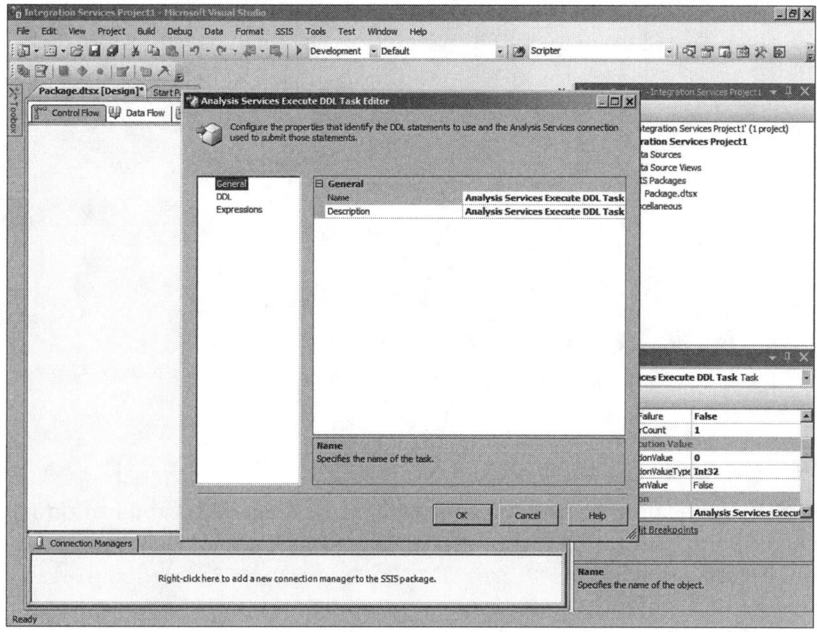

FIGURE 39.3 Use the Analysis Services Execute DDL task editor to get the DDL Statements dialog box.

Enter a name for your task. Next, click DDL in the editor to create a new connection that points to your Analysis Server. Leave `SourceType` as it appears (`Direct Input`). Click SourceDirect and insert your `Backup` command into the DDL Statements box that appears, as shown in Figure 39.4. To refresh your knowledge of the `Backup` command and how to generate a backup script, see the "Using a DDL Command to Back Up Your Database" section earlier in this chapter. Now you can debug your SSIS project to test your backup package.

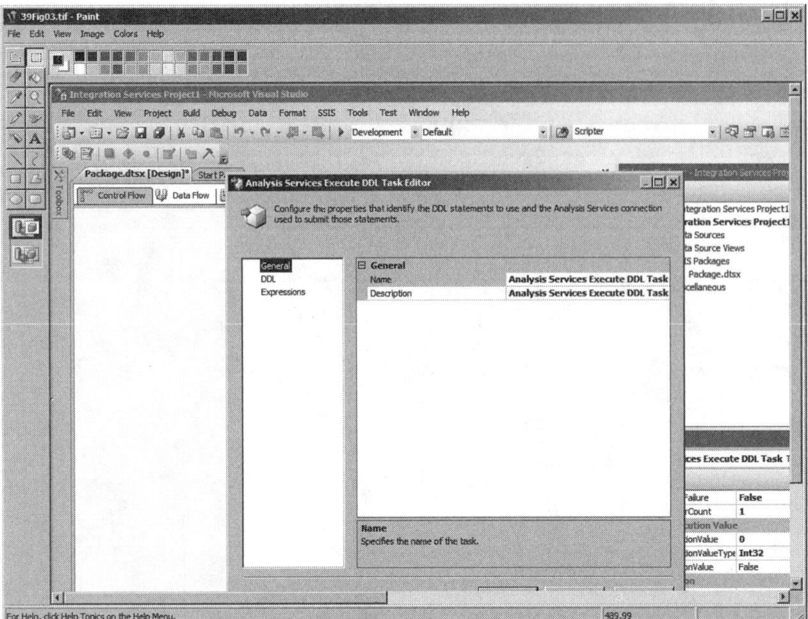

FIGURE 39.4 Insert your `Backup` command into the DDL Statements dialog box.

AMO Application

You can create an AMO application to back up your data. There is an AMO application for backup among the sample applications. If you installed the samples, you will find the backup application in `C:\Program Files\Microsoft SQL Server\100\Samples\Analysis Services\Programmability\AMO\BackupAndRestore`. Just modify the sample project to point to your database. Then, you can compile the application and use any task-scheduling service to schedule it to run.

Restoring Lost or Damaged Data

Backup operations are generally set to run on a regular basis. With regular backups, you can be sure that you'll have something to restore your data from, in case you have to do a restore operation. On the other hand, a restore operation is generally run in response to some event, such as a hardware malfunction or human error.

The `Restore` command reads all the files from a backup file that you specify. It places them into their target locations and, at the end of the transaction, renames the files. If you plan to overwrite your existing database, you will nevertheless see new files appear in the same folders as the existing data files. Your existing files won't be overwritten until the operation has been committed. Therefore, make sure that you have enough storage room for both sets of files.

The primary design goal of the restore operation is to provide a rich set of functionality and to enable you to custom configure your restored database. The restore operation has quite a number of options, according to the various physical layouts of data files.

Using the Restore Database Dialog Box

The Restore Database dialog box is a perfect training tool if you're performing an Analysis Services restore operation for the first time, or if you prefer the ease and convenience of the user interface. Here's how you can use the Restore Database dialog box: Start in SQL Server Management Studio and right-click the Databases folder. Choose Restore from the contextual menu. Figure 39.5 shows what you would see.

The options in this dialog box are arranged in three categories:

- The Restore Target category, where you choose the database you need to restore from the drop-down list in the Restore Database text box. If you want to keep your damaged database alongside the restored one, just type a different name for the restored database. In addition, you supply the name of the backup file you want to use in the From Backup File text box.
- In the Options category, you have two choices to make:
  - Select the Allow Database Overwrite box if you want your newly restored database to replace the damaged one. If you don't want the restored database to overwrite the old one, you must give the restored database a different name.
  - Select the Include Security Information box if you want to skip restoring membership information for Analysis Server security roles.
- Fill in the Encryption category if the database backup file you are restoring this database from was encrypted when it was created. In such a case, in the Password text box, enter the password that was set for the backup file when it was created.

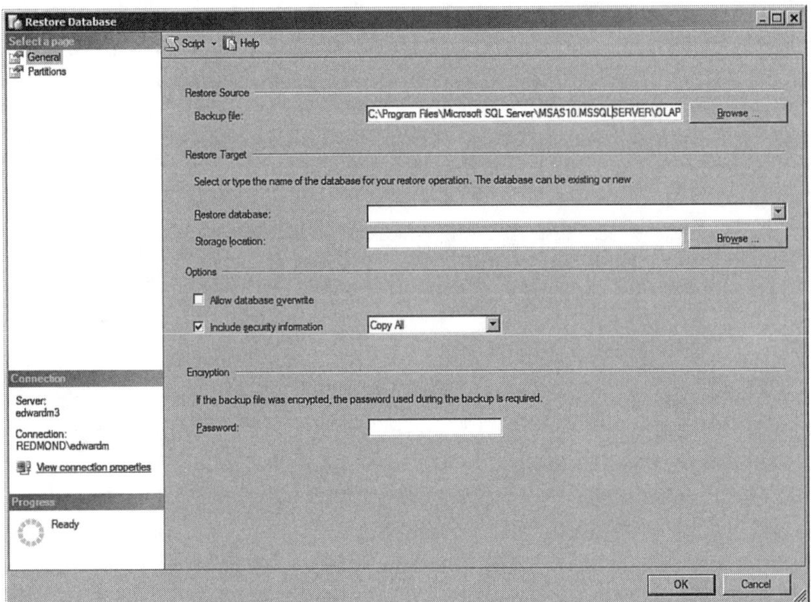

FIGURE 39.5 The Restore Database dialog box offers options for your restore operation.

Using the DDL Command to Restore Your Database

If you prefer, you can work directly with the DDL command to restore your database, instead of using the Restore Database dialog box user interface. The easiest way for us to explain this is to use the Script function of the dialog box.

NOTE

You can also use any text editor to write your own command. If you save it with the extension `.xmla`, you can use SQL Server Management Studio to send your command directly to Analysis Server.

Along the top of the right pane in the Restore Database dialog box, you'll find a series of buttons. Click the button labeled Script. If you move back to SQL Server Management Studio, you'll see a command script that reflects the options you selected in the dialog box.

If you right-clicked Databases and selected Restore from the contextual menu, selected `FoodMart 2008.abf` in the From Backup File box in the Restore Database dialog box options, and then clicked Script, you would see the command shown in Listing 39.4.

LISTING 39.4 A Simple DDL **Restore** Command

```
<Restore xmlns="http://schemas.microsoft.com/analysisservices/2003/engine">
  <File>C:\Program Files\Microsoft SQL Server\MSSQL.1\OLAP\Backup\FoodMart
2008.abf</File>
```

```
  <Security>SkipMembership</Security>
</Restore>
```

Its designers built in to Analysis Services both simplicity (as shown in the preceding example) and power to execute restore for the most complex configurations. Power is provided by the options that you can add to the DDL command. The complete set of options for the `Restore` command appears in Listing 39.5, with the default values in bold.

LISTING 39.5 The Complete Set of **Restore** Command Options

```
<Restore>
<File>BackupFile</File>
[<DatabaseName>DatabaseName</DatabaseName>
<DatabaseID>DatabaseID</DatabaseID>]
[<AllowOverwrite>true/false</AllowOverwrite>]
[<Locations>
          [<Location>
[<File>BackupFile</File>]
<DataSourceID>DataSource ID</DataSourceID>
[<DataSourceType>Remote¦Local</DataSourceType>]
     [<ConnectionString>Analysis Server Connection string</ConnectionString>]
     [<Folders>
          [<Folder>
               <Original>old folder</Original>
               <New>new folder</New>
          </Folder>]
     <Folders>]
     </Location>]</Locations>]
     [<Security> CopyAll¦ SkipMembership </Security>]
     [<Password></Password>]
</Restore>
```

For an explanation of these options, see the previous section, "Using the Restore Database Dialog Box."

Using DISCOVER_LOCATIONS to Specify Alternative Locations for Partitions

When you restore a database with partitions that are not located in the default `Data` folder, you have to find the locations of the partitions so that you can specify the alternative locations. To look into a backup file and find the locations of partitions, you use the `DISCOVER_LOCATIONS` mechanism. You can issue the `DISCOVER_LOCATIONS` request against Analysis Server and restrict it with the name of your backup file. You can get two pieces of important information with `DISCOVER_LOCATIONS`: the location of the database's partitions and their sizes. With this information, you can be sure that each partition will be restored to its correct location.

Because the `Restore` command requires a valid password to access a backup file, a `DISCOVER_LOCATIONS` request will not yield the content of the backup file without a valid password. Be sure that you have the correct password before you begin a `DISCOVER_LOCATIONS` request.

We recommend that you use the Restore Database dialog box in SQL Server Management Studio to make these adjustments. You can, however, write your own DDL command.

When you click Partitions in the tree in the left pane of the Restore Database dialog box in SQL Management Studio, a `DISCOVER_LOCATIONS` request is automatically issued against the backup file you specified. You'll then see a list of all the partitions inside the file so that you can choose locations.

NOTE

Partitions located in the current folder must be in the same folder after the database is restored. You can change the location of the folder, however. This restriction also applies to all the partitions located in the `Data` folder. If the partition is in the `Data` folder before the restore operation, it must be in the `Data` folder afterward.

All this means that your restore operation requires a little preparation. If you plan to have partitions reside on a different drive after the restore operation, it's best to create those partitions in their own folders in the first place, even if they're in the neighborhood of the `Data` folder (see Listing 39.6). Planning ahead gives you some room to play with different locations later.

LISTING 39.6 A **`Restore`** DDL Command for Remapping Partition Locations

```
<Restore xmlns="http://schemas.microsoft.com/analysisservices/2003/engine">
  <File>C:\Program Files\Microsoft SQL Server\MSSQL.1\OLAP\Backup\FoodMart
➥2008.abf</File>
  <Locations>
    <Location>
      <Folders>
        <Folder>
          <Original>C:\tmp\data</Original>
          <New>C:\tmp\data1</New>
        </Folder>
      </Folders>
    </Location>
</Restore>
```

After you issue this command, any partition that was in the `c:\tmp\data` folder is restored into the `c:\tmp\data1` folder.

MDX Extensions for Browsing Your File System

Assume that a database administrator, working from a remote computer, needs to create a backup of a database. This database administrator is not the administrator of the computer running Analysis Services. It's a good idea to restrict the privileges of the database administrator rather than have one person serve as both the database administrator and the computer administrator.

To create the backup file, the database administrator has to specify the path to the backup file to be created, and that path must be valid for the computer running Analysis Services, not the remote computer from which the backup command is issued. Therefore, our database administrator needs limited rights to browse the file system on the server.

There are number of typical approaches—that is to say, approaches other than using Multidimensional Expressions (MDX)—to granting such limited rights. The following list contains just a few of them, along with some of their disadvantages:

- Create a network share and give the database administrator rights to the share.

  The disadvantage of this approach is that it requires the administrator of the server computer to be present and spend a lot of time managing security for network shares. It can make the life of security experts a nightmare.

- Create a virtual directory in a local web server and give the database administrator rights to browse the folders in the virtual directory.

  Creating a virtual directory in a web server might not be a bad idea from the perspective of the network administrator. It's relatively easy to open an HTTP port in the firewall. However, for a number of reasons, companies find it impractical to run and maintain a web server on the computer that is dedicated to Analysis Services operations.

- Give the database administrator full administrative rights to the server computer so that she can connect through default network shares.

  Elevating the privileges of a database administrator to the level of administrator of the Analysis Server is probably the least time-consuming approach from the perspective of the Analysis Server administrator. However, we strongly recommend against this practice from a security perspective. This approach might be tolerated in small organizations, but it really conflicts with a robust multilevel security system.

- Build file-browsing client/server software that enables users to browse the server file system remotely. This is the MDX file extensions approach.

The MDX Extensions

Analysis Services supplies four MDX extensions that you can use to give a database administrator a limited set of rights to browse the file system on the computer running Analysis Services:

- **SystemGetLogicalDrives**—If you issue this request, something like the following would be returned:

  ```
  'C:' , 200
  'D:' , 300
  ```

  The first value in each line represents a drive letter. The second value represents the space (in megabytes) available on that drive.

- **SystemGetSubdirs**—With this request, use an input parameter that is a string that represents a Universal Naming Convention (UNC) path. This command returns a list of all the folders on that drive. You can issue subsequent calls to this function to browse the file system.

- **SystemGetFiles**—Use this request to find all the files in a specific folder.

- **SystemGetFileExists**—Use this request with an input parameter of a filename to determine whether a specific file exists on the system. It returns a value either confirming or denying that the file exists. This command comes in handy in a situation where you need a simple test (for example, to avoid overwriting a backup file).

Security Considerations

When you use these MDX file system–browsing extensions against a default installation of Analysis Server, you won't gain the ability to browse all folders on all drives. If you had a default installation of Analysis Server on the C: drive, you would have access to only two folders:

- `C:\Program Files\Microsoft SQL Server\MSAS10.MSSQLSERVER\OLAP \Backup`
- `C:\Program Files\Microsoft SQL Server\MSAS10.MSSQLSERVER\OLAP\Log`

The purpose of these file system–browsing extensions is to give you access to only the files you need to perform administrative duties. The administrator of Analysis Server has control over which folders are allowed for browsing.

You can use the server property `AllowedBrowsingFolders` to add browsable folders to the default list. The property contains a string that represents the list of folders allowed for browsing, with a vertical separator dividing one folder from another. With a default installation of Analysis Services, you would find a string like this:

```
C:\Program Files\Microsoft SQL Server\MSAS10.MSSQLSERVER\OLAP\Log¦C:\Program
C:\Program Files\Microsoft SQL Server\MSAS10.MSSQLSERVER\OLAP\Backup
```

If you want to give full access to the C: and D: drives, change the value for `AllowedBrowsingFolders` to `C:¦D:`.

CHAPTER 40

Deployment Strategies

IN THIS CHAPTER

- Using the Deployment Wizard
- Synchronizing Your Databases
- Synchronization and Remote Partitions
- Synchronization and Failover Clusters

In a typical application lifecycle, you first manipulate your data in the development environment where you can change any element of the application if you don't like the way it behaves when it works with the data. Then, you move the application (and likely the data) to the test environment, from which it is likely to return to the development environment after the testers find problems. At some point, you're satisfied with the application and are ready to deploy it to a production environment.

Analysis Services 2008 provides a couple of different ways to deploy a database—one of the common tasks performed by database developers and administrators. Analysis Services includes a Deployment Wizard, a step-by-step user interface you can use for performing deployment tasks. However, you can just as easily deploy your project by generating a script. Alternatively, you can deploy your database from a test to a production environment using the `Synchronize` command.

Using the Deployment Wizard

The Deployment Wizard is a step-by-step user interface you can use to deploy the file that results from building an Analysis Services project (`projectname.asdatabase`) to a target server. You start with an Analysis Services project developed in Business Intelligence Development Studio (BI Dev Studio). In the beginning of the wizard, you browse for the database file in your project:

1. You give the wizard the name of the database on the target server that you want to deploy data to. If there isn't a database by that name on the target server, the

wizard creates one for you. The data in an existing database is overwritten in the deployment operation.

It then shows you options for deploying your project to the computer running Analysis Services.

2. First, you specify what you want to do about partitions and roles:
   - For partitions, you can either overwrite existing partitions or keep the partitions for existing measure groups.
   - For roles and members, you can either overwrite the existing roles and members or keep the existing roles and members.
3. Next, you set your configuration properties:
   - For existing objects, we recommend that you retain the configuration and optimization settings.
   - For the remaining options, which are automatically populated for you, we recommend that you stick with the defaults.
4. Then you specify the data source connection strings and impersonation information. The wizard gives you the option of choosing a data source impersonation mode, which allows you to select the most appropriate mode, depending on your security model.
5. Your next step is to specify the processing method you want: Default Processing, which means that Analysis Server will choose the processing mode for each object; Full Processing, which means that every object will be fully processed; or No Processing, which means that your database won't be processed. For more information about processing, see Chapter 26, "Server Architecture and Command Execution."
6. If you specified either Default or Full Processing, you can specify your processing option for writeback: Use the Existing Writeback Table Unless None Exists and Create a New One If Necessary; Create a New Writeback Table (if one already exists, your processing will fail); or Create Always, which means that a new writeback table will be created and any existing writeback table will be overwritten. For more information about writeback, see Chapter 26.

NOTE

You have the option to process all your objects in one transaction instead of processing each object in a separate transaction.

If you're ready to deploy the database to the target server, click Next on the Confirm Deployment screen of the wizard. Alternatively, you can create a deployment script made up of the choices you made in the wizard. All you have to do is specify the location you want to save the script to and click Next. With a script, you can run the Deployment Wizard in silent mode.

NOTE

The Deployment Wizard will not execute the deployment if you select the Generate Script option on the last page of the wizard.

Synchronizing Your Databases

In many situations, you might implement your applications in an environment where the production servers are separate from the testing (staging) servers. Analysis Services gives you a way to deploy changes from the test (or development) environment to the production environment. You can use the `Synchronize` command to keep the two databases in sync.

After you've created your Analysis Services database and then processed and tested it on your test server, you want to be able to click a single button and deploy the database to the production server. You can do your deployment in the different way, by backing up the database from the test server, moving it over to the production server, and then restoring it.

With Analysis Services, you can send a single `Synchronize` command to synchronize the two databases. You send the command to your target server—the one to which you want to copy the data. The target server connects to the source server and pulls data from it. For a more detailed explanation of what is going on, look at Figure 40.1.

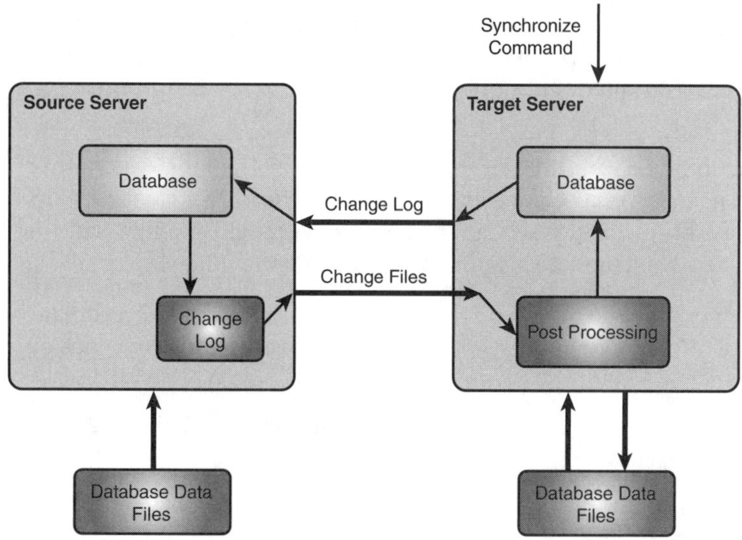

FIGURE 40.1 The sequence of operations during the `Synchronize` command.

First, the target server sends the command to obtain a read lock on the database it needs to synchronize into. This is done to make sure that the source database is not changed during the synchronization transaction. Then, the target server requests from the source server a list of physical files that belong to the database. After it receives the file list, the target server compares the list to its own list—you can think of the target server as comparing the state of the source database to its own state. At this point, the target server comes up with the differences of the state of its own database to the state of the database on the source server and sends the list to the source server. The number of different files can be smaller than the number of files in the database on the source server. The source server sends files delta to the target according to the list.

After it receives the new files (the ones that were different), the target server releases the lock on the source database. At this point, the target server is no longer dependent on the source server and can finish the operation itself. This last stage is called post-processing, and it consists of the following:

- If you specified mapping in the `Synchronization` Data Definition Language (DDL) command, the server remaps the locations of the partitions.
- The database encryption key is regenerated.
- If you chose to rename the database during the synchronization operation, the server regenerates new IDs for the objects.
- The server updates the roles and role members depending on the options specified in the DDL command.

Object definitions, such as cell calculations, are not visible to the end user. In many cases, they represent intellectual property that is guarded under database administrator privileges. Therefore, you need to grant database administrator rights for the source server to the target server's account. The `Synchronize` command is issued under the target server's account because the target server queries not only the data, but also the definitions of the objects.

From a high-level abstraction, you can think of the process as one of pulling data, rather than pushing data. The target server receives a command to synchronize a database with the corresponding database on the source server. The target server begins pulling data from the source server. The advantages of this pull model include the following:

- The pull mechanism is simple. There is no need for the source server to coordinate the transaction. The target server requests data, and thereby acquires a read lock on the source server.
- From a security standpoint, there is no need for the source server to have any specific permissions on the target server.

On the other hand, the pull model is not suited for scenarios in which you need to synchronize a change from the source server to several target servers in a single transaction. In such a situation, the push model works better; the source server is then responsible for coordinating the transaction.

You can use the Analysis Services `Synchronize` command through the user interface or through a DDL command.

Using the Synchronize Database Wizard

To open the Synchronize Database Wizard from SQL Server Management Studio, right-click the Databases node in the tree console and select Synchronize from the contextual menu. Figure 40.2 shows the Synchronize Database Wizard.

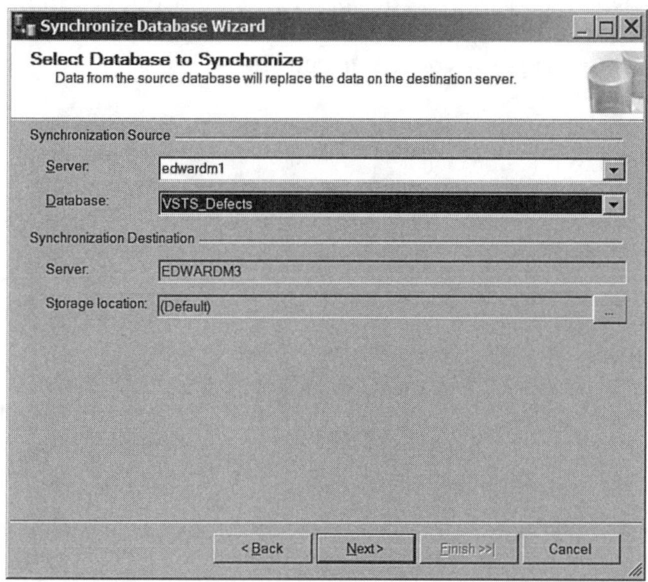

FIGURE 40.2 You can use the Synchronize Database Wizard to synchronize two databases.

1. On this first page, in the Source Server text box, type or select the name of the server that contains the database you want to copy from.

   In the Source Database text box, type or select the name of the database you want to copy from.

   The Destination Server text box is automatically populated for you.
2. Next, you specify your security options. Select Skip Membership if you want to skip the membership information for Analysis Server security roles. Select Copy All if you want all the membership information in the source server to be copied to the target server. If you select Ignore All, the target server keeps all roles and their members as they were before the synchronization operation.
3. For the last step, either you can synchronize your databases now or you can save the script that the wizard automatically created as you made your choices.

Using a DDL Command to Synchronize Databases

If you prefer, you can work directly with the DDL command instead of using the Synchronize Database Wizard user interface to synchronize your database. The easiest way to explain this is to start with the wizard.

NOTE

You could also use any text editor to write your own command and send it directly to the Analysis Server. All you have to do is give your file the extension .xmla.

At the end of the Synchronize Database Wizard, click the option Save the Script to a File, and then open the file in the SQL Server Management Studio. If you used the wizard to make the simplest choices, the `Synchronize` DDL command would be pretty short, as shown in Listing 40.1.

LISTING 40.1 A Simple **Synchronize** DDL Command

```
<Synchronize xmlns:xsi="http://www.w3.org/2001/XMLSchema-instance"
xmlns:xsd="http://www.w3.org/2001/XMLSchema"
xmlns="http://schemas.microsoft.com/analysisservices/2003/engine">
     <Source>
          <ConnectionString>Provider=MSOLAP.3;Data Source=
localhost;ConnectTo=9.0;Integrated Security=SSPI;Initial Catalog=
FoodMart 2008</ConnectionString>
          <Object>
               <DatabaseID>FoodMart 2008</DatabaseID>
          </Object>
     </Source>
     <Locations/>
      <SynchronizeSecurity>SkipMembership</SynchronizeSecurity>
      <ApplyCompression>true</ApplyCompression>
</Synchronize>
```

All the script in Listing 40.1 does is specify the connection string to the source server and the name of the database to synchronize with. The complete set of options for the `Synchronize` DDL command appears in Listing 40.2, with the default values in bold.

LISTING 40.2 The Complete Set of Options for **Synchronize**

```
<Synchronize>
<source>
     <ConnectionString> Connection string</ConnectionString>
     <object>object_ref</object>
</source>
[<Locations>
          [<Location >
               [<DatasourceID>Datasource ID</DatasourceID>]
               [<DataSourceType>Remote|Local</DataSourceType>]
               [<ConnectionString>Analysis Server Connection
               string</ConnectionString>]
```

```
            [<Folders>
                [<Folder>
                    <Original>old folder</Original>
                    <New>new folder</New>
                </Folder>]
            </Folders>]
    </Location>]
</Locations>]
[<SynchronizeSecurity> CopyAll¦ SkipMembership ¦ IgnoreSecurity
</SynchronizeSecurity>]
[<ApplyCompression>true/false</ApplyCompression>]
</Synchronize>
```

NOTE

If you specify <SynchronizeSecurity> as SkipMembership and this is the first time you are synchronizing to the target server, the cubes in your database might become unavailable to users. This happens because the Synchronize command empties all role objects.

You can change the data source by setting <DataSourceID> and <ConnectionString>. Make sure that <DataSourceType> is set to Local. If <DataSourceType> is set to Remote, this portion of the DDL command will specify remote partitions.

If you set <ApplyCompression> to TRUE, you specify that Analysis Services will compress any data sent from the source server to the target server. This option is most valuable in cases where a slow network connects the two servers. The compression algorithm that Analysis Services uses is an advanced one, developed internally at Microsoft. When the compression option is set, synchronization uses the resources of both the source and target servers. You can expect a slight slowdown in performance even if the servers are using minimal resources.

Similarities Between the Synchronization and Restore Commands

There are many similarities between the Synchronize and Restore DDL commands. (The Restore command was discussed in Chapter 39, "Backup and Restore Operations.")

- Both commands have a <Folders> section for you to specify the locations for partitions that are not located in the default Data folder.
- Both commands have properties that you can use to specify behavior in the presence of remote partitions.
- Both commands have similar security issues. In both cases, you specify whether you want to overwrite membership information on the target server.

Synchronization and Remote Partitions

Synchronization in the presence of remote partitions is similar in many ways to a restore process in the presence of remote partitions. Figure 40.3 shows one server (Source Master) with remote partitions on two other servers (Source Slave1 and Source Slave2). If the synchronization operation works with only the database on Source Master and the database on the server Target Master, and doesn't take into account the remote partitions, we run into a problem.

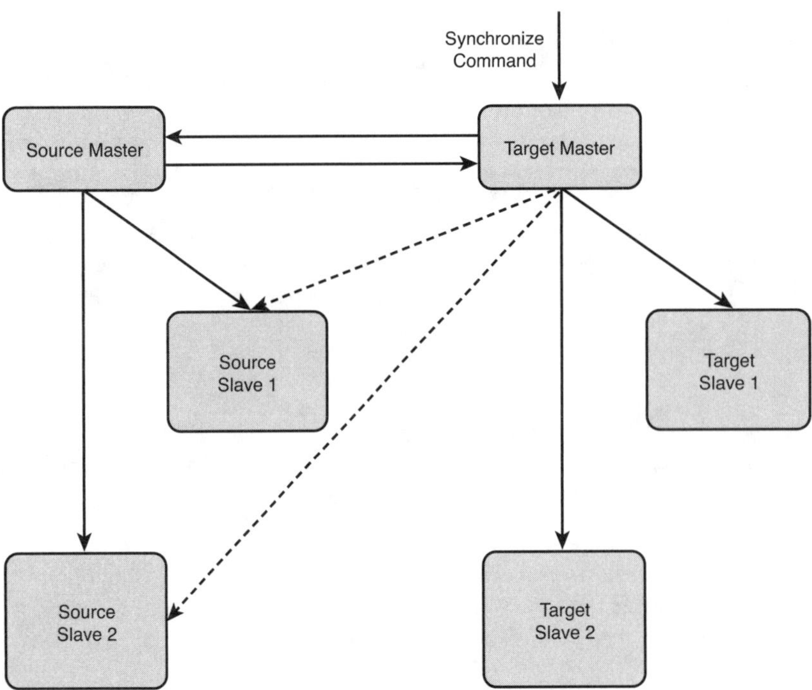

FIGURE 40.3 Synchronizing databases with remote partitions requires special attention.

The resulting database on the target server (Target Master) looks for its remote partitions on the original source servers (Source Slave1 and Source Slave2), represented in the figure by broken lines. Two different master servers cannot reference a single set of remote partitions. With the situation represented by the broken lines, any attempt by the target server to reach the remote partitions will fail.

To avoid this problem, the synchronization operation must synchronize the source slave servers to the target slave servers and adjust the corresponding data sources. To accomplish this, make sure that the `Synchronize` command includes additional information for each source slave server with which a target slave server should synchronize. The functionality in the Synchronize Database Wizard enables you to add this information. In fact, it won't let you proceed if you don't add the information.

Figure 40.4 shows the wizard's Specify Locations for Remote Partitions page, which appears only if there are remote partitions for your database. The wizard lists all the remote partitions for the source server under Source Server (in our example, Source Slave1 and Source Slave2). Under Destination Server, you can browse for the partitions on the target slave servers.

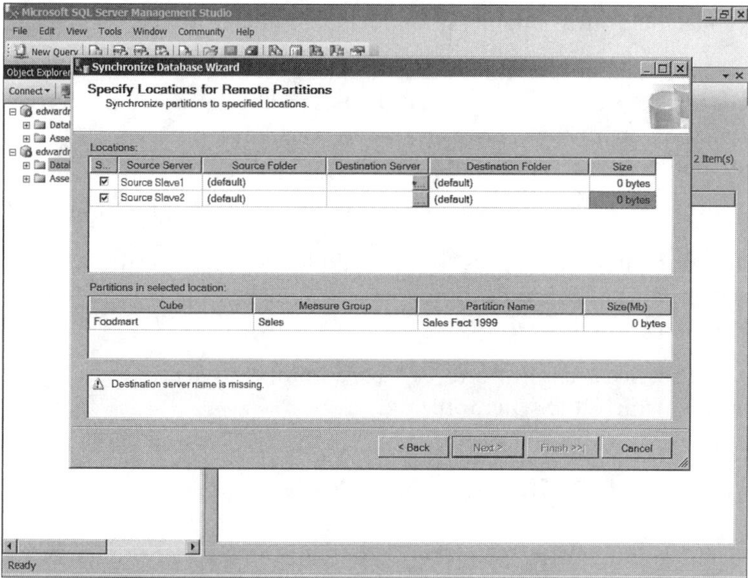

FIGURE 40.4 You can use this page of the Synchronize Database Wizard to map slave servers for synchronization.

You can't advance in the wizard until you have mapped all the source slave servers to the appropriate target slave servers. Behind the scenes, the wizard is composing a DDL command, as most wizards do. The wizard uses the information on this page to compose the part of the command that maps the source slaves to the target slaves. Listing 40.3 contains that part of the `Synchronize` command.

LISTING 40.3 Mapping Remote Partitions

```
<Location>
     <DatasourceID>Slave1</DatasourceID>]
     <DataSourceType>Remote</DataSourceType>]
     <ConnectionString>Provider=MSOLAP.4;Data Source=Target Slave1;Initial
Catalog=Slave1</ConnectionString>
</Location>
```

After it receives a `Synchronize` command that contains this `<Location>` section, the Target Master server connects to the Target Slave1 server and instructs it to synchronize itself with Source Slave1. If several slave servers are involved, the Target Master coordinates the synchronize operation with all the slave servers. Only after all the slaves have finished the synchronization operation does the Target Server commit the transaction.

Coordination between several servers is a complicated task. You must take care of the following details when you synchronize a database that has remote partitions:

- Before you synchronize, make sure that all the target slave servers are set up correctly to contain the slave databases and that the `MasterDataSourceID` property is set. For more information about how to set up slave servers, see Chapter 25, "Building Scalable Analysis Services Applications."
- Use the default locations for your remote partitions; don't use custom locations.
- If the source master configuration changes so that it no longer keeps partitions on one of the slave servers, after synchronization you have to delete the slave database that the target master server no longer uses.
- The target slave server service account needs to have administrative privileges for the source slave server with which it is synchronizing.

Synchronization and Failover Clusters

The synchronization operation is agnostic as to whether either the source or the target server is installed and operating on a failover cluster. If the failover operation occurs during synchronization, Analysis Services automatically rolls back the unfinished synchronization transaction.

You can restart the `Synchronize` command when the failover operation is complete.

CHAPTER 41
Resource Monitoring

IN THIS CHAPTER

- DMVs and SchemaRowsets
- Querying DMVs and SQL Semantics
- Monitoring Connections, Sessions, and Commands
- Monitoring Server State
- Using Perfmon Counters

Monitoring resources of server applications is one of the most important duties of a system administrator. For example, an Analysis Services administrator might need to pinpoint which query caused an overload of server resources and take action to cancel such a query. At any time, an administrator may also need to get a clear picture of resource consumption and various activities on the server. No less important is the need for a server administrator to be able to view an overall snapshot of the health of a server, analyze hardware-utilization trends, and when armed with this information, plan for future upgrades.

Designers of Analysis Services consider the capability to monitor resources a high priority, and so that capability has improved with each release. Through all versions, the designers have implemented performance monitors. Analysis Services 2005 introduced trace infrastructure and integration with SQL Server Profiler (discussed in Chapter 38, "Using Trace and Audit Analysis Services"). Analysis Services 2005 also supported several basic `Discover` (also known as `SchemaRow set` requests) requests for monitoring server activities (for example, `DISCOVER_SESSIONS` and `DISCOVER_CONNECTIONS`).

Analysis Services 2008 introduces an entirely new internal infrastructure for monitoring server resources. It also provides a new interface for exposing Analysis Services management-related information called Dynamic Management Views (DMVs). Currently, DMVs provide the most convenient way to track server resources.

In this chapter, we drill down into DMV functionality and cover a variety of ways to monitor system resources, such as performance counters.

DMVs and SchemaRowsets

Historically speaking, the main resource monitoring application programming interface (API) for Analysis Services has been `Discover` XML for Analysis (XML/A) requests (further discussed in Chapter 32, "XML for Analysis"), also known as `SchemaRowsets` (a term introduced by an OLE DB specification). The new DMVs are an ad-hoc SQL query-based API similar to SQL Server relational services DMVs. Before we discuss the benefits of using DMVs, let's discuss the overall architectural structure of DMVs and the new resource-monitoring infrastructure, as shown in Figure 41.1.

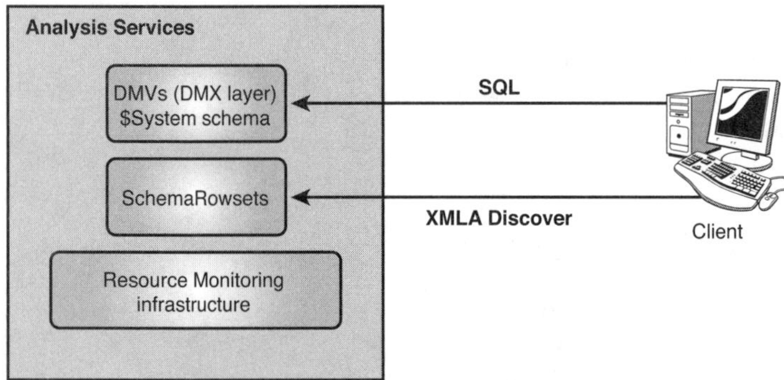

FIGURE 41.1 Different ways of querying server resources.

As you can see in Figure 41.1, under the hood the DMVs are implemented as a layer on top of the `SchemaRowset` infrastructure. DMVs take advantage of a SQL-like query language that is internally supported by the data-mining parser. After a request to the DMV is sent to Analysis Services, it is parsed by the data-mining parser, which then generates an internal `SchemaRowset` request. The system executes the `SchemaRowset` request and performs the necessary post-processing operations such as filtering or sorting.

The new API gives you the power and flexibility of a SQL query language to access system information. In the past, when executing a `SchemaRowset` request, you either needed to write an application (such as the ActivityViewer sample for Analysis Services 2005) or create a long XML document; DMVs enable you to access the same information by just typing a query in SQL Server Management Studio. Any other application that invokes the Analysis Services OLE DB provider or ADOMD.NET provider can query DMVs. Therefore, you can set up a linked server in SQL Server relational services to expose information provided by Analysis Services DMVs by querying SQL Server. You can use reporting services to build reports showing Analysis Services resource consumption and overall system health.

Querying DMVs and SQL Semantics

DMVs are exposed as part of the `$System` schema, and their naming matches the names of the underlying `SchemaRowsets`. For example, if you want to query information about client connections (exposed by the `DISCOVER_CONNECTIONS SchemaRowset` request), you use the `Discover_Connections` DMV by entering the following query in the DMX query editor of SQL Server Management Studio:

```
select * from $system.discover_connections
```

Figure 41.2 shows the results of this query.

CONN...	CONNECTION_...	CO...	CO...	CONNECTION_HOST_APPLI...	CONN...	CONNECTION_...	CONNECTION_...	CONNECTION_...	CONNECTION_
6	REDMOND\ed...		[::1...	MDXSample	10/15/...	45442	10/15/2008 5:4...	10/15/2008 5:4...	45286
8	REDMOND\ed...		[::1...	MDX Studio	10/15/...	24507	10/15/2008 5:5...	10/15/2008 5:5...	15
1	REDMOND\ed...		[::1...	Microsoft SQL Server Manag...	10/15/...	20872	10/15/2008 5:5...	10/15/2008 5:5...	20841
11	REDMOND\ed...		[::1...	Microsoft SQL Server Manag...	10/15/...	7238	10/15/2008 5:5...	10/15/2008 5:5...	46
10	REDMOND\ed...		[::1...	Microsoft SQL Server Manag...	10/15/...	7160	10/15/2008 5:5...	10/15/2008 5:5...	7113

FIGURE 41.2 Connections currently opened by client applications.

Analysis Services does not differentiate between requests related to the resource monitoring and other `SchemaRowset` requests, such as requests for available cubes or dimensions. Therefore, you can use DMVs to access all `SchemaRowsets` provided by Analysis Services. We will not attempt to enumerate every single `SchemaRowset` or DMV available for you to query; instead, you can find all of them by sending the following query:

```
select * from $system.dbschema_tables.
```

To see the columns that are available for each of the DMVs, send this query:

```
select * from $system.dbschema_columns.
```

This query returns a long list. Use a `WHERE` clause to restrict this list only to columns relevant to a specific DMV. For example, to list columns related to the `Discover_Connections` DMV, use the following query:

```
select * from $system.dbschema_tables where table_name = 'DISCOVER_CONNECTIONS'
```

Unfortunately, Analysis Services does not support all constructs of the SQL language for querying DMVs. For example, names of the DMVs are case sensitive; this explains why in the preceding query, we had to spell out the name of the DMV in all uppercase letters.

Among many SQL constructs, Analysis Services supports the following (which are the more frequently used):

- **Conditions**—Use a `WHERE` clause to narrow the query results. You can use `AND`/`OR` operators as part of your condition.

- **`Distinct` clause**—This clause enables you to retrieve a set of distinct values. For example, you can query for a distinct set of users who have opened connections to Analysis Services by using the following query:

```
select distinct Connection_user_name from $system.discover_connections
```

- **`Order by`**—This syntax enables you to sort the result. For example, to get a list of server connections sorted according to the time they were opened, send the following query:

```
select * from $system.discover_connections order by connection_start_time
```

- **Data projection**—You can apply calculations to retrieve results. For example, Analysis Services returns time-related information in Greenwich mean time (GMT), but you can report the connection start time in Pacific standard time (PST) by sending the following query:

```
select connection_start_time - 7/24 as [PST start time] from
$system.discover_connections.
```

- **Function calls**—You can use a variety of functions to manipulate query results. For example, to return dates in a different format, use the `Format` function and send the following query:

```
select Format (connection_start_time - 7/24, 'MM/dd/yyyy/HH/mm') as [PST
start time] from $system.discover_connections
```

Limitations of the SQL constructs include the following:

- The `Group By` clause is not supported, nor are additive functions such as `Count` and `Sum`.
- The `Join` clause is not supported. To work around this limitation and join results of multiple DMVs, use SQL Server linked servers.
- The `Like` statement is not supported.
- Data-conversion functions such as `Cast` and `Convert` are not supported.

Monitoring Connections, Sessions, and Commands

Now that you are becoming familiar with querying DMVs, we will take a closer look at the most useful DMVs (at least in our opinion) and the information they report. As discussed in Chapter 26, "Server Architecture and Command Execution," Analysis Services supports several sessions per connection and can potentially have multiple commands running simultaneously on each session (although having multiple commands per session is not currently implemented in Analysis Services 2008). To monitor information about connections, sessions, and commands, you use three DMVs: `Discover_Connections`, `Discover_Sessions`, and `Discover_Commands`.

In addition to accessing information about the resources being used by the system, these DMVs provide information about the user who initiated the connection and the machine from which these connections were established.

Analysis Services reports information about sessions and commands in the following columns:

- Information about the user appears in the `Connection_User_Name` and `Session_User_Name` columns.
- Information about the machine is provided in the `Connection_Host_Name` column.
- Timing-related information is provided in `Connection_Start_Time`, `Session_Last_Command_Start_Time`, and similar columns.
- The text of the current running query or last completed query is provided in the `Session_Last_Command` column.
- Cumulative session-level I/O is reported in the `Session_Reads`, `Session_Writes`, `Session_Reads_KB`, and `Session_Writes_KB` columns.
- The I/O of the currently executing (or last executed) command is reported in the `Command_Reads`, `Command_Writes`, `Command_Reads_KB`, and `Command_Writes_KB` columns.
- Cumulative CPU is reported on the session level in the `Session_CPU_Time_MS` column. (Cumulative CPU time is reported in milliseconds.) Command CPU time is provided in the `Command_CPU_Time_MS` column.

NOTE

The CPU reported by a DMV is a cumulative CPU time of all threads executing. Therefore, on a multiprocessor or multicore machine, the value reported in this column might be greater than the actual query or command duration.

- Network-related information is reported on the connection level because individual sessions or commands do not have information about the amount of data transmitted over the wire. The following columns contain network-related information: `Connection_Bytes_Sent` (actual bytes sent on the network), `Connection_Data_Bytes_Sent` (reports the amount of data before it got compressed and sent over the wire), `Connection_Bytes_Received`, and `Connection_Data_Bytes_Received` (columns that report statistics about incoming traffic).

NOTE

Associating memory consumption with a particular session or command is a nearly impossible task. Analysis Services uses caches that are shared between commands and sessions (as discussed in Chapter 29, "Architecture of Query Execution—Calculating MDX Expressions"). Therefore, associating shared caches with a particular session makes little sense.

Monitoring Server State

In many cases, it is useful to monitor resource utilization via different Analysis Services objects. For example, you might want to see how much memory a certain dimension consumes. Analysis Services provides `Discover_Object_Activity` and `Discover_Object_Memory_Usage` DMVs to track resources used by a particular object.

The `Discover_Object_Activity` DMV enables you to track CPU and I/O used by an object. In Analysis Services, objects form a hierarchy. For example, to report dimension CPU usage, the DMV returns a record for each attribute of that dimension, enabling you to calculate the total value of a CPU used by a dimension.

If you issue the following query, for instance, the DMV will return the result shown in Figure 41.3.

```
select * from $system.DISCOVER_OBJECT_ACTIVITY
```

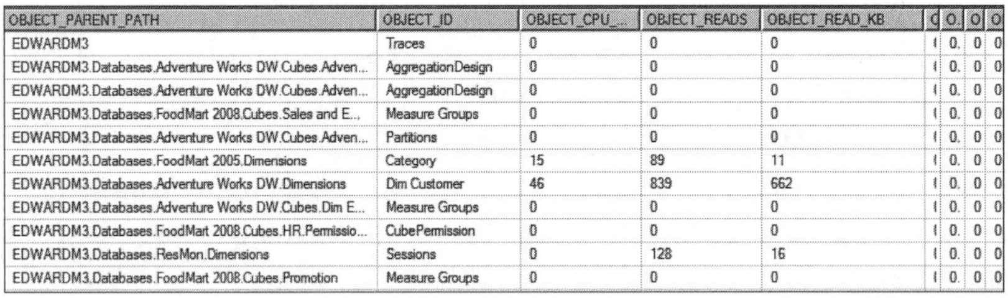

OBJECT_PARENT_PATH	OBJECT_ID	OBJECT_CPU_...	OBJECT_READS	OBJECT_READ_KB	O	O.	O	O
EDWARDM3	Traces	0	0	0	(	0.	0	0
EDWARDM3.Databases.Adventure Works DW.Cubes.Adven...	AggregationDesign	0	0	0	(	0.	0	0
EDWARDM3.Databases.Adventure Works DW.Cubes.Adven...	AggregationDesign	0	0	0	(	0.	0	0
EDWARDM3.Databases.FoodMart 2008.Cubes.Sales and E...	Measure Groups	0	0	0	(	0.	0	0
EDWARDM3.Databases.Adventure Works DW.Cubes.Adven...	Partitions	0	0	0	(	0.	0	0
EDWARDM3.Databases.FoodMart 2005.Dimensions	Category	15	89	11	(	0.	0	0
EDWARDM3.Databases.Adventure Works DW.Dimensions	Dim Customer	46	839	662	(	0.	0	0
EDWARDM3.Databases.Adventure Works DW.Cubes.Dim E...	Measure Groups	0	0	0	(	0.	0	0
EDWARDM3.Databases.FoodMart 2008.Cubes.HR.Permissio...	CubePermission	0	0	0	(	0.	0	0
EDWARDM3.Databases.ResMon.Dimensions	Sessions	0	128	16	(	0.	0	0
EDWARDM3.Databases.FoodMart 2008.Cubes.Promotion	Measure Groups	0	0	0	(	0.	0	0

FIGURE 41.3 Information showing resources used by Analysis Services objects.

Each object in the return result is uniquely identified by its own ID and the ID of its parent reported in the first two columns: `Object_ID` and `Object_Parent_Path`. You can build a multidimensional model on top of the DMV results and use it to analyze resource-consumption information. To model the hierarchical relationships between Analysis Services objects, use a parent-child dimension. (For more information about the parent-child dimensions, see Chapter 8, "Advanced Modeling.") By the time of this book's release, you should be able to download a sample project with the Analysis Services resource-monitoring cube from http://codeplex.com. Figure 41.4 shows examples of memory consumption by an Analysis Services object, exposed by the resource-monitoring cube.

Analysis Services reports objects' resource usage in the following columns:

- Cumulative object I\O is reported in `Object_Reads`, `Object_Writes`, `Object_Reads_KB`, and `Object_Writes_KB` columns. The stats are stored only in memory and not persisted as part of Analysis Services metadata; therefore, after server restart, all numbers are zeroed.
- The number of rows scanned while executing the query is reported in the `Object_Rows_Scanned` column.

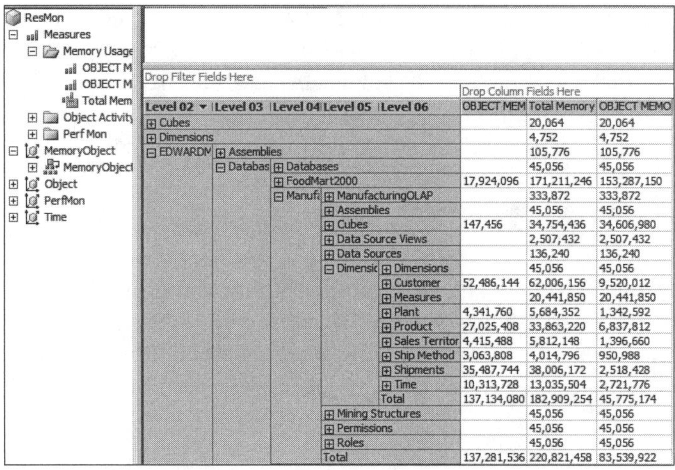

FIGURE 41.4 Memory consumption by Analysis Services objects.

- The number of rows returned as the result of the query is reported in the `Object_Rows_Returned` column. This information is useful when analyzing the performance of a query. For example, sometimes a query needs to read an entire attribute to return just a few members. In this case, you will notice that the number of rows scanned is greater than the total number of rows returned and you might want to optimize the query.
- The number of times aggregation has been hit (or missed) is reported in the `Object_Aggregation_Hit` and `Object_Aggregation_Miss` columns. Armed with this information, you can fine-tune your aggregation design.
- The amount of memory used by the Analysis Services object is reported in the `Object_Memory_Shrinkable` and `Object_Memory_NonShrinkable` columns. (For more information about different memory types, see Chapter 27, "Memory Management.") The shrinkable memory is the one that can be released by Analysis Services, if needed. Nonshrinkable memory is the memory used by metadata objects, for example, which, once loaded into memory, is not released until the object has been deleted.

Using Perfmon Counters

The Windows operating system reports its resource utilization via a performance-monitoring infrastructure. You can use a `perfmon.exe` application to monitor a variety of operating system variables related to the performance of a particular system. The performance-monitoring infrastructure is extensible, and any application can publish its own performance-related statistics. Analysis Services exposes its performance information through the Perfmon counters. If you run `perfmon.exe` from the Run prompt, you can select Analysis Services-specific Perfmon counters.

The main difference between DMVs and Perfmon counters is that the Perfmon counter is a single numeric value reporting the server resource utilization, whereas a DMV reports more detailed information. For example, the `MSAS 2008:Connection\Current connections` counter reports the total number of currently opened connections to Analysis Services. While querying `Discover_Connections`, the DMV returns a list of all connections and information about each one of the connections. DMVs, Perfmon counters, and traces are all complementary mechanisms that enable you to access information about the current Analysis Services state.

The performance-monitoring infrastructure enables you to see counter values in real time using the Perfmon application, and enables you to record Perfmon counter values in the form of a log. After you have collected your Perfmon log, you can use the often-overlooked SQL Server Profiler functionality that enables you to correlate a Perfmon log with a previously recorded trace.

NOTE

For Analysis Services 2005 to record a Perfmon counter log, you need to grant access to the server bin folder (`%program files%\Microsoft SQL Server\MSSQL.2\OLAP\bin`) for the `LocalMachine\Performance Log Users` security group. In Analysis Services 2008, this is no longer required.

To make it easier to access Analysis Services Perfmon counters, we decided to expose the Analysis Services Perfmon counters through DMVs. You can also write your own application to retrieve Perfmon counters using the Perfmon API.

Retrieving Perfmon counters via DMVs is a little tricky because of one of the limitations of the SQL language implementation by Analysis Services. Because multiple Perfmon counters could be available on a single computer, Analysis Services does not allow you to access values of all of them in a single request. You must explicitly specify which counter you need to see. To pass a name of the Perfmon counter to the DMV, use the `systemrestrictschema` function provided by Analysis Services. This function takes its parameter and uses it as a restriction to the underlying internal `SchemaRowset` request. (For more information about the DMV internal architecture, refer back to the material earlier in this chapter.) For example, to query for the value of the `MSAS 2008:Connection\Current connections` counter, you need to send the following DMV query:

```
select * from systemrestrictschema ($system.discover_performance_counters,
PERF_COUNTER_NAME = '\MSAS 2008:Connection\Current connections')
```

You can also query for multiple Perfmon counters at the same time by specifying multiple restrictions in the `systemrestrictschema` function. For example:

```
select *
from systemrestrictschema ($system.discover_performance_counters,
PERF_COUNTER_NAME = '\MSAS 2008:Connection\Current connections',
PERF_COUNTER_NAME = '\MSAS 2008:MDX\Total Cells Calculated')
```

Index

A

B

C

D

E

F

J-K

L

M

N

O

P

R

S